KU-221-859

A Companion to Bioethics

Blackwell Companions to Philosophy

This outstanding student reference series offers a comprehensive and authoritative survey of philosophy as a whole. Written by today's leading philosophers, each volume provides lucid and engaging coverage of the key figures, terms, topics, and problems of the field. Taken together, the volumes provide the ideal basis for course use, representing an unparalleled work of reference for students and specialists alike.

Already published in the series:

Blackwell
Companions to
Philosophy

A Companion to Bioethics

Edited by

HELGA KUHSE
and
PETER SINGER

Blackwell
Publishing

© 1998, 2001 by Blackwell Publishing Ltd

BLACKWELL PUBLISHING
350 Main Street, Malden, MA 02148-5020, USA
108 Cowley Road, Oxford OX4 1JF, UK
550 Swanston Street, Carlton, Victoria 3053, Australia

All rights reserved. No part of this publication may be reproduced, stored in a retrieval system, or transmitted, in any form or by any means, electronic, mechanical, photocopying, recording or otherwise, except as permitted by the UK Copyright, Designs, and Patents Act 1988, without the prior permission of the publisher.

First published 1998
First published in paperback 2001
Reprinted 2002, 2004 (three times)

Library of Congress Cataloging-in-Publication Data

A companion to bioethics / edited by Helga Kuhse and Peter Singer.
        p. cm. – (Blackwell companions to philosophy)
   Includes bibliographical references and index.
   ISBN 0-631-19737-0 (hardback) – 0-631-23019-X (paperback)
   1. Bioethics.   2. Medical Ethics.   I. Kuhse, Helga.   II. Singer, Peter.
III. Series.
   R724.C616   1998
   174'.2 – dc21   97-50242
                                                           CIP

A catalogue record for this title is available from the British Library.

Set in 10.5 on 11.5 pt Photina
by Best-set Typesetter Ltd, Hong Kong
Printed and bound in the United Kingdom
by TJ International Ltd, Padstow, Cornwall

The publisher's policy is to use permanent paper from mills that operate a sustainable forestry policy, and which has been manufactured from pulp processed using acid-free and elementary chlorine-free practices. Furthermore, the publisher ensures that the text paper and cover board used have met acceptable environmental accreditation standards.

For further information on
Blackwell Publishing, visit our website:
www.blackwellpublishing.com

Contents

PART X AIDS

PART XI EXPERIMENTATION WITH HUMAN SUBJECTS

PART XII EXPERIMENTATION WITH ANIMALS

PART XIII ETHICAL ISSUES IN THE PRACTICE OF HEALTH CARE

Contributors

Professor John D. Arras,
Department of Philosophy,
Cabell Hall,
University of Virginia,
Charlottesville, VA, USA.

Professor Margaret Pabst Battin,
Department of Philosophy,
University of Utah,
Salt Lake City, UT, USA.

Professor Joseph Boyle,
St Michael's College,
University of Toronto,
Toronto, Ontario, Canada.

Professor Dan W. Brock,
Department of Philosophy,
Brown University,
Providence, RI, USA.

Professor Baruch Brody,
Baylor College of Medicine,
Center for Ethics,
Houston, TX, USA.

Professor Alexander Morgan Capron,
Law Centre,
University of Southern California,
Los Angeles, CA, USA.

Professor Ruth Chadwick,
Centre for Professional Ethics,
University of Central Lancashire,
Preston, UK.

Professor James F. Childress,
Department of Philosophy,
Cabell Hall,
University of Virginia,
Charlottesville, VA, USA.

Dr Vichai Chokevivat,
Department of Communicable Disease
    Control,
Bangkok, Thailand.

Dr Angus Clarke,
University of Wales College of
    Medicine,
Institute of Medical Genetics,
Heath Park,
Cardiff, UK.

Dr Jan Crosthwaite,
Department of Philosophy,
University of Auckland,
Auckland, New Zealand.

Professor Norman Daniels,
Department of Philosophy,
Tufts University,
Medford, MA, USA.

Professor Leonardo D. de Castro,
Department of Philosophy,
University of the Philippines,
Diliman,
Quezon City, Philippines.

Dr Carlos Del Rio,
National AIDS Programme
(CONASIDA),
Mexico.

Professor Govert den Hartogh,
Faculteit den Wijsbegeerte,
Onderzoekschool Ethiek,
Amsterdam, The Netherlands.

Associate Professor Carl Elliott,
Center for Bioethics,
University of Minnesota,
Minneapolis, MN, USA.

Professor Segun Gbadegesin,
Department of Philosophy,
Howard University,
Washington, DC, USA.

Professor Raanan Gillon,
Analytical Ethics Unit,
Imperial College,
London, UK.

Professor R. M. Hare,
Bywater,
The Street,
Ewelme,
Wallingford, Oxfordshire, UK.

Professor John Harris,
Centre for Social Ethics and Policy,
University of Manchester,
Manchester, UK.

Professor Roger Higgs,
Department of General Practice and
Primary Care,
King's College School of Medicine and
Dentistry,
London, UK.

Associate Professor Nils Holtug,
Department of Education, Philosophy
and Rhetoric,
University of Copenhagen,
Copenhagen, Denmark.

Professor Eike-Henner W. Kluge,
Department of Philosophy,
University of Victoria,
Victoria, BC, Canada.

Professor Jeff McMahan,
Department of Philosophy,
University of Illinois,
Urbana, IL, USA.

**Associate Professor Paul M.
McNeill,**
Department of Community Medicine,
University of New South Wales,
Sydney, Australia

Dr Carlos Magis,
National AIDS Programme
(CONASIDA),
Mexico.

Dr Rita C. Manning,
Department of Philosophy,
San Jose State University,
San Jose, CA, USA.

Sarah Marchand,
Program in Medical Ethics,
School of Medicine,
Madison, WI, USA.

Professor Jonathan D. Moreno,
Center for Biomedical Ethics,
University of Virginia,
Charlottesville, VA, USA.

Professor Timothy F. Murphy,
Department of Medical Education,
University of Illinois College of
Medicine,
Chicago, IL, USA.

Dr Catherine Myser,
Ethics Program,
University of Vermont College of
Medicine,
Burlington, VT, USA.

Dr Justin Oakley,
Centre for Human Bioethics,
Monash University,
Clayton, Australia.

Dr F. Barbara Orlans,
Kennedy Institute of Ethics,
Georgetown University,
Washington, DC, USA.

Professor Laura M. Purdy,
Bioethicist, University Health
  Network and University of Toronto
  Joint Centre for Bioethics,
Department of Philosophy and Wells
  College,
University of Toronto,
Toronto, Canada.

Professor James Rachels,
Department of Philosophy,
University of Alabama,
Birmingham, AL, USA.

Dr Rosamond Rhodes,
Bioethics Education,
Medical Education,
Mount Sinai School of Medicine,
New York, NY, USA.

Dr Paul Robinson,
Freelance Editor,
London, UK.

Professor Bernard E. Rollin,
Department of Philosophy,
Colorado State University,
Fort Collins, CO, USA.

Dr Udo Schüklenk,
Centre for Human, Bioethics,
Monash University,
Clayton, Victoria, Australia.

Professor Bonnie Steinbock,
Department of Philosophy,
College of Humanities and Fine Arts,
SUNY Albany,
Albany, NY, USA.

Dr Brian Stoffell,
Medical Ethics Unit,
Flinders University Medical Centre,
Bedford Park, South Australia.

Professor Michael Tooley,
Department of Philosophy,
University of Colorado at Boulder,
Boulder, CO, USA.

Verena Tschudin,
European Centre for Professional
  Ethics,
Faculty of Science and Health,
University of East London,
London, UK.

Dr Wibren van der Burg,
Schoordijk Institute for Jurisprudence
  and Comparative Law,
Tilburg University,
Tilburg, The Netherlands.

Baroness Mary Warnock,
Axford,
Wiltshire, UK.

Dr Mary Anne Warren,
Department of Philosophy,
San Francisco State University,
San Francisco, CA, USA.

Professor Daniel Wikler,
Program in Medical Ethics,
School of Medicine,
University of Wisconsin,
Madison, WI, USA.

Dr Robert Young,
Department of Philosophy,
Latrobe University,
Melbourne, Victoria, Australia.

Acknowledgements

Now that the work is finished, we wish to thank Alyn Shipton for encouraging us to take on this project – although we had some doubts along the way that we would ever finish what turned out to be a mammoth task. We also thank the following members of the staff of Blackwell Publishers for their support: Steve Smith, Sandra Raphael, Simon Eckley, Mary Riso and Leanda Shrimpton.

Helga Kuhse and Peter Singer
April 1998

PART I
INTRODUCTION

1

What is bioethics?
A historical introduction

HELGA KUHSE AND PETER SINGER

Since the 1960s ethical problems in health care and the biomedical sciences have gripped the public consciousness in unprecedented ways. In part, this is the result of new and sometimes revolutionary developments in the biomedical sciences and in clinical medicine. Dialysis machines, artificial ventilators and organ transplants offer the possibility of keeping alive patients who otherwise would have died. *In vitro* fertilization and related reproduction techniques allow a range of new relationships between parents and children, including the birth of children who are not genetically related to the women who bear them. The development of modern contraceptives, prenatal testing and the availability of safe abortions have given women and couples increased choices about the number and kinds of children they are going to have. These technological breakthroughs, however, have not been the only factor in the increasing interest in ethical problems in this area. Another factor has been a growing concern about the power exercised by doctors and scientists, which shows itself in concern to assert 'patients' rights' and the rights of the community as a whole to be involved in decisions that affect them. This has meant greater public awareness of the value-laden nature of medical decision-making, and a critical questioning of the basis on which such decisions are made. It has become patently obvious during the past three or four decades that, to give just one example, someone has to decide whether to continue life-support for patients who will never regain consciousness. This is not a technical decision that only doctors are capable of making, but an ethical decision, on which patients and others may have views no less defensible than those of doctors.

It was in the climate of such new ethical issues and choices that the field of inquiry now known as 'bioethics' was born. The word was not originally used in this sense. Van Rensselaer Potter originally proposed the term for a 'science of survival' in the ecological sense – that is, an interdisciplinary study aimed at ensuring the preservation of the biosphere (Potter, 1970). This terminology never became widely established, however, and instead 'bioethics' came to refer to the growing interest in the ethical issues arising from health care and the biomedical sciences. It is to bioethics in this latter sense that the present volume forms a *Companion*.

Although the term itself is new, and the prominence of bioethics owes much to recent developments in the biomedical sciences, bioethics can also be seen as a modern version of a much older field of thought, namely medical ethics. Undoubtedly bioethics claims medical ethics as part of its province, but in many ways it takes a distinctly different approach. Traditionally, medical ethics has focused primarily on the doctor–patient relationship and on the virtues possessed by the good doctor. It has also been very much concerned with relations between colleagues within the profession, to the extent that it has sometimes seemed to exemplify George Bernard Shaw's remark that 'all professions are conspiracies against the laity.' Bioethics, on the other hand, is a more overtly critical and reflective enterprise. Not limited to questioning the ethical dimensions of doctor–patient and doctor–doctor relationships, it goes well beyond the scope of traditional medical ethics in several ways. First, its goal is not the development of, or adherence to, a code or set of precepts, but a better understanding of the issues. Second, it is prepared to ask deep philosophical questions about the nature of ethics, the value of life, what it is to be a person, the significance of being human. Third, it embraces issues of public policy and the direction and control of science. In all these senses, bioethics is a novel and distinct field of inquiry. Nevertheless, its history must begin with the history of medical ethics.

Medical Ethics

Medical ethics has a long and varied history (Reich, 1995: 1439–646). While it is often thought that it had its beginning in the days of Hippocrates, in ancient Greece, it is in fact much older. Even tribal societies, without a written language, already had more or less well articulated values that directed the provision of health care by shamans, exorcists, witches, sorcerers and priests, as well as by midwives, bonesetters and herbalists. One of the earliest written provisions relating to the practice of medicine is from the Code of Hammurabi, written in Babylon in about 1750 BC. It stipulates that if a doctor uses a bronze lancet to perform a major operation on a member of the nobility that results in death or leads to the loss of an eye, the doctor's hand will be cut off (Pritchard, 1969). Other early provisions of medical ethics were embedded in a religious tradition. A monument in a sanctuary of Asclepias, for example, tells doctors to be 'like God: savior equally of slaves, of paupers, of rich men, of princes, and to all a brother, such help he would give' (Etziony, 1973); and the Daily Prayer of a Physician, often attributed to the twelfth-century Jewish doctor Moses Maimonides (but now thought to date from the eighteenth century), condemns not only 'thirst for profit' but also 'ambition for renown and admiration' (Veatch, 1989: 14).

The ancient ethical codes were often expressed in the form of oaths. The best known medical oath in the Western tradition is the Oath of Hippocrates, commonly assumed to be from the fifth century BC, and often regarded as the very foundation of Western medical ethics. Despite the oath's continuing appeal, its origins are clouded in mystery. Around 500 BC many different schools of medical practice coexisted, each of them reflecting somewhat different medical, philosophical and religious beliefs. One of these medical schools, on the island of Cos, was headed by the physician Hippocrates. The Hippocratic School produced a large body of writings on medicine, science and ethics. The date of the oath, however, is unknown, with estimates ranging from the sixth century BC to the beginning of the Christian era (Edelstein, 1967). The oath's significance in the history of Western medical ethics is twofold. In affirming that 'I will use dietetic measures to the use and profit of the sick according to my capacity and understanding. If any danger and hurt threatens, I will endeavour to avert it,' the oath establishes the principles of benefi-cence and non-maleficence, that is, that doctors must act so as to benefit their patients and seek to prevent harm. In addition, the oath's prohibition on giving a potion to produce an abortion, or giving any poison to end the life of a patient, is consonant with the view of the sanctity of human life that has dominated medical ethics under Christendom. Other aspects of the oath – like the injunction to honour one's teacher like a parent, 'to share his fate and if occasion arise supply him with the necessaries of life' – are less frequently referred to in modern discussions of medical ethics.

While some scholars hold that the increasing importance of the Hippocratic Oath is linked to the rise of Christianity, this is disputed by others who believe that there are significant differences and tensions in the ethical precepts on which Hippocratic and Christian medicine were built. One obvious difference lies in the two traditions' religious commitment. At different times, various modifications were thus introduced to make the Hippocratic Oath acceptable to Christians. One of the earliest of these dates from the tenth or eleventh century. It is entitled 'From the Oath According to Hippocrates Insofar as a Christian May Swear it'. This oath no longer required Christian doctors to swear to Greek gods and goddesses; rather, those taking the oath addressed themselves to 'God the Father of our Lord Jesus Christ' (Jones, 1924: 23).

Perhaps one of the most significant moral influences of Christianity relates to its emphasis on love for one's neighbour and compassion for the ill. Religious institu-tions, such as monasteries, began to set up 'hospitals' for the ill and destitute, and Christian teaching emphasized that doctors must cultivate the virtues of compas-sion and charity. A treatise, probably dating from the early twelfth century, exhorts doctors not to heal 'for the sake of gain, nor to give more consideration to the wealthy than to the poor, or to the noble than the ignoble' (MacKinney, 1952: 27), and in the thirteenth century Thomas Aquinas considered it a sin if a doctor demanded an excessive fee, or if he refused to give gratuitous treatment to a patient who would die for want of it.

If greed and lack of charity were regarded as sins, so were other practices as well. Navarrus, a leading sixteenth-century canonist, provided a clear statement that condemned euthanasia as sinful, even if motivated by pity. In this, he followed St Augustine's earlier pronouncement, in *The City of God*, that Christians must not choose suicide to escape illness; and Thomas Aquinas' condemnation of the prac-tice on the grounds that it was unnatural and a usurpation of God's prerogative to give and take life.

When it came to another topic still central to contemporary bioethical debate – that of abortion – the historical position of the Church has been somewhat ambiguous. While the practice was standardly condemned in the early Christian literature, its wrongness was often regarded as a matter of degree. Following Aristotle, various thinkers – including Thomas Aquinas – thought that only the abortion of an animated fetus constituted homicide. Animation was presumed to occur at forty days for male fetuses, and ninety days for female fetuses. By and large, this view remained dominant until 1869, when Pius IX declared all direct abortions homicide, regardless of the fetal stage of development.

Over the millennia, many different religious groups have attempted to formulate the central virtues and duties of doctors in various ways. As might be expected, these formulations do not always agree with one another. The Roman Catholic Church is not the only Christian Church to have well-developed views on a range of issues in medical ethics; there are a number of Protestant Churches with distinct positions as well. In addition, there are of course extensive non-Christian religious teachings. Jewish and Islamic medical ethics, for example, articulate the duties and responsibilities of Jewish or Islamic doctors, and in East Asia and the Indian subcontinent, traditions of medical ethics are intertwined with Taoism, Confucianism, Buddhism, Shintoism and Hinduism.

Over the centuries, medical practitioners themselves continued to reflect on the qualities that the virtuous doctor should possess, in particular in his relationship with patients. While these reflections were typically intertwined with prevailing religious trends and teachings, the seventeenth and eighteenth centuries brought some changes. John Gregory, a prominent eighteenth-century Scottish doctor-philosopher, drew on prevailing Enlightenment philosophies to articulate his view that doctors must by 'sympathetic', in the sense developed by the great Scottish philosopher David Hume. In other words, the doctor was to develop 'that sensibility of heart which makes us feel for the distresses of our fellow creatures, and which, of consequence, incites us in the most powerful manner to relieve them' (Gregory, 1817: 22).

Gregory's reflections on the role of doctors and the doctor–patient relationship are still highly relevant today. Not only was he possibly the first doctor who sought to develop a universal moral basis for medical ethics – one that was free from narrow religious and parochial concerns – but his view of the central role played by care and sympathy in the doctor–patient relationship may also be read as one of the first articulations of an 'ethics of care'. In recent times, care approaches to ethics have played an important role in feminist and nursing approaches to ethics.

Nursing Ethics

Medical ethics has not been the only source of ethics relating to health care. Professional nursing had its beginning in nineteenth-century England, where Florence Nightingale established the first school of nursing and laid down some of the ethical precepts that would shape the practice of nursing for a long time. Emphasis was placed on the character of the nurse. Above all else, a good nurse must be a good woman, as Florence Nightingale put it.

By the early 1890s nurses had begun seriously to discuss ethical issues in nursing. In 1899 the International Council of Nurses was established, professional journals, such as *The American Journal of Nursing*, sprang up and in 1901 Isabel Hampton Robb, a leader of nursing at the time, wrote one of the first books on nursing ethics, entitled *Nursing Ethics for Hospitals and Private Use* (Robb, 1901). The vast majority of nurses are women and, until fairly recently, the vast majority of doctors have been men. Not surprisingly, the relationship between doctors and nurses reflected the different roles of women and men, and their relative status in society. One of the manifestations of this was the assumption that the primary responsibility of nurses was to doctors rather than to patients, and that nurses had to show absolute obedience to their medical colleagues. As one American nursing leader put it in 1917: 'The first and most helpful criticism I ever received from a doctor was when he told me that I was supposed to be simply an intelligent machine for the purpose of carrying out his order' (Dock, 1917: 394).

The view that the nurse's primary responsibility was to the doctor prevailed until the 1960s, and was still reflected in the 1965 version of the *International Code of Nursing Ethics*. Item 7 of the *Code* states: 'The nurse is under an obligation to carry out the physician's orders intelligently and loyally.' The revival of feminist thinking in the late 1960s paralleled the developing self-consciousness and self-assertiveness of nurses, and in the 1973 *International Council of Nurses' Code for Nurses* the nurse's 'primary responsibility' is no longer seen to be to doctors but to patients – 'to those people who require nursing care'.

This questioning by nurses of their traditional role and their relationship with doctors and patients eventually converged with a movement by feminist philosophers that challenged the traditional (and therefore male-dominated) view of ethics as a matter of abstract, impartial and universal principles or rules. Instead of this conception of ethics, feminist philosophers like Nell Noddings (Noddings, 1984) conceived of ethics as a fabric of care and responsibility arising out of personal relationships. Building on this 'female' approach to ethics, both philosophers and nurses sought to construct a new ethics for nurses based on the concept of care. Jean Watson, a nurse and a prominent proponent of a nursing ethics of care, applies to the nursing situation Noddings' view that an ethics of care 'ties us to the people we serve and not to the rules through which we serve them' (Watson, 1988: 2).

Bioethics

Perhaps the first 'modern' work of bioethics was Joseph Fletcher's *Morals and Medicine*, published in 1954. Fletcher was an American Episcopalian theologian whose controversial 'situation ethics' approach to ethical questions had more in common with consequentialist ethics than with traditional Christian views. In keeping with this, he later abandoned his religious belief. Although Fletcher did much to stimulate early discussions of ethical issues in medicine, it was only in the 1960s that bioethics really began to take shape as a field of study. This period was one of important cultural and social changes. The civil rights movement focused attention on issues of justice and inequality; the Cuban missile crisis and the Vietnam War led to a renewed questioning of war and nuclear weapons; and the resurgence of feminism, coupled with the availability of safe abortions and modern contraceptives, raised questions about women's reproductive rights. For much of the late 1960s and early 1970s, university authorities were besieged by students, initially in opposition to the Vietnam War, but later also demanding that their courses be relevant to the larger social issues of the day. These changes had their effect on the practice of philosophy too, sparking a renewed interest in normative and applied ethics. While the prevailing orthodoxy among English-speaking moral philosophers throughout the 1960s was that philosophy deals with the analysis of moral terms rather than with practical issues, this attitude began to shift in the 1970s. Increasingly, moral philosophers began to address themselves to such practical ethical issues as abortion and euthanasia, the ethics of war and of capital punishment, the allocation of scarce medical resources, animal rights and so on. They frequently dared to question what had not been questioned before. Since some of these issues related to practices in health care and the biological sciences, this movement in philosophy helped to establish bioethics as a critical discipline.

The other major impetus to the development of the field was the development of new medical technology that threw up questions no one had needed to answer before. One of the first high-profile bioethics issues in the United States shows this clearly. The first machines that could dialyse patients who had suffered kidney failure dramatically saved the lives of patients who would otherwise have been dead in a matter of days; but the machines were very expensive, and there were many more patients who were suffering from renal disease than machines. In 1962 the artificial kidney centre in Seattle, Washington, set up a committee to select patients for treatment. Its life-and-death decisions earned it the name of 'the God committee', and focused attention on the criteria it used. A study that showed a bias towards people of the same social class and ethnic background as the committee itself eventually led to further discussion about the best way to solve such problems.

Of all the medical breakthroughs of this period, the most widely publicized was the first heart transplant, performed by the South African surgeon Christiaan Barnard in 1967. The patient's death eighteen days later did not dampen the spirits of those who hailed a new era of medicine – with its attendant ethical dilemmas. The ability to perform heart transplants was linked to the development of respirators, which had been introduced to hospitals in the 1950s. Respirators could save many lives, but not all those whose hearts kept beating ever recovered any other significant functions. In some cases, their brains had ceased to function altogether. The realization that such patients could be a source of organs for transplantation led to the setting up of the Harvard Brain Death Committee, and to its subsequent recommendation that the absence of all 'discernible central nervous system activity' should be 'a new criterion for death' (Rothman, 1991). The recommendation has subsequently been adopted, with some modifications, almost everywhere.

If the availability of respirators and other powerful life-extending technology raised questions about the time when a patient should be declared dead, it also brought to the forefront questions about the proper limits of employing this technology in attempts to save or prolong a patient's life. While it had generally been accepted that competent patients must not be treated against their will, the situation of incompetent patients was far less clear. This was true not only with regard to patients who had been rendered incompetent by illness, accident or disease, but also the treatment of seriously disabled or premature newborn infants. The question was simply this: if a patient is unable to say 'no', does this mean that his or her life must always be prolonged for as long as possible, even if the patient's prospects are very poor?

In 1973 a leading US medical journal, the *New England Journal of Medicine*, published a study by two paediatricians on the ethical dilemmas they encountered in the special care nursery (Duff and Campbell, 1973). The doctors, Raymond Duff and A. G. M. Campbell, did not think that all severely ill or disabled infants should receive life-prolonging treatment. They thought it important to break down 'the public and professional silence on a major taboo', and indicated that out of 299 infants in the special-care nursery, 43 had died as a consequence of a non-treatment decision. A central question was whether these non-treatment decisions were morally and legally sound.

Questions about the limits of treatment for those who are unable to decide for themselves were raised not only in the United States but in other countries as well. Australian and British doctors, for example, had begun publishing their views on the selective non-treatment of infants born with spina bifida, and thereby contributed to an ongoing debate about the appropriateness of a 'quality of life' or a 'sanctity of life' approach in the practice of medicine (Kuhse and Singer, 1985).

It was not until 1976 that a landmark US case – that of Karen Ann Quinlan – lent support to the view that doctors had no legal duty to prolong life in all circumstances. Karen Ann Quinlan, who had become comatose in 1975, was attached to a respirator to assist her breathing. Her condition was described as 'chronic persistent vegetative state'. When the treating doctor refused to honour the family's wishes that Karen be removed from the respirator, the case eventually came before the New Jersey Supreme Court, which decided that life-support could be discontinued without the treating doctor being deemed to have committed an act of unlawful homicide. The case had implications for future thinking about various issues relating to medical end-of-life decisions, such as the moral and legal relevance of the distinction between so-called ordinary and extraordinary means of treatment, the role of parents or guardians in medical end-of-life decisions, the validity or otherwise of a now incompetent patient's previously expressed wishes regarding life-sustaining treatment and so on.

Important ethical issues had already been raised in the United States with regard to the ethics of human experimentation by writers such as Henry K. Beecher (Beecher, 1966). It had become known that patients at the Jewish Chronic Disease Hospital in Brooklyn had been injected with live cancer cells, without their consent; that, from 1965 to 1971, mentally retarded children at Willowbrook State Hospital in New York had been inoculated with the hepatitis virus; and that a 1930 study aimed at determining the 'natural history' of syphilis in untreated black men continued in Tuskegee, Alabama, until the early 1970s.

The public attention directed at these cases led to important changes in the scrutiny that US agencies henceforth directed at medical research. In 1973 the US

Congress established the National Commission for the Protection of Human Subjects of Biomedical and Behavioral Research, whose members were charged with the task of drawing up regulations that would protect the rights and interests of subjects of research. While the Commission's role was only temporary, its influence was not. Most of the Commission's recommendations became regulatory law, and one of its reports – the Belmont Report – clearly articulated the ethical principles that should, in the Commission's view, govern research: respect for persons, beneficence and justice. Subsequently, principles such as these have been influential in bioethics through their incorporation into a widely used bioethics text – *Principles of Biomedical Ethics* (Beauchamp and Childress, 1994).

By the end of the 1960s, mounting ethical problems in medicine, research and the health-care sciences had already led to the establishment in the United States of the first institutions and centres for bioethics. One of the best known of these centres – the Institute of Society, Ethics and the Life Sciences (the Hastings Center) – was founded by Daniel Callahan and Willard Gaylin in 1969. Its publication, the *Hastings Center Report*, one of the first publications exclusively directed towards the newly emerging discipline of bioethics, is still one of the most widely read publications in the field.

Almost from the beginning, bioethics was an interdisciplinary enterprise. While ethics had been the near-exclusive domain of moral philosophers and religious thinkers, bioethics crossed the boundaries not only of medicine, nursing and the biomedical sciences, but of law, economics and public policy as well. Bioethics in this broad, interdisciplinary sense has since become firmly established as a field of inquiry and of learning – first in the United States, and since then in many other countries as well. It is now taught at universities at both undergraduate and postgraduate levels, and many nursing and medical schools regard bioethics as an integral part of their curriculum. There are more than 200 bioethics research centres throughout the world, and bioethicists are often consulted by government commissions, law reform bodies and professional organizations. Many countries have their own national bioethics associations and the International Association of Bioethics (IAB) links bioethicists from all parts of the world. A number of highly regarded scholarly bioethics journals emanate from different continents, and international congresses on bioethics are now a frequent phenomenon. In short, while bioethics had its beginning in the United States, it is now a global field of inquiry.

References

Beauchamp, Tom L. and Childress, James F. (1994). *Principles of Biomedical Ethics*, 4th edn. New York: Oxford University Press. [First published in 1979.]

Beecher, Henry K. (1966). Ethical and clinical research. *New England Journal of Medicine*, 274, 1354–60.

Dock, Sarah (1917). The relation of the nurse to the doctor and the doctor to the nurse. *American Journal of Nursing*, 17.

Duff, R. S. and Campbell, A. G. M. (1973). Moral and ethical problems in the special-care nursery. *New England Journal of Medicine*, 279, 890–4.

Edelstein, Ludwig (1967). The Hippocratic Oath: text, translation and interpretation. In *Ancient Medicine: Selected papers of Ludwig Edelstein*, ed. O. Temkin and C. L. Temkin. Baltimore, MD: Johns Hopkins Press, 3–63.

Etziony, M. B. (1973). *The Physician's Creed: an anthology of medical prayers, oaths, and codes of ethics written by medical practitioners throughout the ages*. Springfield, IL: Charles C. Thomas.

Fletcher, Joseph (1954). *Morals and Medicine: The moral problems of the patient's right to know the truth, contraception, artificial insemination, sterilization, euthanasia*. Boston: Beacon.

Gregory, John (1817). *Lectures and Duties on the Qualifications of a Physician*. Philadelphia: M. Carey.

Jones, W. H. S. (1924). *The Doctor's Oath: an essay in the history of medicine*. New York: Cambridge University Press.

Kuhse, Helga and Singer, Peter (1985). *Should the Baby Live? The problem of handicapped infants*. Oxford: Oxford University Press.

MacKinney, L. C. (1952). Medical ethics and etiquette in the early Middle Ages: the persistence of Hippocratic ideals. *Bulletin of the History of Medicine*, 26, 1–31.

Noddings, Nel (1984). *Caring: a feminine approach to ethics and moral education*. Berkeley: University of California Press.

Potter, V. R. (1970). Bioethics, science of survival. *Biology and Medicine*, 14, 127–53.

Pritchard, J. B. (1969). *Ancient Near Eastern Texts Relating to the Old Testament*, 3rd edn. Princeton, NJ: Princeton University Press.

Reich, W. T. (ed.) (1995). *Encyclopedia of Bioethics*. London: Simon & Schuster and Prentice Hall International.

Robb, Isabel Hampton (1901). *Nursing Ethics for Hospitals and Private Use*. Cleveland, OH: J. B. Savage.

Rothman, David (1991). *Strangers at the Bedside*. New York: Basic Books.

Veatch, Robert M. (1989). *Medical Ethics*. Boston: Jones and Bartlett.

PART II

QUESTIONS ABOUT BIOETHICS

2

Ethical theory and bioethics

JAMES RACHELS

What is the relation between bioethics and ethical theory? Since bioethics deals with the moral issues that come up in particular cases, and ethical theory deals with the standards and principles of moral reasoning, it is natural to think the relation between them might be something like this:

> *The straightforward-application model.* The ethical theory is the starting-point, and we apply the theory to the case at hand in order to reach a conclusion about what should be done.

Utilitarianism is the leading example of an ethical theory that might be thought to solve bioethical problems by the straightforward application of its ideas. Utilitarianism says that in any situation we should do what will have the best overall consequences for everyone concerned. If this is our theory, and we want to decide what should be done in a particular case, we simply calculate the likely effects of various actions and choose the one that produces the greatest benefit for the greatest number of people.

But many bioethicists reject this model. In the first place, anyone who approaches an ethical problem by announcing 'I hold such-and-such a theory; therefore my conclusion is so-and-so' will be unlikely to get much of a hearing. We want to know what really is best, not just what this or that theory says. Moreover, many investigators doubt that there can be a satisfactory ethical theory of the kind that philosophers have traditionally sought, because, they say, morality cannot be codified in a set of rules. Instead, living morally is a matter of cultivating virtuous habits of action, including, perhaps, the kind of 'caring' behaviour that some feminist writers have argued is central (see chapter 11, pp. 98–105). And in any case, it is said, bioethical controversies are too complicated to be resolved by the simple application of a theory. Theories are general and abstract, while real life is messy and detailed.

If we reject the straightforward-application model, where do we turn for an alternative? One of the most popular options is an approach that focuses on 'case studies' – detailed investigations of specific cases that make use of whatever analytical ideas and principles seem most promising in the circumstances at hand. The case-study approach suggests a different conception of the relation between ethical theory and bioethics:

The physics/car-mechanic model. The relation between ethical theory and bioethics is like the relation between physics and automobile repair. Cars operate according to the laws of physics, to be sure; but one doesn't have to know physics to be a good mechanic, and one certainly does not 'apply' the laws of physics to fix cars. The mechanic's reasoning does not begin with 'For every action, there is an equal and opposite reaction.' Instead, it begins with something like: 'The problem is either electrical or fuel-related. If it's electrical . . .'

So, like the car mechanic, the bioethicist will rely on mid-level principles, ignoring the lofty but unhelpful pronouncements of high-level theory.

Case Studies and Mid-level Principles

At first blush, the case-study approach seems to permit bioethicists to make progress without resorting to ethical theory. But this turns out to be an illusion. In ethics, theoretical issues crop up everywhere. Deciding about abortion requires that we think about the nature of persons; the allocation of health-care resources raises questions of distributive justice; and arguments about euthanasia make critical assumptions about the meaning and value of human life. Without the resources of ethical theory we could make little progress in dealing with such matters. It is also an illusion to think that mid-level principles can, by themselves, yield definitive answers to ethical questions.

Consider the case of Theresa Ann Campo Pearson, an anencephalic infant known as 'Baby Theresa', who was born in Florida in 1992. There are about 1,000 such infants – babies without brains – born each year in the United States, so Baby Theresa's story would not have been newsworthy except for an unusual request by her parents. Knowing that their baby could not live long and that, even if she could, she would never have a conscious life, Baby Theresa's parents volunteered her organs for transplant. They thought her kidneys, liver, heart, lungs and eyes should go to other children who could benefit from them. The physicians believed this was a good idea, but Florida law would not allow it. So after nine days Baby Theresa died, and by then her organs had deteriorated too much to be transplanted. Other children died as well – the ones who would have received the transplants – but because we do not know which children they were, we tend not to think of their deaths as real costs of the decision.

The newspaper stories about Baby Theresa prompted a great deal of public discussion. Would it have been right to remove the infant's organs, thereby causing her immediate death, to save the other children? A number of professional bioethicists joined the debate, but surprisingly few of them agreed with the parents and physicians. Instead they appealed to various principles to support letting all the children die. 'It just seems too horrifying to use people as means to other people's ends,' said one expert. Another explained, 'It is unethical to kill in order to save. It's unethical to kill person A to save person B.' And a third added: 'What the parents are really asking for is: kill this dying baby so that its organs may be used for someone else. Well, that's really a horrendous proposition.'

16

Here we see mid-level principles at work (see chapter 7, pp. 61–71). ('It is unethical to kill in order to save' is a typical mid-level principle). Compared to the abstract pronouncements of ethical theory, mid-level principles are much more like everyday moral rules. They express our commonsense understanding of right and wrong. Therefore, it may be argued, we can have greater confidence in decisions that are supported by widely shared mid-level principles than decisions based on general theories, which are more remote from everyday life and inevitably more controversial.

Of course, these principles are called 'mid-level' because they are derived from, or justified by, higher-level principles. So aren't we just ignoring an important part of the picture if we are content with only the mid-level rules? To this there are two replies. First, it may be maintained that mid-level principles are not derived from higher considerations. They may be viewed as a collection of independent moral principles each of which is valid in itself. (Someone taking this view might like the sort of general ethical theory championed by W. D. Ross in the 1930s.) The problem, however, is that within this approach one has no way of adjudicating conflicts between the independent rules. Suppose a different bioethicist, looking at the case of Baby Theresa, felt that the mid-level rule 'Save as many children as possible' has priority? Or suppose she favoured the rule 'Saving the life of a child with the potential for a satisfying human life is more important than respecting the life of a child without a brain?' Then, of course, the conclusion would be that Theresa's organs should be taken. So the mid-level rules alone cannot provide a definitive answer to the question of what we should do.

Second, and more interesting, it could be pointed out that the same mid-level rules may be endorsed by *more than one* higher-level principle. Kantians, for example, take it as an ultimate principle that people should always be treated as ends in themselves; so they would naturally insist that 'It is wrong to kill person A to save person B.' But utilitarians might also endorse this mid-level principle. They might see it as a useful rule of thumb because following it will have generally good consequences, just as following other familiar rules – don't lie, don't steal and so on – have generally good consequences. Thus these theorists may arrive at the same mid-level rules, despite their different starting-points. If so, we do not need to worry about which starting-point is correct. On the contrary, our confidence in the mid-level principle is increased by the fact that many outlooks endorse it.

Once again, however, a problem arises about how to adjudicate conflicts. Both Kantians and utilitarians would also endorse, as a mid-level rule, that we should save as many children as possible. But when there is a conflict they might have different recommendations about which mid-level rule should be given priority. By establishing priorities, each theory gives an answer to the question of what should be done. But if they ultimately lead to different answers, we cannot avoid the larger issue of which theory is correct.

Of course, the failure to reach a definite conclusion need not be regarded as a defect. There is a way to avoid choosing between theories: when different lines of reasoning lead to different outcomes, we can conclude that we are faced with an unresolvable dilemma. This may appeal to those who dislike appearing dogmatic.

'Not all dilemmas have easy solutions,' it may be said, and the doctors and scientists may be left to fend for themselves, with the bioethicist wishing them good luck. According to taste, this may be considered a realistic acknowledgement of the complexity of an issue or a failure of nerve.

The following episode illustrates an additional way in which ethical theory can aid in the analysis of particular cases. In 1995 an international medical team fought an outbreak of ebola – a devastating virus that destroys cells and causes disintegration of the internal organs as it spreads throughout the body – in Kikwit, Zaire, in which 244 people died. As the epidemic was winding down, a nurse who had worked throughout the crisis was stricken, and the Zairian doctors formulated a desperate plan to save her. This particular strain of ebola did not kill everyone who became infected; one in five victims survived. So the Zairian physicians proposed to save the nurse by transfusing whole blood from one of the survivors, in the hope that whatever antibodies had saved him would be transferred to her.

The foreign doctors adamantly opposed this plan. The donor blood might contain HIV, or hepatitis, or some other harmful agent, they said. And suppose the diagnosis is mistaken – what if she only has malaria or typhoid? By transfusing the blood we might actually be giving her ebola, not curing her of it. Besides, in a similar procedure using animals, the treatment had failed.

The Zairian physicians met privately to discuss these objections. They dismissed the worries about giving the nurse HIV or typhoid; after all, she already had ebola. As for the possibility that the diagnosis was mistaken, this was also dismissed. 'We shouldn't doubt our diagnosis,' said one doctor, 'we've seen so many cases.' They concluded that, although their chances of helping the nurse in this way were slight, it was better than nothing.

With the nurse's consent, the transfusion was given, and she recovered. Eight more patients were then given similar transfusions, and seven of them also recovered. These were the last cases in the epidemic. The foreign doctors did not, however, concede that the treatment had worked. 'We'll never know,' said a physician from the Centers for Disease Control in Atlanta. Other possible explanations for the recoveries were offered – late in the epidemic the virus may have become less deadly, or people may have been getting smaller viral loads when infected.

At first glance, it seems that there was little difference in principle between the views of the Zairian physicians and the foreigners. Both groups were concerned, in a straightforward way, with the welfare of the patients: they merely differed about what strategy would stand the best chance of accomplishing their common goal. Yet, on reflection, we can detect a subtle difference between them. The difference concerned their respective attitudes about action versus inaction. In explaining their unanimous decision to proceed with the transfusion, the head of the Zairian team said 'We felt compelled to try *something*.' And before the procedure was undertaken, he challenged the European and American physicians: 'Tell us if there is something else we can do, and we'll do it.' The one thing not acceptable to them was to do nothing: they couldn't just let the nurse die.

The foreigners, by contrast, were more conservative. When in doubt, their preference was not to act, but to wait and see what would happen. The traditional first

18

principle of medical ethics is 'Do no harm,' and the foreign doctors seem to have been strongly motivated by this thought. It is as though they were thinking: *it is worse to cause harm than merely to allow it to happen.* Or perhaps: *one bears greater responsibility for the consequences of one's actions than for the consequences of one's inactions.* The question of who was right, the Zairians or the foreigners, is partly a question about the soundness of these mid-level principles.

A benefit of doing case studies is that they help us to identify the intuitive principles that influence people. Once exposed, such principles may be subjected to critical examination. Are they, in fact, sound? In practice, however, the critical examination is often skipped, and it is assumed that any principle that seems intuitively plausible is a 'relevant factor' to be taken into account in analysing issues. The chief danger of the case-studies approach is that it can degenerate into nothing more than a systematic description of what people happen to believe.

The mid-level principles we have mentioned – that we may not kill one person in order to save another, that we should save as many as possible and that it is worse to cause harm than to allow it to happen – are among the items often found in the bioethicist's kit-bag. Here is a small sample of additional principles that might be invoked as case studies are pursued:

- that people are moral equals – that no one's welfare is more important that anyone else's;
- that personal autonomy, the freedom of each individual to control his or her own life, is especially important;
- that people should always be treated as ends in themselves, and never as mere means;
- that personal relationships, especially kinship, confer upon people special rights and responsibilities with regard to other people;
- that a person's intention, in performing a given action, is relevant to determining whether the action is right;
- that we may not do evil that good may come; and
- that what is 'natural' is good and what is 'unnatural' is bad.

Obviously, different bioethicists will be attracted to different combinations of these ideas; each investigator will accept some of them and reject others. But on what grounds will they be accepted or rejected? Once again, it is an argument for the relevance of ethical theory that a well-supported theory would provide principled evidence or argument concerning which of these are worthy of acceptance and which are not. Each item on this list can be rationally assessed; it need not be judged simply on its intuitive appeal. But such assessments quickly take one into the more abstract matters of ethical theory.

Justifying the Choice of an Ethical Theory

There are other reasons why bioethicists have doubted the value of ethical theory. Some doubts are prompted by the number of theories available. It is not as though there were only one theory on which everyone agrees. Instead, there are numerous theories that conflict with one another. Confronted with such an array, what is the bioethicist to do? Is there any principled way to choose between the competing theories? Or is the choice merely arbitrary?

This issue was raised in the eighteenth century by David Hume, who argued that morals are ultimately based on 'sentiment, not reason'. Hume knew that moral judgements require reasons in their support, but he pointed out that every chain of reasoning leads back to some first principle that is unjustified. If we ask for a justification of that principle, perhaps one can be given, but only by appealing to still another unjustified assumption, and so on forever. We can never justify all our assumptions; reasoning must begin somewhere. A utilitarian might begin by assuming that what is important is maximizing welfare. Someone else, with a different cast of mind, might make a different assumption. But reason alone cannot justify the choice of one starting-point over another.

Hume is not the only philosopher who has objected to exaggerated claims about what unaided reason can accomplish. A more recent critic, Alasdair MacIntyre, advances a different sort of objection. MacIntyre argues that 'rationality' has meaning only within a historical tradition. The idea of impartial reason justifying norms of conduct binding on all people is, he says, an illusion fostered by the Enlightenment. In reality, historical traditions set standards of inquiry for those working within them. But the standards of rational thinking differ from tradition to tradition, and so we cannot speak of 'what reason requires' in any universal sense. In his 1988 book *Whose Justice? Which Rationality?* MacIntyre writes:

> What the enlightenment made us for the most part blind to and what we now need to recover is . . . a conception of rational inquiry as embodied in a tradition; a conception according to which the standards of rational justification themselves emerge from and are part of a history in which they are vindicated by the way in which they transcend the limitations of and provide remedies for the defects of their predecessors within the history of that same tradition.

Thus, in MacIntyre's view, the reasons that would be adduced by a modern liberal in arguing, say, that slavery is unjust, would not necessarily be acceptable to an Aristotelian, whose standards of rationality are different; and the search for standards that transcend the two traditions is a fool's quest. No such tradition-neutral standards exist, except, perhaps, for purely formal principles such as non-contradiction, which are too weak to yield substantive results.

What are we to make of all this? If these arguments are correct, then no ethical theory can be anything more than an expression of the theorist's sentiments or the historical tradition he or she represents. But before we accept such discouraging conclusions, there are some additional points that should be kept in mind.

First, even if 'reason alone' cannot determine what ultimate principles we should accept, this does not mean the choice must be arbitrary. There are numerous constraints on what principles we may choose, and these constraints provide grounds for hoping that reasonable people will be able to reach agreement. All people have the same basic needs – food, warmth, friendship, protection from

20

danger, meaningful work, to name only a few. We all suffer pain and we are all susceptible to disease. All of us are products of the same evolutionary forces, which have made us at least partially altruistic beings. And we are social animals who live in communities, so we must accept the rules that are necessary for social living. Together, these facts, and others like them, impose striking limits on what sort of principles it is rational for us to accept.

Second, it may be true, as MacIntyre says, that the standards of rational thinking differ from one historical tradition to another. But this does not mean that traditions are immune from criticism. Some moral traditions depend on theological assumptions that are inconsistent or arbitrary. Others make assumptions about the nature of the world that are at odds with what we have learned from modern science. Still others are based on untenable views about human nature. Thus there is no need to assume that all traditions are equal. At the very least, those that do not depend on what Hume called 'superstition and false religion' are preferable to those that do.

Bearing these points in mind, we might be a little more optimistic about what reason can accomplish. We might hope to discover ethical arguments that appeal to rational people generally and not just to some subset of people who have agreeable sentiments or form part of an agreeable tradition. But abstract considerations will take us only so far; the real proof that such arguments are possible is to display one. A test case might be slavery, which, as we have noted, is condemned by modern liberal culture but accepted within other traditions. Is there an argument against slavery that must be acknowledged by every reasonable person, regardless of the tradition of which he or she is a part?

The primary argument against slavery is this: all forms of slavery involve treating some people differently from the rest, depriving them of liberty and subjecting them to a host of evils. But it is unjust to set some people apart for different treatment unless there is something about them that justifies setting them apart – unless, that is, there is a *relevant difference* between them and the others. But there are no such differences between humans that could justify setting some of them apart as slaves; therefore slavery is unjust.

Should this argument be compelling, not only to modern liberals, but to those who live in different sorts of societies, with different sorts of traditions? Consider a slave society such as Aristotle's Athens. According to one estimate, there were as many slaves in Athens, in proportion to the population, as there were in the slave states of America before the civil war. Aristotle himself defended slavery, arguing that some people are 'slaves by nature' because of their inferior rationality. Yet the resources available within Aristotle's own tradition seem to have been sufficient for an appreciation of slavery's injustice. Aristotle reports that 'Some regard the control of a slave by a master as contrary to nature. In their view the distinction of master and slave is due to law or convention; there is no natural difference between them: the relation of master and slave is based on force, and being so based has no warrant in justice.'

Aristotle did not share this enlightened view. Plainly, though, he accepted the principle that differences in treatment are unjustified unless there are relevant differences between people. In fact, this is just a modern version of an idea that he advances in the *Nicomachean Ethics*, namely that like cases should be treated alike and different cases differently. That is why he felt it necessary to defend slavery by contending that slaves possess an inferior degree of rationality. But this is a claim that can be shown to be false by evidence that should be counted as evidence as much by him as by us. Therefore, even on Aristotle's own terms, slavery should be recognizable as unjust. And in saying this we are not simply transporting our standards of rationality back into a culture that was 'different'.

Perhaps, then, we may hope for an ethical theory that will specify norms acceptable to all reasonable people. Justifying such a theory, however, will not be easy. (But then, why should it be? Why should justifying a general theory in ethics be easier than justifying a general theory in, say, physics or psychology?) The process will include assessing our intuitions about particular cases; looking at a host of arguments about individual behaviour and social policy; identifying and evaluating mid-level principles; bringing to bear what we know about human nature and human social systems; considering the claims of religion; and then trying to fit it all together in one unified scheme of understanding. If there is indeed one best overall ethical theory, it is likely to appear as many lines of inquiry converge. The fact that there is still so much disagreement among ethical theorists may be due not to the impossibility of the project but to its complexity, and to the fact that secular ethical theory is still a young subject.

What does this mean for the question with which we started, about the relation between ethical theory and bioethics? We have seen that the physics/car-repair model won't do, because case studies cannot be conducted independently of theoretical concerns. We are now in a position to appreciate more fully why the simple-application model won't do either. It is not that ethical theory is useless, or that real life is too messy and complicated to be approached using its tools. Rather, it is that the simple-application model represents the relation between ethical theory and bioethics as a one-way affair. In reality, however, bioethics contributes to ethical theory as well as benefiting from it. In studying cases and identifying and analysing mid-level principles, bioethicists are pursuing one of the many lines of inquiry that contribute to the development of ethical theory. In this sense, bioethics is part of ethical theory. One flows into the other.

Considering all this, we might try a different analogy that provides a more satisfactory way of understanding the relation between ethical theory and bioethics.

The biology/medicine model. The relation between ethical theory and bioethics is like the relation between biology and medicine. A physician who knew nothing of biology, but who approached her patients in the spirit of a car mechanic with a kit-bag of practical techniques, might do a generally serviceable job. But she would not be as good as the physician who did know the relevant sciences. The difference would come out when new or tricky problems arose, requiring more than the rote application of already familiar techniques. To deal with the difficult problems. she might find herself turning to scientific researchers for help, or even turning temporarily to more fundamental research herself. And what she learns from the cases she encounters in her practice might, in turn, have significance for the further development of the sciences.

At its best, bioethics does not operate independently of ethical theory; but neither does it proceed by simply 'applying' a theory to particular cases. Instead there is an interplay between theory and case study that benefits both.

References

Aristotle (1946). *The Politics*, trans. Ernest Barker. London: Oxford University Press.
Briggs, David (1992). Baby Theresa case raises ethics questions. *Champaign-Urbana News Gazette*, 31 March, A6.
Halpern, Eliott and Jacobovici, Simcha (1966). Plague fighters. *Nova* (Public Broadcasting System), 6 February.
Hume, David (1751). *An Inquiry Concerning the Principles of Morals*, Appendix I.
MacIntyre, Alasdair (1988). *Whose Justice? Which Rationality?* Notre Dame, IN: University of Notre Dame Press.
Ross, W. D. (1930). *The Right and the Good*. Oxford: Oxford University Press.

Further Reading

Beauchamp, Tom L. and Childress, James F. (1994). *Principles of Biomedical Ethics*, 4th edn. New York: Oxford University Press.
Brody, Baruch A. (ed.) (1988). *Moral Theory and Moral Judgments in Medical Ethics*. Dordrecht: Kluwer.
Jonsen, Albert R. and Toulmin, Stephen (1988). *The Abuse of Casuistry: a history of moral reasoning*. Berkeley: University of California Press, 1988.
Various authors (1995). Theories and methods in bioethics: principalism and its critics. *Kennedy Institute of Ethics Journal*, 5 (September).

3

Bioethics and cultural diversity

SEGUN GBADEGESIN

Each people and each culture finds its own dignity within its own cultural identity. Moreover, cultural identities, if properly respected and understood, can offer new richness of thought to the whole human family. Therefore each culture and religion, with its own ethical perspectives, must be respected and appreciated. Our Western culture is not the best: most of the papers and books on Bioethics are still strongly ethnocentric and seem incapable of accepting the simple truth that we Western people are only one of the components of the complex system which is the human family. (Chiavacci, 1992: 99)

Bioethics Today: Present Realities

The present reality is that, for many people from non-Western cultures, bioethics is a Western phenomenon. This view is not limited to people from traditional cultures; some non-Western scholars are suspicious of the foundations and directions of bioethics. A recognition of the cultural specificity of bioethics is shared by some Western scholars, as the quotation from Enrico Chiavacci suggests. The shadow of cultural pluralism looms large on the horizon of any attempt to make ethics a product of reason alone, independent of culture. Merely acknowledging the 'inextricable linkage between culture and morality', as Pellegrino puts it, does not clear that shadow (Pellegrino, 1992). There remains the question of how we are to deal with it. Must bioethics always be culturally specific? Or can it in some way escape the bounds of culture and be universal in a way that makes it acceptable to all reasoning beings?

I once wrote an article on 'The Ethics of Polygyny' in which I argued that the principles of respect for persons, fairness and consideration for the interests of those affected should be applied to judging the morality of the practice in its various manifestations, and I cautioned against an absolute justification or condemnation of the practice. To my surprise, one of the anonymous readers of the paper for a specialized journal to which I had sent it disagreed with my basic framework, on the ground that I was applying a Western philosophical paradigm to assess a non-Western practice. In other words, I was charged with the crime of imposing a Western moral view on an African cultural practice. Naturally, as an African myself I am sensitive to this kind of allegation. In the published version of the paper, I argued that the principles of respect for persons, fairness and interest rely on a Western framework and the question is whether such a framework is in fact adequate for evaluating the institutions and practices of other cultures (Gbadegesin, 1993). Or is it, on the other hand, right to claim that African institutions ought to be evaluated by African moral standards, and only by those standards?

Much as I sympathize with this latter point of view, it is very easy to assume that principles appealed to in Western ethics do not feature at all in traditional African moral discourse. But this would be exaggerating cultural differences. Traditional Africans – men and women – may implicitly appeal, on appropriate occasions, to these principles as well. In this essay I will use the culture of Africa – and more specifically that of the Yoruba people of south-western Nigeria and Benin – as an example of a non-Western culture, simply because it is the one I know best. It is, of course, impossible to generalize from one non-Western culture to all others. The non-Western world has as many differences within its own members as it has between itself and the West. Nevertheless, the traditonal culture of the Yoruba can serve as an illustration of the issues with which we are confronted when we try to grapple with issues in bioethics against the background of a traditional culture.

The communal structure of traditional African society does not guarantee completely harmonious relationships. People occasionally fight. Elders are called upon to resolve disputes, either between husband and wife or between co-wives or between brothers. On such occasions, the elders listen carefully to all sides of the dispute and then, thoughtfully, they point out the faults on the part of each of the parties to the dispute by appealing to the appropriate moral standards. They say, for instance: 'My son, what you have done is wrong because you treat your wife badly. Don't you realize that she has feelings? What do you think her family will think of us?' In other words, the elders appeal to considerations that give meaning to the principles of interest, fairness and respect for others. It would therefore be wrong to suggest that these principles are exclusively Western. True, they are formulated by Western philosophers in their philosophical discourse, but they are also universally recognized principles applicable to interpersonal relationships. We should neither exaggerate nor deny the differences that exist between cultures.

The problem we face with regard to contemporary bioethics does not appear to be insurmountable. There is, as already noted, the perception that bioethics is dominated by the West and by the Western ethos of liberal individualism. This perception applies both to the values that make up the ethos of Western liberalism and to the focus of research in bioethics in the West. So far as this issue of focus is concerned, there seems to be a conflict between what is of concern to the West and its technological breakthroughs, and what is of interest to non-Western cultures. There is a need to resolve these apparent conflicts. The challenge of transcultural bioethics is to underscore the universality of bioethics without undermining the significance of distinct cultural identities.

The Universality of Bioethics

Every culture, even the most traditional one, *must* develop a response to the new technologies in health-care systems. This response may be a rejection or an acceptance of these technologies with their consequences (Pellegrino, 1992). This rejection or acceptance may be based on traditional norms or on a modification of those norms in the face of the requirements of the new technologies. So we have here a sense in which it is true to say that bioethics is universal: it requires, from every culture, a response to new technologies. The technology may be as simple as the existence of a vaccine against smallpox or as complex as that of organ transplantation. What choice to make in such contexts becomes a moral issue since human interests are at stake. Therefore issues raised in bioethics are universal issues. The problem is that while the *problem* is, in this sense, universal, the universality of the *answers* may be challenged.

At the level of principle there are challenges to the universal validity of the principles of autonomy, individualism and secularism. It is not that the concept of autonomy is totally alien to non-Western cultures; only that while the West emphasizes individual autonomy, the non-Western value-system is more likely to value cultural, communal or family autonomy. Thus from Japan to Nigeria, the decision as to the choice of medical procedure is not left to the individual. Instead, depending on the culture, it may be made by the family, the community elders or perhaps by the doctor. On the other hand, non-Western cultures may hold principles that seem alien to the Western view. A patient who objects to the amputation of both legs on the ground that it is better to die than to live without legs may be operating on the principle that 'death is better than loss of dignity'. This makes sense to people living in a culture that has traditionally accepted such an idea.

At the level of practice, there are challenges to the Western focus on high-profile biomedical technology which seems to be the driving force of bioethics in the West. These may be of little theoretical or practical interest to traditional cultures. The lack of resources for new technology limits the theoretical interests of these cultures. Some traditional cultures are pressed by the prevalence of poverty-generated diseases and the shortage of health-care facilities. Therefore issues of social justice in the allocation of resources, and a focus on primary health care and preventative medicine, seem more important than consideration of the ethics of life-support systems or organ transplantation.

The Challenge of Transcultural Bioethics

A transcultural bioethics would be a bioethics that is not specific to any single culture, but forms an arena of discussion in which people from diverse cultures can all take part on an equal footing. The rationale for transcultural bioethics, so defined, seems clear: bioethical issues transcend any single culture. The mapping of the human genome is a paradigm example of a project that has significance beyond any single culture. The tendency of multinational drug companies to do their testing in a variety of different countries also demonstrates that bioethical issues cannot be contained within national boundaries. But as we have already noted above, the same is also true of any new technology or procedure that can or will be taken up around the world. Intercultural understanding is essential for resolving bioethical issues. Transcultural bioethics facilitates intercultural understanding. Therefore transcultural bioethics may also facilitate the resolution of bioethical issues. The question remains, though, of what the conditions for the possibility of transcultural bioethics are, and how, if at all, transcultural bioethics would be different from bioethics today.

I have suggested that bioethical issues and questions cut across cultures, though the answers may vary from culture to culture. The challenge to the development of transcultural bioethics would seem to be posed at these various levels. Can we meet the challenge?

Practice

I start with the easiest: the level of the practice of bioethics itself. Transcultural bioethics should aim at refocusing research by bioethicists all over the world less exclusively on those topics that are primarily of concern to the Western world and towards those issues that are relevant to the most pressing needs in their own cultures. Bioethics can, through its international associations, conferences and electronic discussion forums, serve to coordinate transcultural dialogue on these activities. True, in some countries the need for political stability, democratic institutions and economic advancement is too demanding to allow much attention to issues in bioethics. But justice in the allocation of resources to the health-care sector is equally demanding. If no one is able to investigate the present realities, we will not be informed and nothing will change. Therefore, at the level of practice, the prospect of transcultural dialogue is not a remote one. But it cannot be achieved by exporting the research interests of Western bioethicists to non-Western countries where other interests may be dictated by the realities they face. Such realities may also include the need to mediate in the conflict between the demands of biomedical technology and the beliefs and moral systems of cultures and religious traditions that have, perhaps, had very different ways of relating to people.

Beliefs and values

The most difficult challenge occurs at the level of fundamental ethical values. It is here that the conflict between Western, philosophically inspired ethics and culturally motivated moral intuitions and beliefs appears most clearly. Of course, this way of putting it already signifies a bias in favour of the former. After all, the idea of a culturally motivated intuition suggests that something is lacking, namely the blessing of philosophy. It is on this assumption that the most difficult problem arises: how do we draw on the various conflicting beliefs and values in such a way as to enhance the possibility of a transcultural dialogue? In other words, in the light of these conflicting beliefs and values, what are the conditions for the possibility of a transcultural bioethics? Three approaches to this question may be sketched:

1 Defend and retain 'Western' values and impose them on other cultures. This is the method of cultural imperialism and value absolutism.
2 Reject the universal validity of Western values and recognize a plurality of different culturally embedded values as the basis for a range of equally valid approaches to bioethics. Transcultural bioethics would then be seen as imply-

27

ing respect for cultural identities without the need for a common morality. This is the method of cultural pluralism and value relativism.

3   Examine. meta-culturally, Western and non-Western values (and the princi-ples, rules and practices based on them), looking out for common foundational values which transcend cultures and which could be used to formulate common bioethical principles. This is the method of transculturalism and value reciprocity.

Cultural Imperialism and Value Absolutism

The presentation of Western values, for example, the right to individual freedom and autonomy, as universal values has been historically described as cultural imperialism by some people from non-Western cultures. There is a warrant for this reaction, especially when one recalls the arrogance of colonial administrators and the concept of 'the white man's burden' which they championed. Therefore it is obvious that taking Western values − or the values of any single culture − as absolute cannot be an adequate foundation for transcultural ethics. The suspi-cion of non-Western cultures about bioethics today is, at least in part, a natural reaction based on historical experience. The fact that value bigotry usually accom-panies value absolutism does not help matters either. Therefore transcultural bioethics must seek a more solid foundation than can be provided by cultural imperialism.

This is not to suggest that Western values are necessarily indefensible or inad-equate. The point is that for Western values to ground principles that are universal, their adequacy cannot be based on their cultural specificity or superiority. This is, incidentally, not just a question of Western versus non-Western cultures. Within the Western divide of the cultural landscape, there are varieties of cultural differences. Thus the African-American and Native-American cultures in North American differ significantly from the Euro-American majority culture.

Cultural Pluralism and Value Relativism

The following dialogue between a person who considers himself to be a pluralist, and another who takes a more universalist stance, may help to indicate some of the problems in extreme positions:

Pluralist: Bioethics is a Western phenomenon. As a discipline. it has its origin in the West. It concerns itself with Western issues in medicine and biomed-ical research. It appeals to the Western moral paradigm and to the use of reason as the only means of resolving such issues.

Universalist: Bioethics is a universal phenomenon. It has been brought alive by new developments in medicine and biomedical research which are not confined to Western societies. It deals with these issues from a philosophical perspective, which is the perspective of reason. The only alternative would be to take the perspective of a specific culture, but if that choice is to be justified, then it can only be justified by reason.

Pluralist: I agree that bioethics could be universal, but I do not believe that it is now. For in order to be universal, it has to: (i) deal with or show interest in issues relevant to non-Western cultures; and (ii) accept non-Western moral paradigms as morally valid.

Universalist: I understand your charge in (i): not all issues raised by biomedical research are of particular interest to all societies whose priorities may be somewhere else. The ethics of organ transplantation may not be of interest to a society in which it is not technologically feasible. But the charge in (ii) is difficult to understand, and it seems to me to be at the core of your complaint. For the challenge to accept non-Western moral standards as morally valid could mean (a) accepting them as morally valid after they have been rationally scrutinized or (b) accepting them even when they are known by a Westerner to be wrong. But you know that reason must be the arbiter in this matter, and reason has no cultural bias.

Pluralist: You appeal to reason as if it is so simple. But judgement of rationality is not a straightforward matter. Consider the following cases:

(a) A woman refused surgery for the treatment of her breast cancer because it would leave her without a breast.

(b) A man committed suicide because a bad automobile accident left him paralysed from the waist down.

(c) The daughter of a 90-year-old woman would not give consent to surgery for her mother because she is old enough to die peacefully in her own home.

(d) The relatives of an aged dying woman, concerned about her incoherent utterances bordering on 'confessions' about past 'wickedness', decided to put her to final rest on their own.

There is a standard here, in each of these cases, which can be understood by an average Yoruba person. It is captured in the Yoruba concept of *ikuyajesin*, which can be understood as the view that death is preferable to ridicule or loss of dignity. Is this understandable in the same way as a valid standard by the universalist? Or will it be subjected to 'rational' critique beyond the concept of *ikuyajesin*?

Universalist: Your position is at the opposite pole to cultural imperialism, but no more satisfactory. Your position appears to be non-controversial: there is a plurality of culture groups, and each of them deserves respect. Indeed, the values derived from these cultures are legitimate objects of respect. But our recognition of the plurality of cultures and their values should not be taken to entail value relativism. It does not imply that there can be no objective basis for cross-cultural judgements of values. Indeed, your position is in real danger of incoherence. You call for cross-cultural tolerance; but what basis can you have for this? Is cross-cultural tolerance a value that all cultures already affirm? I doubt it; but unless it is, then on your own showing, cross-cultural tolerance can have no universal basis.

Although the universalist gets the better of this argument, it is important not to throw away the baby of cultural pluralism with the bathwater of value relativism. The point of the cultural pluralist is that it is important to respect and to try to understand differences with regard to ways of life and belief systems; and to avoid jumping too quickly into a judgement of irrationality. There is hardly a cultural belief or practice that has no rational basis as far as the group is concerned. There is always a standard, as in the above cases: *ikuyajesin* – death is preferable to ridicule or loss of dignity. The cultural pluralist's position is that this principle may not be appreciated by the Western universalist; and if not, the latter will find the decision in all the cases puzzling if not irrational. Yet the decision derives from a culturally embedded understanding of what is considered important and fundamental to personhood in the Yoruba community. The point of the pluralist's objection is that 'you cannot understand if you don't belong.'

It is still important, however, to separate cultural from ethical relativism. Though the latter appears to ride on the back of the former, we may affirm cultural relativism while we reject ethical relativism. The fact of cultural differences and the importance of understanding them and bearing them in mind in our judgements of rationality and morality is the emphasis of cultural relativism. The thesis of *ethical* relativism goes beyond this, for the ethical relativist moves from the observation that there are cultural differences to the inference that there can be no valid cross-cultural standards for evaluating conduct. It seems to me that the position of the cultural relativist is compatible with the view that while we may, in the end, judge a particular standard as inadequate, we need to understand and appreciate the viewpoint of the particular standard fully before we do so.

Transculturalism and the Idea of Shared Values

An adequate response to the challenge of transcultural bioethics should reject both the arrogance of cultural imperialism which takes as absolute the dominant values of the West, and the scepticism of ethical relativism which puts the parochial moral values of ethnic and cultural groups as beyond challenge. On the positive side of the response, emphasis must be placed on:

1 serious effort to understand the cultures and values of other peoples;
2 development of a compendium of values and belief systems across cultures;
3 promotion of intercultural dialogue on the critical analysis of those values and belief systems;
4 identification of a set of common core values that transcend particular cultures; and
5 utilization of this set of common values in the development of bioethical principles and standards.

What appears to be the main obstacle to transcultural bioethics is the suspicion that, in its present form, it projects only the dominant values of the West: autonomy, individualism, secularism and privacy. There may, in fact, be no warrant for this charge. However, the fact that bioethics developed in the West in response to the impact of developments in biomedical technology on health-care delivery seems to lend credence to the suspicion. What is needed is a transcultural dialogue on the values that must inform the project of bioethics in a world that is becoming smaller day by day. If such a dialogue can bring out the commonality of shared values and reconcile the apparent differences in outlook, then it may bring the world of bioethics closer than we care to imagine.

References

Chiavacci, Enrico (1992). From medical deontology to bioethics: the problem of social consensus of basis issue within Western culture and beyond it in the human family. In Edmund Pellegrino (ed.), *Transcultural Dimensions in Medical Ethics.* Frederick, MD: University Publishing Group, 99.

Gbadegesin, Segun (1993). The ethics of polygyny. *Quest: Philosophical Discussions,* 7/2, 3–29.

Pellegrino, Edmund (1992). Intersections of Western biomedical ethics and world culture: problematic and possibility. *Cambridge Quarterly Journal of Healthcare Ethics,* 3, 191–6.

Further Reading

Callahan, D. and Campbell, C. S. (1990). Theology, religious traditions and bioethics. *Hastings Center Report,* 20/4, Suppl. 1.

Engeldhardt, H. Tristam (1989). The emergence of a secular bioethics. In Tom L. Beauchamp and LeRoy Walters, *Contemporary Issues in Bioethics.* New York: Wadsworth, 68–9.

——(1991). *Bioethics and Secular Humanism: The search for a common morality.* Philadelphia: Trinity Press International.

Flack, H. (1992). The confluence of culture and bioethics. In *African American Perspectives on Biomedical Ethics,* ed. H. Flack and E. Pellegrino. Washington, DC: Georgetown University Press, xi–xx.

Hoffmaster, B. (1992). Can ethnography save the life of medical ethics? *Social Science and Medicine,* 35, 1421–31.

Ingstad, Benedicte, and Whyte, Susan R. (1995). *Disability and Culture.* Berkeley: University of California Press.

Leisinger, Klaus (1993). Bioethics here and in poor countries: a comment. *Cambridge Quarterly Journal of Healthcare Ethics,* 2, 5–8.

Marshall, Patricia, Thomasma, David, and Bergsma, Jurrit (1994). Intercultural reasoning: the challenge for international bioethics. *Cambridge Quarterly Journal of Healthcare Ethics,* 3, 321–8.

Meleis A. I. and Jonsen, A. R. (1983). Ethical crises and cultural differences. *Western Journal of Medicine,* 138, 889–93.

Murray, Robert F. (1992). Minority perspectives on biomedical ethics. In *Transcultural Dimensions in Medical Ethics,* ed. E. Pellegrino et al. Frederick, MD: University Publishing Group, 35–42.

Veatch, R. M. (1989). *Cross Cultural Perspectives in Medical Ethics: Readings.* Boston: Jones and Bartlett.

4

Gender and bioethics

JAN CROSTHWAITE

The professions and disciplines from which bioethics emerged – medicine, theology, philosophy and law – have long been male-dominated, male-focused and sometimes misogynist. Early bioethical writings, even when addressing issues of primary concern to women, like abortion, rarely considered women's views specifically or engaged with feminist thinking on these issues. They showed little awareness of the patriarchal character of institutions within which bioethical issues arose, or of the possible impact on bioethical issues of cultural assumptions about differences between women and men. Nor was the possibility of gender bias in ethical theorizing itself considered. That fundamental conceptions of human norms and the processes of ethical deliberation might reflect a particular gendered perspective went largely unremarked. Bioethical debate and the principles underlying it were assumed to be open to all rational minds and uncontaminated by such contingencies as gender.

While women have not been absent from bioethical discussions, it is relatively recently that women's voices have being heard as making a distinctive contribution. This largely reflects the increasing recognition of feminist thinking as an important contribution to critical reflection on intellectual traditions and social institutions. The contributions of women and feminists can be both disturbing and enriching: disturbing because they are often critical of health-care institutions and practices, and also of bioethics and its reflections on these; enriching (and essential) because they are disturbing and because they bring to debates the diverse but often distinctive experiences, interests and values of women.

Feminism and Gender

It is feminism which allows the significance of women's voices to be understood. Feminism is not a single viewpoint; feminist thinking is informed by different disciplinary backgrounds, different political frameworks, different race, class, cultural and individual experiences, and different understandings of feminism itself. (Tong, (1989), provides a helpful introduction to a variety of feminisms.) Indeed, a recurrent issue for feminists is whether there is anything which can be held to unify the different feminist voices without thereby disrespectfully diminishing their differences and effectively silencing some.

I think there is a unifying distinctive theme in feminism: the concern to understand and eliminate the oppression of women in all its guises. This underpins feminist concerns to document women's experiences, preferably in their own voices, and to provide theoretical analyses of these experiences, their origins and implications, as the basis for a critique of social institutions.

Feminist concern with the oppression of women provides the framework for understanding the significance of gender. 'Gender' refers to the social elaboration of a biological difference between male and female into two distinct kinds of people, men and women. Feminists have identified both the existence of gender differences and their particular construction in Western civilization as contributing to the oppression of women. Feminist writers in the 1970s distinguished sex, the biological differentiation of male and female, from gender, the social differentiation of masculine and feminine individuals in terms of roles, behaviour and psychological traits. More recent feminists have been critical of the conceptualization and use of any sex/gender distinction. They argue that it presents a false dichotomy, and that accounts of gender often privilege a particular cultural/historical perspective at the expense of recognizing the diversity of ways of understanding differences between men and women to be found across different times, cultures and classes. Emphasis on gender *simpliciter* also obscures the contribution of other factors (including race and class) to the life experiences, social relationships and sense of self of individual women and men.

How to accommodate the multifarious and cross-cutting differences between women (and between social groups in general) is a major issue in contemporary feminist thinking. Recognition of difference complicates feminist social analysis and feminist attempts to eliminate women's oppression, but it also promotes more sophisticated analysis and political theorizing.

Whatever the theoretical standing of the concept of gender, attention to differences between men and women (both assumed and actual) is important to understanding and ethically evaluating any social practice, including health care. It reveals unjust differences in distribution of or access to rights and goods, and it reveals the existence and operation of oppressive relationships and social structures. Attention to gender enriches bioethical understanding and evaluation. It encourages attention more generally to the operation of power relations in health-care institutions and practices, and to the impact of health-related issues on the oppression of social groups. It forces bioethicists to attend more to the political and social contexts of both bioethical issues and the practice of bioethics itself.

Gender and Health Care

Feminists have drawn attention to gender inequality and discrimination within health-care professions, and have pointed out the gendered division of labour and status in health-care institutions (Miles, 1991, chapter 5). Activities of 'care' are women's work, while 'curing' (and the scientific expertise which backs it) is men's province and more valued. This reflects traditional Western stereotypes of femininity and masculinity. It also reinforces a distorted conception (characteristically expressed in war metaphors) of health care as the (masculine) conquest of disease through technological wizardry and the valiant battles of physicians and surgeons against invading organisms and unruly organs.

Feminists have also documented the exploitation and abuse of women patients, from unnecessary hysterectomies to genital reconstructions performed without women's knowledge (Scully, 1980). Even within the practice of beneficent medicine, there are disturbing ethical failures in the treatment of women. Research suggests that women may receive a lesser quality of health care than men with similar conditions (Muller, 1990). But women's most frequent complaints concern failures of respect: not being taken seriously as authorities on their own experience and preferences; not being properly informed about their condition and treatment options; and generally not being accorded the rights of competent adults to decide about their own health care. Gender stereotypes and behaviour patterns foster these failures and reinforce the inequalities inherent in physician–patient encounters (Todd, 1989). Yet while bioethics has been centrally concerned with issues of patient autonomy and power imbalances between health professionals and their clients, it has had little to say about the impact of gender on these issues.

The protection of research subjects is also a major concern of bioethics, but it is feminists who have primarily drawn attention to unethical experimentation on women, including the therapeutic use of drugs which have not been adequately tested for effects on women. Women have been under-represented in and excluded from studies concerning illnesses which affect them as well as men (Bird, 1994). Sometimes gender differences are explicitly used as a reason for excluding women, because incorporating such factors as women's hormonal cycles and the possibility of pregnancy complicates research and adds to its cost. Therapies and illnesses may affect women differently from men, and their exclusion or under-representation in research is medically, scientifically and ethically problematic.

Feminists have attributed much gender bias in health care and research to the assumption that women's health issues are primarily reproductive, a reflection of a long tradition of identifying women with their reproductive biology. They have discerned also the effects of Western culture's identification of human norms with men and men's experience and values (usually men of a particular race and class). Even in those areas where women's physiology and experience are unique, their reproductive biology, traces of an assumption that women are deviations from the human (i.e., male) norm can be found. Women's normal functioning is seen as medically problematic; menopause becomes an 'oestrogen deficiency disease'. Prophylactic removal of healthy but supposedly 'useless' reproductive organs from older women also suggests a narrowly reproductive focus on women's bodies and lives, particularly when not accompanied by any consideration of other possible functions (e.g., in sexual response) of such organs. Feminists have also argued that research into some diseases in women, such as HIV/AIDS, has been more concerned with the implications of women's illness for men and babies than for women themselves (Faden, Kass and McGraw, 1996). Such attitudes can be seen as reflecting and reinforcing oppressive views of women as fundamentally bearers of men's children.

34

Feminists have long criticized medicine as an agent of the social control of women. In areas which significantly affect women's reproductive lives, predominantly male medical professionals control information and access to technologies, and dominate individual and social decision-making. In these areas, and in mental health, medicine has sustained women's oppression through control of their bodies and behaviour, and through its articulation and enforcement of gender roles and characteristics. Gynaecological surgery of various kinds has been used to 'cure' behaviour deemed inappropriate for women. Psychiatry and access to reproductive technology (both conceptive and contraceptive) have been used to enforce socially acceptable (hetero)sexual and maternal behaviour and roles (Miles, 1991; Scully, 1994).

Such analyses are of course disputed. The motivations of health-care professionals for the therapies they offer or the research they undertake rarely include deliberate harm to or exploitation of women. Hence accusations of oppression can be shocking and painful. Moreover, differential treatment of women and men may be justified in terms of the sex-differentiated distribution and implications of diseases (as Mertz and others, 1996, argue in response to feminist accusations of bias in AIDS research), and treatments such as hysterectomy or hormone replacement may be proper and desirable in individual cases. However, feminist analysis is concerned less with conscious motivations than with discerning underlying assumptions, and patterns of thinking and practices, of which people may be quite unaware. Feminists draw attention to the systemic effects of what may be individually well-motivated actions. Nor do all feminists agree about analyses, implications or acceptability of particular health-care practices or policies.

Feminist criticism of health-care professions, practices and policies provides important data for bioethical reflection. The defence of actions and practices against such criticism is therapeutic in that it requires that feminist concerns be explicitly addressed and the possibility of gender as a category of analysis be considered. Relations of dominance between social groups are ethical concerns and should be part of bioethical deliberation. Feminist analyses provide distinctive ways of understanding and evaluating social practices and institutions, including those concerned with health care, and feminist debates stimulate reflection on issues which might otherwise go unstudied. (See also Parts IV (Before Birth) and V (Issues in Reproduction).)

Gender and Ethics

As recent work in feminist bioethics makes clear (e.g., Sherwin, 1992; Wolf, 1996), the importance for bioethics of feminist attention to gender goes beyond the critique of specific health-care practices and institutions. It also prompts reflection on the possibility of gender biases in the theoretical frameworks of bioethics, particularly in conceptions of the nature of moral agents and moral deliberation.

Feminist approaches to ethics and consequently to bioethics are varied. Though sometimes mistakenly identified with feminine ethics of care, they reflect a range of theoretical positions. What they share is the fundamental feminist concern with understanding and eliminating women's oppression, and with ensuring proper attention is paid to women's experiences and interests. These concerns underpin feminist critiques of ethical (and bioethical) theorizing. But feminist ethics move beyond critique to articulating alternative theories and approaches to moral deliberation. (See also Part III (Ethical Approaches), particularly chapter 11 (A Care Approach).)

Such theories often incorporate elements of the ethic of care described by Carol Gilligan, who claimed to hear a distinctive 'ethic of care or responsibility' in women's moral deliberations (Gilligan, 1982). It is characterized by an emphasis on maintaining connection and relationships, on care for others (and self) and on avoiding harm. Care thinkers focus on the particular features and contextual location of moral problems, rather than attempting to abstract features which would allow these to be subsumed under general rules or principles. They seek to resolve problems through communication, appealing to shared understanding of relationships and needs, and prefer the creative exploration of options that might dissipate conflicts to the consistency of universal rules.

Gilligan contrasted this 'moral orientation' with the 'ethic of justice' she saw as dominant in contemporary moral discourse. She argued that the voices of care and justice are gender-inflected, though neither uniquely nor universally found in women and men respectively. An ethic of justice emphasizes values of fairness and equal respect for individuals (particularly their rights to self-determination). It focuses on the impartial adjudication of conflicting claims or obligations through an appeal to rationally derived and universally applicable principles. While this does not adequately reflect the range or subtlety of Western ethical theorizing, it does capture certain dominant themes, which emerge strongly in bioethical debates.

Both the content of an ethic of care and its presentation as an alternative to dominant moral theorizing throw into question the claims of traditional ethical theories to present universal, impartial and gender-neutral moral thinking. This, together with its resonance with many women's experience and values, makes care ethics of particular interest to feminists. But care's characterization as a feminine ethic is problematic, given feminist concern with gender and oppression. A feminine morality embedded in nurture, close personal attachments and emotional response to others, recalls demeaning characterizations of women as morally inadequate. Ideas of women as emotional, lacking a sense of justice and incapable of objective and impartial rationality, have been used in Western culture to justify their exclusion from public life and their subordination to men. Feminists are also justifiably cautious about any ethic generated within a situation of subordination. The inclusion of women's moral thinking in a feminist ethic must be moderated by critical awareness of gender and of the location of women's experiences and values within (usually patriarchal) social structures and contexts.

Many feminists wish to transcend a justice–care dichotomy. They endorse certain aspects of feminine ethics of care, but also appeal to justice values to ground their critique of oppression. Indeed, feminist analyses of oppression suggest reconceptualizing and extending our understanding of justice beyond the dominant focus on distributive justice (Young, 1990). Care-oriented values also support feminist advocacy of individual empowerment as a means to counteracting unequal and oppressive relationships.

Like care ethics, feminist ethics emphasize the importance of attention to context, particularly social context, and to the unique properties of specific individuals and moral problems. They also argue that human relationships, emotional responses, and individuals' understandings of themselves and their situations are essential components of moral reflection and should not be seen as antithetical to it (Sherwin, 1992). Such emphases favour a different account of the nature of moral deliberation and of human beings as moral agents from those dominant in Western ethical and political thinking.

Moral Persons and Moral Deliberation

Susan Wolf attributes part of bioethics' failure to engage with feminism to its 'early embrace of a liberal individualism largely inattentive to social context' and 'its emphasis on deduction from ethical principles rather than induction from concrete cases' (1996: 5). Liberal individualism gives priority to respect for individual self-determination or autonomy. It sees fairness and equality of treatment as requiring the impartial application of universal principles which abstract essential commonalities from the messy specificities of real individuals. This yields a notion of abstract individuals as fundamentally autonomous agents, aware of their own preferences and values, and motivated by rational self-interest (though not necessarily selfish). Their connections to one another are primarily through voluntary contractual relationships mediated by reason-determined codes of rights and obligations. The imposition of any particular conception of what is good or valuable is a failure of respect for the essentially self-determining nature of such individuals. Such a conception has difficulty in recognizing the complex relationships between individuals and social groups, except as these emerge in individual preferences.

Against such abstract ciphers, many feminists present a richer conception of persons as historically and culturally located, socially related and essentially embodied (for example, Diprose, 1994). Individuals are located in and formed by specific relationships (chosen and unchosen) and ties of affection and responsibility. Their preferences and possibilities are affected by membership of social groups with specific concrete and symbolic properties. Such a conception of socially embedded selves refocuses thinking about autonomy, shifting the emphasis from independent self-determination towards ideals of integrity within relatedness. It demands an approach to moral deliberation which does not require detachment from others, nor the idea of a self-transparent 'self'. Respecting autonomy becomes less a matter of protecting individuals from 'coercive' influences than one of positive empowerment, recognizing people's interdependence and supporting individuals' development of their own understanding of their situation and options.

Attention to social groups also shifts ethical emphasis on individual judgement more towards ideals of communicative and collaborative decision-making. The understanding and judgements of concrete individuals are particular rather than universal, and are constrained by personal situation and experience. Many feminists reject the possibility of an unsituated epistemological or moral perspective, arguing that knowledge and morality are products of social negotiation. Current debates in feminist epistemology and feminist ethics address the possibility of recognizing and valuing diverse perspectives without embracing a relativism that would limit the possibility of shared social life and moral standards and undercut the ground from which to condemn oppression.

Against the ideal of objective and impartial moral rationality, many feminists emphasize an engaged moral response. Moral perception and response involve some form of empathic engagement with specific others, rather than detached application of abstract principles. This, together with recognition of the moral significance of emotions and affective relationships, calls into question ideals of impartiality in ethics. While there are clearly contexts in which it is wrong to favour particular others, certain professional and personal relationships may permit or even morally require such preferential treatment. Health professionals are increasingly feeling the tension between obligations to their own patients and the impartiality required of custodians of scarce public resources.

Distinguishing proper responsiveness to the needs of particular others from distorting bias (and harmful self-sacrifice) requires a carefully nuanced understanding of the nature and demands of the variety of interconnected human relationships – personal, professional and political – and a sense of how these fit into a wider social framework. Feminist thinking, with its concern to understand oppression and the many faces of power, both personal and institutional, helps provide such a perspective.

Bioethical Self-reflection

As a discipline with responsibilities for the ethical evaluation of major social institutions, bioethics must be prepared to engage in critical reflection on its own social position, assumptions and practices. Its dominant theoretical frameworks, including the 'four principles', have come under critical scrutiny recently, from inside and outside (Gudorf, 1994). The resultant self-examination is necessary and beneficial, though its outcome is far from clear. But it is clear that the process could benefit from exploring some of the directions and implications of feminist approaches to ethics (and to epistemology).

All professions tend to reflect socially dominant perspectives and values, yet bioethics often needs to represent the interests of those who will be affected by health-care policies and practices, particularly socially disadvantaged groups. The professional context of bioethics makes it difficult for marginalized groups to speak for themselves. Bioethical deliberations are frequently debates between 'experts', carried out in committees, professional or academic institutions and journals. The ethical (and epistemological) problems of speaking for others are obvious and need to be consciously addressed.

Bioethics in the 1990s is increasingly aware of the need to include the perspectives and experiences of marginalized social groups, and frequently includes feminist commentaries in its discussion of issues. However, merely presenting such perspectives is not yet integrating them into the framework of bioethics, and work remains to be done on providing the theoretical structures which can move from multiple, sometimes conflicting, perspectives to defensible resolutions of moral issues.

Given the obvious overlap in interests and possibilities of fruitful interaction, it is surprising that bioethics has not engaged more with feminist thinking. Doing so stretches the focus of bioethics beyond familiar horizons, adding new dimensions to familiar debates and making visible issues previously overlooked. Most important, such engagement offers new conceptual frameworks and fosters a self-critical bioethics, attentive to its relationship to contested social institutions and practices – a large reward for a little attention to gender.

References

Bird, C. E. (1994). Women's representation as subjects in clinical studies: a pilot study of research published in *JAMA* in 1990 and 1992. In A. Mastroianni, R. Faden, and D. Federman (eds). *Women and Health Research: Ethical and legal issues of including women in clinical studies*. Vol. 2. *Workshop and commissioned papers*. Washington, DC: National Academy Press, 157–73.

Diprose, R. (1994). *The Bodies of Women: ethics, embodiment and sexual difference*. London and New York: Routledge.

Faden, R., Kass, N. and McGraw, D. (1996). Women as vessels and vectors: lessons from the HIV epidemic. In S. M. Wolf (ed.), *Feminism and Bioethics: Beyond reproduction*. New York and Oxford: Oxford University Press, 252–81.

Gilligan, C. (1982). *In a Different Voice: psychological theory and women's development*. Cambridge, MA: Harvard University Press.

Gudorf, C. E. (1994). A feminist critique of biomedical principlism. In E. R. DuBose, R. P. Hamel and L. J. O'Connell (eds), *A Matter of Principles? Ferment in U.S. bioethics*. Valley Forge, PA: Trinity Press International, 164–81.

Mertz, D., Sushinsky, M. A. and Schüklenk, U. (1996). Women and AIDS: the ethics of exaggerated harm. *Bioethics*, 10/2, 92–113.

Miles, A. (1991). *Women, Health and Medicine*. Milton Keynes and Philadelphia: Open University Press.

Muller, C. F. (1990). *Health Care and Gender*. New York: Russell Sage Foundation.

Scully, D. (1980). *Men who Control Women's Health: The miseducation of Obstetrician-Gynecologists*. New York and London: Teachers College Press, Teachers College, Columbia University.

Sherwin, S. (1992). *No Longer Patient: Feminist ethics and health care*. Philadelphia: Temple University Press.

Todd, A. D. (1989). *Intimate Adversaries: Cultural conflict between doctors and women patients*. Philadelphia: University of Pennsylvania Press.

Tong, R. (1989). *Feminist Thought: A comprehensive introduction*. Boulder, CO, and San Francisco: Westview Press.

Wolf, S. M. (ed.) (1996). *Feminism and Bioethics: Beyond reproduction*. New York and Oxford: Oxford University Press.

Young, I. M. (1990). *Justice and the Politics of Difference*. Princeton, NJ: Princeton University Press.

Further Reading

Alcoff, L. and Potter, E. (eds) (1993). *Feminist Epistemologies*. New York and London: Routledge.

Cole, E. B. and Coultrap-McQuin, S. (eds) (1992). *Explorations in Feminist Ethics: Theory and practice*. Bloomington and Indianapolis: Indiana University Press.

Cook, R. J. (1994). Feminism and the four principles. In R. Gillon and A. Lloyd (eds), *Principles of Health Care Ethics*. Chichester: John Wiley, 193–206.

Dally, A. (1991). *Women under the Knife: A history of surgery*. London: Hutchinson Radius, 1991.

DeBruin, D. (1994). Justice and the inclusion of women in clinical studies: a conceptual framework. In A. Mastroianni, R. Faden and D. Federman (eds), *Women and Health Research: Ethical and legal issues of including women in clinical studies*. Vol. 2. *Workshop and commissioned papers*. Washington, DC: National Academy Press, 127–50.

Doyal, L. (1995). *What Makes Women Sick? Gender and the political economy of health*. New Brunswick, NJ: Rutgers University Press.

Foster, P. (1995). *Women and the Health Care Industry: An unhealthy relationship?* Buckingham and Philadelphia: Open University Press.

Held, V. (ed.) (1995). *Justice and Care: Essential readings in feminist ethics*. Boulder, CO, and Oxford: Westview Press.

Holmes, H. B. and Purdy, L. M. (eds) (1992). *Feminist Perspectives in Medical Ethics*. Bloomington and Indianapolis: Indiana University Press. [A collection of articles from *Hypatia*, 1989, 4/2 and 4/3, special issues on feminist ethics and medicine, and ethics and reproduction.]

Jaggar, A. M. (1992). Feminist ethics. In L. Becker and C. Becker (eds), *Encyclopedia of Ethics*. New York and London: Garland, 361–70.

More, E. S. and Milligan, M. A. (eds) (1994). *The Empathic Practitioner: Empathy, gender and medicine*. New Brunswick, NJ: Rutgers University Press.

Russell, D. (1995). *Women, Madness, and Medicine*. Cambridge: Polity Press.

5

Religion and bioethics

BARUCH BRODY

Most contemporary bioethical discussions involve purely secular moral principles and modes of reasoning. This is true whether the discussions appeal to mid-level principles of bioethics (such as autonomy, beneficence or justice) or to more fundamental moral theories (such as utilitarian maximization of the good or Kantian respect for persons). This was not always true. Denominationally based bioethics (e.g., Roman Catholic, Jewish) was far more prevalent in earlier periods, and many of the founders of contemporary bioethics (e.g., Joseph Fletcher, Paul Ramsey, Richard McCormick) were theologians who did not see their work in bioethics as involving purely secular moral thinking. A full account of how this change occurred, and an evaluation of it, is beyond the scope of this essay; suffice it to say that both the general secularization of contemporary pluralistic societies and the increasing influence in bioethics of secular disciplines such as medicine, law, analytical philosophy and policy analysis played significant roles in producing these secular bioethical discussions.

This essay will focus on three questions concerning possible roles for religious themes in contemporary bioethics:

1   Are there important modes of reasoning that are prominent in religious bioethical thought and that lead to conclusions different from those reached by contemporary secular bioethical reasoning?
2   Does the invocation of more general concepts that are prominent in religious moral reflection both reinforce and modify the conclusions reached by the secular modes of reasoning which are commonly employed in bioethics?
3   If there are these distinctions between religious and secular bioethical reasoning, how should secular pluralistic communities deal with value conflicts resulting from some accepting and others rejecting religious themes in bioethical reflection.

Because of the limited space available, our discussion of these issues will be illustrative rather than comprehensive.

Rule-based Constraints in Religious Bioethical Thought

Religious ethical discussion is often conducted by reference to moral rules which prohibit or mandate the performance of certain types of actions. They serve as

41

constraints on the actions that may or may not be performed. These may be absolute constraints (to be followed, regardless of what else is at stake) or relative constraints (to be followed, unless other more crucial considerations take precedence). They may be based on such diverse sources as a general divine revelation, the reflections of the religious leadership or of the membership of a religious community or God's response to the prayers of the individual. Whatever their source or their strength, they are seen as at least sometimes taking precedence over more secular mid-level principles or general theories and at least sometimes leading to different practical conclusions.

One example is the prohibition against the innocent being killed even if they agree to being killed or even if they are killing themselves. Secular discussions of assisted suicide and active voluntary euthanasia often conclude that such actions are morally permissible because they respect the autonomous choices of the parties being killed and because they benefit the parties being killed (at least as the consequences are evaluated by those parties). Opponents on secular grounds often wind up appealing to policy concerns about possible abuses or the possible worsening of important relations (e.g., the patient–physician relation) rather than to ethical concerns about the morality of the actions themselves. Those who adopt on religious grounds the prohibition against the innocent being killed as a rule-based constraint are in a different position; from their perspective, assisted suicide and voluntary euthanasia are wrong because of their intrinsic nature.

Several observations about this first example are in place: it is certainly possible to adopt this rule-based constraint as part of a secular moral theory; in fact, however, it is primarily invoked in a number of religious traditions. Second, the rule in question only prohibits killing; it does not mandate doing everything possible to keep people alive. In this way, adherents of respecting this constraint are not committed to any position on the sanctity of life. To avoid that position, however, they are committed to the possibility of drawing a morally meaningful distinction between killing and letting die. Third, as rule-based constraints need not be absolute constraints, adherents of respecting this constraint may allow for morally legitimate assisted suicide or active euthanasia in the most extreme cases.

A second example is the prohibition against separating procreative potential and conjugal intimacy in individual sexual acts. Respecting this rule-based constraint is the basis for the opposition in some religious communities to artificial contraception (conjugal intimacy without procreative potential) and to *in vitro* fertilization (procreative potential without conjugal intimacy). It is otherwise hard to define any basis for opposition to these acts, which augment the possibilities for autonomous choice and which benefit the parties involved (at least as they evaluate the consequences), although some have offered a feminist critique of aspects of *in vitro* fertilization.

Several observations need to be made about this second example. This rule-based constraint is supported almost exclusively by the teachings of the Roman Catholic Church. Our first example is supported by many religious communities. Second, a closely related rule-based constraint accepted in other communities (e.g., the Eastern Orthodox Church) is a prohibition against the separation of those two elements over the entirety of a relationship, rather than over an individual act. Such a modification prohibits the choice of childlessness during an entire relationship, while allowing contraception to be used in particular sexual acts. Similarly, it allows *in vitro* fertilization using gametes from the couple, while prohibiting the use of donor gametes.

A wide variety of these rule-based constraints is advocated in different religious traditions. Some deal with issues relating to the beginning of life, such as assisted reproduction, contraception, sterilization, abortion and the use of fetuses in research or for tissue donation. Others relate to end-of-life issues such as active and passive euthanasia, the definition of death and autopsies and organ donations. Still others relate to medical care between life and death, and range from issues of physicians' deportment (e.g., how to treat patients of the opposite gender) to types of therapies (e.g., blood transfusions) that are unacceptable. As the discussion of these examples suggests, particular rule-based constraints are adopted by some religious communities and not by others. They serve therefore as the basis for Roman Catholic, Eastern Orthodox, Protestant, Jewish or Muslim bioethics, rather than as the basis for general religious bioethics. Finally, as some religious traditions accept more of these constraints than others, some will have more distinctive bioethics than others.

There are two general questions raised by these rule-based constraints for those who are not members of the particular religious traditions that advocate them. The first is the question of responding to them in a secular pluralistic society: in what ways, if any, should clinical practice or social policy be modified to respect those constraints? This question will be discussed below. The second is the question of their secular validity. Is there any reason, independent of the commitments of the tradition in question, for accepting these rule-based constraints? This question deserves at least some immediate attention, even if a full treatment of it lies beyond the scope of this essay.

Some of the religious traditions which invoke these rule-based constraints insist that at least some can be justified in purely secular terms. This is particularly true of those traditions which see at least some of these constraints as part of some universally binding natural law discoverable by human reason. A variety of secular justifications has been invoked to justify these constraints. *Rule utilitarian justifications* suggest that the acceptance and/or the following of these constraints is in the long run socially beneficial, even if better results might follow from violating them in particular cases. Thus it has been argued that physicians must not kill their patients, even if the patients request their physicians to do so to alleviate their unbearable suffering, because accepting and/or following the constraint against killing fosters socially vital respect for the value of human life. *Deductive justifications* see the constraints in question as direct implications of fundamental moral principles. Thus it has been argued that physicians must not kill their patients because doing so violates the fundamental moral principle of treating the existence of each human living being as a valued end, or because doing so violates the fundamental moral principle of respecting the natural desire for life. *Intuitive justifications* suggest that we directly intuit as self-evident truths that these constraints must be followed.

43

Thus it has been argued that the prohibition against killing is a self-evident truth requiring no further justification.

Each of these justifications faces problems. The general logic of rule utilitarian justifications is unclear. If we are concerned about consequences, why should we do what produces worse results in a given case just because generally doing so and/ or accepting a rule generally to do so produces better results? (See chapter 9, pp. 80–5.) The logic of deductive justifications is clearer, but they appeal to fundamental moral principles whose validity seems to be less certain than the validity of the constraints themselves. Intuitive justifications suffer from differences in people's intuitions, differences which become greater as the content of the intuitions becomes more specific and therefore more applicable. I am not claiming that secular justifications cannot be found for at least some of the often invoked rule-based constraints. What I am claiming is that the difficulties with the more common secular justifications explain why these constraints are most often invoked in religiously oriented bioethical thought.

Invoking Broader Religious Themes in Bioethics

Religious medical ethics often invokes broader themes from religious ethical thinking and applies them to problems in bioethics. The results are often consonant with results that are obtainable by secular moral reasoning. Even when this is so, the adherents of the religious tradition in question see their religious themes as deepening the justification of the conclusions in question. In fact, however, there are often subtle but real differences between the conclusions reached by the secular and the religious arguments. We will discuss two examples of this type of religious bioethical reasoning, the appeal to the principle of double effect and the appeal to the notion of covenantal fidelity.

Much religious moral thought assesses actions in terms of the intentions embedded in them rather than in terms of what is done or what results. As a result, the intention embedded in the action can substantially determine the moral licitness of the action. This has given rise in certain religious traditions to the principle of double effect. According to this principle, an action which has two effects, one licit and one illicit, can be morally permissible if the licit effect is the intended effect and the illicit effect is an unintended even if foreseen effect. Thus, for example, while it is morally illicit in warfare to bomb innocent non-combatants, it may be morally licit to bomb a munitions factory located in an area populated by civilians. This is because the intended effect is the licit bombing of the factory while the illicit bombing of the innocent non-combatants is a foreseen but unintended effect.

The use of this principle presupposes both a conceptual and a moral distinction between intended and merely foreseen effects. Whether those distinctions can be defended is a question that lies beyond the scope of this chapter. What we need to note is that this principle has important bioethical implications. One example is the support it offers for providing dying patients with adequate pain relief even if that compromises respiratory functioning and hastens the death of the patients. Secular moralists justify providing that relief because of its beneficial consequence of pain

44

relief or because it is what the patient wants. By contrast, religious moralists often use the principle of double effect to justify providing the pain relief on the grounds that the intended effect is the licit pain relief while the hastening of the death is at best foreseen but unintended. While broadly in agreement with the secular reasoning, the use of the principle of double effect may not support the provision of pain relief in those cases in which the hastening of the death is also intended as a means for eliminating further suffering; the secular reasoning, focusing on the consequences and on the wishes of the subject, may not be troubled by that fact.

Much religious moral thought draws upon theological conceptions to develop an ideal of human relations. One such ideal is covenantal fidelity. Much as God and his people have entered into a covenant of fidelity with each other, which mandates faithfulness to each other, so individuals entering into special relations with each other should feel bound by the mandates implied by the ideal of covenantal fidelity. The relation of spouses is often portrayed as subject to that ideal.

Religious bioethicists have applied this ideal to the patient–physician relation. This has led them to the conclusion that treating physicians must be faithful to the interests of their patients, disregarding (unless the patient agrees to their consideration) social interests in promoting research or in limiting health-care expenditure. Many secular bioethicists have also argued for this faithfulness to patient interests, invoking the many benefits of such relations and the respect for the patient implied by it. While broadly in agreement with much secular reasoning, the invocation of the ideal of fidelity may not concur in those cases in which social needs are very great. The secular arguments may support an exception to physicians' faithfulness to patient interests in such cases; the ideal of covenantal fidelity, modelled on God's faithfulness to His people, may not.

These are only two examples of the invocation of themes from general religious ethics to support, but also to modify, secular bioethical conclusions. Other themes that have been invoked in different settings include the stewardship of social resources, respect for the integrity of nature and compassion for all living creatures. Different religious traditions invoke different themes, thereby leading to more differences in the bioethics of different denominations. These differences, as well as the differences resulting from different rule-based constraints, must be dealt with by a pluralistic society.

Responding to Religious Themes in a Pluralistic World

Modern societies are comprised of individuals with a wide variety of differing religious beliefs, as well as individuals with purely secular belief systems. In areas of concern to bioethics, as well as in other areas, this leads to a need to develop policies that accommodate these differences. Exactly what these policies should be is a very complex issue.

One standard approach, which is particularly helpful in dealing with differences in clinical settings, is the conscience clause. This allows members of a religious community who object to certain actions because they violate rule-based constraints accepted in their community to refuse to perform those actions or to have those actions performed on them. Thus, the 1995 Northern Territory of Australia's Right of the Terminally Ill Act, which permitted acts of voluntary euthanasia and assisted suicide, explicitly allowed health-care providers not to participate in providing such assistance. This avoided conflicts between the mandates of the provider's conscience, whether shaped by religious constraints on action or by secular moral concerns, and the rights of the patient under the Act. Similarly, New Jersey, in adopting a brain-death statute, allowed members of religious communities who oppose brain death, and who see withdrawal of life-support measures from brain-dead individuals as illicit killings, to opt out of the statute and to insist that they be treated as alive if and when they become brain dead.

This approach, while widely supported as a measure of respect for differences in a pluralistic society, is not without its difficulties. Among the questions to be considered are: What should be done if all providers invoke the conscience clause? What happens to the right of assisted suicide, or the right to an abortion, if all the reasonably available providers refuse to participate on the grounds that participation is against their principles? Who should pay for showing this respect? Should the New Jersey family of the brain-dead individual maintained on life-support pay for the extra days of that support, or should it be covered by private/public health insurance? Should families of minor children be able to insist that their religious commitments be respected when health care is provided to their children? Should, for example, Jehovah's Witness families be able to refuse needed blood transfusions for their children on the grounds that society must respect their commitment to the rule-based constraint banning the use of blood products?

The conscience clause approach primarily addresses the issue of respecting differences in individual actions. Much more complex issues are raised by attempts to fashion social policies that respect differences in a pluralistic society. A neutrality approach has often been advocated. On this approach, governmental policies should to the maximum extent possible be neutral on the moral disagreements which divide citizens in pluralistic societies. While this initially sounds very plausible in theory, difficulties arise in practice, and these difficulties reveal fundamental ambiguities in the very idea of a neutral social policy.

A good example of these difficulties is provided by the attempt to fashion a neutral social policy governing the use of fetal tissue after induced abortions. There are few who object to the use of such tissue after spontaneous abortions; however, there are many who object to the use of such tissue from induced abortions because they judge (often on religiously based grounds) that induced abortions are morally illicit killings, and that using tissue resulting from such induced abortions is wrong, either because it will encourage more illicit abortions or because it represents illicit complicity with a moral evil.

The adoption of the conscience clause approach ensures that objecting individuals need not participate in the use of such tissue. To carry this approach out fully, both those who use and those who receive the tissue should be told of its source. But what about the social issue of government funding for research into the use of such tissue or the clinical use of such tissue? Is there some way to adopt a social policy that is neutral on the relevant moral or religious issues?

One attempt to do so is the separation policy which has been adopted in many governmental regulations on these topics. According to that policy, the government may fund such research or such clinical care while remaining neutral on the moral issues if the question of tissue donation is raised only after the decision is made to have the induced abortion. Only if the timing or technique of the induced abortion is not effected by the subsequent tissue donation. In such cases, tissue donation seems to be on all views a morally superior alternative to just discarding the fetal tissue. Some see this as a neutral policy because it limits governmental support to accommodate the moral or religious sensitivities of different groups of citizens. Individuals and/or groups who approve of additional research or clinical care are free to support it on their own, but the government remains neutral on the moral or religious controversies by confining its support to those cases that are broadly acceptable because the issue of tissue donation has been separated from the abortion issue. From this perspective, the only question is whether the separation policy is sufficiently sensitive to those who feel that government support, even with tissue donation being separated from the abortion decision, still involves indirect complicity in illicit abortions.

Others feel that such a policy is not really neutral. The result of the separation policy is that government funding is limited to those cases which meet the moral or religious sensitivities of one group of citizens. The views of other citizens, who support broader governmental funding, are not being respected. Looking at the impact of the separation policy, one cannot help wondering whether it is the adoption of a neutral social policy or the adoption of a restrictive social policy based upon one set of conservative moral or religious views.

A third approach suggests that looking at the impact of a social policy is the wrong way to decide whether it is a neutral policy. The neutrality of a social policy is determined by whether or not it can be justified by neutral reasons. If it can be, then it is a neutral policy regardless of its impact. It is unclear, however, that this neutral reasons approach is really helpful in evaluating the separation policy. The fact that a social policy accommodates the views of a diversity of citizens and helps avoid social conflict over potentially divisive issues is a neutral reason for adopting it. Those who advocate the separation policy have therefore a neutral reason for their policy. Those who oppose the separation policy because it does not accommodate the views of those who support broader social funding can use the same sort of neutral reasons to support their opposition.

The fashioning of a neutral social policy on the question of the use of fetal tissue after induced abortions, and on many other questions which involve moral disagreements based in religious diversity, is therefore more complicated than is often realized. I believe that these complications are rooted in fundamental ambiguities in the idea of a neutral social policy.

Pluralistic societies with members from different faith communities are unlikely to reach consensus on bioethical questions. The invocation by different groups of different rule-based constraints and different broader theological themes is likely to lead to substantial disagreement unless those invocations can be supported by neutral reasoning acceptable to all. The adoption of conscience clauses in clinical policies and of neutral social policies seems to offer a way of respecting differences, but many questions remain about the meaning and the implications of these two approaches.

Further Reading

Brody. B. A. (ed.) (1989). *Suicide and Euthanasia: historical and contemporary themes*. Dordrecht: Kluwer.

Camenish, P. F. (ed.) (1994). *Religious Methods and Resources in Bioethics*. Dordrecht: Kluwer.

Fletcher, J. (1954). *Morals and Medicine*. Boston: Beacon Press.

Lammers. S. E. and Verhey. A. (eds) (1987). *On Moral Medicine: theological perspectives in medical ethics*. Grand Rapids, MI: Eerdmans.

Lustig. A. (ed.) (1991). *Theological Developments in Bioethics: 1988–90*. Dordrecht: Kluwer.

—— (1993). *Theological Developments in Bioethics: 1990–92*. Dordrecht: Kluwer.

McCormick, R. and Ramsey, P. (eds) (1987). *Doing Evil to Achieve Good*. Chicago: Loyola University Press.

Numbers, R. L. and Amundsen, D. W. (eds) (1987). *Caring and Curing: Health and medicine in the Western religious traditions*. New York: Macmillan.

Olick, R. S. (1991). Brain death, religious freedom, and public policy: New Jersey's landmark legislative initiative. *Kennedy Institute of Ethics Journal*, 1, 275–88.

O'Rourke, K. D. and Boyle, P. (eds) (1993). *Medical Ethics: sources of Catholic teachings*, 2nd edn. Washington, DC: Georgetown University Press.

Rahmun, F. (1987). *Health and Medicine in the Islamic Tradition*. New York: Crossroads.

Ramsey, P. (1970). *The Patient as Person*. New Haven: Yale University Press.

Rosner, F. and Bleich, J. D. (eds) (1979). *Jewish Bioethics*. Brooklyn: Hebrew Publishing Company.

Sullivan, L. E. (ed.) (1989). *Healing and Restoring: Health and medicine in the world's religious traditions*. New York: Macmillan.

Verhey, A. and Lammers, S. E. (eds) (1993). *Theological Voices in Medical Ethics*. Grand Rapids, MI: Eerdmans.

6

Law and bioethics

WIBREN VAN DER BURG

There is probably no other field in which law and ethics are so strongly intertwined as in biomedicine. Legal and ethical doctrines on topics like informed consent have been developed through close cooperation between lawyers and ethicists. The work of ethicists is in many ways both oriented towards the law and influenced by the law. Ethicists act as expert witnesses in courts or as advisers on legislative issues, for example, on the regulation of embryo research. In countries where ethics committees or review boards are legally recognized, they seem to have a semi-judicial status. Conversely, legal concepts, like the right to privacy, dominate moral discussions.

Because bioethics and health law are so strongly connected, every bioethicist must have a basic understanding of law. For instance, when an ethicist is asked for advice on legislation, he or she should take account of the institutional character of law, which has its own dynamics, restraints and societal functions. Take, for example, a discussion of prostitution in the context of AIDS policies. Here the practical problems of enforcement and the possible side-effects of legal prohibition alone might produce such bad consequences that the more principled arguments against legal moralism become superfluous.

Law

A general and neutral definition of law seems to be impossible because in various respects law is a highly variable and diverse phenomenon. Of course, a number of defining characteristics have been suggested, especially some criteria that would distinguish law from morality. Among those criteria are the connection of law with political authority or with sanctions, the existence of certain kinds of procedures and the emphasis on external acts rather than on motives. However, as Judith Shklar (1964) has argued, none of the differential features suggested is found in all legal systems or practices, nor are they always absent in morality.

Nevertheless, these and other less than general characteristics are important for a full understanding of the phenomenon of law. When they are present in concrete legal systems – and only in so far as they are present – they influence the internal dynamics and societal functioning of law. Most of these features have to do with the institutionalized character of law, which takes different forms in different historical contexts.

One example may suffice to show the importance of taking these institutional characteristics into account. Law emphasizes, partly for reasons of proof, external acts rather than internal intentions, whereas many ethical theories do the reverse. This difference explains why the distinction between 'active' and 'passive' euthanasia is usually deemed more important in law than in moral theory. A Dutch criminal case against a gynaecologist in Alkmaar, who was accused of the active euthanasia of a severely handicapped and suffering neonate, illustrates this difference in approach. In my view, the crucial moral issue in cases like this is whether or not to start medical treatment when non-treatment will result in the baby's death within months. This is the real decision about life or death. However, the lower court considered this issue to be within the realm of professional autonomy and therefore of no legal relevance. (I should add that the appeal court took a more sophisticated stance.) The legal discussion focused on a different point in the decision process, namely active euthanasia. If the doctor had chosen to let the baby die a 'natural' but slow and painful death, or even if he had intentionally hastened death by administering increasing doses of painkillers, he would not have been prosecuted. Because he actively administered euthanasia, however, he was prosecuted for murder. (In the end he was not convicted.) Most ethicists agreed that, once the non-treatment decision had been taken, this was the most humane way of acting to avoid further suffering for the baby. Thus the ethical and legal discussions focus on different points in the decision process: the non-treatment decision and the active euthanasia respectively. This relative emphasis on external acts rather than intentions is only one of the characteristics of law with a more general though not universal nature. There are many others that are connected only to specific legal cultures or to fields of law in specific phases of their development. This wide variety of characteristics possessed by law in different cultures and fields makes it almost impossible to make general statements about law and bioethics. Positive law takes a different shape in every country and, even if statutory rules seem identical, the differences in legal cultures often result in different interpretations.

A major difference between legal cultures is that between the 'Common Law' countries (the Anglophone world) where judicial precedent constitutes the main body of law, and 'Civil Law' countries (roughly the countries of the European continent and their former colonies) where codification and statutory law form the core of the law. In the Common Law tradition, the basic attitudes towards statutes and legal rules, and hence the interpretative strategies, are generally more restrictive than those in Civil Law countries. A statute on patient rights will therefore be more restrictively interpreted in, for example, England and Wales than in the Netherlands; hence an identical statute (or an international treaty) may have different effects in the two different traditions.

There is even variation within a legal culture. Legal thought and attitudes in the field of contract law differ from those in criminal law. Reference to morality in criminal law is, for instance, generally considered more acceptable if it results in the acquittal of the defendant than if its purpose is to broaden the scope of a legal prohibition. The fact that health law is an amalgam of various fields of law therefore creates many internal tensions and inconsistencies.

There is also a more fundamental plurality in the concept of law. There are two perspectives on law that cannot be consistently grasped in one theory, just as an electron can be seen as a particle and as a wave, but not as both at the same time.

The first approach regards law as a product, as law in the books. Law is, for instance, structured as a collection of statutes, judicial decisions and customary rules, or as a system of rules and principles. This approach to law is, in a sense, the most natural one. Legislators produce law in the form of statutes; judges decide cases on the basis of their understanding of the legal rules and principles. The second approach regards law as a process, as an activity (or, rather, a cluster of processes). Law is seen as an interpretative and argumentative practice (Dworkin, 1978) and legislation as a purposive enterprise (Fuller, 1969).

Both views on law are connected and presuppose each other. Law as a process is in many ways oriented to and structured by law as a product. Law as a product only makes sense because it is continuously interpreted, reconstructed, changed and applied in a great many processes. Interdependent as they may be, it is nevertheless impossible to combine both perspectives at the same time. A unifying theory cannot be found by bringing both dimensions of law under one heading; it can be found only by acknowledging the dialeçtic interplay between them. This unavoidable but rarely explicitly recognized multitude of perspectives inherent in the phenomenon of law itself is, in my view, a major cause of the misunderstandings and quarrels between the various schools of jurisprudence, like natural law and legal positivism.

The distinction between the two perspectives has important practical consequences. In a product view (which is dominant in many legal textbooks) many standard distinctions can be defended, like that between existing law (law as it is) and ideal law (law as it ought to be from a critical point of view) or between law and morality – the product is usually easily identifiable by some test of pedigree. But in a process view, the legal and moral arguments cannot be so neatly separated, as Ronald Dworkin (1978) has argued. When discussing the legality of euthanasia in court, we have no simple criteria to say this argument is a moral one and that one is strictly legal. The two categories fuse, because law is an open system which means that in principle every moral argument can be legally relevant. And as soon as we regard law as a dynamic, ongoing process of competing interpretations, we realize that our views on what 'the law on euthanasia' is are always partly determined by and open to our normative views on what the law on euthanasia ought to be. We should therefore lay aside the simple, static image of existing or positive law in favour of a more dynamic concept in which views on law as it is and views on law as it should be are continually merging into views on law as it is becoming.

Morality

In ethics, a largely analogous distinction can be made between a product view of morality and a practice view. (Process and practice are not fully equivalent, which is largely due to the institutional character of law.) A product approach in ethics focuses on normative theories, principles and guidelines – for instance, on protocols and guidelines regarding medical experiments. We can also regard morality as a practice, as an activity in which we are continually interpreting, reconstructing and realizing our central moral values – for instance, our ideal of being a good doctor or nurse.

Here again, my suggestion would be that we need both perspectives of product and practice, but cannot take both at the same time. The choice of perspective has important consequences. In a product view, Hart's distinction between positive and critical morality is a clear-cut one (cf. Hart, 1963). However, if we reflect from within ethics on ethics as an interpretative practice, this distinction becomes a dialectical interplay, simply because we have no Archimedean point for our critical morality. Our view of ideal morality is always partly determined by our positive morality; and at the same time our positive morality includes the possibility of self-criticism and justification in the light of ideal or critical morality.

From Morality to Law

After this preparatory work, we can now turn to the central theme of this article: the relationships between morality and law in the field of biomedicine. Morality influences law in many ways. Moral opinions on issues like abortion are often expressed in legislation or reflected in judicial decisions. This raises the question: when is it justified to transform morality into law or at least to give legal effect to it? It should be noted that if we phrase the question in this standard way, we implicitly take a product view of both law and morality. We are asking when a moral rule or principle should be incorporated into the law. In a process or practice view, the distinction between law and morality is less strict and therefore the question would get a vaguer and less tangible character.

I will cluster the major issues under three headings.

The integrity of the law (and of its constitutive fields and processes), with its special function and character, should be taken into account. For instance, when discussing euthanasia, we should recognize that law has special problems of enforcement and proof, and that legal rules should be general. It seems impossible to make general rules that fully cover the morally acceptable cases of euthanasia, and to set corresponding standards of proof which only acceptable cases can meet. This implies, in my view, that even though we should legalize some forms of euthanasia, we will be forced to prosecute certain morally acceptable cases in order to avoid tolerating unacceptable cases. Embryo experimentation presents another example: even if, from a moral point of view, individuation at fourteen days after conception were only an arbitrary line, it might be a defensible one in legislation, just because legal rules have to be simple and clear.

Both the intended effects and the unwanted side-effects should be calculated (cf. Skolnick, 1968). Moreover, we should be realistic about the intended effects: legislation is not always effective in influencing people's behaviour. The unpredicted and undesirable side-effects of legislation sometimes even outweigh the actual beneficial effects. The US prohibition of alcohol is a classic example: it made the Mafia flourish, and it led to corruption, blackmail and selective law enforcement. The modern 'war on drugs' has similar effects; if we take these into account we should doubt whether criminalization is a good strategy. A strict prohibition of abortion usually has undesirable consequences, like women dying after undergoing illegal abortion practices.

The side-effects of the existence of a law can yield arguments both for and against legalization of specific practices. Laws against euthanasia may result in a completely uncontrolled, secret medical practice of euthanasia; legalization of euthanasia may make some older people feel that they are under social pressure to request it.

The third cluster of topics is straightforwardly *normative*. According to most normative political theories, some forms of behaviour that are considered morally wrong should nevertheless not be the subject of legal prohibition; but just when and why this is so is an issue of controversy. Some theories construe the sphere of morality in which the law has no business broadly, on the basis of classic ideas like safeguarding private spheres or fundamental rights. Apart from their controversial character, these normative theories seem to be only partly relevant in the reality of modern societies, where states play an active role and where law is a crucial instrument for policy purposes. Moreover, a serious limitation of most of these theories, even of Feinberg's celebrated four-volume analysis and defence of such an approach (Feinberg, 1984–90) is that they deal only with criminal law. In modern states, however, other forms of law may be more important. Medical malpractice rarely leads to criminal cases; the threat of private lawsuits is more substantial. Consider the practice of surrogate pregnancy, for example. (See also chapter 17, pp. 163–72.) Law can deal with surrogacy in many ways other than prohibition: it may establish family relationships and inheritance rights between the child and either the surrogate mother or the commissioning couple; it may give or withhold legal effect to the surrogacy contract; internal hospital regulations can make assisted insemination for such purposes impossible. In modern societies, many morally sensitive issues concern contract or administrative law rather than criminal law. This variety makes it impossible to suggest simple criteria for deciding which part of morality is to be legally regulated, or for the way in which this should be done. Even an outline of a normative theory on this broader theme is still lacking.

From Law to Morality

Conversely, law also influences morality in various respects. Legal styles of argument can influence the style of moral reasoning. If a legal system focuses on cases, morality will probably be *case-oriented* as well. Civil Law legal cultures naturally focus on statutory rules; we may therefore expect moral reasoning in these countries to be more rule-oriented than in the more casuistic Common Law countries. (See also chapter 12, pp. 106–14.)

Furthermore, legal concepts sometimes influence the structure of moral debates. When the theme of abortion is legally structured in terms of conflicting rights, it will be more difficult to encourage an open moral debate in terms other than rights, for example, on whether abortion based on gender is acceptable. If there is a threat of a conservative backlash against legalized abortion, citizens may be unwilling to give up the liberal rights framework, even if it is not adequate for more subtle moral questions.

Finally, law may directly influence the contents of popular morality. For example, legal rules on informed consent may, directly or in the long run, mould medical practice and moral opinion.

A different normative issue is whether law gives rise to moral obligations. Especially in rapidly developing fields such as those of bioethics, the law often cannot keep up with the pace of change. Is a health-care professional morally obliged to obey a law that is inadequate or unjust, like an illiberal abortion law? This theme of political obligation and civil disobedience has elicited a rich literature (cf. Greenawalt, 1989). A word of caution might be in place. Law is more than a set of statutory rules: most legal systems have means (like the defence of necessity) for allowing acts that, though against the letter of the law, are morally justified. It may therefore be unclear whether an act like euthanasia or abortion is really illegal, precisely because moral argument is relevant in interpreting the law (cf. Dworkin, 1978).

Converging Law and Morality

The relations between morality and law usually have the character of mutual interaction rather than that of a one-way influence. We can distinguish three ideal typical developmental phases or models in the development of interaction between health law and bioethics in most Western countries. In the first phase, the emphasis is on ethical practice; only a small number of legal rules exist as a codification of this practice. In the second, law and ethics converge in a product approach and cooperate closely in changing the traditional practice; in the third, they diverge again.

Until the 1960s, neither bioethics nor health law were independent disciplines; guidelines and rules (the 'product') were almost non-existent. The medical profession was largely autonomous and free from external legal regulation; medical ethics was primarily an ethics of good medical practice. The few legal rules that existed usually reflected positive morality, like rules prohibiting abortion, euthanasia and certain sexual activities. In this setting, the relationships between law and morality were primarily discussed under the headings of legal moralism and paternalism. We may therefore call this the moralistic-paternalistic model. The best critical analysis of problems in this model can be found in Feinberg's work, to which reference has already been made (cf. also Dworkin, 1994).

This moralistic-paternalistic model has, in most countries, gradually been replaced by a different one, which I shall call the liberal model. Health law and bioethics have developed into flourishing disciplines that are closely connected. They have a common mission: the search for adequate answers to the many new problems that arose and the struggle to make biomedical practice comply with norms shared by ethics and health law. In interdisciplinary cooperation, ethicists and lawyers are developing doctrines of euthanasia and abortion. Legal case materials are used for illustration in bioethics textbooks; ethical literature is quoted in legal texts and court decisions.

This convergence has been facilitated by a number of closely connected factors that characterize the new liberal model. First, both health law and bioethics take a product view (exemplified in the principlism of Beauchamp and Childress (1994); see also chapter 7, pp. 61–71), trying to develop new theories for the new problems that arise (or for old problems that are seen in a new light): the plight of psychiatric patients, the possibilities and risks of new technologies. Second, both use the same conceptual categories: rules, principles, right, procedures. As a result, translation from legal to moral analysis, and vice versa, seems (at least superficially) simple, which is a precondition for successful cooperation. Third, both focus on what is minimally necessary for decent medical practice rather than on the ideal situation; formulating and realizing minimum standards seems to be a major achievement already. The fourth factor is closely connected to the other three: both use the same liberal substantive theory, in which autonomy and patient rights are central.

These four factors not only facilitate cooperation between the two disciplines, but also contribute to their effectiveness. In modern pluralist societies, an overlapping consensus can more easily be reached on procedures, minimum rules and rights than on the good life. The liberal model offers simple legal solutions to intricate problems like abortion and euthanasia by entrusting individuals with the responsibility for moral dilemmas. The problems that were most urgent in the early years of bioethics and health law – patient rights, abortion, medical experiments – can thus all be fruitfully addressed in the context of a product-oriented liberalism (at least, with respect to abortion, if one starts from the assumption that the fetus does not count as a full person). Moreover, scarce intellectual resources and weak societal powers are thus combined.

Of course, this liberal model has not been equally effective everywhere; in fact, no country has yet fully implemented it. In strongly pluralist societies, like the US and the Netherlands, it has been much more influential than in, for example, Ireland. There are even differences within one country. The US has adopted an extremely liberal stance on patient rights, whereas, so far, it has taken a more moralistic position on various issues in the field of human sexuality.

Diverging Law and Morality: Beyond the Liberal Model

The liberal model has now gained broad support in many countries. Central elements have been legally recognized and sometimes codified in constitutional rights and statutes. (Although, of course, this process of legal recognition is in many countries still far from completion.) Bioethics and health law have become established fields in many universities. The very success of the liberal model, however, now leads to its decline: the advantages become less important and the disadvantages become more visible. Although the criticisms are quite diverse, they have a common implication: developments in health law and bioethics should no longer be parallel and connected. To put it simply: health law is criticized as being too dominant, too rigid and not sensitive enough to the complex problems of health-care practice; bioethics is criticized as being reduced to a minimum rights-oriented morality that neglects broader ethical dimensions. Precisely because and in so far as the liberal model has been realized, we are now in a position to go beyond it.

Trying to predict future developments would be too speculative. Therefore I can only make some tentative suggestions for the way in which a new, post-liberal model of the relations between health law and bioethics should be construed. First, the liberal model has undeniably brought progress; its achievements, especially in health law. should not be discarded lightly. Patient rights. legal abortion. informed consent and so on should be preserved. It should, however, be supplemented, and in some respects corrected, on the basis of a proper understanding of the specific roles and characteristics of law and ethics, and of the differences between them rather than their similarities.

With regard to bioethics, we should acknowledge that the four factors responsible for the liberal success have resulted in a certain one-sidedness. These characteristics were challenged by a host of critics in modern ethics, ranging from MacIntyre (1981) to the advocates of an ethics of care (Gilligan, 1982). To compensate for this one-sidedness, we should supplement them with a richer view of ethics rather than do away with them. Many current topics simply cannot be discussed adequately in terms of the liberal model: we should discuss both product and practice, both the minimally decent and the excellent doctor. When we discuss experiments with human embryos or sex selection, references to autonomy and rights are not sufficient. A full ethical analysis of prenatal diagnosis requires a discussion of topics like society's attitude towards persons with a handicap, and this inevitably leads us to issues that are connected to more personal and even religious conceptions of the good life. These are examples of the ways in which, in ethics, we must go beyond the liberal model.

For health law, the situation is different, and here we should largely stick to the liberal model. Legislating virtues, let alone legislating the full richness of the good life, is not possible and not desirable. Therefore health law in some respects can only follow bioethics in its reorientation towards practice and towards ideals of good health care. But it should, at least, not hinder this ethical reorientation and therefore it should show more self-restraint. Legal rules are sometimes too rigid and general to do justice to the intricate details of health-care practice. As the rise of 'legally defensive medicine' – for example, ordering additional tests primarily in order to minimize the risk of being sued – illustrates, legal rules can adversely influence health care. After a period of rapid expansion of health law, it may therefore now be time for a more modest attitude of legal self-restraint and for the reduction of legal interventions.

As a result, law and ethics will diverge. Precisely because the close cooperation between law and ethics has been so fruitful in the past, it is now time to loosen the bonds in the interests of law and of morality, but especially in the interest of good health-care practice.

References

Beauchamp, T. L. and Childress, J. F. (1994). *Principles of Biomedical Ethics*. New York: Oxford University Press.
Dworkin, G. (ed.) (1994). *Morality, Harm, and the Law*. Boulder, CO: Westview Press.
Dworkin, R. (1978). *Taking Rights Seriously*. Cambridge, MA: Harvard University Press.
Feinberg, J. (1984). *The Moral Limits of the Criminal Law*. Vol. 1. *Harm to Others*. New York: Oxford University Press.
—— (1985). *The Moral Limits of the Criminal Law*. Vol. 2. *Offence to Others*. New York: Oxford University Press.
—— (1986). *The Moral Limits of the Criminal Law*. Vol. 3. *Harm to Self*. New York: Oxford University Press.
—— (1990). *The Moral Limits of the Criminal Law*. Vol. 4. *Harmless Wrongdoing*. New York: Oxford University Press.
Fuller, L. L. (1969). *The Morality of Law*. New Haven: Yale University Press.
Gilligan, C. (1982). *In a Different Voice*. Cambridge, MA: Harvard University Press.
Greenawalt, K. (1989). *Conflicts of Law and Morality*. New York: Oxford University Press.
Hart, H. L. A. (1961). *The Concept of Law*. Oxford: Clarendon Press.
—— (1963). *Law, Liberty and Morality*. Oxford: Oxford University Press.
MacIntyre, A. (1981). *After Virtue*. Notre Dame, IN: University of Notre Dame Press.
Shklar, J. N. (1964). *Legalism: Law, morals, and political trials*. Cambridge, MA: Harvard University Press.
Skolnick, J. H. (1968). Coercion to virtue. *Southern California Law Review*, 41, 588–641.

Further Reading

Blom-Cooper, L. and Drewry, G. (1976). *Law and Morality*. London: Duckworth.
Clouser, K. D. (1994). Morality vs. principlism. In R. Gillon (ed.), *Principles of Health Care Ethics*. Chicester: John Wiley, 251–66.
Devlin, P. (1965). *The Enforcement of Morals*. London: Oxford University Press.
Dickens, B. M. (1994). Legal approaches to health care ethics and the four principles. In R. Gillon (ed.), *Principles of Health Care Ethics*. Chicester: John Wiley, 305–17.
Dworkin, R. (ed.) (1977). *The Philosophy of Law*. Oxford: University Press.
Mason, J. K. and McCall Smith, R. A. (1994). *Law and Medical Ethics*. London: Butterworth.
Raz, J. (1979). *The Authority of Law: essays on law and morality*. Oxford: Clarendon Press.
Skolnick, J. H. (1992). Rethinking the drug problem. *Dædalus: Journal of the American Academy of Arts and Sciences*, 121, 133–59.
Van der Burg, W. (1997). Bioethics and law: a developmental perspective. *Bioethics*, 11/2, 91–114.
Walker, D. M. (1980). Law. In *The Oxford Companion to Law*. Oxford: Clarendon Press.

PART III
ETHICAL APPROACHES

7

A principle-based approach

JAMES F. CHILDRESS

This chapter will analyse and assess several principle-based approaches to ethics, with particular attention to bioethics. It will explore the various forms they take, the kinds of principles they accept and the different ways they relate principles to particular judgements in concrete situations.

A principle-based approach must, at a minimum, hold that some general moral norms or action guides are central in moral reasoning. Some moral norms or action guides may be construed as principles, other as rules. Both principles and rules are 'general action guides specifying that some type of action is prohibited, required, or permitted in certain circumstances' (Solomon, 1978, vol. 1: 408). Although I will sometimes use the term 'principles' as well as the term 'norms' to encompass both principles and rules, I will also construe principles as more general norms and rules as more specific norms. Principles often provide warrants for more specific rules, which specify more concretely the type of prohibited, required or permitted action.

The Variety of Principle-based Approaches

Even if a principle-based approach remains the most influential framework in bioethics – as some commentators maintain – no single approach can be called *the* principles approach. Hence, the criticisms directed against one principle-based approach may not apply to other such approaches. For instance, criticisms aimed at a deontological theory that is principle-based may not be effective against a non-deontological theory that is also principle-based. And yet the language of 'principles' is sometimes mistakenly restricted to deontological theories, that is, to theories holding that some inherent or intrinsic features of acts, such as truthfulness or lying, make them right or wrong. This restriction is a mistake because consequentialist theories, which focus on the probable consequences or effects of actions, may also be principle-based. For example, utilitarianism, which is the most prevalent contemporary consequentialist theory, appeals to the principle of utility in assessing actions or rules (see, for example, the writings of Joseph Fletcher, R. M. Hare and Peter Singer (1993), among others).

Act utilitarians apply the principle of utility directly to different possible acts in a situation to determine which would probably produce the greatest good for the greatest number; that act is then right and obligatory. They further insist that principles and rules other than utility can function only as maxims or rules of thumb without prescriptive, binding power. Such principles or rules can help agents see the tendencies of different acts to produce good or bad consequences. By contrast, rule-utilitarian theories appeal to the principle of utility to shape other principles and rules, which then determine the rightness or wrongness of particular acts. A rule utilitarian might, for instance, defend such rules as truthfulness and confidentiality on the grounds that physicians' adherence to these rules over time will produce the greatest good for the greatest number. Physicians would then follow such rules rather than directly applying the principle of utility. However, they could appeal to the principle of utility to resolve conflicts between such rules as truthfulness and confidentiality in a particular situation. According to act utilitarians, both rule utilitarians and deontologists are more alike than different – both make too much of principles and rules (other than the principle of utility itself) and too little of the consequences of particular acts.

Some principle-based approaches attempt to include both consequentialist and non-consequentialist or deontological considerations, without reducing one to or deriving one from the other, and without appealing to any overarching principle (see Beauchamp and Childress, 1994). For instance, the National Commission for the Protection of Human Subjects of Biomedical and Behavioral Research (1978) justified its policy recommendations by three major principles: respect for persons (which includes respect for autonomy), beneficence (which includes non-maleficence) and justice. Most moral justifications of research involving human subjects invoke the non-consequentialist principles of respect for autonomy, expressed in rules of informed consent, and of justice, expressed in the fair selection of research subjects, along with such consequentialist considerations as the research's probable benefits (to the subject and to others) balanced against its risks (to the subject).

More broadly, in the literature of bioethics, principles represent the following sorts of general moral considerations, here stated as obligations: obligations to respect the choices of competent persons (respect for persons or personal autonomy); obligations not to harm others, including not killing them or treating them cruelly (non-maleficence); obligations to benefit others (beneficence); obligations to produce a net balance of benefits over harms (utility); obligations to distribute benefits and harms fairly (justice); obligations to keep promises and contracts (fidelity); obligations of truthfulness; obligations to disclose information; and obligations to respect privacy and to protect confidential information (confidentiality).

In various principle-based ethical frameworks, some of these obligations appear as principles, others as rules, some as primary and fundamental, others as secondary and derivative. For example, in *Principles of Biomedical Ethics* (1989, 1994, as well as earlier editions), Tom Beauchamp and James Childress identify four primary principles – respect for autonomy, non-maleficence, beneficence (including utility) and justice – and several derivative rules – 'tell the truth,' 'keep your promises,' 'protect the privacy of others' and 'do not pass on to others information given to you in confidence' – along with various other rules, such as the requirement to obtain the informed consent of a patient or experimental subject. On this view, rules are derivative, because they are grounded in the principles. 'Tell the truth,' for example, can be derived from the principle of respect for autonomy because people cannot make autonomous decisions without accurate information. (This is the approach taken by Beauchamp and Childress, sometimes called the 'four principles approach' by defenders (Gillon, 1994) and 'principlism' by critics (Clouser and Gert, 1990).) Robert Veatch's list of principles in *A Theory of Medical Ethics* (1981) is similar in important respects but differs in others: beneficence; contract-keeping; autonomy; honesty; avoiding killing; and justice. He also recognizes several moral rules or intermediate moral requirements, such as informed consent. In a much shorter list, H. Tristram Engelhardt's *Foundations of Bioethics* (1995) accepts as principles only autonomy and beneficence, while reducing justice to these two considerations, but he then also recognizes several derivative obligations.

It is thus evident that one major difference among principle-based approaches is how they sort out different obligations. Some ethicists may encompass several obligations under a few general headings, while others may view them as distinct and even separable obligations. And some theories use the language of rights rather than the language of obligations.

Variety also marks the justification of different ethical principles. To some the language of principles suggests a strictly rationalistic theory that appeals to non-historical foundations, such as natural law. And they argue that principles-based approaches pay inadequate attention to history, convention, community, tradition and the like. Certainly some principle-based approaches do in fact appeal to universal moral norms based on natural law (see, for instance, Pope John Paul II, *Evangelium Vitae*, 1995). However, rationalistic conceptions are not the only versions of principles in ethics or bioethics. For instance, Beauchamp and Childress (1994) appeal to the 'common morality', that is, to principles discerned in a society's laws, policies and practices. Some critics dismiss such appeals to the 'common morality' as relativistic, but principles can still 'transcend the insights and beliefs of many particular groups and traditions, and . . . are often useful for critically examining and restructuring past moral thinking and present moral perplexity' (Beauchamp and Childress, 1989: 24, note 20). Some conceptions of principles and rules thus identify them with the traditions of particular communities, rather than with universal moral norms derived from abstract human reason or human nature.

Connecting General Principles to Particular Judgements about Cases

Principles need bridges to concrete, particular judgements. The same principle may point in different directions – for example, the principle of benefiting the patient may offer ambiguous directives. And any relevant principle may conflict with other relevant principles – for example, the principle of benefiting the patient may conflict with the principle of respecting the patient's autonomous choices. In the light of such ambiguities and conflicts, Henry Richardson (1990) identifies three major ways to connect principles to case-judgements: (1) application, which deduces or derives the right course of action from general principles and rules; (2) balancing, which weights conflicting principles to determine which has priority in the situation; and (3) specification, which proceeds by 'qualitatively tailoring our norms to cases' through specifying such circumstances as who, what and when.

63

Despite the prominence of the metaphor of application – for example, in the phrase 'applied ethics' – it cannot illuminate all or even most significant connections between principles and particular judgements. Not all cases involve the rational deduction of particular judgements from general principles, and particular case judgements may even modify the way principles are formulated and interpreted. Hence, most principle-based approaches reject the metaphor of application as misleading in so far as it suggests a strictly deductivist, mechanical method that appears to flounder in cases of conflict.

The two other possible ways of connecting principles and particular judgements – specification and balancing – address two distinct (but inseparable) dimensions of norms: their meaning, range and scope on the one hand, and their weight or strength on the other.

Specifying the meaning, range and scope of moral norms

We regularly specify the meaning, range and scope of moral norms. First of all, as R. M. Hare (1989: 54) notes, 'any attempt to give content to a principle involves specifying the cases that are to fall under it . . . Any principle, then, which has content goes some way down the path of specificity.' Second, specifications often take the form of rules that provide more concrete guidance. For instance, rules of voluntary, informed consent often specify the principle of respect for personal autonomy. And rules of confidentiality specify the requirements of several principles, including respect for autonomy and utility, the latter because of the value of confidential relations for the provision of effective health care. Third, apparent cases of conflict between principles (and rules) may evaporate when the relevant principles (and rules) are more fully specified.

To take one example, different specifications play a role in different definitions and moral assessments of lying. On the one hand, 'lying' is sometimes defined as making an intentionally deceptive statement. According to this definition, a physician in the US tells a lie when he or she greatly exaggerates the severity of a patient's medical problems in order to obtain full coverage for the patient from an insurance company. The moral debate about such a case would focus on whether the rule against deception could be overridden by a principle of patient benefit or of utility. Whatever the conclusion about this particular case, few if any ethical theories consistently hold that lying, so defined, is absolutely wrong, because it is easy to imagine circumstances where lying would prevent a terrible harm or injustice.

On the other hand, 'lying' is sometimes defined not simply as making an intentionally deceptive statement, but as intentionally deceiving or withholding information from *someone who has a right to the truth*. Under such a definition, the moral debate would focus on whether the physician in the case above actually lied, and the answer would depend in part on whether the insurance company had a right to accurate information, especially if its policies appeared to be unjust. On this second definition of lying, the rule against lying could be viewed as absolute, but all the difficult moral questions would be answered and all the exceptional cases handled by determining who has a right to the truth rather than by balancing the prohibition of lying against other moral considerations.

A process of specification pervades the papal encyclical 'The Gospel of Life' (*Evangelium Vitae*, 1995), which focuses on different ways of taking human life from the perspective of the Biblical commandment, 'Thou shalt not kill.' It would be difficult to defend the prohibition against killing as absolute, and, even in the Bible, it coexists with the divine authorization to kill in self-defence, in warfare and in capital punishment. The Christian tradition over time specified this broad principle in the following rule: do not directly take the life of an innocent human being. And, based on convictions about when human life begins, Roman Catholicism has prohibited abortion as well as active euthanasia.

In general, then, various principle-based approaches specify their principles in more specific, concrete and detailed rules. Often these are quite uncontroversial – for example, specifying the principle of respect for autonomy in rules requiring informed consent or refusal. One important question is whether moral rules can stand on their own and provide sufficient guidance without reference to more general principles. Clouser and Gert (1990) reject moral principles altogether in favour of more specific rules along with some ideals. However, it is not clear that all that is important in moral principles, such as those defended by Beauchamp and Childress (1994 and earlier editions) can always be captured in the ten rules Gert (1989) offers in their place. These moral rules are: don't kill; don't cause pain; don't disable; don't deprive of freedom; don't deprive of pleasure; don't deceive; keep your promise; don't cheat; obey the law; and do your duty. These rules specify the harms that are to be avoided under the general requirement – which others might call a principle – of non-maleficence. All are negative except for promise-keeping, obedience to the law and performance of duty (mainly role-related duty). Gert (and Clouser) find the principles of respect for autonomy, beneficence and justice in principlism most problematic. Yet they bring part of what others include under the principle of beneficence under their ideals, which include positive actions to relieve pain, prevent death and help the needy (Clouser and Gert, 1990: 229, 234). But such actions thereby become praiseworthy rather than prima facie obligatory, as claimed by some principle-based approaches. Furthermore, some argue that the omitted principles perform important moral functions not completely discharged by the rules; for instance, the principle of respect for personal autonomy goes well beyond these specific rules in expressing an important moral obligation.

However, Clouser and Gert (1990), among other critics, charge that the principles identified by Beauchamp and Childress and others do not adequately determine action because they are so general and vague. One attempt within principlism to address these charges further extends the role of specification; examples include 'specified principlism' (David DeGrazia, 1992) and the combination of specification with constrained balancing (Beauchamp and Childress, 1994). Still some philosophers wonder whether specification, which is intended to reduce intuitive judgements, actually falls prey to the same problems its proponents find in efforts to balance moral norms (Arras, 1994).

Balancing moral norms

Balancing moral norms is another way to try to resolve moral dilemmas and conflicts. Balancing presupposes a certain conception of the weight or strength of moral norms. At least four main conceptions of norms' weight or strength appear on a spectrum: (a) viewing maxims or rules of thumb as merely illuminative or suggestive, (b) balancing prima facie binding principles and rules, (c) ranking principles in lexical or serial order and (d) adhering to absolute principles and rules. While it is entirely possible that all four conceptions play some role in ethics and bioethics, much of the debate focuses on which general moral considerations should have how much weight or strength.

At one end of the spectrum are absolutists, who maintain that some moral principles and rules bind moral agents regardless of the circumstances, including countervailing moral factors. However, even absolutists generally recognize only a few absolute principles and often define and specify them so as to reduce or eliminate irresolvable moral dilemmas. To take one example, Paul Ramsey (1968, 1970) often handled hard cases not by overriding or rebutting moral rules but rather by deepening their meaning. Hence, he could view some cases of justified deception – for example, to save a life – not as 'exceptions', but rather as implicit within a deeper understanding of the rule against lying (1968).

It is important to distinguish the debate about *which* principles or rules are absolute from the debate about *whether* there are absolutes. Scepticism about construing some principle, such as the sanctity of life or truthfulness, as absolute, often leads to a general challenge to absolutism. Nevertheless, some principles and rules, particularly specified negative rules, may be absolute or virtually absolute – plausible candidates include moral rules against rape, cruelty and murder. But much of the moral work appears in setting the criteria for these categories – for instance, which kinds of acts count as murder? Once the criteria are set, no competing moral considerations can justify the acts in question.

At the other end of the spectrum, Joseph Fletcher's (1966) 'situation ethics' recognized only one absolute principle – neighbour-love or utility – and then viewed all other principles and rules as mere maxims or rules of thumb. They are all parallel to the maxim in baseball, 'don't bunt on third strike,' which advises rather than obligates managers and players. In Fletcher's 'situation ethics', which is a form of act utilitarianism, principles and rules other than utility merely identify the tendencies of actions, based on past experience, to produce or subvert good consequences. They only illuminate various courses of action; they do not prescribe what ought to be done (Gustafson, 1965). A more thoroughgoing 'situation ethics' might even reject the overarching moral principle of utility in favour of particular judgements based on intuition or conscience.

One intermediate conception of the weight and strength of moral norms views them as prima facie or presumptively binding, rather than as either absolutely binding or merely advisory. For example, Beauchamp and Childress (1994) argue that their four primary principles – respect for autonomy, non-maleficence, beneficence (including utility or proportionality) and justice – along with such derivative rules as telling the truth, keeping promises, not violating privacy and maintaining confidentiality – are only prima facie binding. That is, they are binding at first impression and are sufficient to establish the rightness or wrongness of an act unless they are outweighed or overridden. In so far as an act embodies the characteristics or features identified by the relevant principles or rules, it is morally right or obligatory. However, acts may have several morally relevant features, such as truthfulness and causing harm, which represent conflicting principles or rules. As prima facie binding, all relevant principles and rules have to be weighed and balanced in situations of conflict. However, for Beauchamp and Childress, in contrast to Fletcher, the moral agent has to justify departures from any of these principles – because they are prescriptive, not merely illuminative – by showing that in the situation concerned some other principle has more weight or greater stringency. The assignment of weights or priorities occurs in the situation, not through abstract, a priori formulations.

This approach suffers from the limitations of any pluralistic perspective that does not assign, in advance, weights or priorities to various principles and rules: it appears to be excessively intuitive. While conceding that intuitive judgements cannot be totally eliminated in balancing principles in actual situations, Beauchamp and Childress (1989, 1994) propose – in addition to various specifications – a decision procedure to reduce the reliance upon intuition. They contend that 'the logic of prima facie duties' contains 'moral conditions that prevent just any judgment based on a grounding principle from being acceptable in a moral conflict' (Beauchamp and Childress, 1989: 53). And they identify several conditions for justified infringements of prima facie principles and rules – there must be a realistic prospect of achieving the moral objective that appears to justify the infringement; the infringement must be necessary in the circumstances; the infringement should be the least possible, commensurate with achieving the primary goal of the action; and the agent must seek to minimize the negative effects of the infringement (Beauchamp and Childress, 1989, 1994). They contend that a stronger decision procedure finds no warrant in moral experience and moral theory.

Some critics doubt that balancing moral norms, even within such constraints, can always yield the right conclusion in a serious conflict – for example, between promoting societal welfare through research involving human subjects and protecting the rights of those subjects through voluntary, informed consent. They also suspect the rule utilitarian's appeal to the ultimate principle of utility in order to adjudicate conflicts among various principles and rules. Instead, they offer a set of priority rules that rank different principles and rules in advance of concrete situations.

One major effort to develop a ranking, a lexical or serial order for moral principles appears in Veatch's *A Theory of Medical Ethics* (1981), which gives all the deontological or non-consequentialist principles, such as promise-keeping and honesty, 'lexical priority over the principle of beneficence'. However, when deontological or non-consequentialist principles themselves conflict, Veatch employs a 'balancing strategy'. He thus finds 'a solution to the inevitable unacceptable tension between Hippocratic individualism and the utilitarian drive toward aggregate

67

net benefit'. This solution 'comes from the articulation of other nonconsequential-ist principles that will necessarily have a bearing on medical ethical decisions: contract keeping, autonomy, honesty, avoiding killing, and justice', and from assigning them collective priority over the production of good consequences for individuals (Hippocratic individualism) or for society (utilitarianism). Non-conse-quentialist principles receive 'coequal ranking' in relation to each other and 'lexical ranking' over the principle of beneficence. Similarly Engelhardt (1995) assigns the principle of autonomy priority over the principle of beneficence. Critics of such attempts to provide a lexical order challenge what amounts to an absolute ranking, in the abstract, of one principle over against another or others, contending that it inevitably runs foul of actual human experience in real situations.

Critiques

In the light of the wide variety of principle-based positions, it is not surprising that they regularly attack each other. Beyond these intramural disputes, other critics challenge several or all principle-based approaches.

First, proponents of case-based approaches sometimes rail against the 'tyranny of principles' on behalf of the primacy of particular judgements (Toulmin, 1981; Jonsen and Toulmin, 1988). However, when their claims are examined carefully, these casuists, as they are frequently termed, mainly oppose certain kinds of princi-ples, that is, principles that are absolute, invariant, eternal and so forth. Many principle-based approaches also reject such conceptions of principles and can ac-cept several of the casuists' other claims. For instance, recognizing an important role for general moral norms does not imply that moral knowledge is fundamental-ly general rather than particular. Even if particular case judgements are primary, those judgements imply similar judgements for relevant similar cases. The require-ment of universalizability or generalizability, many philosophers argue, entails that moral agents extend their moral judgement that 'X is wrong' to all relevantly similar 'Xs'. Hence, particular judgements, even if they are primary, still give rise to principles and rules, which can then guide further action. Defenders of general moral norms often stress, against the casuists, that norms are important in identi-fying relevant similarities and differences between cases. One approach that views both particular case judgements and general moral norms as important in moral reasoning holds that they are dialectically or dialogically related – each one may potentially modify and correct the other in an effort to achieve greater coherence (see Beauchamp and Childress, 1989, 1994). Finally, principle-based approaches can recognize the importance of settled cases, so-called paradigm cases about which there is a strong moral consensus, and can reason analogically from such cases to new or controversial ones, just as casuists do.

Some casuists also admit that principles and rules are appropriate and even necessary in interactions among strangers, in contrast to relations between inti-mates and friends (Toulmin, 1981). Hence, a fundamental question in bioethics is whether patients and health-care professionals interact as intimates and friends or as strangers. Holding that, at least in the West, such interactions largely involve moral strangers, Engelhardt (1995) proposes a theory of bioethics for peaceable, secular, pluralistic societies with primary attention to the principle of respect for autonomy.

Several critics of principle-based approaches, particularly what has been called principlism, lament the tiresome invocation of the mantra of principles (Clouser and Gert, 1990: Arras, 1994). This criticism suggests that some principle-based approaches distort bioethics by offering relatively abstract categories, such as autonomy and non-maleficence, which tempt novices to suppose that they have become experts in ethics because they can chant the mantra. These novices then mechanically apply the principles to particular situations. Proponents of principle-based approaches retort that there is good and bad scholarship in ethics and bioethics, whichever approach is taken, and that it is important to compare the best representations of each approach, as well as to criticize deficient versions.

Other critics charge that principle-based approaches reduce ethics and bioethics to the analysis and resolution of moral quandaries and dilemmas. However, principle-based approaches recognize that much, even most, of the moral life is a matter of doing what one recognizes to be right, obligatory or good without any perplexity about what one ought to do and without direct appeal to principles. Nevertheless, when conflicts and novel situations arise, as they sometimes do, principles are important.

A closely related criticism holds that principle-based (and case-based) approaches err in concentrating on 'What ought I/we to *do?*' rather than on the more fundamental question 'What ought I/we to *be?*' The latter question directs us to virtue and character. Proponents of the primacy of virtue and character often hold that a virtuous professional can *discern* the right course of action in the situation without reliance on principles and rules, and/or that a virtuous person will *desire* to do what is right, apart from the threat of moral sanctions. Defenders of principles respond that there is simply no assurance that good people will discern what is right, especially in novel situations of conflict, or that they will always desire to do what is right. For instance, in many cases it is simply unclear what a virtuous physician would do. Thus principles and rules, often backed by moral sanctions, can helpfully guide conduct. Furthermore, principles of action also help to determine which virtues should be developed, particularly because many virtues are correlated with principles and rules – for example, benevolence with beneficence, and truthfulness with the rule requiring us to tell the truth. Several other virtues – such as conscientiousness and courage – are important for morality as a whole, including action in accordance with principles.

A final criticism holds that principle-based approaches tend to speak in male voices about male experiences, while neglecting women's voices and experiences. In her pioneering study, Carol Gilligan (1982) reports that women tend to concentrate on narratives, contexts and relationships of care, rather than on tiers of moral principles, with their logic of hierarchical justification, which males by contrast tend to emphasize. However, as Gilligan herself recognizes, care and principles (which she characterizes in terms of justice) are often complementary rather than opposed. And, in many cases, moral agents have to determine, at least in part through principles and rules, how much weight to give to different relationships; for example, a physician may have to determine whether to breach confidentiality in order to warn a stranger of a patient's threatened violence. Furthermore, principles of justice, particularly in the form of equality, and respect for personal autonomy, strongly support often neglected women's rights. Finally, some feminists, who take seriously the social context of sexist oppression, wonder whether female caring is to a great extent a product of this context and whether it may even help to perpetuate oppression. Nevertheless, the care perspective offers an important corrective to some principle-based approaches by attending to context, narrative, relationships, emotion, compassion and the like. At a minimum, principle-based approaches must be carefully (re)formulated in the light of the whole range of human moral experience, including women's experiences of caring as well as of oppression.

In conclusion, several critiques offer major challenges to principle-based approaches to ethics and bioethics, but many proponents of principle-based approaches believe that they can accommodate the most important and cogent criticisms without abandoning their principles.

References

Arras, J. D. (1994). Principles and particularity: the role of cases in bioethics. *Indiana Law Journal,* 69, 983–1014.

Beauchamp, T. L. and Childress, J. F. (1989). *Principles of Biomedical Ethics,* 3rd edn. New York: Oxford University Press.

—— (1994). *Principles of Biomedical Ethics,* 4th edn. New York: Oxford University Press.

Clouser, K. D. and Gert, B. (1990). A critique of principlism. *Journal of Medicine and Philosophy,* 15, 219–36.

DeGrazia, D. (1992). Moving forward in bioethical theory: theories, cases, and specified principlism. *Journal of Medicine and Philosophy,* 17, 511–39.

Engelhardt, H. T. (1995) *Foundations of Bioethics,* 2nd edn. New York: Oxford University Press.

Fletcher, J. (1966). *Situation Ethics: the new morality.* Philadelphia: Westminster Press.

Gert, B (1989). *Morality: a new justification of the moral rules.* New York: Oxford University Press.

Gilligan, C. (1982). *In a Different Voice: psychological theory and women's development.* Cambridge, MA: Harvard University Press.

Gillon, R. (1994). Medical ethics: four principles plus attention to scope. *British Medical Journal,* 309, 184–8.

Gustafson, J. M. (1965). Context versus principles: a misplaced debate in Christian ethics. *Harvard Theological Review,* 58, 171–202.

Hare, R. M. (1989). Principles. In *Essays in Ethical Theory.* Oxford: Clarendon Press, 49–65.

John Paul II, Pope (1995). *Evangelium vitae.* Rome: The Vatican.

National Commission for the Protection of Human Subjects of Biomedical and Behavioral Research (1978). *The Belmont Report: Ethical guidelines for the protection of human subjects of research.* DHEW Publication No. (OS) 78. Washington, DC: Department of Health Education and Welfare.

Ramsey, P. (1968). The case of the curious exception. In G. Outka and P. Ramsey (eds), *Norm and Context in Christian Ethics*. New York: Charles Scribner's Sons.

—— (1970). *The Patient as Person*. New Haven: Yale University Press.

Richardson, H. (1990). Specifying norms as a way to resolve concrete ethical problems. *Philosophy and Public Affairs*, 19, 279–320.

Singer, P. (1993). *Practical Ethics*, 2nd edn. Cambridge: Cambridge University Press.

Solomon, W. D. (1978). Rules and Principles. In W. T. Reich (ed.), *Encyclopedia of Bioethics*. Vol. 1. New York: Free Press, 407–13.

Toulmin, S. (1981). The tyranny of principles. *Hastings Center Report*, 11/6, 31–9.

Veatch, R. M. (1981). *A Theory of Medical Ethics*. New York: Basic Books.

Further Reading

DuBose, E. R., Hamel, R. and O'Connell, L. J. (eds) (1994). *A Matter of Principles: ferment in US bioethics*. Valley Forge, PA: Trinity Press International.

Gillon, R. (ed.) (1994). *Principles of Health Care Ethics*. New York: John Wiley.

—— (1994). Symposium: emerging paradigms in bioethics. *Indiana Law Journal*, 69, 945–1122.

—— (1995). Special issue: theories and methods in bioethics: principlism and its critics. *Kennedy Institute of Ethics Journal*, 5, 181–286.

8

An absolute rule approach

JOSEPH BOYLE

Several approaches to moral decision-making are recognized by their proponents and others as absolute rule approaches to ethics. Most notably, approaches rooted in the moral philosophy of Kant and approaches rooted in the Catholic natural law tradition whose classic source is the moral theology of Thomas Aquinas are absolutist in a similar and influential way: certain moral rules or precepts are held to be without exception. Biblically based prohibitions against adultery and other sexual behaviour, the Catholic prohibition against intentionally killing the innocent and the Kantian prohibition against lying are well known examples of moral rules taken to be exceptionless. Debates over whether these and other rules and their applications in bioethical contexts are in fact interestingly exceptionless continue to be part of bioethics, as recent debates about mercy killing, artificial reproduction and truth-telling in clinical and research contexts reveal. So the topic of this essay is important for understanding the normative basis of the moral perspective of the many physicians, religious people and others who think some moral rules are absolute.

The Idea of an Absolute Rule

An absolute rule is exceptionless, that is, what the rule prescribes is morally decisive and cannot be overridden by other considerations. This idea is plain enough: one is to follow an exceptionless rule no matter what; such rules are not defeated by other moral considerations.

But various sorts of moral statements are reasonably considered rules, and they can all be absolute or exceptionless in the sense just explained. Most of these kinds of absolute rules do not, upon reflection, contribute to the distinctive approach to moral decision-making evoked by the tag 'absolute rule approach'. This approach is characterized by a claim about a specific kind of rule which I will call a precept, namely a universal prescription which directs that an action of a kind characterized in descriptive, non-moral terms may, should or should not be done.

On this account, three kinds of morally interesting sentences or 'rules' are not precepts and so not absolute rules in the sense to be considered here. First, universal moral principles, for example, the principle of utility or the categorical imperative, are not precepts, but grounds for precepts and other moral considerations. Within some ethical approaches a universal principle may have absolute weight in relation to all other moral considerations. This does not make the principle a precept and does not imply that any precept it grounds will be absolute. Of course, within some moral theories dominated by a single, supreme normative principle, some absolute precepts will be grounded, but even in these cases, it is useful to distinguish ground and precept. A precept requires, in addition to its normative ground, a description of a kind of action (Donagan, 1977: 66–8). Thus, if deception in medical experimentation is held to violate the Kantian principle of respect for rational creatures, the act of deceiving a research subject must be described so as to reveal its incompatibility with that respect. Although Kant and Aquinas would probably agree that the prohibition of such deception is absolute (supposing that it involves lying), there is disagreement among proponents of absolute rule approaches to ethics as to whether this prohibition is exceptionless.

Second, a person's final judgement as to what he or she should do in a particular situation is not a precept, and many might wonder if it is in fact a rule. Whether formulated as a judgement of conscience or as a kind of self-addressed imperative, this prescription is logically singular. Precepts prescribe actions in so far as they instantiate certain action kinds, and people's final moral verdicts about what to do are based on the precepts relevant to the action. But a person's final verdict is that he or she may or should or should not do some individual thing. On the assumption that such final evaluations have taken account of all morally relevant considerations, it is reasonable to consider them absolute. Anything which might change one's moral verdict has already been taken into account. But this kind of absoluteness can characterize many and perhaps all ethical approaches, whereas absolute rule approaches are distinctive among moral theories (Finnis, 1991: 4).

Third, prescriptions of actions already characterized by moral evaluations are ordinarily not precepts but tautologies. I say ordinarily because there are precepts bearing upon actions already morally characterized whose purpose is to round out the moral evaluation of already approved or condemned actions. Calling an act parricide presupposes it is wrongful killing but adds something needed for a full moral evaluation. It is sometimes unclear whether the characterization of the action that is the subject of a prescription or a given moral statement is a precept or a tautology. It seems clear, however, that the role of absolute rules in moral decision-making is reduced to nearly zero if they are no more than a set of tautologies in which we are reminded of the wrongfulness of actions already characterized as wrongful. So, I will not regard as precepts such rules as 'Murder (understood as wrongful killing) is wrong' or 'Lying (understood as deceiving those who have a right to the truth) is wrong.' Any absoluteness such norms might have is simply a function of their tautologous character (Finnis, 1991: 4–6).

The contrast between precepts and other absolute rules points to the sense in which precepts might be distinctively and interestingly exceptionless: a precept is absolute if and only if it prescribes that an action of a certain kind should not be done and that its being of that kind guarantees that no further, true description of the action and its circumstances will remove its impermissibility. In other words a negative precept, a prohibition of a kind of action, is absolute when one knows not only that the action as one has characterized it is wrong, but also that anything else one might discover about that action, its circumstances and consequences will not alter that negative evaluation of the action.

The idea can be exemplified by the traditional Catholic precept against killing humans: no one should intentionally kill an innocent human. In this precept the subject is not killing but intentional killing, and it is the intentional killing of innocents, not humans as such, that is prohibited. The restriction of the precept to 'innocents' has not been understood as rendering it a tautology. Innocents are not defined as those it is wrong to kill but very roughly as those not engaged in or convicted of wrongdoing (Finnis et al. 1987: 86–91; Finnis, 1991: 2). One who understands this precept as an absolute rule will judge that when one knows that an act is an act of intentionally killing an innocent human being, then one knows that the act is wrong, and is wrong in such a way that anything further one might discover about the action will not change its moral valence from impermissible to permissible.

As this example indicates, the route from precept to final moral verdict is much quicker and more direct when the precept is absolute than when it is not. The absolute prohibition establishes the basic moral verdict: an action of a kind excluded by a moral absolute simply cannot morally be done.

Both Kantians and Catholic natural lawyers have emphasized that other precepts than prohibitions are absolute and in some sense exceptionless. For example, Kantian imperfect duties can be considered absolute in the sense that they are always in force even though they sometimes cannot prescribe that a particular action should be done. Moreover, they can be formulated as prohibitions against failing to form and act on some plan of self-perfection and beneficence (Donagan, 1991: 500). Still, the absoluteness of such precepts is not the same as the exceptionlessness of some prohibitions of specifically described actions. The latter, not the former, are what provide the distinctive approach to moral decision-making found in natural law thinking and Kantian ethics. For exceptionless prohibitions of actions like lying and intentional killing of the innocent tell us that some definite things we might have reason to do are simply out of the question morally. Our serious duties to improve ourselves and help others simply do not have this sort of relationship to any definite thing we might choose to do.

The Role of Absolute Rules in Moral Thinking

As already suggested, absolute rule approaches to moral decision-making do not limit moral rules to exceptionless prohibitions. Their defenders believe that there are relatively few moral absolutes and that the principles grounding them also ground other precepts. For example, natural law principles enjoining rational concern for human good not only absolutely exclude a small set of actions which harm people, they also enjoin positive initiatives to support people and their goods (Finnis, 1991: 1–3). Thus we are obliged not only not intentionally to kill, slander and so on, but reasonably to avoid harming these and other human goods incidental to other worthwhile projects, and to promote these goods in ourselves and others.

So moral absolutes are understood by those who accept them as playing a distinctive role in moral thinking within a larger scheme of moral norms and precepts (Anscombe, 1981: 34). A key feature of that role has been noted above: knowing that a proposed action is forbidden by a moral absolute ends moral deliberation (though not necessarily temptation) and immediately establishes the person's moral verdict on the action. Thus, even though absolute precepts have fuzzy edges and generate borderline cases that are difficult to decide, they do provide fixed points in the normative landscape. Since abiding by absolute precepts can be difficult, they do not simplify moral life, but their accessibility as fixed points can help those who wish to avoid rationalization and moral confusion.

Other precepts do not work this way; redescription of the action in question can turn up morally relevant features which can change one's moral evaluation of the action (Grisez, 1983: 256–9). The classical example is that we are ordinarily obliged to return property to the owner upon demand, but not when we discover that the owner intends to use it for seditious purposes. The analogous case of promise-keeping is more applicable to bioethics: promises generally involve an obligation to carry out what is promised. But sometimes it is unreasonable to keep one's promise, since keeping it would be unfair to others or harmful to one's moral self.

Moral Absolutism and Consequentialism

The functioning of moral absolutes within moral deliberation provides a significant block to the introduction of consequentialist considerations into a moral approach which includes them (Anscombe, 1981: 34). Consequentialist considerations cannot overturn an absolute prohibition, even if those considerations would justify the action were it not absolutely excluded. In other words, moral absolutes might be said to dominate the larger moral schemes they are part of because, being exceptionless, they trump other moral precepts.

Donagan has argued that this dominance is justified as structurally necessary in a moral system having as its normative basis the Kantian principle of respect for rational creatures. He claims that this dominance is what is expressed in the Pauline principle that evil is not to be done that good may come of it, that is, that exceptionless precepts are not to be violated so that otherwise mandatory goods can be achieved.

> The Pauline principle, therefore, is not an external stipulation, like the serial ordering adopted by contractarian theorists, for getting rid of conflicts between perfect and imperfect duties. It is nothing but a general statement of a condition implicit in every precept of imperfect duty that is validly derivable from the fundamental principle of morality itself. It is structurally necessary. And it manifestly entails that the precepts of imperfect duty – the precepts that flow from the principles of culture and beneficence – cannot be inconsistent with the prohibitory principles. (Donagan, 1977: 155)

There is a natural law analogue of Donagan's Kantian argument. Natural law thinking is teleological in a way Kantian ethics is not. A rational regard for the good of rational creatures is its basic normative principle. But natural law is not consequentialist; its proponents never supposed that determination of the best state of affairs was the proper conception of rational regard.

The logical coherence of the view that a goods-based moral theory need not be consequentialist is shown by the fact that natural law theory's background is in the theistic, providential world-view of Catholic moral theology. In that conception, humans have a real but limited part to play within divine providence, namely to live their lives responsibly in accord with the precepts which define their role in the divine plan, but the overall outcomes are beyond human reckoning and so are God's responsibility (Finnis, 1991: 12). It follows that following an exceptionless precept will not bring final disaster. The present point, however, is that the providential framework of theism reveals the coherence of a morality that is both goods-based and non-consequentialist.

Furthermore, the possibility of such a morality does not require theistic premises. Perhaps moral absolutism has theistic implications; even if it does, however, those implications are not a necessary part of the justification of the dominance of moral absolutes. Consequentialism has well-known difficulties (Donagan, 1977: 192–208). One need not be a theist to be impressed by these difficulties, including those which emphasize the limits and fallibility of practical knowledge. In particular, one need not be a theist to accept the view that good is composed of diverse and incommensurable elements which provide options for choice that rationally cannot be ranked as higher, lower or tied on the same scale. This view casts doubt on the possibility of making characteristically consequentialist judgements, namely those moral directives based on a determination of what is simply or unconditionally better or best (Finnis et al., 1987: 254–60). Theism aside, wherever and to whatever extent moral directives based on comparative value judgements are not possible, the perspective of moral absolutism becomes more plausible: in all such cases, the greater good does not provide a rational basis for setting aside absolute prohibitions themselves based on a concern for how each of us should respect persons and the elements of their welfare.

Plainly, the preceding account is no more than a sketch of opening moves in a complex philosophical dialectic. The point is simply that the anti-consequentialism of moral absolutism need not be simply a relic of its religious origins or a combination of mistakes and confusions but is part of a coherent, although admittedly controversial, moral view.

The Casuistry of Moral Absolutism

It is sometimes unclear whether an action one is evaluating is prohibited by a moral absolute. For example, it is often unclear whether a decision to act or forgo action which will hasten or cause death is a violation of the absolute prohibition against intentionally killing the innocent. Consequently, the fixed points in the moral landscape which moral absolutes provide are not always defined by bright, clear borders. The absolutes have fuzzy edges and there are borderline cases that are difficult to settle. Thus, within both Kantian and Catholic natural law forms of moral absolutism there is a need for casuistry to determine whether or not a certain kind of action falls within a kind prohibited by a moral absolute. The purpose of this kind of moral analysis is not consequentialist determination of the overall good an action or its alternatives might achieve, but the conceptual clarification needed to know whether a borderline case is an action of a kind prohibited by a moral absolute (Anscombe, 1981: 36). Thus, although the structure of moral absolutist theories is deductive, since precepts are justified in the light of moral principles to which they are connected by action descriptions, much of the philosophical work of absolutist ethics lies in the non-deductive conceptual clarification is needed to reveal precisely the moral kind of the action being evaluated (Donagan, 1977: 71–4).

The casuistry of moral absolutism comes in several varieties which, in contrast to other forms of casuistry, have in common the control of the process of comparing and clarifying actions by a basic moral principle. Donagan develops a distinctive strategy. He seeks to derive prohibitory precepts from the Kantian basic principle that one should never fail to respect rational nature as an end in itself by specifying actions which generally violate that principle. He then considers putative exceptions with a view towards determining whether or not they are inconsistent with the basic principle. Those inconsistent with the basic principle are included within the kind of action prohibited and the others are set aside. So the action absolutely excluded cannot be, for example, killing or lying as such, but killing or lying 'at will', that is, except in those circumstances in which killing or lying is shown to be consistent with the basic principle (Donagan, 1977: 72–3). Here the casuistry is presupposed for the formulation of the absolute precept.

More widespread than Donagan's indirect derivation of precepts is the direct approach of Catholic natural law according to which certain well-formulated absolute precepts, for example, the prohibition against intentionally killing the innocent or against using falsehoods to deceive, are taken as justified. Cases arise in which it is unclear whether a given act is or is not an act of the prohibited kind: whether some ambiguous communications are or are not lies or whether some defensive killings are intentional killings of the innocent. Casuistry seeks to settle such questions.

Casuistry of this kind is well known in bioethics and applied ethics more generally both because of the extent of natural law casuistry and its influence even outside Catholic circles. Much of this casuistry centres on the application of the controversial doctrine of the double effect. The distinction between what is often called 'indirect' killing and direct or intentional killing is perhaps the most influential of these applications of double effect in bioethics and in other areas of applied ethics, such as just war theory.

This doctrine presupposes that a distinction can be made between what is done intentionally and what is voluntarily brought about as a side-effect of an intentional action. It maintains that this distinction has a special moral significance: states of affairs it would be absolutely wrong to bring about intentionally may, if other conditions are met, voluntarily be brought about as side-effects. In other words, the absolute prohibition applies only to the intentional action (Anscombe, 1982: 21).

This doctrine is not an ad hoc device to avoid the disagreeable consequences of Catholic absolutism; it is as controversial for what it forbids as what it allows: it permits a hysterectomy on a pregnant woman having cancer and various other 'indirect' abortions, but it cannot be used to block the application of the absolutist prohibition against intentional killing to any abortion aimed at ending fetal life. Similarly, in end-of-life decisions, double effect allows that life-sustaining treatment may be removed if it constitutes a significant burden on the patient or others. But double effect has no tendency to allow withholding treatment for the sake of ending a life judged no longer worth living. Thus, whatever its legitimate role in other moral outlooks, double effect appears deeply embedded in the absolutism of Catholic natural law theory. A possible explanation is that a non-consequentialist concern for the goods of persons plausibly leads to absolute prohibitions of some voluntary harmings. Intentional harmings can be prohibited since one can always refrain from intentional action. But not all harms brought about as side-effects can be prohibited, since frequently whatever a person chooses to do he or she will bring about harm as a side-effect (Boyle, 1991: 486–8).

As in casuistry generally, the results of absolutist casuistry are likely to be fallible and controversial. But within its absolutist framework, such mistakes can be corrected and, as Anscombe noted, the mistakes of casuistry can cause one to stretch a point on the circumference, but they do not allow one to destroy the centre (Anscombe, 1981: 36).

Absolute rule approaches to ethics, whether in their Kantian or Catholic natural law versions, are not fashionable nowadays, in bioethics or elsewhere. But being out of fashion is not the same as being philosophically disreputable, and much of this contribution is meant to suggest that absolute rule approaches to ethics are not based on superstition or confusion. There is another reason for taking absolute rule approaches to ethics seriously in bioethics. Many distinctions, arguments and analyses originally developed within these approaches have become important elements within bioethical discussions. Questions about the intelligibility of these elements, whether within or independently of their original absolutist framework, can hardly be answered without taking that framework seriously.

References

Anscombe, E. (1981). Modern moral philosophy. In *Ethics, Religion and Politics: Collected papers*. Vol. III. Minneapolis: University of Minnesota Press.

—— (1982). Action, intention and 'double effect'. *Proceedings of the American Catholic Philosophical Association*, 54, 12–25.

Boyle, J. (1991). Who is entitled to double effect? *Journal of Medicine and Philosophy*, 16, 475–94.

Donagan, A. (1977). *The Theory of Morality*. Chicago and London: University of Chicago Press.

—— (1991). Moral absolutism and the double effect exception: reflections on Joseph Boyle's *Who is Entitled to Double Effect? Journal of Medicine and Philosophy*, 16, 495–509.

Finnis, J. (1991). *Moral Absolutes: Tradition, revision and truth*. Washington, DC: Catholic University of America Press.

Finnis, J., Boyle, J. and Grisez, G. (1987). *Nuclear Deterrence, Morality and Realism*. Oxford: Oxford University Press.

Grisez, G. (1983). *The Way of the Lord Jesus*. Vol. I. *Christian Moral Principles*. Chicago: Franciscan Herald Press.

9

A Utilitarian approach

R. M. HARE

The main constituents of any utilitarian theory may be called *'consequentialism'*, *'welfarism'* (Sen and Williams, 1982: 3) and *'aggregationism'*. Consequentialism can be defined, roughly at first, as the view that the consequences of an act are what make it right or wrong. But this by itself is unclear. There is one sense of 'consequences' in which nobody who thinks carefully about the question can help being a consequentialist. That is the sense used here.

A consequentialist is somebody who thinks that what determines the moral quality of an action (that is, determines whether it is right or wrong) are its consequences. A contrast is sometimes drawn between theories which determine the moral quality of actions by their observance or non-observance of rules, and those which determine it by whether they promote valued consequences. But it is obvious that, as we shall see, it is determined by both, and that any adequate theory will take both consequences and rules into account. We normally judge the rightness or wrongness of actions by their conformity to rules or principles, and the principles themselves are judged by the consequences of observing them. If the actions are intentional, we praise or blame the agent for them.

An action is the making of some difference to what happens – to the history of the world. If I make no difference to what happens, I have done no action. In the widest sense, even if I do nothing (do not move a finger), I have done an action (what is sometimes called an act of omission).

I can of course be blamed for doing nothing: someone might say 'You were to blame for not saving the life of the patient when you could have.' It made a difference to the history of the world that I did nothing. We are, in other words, *responsible* for what we fail to do as well as for what we actively do. Suppose, then, that my gun is pointing at somebody and I pull the trigger, and he dies. We say 'I have killed him.' Killing him was what I did – my act. If I did wrong, what made it wrong was the consequence of my pulling the trigger, namely that I killed him. In the light of this example, it is hard to see how people can deny that consequences, in *this* sense, are what make actions right or wrong, and make the people who do them, if the actions are intentional, good or bad. So, in this sense, consequentialism is hard to reject. The people who reject it no doubt have some other sense of 'consequentialism' in mind; but it is seldom clear what sense.

The second constituent of utilitarianism is *welfarism*. Utilitarians think that the consequences that are relevant to the morality of actions are consequences that increase or diminish the *welfare* of all those affected. This means, for a utilitarian, the welfare of all those affected considered impartially. We may define 'welfare' as 'the obtaining to a high or at least reasonable degree of a quality of life which on the whole a person wants, or prefers to have'.

The word 'prefer' is very important, but also ambiguous. It can be used, and normally is used by economists, to mean a pattern of behaviour. In this sense we are said to prefer one sort of thing to another if we habitually and intentionally choose the first sort of thing when we have the choice. On the other hand, it can be used to mean an introspectable mental state of liking one thing more than another. Economists tend to use the first sense, because it makes it possible to determine empirically, by observing people's behaviour, what they prefer. The ambiguity normally causes no trouble, because what we prefer in the introspectable sense we usually also prefer in the behavioural sense; but there can be exceptions where the uses diverge. For example, many people (and not only neurotics) try unsuccessfully to shake off habits which they wish they did not have; so their behaviour does not tally with their introspectable preferences.

There is also a problem about whether, for a utilitarian, *all* preferences have to be counted, or only some. For example, suppose that some child now prefers to go on eating sweets, although it will tend to make him obese, which he will later prefer not to be. This is a fairly easy case to deal with: the utilitarian will aim at the child's preference satisfaction as a whole; its enjoyment of the sweets will count for something, but probably its suffering later from the disadvantages that fat people cannot avoid will count for more.

But there are more difficult problems. How about so-called 'external' preferences? These are preferences that states of affairs should obtain which will never enter into the experience of the preferrer (see Dworkin, 1977: 234). I prefer, say, that in my country people should not indulge in homosexual acts even in private and even if I never see them doing it. Does this preference of mine count for *anything* against the enjoyment they get? There have been many disputes on this point, but it is simplest to say that this and other external preferences do not count (see Hajdin, 1990).

The biggest problem of all about preferences is the problem of *when* the preferences are to be had, if they are to count. It is convenient to use the terms 'now-for-now', 'then-for-then' and 'now-for-then preferences' (Hare, 1981: 101ff.). A now-for-now preference is a preference now for what should happen now; a then-for-then preference is a preference at some later time for what should happen at that time; a now-for-then preference is a preference now for what should happen at some later time. Suppose that I have a preference now that I should not be kept alive if I am seriously handicapped; but that when the time comes I very much want to live. So my now-for-then preference conflicts with my then-for-then preference. Which ought utilitarians to satisfy, if they cannot satisfy both? It seems simplest to say that now-for-then preferences do not count (Hare, 1981: 101ff.; Brandt, 1989).

Moral philosophers dispute about whether preferences of all sentient creatures are to count, or only the preferences of humans. A thoroughgoing utilitarian will take the former view, and defend it by just the same arguments as are used to defend utilitarianism in general (Singer, 1993: chapter 3).

81

So far, then, we have, as constituents of utilitarianism, consequentialism, that is, the view that it is their consequences that determine the morality of actions, and welfarism, that is, the view that the consequences that we have to attend to are those that conduce to the welfare of those affected or the opposite. The remaining constituent is a view about the *distribution* of this welfare. It is the view that when, as usually, we have a choice between the welfare of one lot of people and the welfare of another lot, we should choose the action which maximizes the welfare (i.e., maximally promotes the interests) of all *in sum*, or *in aggregate*. We may call this constituent *aggregationism*.

Aggregationism implies that we should ignore the *distribution* of the welfare that we are bringing about, and simply maximize its total sum in aggregate. That is, if one outcome will produce more welfare, but distribute it very unequally, but another will produce less, but distribute it more equally, it is, according to aggregationism, the first outcome that we ought to choose. This often leads to objections to aggregationism, and therefore to utilitarianism itself, by people of an egalitarian bent, who think that equality of distribution matters in itself, as an independent value, and must not be sacrificed to the maximization of the total welfare.

There are also objections of a different, even opposite kind; it is often held that we have particular duties to, say, a patient or a family member, that we do not have to people in general, and that this person has rights to our attention that other people do not have.

But before we discuss these objections to aggregationism, we must point out that it certainly *seems* to be a simple consequence of a view that is held by many people, including many opponents of utilitarianism, namely the view that in making moral judgements we have to be *impartial* between the interests of the people affected by our judgements. This impartiality is what Bentham was getting at in his famous dictum 'Everybody to count for one, nobody for more than one' (cited in Mill, 1861: last chapter). It is also what is implied by a requirement, which a great many anti-utilitarians (Dworkin, 1977: 182, for example) hold dear, that we should show 'equal concern and respect' for all. It is hard to see what it would be to show equal concern and respect, if not to respect their interests equally. But if we respect their interests equally, we shall give the same weight to the equal interests of each of them. So, for example, if one of them wants some outcome more than the other wants to avoid it, we shall think we ought to bring that outcome about. But this leads directly to aggregationism.

It is easy to see this. If I give as much weight to the interests of person A as to those of person B, and the same weight again to those of person C, what happens when the interests of A and B, on the one hand, preponderate in sum over the interests of C on the other? Obviously, it would seem, the interests of A and B ought to weight more with us than those of C. If we said anything but this, we should *not* be giving equal weight to the interests of A, B and C, and therefore not showing equal concern and respect for A, B and C. So, if one outcome will promote the interests of A and B, and the other will promote the interests of C, and the interests of all these individuals are equal, and we cannot produce both outcomes, it is the first outcome that we ought to produce, if we are to show all three equal concern and respect.

It is therefore surprising that so many anti-utilitarians, who profess to believe that we ought to show equal concern and respect to all those affected, object to aggregationism. The argument just given could be put by saying that if the interests of A and B are stronger *in aggregate* than those of C, we should promote the former rather than the latter. Yet it was based on the requirement to give equal concern and respect to all three.

Another argument commonly used against aggregationsim is also hard to understand (Rawls, 1971: 27). This is the objection that utilitarianism 'does not take seriously the distinction between persons'. To explain this objection: it is said that, if we claim that there is a duty to promote maximal preference satisfaction regardless of its distribution, we are treating a great interest of one as of less weight than the lesser interests of a great many, provided that the latter add up in aggregate to more than the former. For example, if I can save five patients moderate pain at the cost of not saving one patient severe pain, I should do so if the interests of the five in the relief of their pain is greater in aggregate than the interest of the one in the relief of his (or hers).

But to think in the way that utilitarians have to think about this kind of example is *not* to ignore the difference between persons. Why should anybody want to say this? Utilitarians are perfectly well aware that A, B and C in my example are different people. They are not blind. All they are doing is trying to do *justice* between the interests of these different people. It is hard to see how else one could do this except by showing them all equal respect, and that, as we have seen, leads straight to aggregationism.

It must be admitted that often utilitarians argue that we should treat other people's interests as if they were all our own interests. This is a way of securing impartiality. It is implied both by the Christian doctrine of *agape* and by the Kantian categorical imperative, as Kant explicitly says (Kant 1785: BA69 = 430). But this is not to ignore the difference between persons. It is merely to give equal weight to the interests of all persons, as we would do if we gave to all of them the same weight as we give to our own interests; and this is what *agape*, and treating everybody as ends as Kant says we should, require.

This objection belongs to a class of objections to utilitarianism that rest on appeal to common moral convictions or intuitions. In the case we have just been considering it seems counter-intuitive to say that an enormous harm to one person can be outweighed in moral thinking by a larger number of small gains to other people. There are also a tedious number of other objections to utilitarianism based on appeals to intuition. They are to be answered by recognizing that moral thinking occurs at two levels, the critical and the intuitive, and that intuition operates at the latter level, but utilitarianism at the former level, so that the two do not conflict.

We have already mentioned some examples of this kind of objection, such as the objection that we sometimes think we ought to attach an independent value to equality in distribution, or that we ought to favour those near to us, even when utility is not thereby maximized. Other well-worn examples are the alleged requirement of utilitarianism that the sheriff should execute the innocent man to prevent a riot; that one should save an important person from an air crash rather than one's own son if one cannot save both; that one should break promises when even the slightest advantage in preference satisfaction is produced thereby; and that one should kidnap one person, kill him and extract his organs for transplants in order to save the lives of many. (On such objections see Hare, 1981: chapters 8–9.)

They are all easily answered once we realize the importance for moral practice of having firm principles or rules that we do not readily depart from. We cannot often predict the future well enough to be sure what act would maximize utility; and even if we have the information, we do not often have time to consider it fully, and without bias in our own favour. These sound general rules form the basis of our general moral convictions and intuitions, and it is unwise to depart from them lightly. If we do, we shall often be in danger of not acting for the best.

These rules have to be general or unspecific enough to be manageable. For one thing, if they are too complicated we shall not be able to teach them to our children or even learn them ourselves. Also, if they are too specific they may not be of much use. The point – or one of the points – of having moral rules is to cover a lot of cases which, though different in detail, resemble one another in important features.

So there is a good case for having simple general rules. We need therefore some way of putting a limit to the specificity that our rules can have. By 'specificity' I mean the opposite of 'generality'. It is important to notice that generality, in the sense in which it is the opposite of specificity, is not the same as universality (Hare, 1972). Principles can be highly specific but still universal, in the sense of containing no references to individuals. But this is not yet a sufficient answer to the objections we have been considering – the objections from counter-intuitiveness. What shall we do in unusual cases, where we find ourselves wanting to make exceptions to the rules for good moral reasons, as they seem to us?

The way to get over this difficulty is to allow two levels of moral thinking. At the intuitive level we have the general rules, which are simple enough to master. But there will be conflicts between these simple rules. These conflicts are really the source of the objections from counter-intuitiveness. For example, there is a simple rule which bids doctors do the best they can to cure their patients, and another which forbids them to murder people in order to extract their organs. The rules may conflict in unusual cases. If they do, we need a higher level of thinking, which can be much more specific and deal in detail with these cases.

It will be found that real cases, such as we might encounter in practice, are not so difficult to handle as the cases in philosophers' examples. The former will generally be much more complex than the latter, and the additional information available will enable us to reconcile our intuitions with utilitarianism. For example, the abandonment of the rule forbidding murder will inevitably have such serious evil consequences that no saving of patients' lives by giving them murdered people's organs will compensate for the harm done. These murders will not long remain secret; and there can be better ways of securing organs for transplant. And the sheriff will do well to think what will happen in real life if sheriffs do not maintain the rule of law and justice, and so preserve people's rights. Rights certainly have a place in moral thinking, but it is a place easily preserved for them by consequential-ism and utilitarianism (Hare, 1981: chapter 9; Sumner, 1987). Similarly, there are utilitarian reasons why a substantial degree of equality in society is good for every-body (Hare, 1981: chapter 9), and why doctors and parents should look after their own patients and children respectively (Hare, 1981: chapter 8). These partial and egalitarian principles at the intuitive level can be justified by impartial reasoning at the higher or critical level.

It is good enough if utilitarianism tallies with our intuitions in real cases; they do not have to fit cases which are unlikely ever to arise. If such cases do arise in unusual circumstances, most people on reflection will decide that they ought to act for the best (that is, as utilitarianism bids), even if this involves breaking one of the conflicting intuitive rules in order to observe the other.

References

Brandt, R. B. (1989). Fairness to happiness. *Social Theory and Practice*, 15.

Dworkin, R. (1977). *Taking Rights Seriously*. Cambridge, MA: Harvard University Press.

Hajdin, M. (1990). External and now-for-then preferences in Hare's theory. *Dialogue*, 29.

Hare, R. M. (1972). Principles. *Aristotelian Society*, 73. [Reprinted in 1989 in *Essays in Ethical Theory*. Oxford: Oxford University Press.]

—— (1981). *Moral Thinking*. Oxford: Oxford University Press.

Kant, I. (1785). *Groundwork of the Metaphysic of Morals*, cited from the translation by H. J. Paton, *The Moral Law*. London: Hutchinson, 1948, 92. [References are to pages of original editions and to the Royal Prussian Academy edition.]

Mill, J. S. (1861). *Utilitarianism*.

Rawls, J. (1971). *A Theory of Justice*. Cambridge, MA: Harvard University Press.

Sen, A. and Williams, B. (1982). *Utilitarianism and Beyond*. Cambridge: Cambridge University Press.

Singer, P. (1993). *Practical Ethics*. Cambridge: Cambridge University Press.

Sumner, L. W. (1987). *The Moral Foundation of Rights*. Oxford: Oxford University Press.

10

A virtue ethics approach

JUSTIN OAKLEY

The closing decades of the twentieth century have seen a revitalization in ethics of the ancient notion of virtue. The origins of this renewed philosophical interest in the virtues can be traced back to Elizabeth Anscombe's article, 'Modern Moral Philosophy', published in 1958, but the bulk of work on virtue-based approaches to ethics did not begin to appear until the early 1980s, mainly in the writings of Philippa Foot, Bernard Williams and Alasdair MacIntyre. Nowadays, a virtue-based approach to ethics has been developed to the point where it is widely recognized as offering a coherent and plausible alternative to the mainstream consequentialist and Kantian approaches. This revival of virtue-based approaches to ethics has led to a corresponding development of a virtue-ethics perspective on issues in bioethics.

The Rise of Virtue Ethics

While a virtue-based approach to ethics has its intrinsic merits, the turn towards virtue ethics has to a significant extent been motivated by dissatisfaction with certain aspects of mainstream ethical theories. One general complaint which advocates of virtue ethics have made about consequentialist and Kantian theories is that they place too much emphasis on questions about what we ought to *do*, at the expense of dealing with more basic questions about what sort of person we ought to be and what sort of life we ought to lead. Another general criticism which proponents of virtue ethics make of consequentialist and Kantian theories is that they are deficient even as ethics of action, for they are excessively abstract and thus say too little about what agents ought to do in concrete circumstances. A related charge is that these mainstream theories evaluate all acts in terms of 'right', 'wrong', 'obligatory' or 'permissible', and in doing so leave us with an impoverished moral vocabulary. A virtue ethics approach, by contrast, employs such evaluative terms as 'courageous', 'callous', 'honest' and 'just' – as well as the more familiar 'right' and 'wrong' – and thereby provides a much richer and more finely-grained range of evaluative possibilities. More specifically, many have argued that the impartiality characteristic of both consequentialist and Kantian approaches to ethics devalues the ethical importance of personal relationships such as friendship, and that the duty-based approaches of Kantianism and deontology lead to an objectionably minimalist conception of a good life.

86

The development of a virtue ethics approach to bioethics, in particular, while inspired by these general dissatisfactions with standard ethical theories, has also drawn impetus from some more localized targets. To some extent, virtue-based approaches to bioethics have been developed as a reaction to the dominance of bioethics by utilitarianism, which some have thought oversimplifies certain issues in bioethics (see Hursthouse, 1987). But some writers explain the rise of virtue theory in bioethics as a reaction not so much to utilitarianism in particular but rather as a response to the shortcomings of principle-based approaches to bioethics (or 'principlism' see chapter 7, pp. 61–71), which usually claim to be founded on common ground between utilitarian and Kantian or deontological approaches to bioethics. Principle-based approaches (and especially that taken by Beauchamp and Childress, 1994) have become a virtual orthodoxy in discussions of many issues in bioethics (and patient-care issues in particular), but various writers have recently expressed doubts about whether such approaches adequately capture both the contextual nature of decisions in patient care, and the moral importance of a health professional's character (and these doubts echo some of the general criticisms noted above of consequentialism and Kantianism as ethical theories).

However, it can be misleading to contrast virtue-based and principle-based approaches to bioethics, since this implies that virtue-based approaches reject appeals to principles. But there is no reason why a virtue ethics approach cannot endorse certain principles, both generally – such as 'we ought to repay our debts' – and in relation to patient care – such as 'a good general practitioner normally gives priority to his or her own patients over those of other doctors.' Also, since principle-based approaches are usually put forward more as theories telling us how we are to *deliberate* about ethical issues, rather than as accounts of what ultimately *justifies* a certain decision, to contrast principle-based approaches with virtue ethics can create the false impression that virtue ethics is simply a rival theory of deliberation or character, supplementing more fundamental theories of justification.

Further, while there is no essential conflict between a virtue ethics approach to bioethics and the idea (commonly found in principle-based approaches) that patient autonomy is an important value, it is nevertheless possible to see the development of a virtue ethics approach to bioethics as a reaction to the rise of the consumerist movement in health care, which places respect for patient autonomy as the paramount value in health-care decisions. The advance of the consumerist movement has led some writers to assume that the most appropriate role for a health professional is that of the patient's agent, where health professionals have no moral independence from the patients they serve. However, others have expressed concern that such a notion involves a kind of 'deprofessionalization' of health-care workers, and virtue ethics' emphasis on the importance of character (in a morally robust sense) can be seen as an attempt to remedy this tendency.

Some philosophers have regarded the above shortcomings of consequentialist and Kantian approaches as reasons to supplement or modify the accounts of moral motivation and deliberation usually given by those theories, while retaining a basically consequentialist or Kantian criterion of rightness. However, other philosophers have regarded those shortcomings as fatal defects of consequentialism and Kantianism, and have looked to virtue ethics as a thoroughly revisionary theory, capable of providing a criterion of rightness which will replace those given by the standard theories.

Many of virtue ethics' claims have often been put in a negative form, so the approach has become better known for what it is against rather than by what it is for. But focusing only on virtue theorists' critiques of standard ethical theories fails to distinguish the approach from those of others who have made similar criticisms. For example, advocates of feminist approaches to ethics (see chapter 4, pp. 32–40) have also attacked mainstream impartialist ethical theories for their inadequate treatment of personal (and family) relationships, and proponents of particularism have also been critical of the excessive abstraction of conventional principle-based ethical theories. (Particularists argue that the search for general ethical principles leads us to overlook the multiplicity of features which can have moral relevance, and the variations in the moral relevance of those features across different contexts, and so urge us to focus primarily on examining the details of each case as closely as possible.) We therefore need a systematic account of the *positive* claims made by virtue ethics, in order to show what is essential to and distinctive about the approach. In the next section I will sketch a brief account of those positive claims.

What is Virtue Ethics?

There are *six* key claims which are essential to modern forms of virtue ethics. These claims are common to the different varieties of virtue ethics, and also help to distinguish the approach from utilitarianism and Kantianism. The first and perhaps most fundamental claim made by virtue ethics states its criterion of rightness (see Hursthouse, 1991: 225; 1996: 22):

(a) An action is right if and only if it is what an agent with a virtuous character would do in the circumstances.

Thus, according to virtue ethics, reference to character is *essential* in the justification of right action. A right action is one that is in accordance with what a virtuous person would do in the circumstances, and what *makes* the action right is that it is what a person with a virtuous character would do here. For example, Philippa Foot (1977: 106) argues that it is – other things being equal – right to save another's life, where continued life would still be a good to that person, because this is what a person with the virtue of benevolence would do. Likewise, Rosalind Hursthouse (1996: 25) argues that it is ordinarily right to keep a deathbed promise, even though living people would benefit from its being broken, because that is what a person with the virtue of justice would do here.

The primacy given to character in (a) helps to distinguish virtue ethics from standard forms of Kantianism, utilitarianism and consequentialism, whereby actions are justified according to rules or outcomes. However, more recent advocates of Kantian, utilitarian and consequentialist theories have suggested that the relevant criterion of rightness can be understood as an internalized normative disposition in the character of the good agent. Such theories can therefore be put in terms of what a virtuous person would do, where such a person is one whose motivation to act is regulated by the correct rules, or is motivated to maximize utility (see Oakley, 1996: 131–2). How does (a) distinguish virtue ethics from those theories?

Unlike those forms of Kantianism, utilitarianism and consequentialism which tell us what sort of character is recommended by their respective theories, virtue ethics holds that reference to character is *essential* in a correct account of right action. By contrast, most forms of those other theories which tell us to develop a Kantian, utilitarian or consequentialist character allow that the rightness of an action can be determined independently of a reference to the character of a good Kantian, utilitarian or consequentialist agent. For example, act utilitarians hold that an act is right if and only if it results in the most utility of any act the agent could do. They then tell us that the best character to have is the one which would result in the most utility overall. But the sort of human character which can be relied upon to maximize utility overall may not allow the agent in every possible situation to perform the act with the best consequences. So, act utilitarians recognize that a person with the best character may act wrongly on certain occasions.

However, some recent versions of Kantianism, utilitarianism and consequentialism hold that right actions must necessarily be those which are guided by a certain sort of character, and so, like virtue ethics, these accounts give character an essential role in the justification of action. For example, recent revivals of rule utilitarianism have suggested that the aversions in an agent's character can play an analogous role in justifying actions to that played by rules in standard versions of rule utilitarianism. That is, rule utilitarianism standardly evaluates actions in a two-step process, by examining their conformity to a set of rules, and those rules in turn are justified if their being generally followed maximizes utility. Similarly, Richard Brandt has proposed a form of rule utilitarianism which

> orders the acceptable level of aversion to various act-types in accordance with the damage . . . that would likely be done if everyone felt free to indulge in the kind of behaviour in question . . . The worse the effect if everyone felt free, the higher the acceptable level of aversion. (1989: 95; see also Hooker, 1990)

On this sort of view then, the aversions in an agent's character are essential to a correct account of right action, just as rules in standard versions of rule utilitarianism are essential to justifications of right action. Thus, one must look beyond the primacy of character in (a) in order to distinguish virtue ethics from these other forms of character-based ethics.

The distinctiveness of virtue ethics compared to other theories is brought out more fully when we turn to the ways in which advocates of the approach ground the normative conceptions in the character of the virtuous agent. Modern virtue ethicists take one of two broad approaches to filling out the notion of a virtuous character. Many virtue ethicists take the Aristotelian view that the virtues are character traits which we need to live humanly flourishing lives. On this view, developed by Foot (1978) and Hursthouse (1987), benevolence and justice are virtues because they are part of an interlocking web of intrinsic goods – which includes friendship, integrity and knowledge – without which we cannot have *eudaimonia*, or a flourishing life for a human being. According to Aristotle, the characteristic activity of human beings is the exercise of our rational capacity, and only by living virtuously is our rational capacity to guide our lives expressed in an excellent way. There is a sense, then, in which someone lacking the virtues would not be living a *human* life. Another approach to grounding the virtues, developed principally by Michael Slote (1992), rejects the Aristotelian idea that the virtues are given by what humans need in order to flourish, and instead derives the virtues from our commonsense views about what character traits we typically find admirable – as exemplified in the lives of figures such as Albert Einstein and Mother Teresa – whether or not those traits help an individual to flourish.

A second claim made by virtue ethics is:

(b) Goodness is prior to rightness.

Contrary to deontological theories and to traditional forms of Kantianism, virtue ethics holds that the notion of goodness is primary. Thus, no account can be given of what makes an action right without having first established what is valuable or good. This sort of priority of the good over the right is also found in utilitarian theories (and in consequentialist theories generally), and so claim (b) brings out a structural similarity between virtue ethics and those theories.

A third claim made by virtue ethics is:

(c) The virtues are irreducibly plural intrinsic goods.

The intrinsic goods embodied in the virtues cannot be reduced to a single underlying value, such as utility, but are plural. While this claim distinguishes virtue ethics from older, monistic forms of utilitarianism, it does not distinguish the approach from modern, pluralistic forms of preference utilitarianism. For preference utilitarians can allow that there is a plurality of things which have intrinsic value, at least in so far as people desire to have certain things (such as knowledge, autonomy and accomplishment) in themselves, and not merely for their good consequences.

Nevertheless, a further claim helps to distinguish virtue ethics from a preference utilitarian approach:

(d) The virtues are objectively good.

Virtue ethics sees the virtues as objectively good in the sense that they are good independent of any connections they may have with desire. The goodness of the virtues is based on their connections with essential human characteristics, or with what we consider admirable, and they remain good, whether or not the agent who has them desires (or would, if suitably informed, desire) to have them. By contrast, a preference utilitarian who accepts the plural value of the different virtues derives their value from the fact that the agent desires (or would, if suitably informed, desire) to have them.

However, some consequentialists allow that there can be plural intrinsic and objective values. On this view, it is valuable for agents (for example) to be autonomous, even if they do not (and would not, if suitably informed) desire to be autonomous. Two further claims help to distinguish virtue ethics from these forms of consequentialism:

(e) Some intrinsic goods are agent-relative.

Standard forms of consequentialism claim that all goods are *agent-neutral*. Roughly speaking, this means that a particular intrinsic good counts for the same in justification, whether it is *my* good or someone else's. So, for example, pluralistic consequentialists who accord intrinsic value to friendship and integrity tell me to maximize friendship and integrity *per se*, whether or not doing so is at the expense of my own friendships or integrity. By contrast, virtue ethics holds that certain goods, such as friendship, have *agent-relative* value. That is, the fact that a relationship is *my* friendship is itself a morally relevant feature, and carries additional moral weight in justifying what I do. Thus, if I find myself in circumstances where I must choose between performing a friendly act towards my friend and promoting friendships between others (for example, if my friend asks me to help him move house on the day I had been planning to throw a party to welcome new colleagues), virtue ethics would allow that I would be justified in acting for my friend.

Finally, unlike standard forms of consequentialism, which hold that we must maximize the good, virtue ethics claims that:

(f) Acting rightly does not require that we maximize the good.

Virtue ethics holds that acting rightly does not require agents to bring about the very best possible consequences they can. Rather, many virtue ethicists argue that we ought to aspire to a level of human *excellence*. For example, instead of being required to have the very best friendships we can have. virtue ethics tells us that we ought to have excellent friendships.

These six claims do not themselves add up to a substantive ethical theory; they need to be filled out with some account of the virtues themselves before the theory can be applied to practical problems.

Virtue Ethics Approaches to Bioethics

As is becoming clear from the writings of its contemporary exponents, virtue ethics has a great deal to contribute to bioethics. Virtue ethics provides a distinctive new perspective on many familiar issues in bioethics, and it addresses some important questions which standard utilitarian and deontological approaches have shown themselves ill-equipped to deal with, or have neglected altogether. Among the areas of bioethics which have received considerable attention from virtue ethicists are abortion, euthanasia and the practice of health care.

An excellent example of a virtue ethics approach to bioethics is Rosalind Hurst-house's ground-breaking book on the ethics of abortion, *Beginning Lives* (1987). Hursthouse argues that the traditional debate about the competing rights of the mother and the fetus is fundamentally irrelevant to the morality of abortion. Individuals can exercise their rights virtuously or viciously, and Hursthouse argues that the morality of a woman's decision to have an abortion depends importantly on the sort of character which a woman manifests in deciding to have an abortion in her particular circumstances. For example, deciding to terminate a seven-month pregnancy in order to have a holiday abroad would be callous and self-centred, and aborting a fetus because one is fearful of motherhood is cowardly, if one is otherwise well-positioned to become a parent; however, an adolescent girl who has an abortion because she does not feel ready for motherhood yet would thereby show a proper humility about her present level of development. Hursthouse argues that these judgements are appropriate because 'parenthood in general, and motherhood and childbearing in particular, are intrinsically worth-while, [and] are among the things that can be correctly thought to be partially constitutive of a flourishing human life' (1991: 241; see also 1987: 168–9, 307–18). These virtue-based evaluations of women's abortion decisions also reflect the fact that terminating a pregnancy (unlike, say, having a kidney removed) involves cutting off a new human life, which in most circumstances should be regarded as a morally serious matter (Hursthouse, 1991: 237; see also 1987: 16–25, 50–8, 204–17, 331).

Hursthouse's virtue ethics approach to abortion brings out *two* broad sorts of reasons why a woman may in some circumstances be acting wrongly in deciding to terminate her pregnancy. First, she may be showing a failure to appreciate the intrinsic value of parenthood, and its importance to a flourishing human life. And second, she may be taking the decision to cut off a new human life without due seriousness. Hursthouse discusses briefly how these sorts of failings may also be shown by individuals in making decisions about allowing severely disabled infants to die, and in decisions about experimentation on human embryos.

Another example of a virtue ethics approach in bioethics is Philippa Foot's (1977) influential discussion of euthanasia. Foot analyses the concept of euthana-sia, and argues that wanting to die does not necessarily make death a good for that person; rather, death can be a good to a person only when their life lacks a mini-mum of basic human goods, such as autonomy, friendship and moral support. Foot argues that the virtues of justice and charity allow one to fulfil a competent individ-ual's request to be killed, where such basic human goods are absent. Foot also argues that analysing end-of-life decisions in terms of these virtues can bring out an important moral difference between killing and letting die. In normal circum-stances, both justice and charity require us not to kill people, and both virtues require that we do not let people die when we could reasonably have helped them. Further, where someone whose life lacks a minimum of basic human goods ex-presses a sincere request to be killed, both justice and charity would permit such an action to be carried out. However, where such a person demands *not* to be killed, and, say, wishes to be left to die in agony, the requirements of these virtues diverge – that is, justice would forbid us from carrying out the act of killing which charity would normally permit us to perform in such circumstances.

Virtue ethics also offers a promising and insightful approach to many issues in patient care. For example, Edmund Pellegrino and David Thomasma (1993) show how an account of the virtues in medical practice is necessarily based on a philosophy of medicine, in a way that demonstrates what goals are appropriate to and distinctive of medicine as an important human endeavour. Virtue ethics approaches to medical practice typically examine issues in patient care by looking at the doctor–patient relationship, and at the sorts of character traits which are crucial for a doctor in that relationship, such as honesty, compassion, integrity and justice. Thus, according to this approach, doctors ought to tell the truth, not so much because of the importance of informed consent and respect for patient autonomy, but rather because that is what is involved in their having the virtue of truthfulness (see Pence, 1980; Shelp, 1985; Drane, 1988: 43–62; Hauerwas, 1995). However, some who acknowledge the importance of virtuous character traits in good medical practice do not take a virtue-*based* approach, but rather see such accounts as providing a necessary practical supplement to a fundamentally deontological or utilitarian morality (see e.g., Pellegrino and Thomasma, 1993; Beauchamp and Childress, 1994; Hare, 1994).

Criticisms of Virtue Ethics

A number of criticisms have been made of virtue-based approaches to ethics. I will describe two criticisms which I take to be particularly important, and outline how a virtue theorist might respond to them. Both of these objections centre on virtue ethics' appeal to 'what the virtuous agent would do' as the determinant of right action (as in (a) above).

The first criticism raises doubts about whether the notion of virtue is clear or detailed enough to serve as the basis of a criterion of rightness. Many writers argue that this criterion of rightness is too *vague* to be an acceptable basis of justification in ethics. How do we determine what the basic virtues are, and so what a virtuous agent would be like? Is it possible to establish what a virtuous agent would be like without knowing what actions are right? And even if we could establish the character of a virtuous agent, the practical applications of such a model are unclear. What would a virtuous agent do in the great variety of situations in which people find themselves? Further, there is a plurality of virtuous character traits, and not all virtuous people seem to have these traits to the same degree, so virtuous people might not always respond to situations in the same way. For example, is the right action in a given a set of circumstances the action which would be done by an honest person, a kind person or a just person? And even if the range of possible virtuous characters is narrower than this suggests, how do we *know* what a virtuous person would do in a particular situation? As Robert Louden (1984: 229) puts it:

> Due to the very nature of the moral virtues, there is . . . a very limited amount of advice on moral quandaries that one can reasonably expect from the virtue-oriented approach. We ought, of course, to do what the virtuous person would do, but it is not always easy to fathom what the hypothetical moral exemplar would do were he in our shoes.

Now, to the extent that the criticism here expresses a general worry about appeals to 'what a certain person would do', it is worth remembering that such appeals are quite commonly and successfully used in justifications in a variety of areas. For example, novice doctors and lawyers being inducted into their professions sometimes justify their having acted in a certain way by pointing out that this is how their professional mentor would have acted here. Also, courts often rely significantly on claims about what a reasonable person would have foreseen, in determining a person's legal liability for negligent conduct. Moreover, any general worry about such appeals would also apply to many modern consequentialist theories, which hold that the rightness of an action is determined partly by appealing to what consequences would have been foreseen by a reasonable person in the agent's position.

However, those who accept reliance on such appeals in other areas might well have misgivings about the particular sort of appeal to such a standard which is made by virtue ethics. For establishing what counts as having reasonable foresight of the consequences of actions may be far easier than establishing what counts as having a virtuous character. And it may be considerably more difficult to determine which of the variety of virtuous character traits a virtuous person would act on in a given situation than it is to determine which consequences of a given action a reasonable person would actually foresee (see Rachels, 1993: 178).

Now, establishing the nature of a virtuous agent's character is indeed a complex matter, but it should be remembered that virtue ethics does not derive this from some prior account of right action. Rather, which character traits count as virtuous is determined by their involvement in human flourishing or their admirability, as explained above. It is true to say that virtue ethics does not deliver an 'algorithm' of right action (as Aristotle put it), and that a virtue ethics criterion of rightness is perhaps less precisely specifiable and less easily applicable than that given by consequentialist theories (although perhaps not compared to those given by Kantian theories). But it is perhaps an overreaction to argue that this undermines virtue ethics' claim to provide an acceptable approach to ethical justification. For virtue ethicists often given considerable detail about what virtuous agents have done and would do in certain situations, and these details can help us to identify what it is right to do in a particular situation. (We might not gain any more precision from the directives of contemporary Kantian and consequentialist theories which advise us to do what a good Kantian or consequentialist agent would do.) And further, virtue ethics need not claim that there is only one true account of what a virtuous person would be and do, for it can allow that, sometimes, whichever of two courses of action one chooses, one would be acting rightly. In some situations, that is, whether one does what a kind person would have done, or what an honest person would have done, one would still have acted rightly (see Hursthouse, 1996: 34).

The second major criticism of virtue ethics is more fundamental than the first, as it focuses on the plausibility of a purely character-based criterion of rightness, such as that given by virtue ethics in (a) above. That is, many have argued that reference to what an agent with a virtuous character would have done (no matter how precisely specifiable and unitary virtuous character traits are) is not sufficient to justify actions. In support of this criticism, many writers argue that people with very virtuous characters can sometimes be led by a virtuous character trait to act wrongly. For example, a benevolent doctor may be moved to withhold a diagnosis of terminal cancer from a patient, although the doctor reveals the news to the patient's family, and asks them to join in the deception. Or a compassionate father might decide to donate most of the family's savings to a worthwhile charity, without sufficiently thinking through how his action is likely to result in severe impoverishment for his family in the long term. Likewise, a compassionate nurse caring for a convicted murderer in a prison hospital might be so moved by the story of the patient's deprived upbringing that the nurse may deliberately fail to raise the alarm when the patient makes a dash for freedom. As Robert Veatch (1988: 445) puts the worry: 'I am concerned about well-intentioned, bungling do-gooders. They seem to exist with unusual frequency in health care, law, and other professions with a strong history of stressing the virtue of benevolence with an elitist slant.' If we agree that thoroughly virtuous people can sometimes be led by their virtuous character traits to act wrongly, then this seems to cast strong doubt on the plausibility of virtue ethics' criterion of rightness in (a) above. Many critics have been led by such examples of moral ineptitude to claim that virtue ethics is incomplete, and must therefore be underwritten by a deontological or a utilitarian criterion of rightness (see Frankena, 1973: 63–71; Pellegrino and Thomasma, 1993; Rachels, 1993; Beauchamp and Childress, 1994: 62–9; Hare 1994; Driver, 1995).

Now, some virtue theorists would question whether the agent does act wrongly in these sorts of cases (see e.g., Slote, 1995). However, suppose it is granted that the agent concerned does indeed act wrongly in some such cases. There is no reason to think that virtue ethics is committed to condoning such moral ineptitude. For most virtues are not simply a matter of having good motives or good dispositions, but have a practical component which involves seeing to it that one's action succeeds in bringing about what the virtue dictates. Therefore, we might question the extent to which the agent really does have the virtuous character trait which we are assuming he does here. Is it really an act of benevolence to withhold a diagnosis of terminal cancer from a patient, leaving that patient to die in ignorance of his or her true condition? Alternatively, in cases where the action does not seem to call into question the degree to which the agent has the virtuous character trait under scrutiny, it might be that the agent was lacking in some other virtue which was appropriate here. Thus, the father seems to have an inadequate sense of loyalty towards his own family, and the nurse's sense of justice seems defective. However, in some cases, these sorts of responses may not be very plausible, and to that extent, the virtue ethics criterion of rightness in (a) may need to be re-examined.

Conclusion

Because contemporary virtue ethics is a relatively recent arrival in ethical theory and bioethics, it is difficult to assess its future prospects. A virtue ethics approach has already made significant contributions in both areas, but more remains to be done, both to develop the approach itself and to investigate its applications to ethical issues in health care and reproduction. Nevertheless, it is clear that the renaissance of virtue theory has enriched normative ethics considerably, and the emergence of virtue-based approaches to issues in bioethics has created a promising alternative to the rather formulaic methods of the more established approaches.

References

Anscombe, E. (1958). Modern moral philosophy. *Philosophy*, 33.

Beauchamp, T. L. and Childress, J. F. (eds) (1994). *Principles of Biomedical Ethics*. New York, Oxford University Press.

Brandt, R. (1989). Morality and its critics. *American Philosophical Quarterly*, 26.

Drane, J. F. (1988). *Becoming a Good Doctor: the place of virtue and character in medical ethics*. Kansas City: Sheed and Ward.

Driver, J. (1995). Monkeying with motives: agent-basing virtue ethics. *Utilitas*, 7, 281–8.

Foot, P. (1977). Euthanasia. *Philosophy and Public Affairs*, 6, 85–112. [Reprinted in *Virtues and Vices*, 1978.]

—— (1978). *Virtues and Vices*. Berkeley: University of California Press.

Frankena, W. (1973). *Ethics*, 2nd edn. Englewood Cliffs, NJ: Prentice-Hall.

Hare, R. M. (1994). Methods of bioethics: some defective proposals. *Monash Bioethics Review*, 1, 34–47.

Hauerwas, S. (1995). Virtue and character. In W. Reich (ed.), *Encyclopedia of Bioethics*, 2nd edn. Vol. 5. New York: Macmillan, 2525–32.

Hooker, B. (1990). Rule-consequentialism. *Mind*, 99, 67–77.

Hursthouse, R. (1987). *Beginning Lives*. Oxford: Blackwell.

—— (1991). Virtue theory and abortion. *Philosophy and Public Affairs*, 20, 223–46.

—— (1995). Applying virtue ethics. In R. Hursthouse, G. Lawrence and W. Quinn (eds), *Virtues and Reasons: Philippa Foot and moral theory: Essays in honour of Philippa Foot*. Oxford: Clarendon Press, 57–75.

—— (1996). Normative virtue ethics. In R. Crisp (ed.), *How Should one Live? Essays on the virtues*. Oxford: Clarendon Press, 19–36.

Louden, R. (1984). On some vices of virtue ethics. *American Philosophical Quarterly*, 21, 227–36.

Oakley, J. (1996). Varieties of virtue ethics. *Ratio* 9, 128–52.

Pellegrino, E. D. and Thomasma, D. C. (1993). *The Virtues in Medical Practice*. New York: Oxford University Press.

Pence, G. (1980). *Ethical Options in Medicine*. Oradell: Medical Economics Company.

Rachels, J. (1993). *The Elements of Moral Philosophy*, 2nd edn. Englewood Cliffs, NJ: Prentice-Hall.

Shelp, E. (ed.) (1985). *Virtue and Medicine*. Dordrecht: Reidel.

Slote, M. (1992). *From Morality to Virtue*. New York: Oxford University Press.

——(1995). Agent-basing virtue ethics. In P. French, T. E. Uehling and H. K. Wettstein (eds), *Midwest Studies in Philosophy*. Vol. 20. *Moral Concepts*. Notre Dame, IN: University of Notre Dame Press.

Veatch, R. (1988). The danger of virtue. *Journal of Medicine and Philosophy*, 13.

Further Reading

Aristotle (1980). *The Nicomachean Ethics*, trans. W. D. Ross. Oxford: Oxford University Press.

Baron, M., Pettit, P. and Slote, M. (1997). *The Methods of Ethics: A debate*. Oxford: Blackwell.

Crisp, R. (ed.) (1996). *How Should one Live? Essays on the virtues*. Oxford: Clarendon Press.

Crisp, R. and Slote, M. (ed.) (1997). *Virtue Ethics*. Oxford: Oxford University Press.

Flanagan, O. and Rorty, A. (eds) (1990). *Identity, Character, and Morality: essays in moral psychology*. Cambridge, MA: MIT Press.

French, P., Uehling, T. E. and Wettstein, H. K. (eds) (1988). *Midwest Studies in Philosophy*. Vol. 13. *Ethical Theory – Character and Virtue*. Notre Dame, IN: University of Notre Dame Press.

Hurka, T. (1992). Virtue as loving the good. In E. F. Paul, F. D. Miller and J. Paul (eds), *The Good Life and the Human Good*. Cambridge: Cambridge University Press.

Kruschwitz, R. and Roberts, R. C. (eds) (1987). *The Virtues: contemporary essays on moral character*. Belmont: Wadsworth.

MacIntyre, A. (1984). *After Virtue*, 2nd edn. Notre Dame, IN: University of Notre Dame Press.

Pence, G. (1984). Recent work on the virtues. *American Philosophical Quarterly*. 21, 281–97.

—— (1991). Virtue theory. In P. Singer (ed.), *A Companion to Ethics*. Oxford: Blackwell.

Pincoffs, E. (1986). *Quandaries and Virtues*. Lawrence: University Press of Kansas.

Statman, D. (ed.) (1997). *Virtue Ethics*. Edinburgh: Edinburgh University Press.

Williams, B. (1973). A critique of utilitarianism. In J. J. C. Smart and B. Williams. *Utilitarianism: For and against*. Cambridge, Cambridge University Press.

11

A care approach

RITA C. MANNING

An ethic of care has emerged as a new way to conceptualize some deeply held moral intuitions. It provides an important tool for analysing, discussing and ultimately shaping practice in bioethics. In what follows, I shall briefly describe an ethic of care as I understand it and then apply it to some difficult issues in bioethics.

Caring as an Ethical Perspective

An ethic of care is a way of understanding one's moral role, of looking at moral issues and coming to an accommodation in moral situations. There are five central ideas in an ethic of care: moral attention, sympathetic understanding, relationship awareness, accommodation and response. I will discuss each in turn.

Moral attention

Moral attention is the attention to the situation in all its complexity. When I am morally attentive, I wish to become aware of all the details that will allow me to respond to the situation with sympathetic understanding. In this case, I attend carefully to my patient in order to ascertain how she is feeling.

Sympathetic understanding

When I sympathetically understand the situation, I am open to sympathizing and even identifying with the persons in the situation. I try to be aware of what the others in the situation would want me to do, what would most likely be in their best interests and how they would like me to carry out their wishes and interests. I call this attention to the best interests of others maternalism. It is done in the context of a special sensitivity to the wishes of the other and with an understanding of the other's interest that is shaped by a deep sympathy and understanding. To return to my patient – I try to see her sympathetically. If I feel it hard to be sympathetic, I may try several strategies – perhaps imagining her as myself in an earlier medical crisis. As I adopt this sympathetic attitude I become aware of what she wants and needs from me. Finally, I look to satisfy her need in a way that will preserve her sense of competence (when the patient is relevantly competent) and increase her comfort.

98

Relationship awareness

There is a special kind of relationship awareness that characterizes an ethic of care. I recognize that the other is in relationship with me. First there is the most basic relationship, that of fellow creatures. Second there is the immediate relationship of need and ability to fill the need. Finally, I may be in some role relationship with the other that calls for a particular response, such as health care worker–patient. I am aware of all these relationships as I survey a situation from the perspective of an ethic of care. But there is another kind of relationship awareness that is involved as well. I am aware of the network of relationships that connects humans, and I care about preserving and nurturing these relationships. So I see my patient as a fellow fragile human. I recognize that she is in need of my help and that I am able to give it. I recognize my role as a health-care professional and the special obligation this implies. Next, I see her as a member of the appropriate health-care setting. Finally, I acknowledge the web of personal relationships that can either support or undermine her health and well-being. As I search for ways to help her, I do so with the desire to strengthen all these relationships.

Accommodation

Related to the notion of relationship awareness is accommodation. Many times there are many persons involved and how best to help is not obvious. In this case, my desire to nurture networks of care requires that I try to accommodate the needs of all, including myself. It is not always possible, or wise, to do what everyone thinks they need, but it is often possible to do what you think is best while at the same time giving everyone concerned a sense of being involved and considered in the process.

Response

Finally, an ethic of care requires a response on my part. It is not enough to stare at my patient and imagine her in a sympathetic way, to see our relationship as well as the myriad of relationships that connect her to others. I must make my caring concrete in the actions that I take to respond to her need.

The Care Voice and the Justice Voice

Carol Gilligan's pioneering work, *In a Different Voice* (1982), was the first systematic attempt to describe the voice of care and to distinguish it from what she called the voice of justice. Since then, psychologists and philosophers have been busy elucidating the central concepts and testing for various aspects of the two voices. I begin with a brief history.

Lawrence Kohlberg (1981) developed a theory about how people reason and develop morally. His theory of moral reasoning posited that people reason morally by applying principles to cases, thus yielding judgements about what they ought to do. Moral progress, on Kohlberg's account, is cognitive and proceeds to progressively more general principles, with ideal moral progress culminating in principles that are universal and binding on all persons.

Carol Gilligan noted that Kohlberg's subjects, though culturally diverse, were all male. She began to apply his tests to female subjects of various ages. Her conclusion was that some people, notably females, used a different reasoning strategy from that described by Kohlberg and that they progressed by moving through a different set of stages.

Gilligan theorized that some of her subjects appealed to an ethic of care. This involves a through understanding of the context, and a willingness to balance the needs of self and other in a way that preserves both. For Gilligan, moral progress was both cognitive and emotional – the growth in the ability to see the situation from the perspective of self and other and to care about one's self as well as others.

She illustrated the differences in moral reasoning with two 11-year-olds, Jake and Amy. Jake and Amy are both given Kohlberg's Heinz dilemma to solve. A druggist has invented a drug to combat cancer. Heinz's wife needs the drug but Heinz does not have the money to buy it and the druggist will not give it to him. The children are asked whether Heinz should steal the drug. Jake quickly answers affirmatively and defends his answer by appealing to the relative importance of life over property. Amy begins by saying that it depends. She points out all the things that could go wrong if Heinz steals the drug – perhaps he will get caught and go to jail and his wife will be worse off. She suggests instead that Heinz and the druggist should sit down and work it out to everyone's satisfaction.

Jake fits easily into Kohlberg's schemata: he imagines himself in Heinz's position and applies a principle that quickly yields an answer. He does not need any more information about Heinz, the druggist, Heinz's wife, etc. Amy, on the other hand, is virtually impossible to analyse on Kohlberg's scale because she never states or even implies a principle that will yield an answer. Instead, as she imagines herself in Heinz's shoes, she sees the complexity of the situation and realizes that its solution requires that Heinz and the druggist and Heinz's wife recognize their involvement in a relationship and that they honour this awareness by working out a solution that will enable them all to survive and, if possible, flourish.

For Jake the solution is cognitive: Heinz merely reasons about the situation and can take action on the basis of that reasoning. Amy sees a real solution as necessarily involving growth in moral sensitivity and commitment.

On the basis of such differences in her subjects' responses, Gilligan posited a moral orientation, which she calls the voice of care, in addition to the justice orientation of Kohlberg. I propose we sort out the differences by seeing how each voice answers two questions: What are moral agents like? What is the moral standing of persons and communities?

The justice voice says that moral agents are or should be isolated, abstract individuals who follow abstract rules in a cool and impartial manner. Moral agents are isolated in the sense that they are both independent of others and free to choose what relationships to have with others. The model of interaction is contractual – the moral agent chooses to whom she or he will be related and the conditions of the relationship. They are abstract in the sense that their moral obligations are specified independently of the particular facts about them and about the situations they find themselves in. Rather, their moral obligations are spelled out in abstract rules, rules that are general enough to bind all others similarly situated. In following these general rules, they must be cool and impartial. This requires unemotionally applying the rules in the same fashion, regardless of the ties of affection and/or enmity that call on them to be partial.

The voice of care, on the other hand, understands moral agents as embedded in particular social contexts, relationships and personal narratives, who direct their moral attention to real others and are open to sympathetic understanding and identification with those others.

In part because the justice voice conceives moral agency in the way it does, it gives the following answer to the question of the moral standing of persons and communities. All persons are equally valuable – hence there are no special obligations to particular others. Communities and relationships have no moral standing on their own account.

The care voice, on the other hand, agrees that though all persons are valuable, there are special obligations: those imposed by actual and potential relationships and those imposed by roles. Since it understands communities as more than mere aggregates of individuals, and relationships as more than properties of individual persons, it is committed to saying that communities and relationships have moral standing.

Care, justice and self-understanding

There is an additional way to sort out the differences between the care and justice voice and that is in terms of self-understading. This was suggested by Nona Lyons, who argued that a particular self-understanding, a 'distinct way of seeing and being in relation to others' explains the moral agent's preference for a particular moral voice (Lyons, 1983). She identifies two different self-understandings: what she calls the separate/objective self and the connected self. Persons who fit the separate/objective self model describe themselves in terms of personal characteristics rather than connections to others. Connected selves, on the other hand, describe themselves in terms of connections to others: granddaughter of, friend of, etc. This suggests that the separate/objective self sees him- or herself as distinct from others in a more profound sense than does the connected self. The separate/objective self might, for example, see him- or herself as connected to others only through voluntary agreements. The separate/objective self might value autonomy more highly than good relationships with others.

Lyons describes further differences. Separate/objective selves recognize moral dilemmas as those which involve a conflict between their principles and someone else's desires, needs or demands. Connected selves, on the other hand, identify moral dilemmas as those which involve the breakdown of relationships with others. Separate/objective selves fear connection and dependence, and hence value autonomy and independence. Connected selves fear separation and abandonment, and hence value connection and responsiveness.

We can see then how these self-understandings support different moral orientations. Separate selves understand themselves as distinct from others. They conceive moral dilemmas as arising from the conflict between their moral principles and the needs, demands, desires and principles of others. As such, they must mediate their interaction with others in the voice of justice – in terms of ground rules and procedures that can be accepted by all. This is the only foundation for interaction at all, since ties of affection are not seen as strong enough to provide a basis for interaction, especially in persons who fear connection and dependence. This fear of dependence and attachment also explains why they value the objectivity and impartiality that can stand between them and intimates. At the same time, separate/objective selves recognize that interaction with others plays a role in one's satisfaction, so they value community and relationship in so far as these play a role in individual satisfaction.

Connected selves see themselves in terms of others, so relationship, rather than seen as voluntary and incidental to self-identity, is central. The problem of interaction is not then conceived of as how to get others to interact with oneself on terms that would be acceptable to all, but how to protect the ties of affection and connection which are central to one's very self-identity. Moral dilemmas arise over how to preserve these ties when they are threatened, and these dilemmas are mediated by the voice of care. Since the primary fear is of separation and abandonment, a strong value is placed on community and relationships.

Some Implications of an Ethic of Care for Bioethics

An ethic of care has many implications for bioethics. First, the comments on self-understanding suggest that before we insist on one standard of moral practice for all practitioners and patients, we should be sensitive to the diverse self-understandings that we are bound to encounter. Second, the ethic of care can itself be applied to virtually every issue in bioethics. I will discuss just two – its implications for the organization of health-care practice, and its implications for the treatment of terminally ill patients.

A caring model of health-care practice

Recall the central features of an ethic of care: moral attention, sympathetic understanding, relationship awareness, accommodation and response. What implications might these features have for the organization of health-care practice? I shall focus on two features that have a special significance for the organization of health-care practice: moral attention and sympathetic understanding.

Moral attention would imply that practitioners have the time to attend to all the relevant details – in other words, to treat the whole patients and to do so in an unhurried manner. Sympathetic understanding is developed as information is gathered and understanding is developed about how the patient feels, what he or she desires, and what would be best for him or her. This also requires time with the patients.

Relationship awareness too takes time to develop. An ethic of care works best when the relationship is characterized by mutual trust. The other side of relationship awareness, the awareness of the other relationships that might sustain and nurture patients, must also be engaged. Here we must look to the effects on the patient's condition of the network of relationships that surround him or her. If such networks are too fragile or non-existent, we must do what we can to create them. Obviously policies that mandate that a patient be released from the hospital in a specific time, whether or not adequate aftercare is provided, would be incompatible with an ethic of care.

Medical practice in the West can be divided (though not neatly) into two tasks: the doctor/diagnostician/chief decision-makers diagnose the problem and provide instructions for responding to it. Other health-care professionals carry out the orders of the decision-maker (usually a doctor, hopefully in coordination with the patient). Practitioners in both groups are increasingly specialized and the increasing use of medical technology creates further distance between health-care provider and patient. This is surely not the most effective way to practice caring health care. The doctor does not have the time and often does not feel any obligation to get to know enough about patients to offer sensitive care. The increasing specialization of other health-care providers means that they too find it difficult to get to know their patients. In the United States, where medicine is by and large a profit-making industry, patients are paradoxically faced with less care and more caregivers. The nursing staff is often caught in the middle. Nurses, themselves overworked and economically insecure, become ever more important to the patients. Obviously, this is incompatible with an ethic of care. But, in the very real world in which we live, what are nurses to do? If they take an ethic of care seriously, they will feel continually inadequate. It will simply not be possible for them to care adequately for patients.

Some people see this as a criticism of an ethic of care: traditional caregivers (most often women) are faced with impossible demands to give care. I think there are two responses here. First, we must note that we all have an obligation to be caring persons, not in virtue of our gender or our job description, but because we are human beings. Nurses, then, do not have a special obligation to care, though health-care practice has often been organized in such a way that they were the ones most able to be genuinely caring. We all have an obligation to join the political fight for health care that is genuinely caring. Second, we all have obligations to care for ourselves. This obviously includes nurses.

Justice and care

There will be times when a patients' rights model and a care model will be in tension (notably in the patients' rights conception of the autonomous, competent patient versus the care conception of the patient in need who may require maternal assistance). Still they can often work in tandem, and in my opinion they ought to be so wedded. Care and rights should be foundational values for medical institutions and the professionals working in these settings. I envision the marriage of justice and care in the following way. First, we must be sensitive to the self-understanding of those entrusted to our care. Some patients will feel more comfortable in some situations with one or another model of health-care practice. Second, respecting rights is a moral minimum below which we ought not to fall, but care is the moral ideal. Respecting patient rights, then, is a minimal moral requirement, but health-care professionals have not completely discharged their responsibilities until they treat their patients (and fellow professionals) in a genuinely caring way. There is a further amendment to the patients' rights model which must be made to make this a successful marriage. We should no longer assume that all patients are always capable of asserting and defending their rights in an autonomous way. Rather, we should recognize that they may be in need of care, and temporarily (and in some cases permanently) unable to assert and defend their rights. In this case, we care for them and see returning them to full autonomy as part of our obligation rather than as an assumption about their present status.

I want to anticipate one objection here – that my two reasons for insisting on a marriage of justice and care are incompatible. If some patients want to be treated in a justice way – merely having their rights respected – then, it will be said, we should not bring care in to the situation. My response is that treating these patients in this fashion can be either a caring or a non-caring act. One might recognize the person-hood and uniqueness of patients and be content not to violate their rights without really caring about patients. I regard this as morally defective patient care. A caring response would involve respecting rights in a richer sense. It would require sympa-thetic moral attention, time spent with patients and their intimates and responses based on the insight thereby gained. But even if a health-care professional cannot summon up the energy or find the time to care, not violating the patient's rights is still a moral minimum.

So much for the blending of justice and care. I now want to turn to an example of the implications of an ethic of care for treating patients. Though it has implica-tions for every area of health-care practice, I will focus just on care for terminally ill patients.

Caring patient care

My grandfather's final months were spent between a nursing home and the hospi-tal, both far from ideal environments for sensitive care. In both the hospital and the nursing home, rapid staff turnover and divided responsibilities for his care left him feeling uncared for, though he was kept physically comfortable. The fairly rigid visiting hours made it difficult for family members to spend as much time with him as we wished. But in some ways the most troubling lack for me was our inability to communicate honestly as his end neared. I visited him daily and we talked, though only about the most trivial things. When there were two or more visitors, we talked to each other as though he were not there. I suspect that this is a fairly common reaction to dying in our culture, but I think that the institutional settings reinforced it. The parade of attendants who interrupted us with their casual cheerfulness, and the denial that permeated the atmosphere, created a sense of unreality for us both.

I think that my experience was fairly typical. These particular institutional settings made it very hard to practice caring medicine for terminally ill patients. Hospice care, on the other hand, with its emphasis on treating the whole dying patient, might be the most caring way to deal with terminally ill patients. Of course, there are in reality hospices that are genuinely caring and those that are not. In addition, hospices are not immune from rapid turnover and distracted staff. But a hospice with a committed staff, working closely with patients and their families, without the wide range of responsibilities a hospital has and with an acceptance of the patient's imminent death, can provide a more caring atmosphere for dying patients. But in providing the care, it is important to help the patients and their intimates care for each other and for themselves.

Conclusion

An ethic of care is a moral orientation that is sorely needed in our increasingly fractured society. Whether we are teachers or health-care providers, an ethic of care provides guidance about how to live our lives. But it is not just a moral philosophy; it has a political dimension as well. If we are to meet our fellow creatures as caring individuals, we must rethink and, when necessary, restructure our institutions to make this possible.

References

Gilligan, Carol (1982). *In a Different Voice.* Cambridge, MA: Harvard University Press.
Kohlberg, Lawrence (1981). *The Philosophy of Moral Development.* New York: Harper and Row.
Lyons, Nona (1983). Two perspectives on self, relationship, and morality. *Harvard Educational Review,* 53, 125–45.

Further Reading

Battin, Margaret Pabst (1994). *Least Worst Death.* Oxford: Oxford University Press.
Buchanan, Allen and Brock, Dan (1989). *Deciding for Others.* Oxford: Oxford University Press.
Fry, Sara (1989). The role of caring in a theory of nursing ethics. *Hypatia,* 4/2, 88–103.
Held, Virginia (1993). *Feminist Morality.* Chicago: University of Chicago Press.
Holmes, Helen Bequaert and Purdy, Laura (eds) (1992). *Feminist Perspectives in Medical Ethics.* Bloomington and Indianapolis: Indiana University Press.
Kuhse, Helga (1997). *Caring: Nurses, women and ethics.* Oxford: Blackwell.
Larrabee, Mary Jeanne (ed.) (1993). *An Ethic of Care.* New York and London: Routledge.
Manning, Rita (1992). *Speaking from the Heart: a feminist perspective on ethics.* Lanham, MD: Rowman and Littlefield.
Murdoch, Iris (1971). *The Sovereignty of the Good.* New York: Schocken.
Noddings, Nel (1984). *Caring: a feminine approach to ethics and moral education.* Berkeley: University of California Press.

12

A case approach

JOHN D. ARRAS

Top-down vs Bottom-up

In its broadest definition, 'casuistry' is the art of applying abstract principles, maxims or rules to concrete cases. Our morality may tell us, for example, that 'killing is wrong,' but we are then left with the difficult task of determining in concrete circumstances whether a particular act amounts to a form of killing and, if so, whether the killing might possibly be excused or justified. Although just about every moral viewpoint will condemn the killing of an innocent child for selfish motives, for example, other more problematic cases challenge our understanding and deployment of this rule. Is disconnecting a patient from a ventilator a form of killing, or does it just amount to 'letting die'? Is it permissible to kill an animal for food, a fetus for economic reasons or a terminally ill cancer patient at her own request? In order to answer these more complicated questions, we need to develop a complex 'casuistical' account of the rule and its application to particular cases. Defined in this broad way, just about any traditional approach to morality – including Christian, Jewish, Kantian, utilitarian or the 'principlist' amalgam so dominant in contemporary bioethics (Beauchamp and Childress) – will require a casuistical tradition by virtue of which its abstract norms are fitted to concrete cases.

Although casuistry has a long and controversial history as an approach to ethics (Jonsen and Toulmin, Keenan and Shannon, Leites), it has emerged in recent bioethical discussions primarily as an alternative to more 'top-down' or 'theory-driven' methods. Thus, whereas the dominant approach to bioethics has tended to emphasize the importance of moral principles – such as beneficence, autonomy and justice – or the application of moral theories (such as utilitarianism or Rawlsian contractarianism) to concrete dilemmas at the bedside or in social policy, the defenders of casuistry advocate an approach that works from the 'bottom up', starting with our responses to concrete cases and then proceeding, as desirable or necessary, to the development of more abstract principles or moral rules. In this narrower sense, contemporary casuistry has much in common with other 'particularist' or 'interpretivist' criticisms of more principle- or theory-driven methods, such as feminism, pragmatism, hermeneutics and virtue ethics (Arras, 1994).

106

Core Elements of Casuistical Analysis

In order to explicate the more salient features of contemporary casuistry in bioethics, we shall begin, appropriately, with a case drawn from the experience of a neonatal intensive care unit:

> Baby Boy Johnson was the "lucky" one. Ten months ago, he and his twin brother had been born prematurely at 28 weeks to their drug-addicted mother. His brother had died shortly after birth, but Robert had survived, barely, languishing all this time in the pediatric intensive care unit (NICU). "Failure to thrive" is the generic medical description: Born at a mere 2.6 pounds, he now weighed only 6.6 pounds after months of intensive treatment.
>
> Robert was a flaccid, immobile encyclopedia of pediatric ailments. Early on, he had developed a severe lung disorder requiring mechanical ventilation, followed by the usual litany of neonatal catastrophe: a serious intracranial bleed, damaging strokes, seizures, episodes of sepsis, and failure to absorb nutrients. To address the latter problem, a gastrostomy tube was surgically inserted but proved insufficient. Then the surgeon tried to bypass the failing gut with a catheter designed to deliver artificial nutrients directly into the bloodstream; but after two hours of pounding on Robert's skeletal frame, he gave up in frustration. A resident summed up the case: "No body mass, no lungs, no calories to the brain . . . no hope."
>
> Given Robert's dismal prognosis, the doctors began to feel that they were torturing him for no good reason. A nurse told the group that she had to apologize to Robert each time she had to stick him with a needle, which was all-too-frequent. In spite of the caregivers' desire to release Robert from his suffering, his poor, unsophisticated mother and father continued to hope for a "miracle" in this temple of high-tech medicine. The father asks, "Will my son play football?" The mother, perhaps haunted by the likely possibility that her drug habit had damaged her son, asks, "When will my child get off the machine and come home?" Denying the inevitable, Robert's parents steadfastly demand of a horrified staff that "everything be done" for their devastated child.

Paradigm, analogy, taxonomy

Rather than viewing such a case primarily as a site for the immediate deployment of various abstract bioethical principles, the modern casuist must first provide a robust and detailed description of the case, while fitting it under a certain rubric, such as 'termination of treatment'. This description will usually include an inventory of the likely moral reasons or 'maxims' that might typically be invoked in such circumstances. Thus, the casuist would be attentive to what was going on in the case – that is, the interests and wishes of the various parties, the child's medical condition and prognosis, the distinct histories that brought each of the parties to this impasse – as well as to the variety of maxims or middle-level principles triggered by situations of this type, such as 'Parents should normally make medical decisions for their children' and 'Medically futile treatment need not be offered' (Jonsen, 1991).

The next step is to fit the case as described into a *taxonomy*, a structured reservoir of responses to similar cases that contains various *paradigm cases* of conduct judged to be manifestly right or wrong, virtuous or shameful (Jonsen and Toulmin, 1988; Jonsen, 1991). The casuist argues that if moral certitude is to be located anywhere, it resides in our responses to such cases. We know, for example, that it is wrong to kill people without their consent, a paradigmatically wrongful act. We know this, moreover, with greater certitude than we know exactly *why* killing is wrong or which moral theory best explains why it is. Indeed, were a seemingly attractive principle to call for a different response to one of these paradigm cases, that would usually be a good reason to jettison the proposed principle. Thus, casuists are fond of saying that whatever moral certainty we have is to be found at the level of the case, not at the level of abstract principles or theory.

The casuist then tries to locate the new and problematic case on a continuum of cases stretching from a paradigm of acceptable conduct at one end of a spectrum to a paradigm of unacceptable conduct at the other end. Thus, in our case, she might fix on the standard sort of case involving well-educated, well-meaning parents who are generally agreed to have a right of parental decision-making. At the other end of the spectrum, she might conjure up the sort of case where the parents' putative right to make decisions might be effectively overridden. In this particular NICU, there was such a case. Several years before, a case involving a child with a fatal diagnosis (trisomy 18) and a horribly externalized gut (gastroischesis) had provided a defining moment for the unit's evolving moral taxonomy. The surgery to repair the gut would have involved significant and protracted pain and suffering for a child with an already fatal prognosis, but the child's parents had insisted on treatment, saying that surgery was 'God's will'. In this case, the entire medical team had reached consensus that they would not honour the usual maxim of deferring to parental wishes because the treatment would have been painful, futile and unaccompanied by compensating benefit.

The crucial task of the casuist, then, is to determine where along this spectrum of paradigmatic cases the present case falls. Indeed, for the casuist, to say that someone 'knows bioethics' is in large measure to say that he or she is thoroughly familiar with all the 'big' or paradigmatic cases and knows how to reason from them to a suitable result in new and perplexing cases. This is done by means of *analogical thinking* (Jonsen, 1991; Sunstein, 1993). The casuist must compare the case at hand with the paradigm cases in order to determine how they are alike and how they differ in morally relevant respects. In our ICU case, the casuist asks whether the situation involving the patient is closer to the paradigm cases in which parents' right of decision-making are honoured, or rather to the case of the child with trisomy 18. In spite of the evident differences between the Johnson case and the trisomy case, the medical team felt that the similarities were powerful and outweighed the differences. In both cases, treatment was deemed both 'medically futile' and extremely burdensome for the child. In this way, casuistical reasoning gives a concrete significance to the abstract criterion of 'excessive burden'.

This process of reasoning has much in common with the common law. In contrast to normative systems founded on explicit codes and pre-established principles, both the common law and casuistry work from the bottom up, inductively and incrementally developing new principles to deal with problematic cases. Accordingly, casuistry is often referred to as a kind of 'common law morality'.

The role of principles in casuistry

Casuists disagree among themselves about the normative status and derivation of principles in moral reasoning. Some espouse a radically particularist position, claiming that moral principles are mere inductive generalizations based upon our intuitive responses to cases (Toulmin, 1982, 1988). These principles, it is claimed, merely raise our intuitions about cases to a higher level of abstraction and thus do not really tell us anything new. As such, principles have no independent normative force and thus cannot be used to criticize our fundamental responses to paradigmatic cases.

Other casuists, while acknowledging the dependence of principles on our history of moral experience, claim nevertheless that these principles can have an action-guiding or normative force (Jonsen, 1995). For these more moderate casuists, paradigm cases are precisely those that most clearly, powerfully and unambiguously embody the truth of a given moral principle or maxim. They argue that casuistry, properly understood, is not so much an alternative as a necessary complement to the development and deployment of principles (Arras, 1991; Beauchamp and Childress, 1994: 92–100).

In spite of this fundamental difference, both the radical particularists and the moderate casuists agree that whatever meaning a particular principle might have crucially depends upon the role it has played in the history of our previous interpretations. They agree that principles do not emerge from some celestial vault, fully articulated and ready for application to cases. Rather, their meaning is slowly developed and refined as we move from one set of important cases to another. Thus, the right to refuse medical treatment is not simply equivalent to an abstract right to liberty; its precise meaning is forged in the process of working through a large number of treatment refusal cases, each posing some new twist or nuance.

Likewise, both casuistical factions agree that the weight of any given principle cannot be determined in the abstract; like meaning, weight must be gauged in the context of the case. Casuists thus agree with the defenders of ethical 'intuitionism' who reject the possibility of a pre-established hierarchy of values and principles. Eschewing any such 'lexical ordering' (Rawls, 1971: 42) of principles, casuists insist that the details of each case will determine the precise weight of all the relevant yet conflicting moral principles at stake. Thus, the principle of autonomy may prevail in one treatment refusal case where the patient's choice is deemed to be competent, well informed and no threat to the welfare or resources of others; but it may be trumped in other cases where the claims of autonomy are weaker or the rival claims of others to scarce resources are stronger. Casuists caution that there is no rule that would allow us to determine, ahead of time, which value ought to prevail in any given case. Echoing a familiar Aristotelian theme, they insist that there is no substitute for good judgement (*phronesis*) based upon the particulars –

the who, what, where, when, how much – of the case (Jonsen and Toulmin, 1988: 19, 58–74).

Casuistry as rhetoric

In contrast, then, to methodological approaches that view ethics as a quasi-scientific enterprise bent on deductive demonstration of particular truths, casuistry emerges as a thoroughly *rhetorical* mode of inquiry (Jonsen and Toulmin, 1988: 326; Jonsen, 1995). Whereas the partisans of a geometric approach attempt to convince through long chains of reasoning finally punctuated by the claim, 'You cannot think otherwise on pain of inconsistency!' casuists attempt to persuade by adducing numerous and often disparate considerations. Thus, instead of basing their argument for a right to health care on any single principle, such as utility, casuists typically invoke a cluster of complementary considerations including not just utility but also equal opportunity, communitarian themes and the historical commitment of the medical profession to serve the poor. Although this method lacks the theoretical simplicity and aesthetic allure of more monistic approaches, it is much more likely to convince a larger number of people, many of whom may not embrace a theorist's preferred foundational principle. This kind of multifaceted, rhetorical appeal typically yields moral conclusions that are admittedly only probable, not apodictic; but the casuist argues, again following Aristotle, that this is the best we can hope for when arguing about particulars.

Advantages of a Casuistical Approach

Casuistry's close reliance on context gives it a distinct advantage over more theory-driven approaches in the practical worlds of policy formation and the medical clinic. It is a method of thinking especially well-suited to busy physicians and nurses whose clinical outlook is already thoroughly case-oriented and who have neither the time nor the inclination to bother with too much theory. Although casuists must clearly presuppose a fair measure of social agreement on which to base their proposed solutions, they stress that usually there is no need for agreement at the level of deep theory or principle. Consensus can often be reached at a relatively low level of analysis between the invocation of 'middle-level' principles (e.g., the principle of informed consent) and the particulars of the case (Jonsen and Toulmin, 1988; Sunstein, 1995). Thus, while the members of a bioethics commission might advance competing theories of *why* a certain practice, such as surrogate parenting, might be wrong, they might all be able to reason analogically to the conclusion that surrogate contracts constitute a form of 'baby selling', and this might be all the agreement they need for the practical task at hand.

Like the common law, which also eschews appeals to deep theory, casuistry thus appears particularly well-suited to the resolution of conflicts within a pluralistic, democratic society (Sunstein, 1995). In the absence of a single, state-sponsored vision of the good life, casuistry seeks an 'overlapping consensus' between groups with disparate and often conflicting views. But whereas a theorist like John Rawls

(1993) seeks such consensus at the level of overarching, abstract principles, the casuist seeks it at the lower level of responses to paradigmatic cases, responses that might be explained or justified quite differently by different groups.

Seeking consensus at this lower, less theoretical level has an additional benefit for life in a pluralistic society. Whether the competing voices in a public debate take the high road of elevated principle or the low road of analogical reasoning, there are bound to be winners and losers. But if an issue is resolved at the lower level, the losers are likely to feel far less offended and aggrieved than if they had lost on the higher plane of their most cherished principles. In the area of abortion, for example, the so-called 'pro-life' faction might have reacted in a much more temperate and measured fashion had the Supreme Court decided *Roe v. Wade* in a way that did not completely nullify their deeply-held belief that all human life is somehow sacred. An approach more closely tailored to the factual circumstances of that case might possibly have been less polarizing and thus more hospitable to future compromises.

Objections and Replies

Casuistry is insufficiently critical   A common objection to casuistical approaches is that, precisely because they work from the 'bottom up' – because they begin already immersed in current intuitions, convictions and practices – they are unable to provide a critical standpoint from which those very practices might be judged (Arras, 1991: Wildes, 1993; Tomlinson, 1994). It may well be that some of our most strongly felt convictions, far from being obviously right, are actually the fruit of profoundly unjust social practices and institutions. If we could just step back and gain some critical distance, the injustice might become visible; but because casuistry anchors itself in paradigm cases, which are themselves based upon deeply entrenched social practices and attitudes, it will often leave such systemic injustices undetected and unchallenged.

In response, the casuist can and should admit that this approach, which is essentially backward-looking, may have some conservative tendencies. It remains true, however, that the overall direction of casuistical thought, whether conservative or progressive, will ultimately depend upon who is judging and which principles and values animate their analogical reasoning. Progressive social critics using progressive social norms will reason analogically to progressive conclusions.

Second, the casuist will note that most mature cultures will contain resources for robust self-criticism. Even at those moments when the values of the philistines, the hypocrites and the unjust majority seem unshakeable, untapped resources for potentially subversive cultural criticism can often be identified (Walzer, Kuczewski). Martin Luther King, for example, spoke to white racists not as an outsider but rather as a fellow Christian, and he invoked values embedded in his culture's rich traditions and taxonomy to devastating effect.

It would also be fair for the casuist to respond here that even if casuistry is susceptible to the lure of common opinion and ideology, other rival methodological approaches often fare no better. Although principlists or theorists might think

111

themselves better equipped than casuists to recognize and criticize lines of case judgements that deviate from the road of justice, they are often just as blind to the deeply entrenched prejudices of the day.

Reasoning by analogy is too indeterminate A second criticism alleges that casuistry might work well within cultures featuring pervasive agreement on fundamental values, but that it must founder in highly pluralistic or even 'post-modern' cultures like our own (Wildes, 1993). Whether or not this criticism has merit, it does highlight the important fact that casuistry is more a method than a doctrine, more an engine of thought than a moral compass. The direction that this engine takes will invariably depend upon the value commitments of a community of inquirers (Kuczewski). Thus, it makes perfect sense to talk about an Orthodox Jewish casuistry embedded in Halakah (Jewish law), a Roman Catholic casuistry or even the casuistry of a particular neonatal ICU or hospital ethics committee.

The objection, then, is that casuistical reasoning depends upon deep-seated agreement on fundamental values and will necessarily fail to reach determinate conclusions when deployed in modern, pluralistic societies where such agreement is lacking. In contrast to the similar methodology of common law, which enjoys the advantages of having clearly defined decision-making authorities (judges) and paradigm cases that legally bind all subsequent interpreters (legal precedents), casuistry as practised in secular, pluralistic societies features no clearly authoritative 'moral experts' and its precedents (paradigms) are always subject to revision and reinterpretation at the hands of rival commentators.

In response, the casuist might first note the point made above, that casuistry may often be able to help forge consensus at the shallow level of responses to cases even when consensus at the deeper level of principle or theory is unlikely. Secondly, the casuist can resist the implication that modern societies are hopelessly Balkanized into small, hermetically sealed interpretive communities. Increasingly, in spite of the differences between regions and groups, modern societies are becoming increasingly *cosmopolitan*, increasingly marked by the overlap and interpenetration of disparate cultural and linguistic subgroups. Finally, it might be noted that, in spite of our manifest differences, the various interlocking communities of hospital clinicians, academics, judges and juries, medical societies, policy centres and grassroots movements somehow manage to grope their collective way towards an overlapping consensus on a number of fronts in bioethics – even on the highly contested terrain of death and dying – largely with the aid of casuistical reasoning. While it would be overly sanguine to view casuistry as a kind of universal solvent for bioethical disputes, it would be overly pessimistic to ignore the ability of analogical reasoning at least to narrow the range of legitimate disagreement even when it cannot effect consensus.

Conclusion

Although casuistry has emerged in recent years as a rival approach to the dominant strain of principlism in contemporary bioethics, it is best viewed as a more modest but indispensable contribution to a more inclusive, holistic approach to ethical reasoning. Analogical thinking is usually a necessary component both in moral problem-solving and in the gradual development of moral principles and theories. Reasoning by means of paradigm and analogy provides the kind of specificity often lacking in more theory- or principle-driven approaches, allowing us to connect more abstract concepts with familiar fact patterns. And casuistical analysis also allows parties divided at the level of principle to converge on responses to specific paradigms and cases – a distinct advantage in pluralistic, democratic societies.

But casuistry also has familiar limitations that prevent it from being considered a self-sufficient method. Like the common law, it is inherently backward-looking and can be insufficiently attentive to a more systematic and scientific assessment of consequences (Tomlinson, 1994; Posner, 1995: 171–98). Likewise, due to its focus on proximate paradigms, casuistry can also fail to pay adequate attention to larger, overarching social questions, such as what kind of society we wish to live in (Arras, 1991). And finally, relying as it does on settled convictions and common responses to cases, casuistry always risks a facile accommodation to the prejudices of the day. For these reasons, casuistry must be supplemented with an account of action-guiding principles and theories, with a concern for larger questions of the good life within a community, and with a critical eye for deep-seated and pervasive social injustices that distort our interpretation of cases.

References

Arras, J. D. (1991). Getting down to cases: the revival of casuistry in bioethics. *Journal of Medicine and Philosophy*, 16, 29–51.

—— (1994). Principles and particularity: the roles of cases in bioethics. *Indiana Law Journal*, 69, 983–1014.

Beauchamp, T. L. and Childress, J. F. (1994). *Principles of Biomedical Ethics*, 4th edn. New York: Oxford University Press.

Jonsen, A. R. (1991). Casuistry as methodology in clinical ethics. *Theoretical Medicine*, 12, 295–307.

—— (1995). Casuistry: an alternative or complement to principles? *Kennedy Institute of Ethics Journal*, 5, 237–51.

Jonsen, A. R. and Toulmin, S. (1988). *The Abuse of Casuistry: a history of moral reasoning*. Berkeley: University of California Press.

Keenan, J. F. and Shannon, T. (1995). *The Context of Casuistry*. Washington, DC: Georgetown University Press.

Kuczewski, M. G. (1997). *Fragmentation and Consensus: Communitarian and casuist bioethics*. Washington, DC: Georgetown University Press.

Leites, E. (ed.) (1988). *Conscience and Casuistry in Early Modern Europe*. Cambridge: Cambridge University Press.

Posner, R. (1995). *Overcoming Law*. Cambridge, MA: Harvard University Press.

Rawls, J. (1971). *A Theory of Justice*. Cambridge, MA: Harvard University Press.

—— (1993). *Political Liberalism*. New York: Columbia University Press.

Sunstein, C. R. (1993). On analogical reasoning. *Harvard Law Review*, 106, 741–91.

Tomlinson, T. (1994). Casuistry in medical ethics: rehabilitated, or repeat offender? *Theoretical Medicine*, 15, 5–20.

Toulmin, S. (1982). The tyranny of principles. *Hastings Center Report*, 11, 31–9.

—— (1988). The recovery of practical philosophy. *American Scholar*, 57, 337–52.

Walzer, M. (1987). *Interpretation and Social Criticism*. Cambridge, MA: Harvard University Press.

Wildes, K. W. (1993). The priesthood of bioethics and the return of casuistry. *Journal of Medicine and Philosophy*, 18, 33–49.

Further Reading

Brody, B. A. (1988). *Life and Death Decision Making*. New York: Oxford University Press.

Miller, R. B. (1996). *Casuistry and Modern Ethics: A poetics of practical reason*. Chicago: University of Chicago Press.

Strong, C. (1988). Justification in ethics. In B. A. Brody (ed.) *Moral Theory and Moral Judgments in Medical Ethics*. Dordrecht: Kluwer, 159–84.

Sunstein, C. (1996). *Legal Reasoning and Political Conflict*. New York: Oxford University Press, 35–61.

Wallace, J. (1996). *Authoritative Practice: The case for particularism in ethics*. Ithaca, NY: Cornell University Press.

PART IV

BEFORE BIRTH: ISSUES INVOLVING EMBRYOS AND FETUSES

Tooley argues that...

Potentiality does not + personhood.

(close to reductionist argument)

Species membership ≠ personhood

Means abortion acceptable

→ most likely kid or scenario that we envisage)

→ Does not preclude disabilities that are incompatible with personhood (cleft palate?)

If awareness / comprehension / reason / thought / feelings are required for personhood, then abortion is ok.

But if we apply this more precisely...

Tooley argues that...

13

Personhood

MICHAEL TOOLEY

Basic Moral Principles and the Concept of a Person

In everyday discourse, the term 'person' is used in two rather different ways. Sometime its meaning is purely biological, and it is used to refer simply to individuals belonging to our own species, *Homo sapiens*. Often, however, people refer to entities that are not humans – such as gods, angels, possible extraterrestrials – as persons. Or they wonder whether certain animals, such as whales, dolphins and primates, may not be persons. The term 'person' is then being used in a very different way – namely to refer, not to individuals belonging to a certain species, but instead to individuals who enjoy something comparable, in relevant respects, to the type of mental life that characterizes normal adult human beings.

It is the latter concept that has come to play a central role in ethics, and the reason is that a number of considerations strongly support the idea that the concept of a person is crucial for the formulation of many *basic* moral principles, including ones concerned with the morality of killing. For, first of all, consider two different fates that might befall one – on the one hand, being killed, and on the other, having one's upper brain completely destroyed, while one's lower brain remains intact. Since the upper brain, consisting of the cerebral hemispheres, contains the neurophysiological basis not only of higher mental functions such as self-consciousness, deliberation, thought and memory, but also of consciousness of even the most rudimentary sort, the destruction of the upper brain means the destruction of the capacity for any sort of mental life. But in addition, the upper brain also contains the basis of the specific memories, beliefs, attitudes and personality traits that make one the unique person one is. Consequently, the destruction of the upper brain involves the destruction not only of certain general capacities, but of the states that underlie personal identity. Provided that the lower brain, or brainstem, is not damaged, however, there will still be a living member of our species, since it is the lower brain that controls life processes, including respiration. In a case of killing, by contrast, one no longer has a living member of our species. Nevertheless, the two outcomes seem equally bad. Furthermore, if one considers someone intentionally bringing about either outcome, each action seems as wrong as the other.

A second and related consideration involves the idea of reprogramming. Suppose that, rather than being killed, one undergoes *total* reprogramming in which all of one's memories, beliefs, attitudes, preferences, abilities and personality

117

traits are destroyed, and replaced with completely unrelated pseudo-memories, beliefs, attitudes, preferences, abilities and personality traits. If this were done, an entity would still exist that would be not only a living member of our species, but also a psychologically normal, adult human being. But would this outcome be any less unwelcome from the point of view of the individual involved than the two just considered? Or would performing such an action be any less wrong than killing or completely destroying the upper brain of a normal, adult human being? Most people, it seems, do not think so, on the grounds that, though one is left, in the reprogramming case, with a living and quite possibly normal adult human being, the individual who once existed has been destroyed.

A third consideration is this. Suppose that, after one person destroys your upper brain, a second person, knowing that this has been done to you, proceeds to destroy your lower brain. Are you worse off as a result of the latter action, and has the person who performed that action done something that was morally on a par with what the first person did? In order to hold that you would be worse off, it would seem that one would have to hold that the destruction of all of someone's brain was morally worse than the destruction of just the upper brain. If, as many people feel, this consequence is not plausible, one is forced to conclude that although the action of the second person involves killing a living member of our species, while the action of the first person does not, it is the first action, and not the second, that is seriously wrong.

One can make sense of these intuitions only if one concludes, first, that it is a basic moral principle that the destruction of a person is at least prima facie seriously wrong, and secondly, that the wrongness of killing normal adult human beings derives from the fact that killing in such cases involves the destruction of a person. For when this view is adopted, one can explain, on the one hand, why having one's upper brain completely destroyed, or being completely reprogrammed, is morally on a par with being killed: all three acts involve the destruction of a person. One can also explain why one is not made worse off by the destruction of one's lower brain, once one's upper brain has been destroyed – namely that although this action results in the death of a living member of our species, it does not involve the destruction of a person.

The above considerations all turn upon cases involving human beings. The fourth and final line of thought focuses instead upon animals belonging to other species. One way of developing this final point is by raising the question of the morality of killing in the case of some animals with which we are actually acquainted. Thus one might focus, for example, on a chimpanzee that has learned sign language, and ask whether the painless killing of such an animal would be morally problematic, and, if so, to what extent. But given that what we are interested in are *basic* moral principles concerned with killing, there is another way of developing the argument. It arises because basic principles must apply not merely to situations of sorts that we have already encountered, but also to types of situations that, although they have not yet arisen, might very well do so. As a consequence, rather then confining one's consideration to species that are at present known to exist on earth, one can focus instead upon a possible extraterrestrial – one

118

whose mental life is, by hypothesis, in no way inferior to our own. If there were such a being, would killing it be seriously wrong, or would it be morally comparable to killing, say, a plant or an insect? Most people, it appears, feel that the killing of such a being who was not a member of our species, but who had a comparable or superior mental life, would be seriously wrong. If this view is right, then one is forced to conclude, once again, that a fundamental principle that is crucial for setting out an account of the morality of killing is that the destruction of persons is at least prima facie very seriously wrong.

The Concept of a Person and the Wrongness of Killing

The principle that the destruction of persons is very seriously wrong is not itself very controversial: very few philosophically informed people, thoroughly acquainted with the sorts of considerations briefly sketched above, would wish to reject it. There are, however, a number of other issues, in the neighbourhood of this principle, which are far from uncontroversial. One of the most important, for example, is the following. If something is a person, then, other things being equal, its destruction is seriously wrong, and intrinsically so. But in addition, if one destroys a person, one does something wrong *to* the entity that one destroys. Is it only persons of which this is true? Or is personhood a prima facie *sufficient* condition, but not a *necessary* condition, of an entity's possessing this sort of moral status?

What other types of entity might be thought to have the same moral status as that of persons? Two candidates that certainly need to be considered are suggested by discussions of the morality of abortion. First, there are potential persons – where the concept of a potential person is the concept of an entity that, though not a person, contains within itself all of the positive factors that are needed in order for it to become a person. Second, there are entities that, though neither persons nor potential persons, belong to a species whose normal adult members are persons. (Examples of the latter are anencephalic human babies, which, because of severe congenital malformation of the brain resulting in the possession of at most rudimentary cerebral hemispheres, are in a permanent vegetative state, and thus are not even potential persons.)

A second controversial issue concerns the boundaries of personhood. For while there is widespread agreement that certain combinations of psychological properties – such as those that one finds in normal adult members of our own species – suffice to make something a person, there is considerable disagreement among philosophers both concerning which of those properties are the morally significant ones, and concerning which properties constitute a *minimum* basis for personhood.

A final important issue is whether personhood is an all-or-nothing matter, so that all persons, qua persons, have precisely the same moral status, or whether, on the contrary, personhood admits of degrees. On this matter, by far the dominant view has been that personhood does not admit of degrees. As we shall see below, however, there are reasons for questioning this opinion.

119

MICHAEL TOOLEY

What Makes Something a Person?

What properties suffice to make something a person? That certain clusters of properties are sufficient is almost universally accepted among philosophers. Consider,
for example, a being that possesses consciousness, has preferences, has conscious
desires, has feelings, can experience pleasure and pain, has thoughts, is self-
conscious, is capable of rational thought, has a sense of time, can remember its own
past actions and mental states, can envisage a future for itself, has non-momentary
interests, involving a unification of desires over time, is capable of rational deliberation, can take moral considerations into account in choosing between possible
actions, has traits of character that undergo change in a reasonably non–chaotic
fashion, can interact socially with others and can communicate with others. Few
would disagree that such an entity is a person. But what is one to make of this list
of seventeen properties? Some of the properties are rather closely related, so one
may be able to shorten the list somewhat. One will still be left, however, with a large
collection of significantly different properties. Are all of those properties relevant
with respect to whether an entity is a person? Among those that are relevant, are
any of them sufficient on their own to make something a person?

Once these questions are raised, quite different answers are likely to be advanced, and on the whole, relatively little consensus is likely to exist. Thus, with
regard to the issue of what properties, on their own, make something a person,
some important alternative views are that self-consciousness is sufficient, that the
capacity for rational thought is sufficient, that being a moral agent is sufficient, that
being a subject of non-momentary interests is sufficient, that having a mental life
that involves an adequate amount of continuity and connectedness via memory is
sufficient and that simple consciousness is sufficient. How is one to decide on the
correctness of these claims? In this area, appeal to mere intuitions seems especially
unpromising, and there would seem to be little hope of resolving this issue without
making out a case for a systematic moral theory. The question, moreover, is a very
pressing one. For while the choice among the first five views just mentioned might
very well not make too much difference with regard to our present decisions, since
all five views would seem to entail that one does not have a person until one has an
entity whose mental life is unified over time in quite significant ways. if it turned out
that mere consciousness was sufficient to make something a person, that would
obviously have very significant implications with regard to the moral acceptability
of many of our present practices. For adult members of many animal species,
certainly including all mammals, would then have to be classified as persons, and
so their use either as a source of food or in many scientific, medical and commercial
experiments, would be seriously wrong.

Another deeper issue that needs to be addressed by ethical theorists is
whether the possession of certain general *capacities* – such as the capacity for self-
consciousness or for rational thought – makes something a person. Many philosophers in the area of ethics have tended to assume, without offering any supporting
argument, that this is so. Within philosophy of mind, however, it is often held that
a person does not exist until there is a series of actual, conscious experiences that

120

are psychologically interconnected in certain ways. If the latter view is correct, then neither the mere possession of certain unexercised capacities, nor even the combination of conscious experience plus unexercised capacities, suffices to make it the case that one has a person: it is crucial that the relevant capacities be ones that either have been, or are being, exercised.

But can one have, say, a capacity for thought that has never been exercised? It would seem that one can. For given that an organism will have a capacity for thought if it has a brain containing certain complex neuronal connections, it is possible that the necessary neurological development might be completed at a time when the organism is not conscious, so that there would be, at a certain time, a capacity for thought that has never been exercised in any way.

There is a genuine theoretical issue, accordingly, whether something becomes a person as soon as it acquires a relevant capacity, or only later, when it first exercises the capacity. Unlike the preceding issue, however, this one does not have substantial practical implications, as the question of killing rarely arises in such cases. A satisfactory resolution of this issue is essential, however, if one is to have a comprehensive moral theory concerning the basis of personhood and the morality of killing.

Is Personhood a Matter of Degree?

If, in thinking about personhood, one focuses only upon human persons, it is very easy to take it for granted that all persons, qua persons, have the same moral status. But once one considers the possibility of entities that have only some of the psychological properties possessed by normal adult human beings, or that have some of those properties only to a markedly lesser degree, it then becomes clear that it is important to ask whether all persons necessarily have the same moral status, or whether, on the contrary, personhood is a matter of degree.

This issue is also one that it may be very difficult to resolve in the absence of a general moral theory. One way of thinking about this question that may be helpful, however, in the absence of such a theory, is this. First, is the wrongness of destroying a person connected in some way with the value that an individual's life has, or potentially has, *for that individual*? Second, if it is, are there properties that make for personhood such that the extent to which one possesses those properties makes a difference with respect to the value that one's life has for oneself? If the answer to both of these questions is in the affirmative, then one has a reason for concluding that personhood is a matter of degree.

Assume, for illustration, that the ability to remember one's past actions and mental states, and the ability to envisage a future for oneself, and to pursue goals and projects, are properties that make for personhood. Organisms might vary greatly, presumably, in the extent to which they have those abilities. Imagine, then, having those abilities to a much more limited degree – so that, say, one could not remember more than a minute of one's prior life, nor envisage a future extending more than a minute beyond the present. What difference would such a change make to the value that an individual's life would have for that individual? If the

121

answer is that the value would be significantly reduced, and if the wrongness of destroying a person is related to the value that life has, or could have, for the individual in question, then the destruction of a person with such very limited abilities to remember the past and envisage a future will not be as seriously wrong as the destruction of a person who possesses the much less limited abilities characteristic of normal human persons. Not all persons, then, would have the same moral status.

If this is right, there are some significant consequences. First, the fact that an animal belonging to another species has certain crucial characteristics only to a much lesser degree than normal human beings will not mean that the animal has no moral status at all. Second, within our own species, the acquisition of personhood may very well be a gradual process, and similarly for the loss of it, in at least some cases – such as, for example, Alzheimer's disease, which ultimately results in a permanent, degenerative, vegetative state.

Is Potential Personhood Morally Significant?

With regard to the question of whether there are non-persons that have the same moral status as persons, the most important candidates are potential persons. In considering this issue, it is crucial to distinguish between passive potentialities and active potentialities. Thus, while an unfertilized human ovum together with a neighbouring, human spermatozoon are, in a sense, potentially a person, the potentiality is a passive one, since it requires outside intervention to start a process that will ultimately give rise to a person. By contrast, once the unfertilized human ovum is united with the spermatozoon, one has – or so, at least, it might initially seem – an active potentiality for personhood. A potential person is to be understood, therefore, as something that involves an active potentiality for personhood, and it is the destruction of such a potentiality that some have claimed is morally on a par with destroying a person.

Why should the small change in location involved in uniting the ovum and the spermatozoon make such a great moral difference? If this purely physical change were accompanied, for example, and as some people believe, by the creation of an immaterial, immortal soul which was attached to the fertilized human ovum, and which possessed, from the very beginning, the *capacity* for self-consciousness and rational thought, then it would be easy to see why one might hold that a morally significant change had taken place. But this line of thought, whatever its merits, has no connection with the claim that potential persons have the same moral status as persons, since it involves the idea that one really has a *person* – and not merely a potential person – from the very beginning of life.

Does the physical change in itself, then, have moral significance? There are at least two reasons for holding that it does not. First, compare the situation involving the unfertilized ovum and spermatozoon with that of the fertilized ovum. In both cases, genetic material is present that will completely determine the genetic characteristics of any resulting individual. But what of the difference between a passive potentiality and an active one? The answer is that in neither case does one have a *fully* active potentiality – that is, a potentiality that will actualize itself if not interfered with. For unless the fertilized ovum is in an appropriate environment that supplies warmth, nutrients, etc., the development of the fertilized ovum is going to be very limited indeed. In both cases, accordingly, very significant outside assistance is required if a person is ultimately to result, and so it seems very implausible to assign a significantly different moral status to the two situations.

Secondly, consider the following case where there *is* a fully active potentiality. An artificial womb has been perfected, and it now contains an unfertilized ovum, along with a spermatozoon. There is also a device, however, which will ensure that fertilization will soon take place, so that if there is no interference, the result will be the emergence, in nine months' time, of a normal human baby, who will then receive appropriate care so that it can continue to develop. This situation involves accordingly, a fully active potentiality, by contrast with the case of the isolated, fertilized human ovum. The crucial question, then, is this. What is the moral status of destroying the fully active potentiality by, say, turning off the machine before fertilization has taken place. Very few people, it seems, would hold that such an action is morally wrong. If this is right, then the destruction of a fully active potentiality for personhood, rather than being morally comparable to the destruction of a person, is not morally wrong at all.

Is Species Membership Morally Significant?

A second suggestion that is sometimes advanced concerning entities that might have the same moral status as persons is that if something, while neither a person nor even a potential person, belongs to a species whose normal adult members are persons, such an entity has the same moral status as a person. On this view, then, the killing of an anencephalic human infant would be morally on a par with the destruction of a person.

This view appears unsatisfactory, however, for a number of reasons. First, it seems plausible to base an entity's moral status upon its intrinsic properties, rather than upon its relations to other individuals. Thus, for example, whether an entity is a person should not be a matter of how others do or do not regard it, or how they do or do not treat it. Nor should it be in any way dependent upon what other entities happen to exist. Moral status is intrinsic to an individual. Secondly, why should the purely physical relation of belonging to the same species make a difference with respect to one's moral status, when other purely physical properties and relations do not appear to do so? Thirdly, it seems natural to connect having moral status with having interests that need to be protected. The term 'interest', however, can be used in quite different ways. In one sense of the term, anything that contributes to the proper functioning of something is in that thing's interest. So interpreted, it is, for example, in the interest of a computer not to be exposed to extremes of temperature. This sense, however, applies to things that have no moral status. The morally significant concept of interest is, by contrast, one that connects up with being a conscious being, and being capable of having desires. In this sense of 'interest', an anencephalic human infant, for example, does not and cannot have

123

any interests at all, since it can never be conscious. Accordingly, if moral status is connected with having interests in the relevant sense, species membership cannot suffice to bestow moral status. Finally, the proposed principle is exposed to counter-examples. That is to say, there are cases that fall under the principle, and where it therefore implies that a certain entity would have the same moral status as a person, but where this is not intuitively plausible. Thus, for example, the principle implies that a member of our species whose upper brain has been completely destroyed has the same moral status as a person, and this seems incorrect. There would seem to be good reasons for concluding, then, that species membership is not itself morally significant.

If this conclusion is correct, it has some very important implications. The most immediate concerns anencephalic and severely brain-damaged humans. At present, such individuals are sometimes kept alive by medical intervention, and not infrequently at substantial cost. If, however, species membership is not morally significant, there is no moral reason to prolong, often at great cost, the lives of individuals that neither are, nor even can be, persons.

The Moral Status of Human Embryos, Fetuses and Newborn Infants

If the preceding conclusions are correct, then neither the fact that human embryos, fetuses and newborn infants belong to a certain species, nor the fact that they are potential persons, gives them a special moral status. It would seem, then, that their moral status must turn on whether they are persons. In the case of human embryos, even the very modest claim that something cannot be a person unless it possesses at least the capacity for rudimentary consciousness leads to the conclusion that human embryos are not persons. In the case of human fetuses and newborn infants, the issue is less clear-cut; however, there are at least two lines of thought that may prove helpful. In the first place, once potentialities have been set aside, and the focus is upon the type of mental life that an entity is capable of enjoying at present, it seems likely that any criterion of personhood that classified newborn human infants as persons would also classify adult animals of *many* other species as persons as well, and so would necessitate a very significant revision of our ordinary moral opinions. Secondly, many of the criteria of personhood that have been traditionally proposed entail that something is not a person unless it possesses, or has possessed, the capacity for thought, and this means that if any of those traditional criteria is even roughly correct, then human fetuses and newborn infants cannot be persons unless the capacity for thought is something that develops at some point prior to birth – a possibility that does not seem very likely, given our current knowledge of early human behaviour and neurophysiological development.

The conclusion that normal newborn humans are not persons, if correct, has very important consequences concerning our responsibilities to newborn humans. For if potential personhood is not morally significant, and if normal newborn humans are not persons, then the intrinsic moral status of such individuals does not differ from that of anencephalic infants. This in turn means that if one considers the

124

case of human infants that are neurologically normal, but physically severely disabled, the question arises as to whether painless termination of life may not be morally best in many such cases.

Summing Up: Ethics and the Concept of a Person

Many of the most controversial issues that society faces involve either killing or letting die. These include such questions as that of how the concept of death is best defined, of when non-voluntary euthanasia is morally justified, of the moral status of abortion and of our responsibilities with regard to newborn human infants – both anencephalic and severely brain-damaged ones, and also ones that are neurologically normal but severely disabled. A resolution of these problems is likely to remain very difficult until there is a more widespread appreciation of the fact that basic moral principles dealing with killing and letting die need to be formulated in terms of the concept of a person.

A final area where the concept of a person is obviously crucial concerns the moral status of animals belonging to other species. In some cases, given our increasing knowledge of the psychological capabilities of non-human animals, our present understanding of the concept of a person probably provides a sufficient basis for concluding that some non-human animals are persons. In other cases, however, where one is dealing with animals whose psychological capabilities are much more limited, a satisfactory answer may very well require a more subtle understanding of precisely what properties do, and do not, suffice to make something a person.

Further Reading

Blumenfeld, J. B. (1977). Abortion and the human brain. *Philosophical Studies*, 32, 251–68.
Brandt, R. B. (1972). The morality of abortion. *Monist*, 56, 503–26.
Brody, B. (1975). *Abortion and the Sanctity of Human Life: a philosophical view*. Cambridge, MA: MIT Press.
Donceel, J. F. (1970). Immediate animation and delayed hominization. *Theological Studies*, 31, 76–105.
Engelhardt, H. T. (1978). Medicine and the concept of a person. In T. Beauchamp and S. Perlin (eds), *Ethical Issues in Death and Dying*. Englewood Cliffs, NJ: Prentice-Hall.
English, J. (1975). Abortion and the concept of a person. *Canadian Journal of Philosophy*, 5, 233–43.
Gillespie, N. C. (1977). Abortion and human rights. *Ethics*, 87, 237–43.
Glover, J. (1977). *Causing Deaths and Saving Lives*. Harmondsworth: Penguin.
Hare, R. M. (1975). Abortion and the golden rule. *Philosophy and Public Affairs*, 4, 201–22.
Ladd, J. (ed.) (1979). *Ethical Issues Relating to Life and Death*. New York: Oxford University Press.
McCloskey, H. J. (1975). The right to life. *Mind*, 84, 403–25.
Parfit, D. (1984). *Reasons and Persons*. Oxford: Clarendon Press.
Sumner, L. W. (1981). *Abortion and Moral Theory*. Princeton, NJ: Princeton University Press.
Tooley, M. (1972). Abortion and infanticide. *Philosophy and Public Affairs*, 2, 37–65.

MICHAEL TOOLEY

—— (1979). Decisions to terminate life and the concept of a person. In J. Ladd (ed.), *Ethical Issues Relating to Life and Death*. New York: Oxford University Press.
—— (1983). *Abortion and Infanticide*. Oxford: Oxford University Press.
Warren, M. A. (1973). On the moral and legal status of abortion. *Monist*, 57, 43–61.

14

Abortion

MARY ANNE WARREN

The world remains divided between jurisdictions in which abortion is legal and those in which it is not. It has long been permitted in China, India and most of the rest of Asia. During the nineteenth century, it was prohibited in many of the industrialized nations where it had previously been legal, at least during the earlier stages of pregnancy. These prohibitions have now been removed in most of Europe and North America, and in most other industrialized nations. However, the World Health Organization reports that there are fifty-two countries, with 25 per cent of the world's population, which permit abortion only when the woman's life is in danger (WHO, 1992). These include many in Africa and Central and South America, some in the Middle East and a few in Europe, such as Ireland and Poland.

Even where abortion is legal, there is often vigorous pressure against it from national and international organizations that seek the return of prohibition. In the United States, there have been numerous bomb and arson attacks upon medical clinics providing legal abortions, and several physicians and clinic workers have been murdered by abortion opponents. While most abortion opponents do not condone this violence, some decline to condemn it, because they regard abortion as an even greater evil.

Under these circumstances, it is very important to examine carefully the arguments for and against the moral permissibility of abortion. I begin with some of the arguments in support of a moral right to choose to terminate one's own pregnancy. These arguments focus, first, upon the harmful consequences – especially for women and children – of denying women effective means of controlling their own fertility; and, second, upon the infringement of women's basic moral rights which this denial entails. Next, I consider the primary arguments against permitting women to choose abortion. The first and most important of these is that human fetuses, from conception, are human beings, and thus have the same moral right to life as other human beings. This is the official position of the Roman Catholic Church, which holds that abortion is never morally permissible, even when it is the only way to save the potential mother's life. Another argument against abortion is that fetuses have a right to life by virtue of their potential to *become* human beings. There are also arguments against unfettered access to abortion that do not depend upon the claim that fetuses have a right to life. For instance, some argue that to permit abortions to be done for any reason that the woman herself considers adequate is an objectionable cheapening of human life. I shall consider these arguments in turn.

MARY ANNE WARREN

The Arguments for Freedom

The case for freedom of choice must begin with a review of some of the obvious factors that make unwanted pregnancies often extremely difficult to avoid. First, the majority of women are involved in sexual relationships with men, with or without a marriage contract, during at least some of their fertile years. Most women (like most men) want such relationships, and consider them a normal part of life. They cannot be expected to avoid them whenever pregnancy is undesired. Heterosexual relationships are both socially encouraged and economically important to women and children, since throughout the world women usually have the primary responsibility for child-rearing, yet their earning power is usually significantly less than men's.

Second, even the most careful use of contraception is not a guarantee against pregnancy. All contraceptives have a substantial failure rate, and some of the most effective (such as Depro-Provera, Norplant and the Pill) are medically unsafe for many women, particularly if they have little or no access to competent medical care. Third, not all women have the liberty or the material resources to make effective use of contraceptives. Even the least expensive contraceptives are beyond the economic reach of much of the world's population. In rural areas, women often lack means of transportation to and from medical clinics where contraceptives could be obtained. Some men prohibit their wives from using contraceptives; and some religions, including Roman Catholicism, teach that any use of artificial means of contraception is sinful. Finally, some pregnancies are the result of incest or rape.

Under these circumstances, women who lack access to safe abortion cannot reliably decide whether and when to have children, or how many to have. Without this freedom, they are often unable to protect their own lives and health, and those of the children they already have. Families often lack the resources to rear all of the children who would be born if abortion were not available. Women who give birth too often, and who lack good nutrition or good medical care, are more likely to die in childbirth; and their children are more likely to die in infancy. In some cultures, single women face severe penalties – sometimes death – if found to be pregnant. Even in more tolerant cultures, a woman who has children she cannot support may be condemning them and herself to dire poverty.

These are among the reasons why women often experience unplanned pregnancies, and often judge it necessary to end them. This need is so compelling that where abortion is illegal many women risk criminal penalties, as well as death or permanent injury, from clandestine surgical or pharmacological abortions. The World Health Organization estimates that 500 women die each day from abortions induced under unsafe conditions (WHO, 1992).

It is not only individual women and families who suffer from the lack of safe and legal abortion. The earth cannot indefinitely support a rapidly growing human population. Climatic instability due to global warming, and the loss of agricultural land to drought, erosion and development already seriously threaten many countries' ability to feed their populations at present levels. Yet many of the poorest nations are still experiencing rapid population growth – many in part because the

128

lack of access to contraception and abortion forces many women to have more children than they would have chosen to have.

These are consequentialist arguments for the freedom to choose abortion, that is, arguments that focus upon the harmful consequences of the absence of that freedom. There are also rights-based arguments, which focus upon the diminution of autonomy that is inherent in the prohibition of abortion. The right to control what happens to one's own body – within the limits of medicine – is a fundamental part of human liberty. To deny women this right is to infringe many of their other moral rights, including the rights to life, health and the pursuit of a satisfactory life for themselves and those for whose for whom they are responsible. Most (though not all) feminists and civil libertarians regard these infringements as incompatible with women's own moral status as human beings with full and equal basic moral rights.

Unless fetuses are human beings with a right to life, these arguments ought to be highly persuasive. However, they are unlikely to persuade those who believe that fetuses have exactly the same right to life as the rest of us. It is, at best, morally problematic to allow human beings who have a right to life to be killed simply to prevent bad consequences to other human beings. Surely no one is entitled deliberately to kill an innocent human being who has done nothing to waive or forfeit his or her right to life. But are there sound reasons to believe that fetuses are human beings with a full and equal right to life?

Fetal Life and Humanity

It is often said that human life begins at conception. The incorporation into the ovum of the DNA contained in the spermatozoon provides the newly fertilized ovum (or zygote) with a unique human genotype, thereby making possible its development into a mature human being. From the moment of conception, this development is gradual and continuous. Thus, it is sometimes argued, there is no other point in time that can plausibly be identified as that at which a human being begins to exist. If all human beings have an equal right to life, then on this line of argument the zygote must be seen as having the same right to life as any other human being. Neither its early stage of development, nor its social invisibility, nor its dependence upon the woman's body for life support can justify the denial or diminution of its basic human rights, including the right to life (Noonan, 1970). If embryos and fetuses have a right to life, then it would seem to follow that they may not be killed, except under conditions that would equally justify the killing of an older human being. We do not permit parents to kill their already born children on the basis of economic need, threats to the parents' lives or health or concern about the effects of overpopulation; and if fetuses have a right to life then neither should abortion be permitted for such reasons.

But is it true that human life begins at conception? This claim is highly ambiguous. If it means that the biological life of the ovum begins at that point, then it is certainly false. Ova are formed in the ovaries of human females before the latter are born; hence, those ova that are eventually fertilized have already been alive for a long time. And if it means that the ovum becomes biologically human at conception, then it is still false. An unfertilized human ovum is as biologically human as any other living cell that is a normal part of a living human being. It differs from most human cells in being haploid rather than diploid (having twenty-four rather than forty-eight chromosomes); but this is standard for human sperm and ova, and does not belie their species membership. All of the billions of cells of which our bodies are composed are, in this respect, human. If mere biological humanity were sufficient to endow an entity with a right to life, then brushing one's teeth would be the moral equivalent of mass homicide.

A more plausible interpretation of the claim that human life begins at conception is that a particular human organism begins to exist at that time. Most of the cells of which our bodies are composed are obviously not human organisms, but only parts thereof. Fertilized ova are different, in that they are genetically unique (unless twinning occurs), and many of them have the potential eventually to become mature human beings. They may therefore be regarded as individual human organisms.

But even on this interpretation, the claim that life begins at conception can be disputed on empirical grounds. Some ethicists argue that the very early conceptus cannot be identified with the embryo that may develop from it. This is because, for about the first two weeks of its existence, it consists of a set of undifferentiated cells, any one of which could give rise to an embryo under certain circumstances. This 'pre-embryo' may spontaneously divide, resulting in twins or triplets; alternatively, it may combine with another pre-embryo, giving rise to a single fetus. Thus, it seems that the very early conceptus is not, after all, an individual human organism (Ford, 1988). The point is relevant to the abortion debate because, although most deliberately induced abortions take place more than fourteen days from conception, some contraceptives – such as the Pill and the IUD – are thought to work (sometimes) by preventing the implantation of a fertilized ovum: and for that reason some abortion opponents regard them as abortifacients, and hence as morally impermissible.

Although the human pre-embryo may not be an individual human organism, the embryo that develops from it presumably is. The question then becomes, do all human organisms have a right to life? It is not self-evident that they do. Human embryos and fetuses, at least through the first trimester, are so unlike more developed human organisms that it is far from clear that they should be regarded as human beings or accorded the same moral rights. There are, to be sure, some striking physical resemblances: by the end of the first trimester a fetus has a face, hands, feet and many other physical features that are recognizably human. But in the mental and experiential realms there seem to be no resemblances at all. Prior to the latter part of the second trimester, and probably somewhat later (Burgess and Tawia, 1996), a fetus almost certainly lacks the neurophysiological structures and functions which are necessary for the occurrence of conscious experience, as well as for thought, self-awareness and other more complex mental capacities. Consequently, the early fetus cannot suffer pain or be deprived of anything that it wants. It has a biological life, but not what James Rachels has called a 'biographical' life –

130

that is, a life that it has already begun to experience. Thus, while we may value its life, it cannot as yet value its own life; and this fact may cast doubt upon the claim that it has a right to life comparable to our own.

The Argument from Fetal Potential

Some argue that abortion is immoral not because fetuses are already human beings, but because they have the potential to become human beings. If the lives of all human beings have value, then it might seem only reasonable to ascribe a similar value to entities that have the potential to develop into human beings. After all, most of us greatly value our own lives and futures, and fetuses may develop into human beings who will value their lives just as much. Why, then, should their potentially valuable human futures not give them the same right to life that ours do (Marquis, 1989)?

One response to the argument from potential is that, in other contexts, we often treat a particular property as sufficient for the possession of a certain right, without treating the potential to develop that property as also sufficient. For instance, the right to vote in political elections may be granted to citizens who have reached the age of 18, but not to pre-adolescents – even though most of them clearly have the potential to reach the age of 18. This distinction is reasonable, since there are differences between most 18-year-olds and most 8-year-olds that justify giving the franchise to one and not the other. Similarly, there may be differences between potential human beings and actual ones that justify differences in their legal and moral status.

The claim that a fetus's human potential gives it a right to life is also subject to a *reductio* argument. If this claim were true, then it would also have to apply to unfertilized human ova, which also have the potential to become human beings under certain circumstances. These circumstances normally include the timely arrival of enough human spermatozoa to bring about fertilization. But this is just one of a large number of biologically necessary conditions for the eventual birth of an infant. Thus it is odd to assert that the ovum is a potential human being only with the arrival of the male's genetic contribution. It follows that, if potential human beings have a right to life, then not only is abortion morally wrong, but so is using contraceptives and avoiding sexual intercourse when conception is possible. If we wish to reject these conclusions, then we must reject the claim that all potential human beings have a right to life.

It is true that potential human beings are often highly valued, particularly by persons who wish to have children. If a pregnancy is wanted, then the fetus will be valued for its human potential. But if the pregnancy is unwanted or medically dangerous, or if the fetus is found to be severely abnormal, then its value as a potential human being may be outweighed by the needs of actual human beings. It is neither biologically possible nor morally desirable for all potential human beings to become actual ones. Human reproductive biology ensures that most ova never become zygotes; and it is probable that most zygotes never become viable embryos (Grobstein, 1988). Moreover, it is a good thing that this is so, since women's capacity to bear and rear children is limited, as is the earth's capacity to support more human beings.

Abortion and Fetal Development

The argument so far suggests that neither the biological humanity of the early fetus nor its human potential can provide a sound reason for according it an equal right to life. However, as pregnancy progresses it becomes more difficult to regard the fetus as only a *potential* human being. Not only does it come to look more like a baby, but it may begin at some point – probably in the late second or third trimester – to have a rudimentary form of consciousness. This is one reason for regarding early abortion as morally preferable to late abortion. Another is that early abortion is considerably less medically dangerous for the woman, and much less physically and emotionally traumatic. Where early abortion is available, most women who wish to end a pregnancy will strongly prefer to do so well before the end of the second trimester. Nevertheless, circumstances can sometimes justify late abortions. Although most US states do not legally prohibit late abortion, very few abortions are performed after twenty-four weeks – about 0.01 per cent, according to one study (Henshaw et al., 1985: 91). These very late abortions are most frequently done when the fetus has a disastrous abnormality, such as anencephaly (the absence of all or most of the brain), which guarantees that it will either be stillborn or die soon after birth. In such cases, the woman's health and future fertility may require that the pregnancy by aborted.

Making Abortion Difficult to Obtain

Some people doubt that fetuses have a right to life, yet reject a policy of 'abortion on demand'. In their view, when abortion is easy to obtain too many abortions are performed, and too often for morally inadequate reasons. Consequently, they support legislation designed to make obtaining an abortion more difficult. Some argue that abortion should be permitted only in the case of serious medical danger to the woman, or exceptional economic or personal hardship. Some hold that a married woman should be required to obtain the consent of her husband before obtaining an abortion, or that a girl who is a legal minor should be required to have the consent of her parents. Some support mandatory counselling for women requesting abortion, and/or a mandatory waiting period between the request for an abortion and the procedure itself. All of these restrictive policies have been enacted into law in some jurisdictions.

Those who say that abortion should be difficult to obtain believe that to leave the decision in the hands of women, and possibly their physicians, is to devalue human life. In their view, human life should be regarded as precious even when the individual in question has no moral right to be kept alive. This argument assumes that, if free to do so, many women will decide to end pregnancies for trivial reasons. But the magnitude of a woman's personal stake in the outcome of the decision makes this presumption implausible. Laws and regulations that create obstacles to the volun-

132

tary choice of abortion can only make what is already a very difficult personal situation even more difficult. There laws impose the greatest hardships upon women who are young, poor, disabled or otherwise particularly vulnerable. If the goal is to express reverence for human life by reducing the total number of abortions, a fairer and more effective approach is to support improved sex education, universal access to contraceptives and more research aimed at developing safer and more effective contraceptives.

Ideological Bases of the Abortion Debate

Abortion is controversial in our time, not only because many people believe that fetuses have a right to life, but also because it has become a potent symbol of the ancient debates over sexual morality and the proper social roles of women. As Kristen Luker (1984) has documented, Americans who oppose abortion tend to have relatively conservative views on these matters; and the same is very often true elsewhere. Abortion opponents often fear that women, children and society as a whole will suffer if women and men abandon their traditional familial roles. They believe that legal abortion undermines these gendered familial roles, in part by making extramarital sexual activities less perilous for women, and giving men an easy rationalization for not supporting their children. In contrast, those who favour legal abortion are much less likely to believe that women and men require separate and distinct social roles, or that sexual activity is always morally objectionable, unless there is a mutual commitment to having children.

It is difficult to produce evidence in support of the view that safe and legal abortion results in harm to society. On the contrary, the empirical evidence points strongly to the conclusion that, for now at least, access to abortion is important for the well-being of women, families and humanity as a whole. The belief that voluntary abortion harms society, like the belief in the moral equality of the pre-sentient fetus, involves a strong element of faith – usually, though not always, religious faith. The classical liberal view is that personal freedom should not be limited on the basis of religious or other beliefs which lack empirical support, and which are not universally accepted. Abortion cannot be shown to be morally objectionable on strictly secular grounds; and many people (the majority, in many societies) hold moral and religious beliefs that are supportive of women's right to choose abortion. For these reasons, it may reasonably be argued that unimpeded access to abortion is an important part of religious as well as reproductive freedom (Wenz, 1994).

Conclusion

Women often have compelling reasons for choosing abortion, reasons that are morally sufficient to justify killing an embryo or a fetus that has not yet begun to have experiences. Late abortion is morally more troubling, and not something that many women want, given the choice of early abortion. Nevertheless, it is justifiable in some cases, such as when the fetus is disastrously abnormal, or the woman's life

133

MARY ANNE WARREN

or health is seriously endangered. Because abortion is at best an extremely unpleasant experience, and because many people are troubled by it, reducing the total number of abortions that occur is a defensible societal goal. However, respect for women's autonomy and well-being demands that this reduction be brought about through means that enable them better to avoid unwanted or medically dangerous pregnancies, rather than through legal prohibitions or regulatory practices that make abortions needlessly difficult to obtain.

References

Burgess, J. A. and Tawia, S. A. (1996). When did you first begin to feel it? – Locating the beginning of human consciousness. *Bioethics*, 10/1, 1–26.

Grobstein, Clifford (1988). *Science and the Unborn*. New York: Basic Books.

Henshaw, S. K., Binkin, N. J., Blaine E. and Smith J. C. (1985). A portrait of American women who obtain abortions. *Family Planning Perspectives*, 17, 90–6.

Luker, Kristen (1984). *Abortion and the Politics of Motherhood*. Berkeley: University of California Press.

McCauley, Ann P. et al. (1994). Opportunities for women through reproductive choice. *Population Reports*, 22

Marquis, Don (1989). Why abortion is immoral. *Journal of Philosophy*, 86/4, 183–202.

Noonan, John Jr (1970). An almost absolute value in history. In *The Morality of Abortion*. Cambridge, MA: Harvard Univerisity Press, 51–9. [Reprinted in *Contemporary Issues in Bioethics*, ed. Tom Beauchamp and LeRoy Walters. Belmont, CA: Wadsworth, 1994, 279–82.]

Rosenfeld, Allan (1989). Maternal mortality in developing countries: an ongoing but neglected 'epidemic'. *Journal of the American Medical Association*, 21 July, 376.

Wenz, Peter S. (1994). *Abortion Rights as Religious Freedom*. Philadelphia: Temple University Press.

World Health Organization, Division of Family Health (1992). *Reproductive Health: a key to a brighter future*. Geneva.

15

Mother–fetus conflict

BONNIE STEINBOCK

Prior to the 1940s, the fetus was considered to be largely protected within the uterus from external harm. Today it is recognized that a range of behaviours by a pregnant woman can affect the developing fetus or the born child. For example, if the pregnant woman contracts rubella, her fetus may be stillborn, or born deaf, blind or mentally retarded. If she fails to get proper nutrition or smokes cigarettes, her baby may have a low birth-weight, a condition correlated with a significantly higher infant mortality rate. Drinking alcohol, using illicit drugs or even taking over-the-counter drugs can all adversely affect fetal health and development. The recognition that maternal behaviour during pregnancy can have detrimental effects, not only on the fetus *in utero*, but on the child after birth, raises important questions for biomedical ethics: what obligations does a pregnant woman have to her developing fetus? How are her interests to be weighed against those of the fetus and future child? Who should resolve mother–fetus conflicts and what role, if any, ought the state to play?

This chapter attempts to provide a conceptual framework for thinking about mother–fetus conflict. I begin by distinguishing the issue from the abortion debate, arguing that women have prima facie moral obligations to avoid inflicting prenatal harm regardless of whether they have an obligation to refrain from abortion. I then apply the framework to an area that has the greatest relevance to the behaviour of medical practitioners: the so-called 'obstetrical cases', in which women reject proposed medical interventions of various kinds, such as Caesarean delivery or fetal surgery, deemed necessary for the health of the fetus. What are the moral obligations of pregnant women, of health-care providers and what role, if any, should the state play?

Abortion and Mother–Fetus Conflict

Abortion is often considered to be an example – even a paradigm example – of a mother–fetus conflict (Rhoden, 1987). This makes sense only if it is assumed that abortion pits the interests of the pregnant woman against those of the fetus. However, many scholars reject this assumption. They do so because they consider there to be morally important differences between human fetuses and born human beings. Fetuses, through most of gestation, are not conscious or aware or sentient. They cannot think or feel or experience anything. They can be *killed*, as any living thing can be killed, but they are physiologically incapable of feeling pain or having any other experiences at least during the first trimester and probably through most of the second trimester, when 90 per cent of abortions occur. (Fewer than 1.5 per cent of all abortions in the United States take place after twenty weeks; most are done within twelve weeks.) Because they are non-conscious and non-sentient, early-gestation fetuses cannot want anything. Although some philosophers (Regan, 1976) maintain that beings that cannot have wants can nevertheless have interests and rights, others (Feinberg, 1974; Sumner, 1981; Singer and Kuhse, 1986; Steinbock, 1992) argue that sentience and the capacity for at least rudimentary wants are a necessary condition for having interests.

The restriction of interests to beings capable of wanting things stems from a certain conception of what it is to have interests, namely that interests are composed out of our desires, concerns and goals. Interests are, as Joel Feinberg (1984) has suggested, those things in which one has a stake. If we think of interests as stakes in things, and understand what we have a stake in as defined by our concerns or by what matters to us, then the connection between interests and the capacity for conscious awareness becomes clear. Without awareness, beings cannot care about anything. Without the ability to care about anything, beings cannot have desires, preferences, hopes, aims and goals. Without desires, preferences, etc., they cannot have interests. There may be all kinds of reasons, including moral reasons, for preserving or protecting non-conscious beings, but such reasons cannot derive from *their* interests, since non-conscious beings do not have any interests. Accordingly, non-conscious, non-sentient fetuses do not have interests. Therefore abortion, throughout most of gestation, does not pit the interests of the pregnant woman against the interests of the fetus.

Once the fetus becomes sentient, probably towards the end of the second trimester, it has at least one interest, namely an interest in not being subjected to painful stimuli. At least some of the debate about late-term abortions focuses on the pain they allegedly cause sentient fetuses. For example, in the United States, Congress passed the Partial Birth Abortion Ban Act of 1995, which criminalized a rare late-term abortion procedure, technically known as intact dilatation and extraction (D&E). During the procedure, the physician pulls the fetus, often still alive, feet first from the birth canal until only the head remains inside the mother's body. An instrument is then inserted into the fetal skull, the brains are suctioned out and the cranium is collapsed to allow the head to pass through the birth canal.

Most people, even those who are fervently pro-choice, are distressed by late-term abortions, partly because of the risk of inflicting pain and partly because the late-gestation fetus is so close to being a full-term infant that all of the reasons for the social protection of infants are present (Rhoden, 1986b). Yet sometimes such abortions are medically indicated. As Allan Rosenfield, dean of the Columbia School of Public Health, commented in an op-ed piece, 'The anguished decision to use dilatation and extraction is usually reached when a woman's life or health would be jeopardized if the pregnancy is continued or if there is a fetal abnormality incompatible with life.' The choice of method should be based on what is best for the patient and should be chosen by her doctor, not legislators. It was for this reason that President Bill Clinton vetoed the bill on 10 April 1996.

Such abortions are not chosen because the pregnant woman does not want to have a baby; they are typically the tragic outcomes of wanted pregnancies. The women who have them are faced with the death of the baby and a risk to their own life or health, including future sterility, if they attempt to give birth. Presumably every attempt is made to ensure that the fetus does not experience pain during the procedure. If for some reason this is not possible, the long-term interests of the pregnant woman in preserving her life and health surely outweigh the interests of a doomed fetus in temporarily experiencing unavoidable pain.

Leaving aside rare late-term abortions with involve sentient fetuses, what are the implications of the abortion debate for mother–fetus conflict? First, a word about terminology. Those who oppose abortion call themselves 'pro-life' while those who support liberal abortion laws call themselves 'pro-choice'. Neither term is entirely satisfactory; both beg the question in different ways. The 'pro-life' label assumes that the kind of life to be protected is human life; rarely are 'pro-lifers' vegetarians. The 'pro-choice' label assumes that the choice is a morally permissible one. avoiding the question of the moral status of the fetus. Nevertheless, despite these deficiencies, I will use the terms 'pro-lifers' and 'pro-choicers' for two reasons. First, they are shorter and more graceful than the likely alternatives, such as 'opponents of abortion' and 'supporters of liberal abortion laws'. Second, it shows respect to those who identify themselves by these terms to call them what they prefer to be called.

Pro-lifers, who regard embryos and fetuses as 'pre-born children', consider pregnant women to have the same moral obligations to their fetuses as they do to their born children. Abortion is morally as wrong as killing a child would be. It is also morally wrong to engage in behaviours likely to result in fetal harm or death. Thus, pro-lifers will condemn behaviours such as using illicit drugs, abusing alcohol or smoking during pregnancy because of the risk these pose to the developing fetus, without providing any significant or morally important benefit to the pregnant woman.

Pro-choicers who view the early fetus as incapable of being harmed obviously cannot condemn such behaviours during pregnancy on the ground that these harm the fetus. Does this mean that pro-choicers should regard behaviour during pregnancy as a matter of personal choice? Some pro-choicers in the United States have taken this position, vigorously opposing 'fetal rights' legislation (limited, it appears, to US jurisdictions), often seeing it as part of a larger political agenda to make abortion illegal.

In my view, this ignores an important difference between the behaviour of a pregnant woman who is going to term and the behaviour of a pregnant woman who aborts her pregnancy. If a woman does not abort, her conduct during pregnancy may have adverse effects not simply on the fetus, but on the future child. Whatever the status of the fetus, children have interests and rights, including the fundamental moral and legal right not to be injured. Admittedly, the child who has been harmed by maternal behaviour did not exist as a child at the time the injury was inflicted, but that does not lessen the obligation to avoid causing the child who is going to come into existence foreseeable injury.

137

Strictly speaking, then, the term 'mother–fetus conflict' is misleading, since the obligation is not to the fetus *per se*, but to the future child. However, the term 'mother–fetus conflict' emphasizes the fact that the conflict occurs when the woman is pregnant and the child still a fetus. Efforts to protect the fetus must be achieved through the body of the pregnant woman, raising the same sort of issues regarding privacy and bodily autonomy that are present in the abortion debate. Therefore, while it is important to distinguish abortion and mother–fetus conflict, it is equally important to acknowledge the similarities. Otherwise, we run the risk of forgetting the impact of restrictive measures on the pregnant woman, who is a person with her own needs and interests. We run the danger of treating her, as Annas (1986) has expressed it, as a 'fetal container'.

Some people profess to be baffled by the idea that a person can have obligations not to harm individuals who have not yet been born. However, this is not a bizarre idea. Examples abound both in law and in ordinary life. A wrongful act done today may harm someone in the future who is not yet born or even conceived. As one of the authors of a leading book on torts expresses it, 'the improper canning of baby food today is negligent to a child born next week or next year, who consumes it to his injury' (Harper and James, 1956: 1030). Similarly, we can condemn a careless or selfish use of resources that will adversely affect our children or grandchildren. It is equally possible to ascribe responsibility on the part of pregnant women who plan to bear children to avoid behaviour likely to injure them.

Others, who accept the idea of responsibility to not yet existing persons, are puzzled by the claim that women have moral obligations to prevent illness or disability in their 'not-yet-born children' (Murray, 1987), but no obligation to refrain from killing them. This seems paradoxical since ordinarily death is a greater harm than illness or disability. However, the paradox is removed when it is remembered that the victim of the illness or disability is a child who will suffer from the injury, while the entity that is killed by abortion is a fetus that has no interests and cannot be harmed.

Pitting the mother against the fetus

Some people object to the characterization 'mother–fetus' *conflict* as being unnecessarily adversarial. Undesirable behaviours, such as binge-drinking or drug-using, which endanger fetal health also endanger maternal health. They recommend that health-care professionals treat both mother and fetus as a unit with common interests.

This objection to the 'conflict characterization' has a great deal of truth to it. However, it must be recognized that a pregnant woman can have interests that may conflict with what will protect the life or health of her fetus. For example, cancer treatments that give a pregnant woman the best chance of survival may kill or deform her fetus. Fetal surgery which is the fetus's only chance of survival may impose considerable risks on the pregnant woman. It is wishful thinking to pretend that what is best for the pregnant woman is necessarily best for the fetus or future child, or that what is best for the fetus always promotes the pregnant woman's interests. The possibility of conflict remains.

Moral Obligations to the Unborn

The above analysis suggests that women have prima facie moral obligations to avoid inflicting prenatal harm. However, it does not follow that these moral obligations should be made into legal ones. The question of legal obligation and responsibility raises a host of additional questions, including the harms created by legal coercion and the effectiveness of a punitive approach in protecting future children. These considerations have led the majority of commentators to reject the legal prohibition of 'prenatal child abuse' and forced medical treatment of pregnant women.

Confining ourselves to moral responsibility and obligation, the next question is, what are their nature and extent? For example, are pregnant women morally required to avoid only behaviours that will cause harm to the surviving child, or can there be an obligation to avoid fetal death or stillbirth? The answer is obvious for those who consider fetuses to have the moral status of born children, but what should be the view of pro-choicers? It may seem that, to be consistent, pro-choicers should maintain that the woman's obligation is only to the child, if it survives. Behaviour that results in fetal death is not wrong, since abortion is morally permissible. However, there are two complications which make this answer problematic. First, it is rarely possible to separate the risk of causing fetal death from the risk of causing postnatal harm. Smoking, for example, increases the risk of stillbirth and is also associated with learning disabilities. Probably any behaviour that risks killing but does not in fact kill the fetus may harm the future child, and should be avoided for that reason.

A second complication concerns the developmental stage of the fetus. A first-trimester fetus lacks interests, but the same cannot be said of a third-trimester fetus that is conscious and sentient. Such a fetus presumably has all the interests ascribable to a newborn, including the interest in continued existence. Although some philosophers think that this is impossible (e.g., Tooley, 1983), I maintain that sentient beings can have an interest in continued existence (Steinbock, 1992: 57–8). A sentient being can experience pleasure as well as pain and therefore has an interest in having more pleasurable experiences, that is, in continued existence. For this reason, I maintain that both newborns and sentient fetuses ordinarily have an interest in continued existence. (The exception would be when continued existence provided little but suffering.) The refusal by a pregnant woman of a Caesarean section which results in a stillbirth would, on this analysis, constitute a harm to the fetus.

Do sentient fetuses have a right to life, indeed the same right to life as the mother? If so, does this mean that late-term abortions are never permissible, even to save the life of the pregnant woman? I do not think that this follows from acknowledging the sentient fetus's interest in life. Even if it has a right to life, this does not impose on the pregnant woman an obligation to allow it to remain inside her body at the sacrifice of her own life or health (Thomson, 1971), although it would impose a moral obligation on her not to abort for less than pressing reasons. Alternatively, one could argue that the unique situation of the fetus, that is, its dependence and impact on the pregnant woman, make it impossible to ascribe to it a full-fledged right to life, even after it becomes sentient.

The next question is the scope of women's obligations to their 'not-yet-born children'. The danger here is to sentimentalize the relationship between the pregnant woman and her fetus; to think that the fact that the woman is pregnant is the only morally important thing about her; to regard the pregnancy as trumping all other considerations. A better way to conceptualize women's obligations to their not-yet-born children is to think in terms of what is required of parents of born children. As Murray (1991: 107) puts it, 'Our moral obligations to our children may be particularly broad and deep, but they do not overwhelm all other moral considerations in all circumstances.' Moreover, we do not require parents to protect children from all risk of harm, only to take necessary steps to protect children from substantial risks of serious harm. Interpretation of all of these features is obviously something on which reasonable people can disagree. Consider, for example, drinking during pregnancy. There is no known minimum safe level of alcohol consumption. It is possible that any consumption of alcohol could harm the developing fetus. (Recent research suggests that consumption of any amount of alcohol at any time during pregnancy increases the risk – admittedly very small – of infant leukaemia.) Therefore, many doctors recommend that women totally abstain from alcohol throughout pregnancy. Others believe that an occasional glass of wine, especially after the first trimester when the vital organs are being formed, is extremely unlikely to do any harm. Given the disagreement among experts and the low level of risk in any case, a moral obligation totally to abstain from alcohol during pregnancy cannot be established. Instead, low to moderate alcohol consumption is a matter of personal discretion, to be decided by the individual woman in conjunction with her physician.

By contrast, heavy and prolonged maternal alcohol abuse during pregnancy can cause fetal alcohol syndrome (FAS), which is typically marked by severe facial deformities and mental retardation. Drug use during pregnancy is also risky. The effects of fetal exposure to cocaine, for example, include growth retardation in the womb and subtle neurological abnormalities, leading to extraordinary irritability in infancy and learning disorders later. In more extreme cases, cocaine can cause brain-damaging strokes. The difficulty with maintaining that pregnant women have a moral obligation to stop abusing alcohol or using cocaine is that these are usually addictive behaviours and ones that are not fully voluntary. It is perhaps unrealistic to say that a pregnant addict should just stop drinking or smoking crack; most addicts need some sort of treatment to overcome their addiction. However, such help is often not available. Many in-patient alcohol rehabilitation programmes in the United States exclude pregnant women, largely due to a fear of liability. The situation is even worse for drug addicts (Chavkin, 1990). Therefore, even if we maintain that pregnant addicts have a moral obligation to overcome their addictions for the sake of their not-yet-born babies, we should also recognize

140

a societal obligation to provide treatment programmes. In the absence of sufficient voluntary programmes, calls for mandatory substance abuse programmes for pregnant women seem premature.

I have based women's obligations to their not-yet-born children on the decision not to terminate the pregnancy. But what if the failure to terminate is not a decision at all, but rather the result of lack of access to abortion? Does a woman have the same responsibility to safeguard fetal health if she would have chosen abortion, if available? Certainly risky behaviour on the part of a woman who has chosen to bear a child is more callous and blameworthy than similar behaviour from a woman who is undergoing a 'compulsory' pregnancy. Nevertheless, the impact on the child is the same. For that reason, any woman who will bear a child, voluntarily or not, is morally required to avoid inflicting prenatal injury on it, if she can do so without sacrificing important interests of her own.

The Obstetrical Cases: Forced Caesareans

Most women are willing to undergo considerable risk and pain to ensure that their babies are born healthy. Occasionally, however, a woman rejects a medical intervention, such as a Caesarean delivery, recommended by her doctor. Whether her refusal is morally permissible depends on the strength of her reasons. Certainly reasons that are normally trivial (like not wanting to have an ugly scar above the bikini line) would not justify letting a nearly-born fetus die. Refusals for such reasons are rare, if they exist at all. More typical are refusals based on religious or cultural beliefs, a fear of surgery or rejection of the doctor's prognosis. These are not necessarily unimportant or selfish reasons, and refusals based on such considerations are not obviously unjustified.

A separate issue is the appropriate physicians' response. Should doctors respect the patient's refusal of medical intervention if this means letting a nearly-born baby die? Should physicians' responses be based on the validity or strength of the patient's reasons for rejecting the intervention? When, if ever, should doctors resort to the courts?

One issue is whether the patient is competent to refuse treatment. Traditionally, doctors have been able to override patient refusal if surgery is in the patient's best interest and the patient is incapable of giving or withholding consent. A determination of competence depends on the patient's ability to understand her condition, the proposed treatment and the risks and benefits of treating or not treating. The mere fact that the patient refuses treatment her doctors consider necessary does not establish inability to give or refuse consent. However, the line between a competent but idiosyncratic refusal of treatment and an inability to consent is often a very fine one, as illustrated by a recent English case. In March 1997 a woman with a phobia about needles was forced to have her baby delivered by Caesarean section after a highly unusual midnight emergency sitting of the Court of Appeal. The unborn baby's breech position posed no danger to the mother, but doctors told her that the baby could die or be brain-damaged if delivered vaginally. The woman at first agreed to have the anaesthetic administered by needle, and then by mask, but

141

changed her mind both times. Her doctors feared she was going into labour and asked the High Court to approve the operation. The judges accepted arguments that the woman was not mentally competent to make the decision. After being told the Caesarean was approved by the court, the woman agreed to the operation and the baby was delivered safely.

Refusals of Caesarean deliveries present physicians with a dilemma only if two conditions obtain. First, there must be a generally accepted right of competent patients to refuse medical treatment deemed necessary for the welfare of the nearly-born child. If decisions about treatment are for doctors to make, then doctors can simply ignore refusals they consider to be harmful or irrational. In countries where physicians' paternalism is still the norm, the fact that the patient does not consent to a Caesarean would scarcely be a consideration, much less an obstacle to proceeding. It would not occur to obstetricians in such societies to get a court order overriding the woman's refusal. They would simply perform the Caesarean they deemed necessary over the woman's objections. Second, the fetus must lack the status of a full legal person. In some countries (for example, Spain), the fetus is considered to be a person as regards treatment that is of benefit to it. Abortion is generally not permitted, except in the case of severe fetal deformity or to prevent a grave risk to the woman's life or health. Few Spanish obstetricians would permit a nearly-born fetus to die simply because its mother refused a Caesarean delivery. Although this type of case has never reached the Spanish courts, it seems very likely that if such a case were to be heard, Spanish courts would rule in favour of the fetus.

Refusals of Caesarean delivery pose agonizing dilemmas for physicians who respect the patient's right to refuse treatment, but who feel that they cannot sit back and let a nearly-born baby die or be born extremely damaged, especially if the woman's refusal seems irrational. Moreover, doctors are not 'hired hands' who do whatever their clients want. They are supposed to use their professional judgement to determine the right way to manage a particular pregnancy, labour and delivery. If a patient wants the doctor to do something contrary to good clinical practice, the doctor has no obligation to comply.

On the other side, there is increasing consensus, at least in the United States and Canada, among members of the legal profession, bioethicists and professional medical societies that overriding a competent woman's refusal of a Caesarean delivery is almost never justified. This consensus is based on several considerations. First, there is the risk to the woman. Caesarean deliveries, while quite safe, have a higher maternal morbidity and mortality than do vaginal deliveries. (The mortality rate for Caesareans is approximately four times higher than for vaginal delivery.) Thus, if court-ordered Caesareans are performed, increased physical risks are imposed on one person for the sake of another. No court has, for example, ever ordered a parent to surrender a kidney, bone marrow or any other body part for donation to a child, another relative or anyone else. In fact, it is doubtful that a parent could be legally compelled to donate a pint of blood necessary to save his or her child's life. If parents do not have a legal duty to take even minor health risks to benefit their children, why should a pregnant woman be compelled to undergo major surgery for the sake of the fetus?

142

Second, the imposition of compulsory surgery has unsettling implications for the doctor–patient relationship. What if the woman continues to refuse, even after a court order is obtained? Are doctors prepared to hold down, forcibly anaesthetize and cut open a non-consenting woman? A third factor is the possibility the doctors are wrong about the need for a Caesarean. In a number of cases in the United States in which court-ordered Caesareans sections were sought, the women delivered vaginally and the babies were born healthy (Rhoden, 1986a). Compulsory Caesareans therefore may subject women to unnecessary surgery.

Some doctors think that a case can be made for compulsory Caesareans in one case: well-documented complete placenta previa. This is a serious condition that can result in the detachment of the placenta from the uterus, causing haemorrhaging and endangering the lives of both the mother and fetus. According to McCullough and Chervenak (1994: 249–50):

> the only obstetric management strategy consistent with promoting the social-role interests of the fetus is cesarean delivery, because vaginal delivery dooms the social-role interests of the fetus, while cesarean delivery dramatically protects and promotes those interests . . . cesarean delivery, despite its morbidity and mortality risks for the woman and despite its invasiveness, unequivocally produces net medical benefit for the pregnant woman. Any clinical judgment to the contrary borders on the irrational.

McCullough and Chervenak acknowledge that there have been a few cases, even of allegedly well-documented complete placenta previa, when the doctors were wrong in their predictions of fetal death and a vaginal birth was successful. However, they dismiss this as irrelevant. There will always be errors in medicine. The question is not whether doctors can be *certain* that a Caesarean is indicated, but whether their clinical judgement is *reliable*. All the evidence indicates that a Caesarean delivery is indicated for well-documented complete placenta previa.

Moreover, they argue, the pregnant woman is ethically obligated to take reasonable risks on behalf of the fetus in the management of her pregnancy. Furthermore, if her refusal of surgery is based on an irrational fear, overriding her refusal does not violate her autonomy, because false beliefs and irrational fears are not an expression of autonomy. Nor is the woman being used as a mere means to save the fetus, as in the case of forced bone marrow or organ donations, since the surgery can be reliably predicted to benefit her as well as her baby.

However, the legal right to refuse treatment is not limited to sensible, reasonable beliefs. Of course, not every society recognizes the right to refuse treatment. In many countries, physicians' paternalism is still prevalent, and doctors, not patients, decide what treatment patients should have. In such societies, the doctrine of informed consent does not exist. Where informed consent is an essential part of medical practice, it is believed that people should be able to make their own decisions about surgery, even if their choices are idiosyncratic or harmful. As Justice Warren Burger, of the United States Supreme Court, said in his dissent in *Georgetown*, the right to refuse treatment is not limited to 'sensible beliefs, valid thoughts, reasonable emotions, or well-founded sensations'. Moreover, the claim that compulsory Caesareans for complete placenta previa provide a 'net benefit' to the woman is based solely on physical benefit. A Christian Scientist who has spiritual objections to a Caesarean delivery does not regard a compulsory Caesarean as a 'net benefit'. The dangers implicit in allowing doctors to step in and weigh the risks of surgery for someone who has competently chosen to forgo them should lead us to reject even a carefully circumscribed exception to the doctrine of informed consent.

A better solution to the problem of mother–fetus conflict is to prevent its occurrence. A woman may fail to comply with medical advice, such as taking medication, because it makes her sick or because she does not understand the risk to her baby or herself. She may be unable to stay off her feet or remain in the hospital, as her doctors recommend, because of her obligations to her other children. A concerted effort on the part of health-care professionals and social workers to try to help her solve these problems will often do more to protect her fetus than prosecuting her after the harm is done. Effective substance abuse programmes for pregnant women and the provision of adequate prenatal care for all women would be more likely to protect not-yet-born children than a punitive approach.

Fetal Surgery

Over the past decade there have been revolutionary developments in the diagnosis and treatment of fetal anatomical abnormalities. Prenatal surgery has saved some fetuses that would have died *in utero* (Harrison and Adzick, 1991). At the same time, such surgery imposes considerable risks on the pregnant woman. Her womb must be cut open twice, first when the fetus is temporarily removed from the womb to be operated on, and again for a Caesarean delivery. After the fetus is replaced in her womb, she must take powerful drugs daily to prevent labour. There is also the danger of uterine rupture because of the two operations. Moreover, there is no guarantee of a successful outcome for the fetus. Fetal mortality is high and some of the survivors will be born with serious defects.

If the case against forced Caesareans is strong, the case against forced *in utero* surgery is much stronger. Most of the therapies are still experimental. They carry significant risks for the woman and, unlike Caesarean delivery for complete placenta previa, there is no direct benefit to the pregnant woman. There is no guarantee of success, and the result may be a severely handicapped baby. The decision as to whether fetal therapy is 'worth it' must remain a personal and individual one.

Conclusion

Women have moral obligations to avoid inflicting prenatal harm. Just as parents have obligations to avoid exposing their born children to substantial risks of serious harm, so pregnant woman have comparable obligations to the children they will bear. The avoidance of prenatal harm may require women to make sacrifices and take risks. However, the obligation to avoid prenatal harm should be balanced against other obligations and interests. While some behaviours, such as recreational use of crack cocaine, are clearly morally wrong, others, such as refusal of a Caesarean due to fear of surgery, are morally debatable, while still others, such as rejection of experimental fetal surgery, are clearly morally permissible. In resolving mother−fetus conflicts, women's rights to privacy, bodily integrity and autonomy must be considered along with the welfare of the fetus and surviving child.

References

Annas, G. (1986). Pregnant women as fetal containers. *Hastings Center Report*, 16, 13−14.
Brazier, M. (1992). *Medicine, Patients and the Law*, 2nd edn. Harmondsworth: Penguin. [Chapter 11, Pregnancy and Childbirth.]
Chavkin, W. (1990). Drug addiction and pregnancy: policy crossroads. *American Journal of Public Health*, 80, 483−7.
Feinberg, J. (1974). The rights of animals and unborn generations. In W. T. Blackstone (ed.), *Philosophy and Environmental Crisis*. Athens, GA: University of Georgia Press, 43−68.
—— (1984). *Harm to Others*. New York: Oxford University Press.
Harper, F. V. and James, F. (1956). *Law of Torts*. Vol. 2. Boston: Little, Brown.
Harrison, M. R. and Adzick, N. S. (1991). The fetus as patient: surgical considerations. *Annals of Surgery*, 213, 279−91.
McCullough, L. and Chervenak, F. (1994). *Ethics in Obstetrics and Gynecology*. New York and Oxford: Oxford University Press.
Mason, J. K. and McCall Smith, R. A. (1994). *Law and Medical Ethics*, 4th edn. London: Butterworths. 'The rights of the fetus', 136−40.
Murray, T. (1987). Moral obligations to the not-yet-born: the fetus as patient. *Clinics in Perinatology*, 14, 329−43.
—— (1991). Prenatal drug exposure: ethical issues. *Future of Children*, 105−12.
Regan, T. (1976). Feinberg on what sorts of beings can have rights. *Southern Journal of Philosophy*, 14, 485−98.
Rhoden, N. (1986a). The judge in the delivery room: the emergence of court-ordered cesareans. *California Law Review*, 74, 1951−2040.
—— (1986b). Trimesters and technology: revamping *Roe v. Wade*. *Yale Law Journal*, 95, 639−97.
—— (1987). Cesareans and samaritans. *Law, Medicine and Health Care*, 15, 118−25.
Singer, P. and Kuhse, H. (1986). The ethics of embryo research. *Law, Medicine and Health Care*, 14, 133−8.
Thomson, J. (1971). A defense of abortion. *Philosophy and Public Affairs*, 1, 47−66.

Further Reading

American Academy of Pediatrics, Committee on Biothics (1988). Fetal therapy: ethical considerations. *Pediatrics*, 81, 898−9.
American College of Gynecologists and Obstetricians Committee Opinion Number 55. (1987). Patient-choice: maternal−fetal conflict.
Annas, G. J. (1982). Forced cesareans: the most unkindest cut of all. *Hastings Center Report*, 12, 16−17.
—— (1988). She's going to die: the case of Angela C. *Hastings Center Report*, 18, 23−5.
Bays, J. (1990). Substance abuse and child abuse: impact of addiction on the child. *Pediatric Clinics of North America*, 37, 881−904.

Daniels, Cynthia R. (1993). *At Women's Expense: state power and the politics of fetal rights.* Cambridge, MA: Harvard University Press.

Elias, S. and Annas, G. J. (1987). *Reproductive Genetics and the Law.* Chicago: Yearbook Medical Publishers.

Fleischman, A. and Macklin, R. (1987). Fetal therapy: ethical considerations, potential conflicts. In William B. Weil and Martin Benjamin (eds), *Ethical Issues at the Outset of Life.* Boston: Blackwell Scientific Publications, 121–48.

Ginn, D. (1994). Pregnant women and consent to medical treatment. *Health Law in Canada,* 15, 41–8.

Jackman, M. (1995). The status of the foetus under Canadian law. *Health Law in Canada,* 15, 83–6.

Mathieu, D. (1991). *Preventing Prenatal Harm: should the state intervene?* Dordrecht: Kluwer.

Moss, K. (1990). Substance abuse during pregnancy. *Harvard Women's Law Journal,* 13, 278–99.

Nelson, L. J., Buggy, B. P. and Weil, C. J. (1986). Forced medical treatment of pregnant women: 'compelling each to live as seems good to the rest'. *Hastings Law Journal,* 37, 703–63.

Nelson, L. J. and Milliken, N. (1988). Compelled medical treatment of pregnant women. *Journal of the American Medical Association,* 259, 1060–6.

Robertson, J. A. (1982). The right to procreate and *in utero* fetal therapy. *Journal of Legal Medicine,* 3, 333–66.

Steinbock, B. (1992). *Life before Birth: the moral and legal status of embryos and fetuses.* New York and Oxford: Oxford University Press.

—— (1994). Maternal–fetal conflict and *in utero* fetal therapy. *Albany Law Review,* 57, 781–93.

Sumner, L. W. (1981). *Abortion and Moral Theory.* Princeton, NJ: Princeton University Press.

Tooley, M. (1983). *Abortion and Infanticide.* Oxford: Clarendon Press.

146

PART V

ISSUES IN REPRODUCTION

16

Population issues

MARGARET PABST BATTIN

Issues concerning global population growth are among the most vigorously argued of contemporary conflicts. On one side, the so-called neo-Malthusians warn that failure to limit population growth will mean environmental and hence human disaster; on the other, at least three groups of critics – each with different reasons – resist the Malthusian warning and its mandate of population control. While population size and growth rates affect virtually all areas of health, bioethicists have so far given insufficient attention to these problems. Nevertheless, it is possible to see the outlines of at least a partial solution to population problems, though it is a controversial one.

The Malthusian Warning

In 1798, Thomas Malthus warned that human beings, like other species, may reproduce at a rate that outstrips the carrying capacity of the site they inhabit and so doom themselves to destruction. Malthus' idea is a simple one: since human beings can have more children than simply replace themselves, and since these children in turn can also have more children than replace themselves, the growth of the human population tends to be exponential; but their food resources are ultimately limited by the productive capacity of the land. When a species does exceed the carrying capacity of its site, according to Malthusian theory, it 'crashes' or dies back, either partially or completely. Widespread starvation, epidemics of disease exacerbated by the poor nutritional status of the population, pathological or aggressive behaviour aggravated by overcrowding and other factors lead to dramatic, involuntary population loss.

The human population now – at the transition from the twentieth to the twenty-first century – stands at around 6 billion. In the year 10,000 BC, there were somewhere between 2 and 20 million people in the world; by AD 1, 10,000 years later, there were still only about a quarter billion people. By 1600 there were half a billion; 200 years later the population had doubled; by 1930 it had doubled again. Adding the third billion took thirty years, from 1930 and 1960, the fourth billion from 1960 to 1974 – just fourteen years – and the global population reached five billion only twelve years later, in 1986. Adding the sixth billion, which is occurring now, is taking just ten years, and the seventh billion will begin to be added before the year 2000.

Population growth rates have declined somewhat in many parts of the world.

149

But slowed growth is still growth, and due to population momentum as large numbers of young people reach reproductive age, total global population is still increasing very rapidly. Population estimates for the year 2050 range from a 'wishful-thinking' 7.78 billion estimate, representing the original goals of the United Nations International Conference on Population and Development held in Cairo in 1994, to 12.5 billion or more. As Joel Cohen points out, were global population growth to continue to increase even at its current (slowed) rate, by 3050 there would be six sextrillions. But such an increase is impossible; there is not enough land area for this many people to occupy even a single square inch, let alone raise foodstuffs or produce any other goods.

Malthus himself did not advocate 'population control' programmes; he thought moral restraint might serve as some check, but, as a pessimist, he also assumed that the human population, like any overproducing animal species, would go through cycles of expansion and die-back. But contemporary neo-Malthusians, following pioneer Paul Ehrlich, point on that 'die-back' means intense suffering and devastating loss of life for human beings, and warn that the sole way to avoid such a cataclysm is the resolute practice of population control.

Population Control and its Critics

Active concern with population control began in the 1960s, fortified by the development of 'the Pill'. Beginning with India's vasectomy incentive campaign, family-planning programmes have been developed in some 200 countries in the world – some desultory, some completely ineffectual and some very aggressive, like China's one-child programme. Early programmes relied primarily on permanent sterilization, either male or female; newer programmes have stressed reversible contraception, including condoms, oral contraceptives (the Pill), intrauterine devices (IUDs), subdermal implants (Norplant), depot injectibles (DepoProvera) and others, using contraception both to delay the onset of child-bearing and yield greater spacing between children as ways of decreasing total family size. But family planning and population control programmes have been assailed by critics of at least three different sorts.

Religious critics

Among religious groups, two have been most conspicuously opposed to population control: the Catholic Church and Islam. The bases of their opposition are rather different: Catholicism's opposition to population control is primarily based on opposition to 'artificial' contraception, while Islam's opposition is essentially pro-natalist in character: it favours large family size.

Drawing on earlier roots but first articulated well after Vatican II, Catholic teaching, which permits sex only within marriage, insists that the marital act must be both 'unitive' and 'procreative' – that every act of sexual activity must be open to the transmission of new life. This teaching was a direct response to questions raised by the development of the Pill, and issued in a more general teaching about contraception: the use of all forms of 'artificial' contraception is forbidden, as is sterilization. Catholics may licitly use only 'natural family planning', that is, only rhythm methods (including calendar-based schedules and those involving temperature measurement and self-inspection of the cervical mucus), which rely on abstinence during the woman's fertile period. Because they involve periodic abstinence, these methods all require the cooperation of the male.

This teaching (it is a teaching, not doctrine, and it is not articulated as infallible) has had quite different consequences. When first promulgated, it produced what was described as 'the month of theological anger' by clerics opposed to the Church's position. In much of Latin America, however, it has heavily influenced public policy, and family-planning programmes, abortion, sterilization and the distribution of contraception have been prohibited, underfunded or in other ways impeded by governments. In the United States and much of Western Europe, in contrast, it was largely ignored: Catholic women practise contraception at about the same rate as non-Catholic women. Yet Catholic opposition to population control has played a major role in international policy in two ways: it has at times influenced governments to discontinue funding for family-planning programmes; but it has also reinforced attention to issues of unequal distribution of resources and disparate levels of development as a way of understanding how economic injustice can contribute to population pressures.

Islam too has been concerned about the permissibility of contraception, though its theological disputes have focused on the permissibility or impermissibility of male withdrawal during intercourse. Some authorities allow withdrawal; some prohibit it; and some adopt a position of conditional acceptance, permitting it, for instance, only with the wife's consent. Most authorities accept withdrawal and also allow the use of other forms of contraception, including the condom, the diaphragm and the IUD, often emphasizing, however, that the latter should preferably be fitted by a woman physician. Spermicides and oral contraceptives or other hormonal methods are considered permissible only if it can be shown that they do not harm the woman. Islam has also strongly emphasized the importance of children.

Both Catholicism and Islam are undergoing considerable evolution in response to population issues. Although Catholicism still prohibits all 'artificial' contraception and sterilization, it places increasing emphasis on responsible planning of family size, made possible through the use of natural methods of fertility control. Some Islamic countries, like Indonesia, have had very successful family-planning programmes, with dramatic drops in population growth. Others, particularly in the Middle East, are only now introducing family-planning programmes or tolerating non-governmental programmes: several of these seek to introduce concepts of condom use and responsible family-size planning to males rather than females, on the assumption that this is both more in accord with basic Islamic religious teachings and with the realities of reproductive choice in male-dominated societies.

For both religious traditions, critics often suggest that opposition to family planning and population control cloaks a politics of population size: the greater the population, it is assumed, the more adherents a religious group will have and the greater a nation's economic, military and political strength. Sceptics denounce this as a merely political strategy; loyalists defend it as a way of protecting the inherent value of continuation of the family, the religious tradition and society. But change is occurring. While religious groups for the most part continue to see strength in numbers, many countries are beginning to see it the other way around: too large a population is a liability, not an asset. This sets up a new tension: between countries as economic and political units, on the one hand, and on the other the majority religions which inform their cultures and guide the reproductive behaviour of their peoples.

Feminist critics

Meanwhile, feminist critics like Betsy Hartmann have examined the nature and methods of programmes designed to control population growth. Controlling population growth means controlling people, they argue, and it means especially controlling women. Population programmes have typically operated by targeting 'acceptors' – women who can be pressured into accepting contraception or sterilization – and have paid little or no attention to women's subordinate situations in patriarchal societies, their precarious economic circumstances, their lack of education and familiarity with modern medicine, their compromised nutritional status and their desperate need of other health care. Furthermore, the feminist critique adds, population-control programmes have had little sense of women's reproductive rights.

Early population-control programmes in India, Indonesia and other developing countries have sometimes been conducted in inept, irresponsible ways. For instance, these programmes have sometimes encouraged the implantation of various kinds of long-acting contraceptives, especially the IUD and Norplant, without regard to side-effects and with no provisions for removal of the implant should the woman experience side-effects or wish to have a child. Contraceptive testing has variously been conducted without informed consent, with placebo controls (the woman who gets the dummy pill risks a pregnancy she does not want), as in Puerto Rico; and with drugs of which the long-term effects are not known, such as the antifertility vaccines. Compounding the damage, feminists have argued, population-control programmes seem to have committed a conceptual error as well: these programmes appear to *blame* poor, uneducated women in the Third World for unrestrained, 'excess' fertility, as if problems of global population growth, including environmental degradation and immigration pressures on wealthy nations, were exclusively their fault.

Ineptly and irresponsibly managed population-control programmes pursued in the absence of adequate health-care systems in many developing countries have been one target of feminist rage. But the spectre of China's effectively imposed one-child policy has been another. Although it has produced a dramatic reduction in China's enormous growth rate (though because of population momentum, China's population continues to grow), the one-child policy has been condemned by feminists and others for its policies of required contraception, forced abortion and mandatory sterilization. The one-child policy has also been denounced as well for its consequences for women: in a cultural tradition with a pronounced preference for sons, China has seen widespread selective sex-based abortion, concealment and abandonment of female children and, in some cases, female infanticide.

Cornucopian critics

In the debates over population among religious and feminist thinkers, a third school of critics, usually dubbed the Cornucopians, has attempted to show that the supposed limits on population growth are not well founded and hence that population control is not needed. Cornucopianism claims that the earth's resources are not in danger of depletion or disruption by pollution to the point of failing to support the human population. Julian Simon has been particularly vocal among this group, pointing out there is no agreement on the actual 'carrying capacity' of the globe and insisting that human ingenuity can be counted upon to develop new food production techniques and new ways of exploiting and conserving resources. Many researchers have focused on specific areas such as agriculture, fisheries, fresh water, fuels, air quality and so on to try to demonstrate that substantial increases in global population can still be accommodated. For example, Dennis Avery has claimed that improvements in agricultural science will permit the earth to feed as many as 1,000 billion people. But, as critics point out, it is irresponsible to rely on partial Cornucopianism – that is, to argue that some one resource will not be depleted. Even if it were possible to produce food for 1,000 billion people, this does not entail that it is possible to dispose of the domestic and industrial wastes of 1,000 billion people and their engines; or, as Paul Waggoner points out, though there might be water for 400 billion, there may only be resources for fertilizer for 80 billion. Furthermore, some resources are affected by our uses of others. Fresh-water resources for human consumption and agriculture are under increasing stress, partly due to use without purification and re-use and partly due to pollution. Cornucopianism is limited by the weakest essential link.

Surveying some sixty-six past and current estimates of how many people the earth can support, Joel Cohen notes that they range from 1 billion (a sixth of the earth's current population) to a fanciful billion billions (a humorous estimate made by Fremlin in 1964, where the removal of body heat, at 120 persons per square metre, is the sole limitation), but they are narrowing towards a much closer range, between 4 billion (a mark passed in about 1974) to 16 billion, or when ranges of estimates were given, between about 7.7 billion and 12 billion. But a global population of 7.7 billion is virtually inevitable within the next few years, and 12 billion less than one doubling away. Everyone over 40 has already lived through one doubling of the global population; and many may see two doublings within a human lifespan. The issue is not just how high population growth can climb, but at what level population size can be sustained over time.

Observers also point out that many other factors exacerbate population pressures, leading to famine, urban crowding, immigration pressures and so on. Chief among these are the inequitable distribution of goods and resources and disproportionate patterns of consumption between the poor nations and the rich ones. Of the current global population of about 6 billion, about a fifth is affluent (largely in the European and North American countries, and in Australia and Japan), three-fifths are poor (primarily in Asia and Central and South America) and one-fifth lives in absolute poverty (particularly in sub-Saharan Africa), suffering from malnutrition or in the process of starvation. But these patterns are exacerbated by inequities in distribution and consumption. For some resources, inhabitants of the rich northern nations consume as much as seventy-five times as much as inhabitants of the poor, southern ones, though inhabitants of the poor countries are sometimes thought of as greater threats to resources such as forests, for example, because of land-use techniques like slash and burn. The inhabitants of rich nations also produce far more environmental pollution than inhabitants of poor nations. Political power can exacerbate problems of distribution of food and other goods, so that famine occurs as a result of inequitable political processes and the control of resources by powerful groups, not a genuine lack of food. Amartya Sen has argued that there has never been famine in any nation with a free press. Yet the threat of famine and the failure of other resources looms large in the consciousness of many areas of the world, including monumental China.

Many thinkers have urged attention to development and consumption patterns in order to resolve population pressures. But even this has had paradoxical results. Structural adjustment programmes required of poor nations by international lenders like the World Bank and the International Monetary Fund have themselves exacerbated population stresses, it is claimed, as they undercut traditional agriculture by emphasizing export production, decrease the economic power of women and in general disrupt traditional economies in order to promote Western-style economic development. Not only have these pressures disrupted traditional economies, but in many places increased consumption.

'Levelling Off': The Demographic Transition

Much thinking about population issues has been shaped by the assumption that global population growth will 'level off' in the middle of the next century. It is assumed that current declines in growth rates will continue, that population momentum will be slowed and that the average total family size will stabilize at about 2.1 children per woman, on average, around the globe. This is the assumption; the question is whether it is a realistic prediction, or an unsupported and dangerous fantasy. Furthermore, there continues to be disagement about the predicted size of the global population when – or if – levelling off occurs.

The 'levelling-off' assumption relies on projections concerning what is known as the demographic transition, that pattern of four distinct stages a society goes through in moving from an undeveloped, agrarian economy to an industrialized, developed one. In the first stage of the demographic transition, that characterizing pre-modern, undeveloped, non-industrial, agrarian economies, birth rates are high, but so are death rates: in the absence of modern medicine and many other factors, life is hard, infant mortality is high, maternal mortality in childbirth is also high and the average lifespan is short. Thus population size remains comparatively stable: there are many births, but many early deaths. In the second stage, the introduction of immunization programmes, clean water supplies, antibiotics and other developments from the technologically advanced nations leads to a sharp drop in death rates, but traditional social patterns continue to favour high birth rates. With high birth rates and low death rates, the population soars. (This is the current picture in many developing countries, especially in sub-Saharan Africa.) With increasing development, however, a third stage begins: as women are increasingly educated, as infant mortality drops and families find they do not need many children born to assure that a few survive, as social insurance systems mean that parents do not need to rely on their children for support in their old age and as additional children no longer mean an additional source of labour in tasks like wood-gathering, water hauling and farmwork but instead begin to represent a liability in schooling costs, clothing costs, entertainment and supervision in an urban environment, birth rates begin to decline: thus population growth rates slow. In the fourth stage, which characterizes industrialized nations like those of Europe, both birth and death rates are low – births are fewer but lifespans longer – and the population size 'levels off' or stabilizes. Indeed, in some countries – notably Italy, Spain, the former East Germany and Russia, population growth has dropped below the replacement rate.

This pattern of demographic transition has been exhibited in many countries. Projections concerning global population assume that, on the whole, the global population will also exhibit this pattern, moving from a current position in which birth rates for the globe remain high (though low in some areas) but death rates have already been substantially lowered, through declines to the point where both birth and death rates are low. This assumption, that population growth rates will stabilize during the next century, has lulled many thinkers into concluding that there is no real problem, and certainly no justification for coercive population control.

But there are two substantial problems with this conclusion. For one thing, the prospect of 'population entrapment' suggests that, for some societies now experiencing very high growth rates, societal infrastructures will fail very rapidly as the population outstrips their capacity, and will in effect reverse any prospects of development. It will become more difficult to ensure food supplies, to provide education and health care, to offer jobs (especially to women), to maintain social security systems and, as survival becomes increasingly threatened and people retreat to precarious rural and urban foraging lifestyles, people will have more children rather than fewer in the hope that some survive. Population entrapment is most likely in the least developed nations with the most rapid current population growth and greatest population momentum, those nations that Paul Kennedy predicts will be losers, not winners, in the twenty-first century. In these countries, the demographic transition may not take place after all, and population growth will be limited by crash and die-back, especially if immigration restrictions are maintained by the wealthier nations.

A second problem challenging the assumption that the demographic transition will solve population problems lies in the mechanism of the transition: declines in

155

birth rates are associated with economic development. Indeed, economic development has been a strategy actively pursued as a means of population control. The goals associated with it have included increased education, both for women and children, especially female children, lowering infant mortality rates, enhancing the status of women, the creation of jobs for women, etc.: these are the strategies explicitly favoured in the Cairo proposals of 1994. But economic development brings with it dramatic increases in rates of consumption: diets consisting of more fats and meats (less efficient foodstuffs than grains), more extensive energy uses, more uses of consumer and industrial products that pollute or exhaust environmental resources. The spectre here is sometimes pictured as more than a billion inhabitants of China (a fifth of the world's population), all having just one child, maybe two, but, like the inhabitants of the United States, all wanting refrigerators and automobiles. Emulating Western economic models may also mean emulating Western domestic models as well, with low family size but huge uses of resources. Economic development risks increasing rather than decreasing strains on the carrying capacity of humankind's site, the earth, and hence offers an enormously problematic solution to population problems.

Thus we see the real dilemma at the core of the population issue. Current high birth rate/low death rate population patterns of very rapid growth could be allowed to continue as they are, fomenting rigorous immigration controls elsewhere in nations with more stable populations, though these patterns of very rapid population growth risk imminent crash and extensive die-back. Or strategies can be adopted to control population growth, limiting reproductive rights but preventing the human suffering associated with die-back. Or – this is perhaps the most common response among those unfamiliar with the issues – attention can be diverted from the problem, either through denial that any problem exists, or blind trust that one or another of the Cornucopian promises of heightened technology will prove sufficient to save all. This too risks population crash and die-back.

Methods of Population Control

Debate over population is focused not only on issues of maximal and optimal population size, but on methods of population control. Most nations now have family-planning programmes, though these vary tremendously in character, methods and effectiveness; some are governmental, some are conducted by NGOs or non-governmental organizations; and some rely entirely on local private groups. They variously stress education and the provision of family-planning information, access to contraception, the provision of contraception and other health care; they rely to differing degrees on local funding and international assistance; and they are subject in differing ways to interference or support from religious and cultural institutions. Despite their enormous variety, virtually all of them face two basic ethical dilemmas.

Incentives and disincentives   What moral limits are there on the use of incentives and disincentives to control population size? Which are preferable? How strong

156

might they be? Perhaps most notorious for its use of problematic incentives, India's vigorously pursued population-control policy of 1975–6 used, among other incentives, transistor radios: they were offered to any man who would consent to a vasectomy on the spot. Financial incentives were also offered to local officials who could persuade villagers to accept sterilization, often at the mobile 'vasectomy camps' created around the country. At the same time, disincentives were used as well: fines, denial of benefits, denial of medical treatment for government officers, denial of government quarters for civil servants, denial of accommodation in housing projects for the public and disqualification for most government scholarships were threats used to secure compliance with sterilization programmes.

The use of incentives and disincentives to influence reproductive behaviour has occurred in many other areas, in a wide variety of forms. The Nazis used bronze, silver and gold medals to reinforce large family sizes for Aryan women: four, six and eight children respectively. Ceaucescu's Romania used a variety of harsh disincentives and penalties for abortion or failure to have an adequate number of children. Singapore's 1983 combination pronatalist/antinatalist programme provided a wide array of benefits and preferences to encourage educated women to have large families, but also used huge incentive payments for sterilization to decrease fertility among uneducated women. And China's one-child programme has used a wide range of incentives – better jobs, better housing, better pay – for couples with only one child, together with disincentives – fines, demotions, penalties, even house-burnings – to discourage those having more than the permitted number of children.

Both incentives and disincentives can violate fundamental principles of autonomy: incentives by being too big or too attractive to resist, especially for someone in precarious economic circumstances, disincentives by being too dangerous to incur. In both cases, a basic principle of reproductive liberty would require informed, voluntary choice about matters relevant to procreation, but the voluntariness of such choices can quite easily be infringed. India's notorious transistor radios compromised voluntariness in two ways: not only were they too attractive to resist for poor villagers, but the 'point-of-purchase' way in which they were often offered tended to undercut the possibility of reflective deliberation for a man or the possibility of discussion with his wife.

Contraception mandates vs family size ceilings At the same time, ethical issues are also posed by the differing uses of contraception mandates and family size ceilings. India's vasectomy programme emphasized promoting contraception, loosely tied to family size; China's programme, on the other hand, has promulgated a family size limit, coupled with the supply and surveillance of contraception to maintain this limit. While in practice contraception mandates and family size ceilings are often intertwined, they are conceptually different. Contraception mandates may alter the decisional structure of child-bearing choices but still recognize individual preferences in choices about family size; family size limits may impose a ceiling but can leave it to the couple to determine how to prevent child-bearing so as to stay within the limit. Both are often used in ways that openly restrict reproductive liberty; the

157

question is which form of interference is morally more tolerable? Contraceptive mandates seem particularly problematic where the contraceptive employed poses health risks to the user, involves unacceptable side-effects or is irreversible; family size limits are problematic where they are very severe (as in a one-child policy), are inequitably imposed or are not necessitated by a country's demographic situation. Contraceptive mandates tend to impose burdens of restricted child-bearing on just some individuals, the 'acceptors'; family size limit policies often tend to punish violators after the fact.

However, both contraceptive mandates and family size limits may be acceptable in some situations. China provides a good example, it may be argued, of both: it has effectively mandated contraceptive use, though it employs methods appropriate to the user's situation – short-acting methods before child-bearing, the IUD after the birth of the first child and sterilization after the birth of a second or third child, so that even if the first child is lost, an additional pregnancy can be initiated. It has imposed these mandates on *all* women. At the same time, its family size ceiling has been comparatively egalitarian, though it is beginning to undergo some erosion: the policy is one child for all couples (with the exception of two in some rural provinces and no ceiling in non-Han ethnic areas around China's perimeter), not, say, five children for Party members and no children for non-members. It is also clear that China's population situation has been approaching emergency proportions, and that the imposition of stringent growth restrictions has been a demographic necessity.

Even in countries with less acute population problems, family-planning programmes may exhibit some of the same issues. In some countries, family-planning schemes are targeted at groups, segregated by income, ethnicity or race, perceived to be at higher risk of excess child-bearing; even if contraceptive mandates do not violate canons of voluntary choice, these schemes may be inequitable solely in view of their targeted character. Other issues include adherence to veiled family size limitations: target ceilings entertained by programme officials or governments, but not known to recipients of family-planning services or available for public discussion. And family-planning programmes may often violate canons of informed consent by withholding information about the contraceptive measures it makes available, including information about risks, reversibility and side-effects. Nevertheless, it is fair to say that there is a much greater awareness in global family-planning programmes of the ethical issues they raise than in the early days of population-control programmes, thanks in large measure to political surveillance and especially feminist critique, and the abuses evident in many early programmes are diminishing.

Optimal Population Size: Fewer with More or More with Less?

Dire predictions about overpopulation, about sustainable patterns of consumption, about future generations and about the threat of die-back and crash presuppose a set of theoretical reflections most vigorously pursued by Derek Parfit. Although

Parfit's concern is presented in a philosophically sophisticated form, the question he poses is at root a simple – though troublingly difficult – one. Which is to be preferred, when speaking of populations, that situation which yields the highest average level of welfare, or that which yields the greatest aggregate total of welfare? Put in another way, which is to be preferred, a situation in which there are fewer people though their quality of life is high, or one in which there is just as much happiness altogether, but there are more people although their quality of life is lower? Such questions of course raise issues about how 'welfare' is to be measured and what factors 'quality of life' assessments should take into account, such as adequate nutrition, housing, freedom from grinding labour, adequate health, some measure of personal autonomy and leisure and whatever else contributes to human happiness and flourishing, but the central problem is about numbers. When we think about population size in general, should there be fewer people better off, or more people, but worse off? After all, the sum total of welfare or happiness in the world might be the same. Translated into the context of the actual world, with its actual population of about a fifth rich, three-fifths poor and a fifth in absolute poverty, the problem might look like this: would it be a better world in which everyone lives as the rich do – with houses, cars, refrigerators and the ample use of resources? Then there would have to be many fewer of them, if the population is to survive. Or would it be better if the rich had much, much less, and lived at the levels of subsistence that the poor and very poor now do? Then there could be many, many more people alive, with just the same use of resources. The problem is replicated at the individual level. Take any two people in absolute poverty: would it be better if there were just one of them, poor, but not on the edge of starvation? Instead of any five in absolute poverty, one who was rich? Or instead of one comfortable, well-nourished, well-equipped person with all the resources one needs to function well in the world, three who are poor, but surviving? There is no easy answer to these questions, but they are central to issues in population theory and population policy.

A Conjectural Partial Solution to the Population Problem

Neither coercive population control, nor cavalier acceptance of die-back, nor naive acceptance of optimistic but unfounded Cornucopian hopes is a satisfactory solution. The population issue is a real one, with massive human consequences. But I think there is at least a partial solution, a surprisingly easy one, readily seen in the form of a conjecture. What if, we might ask, instead of continuing reproductive patterns in which fertile individuals either accept pregnancy as the consequence of sexual intercourse, or decide whether and how to practice contraception, the default mode of human biology were such that conceiving or siring a child required a *positive* decision, followed by deliberate action intended to allow pregnancy to occur? This shift is what occurs with so-called long-term reversible contraception – like the IUD or the subdermal implant – which maintains a condition in which a woman is infertile, or incapable of pregnancy unless she has the contraceptive

159

neutralized or removed. Of course, the technologies now available for women are far from perfect, and such technologies are not yet available at all for men, though research on long-term contraception for men is in progress in many countries. But we can still entertain the conjecture: what if everybody, both male and female, were to use long-term, reversible, 'automatic' contraception, so that the sustaining or siring of pregnancy required a positive choice, rather than simply a negative choice to prevent it? Such a picture would be morally acceptable only with adequate guarantees of reversibility, and only if it were genuinely universal, not targeted at groups perceived to be overreproducing, since it is only thus that reproductive choice is fully protected – one can always choose to have a child. But with these guarantees, we can imagine further development of contraceptive technologies of high safety, high reliability and immediate reversibility, free of side-effects, nuisance or risks, technologies that would offer 'automatic' but reversible contraception without requiring user compliance but always permitting a positive choice of conception. If *everyone* routinely used automatic contraception, then all child-bearing would require a simultaneous choice by both male and female to try to produce a child. Since people will *accept having* more children than they would *choose to have*, reversing the default, so to speak, in choices about child-bearing will mean that the greatest possible drop in unintended child-bearing occurs that is consistent with full reproductive choice. This change might not solve all population problems, but it would go a long way indeed towards reducing growth without infringement of reproductive rights.

The alternative is China. Given what may seem to be an association between China's very rapid economic growth and its effective adherence to a one-child policy, we can worry that other nations will begin to copy such programmes. Whether they will be as comparatively egalitarian as China's and whether they will involve as great a degree of apparent popular assent is hard to predict; but it is possible that stark population control policies will be enforced in far more biased ways in many other countries. China's policy has involved dramatic infringements of reproductive liberties in some cases; other nations, still more threatened by population pressures, might move to population control – especially of disfavoured minorities – in still more ruthless ways.

Unless, of course, no effective effort is made to control population at all. This is the third alternative. It is potentially starker and more cruel than any form of rigorous population control, since it involves widespread crash and die-back – that is, human death or non-reproduction on a widespread scale, either from starvation or other population-related causes. The neo-Malthusian advocacy of population control is to some degree rejected by religious, feminist and Cornucopian thinkers, but the wholesale rejection of attention to population size at all may invite still worse consequences, though it often seems to be the direction in which we are headed.

Yet there is some accommodation already. Catholicism now supports, even urges, responsible family-size planning, provided it uses 'natural' methods, and in some countries tolerates, although officially prohibiting, modern contraception. Some Islamic countries, like Indonesia, have very effective family-planning programmes, and many Middle Eastern Islamic countries are introducing male-centred family planning programmes. Feminists continue to defend fertility choices, including a wide range of contraceptive modalities as well as abortion, though they have been suspicious about certain long-term, provider-controlled methods. Even the Cornucopian thinkers have been forced to recalculate their forecasts, recognizing that population issues are to be taken seriously and that environmental systems are interdependent: that food is not enough without water, that water is not enough without air, that air is not enough without energy sources and so on, and that population size has substantial effects on all these.

Bioethicists have attended very little to the issues of population. But they might have a good deal to say about which is worse: unrestrained population growth, followed by crash and die-back; or stringently imposed population control limiting reproductive rights. Given that neither of these alternatives is attractive, it remains to be seen whether there is still some other alternative. Long-term, reversible, 'automatic' contraception, in continuous use for both men and women except when they actively choose to have a child, will, I believe, go a long way to finding a route between these two undesirable alternatives.

References

Avery, Dennis T. (1995). *Saving the Planet with Pesticides and Plastic: the environmental triumph of high-yield farming*. Indianapolis: Hudson Institute.

Cohen, Joel E. (1995). *How Many People Can the Earth Support?* New York and London: W. W. Norton.

Dixon-Mueller, Ruth (1993). *Population Policy and Women's Rights: transforming reproductive choice*. Westport, CN and London: Praeger.

Ehrlich, Paul R. (1968). *The Population Bomb*. New York: Ballantine Books.

Ehrlich, Paul R. and Ehrlich, Anne H. (1990). *The Population Explosion*. New York: Simon and Schuster.

Gore, Al (1992). *Earth in the Balance: ecology and the human spirit*. New York: Houghton Mifflin.

Hardin, Garrett (1993). *Living Within Limits: ecology, economics, and population taboos*. New York and Oxford: Oxford University Press.

Hartmann, Betsy (1995). *Reproductive Rights and Wrongs: the global politics of population control*. Boston: South End Press.

Kennedy, Paul (1993). *Preparing for the Twenty-First Century*. New York: HarperCollins.

Malthus, Thomas Robert (1798). *An Essay on the Principle of Population, as it Affects the Future Improvement of Society*. [Complete 1st edn and partial 7th edn (1872), reprinted in 1960 in *On Population*, ed. Gertrude Himmelfarb. New York: Modern Library.]

Parfit, Derek (1984). *Reasons and Persons*. Oxford: Clarendon Press.

Sen, Amartya (1992). *Inequality Reexamined*. Cambridge, MA: Harvard University Press.

Simon, Julian L. (1981). *The Ultimate Resource*. Princeton, NJ: Princeton University Press.

Further Reading

Athanasiou, Tom (1996). *Divided Planet: the ecology of rich and poor*. Boston: Little, Brown.

Brown, Lester R. (1997). *State of the World. A Worldwatch Institute report on progress toward a sustainable society*. New York and London: W. W. Norton. [Annual volume.]

161

Nussbaum, Martha, and Glover, Jonathan (eds) (1995). *Women, Culture, and Development: a study of capabilities*. Oxford: Clarendon Press.

Sen, Gita, Germain, Adrienne and Chen, Lincoln C. (eds) (1994). *Population Policies Reconsidered: health, empowerment, and rights*. Harvard Series on Population and International Health. Cambridge, MA: Harvard School of Public Health and International Women's Health Coalition, distributed by Harvard University Press.

United Nations (1987). *World Population Policies*. Vols 1, 2. New York: United Nations.

17

Assisted reproduction

LAURA M. PURDY

Interest in assisted reproduction has sky-rocketed in the last fifteen or so years, promoted by social values and advancing reproductive technologies. Assisted reproduction includes specific approaches to reproduction that involve a third party in the normally two-person enterprise of making a baby. Current techniques include AID (artificial insemination by donor) and egg donation, IVF (*in vitro* fertilization) and the related technologies of GIFT (gamete intrafallopian transfer) and ZIFT (zygote intrafallopian transfer), as well as various forms of so-called surrogacy; some of these approaches may involve cryopreservation (freezing) (Robertson, 1994).

Social values that promote assisted reproduction are many. First, it is widely believed that having children is a natural and normal part of life, and individuals unable to conceive on their own often feel pressure to reproduce anyway; assisted reproduction may thus benefit the infertile. Some techniques (such as AID or egg donation) can also prevent the birth of children at risk of congenital diseases known to be carried by one of the parties who wishes to parent; other approaches, such as surrogacy, can protect women at special risk of harm from pregnancy. Unfortunately, infertility seems to be increasing. Among its causes are environmental pollution, poverty and poor health, sexually transmitted diseases, sterilization, illegal abortions, unnecessary hysterectomies and employment patterns that lead women to delay child-bearing (Warren, 1988). Second, social attitudes are becoming more open to new approaches to reproductive difficulties. Consequently, many people are willing to seek help with reproduction.

General Assessments of Assisted Reproduction

Some people oppose assisted reproduction in principle. This opposition may arise from conservative premises or feminist ones. Let us consider them in turn.

Conservative objections can be traced to two basic facts. One is that assisted reproduction often separates sex and reproduction. The other is that assisted reproduction radically alters traditional assumptions and relationships (Reich, 1978). Resistance to separating sex and reproduction is generally based either on some version of natural law theory or on explicit religious principle, such as the view that non-procreative sex is sinful. Because natural law theory tends either to commit the naturalistic fallacy or beg questions, it cannot provide a strong moral basis for prohibiting the separation of sex and reproduction. Religious principle is, in turn, an unacceptable basis for social policy in pluralistic societies, although individuals who adhere to the relevant religion are free, other things being equal, to order their lives according to it. Assisted reproduction does alter traditional ways of doing things, but unless one posits the dubious premise that traditional ways are always best, it does not follow that innovations should be rejected wholesale.

Feminist objections can be traced to the fear that assisted reproduction will help men to subjugate women. Feminists emphasize that social pronatalism leads many women to undertake costly and potentially risky procedures to remedy infertility that would not otherwise trouble them. Furthermore, since men still run society, and are especially prominent in science and medicine, women's quest for help with reproduction adds to men's power over them. A few feminists have claimed that if additional techniques, such as ectogenesis or cloning, were perfected, men might seek to eliminate women from society altogether; other developments might also lead to morally objectionable forms of eugenics. Feminists also see assisted reproduction as precluding social reforms that would prevent infertility and provide alternative satisfactions for the infertile (Spallone and Steinberg, 1987). These claims raise genuine concerns that need to be evaluated on an issue by issue basis; however, given the implausible nature of the underlying premise (that men as a group want to subjugate or eliminate women) it would not make sense to reject assisted reproduction in principle on these grounds.

Given that neither conservative nor feminist claims seem sufficient for rejecting assisted reproduction without further argument, let us consider specific types of assisted reproduction.

AID and egg donation

In AID, sperm is obtained from a man who is not the prospective mother's husband, and is placed in her with the aim of initiating conception. AID is widely accepted; it is estimated to produce some 30,000 babies yearly in the United States alone. AID *per se* does not appear to harm the individuals it produces. However, inadequate screening for sexually transmitted diseases like AIDS (acquired immunodeficiency syndrome) or genetic disease is a serious problem that can have catastrophic consequences for the woman or any resulting child. Lack of screening capacity is the principal drawback of do-it-yourself AID. Using a physician's services should in principle guarantee good screening, although this promise may be unmet. However, using a physician to carry out the procedure for AID renders it more costly, and may allow physicians to impose their social values by denying care to single people or lesbian couples. It also opens up the potential for abuses, as when a physician uses his own sperm to initiate a pregnancy without the consent of the woman. AID could theoretically cause marital problems if men are less attached to children who are not genetically related to them. Additional problems that crop up where legal regulation of rights and duties is inadequate are custody claims by donors or demands for financial support by recipients. However AID appears generally to be a beneficial and well-established practice that can make up for male infertility and prevent serious genetic disease (Mahowald, 1992).

164

Egg donation is more complicated. Whereas sperm for donation is obtained by masturbation, obtaining eggs is unpleasant and risky for the donor. Currently egg donation requires women to be hormonally stimulated to produce multiple eggs; monitoring this development requires frequent blood tests and sonograms. If the stimulation is successful, the eggs are then retrieved from the donor by passing a needle through her vaginal wall. The risks include overstimulation by the hormones, possible damage from the needle and potentially harmful long-term effects of these procedures, including a suspected risk of ovarian cancer (Holmes, 1988). In addition, because the procedure is so new (having started with the development of IVF in the early 1980s) the law in many countries is still murky and provides participants with little protection. Given these risks, it seems doubtful that it is in women's interest to donate eggs, although it does not follow that the practice should be prohibited. In any case, new approaches that avoid the use of hormones by harvesting immature eggs or ovarian tissue will reduce these risks, and the legal situation could be clarified by further regulation.

IVF and its relatives

I will concentrate on the moral issues raised by IVF since most of those raised by GIFT and ZIFT are similar. IVF provides a detour around ill-functioning organs. It requires a woman who desires a child either to undergo egg retrieval or to acquire an egg from a donor. Sperm (usually the husband's sperm) is then introduced to the egg in a Petri dish (Walters and Singer, 1982). To increase fertilization rates, especially where sperm is known to be deficient in some way, a single sperm may be injected through the outer membrane of the egg wall. Any resulting embryos are placed in the woman's uterus when they have grown to four or eight cells; often multiple embryos are introduced to raise the odds in favour of pregnancy. If the woman becomes pregnant, she receives frequent injections of progesterone until the twelve-week point. Women undertaking IVF face an elevated risk of ectopic pregnancy, miscarriage and multiple births. The success rate is low, about 19 per cent for women under 40 and 7 per cent for women over 40, although different clinics have different rates of success, and some versions of IVF (such as that undertaken with egg donation) have better results (*Consumer Reports*, 1996: 50).

One major source of moral concern is the welfare of the offspring of IVF. Some people believe that the right to life begins at conception. Because IVF may lead to the production of 'extra' individuals that may be discarded, such people believe that it is tantamount to murder. As the status of embryos is discussed elsewhere in this volume, there is no need to enter the debate here.

Concern about IVF harming any resulting children is appropriate even if one does not share the view that moral personhood begins at conception. Minor harm might be outweighed by the benefit to the child of existence; more serious ones would raise doubts about the morality of IVF. At present there seems to be some increased risk of damage to IVF babies, and more problems might turn up as they develop (Holmes, 1988: 140). The procedure is still quite new (the first IVF baby, Louise Brown, was born only in 1978) so the long-term evidence of its safety is

165

scant. Yet more IVF babies are born every year. Perhaps the high rate of unsuccessful pregnancies is weeding out most serious health problems (Robertson, 1994: chapter 5).

Women are also at risk from IVF. If they provide their own eggs, they may be harmed by the retrieval process. If they become pregnant, their pregnancies may fail; ectopic pregnancies are life-threatening if undetected. If their pregnancy fails, they may try again, compounding both psychological and physical risks. Some women seem to feel driven to try again and again, enmeshed in a cycle of hope and despair. IVF can be costly where it is neither included in a national health insurance system nor covered by private insurance plans. Furthermore, successful pregnancies are much more likely than an ordinary pregnancy to end in a Caesarean section, in part because they are regarded as 'precious' and in need of especially close physician management. However, Caesarean deliveries are riskier and more costly than a vaginal delivery. Given these facts, one might question whether women who undertake IVF fully understand its risk/benefit ratio (Sherwin, 1992).

Women's consent might also be questioned on feminist grounds. Pronatalism is pervasive in human societies, as is the attitude that women who do not have children are necessarily unfulfilled, or even worthless. We cannot know how many feel pressured to produce children at any cost, to live up to these standards (Warren, 1988). The onus of barrenness is so great that some women will even undertake IVF when it is their husbands who suffer from a reproductive problem. Although these points suggest that women considering IVF should have lengthy counselling, they do not support a ban on the practice. Doing so 'to protect women against themselves' would treat women as legal incompetents, damaging women more than unwise reproductive treatments.

The risks and costs of IVF have elicited additional objections. Many people are concerned about using scarce resources to create more children when many existing children need good homes; overpopulation is another concern. Both are genuine worries, although they do not, by themselves, show that a legal ban would be appropriate. First, adoption raises moral questions of its own. Adopting babies may contribute to the exploitation of poor young women; interracial adoptions pose special difficulties. Adopting older children with serious problems may require quitting work or virtually abandoning other life projects; while taking on such a project is admirable, it is unfair to expect only the infertile to be responsible for these children while the fertile are morally free to ignore their plight and have any number of genetically related children. It is also true that the human population is outstripping our ability to make sure that people are even minimally provided for. There is evidence that reproduction rates go down when intelligent economic development takes place, but it seems doubtful that such development will occur quickly enough to avoid further famines and plagues. However, because of negative social views of infertile women and inadequate social security programmes that lead to older people's dependence on their children, it would be unfair to expect the infertile to bear the brunt of measures to reduce population growth; nor would this policy reduce population growth by much. It would be much more sensible to undertake programmes to reduce births that spread the burden more fairly. A related issue is the scarce health-care resources used on IVF at a time when many people lack basic care, either because, as in Britain, their national insurance scheme is underfunded or because, as in the United States, there is no such scheme. However, market forces seem to work strongly against the principle that basic needs should have priority (Purdy, 1996).

Feminists raise additional worries about the overall consequences of having IVF available. Some argue against having the procedure available at all whereas others lament that it is not equally available to all. There is some substance to both these approaches although it is unclear that the remedy is in either case to make IVF unavailable to anybody.

IVF's existence means that the infertile do not have to accept their fate: there is always another procedure to try. Social attitudes towards the infertile, especially women, may thus coerce them into IVF programmes, instead of getting on with their lives. This state of affairs reinforces sexism and pronatalism. The answer to this objection is public debate that alerts women to their options and empowers them to say no to IVF, or to repeated cycles of IVF (Sherwin, 1987). It is true that some technologies, like fetal monitoring, may become part of the standard of care, so that women can hardly refuse them; however, there is no reason to believe that IVF will do so, especially if it is expensive. Some feminists are concerned that IVF could contribute to a slippery slope to a stringent eugenic programme that insists on examining every embryo before implantation. But the objection is then to the eugenic programme. Unfortunately, any innovation that starts out only as an option could be made mandatory by an oppressive state, but that is not sufficient reason to attempt to quell all innovation. A lingering question is why reproductive technologies like IVF continue their steady development. While the extremist worry that men are plotting to replace women with test-tubes seems untenable, the scientific and medical establishment does not have a particularly good record of meeting women's needs. Continued advances in reproductive technology might reinforce the view that women's only legitimate desire is to have children, and that they should be willing undertake any risk to achieve that aim. This possibility is a serious concern that needs thorough public airing.

An additional worry is that the technology, because of its reliance on the scientific and health-care establishments, provides yet another site of discrimination against already disadvantaged groups like single women, poor women and lesbians (Overall, 1993). Some people believe that these women should not be having children and thus cannot have any right to assistance. However, there is no reason to think that they are worse parents than heterosexual couples. This kind of discrimination should be countered by eradicating discrimination, not the service itself.

A further moral concern is that it is often convenient to produce more genetic material than can be used fresh so that genetic materials are now often frozen before use. This practice is disturbing to those who believe it is wrong to manipulate such materials, although it is not clear that their objections are justifiable. A more substantive worry is that such cryopreservation is experimental in humans and the possible long-term risks are unknown. In addition, freezing genetic materials may

167

exacerbate problems about ownership. For example, the materials belonging to a given person or couple may be given to others, couples may come to disagree about what to do with their materials or materials may be left 'ownerless' because of unexpected deaths (Robertson, 1994: 104–14). These problems can be avoided by contracts that determine the disposition of these materials.

IVF also increases the frequency of multiple pregnancies. These pregnancies can pose serious risk to the fetuses and for the prospective parents if they already have children or if the number of fetuses is more than they think they can handle. Selective abortion of healthy fetuses is considered morally dubious by many (Overall, 1993).

Last but not least, IVF with egg donation opens up the potential for pregnancy in post-menopausal women. This use of IVF has been highly controversial, although it is not clear that it warrants the outcry it has provoked. A realistic worry, however, is the prospect of elderly parents who do not live long enough to rear their children to adulthood. This objection is morally tenable only if similar arguments are used against men fathering children in late middle age and beyond.

Surrogacy

Surrogacy involves impregnating one woman to gestate a baby who is to be raised by another. Friends or relatives may carry babies for each other, or the arrangement may be a commercial one undertaken for pay; most of the controversy revolves about this latter practice.

Given that ordinary surrogacy fertilizes the surrogate's own egg, the term 'surrogacy' suggests bias against the so-called surrogate in favour of the sperm provider. After all, she provides both genetic material and gestation; he provides only genetic material, so why should she be described as a surrogate? It would make sense to use a more accurate and objective term like contract pregnancy. A more complicated form of contract pregnancy, so-called gestational surrogacy, proceeds by implanting a fertilized egg (rather than just sperm) into the woman who will become pregnant. It raises the question whether genetic relationship or gestation bestows motherhood on a woman; however, one might want to argue that neither constitutes motherhood and that child-rearing is what turns women into mothers. This deconstruction of motherhood creates serious tensions, especially for feminists (Stanworth, 1987). Feminists surely want to underline the importance of child-rearing, while not devaluing biological links; however, neither do they want to reduce motherhood to biology.

Simple contract pregnancy is morally problematic; additional concerns about IVF and the deconstruction of motherhood come into play with gestational contract pregnancy. Simple contract pregnancy raises questions about the welfare of the resulting children, about its effect on women, both as individuals and as a disadvantaged group and about the integrity and harmony of families (Mahowald, 1992). It also raises the spectre of heartbreaking legal cases where either too many or not enough people want a given child.

Open and widespread contract pregnancy is a new phenomenon and thus it is difficult to know what its effect on children might be. The chief concerns are psychological and emotional since there is no reason to think that ordinary contract pregnancy disadvantages children physically. Children might be disturbed to think that they weren't born the usual way, but the more common the practice, the less problematic that would be. Some people believe that the potential for such problems implies that contract pregnancy is wrong. But it is difficult to see why that would be so, given that many of the same people also believe that it is morally permissible to bring new persons to life even when they are at risk of serious disease or disability, since otherwise they would not enjoy any life at all. Also of concern is the effect of contract pregnancy on the woman's already existing children: they may bond with the fetus and then have to watch a sibling being given away. The question is whether it is possible to explain to young children that their mother is so delighted with motherhood that she wants to make it possible for others who could not have children (or healthy children) without her help. If not, would siblings' emotional difficulties constitute sufficient grounds for banning contract pregnancy? The answer must surely depend on some sort of moral cost-benefit analysis, taking into account the often intense unhappiness of the infertile and the desirability of their other goals such as bypassing problematic genetic materials or reducing risk (Purdy, 1996).

One line of argumentation objects to contract pregnancy on the grounds that it involves the commodification of human life, or baby-selling (Radin, 1987). Some proponents of the practice might argue that there is nothing wrong with commodification; others would deny the charge, arguing that what is at issue is the sale of a right to a parental relationship to a child. This latter response would also suffice against the claim of baby-selling.

A more serious problem is raised by those cases where something goes awry and either too many or not enough people want to raise the resulting baby (Alpern, 1992). The notorious Baby M case, where the gestating woman fought to retain custody, raises the spectre of a child torn between conflicting parties. Cases where a baby is deformed or ill raise the possibility that nobody will take responsibility for it. Neither situation is in a child's best interest, and the practice clearly needs to be regulated to eliminate such possibilities.

What about the consequences of contract pregnancy for women? Opponents argue that the practice exploits the women who undertake pregnancy for pay and may coerce the wives of men who engage outside women to carry pregnancies for them. It is also argued, as with IVF, that the practice reinforces undesirable stereotypes of women as breeders and promotes pronatalism; the issues are similar and will not be pursued further here.

The argument that contract pregnancy exploits women rests on a questionable definition of coercion and on a view of women that doubts whether they can be competent to undertake this kind of activity. Coercion is alleged because the women who undertake contract pregnancy for pay are usually poorer than the contracting couple and the standard $10,000 (US) plus expenses is claimed to constitute an irresistible attraction. However, it turns out that it is not usually impoverished women who undertake such pregnancies, but married lower middle-class or working-class women. Furthermore, although $10,000 is a nice sum, some people argue that it is in fact insufficient compensation for such a major enterprise, considering that the lawyers who help arrange these transactions earn at least as much. The fact that the woman is poorer than the couple is unsurprising, given that the practice is a luxury good, and luxury goods are usually provided by the poor for consumption by the wealthy. Without a fuller critique of capitalism and/or a demonstration that there is something unique about such transactions that makes them illegitimate even in a capitalist context, this allegation fails. The possibility of exploitation seems more plausible in the case of gestational contract pregnancy (Holmes, 1992). First, a contracting couple might be more willing to employ a very poor woman with health problems since the quality of the egg is not at issue; for such women the compensation might indeed be almost irresistible even though pregnancy might seriously harm them. Second, gestational contract pregnancy opens up the possibility of hiring a minority woman who would be unlikely to sue successfully for custody in a racist society, should she change her mind about giving up the baby. None the less, it remains to be shown that the practice could not be regulated to avoid these problems.

Are women incompetent to consent to contract pregnancy? Brokers now try to hire only women who have children, but some object that each pregnancy is different from the last. Thus a woman can never be expected to know how she will react to a new pregnancy. It is hard to judge whether this claim is true, but even if it is, one might want to argue that it makes any pregnancy a morally dubious undertaking, given the possible negative consequences of the failure to bond to the resulting child. Given the long history of belief in women's incompetence, it is important to demand the highest standards of evidence and reasoning for any such claim; it seems dubious here. The moral concern could be taken care of in any case by ensuring that women have a period of grace during which they can decide to keep the child, returning all payments by the contracting individuals.

Some allegations involve possible harm to both individual women and to women as a group. One important issue is the *laissez-faire* environment that subjects women who undertake contract pregnancy to stringent health practices or that requires them to abort the fetus at the behest of the contractors. There is still much controversy about what a pregnant woman owes her fetus, but although it is reasonable to think that morality requires a high standard, enforcing it legally is another matter. Contracts that give control over a woman's body to outsiders are morally suspect and may constitute a first step onto a slippery slope that gives society oppressive social control over their bodies and their lives (Spallone, 1989). Also, some current practices are clearly unfair to women, especially where they deliver a stillborn child and are deprived of some portion of their fee. After all, many workers (among them dry-cleaners and physicians) are fully paid, even where their efforts are unsuccessful. Allowing contract pregnancy to proceed under such conditions seriously harms women and society should seriously consider banning the practice if it cannot protect women from them.

Additional questions about women's welfare are raised if men can engage in contract pregnancy without the consent of their wives (especially since AID generally requires the consent of the husband). Thus women may be saddled with children they do not want (Overall, 1987). Nor do wives have automatic legal protection of their relationship to children they do want if the marriage fails. These are serious harms to women and raise the possibility that contract pregnancy should be banned unless wives can be protected from these dangers by regulation.

References

Arditti, Rita, Duelli Klein, Renate and Minden, Shelley (eds). (1984). *Test-tube Women*. London: Pandora Press.

Alpern, Kenneth D. (ed.) (1992). *The Ethics of Reproductive Technology*. Oxford: Oxford University Press.

Boston Women's Health Book Collective (1992). *The New Our Bodies, Ourselves*. New York: Simon and Schuster.

Consumer Reports (1996). Fertility clinics: what are the odds? (1996). *Consumer Reports*, 61/2, 51–4.

Holmes, Helen Bequaert (ed.) (1988). In vitro fertilization: reflections on the state of the art. *Birth*, 15/3, 134–45.

—— (1992). *Issues in Reproductive Technology*. New York: New York University Press.

Mahowald, Mary (1993). *Women and Children in Health Care: An unequal majority*. Oxford: Oxford University Press.

Overall, Christine (1987). *Ethics and Human Reproduction: A feminist analysis*. Boston: Allen and Unwin.

Purdy, Laura (1996). *Reproducing Persons: Issues in feminist bioethics*. Ithaca, NY: Cornell University Press.

Radin, Margaret (1987). Market inalienability. *Harvard Law Review*, 100, 1849, 1921–36.

Reich, Warren T. (ed.) (1978). *Encyclopedia of Bioethics*. New York: Free Press.

Robertson, John (1994). *Children of Choice*. Princeton, NJ: Princeton University Press.

Sherwin, Susan (1992). *No Longer Patient*. Philadelphia: Temple University Press.

Spallone, Patricia (1989). *Beyond Conception: The new politics of reproduction*. Massachusetts: Bergin and Harvey.

Spallone, Patricia and Steinberg, Deborah Lynn (1987). *Made to Order: The myth of reproductive and genetic progress*. Oxford: Pergamon Press.

Stanworth, Michelle (ed.) (1987). *Reproductive Technologies: gender, motherhood and medicine*. Minneapolis: University of Minnesota Press.

Walters, William A. W. and Singer, Peter (eds) (1982). *Test-tube Babies: A guide to moral questions, present techniques and future possibilities*. Melbourne: Oxford University Press.

Warren, Mary Anne (1988). IVF and women's interests: an analysis of feminist concerns. *Bioethics*, 2/1, 37–57.

Further Reading

Andrews, Lori (1989). *Between Strangers: Surrogate mothers, expectant fathers, and brave new babies*. New York: Harper and Row.

Atwood, Margaret (1986). *The Handmaid's Tale*. Boston: Houghton Mifflin.

Baruch, Elaine Hoffman, D'Adamo, Amadeo F. and Seager, Joni (eds) (1988). *Embryos, Ethics and Women's Rights: Exploring the new reproductive technologies*. New York: Harrington Park Press.

Bayles, Michael (1984). *Reproductive Ethics*. Englewood Cliffs, NJ: Prentice-Hall.

Chesler, Phyllis (1988). *Sacred Bond: the legacy of Baby M*. New York: Times Books.

Corea, Gena (1985). *The Mother Machine: Reproductive technologies from artificial insemination to artificial wombs*. New York: Harper and Row.

Coughlan, Michael J. (1990). *The Vatican, the Law and the Human Embryo*. Iowa City: University of Iowa Press.

Field, Martha (1988). *Surrogate Motherhood: The legal and human issues*. Cambridge, MA: Harvard University Press.

Gostin, Larry (ed.) (1990). *Surrogate Motherhood: Politics and privacy*. Bloomington: Indiana University Press.

Holmes, Helen B., Hoskins, Betty B. and Gross, Michael (eds) (1981). *The Custom-made Child?* Clifton, NJ: Humana Press.

Hull, Richard T. (1990). *Ethical Issues in the New Reproductive Technologies*. Belmont, CA: Wadsworth.

Kass, Leon (1979). Making babies revisited. *Public Interest*, 54, 32–60.

Keane, Noel P. and Breo, Dennis L. (1981). *The Surrogate Mother*. New York: Everest House.

Macklin, Ruth (1994). *Surrogates and other Mothers*. Philadelphia: Temple University Press.

Pretorius, Diederika (1994). *Surrogate Motherhood: A worldwide view of the issues*. Springfield, IL: C. C. Thomas.

Purdy, Laura (ed.) (1989). *Ethics and Reproduction*. Special issue of *Hypatia*, 4/3.

Ramsey, Paul (1970). *Fabricated Man*. New Haven: Yale University Press.

Rothman, Barbara Katz (1989). *Recreating Motherhood: Ideology and technology in a patriarchal society*. New York: Norton.

Shalev, Carmen (1989). *Birth Power: the case for surrogacy*. New Haven: Yale University Press.

Shannon, Thomas A. (1988). *Surrogate Motherood: The ethics of using human beings*. New York: Crossroads.

Singer, Peter and Wells, Deane (1985). *Making Babies: The new science and ethics of conception*. New York: Scribners.

Stephenson, Patricia and Wagner, Marsden G. (eds) (1993). *Tough Choices: In vitro fertilization and the reproductive technologies*. Philadelphia: Temple University Press.

Warnock, Mary (1985). *A Question of Life: The Warnock report on human fertilisation and embryology*. Oxford: Blackwell.

Whitbeck, Caroline (1991). Ethical issues raised by the new medical technologies. In J. Rodin and A. Collins (eds), *Women and New Reproductive Technologies: Medical, psychosocial, legal, and ethical dilemmas*. Hillsdale, NJ: Lawrence Erlbaum, 49–64.

Wood, Carl (1984). *Test-tube Conception*. Englewood Cliffs, NJ: Prentice-Hall.

18

Prenatal screening, sex selection and cloning

PAUL ROBINSON

Between conception and birth, and assuming that monozygotic twinning does not occur, the fertilized ovum develops from zygote to infant. Today a range of more or less sophisticated enquiries and tests can be used to investigate the health and other characteristics of the cluster of human cells which passes, in this process of development, through pre-embryonic, embryonic and fetal incarnation. Prenatal screening is the pursuit of these enquiries and tests in connection, usually, either with all or a targeted subclass of pregnant women in a population. Its governing aims are to reduce the incidence of congenital abnormalities for which no treatment is available and to produce information of use in the pre- and postnatal treatment or management of other disorders. Although it seems likely that the first of these aims will be met to some extent in future by gamete screening and selective *in vitro* fertilization, prenatal screening is currently post-conceptional. Consequently, the incidence reduction just mentioned is achieved chiefly through therapeutic abortion.

Prenatal screening is sometimes identified with the kind of removal and examination of tissue and bodily fluid involved in amniocentesis, chorionic villus sampling (CVS) and fetal blood sampling and tissue biopsy. But while prenatal *diagnosis* frequently involves procedures of this kind, screening, as characterized above, need not do so. At antenatal clinics women will normally encounter a range of questions about previous pregnancies and menstruation, general health, family health, age and so on, designed to assess in a very general way the probability of developmental abnormality in the fetus. Maternal blood pressure, as well as height and weight, are measured, and from these measurements inferences concerning the management of the pregnancy are tentatively drawn. Again, maternal urine and blood are sampled and tested in order to anticipate, among other things, pre-eclampsia and fetal rubella, and to prevent haemolytic disease resulting from a mother's rhesus status. Later in the pregnancy, abdominal palpation (that is, manipulation of the abdomen by hand) and visualizing techniques, such as ultrasound, allow morphological aspects of fetal growth and development to be monitored. All of these procedures are parts of prenatal screening as it is practised in developed countries today (Tucker, 1992).

The *conditions* identified in prenatal screening also display greater diversity than one might at first assume. Such screening need not be directed at disease. Gender

has been, and continues to be, screened for in communities where certain religious needs, and socio-economic advantages, are met and arise out of the birth (typically) of a son; and some commentators think that in the future we shall use prenatal screening to *enhance* the physical and perhaps psychological aptitude of the new-born to levels beyond that required by health. Intuitively, where disease is not the focus of a screening programme, any moral objections to the programme are likely to cut more ice.

I have made a distinction between screening on the one hand, and diagnosis on the other. The difference is as follows: medical practitioners and writers distinguish between an inconclusive presumption that a patient has a disorder and proof of that disorder. Screening programmes generally involve both initial investigations which raise presumptions and further tests intended to confirm or disconfirm these. In *prenatal* programmes, as is apparent in the remarks of the previous paragraphs, initial investigation will usually focus on the pregnant woman. Following this, assuming there is cause for concern, a number of options are available, for example, if a single gene disorder is at issue, the father of the child may be asked to undergo a genetic test. Alternatively the fetus's health or genetic status may be ascertained directly. (In a neat coinage these processes of investigation are called 'screening cascades'.) In any event, only the confirmatory tests with which an enquiry identifying fetal abnormality concludes are *diagnostic*, and in recognition of this the term 'screening test' is often reserved for inconclusive initial tests.

Here are two examples. Maternal serum alphafetoprotein (AFP) estimation is a screening test (in the above sense) now offered routinely in Britain at sixteen to eighteen weeks' gestation. Lower than normal levels of AFP correlate significantly with Down's syndrome and elevated levels are found in women carrying fetuses with neural tube defects (NTDs, examples are spina bifida and anencephaly). Any abnormal levels of AFP have to be investigated further by ultrasound and/or amniocentesis. An 'abnormal' level of AFP can be explained by the carriage of twins or triplets; it can also be explained by the fact that the relevant gestation is more or less advanced than the testing clinician has assumed. The relevant correlations thus accommodate false positives and are too weak to ground diagnosis. Cystic fibrosis (CF) is a recessive genetic disorder and as a result an unaffected pregnant women who tests positive for the CF gene is unlikely to have an affected child. She will do so only if her (let us assume, unaffected) partner is also a carrier – and in Caucasian populations, where CF is more prevalent than elsewhere, one in twenty-five men carry CF – and even where this is so there is a residual, Mendelian, three in four chance that the child will be unaffected. Obviously then, initial tests for CF carrier status, whether they are performed upon pregnant mothers alone or upon expectant couples, are of little use unless followed up with diagnosis by fetal DNA analysis.

The principal, certainly most visible, focus of moral argument about prenatal screening – termination – is typically offered to women only after the diagnosis of serious fetal abnormality. Before we turn to the ethics of termination, however, it is worth pointing out that the seriousness of a number of other ethical issues is in many ways increased by the fact that prenatal screening normally involves

174

more extended and initially inconclusive forms of investigation than one-step testing.

First, it is widely agreed that health-care procedures, other things being equal, ought ideally to respect patient autonomy. It is true, of course, that where prenatal screening is concerned the practice implications of this view are unclear: autonomy is *self*-governance; its being properly respected does not obviously imply that a pregnant woman, or couple, ought to be given *carte blanche* to make decisions the principal beneficiary or victim of which will be, not them, but an unconsulted fetus. I shall return to this issue below. For the moment let us grant, as the law in the common-law world does, that parents should indeed have discretion to direct pre-natal examination by giving or refusing their consent. Very few people would maintain that the sort of autonomy we are concerned with accommodating here is necessarily present in *actual* choice; and everybody would agree that it is obliterated in *manipulated* choice. Instead – and for reasons which seem to have as much to do with the likelihood of deliberation issuing in decisions which genuinely promote the agent's interests as the value of acting as one wishes as such – what we care about are choices which are *informed* but *free of undue influence*. But just how realistic is it to expect choices of this kind to be available to pregnant women and fathers caught up, usually in a state of greater than normal anxiety, in rapidly evolving screening cascades?

In part this is an empirical question and, clearly, the answer to it will vary, depending on the particular character of the screening programme being consid-ered. In advance of any empirical research we know, however, that the medical and statistical interpretation of a screening test can require considerable sophistication – something bound to grow in significance as antenatal clinics attempt to tackle more multifactorial and late-onset diseases. When one adds to this the further difficulty of imagining, let alone evaluating, a future supporting a seriously disabled dependant, it is easy to see how the goal of ensuring that there is autonomous participation in prenatal screening might be imperfectly achieved.

Behind the empirical question lies a more basic conceptual issue about what autonomy is – or rather about what, in the context of health care, we value in autonomy. Suppose a woman is told that there is a 50 per cent chance that the fetus, F, she is carrying has a condition, C. If C is present, there is a 10–25 per cent probability that it will kill during the first twenty years of F's life and more generally a 70 per cent probability that it will cause premature death. Amniocentesis or CVS can be used to confirm C, but the first carries a 0.5–1 per cent and the second, a 2–4 per cent risk of causing miscarriage. After consideration, the woman – call her Jennifer – might, in these circumstances, choose to do whatever the consultant suggests. She might judge, correctly as we can suppose, that the consultant is conscientious, appreciates her values, is less paralysed by anxiety and so on. Alternatively, Jennifer might think about the matter and make a decision, but one which – as, perhaps, she later comes ruefully to see – is quite out of line with her values. In the first of these scenarios was the *opportunity* to decide and uncoerced delegation finally opted for enough to secure what we want of patient autonomy in health care. In the second, does Jennifer act autonomously? And if she does, does that show that an ideal maternal decision after screening ought to be more than autonomous – not just self-governing, but also in some sense properly self-expressive? – *[handwritten annotation]*

A second issue, intensified by the complexity of screening cascades, is that of *cost*. This has two dimensions since it is necessary both to compare the prenatal screening response to congenital malformation with alternative approaches which do not involve antenatal testing; and, where a case for some form of prenatal screening can be made, to assess competing programmes for relative cost-effectiveness. Let me expand briefly on the first of these subissues. Here, as prenatal screening technology develops, a good deal of programme-by-programme audit will need to be carried out, particularly in connection with conditions with less serious pathology than those currently screened for. For one alternative to prenatal screening with a view to termination is simply to ensure that the lives of sufferers of a given congenital disease are as comfortable as it is, in some sense, reasonable to expect. Not surprisingly, recent studies have suggested that *current* prenatal intervention comes off well in this sort of comparison. One study of maternal serum screening for Down's syndrome, published in 1992, estimated the cost of avoiding a birth with Down's through serum screening and termination at £28,000. This figure did not reflect research and development costs and assumes, artificially, a 100 per cent take-up of amniocentesis and termination. But even so it is impressive: the same study reports that in 1987 the (presumably, average) cost of lifetime care for a Down's sufferer after appropriate discounting was calculated at £120,000. If annual inflation were to run at 3 per cent this cost would have grown to about £140,000 by 1992.

Thirdly, it is well known that prenatal screening *as such* (that is, independently of diagnosis or offer of termination) sometimes raises levels of maternal anxiety. The importance of this problem is hard to gauge, and impossible to generalize about, because significantly different forms of investigation – from casual enquiry to anxious, swiftly scheduled, trans-abdominal amniocentesis – might be pursued at one stage or another of a prenatal screening programme; and more important, because, even in an individual case, it will often be extremely difficult to ascertain just how anxious the relevant woman would have been had she never been made aware of screening. At any rate, there can be little doubt that women experience material unease in the course of screening commonly enough; and it seems likely that this unease will arise more frequently, and be more serious, in a prolonged, step-wise form of screening than a one-off test. Clearly this ought to be borne in mind when screening proposals are being contemplated.

These three issues are interrelated. An obvious way to alleviate maternal stress is by ensuring that there is effective information provision and counselling. A less obvious, and dubious-looking, way to achieve the same result would be by representing tests in a way which suggests there is no cause for alarm, everything is merely routine. The first of these strategies, which becomes more attractive as the known risk of a woman giving birth to a child with abnormality grows, arguably increases the screenee's autonomy, but drives up costs. The second, which could be pursued without institutional dishonesty only during the early stages of screening,

176

cuts costs but, as the patient passes through a cascade of screening tests, increasingly fails to respect maternal autonomy.

I want now to set out and comment on some ethical issues which arise once screening discloses a serious fetal abnormality. This occurs, depending on what one thinks of as serious, in only a few cases. It has been estimated that genetic disease and/or congenital malformation affects approximately 3–5 per cent of live births, and many of the conditions recorded in this figure are minor.

Currently the range of prenatally diagnosable conditions which can be corrected by fetal therapy is relatively small. Doubtless this will change, but for the time being the principal response – both offered and taken – to diagnosis of serious fetal abnormality is abortion. A comprehensive discussion of abortion is provided elsewhere in this *Companion* (see chapter 14, pp. 127–34). Here theoretical implications of the suggestion that abortion can be licensed *by disability* are explored. Contrast the submission that abortion after conception through rape is ethical.

It should be borne in mind as we proceed that in the future antenatal clinics are likely to prevent some forms of untreatable fetal anomaly, without resorting to abortion by using artificial cloning techniques. Two techniques, both of which are performed *in vitro*, deserve mention. In the first, which has already been performed, the pre-embryonic cell cluster which develops after fertilization is biopsied (cell-sampled) and, because the cells which comprise it are totipotential (that is, inchoate and undifferentiated, rather like fertilized ova), this causes monozygotic twinning to occur. Of the two genetically identical individuals which result, one may now be cryogenically preserved, while the other is stimulated to grow in preparation for tests for abnormality. These tests will have the effect of destroying the embryo upon which they are performed, but this does not deprive the data they produce of value, because any findings can be read across to the preserved twin. That twin can then either be destroyed or implanted in a routine IVF procedure, depending on the disclosure of serious anomaly. The second cloning technique involves taking an oocyte, removing its nucleus, and replacing this with the nucleus of a *somatic* cell taken from a healthy donor. The resulting composite cell, which (once the nucleic DNA settings have been reversed) is to all intents and purposes a zygote, can now be implanted, again using IVF technology, and allowed to develop into a 'carbon copy' of the donor – free, of course, of any hereditary disease he or she was free of.

Until very recently cloning of the second kind was largely the stuff of science fiction. It had been achieved with frog ova, but the offspring died as tadpoles. In February 1997, however, 'Dolly' the sheep, a Dorset ewe, was created by British researchers by nucleic substitution. The scientific progress of this development is considerable: Dolly is a mammal; she is also, so her makers claim, the product of DNA derived from a fully differentiated mature udder cell; and she has survived into adulthood.

The first cloning technique, as described, is in effect an elaborate form of prenatal testing for genetic disease. It is like ordinary *in utero* testing in that it assumes our readiness to destroy embryos carrying genetic disorder; but, uniquely, it involves the destruction of an embryo – the tested twin – where test findings are

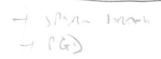

1ˢᵗ *EMBRYO* ...though perhaps, perfect, ...always done)

genetically *favourable*. This second feature commits those who adopt the technique to the view that perfectly healthy embryos may or should be destroyed in order to ensure that other, again healthy, embryos *are* healthy. That is not something to which advocates of traditional prenatal testing are committed. Among the advantages of cloning here, are the fact that it does not involve the ordeal of abortion, and the fact that any embryonic disposals it does involve will occur at an early stage of development.

Nucleic substitution *could* be used to screen out unwanted genetic characteristics, or (the point is better made this way) to guarantee wanted genetic characteristics; and for this reason it will no doubt be exploited in animal breeding – for agricultural purposes or, raising nice questions for those involved, perhaps to secure or prolong competitive advantage in sports such as horse-racing and dog-showing. It could also be employed to preserve red-list animal species whose remaining members refuse to breed in captivity. However, it is hard to envisage circumstances in which a couple resort to nucleic substitution *purely* in order to ensure that their children are free of genetic disorder. Too many other, less costly, less invasive and more convenient means to that end are available – means which would result in children of mixed genetic origin. Most people do not particularly want carbon copies of themselves to bring up.

Putting the prevention of genetic diseases to one side, how should we react to the apparently rapid approach of feasible nucleic human cloning? Some objections to it are objections not to human cloning as such, but (something envisaged as) its misuse: the prospect of excessive replication leading to 'armies of clones' has been worried about, for example, and one might well have misgivings about the motivation of someone who approaches a cloning clinic with the thought, simply, that it would be fascinating to watch a version of himself growing up. Concerns of this kind argue for regulation, not against cloning. However, some people feel strongly that human cloning is inherently wrong or repugnant – others, that it is a good to the clonee, because it delivers a kind of extended longevity or, if repeated forever, immortality. These attitudes require careful examination. The first can be bolstered by failure to separate it from complaints about misuse. The second, which was latent in a great deal of the reportage of Dolly, can be dealt with more expeditiously, since it is patently a mistake to suppose that *you* exist or persist in a cloned 'version of yourself'. One way to see this is to ask yourself how many people there would be in a room containing yourself and your clone.

I return now to abortion for disability. Many people believe that the deliberate destruction of innocent human life is, in itself, wrong. They assert the *sanctity* of (human) life. If this is correct, and if it is accepted, as proponents of sanctity usually do accept, that the fetus is an innocent human being, there is no avoiding the conclusion that abortion for disability is wrong. *How* debilitating the disorder is is irrelevant, and fetuses do not divide into those with serious impairment, which we may, and those in good or better health, which we may not, destroy.

Difficulties with this position emerge when we try to square it with the widely accepted view that it is not necessarily immoral to kill a non-human animal, such as a pig. Why, on the sanctity of life view, are innocent human beings, but not innocent pigs, necessarily wronged by fatal attack? Can membership of a *species* really be as important as is being urged here? It should be emphasized that the sanctity of life doctrine attaches moral significance not to *quality* of life, but *being* alive, and *being* human, as such. That attachment is typically underwritten by religious commitments, but if it is thought of as basic, a moral axiom, it is difficult to accept.

A principle which avoids arbitrary speciesism by committing us to the sanctity of *all* life, or of all *animal* life, would generate the same position on abortion as the view that human life is sacrosanct. But, supposing that we want both to avoid speciesism *and* reject the claim that killing farm pigs is morally wrong, we have to hold that killing (even where intentional, even of innocents) is not *necessarily* wrong. Let us accept this claim *pro tem*. We can now ask whether suggestions as to the conditions under which killing *is* wrong have any noteworthy implications for the view that fetal anomaly warrants termination.

The death of a human being normally entails that certain desires and preferences go unsatisfied, that certain interests are not catered to and that good experiences are missed, bad experiences, sometimes, had; and it has often been suggested by those who reject the sanctity doctrine that morally wrong conduct, including (where wrong) killing, ought to be understood in terms of these thwartings and disappointments. No great insight is required to see that this proposal might well be fleshed out in such a way as to imply that disability *is* relevant to the ethics of abortion, but quite what this relevance might be is at this point obscure, since the proposal can be developed in two quite different ways. The first, which we shall call the *restricted* view, focuses on the impact of a killing on the victim alone. The second, *unrestricted* view, takes into account the effects of killing on all concerned. Exactly who is concerned, we shall turn to below.

The restricted view, in the form to be considered here, claims that fetal disability either leaves a life worth living, because in that life well-being outweighs any suffering, or spoils a life to such an extent that it is not worth living. The idea is that only a life of the second sort can be terminated ethically on grounds of disability. This view clearly seeks to promote the best interests of the fetus. It also mirrors closely the way non-competent adults and neonates are regarded in law throughout the common-law world – although where infants and adults with no prospect of worthwhile life are concerned only passive termination, or *allowing* the patient to die, is lawful (see Part 7). Significantly though, restricted welfarism has been eschewed where the law of abortion for handicap is concerned: here, to avoid criminal prosecution it is not in general necessary to prove that the foreseeable life of the fetus would not have been worth living.

In attaching this significance to whether an individual is *in* or *ex utero* the law is, arguably, seriously defective. However, it cannot be argued that, because we adopt a restricted welfarist attitude to neonates, we must adopt the same attitude towards fetuses. Such argument would presuppose that we are *correct* to take the restricted view of neonates, and once the moral significance of birth has been called into question this is very much at issue.

In fact, in connection not just with therapeutic abortion but other kinds of treatment decision arising from incapacity as well. restricted welfarism is

179

incoherent. The welfare of a disabled person can invariably be increased by assistance. Most people believe that we have a duty to assist others, but on any view this duty has limits. So the question the restricted view needs to ask cannot be, 'Will this person have a life worth living?' Instead, it has to be, 'Would this person have a life worth living *if* an acceptable level of support is provided?' We cannot answer this unless we know *already* what our obligations to the disabled are – as citizens of the state, members of the relevant family and individuals. The only exception to this occurs where the prospects of a life having positive value are unaltered by the extent of care, either because the life is irremediably poor, or because it can be confidently predicted that, without assistance, the life will be worth living. The notion, moreover, that we should focus, as the courts appear usually to do, on whether a life *could* be worth living, while suggestive of an extensive collective duty of rescue, cannot be regarded as a serious clarification – as is revealed by the enquiry, 'Could it, given *what*? That the mother takes out a second mortgage? That charities for the relevant disability flourish? That the government will raise annual expenditure on health in line with inflation?'

From a welfare-consequentialist perspective it is natural to address this difficulty by moving to a form of *unrestricted*, or at any rate, less restricted, welfarism – to shift the focus, that is to say, to some such matter as the impact of abortion upon a *group* of persons to which the disabled individual belongs. The immediate family, and the totality of people affected by the relevant disability, are two often mentioned constituencies of this kind. Crudely, the idea is that our moral obligations to the disabled cannot be such that in meeting them we ignore a more important aim regarding group welfare: for example, the aim (as adopted in utilitarianism) of maximizing that welfare, or maximizing its average level.

Moves of this kind can certainly deliver answers to the question with which I tried to embarrass the restricted welfarist above, but it is very important to see, and notice the dialectical implications of the fact, that there are theoretical *choices* to be made between the forms of less restricted theory, and that any such choice will automatically involve assumptions about *who* has responsibility for disability and how *heavy* their responsibilities are. To opt, for example, for a family-centred, or predominantly family-centred, welfarist approach is to assume already that the legitimacy of a disabled individual's demand for a life worth living is independent of whether you or I, in another family, are squandering our wealth.

These are issues about constituency in welfare consequentialism. An exceptionally complex question of this kind is whether, where a woman would have another child if she had a disability-related abortion, it would be reasonable in assessing the *ethical* status of the abortion to take into account the interests of that child – the curiously named 'next child in the queue'. This question is complex, as I say (see Parfit, 1976, 1984; and Part V of this book). Here I can discuss it only briefly, without addressing the several issues other than abortion for disability with which it is entangled.

The notion that the interests of a *replacement child* might justify an abortion for disability, so that such an abortion may, or may not, be acceptable, depending on the ability or willingness of the parents to conceive a more healthy child, strikes most people as bizarre. Where termination and a subsequent child are considered after diagnosis of fetal abnormality, this will probably be because the parents realize that a healthy child would diminish *their* welfare less – a matter of ethical interest certainly, but one lacking the apparently outlandish quality of the suggestion that the same parents ought to ask whether they are giving due weight to a replacement child's interests.

Disquiet at this latter suggestion can be readily explained if the sanctity of life doctrine is presupposed, but once it is allowed, as it is in less restricted forms of welfarism, that the interests of those other than the potential abortus can bear on the question of an abortion's acceptability, it becomes hard to see why the interests of the next child should not also carry weight. To explain why abortion cannot be justified by a replacement pregnancy the welfare consequentialist needs to claim that replacement welfare is either of no value at all, or valuable but insignificant where moral justification is concerned. But neither of these options is plausible in itself. Both are *ad hoc* adjustments which fail to emerge naturally from, and arguably are at odds with, the theoretical structure to which, it is being suggested, they should be added.

By way of mitigating this artificiality it is occasionally suggested that, just as a potential child is not harmed by not being conceived, so an actual child cannot be said to benefit from its own conception, the thought being that welfarists need only hold that *beneficial* acts have positive moral worth. But this attempt to free welfarism of its apparent commitment to replaceability looks unsuccessful. Doubtless, from a welfarist perspective the claim that morally worthy acts must be beneficial will seem plausible, but it does not follow, nor is it credible to maintain, that a rise in welfare might somehow fail to be beneficial. It is more attractive to suppose that where net welfare rises there has to be someone who benefits from that rise. The idea that a conceptus cannot benefit from its own conception, while intriguing, is a distraction. The issue at this point is not whether it is intelligible to suppose that a child is benefited by coming into existence: in welfarist terms, that supposition must be false. It is whether the having of a child whose prospects include both good health and a normal lifespan would benefit anyone. And this issue has a clear answer because *a child like this* would benefit from being a child like this. (Needless to say, its parents would benefit too.)

A number of approaches to abortion in which properties of the fetus, such as sentience, personhood and potential personhood, are claimed to possess intrinsic, welfare-*independent* moral significance might be explored at this point; but I want to turn instead to two topics as yet unaddressed: sex selection, the suggestion that we have an *obligation* to prevent birth defects by prenatal screening and therapeutic abortion. Let me explain briefly, however, why I have concentrated on welfarist theory.

To claim, in connection with an impaired fetus, F, that abortion for abnormality is justified is not to say that the relevant abnormality *justifies* F's abortion. For it is possible to allow that the abortion of a fetus with impairment is morally acceptable

181

in certain conditions, but insist that in these conditions the acceptability derives totally from factors independent of the relevant impairment. Disability here might provide one with a reason to abort, and because of this we can speak of abortion *for* disability, but the abortion is not *rendered* permissible by fetal imperfection. A view of this kind, albeit concerning non-abortive destruction, might seem credible where pre-implantation screening is concerned. One might acknowledge, I mean, that imperfections in the early embryo provide a (not always conclusive) reason to destroy it, but urge that the moral status of the embryo – including the fact, if it is a fact, that we may dispose of it – is unaffected by the imperfections.

It is nevertheless true that the principal problem with abortion for disability lies in the more specific question whether abnormality can make an abortion moral, that is, render acceptable an act which would otherwise be morally objectionable. But now the reason for focusing on welfarism ought, I hope, to be apparent. For on what basis could a positive answer to this question be argued, if not a welfarist one? Despite the film-making industry's tendency to assume the contrary, we no longer think of disability as something conferring wickedness of character on the sufferer. We think, instead, that disability has the capacity – in some cases slight, in others very serious – to spoil people's well-being; and this is the argument, if there is one, for preventing it.

Since antiquity at least people have sought more or less strenuously, and with various degrees of success, to ensure that they have sons and daughters in proportion as they would wish. This practice prompts a number of anxieties. Of those considered here, some concern the justifiability of selective *methods* and some concern unattractive *outcomes* of their successful application. I shall take these up in turn.

Doubts about methods of sex selection are common. For example, the vast majority of people, particularly in the developed world, would say that preferences regarding the sex of children are insufficiently urgent to render infanticide acceptable. Equally, reservations might be had about the abortion of 'wrong-sex' fetuses whose sex was disclosed by amniocentesis at sixteen to twenty weeks, as they may also be about the systematic disposal of early embryos involved in a pre-implantational approach. And of course, *vis-à-vis* any technique, including those currently being developed, in which efforts are made to separate androgenic (Y-bearing) and gynaecogenic (X-bearing) sperm prior to selective fertilization, it can be urged that sex preference does not warrant the allocation of resources it requires.

These anxieties raise a *distinctive* problem about sex selection, one which does not arise in the same form where other bases of selection are concerned, only to the extent that preferences regarding the sex of one's children are taken to be in some way frivolous. Of course, this attitude cannot be sustained where interest in the gender of an infant is explained by a more basic concern to avoid giving birth to children with X-linked recessively inherited diseases, like Duchenne muscular dystrophy. It is more likely to carry conviction, however, where serious disease is not the fundamental concern – for example, and most dramatically, where a gender preference is basic, like having a favourite colour. The really difficult questions here arise where preferences are the result of elective cultural or religious arrangements which, because of their widespread acceptance, confer undeniable value on children of a particular sex. I cannot deal with these issues here. They ask, essentially, for a reasoned response, at both the individual and the collective level, to deeply integrated outlooks which, whatever merits they have, seem to punish and reward gender as such.

I shall sketch two points about the outcome of sex selection – one positive, one negative. The positive point is that sex selection can inhibit population growth, enabling people to have a child of the sex they desire without making several attempts. It hardly needs adding that in societies like those just described, overpopulation tends to be a very real problem. The negative point is this. In societies where most people share a common gender preference, sex selection could produce a demographic sex imbalance. Noticing this, bioethicists have asked whether societies in which there are not roughly the same numbers of men and women should be discouraged. Discussions of this question tend to be quite speculative where the empirical issue of demographic change is concerned: we know a fair bit about current gender preferences, but not much about the way in which changes in gender distribution might temper these. Nor is it clear, to me at least, how to characterize features of an imbalanced society in which ethical concerns, properly so called, let alone discouragement, might be grounded. Sexual loneliness could be the cause of widespread and deep unhappiness in a society with a significant gender imbalance, but the notion (which has been raised) that reduced participation in bourgeois family life and an accompanying rise in homosexuality might form the basis of a serious objection to sex selection would need argument.

I turn, finally, to an issue quite different from those considered so far. Screening programmes provide benefits – to the newborn, their families and ultimately, through savings on health-care costs, all of us. This means that where screening could be but is not offered, or where a diagnostic test is executed ineptly, and even (to pick up a thread left hanging when autonomy was discussed above) where a mother or couple refuse to undergo screening, accusations of recklessness or negligence against a clinician, or parent, or health authority, might be made. There is nothing remarkable about this as such. The notion that, where they are provided to patients, medical services should be delivered with proper care, and the wider view that we should develop clinical care for the unborn, are hardly controversial. However, two distinctive issues deserve brief elaboration.

The most enthusiastic supporters of individual liberty usually accept that our right to cause others harm without their consent has limits: that right is normally thought, for example, not to cover my injuring you by reckless driving, even if it does cover my making you worse off by buying the remaining cinema ticket we both want. If this view is accepted it must surely limit maternal, or parental, discretion to decline screening tests, for the purpose of these tests is to reduce the frequency and severity of fetal anomaly. It might be said that this 'harm principle' (as it is sometimes called) condemns the *active* causation of harm, not its allowance through omission or refusal to participate. But unless it is claimed that omissions are in general blameless, this reaction is very unlikely to wash. The relationship of

183

dependence, and associated duty of care, between parents and child ensure that. Hard questions here concern such matters as whether a parent might be morally required to have a test in the fetus's best interests, and whether the state can enforce that requirement justly by legal sanction (see chapter 15, pp. 135–46). Conscientious objection to abortion complicates these questions.

The second issue focuses, in effect, more closely on the nature of harm. In law tortious negligence is the breach of a duty of care owed to somebody who suffers loss or injury as a result. For many years now the courts have struggled with negligence actions, alleging 'wrongful life', in which a handicapped plaintiff complains that he would have been aborted in an effective prenatal screening programme (Markesinis and Deakin, 1994). The central difficulty here concerns, not duty of care, nor the breach thereof, but *loss* – to be more precise, the notion that a disabled person could have sustained loss in not being aborted. For this notion implies (a) that a life can have net negative value; and (b) that failure to abort a fetus whose life is certain to possess negative value is a cause of loss or injury.

I want to accept (a), which undoubtedly needs clarification and support and has caused the courts alarm, and end by commenting on (b). The idea that loss can be caused by a failure to abort has troubled commentators, even where qualms about lives of negative value have been set aside, because loss appears to involve a reduction in the well-being of a loser, and it is clear that no one's well-being could *decline* as a result of their not being prevented by abortion from starting a life, no matter how awful that life. This worry assumes, of course, that, at the time of failure to abort, the relevant individual's life would not already have begun – something we might query, especially where late abortions are concerned – but I suggest we let that pass here: the claim that loss cannot be the basis of a duty to prevent a life from starting remains sound.

It follows, if wrongful life situations involve dereliction of duty, either that the relevant duty (to prevent a life with negative value from starting), or its basis (the prevention of loss), is other than we have supposed; and I want to conclude by mentioning two positions which explore these possibilities. The first claims that the basis of the duty is the prevention not of loss, but *suffering*. A life of misery, considered *en bloc*, and relative to no life at all, is not a loss to the liver, but the liver none the less suffers during it. The second position, which continues to treat loss as the basis of duty, claims that this duty is to prevent a life with negative value, not from starting, but *continuing*. For the longer a life with negative value is, the worse, overall, it is for the liver, and in this sense someone living an awful life loses more as each day passes.

References

Markesinis, B. S. and Deakin, S. F. (1994). *Tort Law*, 3rd edn. Oxford: Oxford University Press.

Parfit, D. (1976). Rights, interests, and possible people. In S. Gorovitz, (ed.), *Moral Problems in Medicine*. Englewood Cliffs, NJ: Prentice-Hall, 369–75.

—— (1984). *Reasons and Persons*. Oxford: Clarendon Press.

Tucker, G. (1992). *The National Childbirth Trust Book of Pregnancy and Birth*. Oxford: Oxford University Press.

Further Reading

Brock, D. J. H., Rodeck, C. H. and Ferguson-Smith, M. A. (1992). *Prenatal Diagnosis and Screening*. Edinburgh: Churchill Livingstone.

Glover, J. (1990). *Causing Death and Saving Lives*. Harmondsworth: Penguin.

Heyd, D. (1992). *Genethics*. Berkeley: University of California Press.

Steinbock, B. (1992). *Life before Birth*. New York: Oxford University Press.

PART VI

THE NEW GENETICS

19

Gene therapy

RUTH CHADWICK

Somatic and Germ-line Therapy

Gene therapy aims to treat disease by modifications at the genetic level. A primary goal of gene therapy, of course, is to treat diseases recognized as being genetic such as cystic fibrosis. A distinction is commonly drawn, however, between single gene disorders, where one gene brings about the condition, such as Huntington's, and multifactorial conditions, where a number of genes may be involved, such as breast cancer; or where genes may predispose, but not predetermine, a person to have a tendency to develop, say, heart disease in certain environmental conditions. Clearly in such cases the development of gene therapy will be much more complicated than in the case of single gene disorders. But gene therapy could also be used to treat such common, multifactorial conditions in so far as they have a genetic component which could be successfully affected by gene therapy. In the case of genetic diseases themselves, gene therapy offers the only hope of cure. Other therapies at best alleviate symptoms. Attempts are now being made to develop and test genetic therapies for a range of conditions. At present what is envisaged is the addition of a functioning copy of a normal gene to a person who lacks one, the mode of delivery of the gene varying according to the condition in question. It might, for example, be inhaled in a nasal spray, in the case of cystic fibrosis, or mixed with cells (e.g., bone marrow) removed from a patient and replaced as in thalassaemia.

Of the two broad categories of gene therapy, germ-line therapy is normally contrasted with somatic gene therapy on the basis that while the latter affects the body cells of an individual, germ-line therapy also affects the reproductive cells, thereby having an impact on that individual's children and ultimately on the gene pool of the species.

The difference between, them, however, is not entirely clear-cut. It is conceivable that cells being introduced into the body in the course of somatic therapy (e.g., via a virus used to transport genes into the body) could recombine with other viruses and infect the germ cells. Further, somatic therapy, like conventional treatment of genetic disease, which may alleviate symptoms but not act at the genetic level, leads to a greater concentration of the mutant gene in the gene pool, through allowing patients to survive and reproduce who would otherwise die. Thus while germ-line therapy would change the gene pool directly, somatic therapy would have an indirect effect. It may not be the case that we are left simply distinguishing the two on the basis of their directness or indirectness, however, as the consequences of germ-line therapy may be thought to have the potential for greater control over and impact on the gene pool than somatic therapy. There is at least a considerable difference of degree. Bernard Davis (1990: 84) has suggested that this prospect too is illusory.

> the techniques now in sight add the corrective gene rather than replace the defective one, and so the latter is still perpetuated; and in such individuals some of the germ cells in the next generation would be expected to segregate the defective gene from the correction, thus allowing the defect to reappear.

In the longer term, however, if research continues, it may be possible to carry out gene therapy that will not only add functioning genes but also replace malfunctioning ones. This would enable the problem identified by Davis to be avoided.

In discussing the ethics of gene therapy there are several issues to be addressed: the place of gene therapy in relation to the goals of medicine; whether there is a moral difference between somatic and germ-line therapy; issues of personal identity; whether gene therapy is a public or a private matter.

Is there a Medical Need for Gene Therapy?

Research or therapy?

The Clothier Committee, set up in the United Kingdom to consider the ethics of gene therapy, identified the following two principles as governing its deliberations:

- the obligation inherent in human nature to enquire, to study, to pursue and apply research by ethical means; and
- in the sometimes inescapable tensions between the pursuit of knowledge and the protection of patients' interests, the latter must prevail (Clothier, 1992: paras 3.4, 3.6.).

The fact that the first principle speaks of the obligation to pursue research rather than to relieve suffering may be explained by the Committee's view that gene therapy should, initially at least, be regarded as research involving human subjects, rather than as therapy, and should accordingly be subject to the requirements for ethically acceptable research.

While it may be understandable to want to regulate the introduction of gene therapy by classifying it as research, this does not settle the questions either of what it is or the motive for doing it. To describe the motive for doing it as the pursuit of knowledge rather than the search for a cure rules out from the start the possibility of classifying gene therapy as innovative treatment, for example. The Clothier Committee has been criticized for its uncritical acceptance of the notion of scientific 'progress' (Consumers for Ethics in Research, 1992); but arguably it is also insufficiently attentive to curative goals, although it does accept that somatic therapy, at least, is a proper goal for medical science.

The arguments for somatic therapy are clear: genetic disorders cause suffering; treatment other than gene therapy can at most alleviate symptoms; somatic gene therapy offers the prospect of a cure. It might be thought that the extension of these arguments to germ-line therapy, and its potential benefits to the unborn, offer support for germ-line therapy. This argument, however, has not been widely accepted. If what is wanted is the absence of children with genetic disorders (and this is highly controversial), it is not clear that germ-line therapy is the method of choice.

First, germ-line therapy is likely to remain for the foreseeable future very difficult, technically speaking. Second, most couples can produce what the British geneticist Marcus Pembrey has called a 'winning combination' of genes without engaging in germ-line therapy (Pembrey, 1992). *In vitro* fertilization and embryo selection offer a way to do this, by testing the embryos and selecting the best to return to the womb. As Pembrey has admitted, however, there is a small number of couples who could not do this, and for them germ-line therapy might provide the only chance of producing a child of their own without genetic disease, for example, in the case of mitochondrial disease, where all of a woman's offspring are at risk. Unlike the DNA in the nucleus, which divides and recombines with that of the other parent, the mitochondrial DNA exists outside the nucleus and is passed on to all a woman's children, thus any disorder there is passed on. What counts as a winning combination is, of course, a matter of dispute, as is shown by current controversies concerning whether deafness is a genetic disadvantage or a cultural difference (see, e.g., Grundfast and Rosen, 1992).

One option, where a winning combination is impossible, would be gamete donation of sperm or egg, where one partner is wary of reproducing, or of embryo donation, thus avoiding the gametes of both partners, but there is a possibility that parents may prefer to have gene therapy on their own embryos. This may be perceived as having a child 'of their own' – genetically related to both partners, rather than a child that is the genetic inheritor of the genes of only one of them, or neither. Of course it can be argued that in germ-line therapy they would be accepting external genetic material, but it is perhaps not so much the threat of external material that would be found undesirable but the disappointment at not having the genetic material of one or both of them passed on to the next generation that would be significant there. Let us suppose that there *is* a demand for germ-line therapy. There remains a question as to whether, in the light of this, germ-line therapy should be practised.

There is a developing consensus that whereas somatic therapy is morally acceptable, germ-line therapy is not, at least for the foreseeable future. This is because somatic therapy is regarded as raising no new issues of principle and as subject to the same ethical constraints as other forms of medical intervention, such as informed consent and confidentiality. Germ-line therapy, on the other hand, *is* said to raise new issues of principle, primarily because it will affect future generations.

191

Arguments against Germ-line Therapy

The standard arguments used against germ-line therapy include the claim that there is a right to an unaltered genome, concerns about unconsenting future generations and worries about loss of genetic diversity. However, despite widespread acceptance of these arguments there are arguments in its favour.

Arguments for Germ-line Therapy

Reproductive autonomy

Suppose that it becomes possible to offer gene therapy for Huntington's disease. Somatic therapy is offered to a woman who has been found to carry the offending gene, prior to her developing symptoms of the disease. She says, however, 'No, I want to make sure that my children do not have to face this: I want germ-line therapy on my embryos as well.'

How far reproductive autonomy should be taken is controversial. Should we understand it to include freedom to make decisions not only about whether or not to reproduce, but also about what kind of children we have? If so, should people be allowed to choose to have children who *do* suffer from a genetic disorder, for example, when deaf parents want a deaf child? This is the type of example in which some people might argue that reproductive autonomy has limits which are set by consideration of the welfare of future children.

The welfare of future people

It might be argued that where we have the possibility of avoiding harm we have a duty to do so, and that in the example of mitochondrial disease there is a possibility of avoiding offspring affected by this through germ-line therapy. Is there then an obligation to practice germ-line therapy in such cases, for the sake of future people?

One preliminary point is that the avoidance of harm could be met not only by germ-line therapy but also by the avoidance of reproduction altogether, at least by one partner. Reproductive autonomy *and* the avoidance of harm, however, can arguably best be accommodated by the practice of germ-line therapy, if that is what the couple wants.

Gene Therapy and Personal Identity

The issues of identity which gene therapy, in particular germ-line therapy, are said to raise, deserve attention. The implications of germ-line therapy for personal identity questions might be raised by either a proponent or an opponent of the technology.

In what sense might identity be at stake in thinking about germ-line therapy and future generations? As Ronald Dworkin has argued in *Life's Dominion*, in thinking about our responsibility to future generations we are normally considering

192

'descendants whose identity is in no way fixed, but depends on what we must consider billions of accidents of genetic coupling' (Dworkin, 1993: 77). Although we can affect, by actions taken now, who these people will be, we are not, it seems, *changing* the identity of specific individuals.

There are those, however, who hold that germ-line therapy does raise questions of identity, as follows:

1   Is the person who is produced as a result of germ-line therapy the *same* person as the one who would have existed without the intervention?
2   Does it matter?

On the first question, some might want to draw a distinction between the case where therapy is carried out on the embryo and the case of gamete alteration, because of different views about when a person's life story begins. Bernard Williams, for example, put forward a zygotic principle (ZP) which holds that 'A possibility in which a given human being, A, features is one that preserves the identity of the zygote from which A developed' (Williams, 1990: 169). John Harris (1992), however, has argued against ZP that a person's life story begins at the gamete stage, so that a future person might have cause to express a grievance on the grounds of interventions that did or did not take place at the gamete stage. Whenever a person's life story begins, however, Zohar (1991) and Elliott (1993) assume that it is likely that some genetic alterations are identity-preserving while others are not. Proceeding on this assumption, the second question – does it matter? – forces us to reflect whether a future person could have a legitimate *grievance* that his or her identity had been changed by germ-line therapy.

Bernard Williams (1991) has suggested that there are only two grievances that could legitimately be expressed by a future person: 'I should have had a nicer time' and 'It would have been better if I had never existed.' There are other possibilities, however, as follows:

I should not have had my genome altered;
I should have been someone else;
I should have been free of this genetic disorder;
I should have been given genetic immunization;
I should not have been brought into existence.

I should not have had my genome altered

The way in which this grievance is expressed, namely '*I* should not have had *my* genome altered,' presupposes that identity has been preserved. In that case the source of any grievance must lie elsewhere than in an identity issue.

I should have been someone else

Unlike the first, this grievance presupposes either that an identity-changing intervention has taken place and should not have, or that an identity-changing intervention has not taken place and should have. This (as Williams says) is incoherent,

193

because *I* could not have been someone else; what might have been the case is that I did not exist and someone else did.

I should have been free of this genetic disorder

This appears to be a coherent grievance that a future person was not given (available) treatment to relieve him or her from genetic disorder. It presupposes the possibility of sameness of person but absence of pathology.

I should have been given genetic immunization

It might be possible to produce people who have been genetically immunized against certain diseases, for example, those that might have been triggered by environmental pollutants. If we could offer such genetic protection and did not, the future person could coherently express a grievance, 'I should have been genetically immunized.' Like the previous grievance, it presupposes identity. It also, however, raises the issue of therapy versus enhancement (see below).

I should not have been brought into existence

This is either a wrongful life claim, that a person has been harmed by being brought into life, or an impersonal claim that it would have been better if I had not existed. It might be expressed by a person who results from an identity-changing intervention (for example, where the intervention is unsuccessful in terms of therapeutic effect). He or she might take the view that it would have been better if the original person had come into existence but that is not a claim that *his* or *her* identity has changed and that this is the source of the harm. In such a case the harm would be the effect of the change rather than the identity change itself.

On the basis of the discussion above, it seems that there is no coherent grievance that a future person can make on the grounds of having been subjected to an identity-changing intervention. On the other hand, if we suppose that an identity-changing intervention has taken place, could the future person be benefited? The answer to this is yes, if it can be a benefit to be brought into existence and to be free of genetic disorder. This person would not have existed without the identity-changing intervention, but he or she has the benefit of existence.

It might be objected that in such a case the original person has been killed, or that he or she has been prevented from coming into existence. In the case of intervention at the embryo stage, for example, the original embryo would have led to the development of a person who will now never exist. But precisely because of that, there is no one to express a grievance.

Private and Public

So far we have been considering gene therapy as a matter for clinical decision-making in the case of individuals and in relation to the personal identity of individuals, but there are arguments to suggest that gene therapy raises issues that are of public concern. These include public health issues and eugenics; resource allocation and equity; and issues of collective identity. In particular, it might be argued that germ therapy, unlike somatic therapy, is a public matter, in so far as it has the greater potential to affect the gene pool.

Public health issues and eugenics

The public health interest in gene therapy has several aspects. First, there is a safety question. Thus Maurice de Wachter (1993: 18) has said:

> as the gene pool is a matter that surpasses the individual patient, public health is a prime concern in matters of gene therapy. Thus, in cases where retroviral vectors are being used, the exposure of the patient and people in close contact with the patient to infectious viruses resulting from the therapy, constitutes one of several possible types of harm . . . The population rightly expects to be protected against risks.

In this respect, however, gene therapy raises no issue of principle different from any other case in which the health status or treatment of an individual has implications for other members of the population, and safety is not the public health issue that has given rise to most concern.

What has caused worry is the link with eugenics. The claim that an intervention would amount to eugenics is sometimes voiced as if it is thought to be a knock-down argument against that intervention. This cannot be assumed: what exactly is found objectionable? One aspect is the implication that some lives are more valuable than others. The attempt to reduce the incidence of genetic disorders in the population is sometimes criticized on the grounds that it embodies inappropriate attitudes towards people currently alive who suffer from those disorders. Another is that eugenics represents interference, whether openly or subtly, with personal freedoms in the area of reproduction.

Historical examples of the abuse of genetics, and more recent attempts by governments to improve the levels of intelligence in their population, for example, in Singapore (Chan, 1992) lend credence to the view that gene therapy, especially germ-line therapy, could become a tool in the hands of a government with eugenic ambitions. One possible response to this is to point to the importance of controlling the use of the technology rather than avoiding it altogether, placing an emphasis on leaving decisions as much as possible to individuals to choose therapy for themselves and their descendants, rather than to government control. A distinction may also be drawn between beliefs that a particular disorder is undesirable, and negative attitudes towards the persons who suffer from that disorder. The latter do not necessarily follow from the former. For some critics, however, the argument that we should concentrate on the control of abuses is naive; they argue that the possible harms are so great that, for example, the genetic basis of characteristics such as intelligence should not even be the subject of research (Shickle, 1997).

Another criticism is the genetic reductionism involved in eugenic thinking. The Clothier Committee, in supporting (somatic) gene therapy, was criticized for ignoring the importance of social context – for example, attitudes towards disability and

195

the link with reductionist social policies. The latter are envisaged as dangerous in so far as they reduce human problems to genetic causes. Where the search for genetic causes is given priority. there is the possibility that energies will be directed towards finding genetic solutions in preference to exploring what social policies can be helpful. This would seem attractive in the light of desires to reduce expensive social policies. Knoppers, for example, has suggested that 'economic incentives could lead to a new eugenics based, not on undesirable characteristics, but rather on cost-saving, a form of economic social justice rather than "genetic justice"' (Knoppers, 1991: 3).

A further problematic aspect is the use of the techniques of gene therapy for enhancement, rather than to cure disease. Popular coverage of this possibility has tended to concentrate on 'designer babies' – couples choosing the characteristics of their children to suit their own whims or expectations for their children's future, such as eye colour or musical ability – but an alternative possible application of enhancement is the kind of preventive vaccination referred to above in the discussion of identity. This would seek to confer resistance to particular diseases by introducing certain genes. The objections to 'improvement' rather than therapy are not always clear (cf. Chadwick, 1988) but one issue relates to social justice.

Decision-making, resource allocation and equity

Even in the use of gene therapy to cure disease there is a problem about resource allocation, related to the selection of candidates for treatment. What is envisaged and feared by some, however, is a free market in genes, for example, to add some hitherto unavailable advantage to offspring. If this were allowed to develop it might appear to open the way to the reinforcement of differences between the wealthy and the poor, by enabling the wealthy to acquire better genes. This would be the case both within developed societies and between developed and developing countries (Holm, 1994). Much depends here, of course, on what is considered to be a good gene and the extent to which genes, as opposed to environment, are supposed to be influential in determining an individual's life chances.

Collective identity

Some critics take the view that in engaging in germ-line therapy we should be losing something that is essentially human. It is not always clear what this objection amounts to. Ronald Dworkin, in *Life's Dominion*, examines the question of what is sacred. He argues that the notion of the intrinsic value of human life is widespread, but that there are different interpretations of what this means. One element in it is the value accorded to the outcome of evolutionary processes. He holds, therefore, that the value of a plant species that is the result of evolution is of a different kind from that of a genetically engineered plant species. If this is the case, it might explain the value accorded to the unengineered species as opposed to one that is the result of germ-line therapy. While it is sometimes seen to be incompatible with the dignity of human beings to try to control their reproduction or their evolution, this is not an objection that applies only to germ-line therapy. The case for the consensus against germ-line therapy, while accepting other interventions, such as somatic therapy, has not been adequately made out.

References

Chadwick, R. (1988). Genetic improvement. In D. Braine and H. Lesser (eds), *Ethics, Technology and Medicine*. Aldershot: Avebury.

Chan, C. K. (1992). Eugenics on the rise: a report from Singapore. In R. Chadwick (ed.), *Ethics, Reproduction and Genetic Control*, rev. edn. London: Routledge.

Clothier, C. (1992). *Report of the Committee on the Ethics of Gene Therapy*. London: HMSO.

Consumers for Ethics in Research (1992). Consumer response to Clothier. *Bulletin of Medical Ethics*, 79, 13–14.

Davis, B. D. (1990). Limits to genetic intervention in humans: somatic and germline. In D. Chadwick et al. (eds), *Human Genetic Information: Science, law and ethics*. Chichester: John Wiley.

de Wachter, M. (1993). *Experimental (Somatic) Gene Therapy: Ethical concerns and control*. Maastricht: Institute for Bioethics.

Dworkin, R. (1993). *Life's Dominion: an argument about abortion and euthanasia*. London: Harper Collins.

Elliott, R. (1993). Identity and the ethics of gene therapy. *Bioethics*, 7, 27–40.

Grundfast K. and Rosen J (1992). Ethical and cultural considerations in research on hereditary deafness. *Molecular Biology and Genetics*, 25/5, 973–7.

Harris, J. (1992). *Wonderwoman and Superman: the ethics of human biotechnology*. Oxford: Oxford University Press.

Holm, S. (1994). Genetic engineering and the North–South divide. In A. Dyson and J. Harris (eds). *Ethics and Biotechnology*. London: Routledge.

Knoppers, B. M. (1991). *Human Dignity and Genetic Heritage*. Ottawa: Law Reform Commission of Canada.

Pembrey, M. (1992). Embryo therapy: is there a clinical need? In D. Bromham et al. (eds), *Ethics in Reproductive Medicine*. London: Springer-Verlag.

Shickle, D. (1997). Do 'all men desire to know'? A right of society to choose not to know about the genetics of personality traits. In R. Chadwick et al. (eds), *The Right to Know and the Right not to Know*. Aldershot: Avebury.

Williams, B. (1990). Who might I have been? In D. Chadwick et al. (eds), *Human Genetic Information: science, law and ethics*. Chichester: John Wiley, 167–73.

Zohar, N. J. (1991). Prospects for 'genetic therapy' – can a person benefit from being altered? *Bioethics*, 4.

20

Mapping the human genome

TIMOTHY F. MURPHY

The Human Genome Project (HGP) is an international scientific project that has as its primary goal the mapping and sequencing of the human genome. The term genome refers to the entire complement of genes in an organism. Mapping refers to the process of identifying the chromosomal site of each gene, while sequencing refers to identifying the molecular composition of each gene, its deoxyribonucleic acid (DNA) base pairs. Genes are the protein units that direct an organism's biological processes and thereby its traits, though the expression of genetic traits will always be influenced by physiological and environmental circumstances. Officially begun in 1990, the project is expected to last about fifteen years and have profound implications for biomedicine, technological and computational science, and the social uses of genetic information. Due in part to the fact that a portion of the project's budget is specifically devoted to a consideration of its ethical, legal and social implications, this latter issue has already generated considerable attention. Given the objectionable goals and applications of genetic science that have occurred in the past, there is good reason to pay attention thoughtfully to a project that opens the elemental units of biological causality to inspection and possible intervention. It is to be remembered that the most objectionable applications of genetic science occurred in the most advanced nations of their time. There is, therefore, no automatic assumption possible that the advanced nations currently involved in the HGP will necessarily make proper use of the genetic data or technologies the HGP will produce.

Origins and Ambitions of the Project

Because of its ambitions, the HGP has sometimes been described as the biological equivalent of the Manhattan Project, the concentrated research that produced the atomic bomb during World War II. In a way, the two projects are indeed related. One of the original incentives for the HGP emerged from the desire to have better methods of assessing genetic variations in people exposed to radioactive fallout (Beatty, in press). Having a baseline understanding of genetic normalcy would be an ideal first step towards that goal. Following a political campaign orchestrated by researchers and politicians, legislatures were convinced that the encyclopaedic task would have sufficient benefits to justify its billion-dollar cost. With the United States taking the lead, other nations joined the effort, including Japan, Australia and a number of European nations. In each case, the merits and drawbacks of the project were debated differently around the globe. There was not, for example, universal consensus that the project was justified. Some researchers and commentators argued that it would be more useful to track genetic data in a conventional way: using familial pedigree studies to trace specific diseases back to their genetic origin. By contrast, the genetic atlas to be achieved by the HGP will identify a great deal of data without describing its function or tying it to useful clinical interventions. Many researchers also feared that the project would siphon money away from other worthwhile scientific projects. These sorts of criticisms have become more muted as the HGP has proceeded, especially since the costs of conducting this research have decreased because of technological advances that will help in other research domains.

In the mind of the public, it was not the scientific merit of the project that attracted attention so much as the haunting spectre of eugenics. The history of genetics bears indelible scars of misguided efforts to breed racially and otherwise superior human beings. Would the HGP raise up a new and more powerful science of eugenics serving questionable social ideals? Even if there were no state-sponsored programmes of eugenics, would genetic probes and profiles empower a more discreet but nevertheless invidious genetic intolerance? These questions remain at the centre of the study of the meaning of the HGP, though it is far from clear that genetic science need be confined by the most malignant chapters of its past. The molecular characterization of human beings that the HGP will produce will hardly be definitive in regard to conclusions about the ideal genetic traits of an individual let alone those of a population. The characterization will nevertheless offer a standard of comparison and, as such, there exists the risk that it may be interpreted as coextensive with human normalcy, genetic variations being interpreted as deficient or defective by comparison. This interpretive effect may especially prejudice not only people whose genetic traits are markedly different from the norm but also those people who suffer some kind of social marginalization or stigmatization. Rightly or wrongly considered as a genetic exemplar, the HGP genetic atlas will spark debate about the range of human normalcy, genetic integrity and the meaning of genetic difference. It remains a matter of concern how debate on these matters should go forward: by each nation in light of its own history and social goals or in light of internationally recognized moral principles (Knoppers and Chadwick, 1994).

Genetic Health and Disease

Having a genetic atlas of human genes will open research agendas not only in diseases with simple genetic bases, such as Huntington's disease, but also polygenic disorders and genetic dispositions towards disease (see chapter 19, pp. 189–97). In the first instance, the HGP will make it increasingly possible to produce genetic probes for many disorders and diseases. For the foreseeable future, the diagnostic capacities of genetic medicine will far outstrip the abilities of genetic medicine to offer therapies. Genetic therapy involves introducing recombinant DNA into somatic cells of an organism for the purpose of treating one or another cell deficiency.

For all the vaunted rhetoric and the familiar ease with which genetic therapy is discussed, the accomplishments of genetic therapy can at best be called modest and suggestive (Leiden, 1995). In the interim, it is a matter of considerable ethical interest whether and under what circumstances genetic testing should go forward for conditions for which there is no therapy available (see chapter 22, pp. 215–28). Nevertheless, biomedical researchers are rightly confident that genetic research will open new doors for new if experimental therapeutic interventions, and accurate diagnosis is important in its own right even if no therapy exists (Walters and Palmer, 1997).

As more and more people submit to genetic testing, society may also expect to face sharp questions of resource allocation. Genetic study will necessarily increase the costs of health care in regard to diagnosis and research. How those costs are to be borne, while continuing to meet other health-care costs, will remain an abiding question for any nation's medical system. The philosopher Leonard Fleck has argued that those with profoundly disabling genetic diseases should have a priority in health-care research because these people are often the most disadvantaged relative to typical human capacities and because there are no alternate means of avoiding ill health of genetic origin (Fleck, 1994). Other commentators have argued that the primary focus in resource allocation ought to be on patterns of disease distribution that are the result of human artifice and social injustice. Even so, not all people may be at the same risks from social policies and injustices. Because of genetic dispositions, members of one ethnic group, for example, may be especially susceptible to toxins in the environment or workplace. If so, the question of compensation or some other form of social redress to those workers will be raised, the natural genetic lottery notwithstanding.

Though there exists a wide range of opinions about standards of resource allocation and compensation for people with genetic disadvantages, there is fairly wide agreement that a focus on genetic bases for ill health may distract policy-makers and the public from keeping the environment and workplaces free from health hazards. Biases about the genetics of disease may, that is, 'blame' the individual for ill health that is ultimately as much social in origin as personal. There is also considerable agreement that the development of new genetic health technologies will broaden the divide between people who enjoy fairly unrestricted access to health care and those people who, for economic and social reasons, have substandard or virtually no health care. Unless there are political interventions to the contrary, any benefits to emerge from the HGP and genetic medicine will be distributed along existing patterns of access to health care. The philosopher Philip Kitcher has pointed out that if the HGP is defended in the name of improving human life, serious questions of moral consistency arise when contemporary social injustices just as damaging as those attributed to genetic disorders are tolerated and neglected (Kitcher, 1996). It remains to be seen, however, whether an era of genetic testing and medicine will force political or moral reconsideration of existing health-care systems.

For health-care providers, questions of resource allocation will be less pressing than practical questions involved in the clinical integration of genetic tests and technologies. As more and more diseases are reconceptualized in terms of their genetic components (AIDS can be thought of as a genetic disorder of certain somatic cells, for example), health-care providers will face important challenges in identifying the appropriate standards that ought to govern genetic testing and experimental medicine. Due ethical and scientific attention must be given to ensuring that genetic tests offer meaningful benefit to patients, as individuals and as populations. In the first instance, as a matter of social justice, patients will have to be protected against prejudicial social uses of their medical diagnoses. In the second instance, as a matter of respecting autonomy, health-care providers will have to identify meaningful ways in which to obtain informed consent for genetic tests and experimental treatments. Lastly, as a matter of beneficence towards both practitioner and patient alike, there will have to be research into ways of dealing with genetic conditions for which there are no treatments and with genetic tests whose results are ambiguous about susceptibility to disease.

Social and Legal Ramifications

On the assumption that genetic probes will increasingly reveal information about disposition to disease, employers and insurers will have an abiding economic interest in access to this information. In countries where health care is offered primarily as a benefit of employment, employers will be interested in screening people with genetically detectable dispositions towards disease and declining to employ those with significant risks, in order to contain costs of health-care benefits. Insurance systems spread health-care costs across large groups of people; to the extent they operate for profit they will be under considerable pressure to reduce coverage for people who are predictably likely to fall ill or to increase costs of coverage to protect the economic viability of the corporation. For reasons like these, it is expected that medical confidentiality will come under increasing assault unless specific legislation governs the extent to which genetic conditions are used as conditions of employment and insurance. In those nations where health care is offered as a civic benefit independent of employment, the question of access to personal genetic data may be less pronounced as an ethical question. though even those nations will still face important questions about meeting health-care costs related to genetic testing and therapy. The HGP will in all instances intensify questions about access to individual genetic records or even to genetic samples for eligibility for employment or insurance, scientific research and forensic purposes in criminal and civil legal actions.

Though some commentators have proposed various recommendations in regard to the banking of genetic records and samples, the question of access to them is far from resolved. The attorney George Annas has proposed, for example, that all banking of data and samples be preceded by public notice and discussion about the policies that ought to govern the banking (Annas, 1994). At the very least, he says, banking should be governed by informed consent agreements that outline the intended purpose of the samples. According to this view, no samples should be used for purposes for which they are not collected unless consent is obtained for that secondary purpose. The question of criminal and civil uses of genetic samples will unfold in the context of legal precedent, judicial decisions and any statutes that may be adopted in a particular country. As it stands now, some convicted criminals are required to leave tissue samples as a condition of their parole, and some accused suspects are required to offer genetic samples in the course of criminal investigations. The judiciary has a certain latitude about the use of genetic data in court cases, but the standards governing the use of genetic data in these settings are still evolving.

Genetic research also raises questions for the law in the domain of patents (see chapter 21, pp. 206–14). Genetic research is expected to yield commercial products in three main areas: genetic tests, pharmaceutical products relying on genetic technology for production or delivery and gene therapies. When fully developed, products of these kinds could have enormous financial value so there is considerable interest in securing patents. Patents secure rights of monopolistic control to an inventor for a specified period of time. The human genome is by itself a product of nature and not patentable any more than the human skeleton would be. The patent debate is thus not about patenting the genome but its DNA sequences as these are identified through the use of particular technologies. To argue against patenting these sequences, the physician Alain Pompidou drew a distinction between discovery and invention: whereas discovery observes what is already in nature, invention requires the construction of forms that do not occur in nature (Pompidou, 1995). Unfortunately, this neat distinction between discovery and invention is not so decisive as Pompidou makes it. Some of the mechanisms of gene mapping and sequencing might lend themselves to patents because they involve the production of isolates that do not occur in nature.

For example, cDNA is a partial copy of a naturally occurring DNA sequence and is achieved through an intervention that excludes introns, namely DNA sequences without any known function, so-called 'junk DNA'. cDNA sequences do not occur in nature yet they reveal the essential protein sequences of a gene. cDNA production methods are now highly efficient and inexpensive and have therefore increased the pace of patent applications. The historian Daniel J. Kevles and the geneticist Leroy Hood have objected to patent rights of exactly this kind, saying 'It would be a perversion of the patent system to allow the patenting of cDNAs as such, independent of any utility except the trivial and obvious one of obtaining the gene that it encodes.' Such a conclusion, they fear, would 'pervert the fundamental purpose of the patent system because it would raise obstacles to further research and technological development' (Kevles and Hood, 1992). They worry that the threshold of patent rights will be set too low and that individual researchers will restrict access to gene products or processes, for example, DNA sequences and/or sequencing techniques. It is feared that such a divided ownership of gene information and research technology will work against the presumption common in research communities that research results belong to all humanity in a common storehouse of knowledge. It is also feared that the withholding of information during periods of patent application would restrict access to genetic data, thereby impeding science generally.

It appears that some processes and products of genetic research will be patentable to the extent that they satisfy criteria of novelty, non-obviousness and utility. Patents may be granted for purified proteins, recombinant proteins, cloning techniques and so on. International policies in this area are still emerging and will involve some mix of public opinion, statute and judicial interpretation. In some respects, many of the worries about patents mentioned above will be clarified only in the light of empirical study and actual events. It may be that worries about the retarding of scientific progress will prove exaggerated. Some patented processes, like the polymerase chain reaction, have become instruments of research rather than impediments to it. The logic of the patent process itself may reduce the significance of the debate about the proper domain of patentability; patent rights depend on a demonstration that a particular product or process is not obvious within the domain of a particular field, that it represents an advance on the field's prior art and that it demonstrate utility. As genetic research advances, many of its products and processes may be increasingly recognized as obvious, and it may become more difficult to patent the products and processes of genetic research, especially since cDNA sequences are not tied to a specific technological or biomedical use. The requirement that inventions be non-obvious and demonstrably useful in order to be patented might, therefore, diminish the number of sequences or processes eligible for patents. The logic of the patent process may ultimately keep gene sequences entirely within the public domain, though again this interpretation is subject to legislative and judicial action.

Conclusions

The HGP has received more simultaneous analysis and commentary than any scientific project of its scope in history. After emerging in the 1970s as a discipline in its own right, bioethics was in many ways sufficiently mature to offer meaningful analysis of the HGP. A great deal of that analysis has stressed the challenges posed by the use of its expected results, and in outlining expected problems, the ethical, legal and social study of the HGP has been an unqualified success even if specific policy recommendations are still evolving. A great deal of commentary has nevertheless been guilty of speculative excess in, for example, trumpeting the proximity of all manner of genetic therapies or in overstating the novelty of the questions it will engender. The HGP raises no new ethical question in kind even as it deepens many of the questions already faced by society in regard to the production and use of information about individuals (Murray, 1993). Indeed, the HGP is entirely continuous with human efforts to rationalize our lives through scientific explanation. What is especially important about the HGP is not that it will produce genetic maps and sequences for that was already being done but that it will do so in an orchestrated and concentrated fashion and that its results will open new vistas for biomedicine and technology. Scientifically speaking, the HGP is business as usual, ambitious in the extreme, with expectations of biomedical and social progress. This project is perhaps only the first rung on a ladder of more ambitious projects. It is now entirely feasible to map and sequence the genome of any living organism. Perhaps computer libraries in the future will contain genetic maps of all living species known or of interest to human beings. Whether this will happen will depend on whether information on that scale would be useful to researchers and justified in its costs. Economic interests in animal and plant production and development may provide exactly those justifications. It is therefore clear that the kind of analysis that began with the HGP will remain useful well after the project is completed.

As with other human enterprises that seem to augur a new kind of future, the HGP has not failed to raise philosophical questions about human nature. Genetic explanations have sometimes been seen as at odds with philosophical doctrines of free will and responsibility. Even if moral philosophy is not undermined by genetic explanations (which it is not – see Warnock, 1992), a challenge to notions of identity and responsibility may come from a specific reading of genetics. If people believe that they are healthy or ill only by reason of genetic endowment, they may suspend efforts to maintain their health. If people believe that criminals are genetically prone to illegal acts, they may look unfavourably on penal sanctions as remedies and seek recourse in eugenic responses to crime. Genetic science that increasingly demonstrates continuity between human beings and other animals may even sharpen and provoke questions about the nature and extent of human dominion over those animals.

There is a seamless continuity of the HGP with its scientific heritage, yet the very ambition of the HGP, combined with a history that has used badly some genetic accounts of human traits and difference, invites reflection on that heritage. Though there are questions to be asked about the meaning of the HGP itself, it is proper that most analysis focuses on the ability to preserve standards of equity and justice in an age where genetic data are often understood as genetic destiny. The temptation towards genetic fatalism is alluring, especially when it comes to explaining and controlling traits and behaviours thought inimical to individual persons or society. One telling example in this regard is the attempt to identify a genetic basis of homosexuality. Media accounts often treat genes as if they were simply behaviours waiting to happen. There is no doubt that there are genetic contributions to all behaviour and human traits, erotic interests included, but it is equally without doubt that physiological, environmental and social circumstances play determining roles as well. Among some cultures, for example, homoerotic behaviour is manifestly the product of developmental experiment, social ritual and custom; no genetic cause is conceptually necessary for its explanation, and it would be a mistake to look for one. We already know that genetics can be put to objectionable social purposes: historical testimony and moral reflection keep those lessons alive. It is important to keep in mind that without attention to the complexity of human behaviour and development, genetic explanations can end in illusionary genetic reductionism. It is equally important to resist looking for easy genetic solutions to complex social ills involving human disease and difference, especially when the most important social ills are not the result of flawed genetic endowments.

204

References

Annas, George (1994). Rules for gene banks: protecting privacy in the genetics age. In Timothy F. Murphy and Marc A. Lappé (eds), *Justice and the Human Genome Project*. Berkeley: University of California Press, 75–90.

Beatty, John (in press). Origins of the U.S. Human Genome Project: changing relations between genetics and national security. In Phillip R. Sloan and Edward Manier (eds), *Controlling our Destinies: humanistic perspectives on the Human Genome Project*.

Fleck, Leonard (1994). Just genetics: a problem agenda. In Timothy F. Murphy and Marc A. Lappé (eds), *Justice and the Human Genome Project*. Berkeley: University of California Press, 133–53.

Kevles, Daniel J. and Hood, Leroy (eds) (1992). *The Code of Codes: Scientific and social issues in the Human Genome Project*. Cambridge, MA: Harvard University Press, 314, 315.

Kitcher, Philip (1996). *The Lives to Come: Genetic revolution and human possibilities*. New York: Simon and Schuster.

Knoppers, Bartha Maria and Chadwick, Ruth (1994). The Human Genome Project: under an international microscope. *Science*, 265, 2035–6.

Leiden, Jeffrey M. (1995). Gene therapy promise, pitfalls, and prognosis. *New England Journal of Medicine*, 333, 871–3.

Murray, Thomas H. (1993). Ethical issues in human genome research. In Ruth Ellen Bulger, Elizabeth Heitman and Stanley Joel Reiser (eds), *The Ethical Dimensions of the Biological Sciences*. Cambridge: Cambridge University Press, 283–94.

Pompidou, Alain (1995). Research on the human genome and patentability: the ethical consequences. *Journal of Medical Ethics*, 21, 69–71.

Walters, LeRoy and Palmer, Julie Gage (1997). *The Ethics of Human Gene Therapy*. Oxford: Oxford University Press.

Warnock, Mary (1992). The Human Genome Project: ethics and the law. In *The Uses of Philosophy*. Oxford: Blackwell, 54–69.

Further Reading

Andrews, Lori B. (ed.) (1994). *Assessing Genetic Risks: implications of health and social policy*. Washington, DC: National Acdemy Press.

Cook-Deegan, Robert M. (1994). *The Gene Wars: science, politics, and the Human Genome Project*. New York: Norton.

Macer, Darryl (1991). Whose genome project? *Bioethics*, 5, 183–211.

Office of Technology Assessment (1988). *Mapping Our Genes: genome projects; how big, how fast*. Baltimore, MD: Johns Hopkins University Press.

Rix, Bo Andreassen (1991). Should ethical concerns regulate science? The European experience with the Human Genome Project. *Bioethics*, 5, 250–6.

Wilkie, Tom (1993). *Perilous Knowledge: the Human Genome Project and its implications* Berkeley: University of California Press.

21

Creating and patenting new life forms

NILS HOLTUG

Genetic engineers are able to carry out transfers of genetic material from one organism to another, even crossing species boundaries, and thus create new kinds of beings and life forms. Among their more spectacular achievements is the so-called 'Mighty Mouse', who is twice the size of her unmodified sisters. More important, they have enabled us to manufacture large amounts of therapeutic drugs, such as insulin, and a vaccine against hepatitis B by inserting new genes into bacteria. Furthermore, many scientists believe that they are on the verge of developing gene therapy for human diseases such as cystic fibrosis and muscular dystrophy.

This gives rise to all sorts of ethical questions regarding whether and when it is morally permissible genetically to modify living organisms. It also raises questions regarding the moral permissibility of patenting these organisms, once they are created.

In answering such questions, many ethicists have adopted a broadly consequentialist approach, according to which the moral permissibility of using the new technologies to modify biological organisms and of patenting should be assessed solely in terms of the consequences of doing so, particularly (if not exclusively) in terms of human (and animal) welfare.

Other ethicists, and a large section of the general public, have responded rather differently. Dissatisfied with the pragmatic nature of the consequentialist reasoning about genetic engineering, they have suggested that there are categorical objections to be raised against this technology or parts of it. Thus, applications of genetic engineering should be assessed in terms of whether they are wrong (or right) *in themselves*, as well as (more contingently) in terms of their ability to promote welfare.

In my discussion I will focus on genetic engineering, but it is also relevant for other biological technologies that may be used to create new life forms. I shall discuss genetically modified organisms quite generally, and thus set aside the notoriously complex issue of what, exactly, a 'new life form' is.

Values

Essential to different approaches to ethical issues in genetic engineering are the values they invoke. One important view, 'welfarism', may be defined as the claim that (a) the moral value of an act should be based exclusively on how good an

206

outcome it brings about, and (b) the goodness of an outcome should be based exclusively on the welfare it contains and (possibly) on how it is distributed. Utilitarians are welfarists in this sense, since they believe that in order for an act to be right, it must bring about an outcome with at least as large a total of welfare as that of any alternative act. However, welfarists need not be utilitarians. They may want to take account of the way welfare is distributed. For example, given a situation in which welfare is distributed in a highly unequal way, they may prefer a situation in which there is less total welfare, but it is distributed more equally.

According to welfarists, all we have to care about when morally assessing genetic (or other) manipulations on living organisms is what the consequences will be in terms of welfare. However, since we cannot always know these with certainty, the assessment will consist in weighing the expected welfare benefits against the welfare risks.

As pointed out above, many people find welfarism seriously inadequate when applied to the question of creating and patenting new life forms. Welfarism, it is claimed, does not at all accord with our intuitive responses to these issues. We are struck by a sense of unease; by the thought that scientists are playing God, or in some other way not respecting the special dignity and worth of living organisms.

The values underlying these responses are often construed as deontological constraints on when it is permissible to bring about good outcomes, that is, outcomes that are good in welfarist terms. There are certain things we must not do – for instance, violate an animal's genetic integrity – even if doing so would bring about a better outcome. This deontological approach differs from welfarism both in the choice of values and in the insistence that (some) values should be respected rather than promoted. (For example, deontologists may insist that it is always wrong to kill an innocent human life, even if killing an innocent human being were the only way in which one could stop a very large number of innocent humans being killed.) Another alternative to welfarism is the view that there are some values – for instance, biological diversity – that in themselves make outcomes better, and so should be promoted along with welfare. This view differs from welfarism only in its choice of values.

Micro-organisms and Plants

Creating new strains of micro-organisms and plants may in different ways involve substantial benefits to humans. Consider, for example, bacteria that produce life-saving medicine and new strains of plants that require less fertilizer, insecticide and pesticide. On the other hand, there are also risks involved in creating these new strains, which should be weighed against the benefits. But, at least in some cases, it seems plausible that genetic interventions are beneficial overall.

We have seen that many people do not believe that such welfarist considerations exhaust the moral realm. One objection is that genetic engineering involves playing God, and is for that reason wrong. Sometimes, I suspect, the point of this objection is to remind us that, unlike God, we are neither omniscient nor omnipotent. Therefore we should be careful not to overestimate our ability to predict and control the consequences of genetic engineering.

However, surely welfarists will agree. In order for the objection to go beyond this view, it must be interpreted differently. On one (literal) interpretation, scientists should not modify the genetic make-up of living organisms since this is God's prerogative. The problem with this interpretation is how we can know that God does not want scientists to do so.

On another interpretation, it is claimed that genetic engineering is *unnatural* and therefore wrong. This view may seem more promising, but it faces two challenges. First, the meaning of 'unnatural' must be specified in a way that satisfies three requirements; (a) it should apply to genetic engineering, (b) it should not apply to the intentional genetic modification of organisms through selective breeding (since even proponents of the 'playing God' objection want to allow this technology) and (c) it should not be ad hoc. Second, it must be explained why, according to the favoured specification, what is unnatural is also immoral. In one sense, all of medicine is 'unnatural', since it seeks to prevent illnesses taking their natural course. It is not obvious how either of these challenges could be met.

Another class of objections takes as its point of departure the claim that we should respect all living organisms. Some people argue that therefore we ought not cross (natural) species boundaries. This can be seen as an attempt to point out a relevant difference between selective breeding and (some instances of) genetic engineering. Genetic engineering often involves inserting a gene taken from one species into an organism from a different species. Therefore (some instances of) genetic engineering will cause the distinctions between species to be blurred, thus violating the integrity of living organisms. Other people argue instead that in genetic engineering, organisms are not respected since they are treated as mere means to satisfy human desires.

There is, however, a question that needs to be addressed regarding these objections. Are micro-organisms and plants really the sort of beings that can be violated and should be respected? Do they have moral standing, either as individuals or as species?

The view that all biological organisms have moral standing is usually supported by the claim that even non-sentient organisms, for example, trees, have a 'good of their own' (Attfield, 1991) or a 'will to live' (Schweitzer, 1929). But as Peter Singer (1993: 279) points out, we should be careful when assessing such claims:

> once we stop to reflect on the fact that plants are not conscious and cannot engage in any intentional behaviour, it is clear that all this language is metaphorical; one might just as well say that a river is pursuing its own good and striving to reach the sea, or that the 'good' of a guided missile is to blow itself up along with its target.

The difficulty is to explain why the sense in which micro-organisms and plants have a good is morally relevant. Trees, like guided missiles, do not really have a *perspective* on the world, according to which things can be good or bad for them. In other words, it cannot make a difference to them what happens to them, since they

208

cannot desire things to go one way or the other or experience such events. Some, therefore, search for other properties on the basis of which non-sentient organisms may acquire moral standing. But to others, these considerations of interests suggest an alternative view, namely that only sentient beings have moral standing. This view, called sentientism, implies that genetic interventions cannot wrong micro-organisms and plants (or species). Obviously, such interventions can be wrong nevertheless, if they are contrary to the interests of humans or animals. But, as pointed out above, there seem to be cases in which a concern for welfare would support creating new strains of micro-organisms and plants.

Animals

A transgenic animal is a genetically modified animal. Such animals can be used as disease models for medical research, as 'bioreactors' that produce proteins to be used in pharmaceuticals or as improved livestock in agriculture. Thus, mice have been designed to develop cancer so that they can be used in cancer research, sheep have been designed to produce Factor IX in their milk and attempts have been made to make pigs grow faster.

Unlike micro-organisms and plants, (many) animals are sentient. This means that there are clear welfarist reasons to take their interests into account, in so far as our acts (or omissions) affect them (see chapter 39, pp. 411–22). Traditionally, this moral concern has been considered only in the context of animals already in existence. However, as the case of genetic engineering brings out, we are sometimes involved in their creation. And it would seem that by creating them, we may affect their interests for better or worse. If, for instance, a transgenic animal is created such that it will experience nothing but severe pain, it seems that this animal has been harmed by being caused to exist in such a dreadful condition.

Some philosophers deny that we can harm or benefit animals (or humans for that matter) by causing them to exist. They believe that the relevant alternatives – existence and non-existence – are evaluatively incomparable. I am sceptical about this line of argument myself, but it is worth pointing out that even if creating an animal cannot harm or benefit it, there may still be an (impersonal) welfarist concern to be taken into account when morally assessing transgenic animals. It may be claimed that it is better that there is more rather than less welfare in the world, and that it is better, other things being equal, if the animals that are created have a high rather than a low welfare.

Welfarists hold that it is prima facie wrong to create transgenic animals if (a) they will experience more suffering than positive welfare or (b) they will replace animals with better lives. (This is why the objection that welfarism does not rule out redesigning farm animals as insentient 'vegetables' is misguided. Most welfarists believe that we should try to prevent animals from suffering *and* ensure that they experience positive welfare.)

Perhaps, in some cases, the bad consequences referred to in (a) and (b) can be counterbalanced by benefits to humans (or other animals), for example, if animal experiments are necessary to make progress in cancer research. If so, transgenesis

209

will be acceptable from a welfarist point of view, even if the animals have lives that are worse than nothing or replace happier animals. Transgenesis will, of course, also be acceptable if it has either no impact on them or a positive impact.

Some proponents of animal rights have argued that since sentient animals have inherent value, they should not be used as a mere means to benefit humans (Regan, 1984). Therefore, it is wrong, for example, to create transgenic mice designed to develop cancer. (For a discussion of this view, see chapter 39.)

A more sweeping objection against creating transgenic animals is to invoke the concept of 'genetic integrity': 'We can define the genetic integrity of an animal as the genome being left intact' (Vorstenbosch, 1993: 110). Defined in this manner, 'integrity is a respect- or constraint-related concept and not a "grading" concept like welfare that suggests from an ethical point of view an "optimizing" approach' (111–12). This objection, it should be noted, is just as much an argument against selective breeding as it is against genetic engineering. Suppose, however, that we bite the bullet and accept the implication for selective breeding.

We might want to know more precisely what the value of genetic integrity is supposed to be. On the face of it, this concept seems to express a concern for animals. But does it really refer to something that is valuable from the *animal's* point of view? Suppose that an animal is genetically modified so that it will not develop a severe disease. In what way is this supposed to be of no value to the animal?

A different concern sometimes claimed to be important when assessing transgenic animals is respect for their *telos*. According to Bernard Rollin, to violate an animal's *telos* is to prevent it from fulfilling its natural desires or inclinations (what matters most to it). This does not make it inherently wrong to alter the *telos* of an animal. It is wrong only if it involves an infringement of the new *telos*. More precisely, 'it is only wrong to change a *telos* if the individual animals of that sort are likely to be more unhappy or suffer more after the change than before' (Rollin, 1986: 89). This view, then, seems to coincide with welfarism.

A different proposal, however, is that 'The *telos* or "beingness" of an animal is its intrinsic nature coupled with the environment in which it is able to develop and experience life' (Fox, 1990: 32). To disrupt the harmony between the animal and its environment is to harm the animal.

Part of what motivates this view is a reaction against the claim – implied by welfarism and Rollin's view – that one way of benefiting animals is by genetically designing them to be happy in the environment in which we put them (e.g., on the factory farm). But it is not clear how this view avoids that claim itself. If the value proposed consists of a fit between the animal and its environment, then what is the problem with creating an animal that has an optimal fit with the environment in which we put it?

Maybe the point is that it is the fit between the animal and its environment that we find in nature (laid down by evolution) which must not be disrupted. This would explain why it is wrong to modify animals to fit the environment on the factory farm. But then another question emerges. How can it *harm* an animal to be created with a different fit with its environment from the one its ancestors had, if its new fit is in fact a good one? Again, the problem is that it may be difficult to see what kind of disvalue is involved from the animal's point of view.

Humans

Most of the uses of somatic and germ-line gene therapy that have been discussed involve treating or preventing genetically determined diseases by inserting the normally functioning gene that healthy people have. (For further discussion, see chapter 19, pp. 187–97.) Here, however, I want to consider gene therapy that aims to insert genes that are not found in the human gene pool into human beings. What should we think of this kind of gene therapy for enhancement?

It is a widely held view that there is a morally relevant difference between using gene therapy to correct a defect and using it to enhance characteristics above what a person would otherwise have had. The latter use is more questionable, if not outright impermissible. This view may seem quite plausible.

However, there are also intuitions that tell against it. Consider the following case. Jane is infected with HIV. Her immune system is starting to give in and she is about to develop AIDS. Fortunately, there is a new kind of gene therapy available – call it therapy A – that will boost her immune system and bring it back to normal, so that she will in fact never develop AIDS. By performing the therapy, we are *correcting* her (or her immune system). Now consider Helen. She has not yet been infected with HIV, but she is a haemophiliac and, since blood reserves at the hospital have not been screened for HIV, we know it is only a matter of time before she is infected, unless she receives a new kind of gene therapy – call it therapy B – that will make her immune. (Unfortunately, therapy B only works on haemophiliacs, so it cannot be used on Jane.) By performing the therapy, we are *enhancing* her (or her immune system), since we are giving her a desirable property that people do not normally (or naturally) have.

The point is that, intuitively, it does not seem more problematic or less urgent to perform therapy B on Helen than to perform therapy A on Jane. But, according to the view that enhancing is more dubious, it must be so (since the cases are relevantly similar in other respects). Thus, the intuitive case for this view is not as clear-cut as it initially seems.

A different view is that gene therapy is only permissible in so far as it is used to treat diseases or prevent them from developing. This view would allow us to perform therapy B on Helen, since we would then be preventing her developing AIDS. But why stop here? As some ethicists point out, there are more ambitious enhancements that could be claimed to benefit people substantially. For instance, John Harris argues that if (though it may not be possible at all) we could genetically engineer better health and a disposition for high intelligence into our children, we ought to do so. After all, we would not hesitate to send our children to a school that achieved these same ends (Harris, 1992: 140–2).

It is, of course, not obvious that a scheme of genetic intelligence enhancement would be a good idea, even if it could be performed safely. It might increase competition and the pressure on children for them to do well. Another worry is that we would experience a loss in terms of equality, since the social gaps between people who are able to pay for this treatment and those who are not so fortunate would widen. Even assuming that the treatment was offered to everyone in a publicly funded health-care system, there might still be a problem of fairness, if it meant that resources were drawn away from people who were seriously ill and thus had a stronger claim on the health-care budget. Finally, the risk of a slippery slope should be considered (see also chapter 28, pp. 280–90).

These reservations may all be accounted for in terms of welfarism. However, many people believe that deontological objections should also be raised. Thus, Hans Jonas (1984: 34) argues that:

> when it comes to this core phenomenon of our humanity, which is to be preserved in its integrity at all costs, and which has not to await its perfection from the future because it is already whole in its essence as we possess it . . . then indeed the well-enough founded prognosis of doom has greater force than any concurrent prognosis of bliss.

Jonas' view raises several questions of interpretation. These questions aside, some will find it objectionable because holding that human nature must be preserved at *all* costs implies that one must be very insensitive towards other values. Thus, a strikingly different view is taken by a somewhat ironical Jonathan Glover (1984: 56):

> It is easy to sympathize with opposition to the principle of changing our nature. Preserving it as it is will seem an acceptable option to all those who can watch the news on television and feel satisfied with the world. It will appeal to those who can talk to their children about the history of the twentieth century without wishing they could leave some things out.

On this view, it would be unreasonable to rule out the possibility of changing human nature *as a matter of principle*. But, of course, in the light of our own fallibility and unfortunate tendency to let our own interests outweigh those of future generations, it is quite possible that the *risks* of ambitious (non-health-related) changes of human nature will always outweigh the expected benefits.

Patents

A further question is whether it is morally permissible to patent new genes and life forms. Here it is crucial to understand what a patent is. A patent may be issued to anyone who invents or discovers any new, useful and non-obvious process, machine, manufacture, composition of matter or any new and useful improvement of these items (35 USC 101). The right obtained by a patent owner is to exclude others from making, using or selling the invention. Importantly, the patent does not automatically give him or her the right to make, use or sell it himself or herself.

Patents on life forms are often opposed partly on the basis of metaphysical views. It is argued that, if life forms are patented, life is thereby reduced to 'a composition of matter' since it is only patentable as such. Obviously, this is not the place to try to resolve the dispute between materialists and their opponents. Instead, we may note that the more it is stressed that life is not just 'a bag of chemicals', the harder it is to see what the moral problem is with patenting this bag of chemicals (which is all that *can* be patented), because we are then not really patenting life itself.

Another, related objection is that patents on life forms are incompatible with having 'reverence for life'. We then need an account of what the relevant difference is between patenting a life form and owning individual members of that life form. After all, having 'reverence for life' is not usually thought to imply that we may not own pets, livestock or crops.

Also, in the case of micro-organisms and plants, the sentientist challenge must be answered. Since these organisms cannot have experiences or want things to go one way or the other, in which sense can they be violated by being patented? In the case of animals, a similar question arises. Even if an animal is sentient, it has no desires regarding being patented, nor does it experience this event. So, although arguably the so-called Harvard mouse was harmed by being created, it is less clear that it was harmed or violated by being patented.

What, then, about welfarist concerns? For welfarists, the question of patents is quite complex. On one hand, patents stimulate important research. On the other hand, patents may tend to increase the prices of therapeutic drugs and other important products. And they may negatively affect the way in which we relate to life, both our own and that of animals, by increasingly commercializing it. Furthermore, they may disadvantage farmers by forcing them to pay royalty fees on the offspring of their herds, and they may disadvantage developing nations because they could not afford to buy biotechnological products once they are patented, and would experience a loss in terms of competitiveness. (These distributional consequences may seem particularly unfair in the light of the fact that more than 75 per cent of the genetic resources in the world are to be found in developing nations, but are used free of cost by biotechnological companies.)

There are, of course, special concerns relating to patents on humans. Patents that would interfere with human autonomy or freedom would be quite dubious according to almost any moral view, whether they were issued on human genes, organs, or even on entire human beings (for additional discussion of patents on human genes, see chapter 20, pp. 198–205).

References

Attfield, R. (1991). *The Ethics of Environmental Concern*, 2nd edn. Athens: University of Georgia Press.

Fox, M. (1990). Transgenic animals: ethical and animal welfare concerns. In P. Wheale and R. McNally (eds), The *Bio-revolution: Cornucopia or Pandora's box?* London: Pluto Press, 31–45.

Glover, J. (1984). *What Sort of People Should There Be?* Harmondsworth: Penguin.

Harris, J. (1992). *Wonderwoman and Superman: the ethics of human biotechnology.* Oxford: Oxford University Press.

Jonas, H. (1984). *The Imperative of Responsibility: in search of an ethics for the technological age.* Chicago: University of Chicago Press.

Regan, T. (1984). *Animal Rights.* London: Routledge.

Rollin, B. (1986). On telos and genetic manipulation. *Between the Species*, 2, 88–9.

Schweitzer, A. (1923). *The Philosophy of Civilization*, 2nd edn. London: A. and C. Black.

Singer, P. (1993). *Practical Ethics*, 2nd edn. Cambridge: Cambridge University Press.

Vorstenbosch, J. (1993). The concept of integrity: its significance for the ethical discussion on biotechnology and animals. *Lifestock Production Science*, 36, 109–12.

Further Reading

Brody, B. A. (1989). An evaluation of the ethical arguments commonly raised against the patenting of transgenic animals. In W. H. Lesser (ed.), *Animal Patents: the legal, economic and social issues.* New York: Stockton Press, 141–53.

Donnelley, S., McCarthy, C. R. and Singleton, R. Jr (1994). The brave new world of animal biotechnology. *Hastings Center Report*, special supplement, 24, S2–S31.

Engelhardt, H. T. Jr (1990). Human nature technologically revisited. *Social Philosophy and Policy*, 8, 180–91.

Hare, R. M. (1991). Moral reasoning about the environment. In B. Almond and D. Hill (eds), *Applied Philosophy.* London: Routledge, 9–20.

Holtug, N. (1997). Altering humans: the case for and against human gene therapy. *Cambridge Quarterly of Healthcare Ethics*, 6, 157–74.

Kass, L. (1985). Patenting life. In *Toward a More Natural Science.* New York: Free Press, 128–53.

Rifkin, J. (1983). *Algeny.* New York: Viking Press.

Rollin, B. (1995). *The Frankenstein Syndrome: Ethical and social issues in the genetic engineering of animals.* Cambridge: Cambridge University Press.

Sandøe, P., Holtug, N. and Simonsen, H. B. (1996). Ethical limits to domestication. *Journal of Agricultural and Environmental Ethics*, 9, 114–22.

Suzuki, D. and Knudtson, P. (1990). *Genethics: The ethics of engineering life.* London: Unwin Hyman.

Wheale, P. and McNally, R. (eds) (1990). *The Bio-revolution: Cornucopia or Pandora's box?* London: Pluto Press.

22

Genetic screening and counselling

ANGUS CLARKE

Genetic counselling has been defined as 'the process by which patients or relatives at risk of a disorder that may be hereditary are advised of the consequences of the disorder, the probability of developing and transmitting it and of the ways in which this may be prevented or ameliorated' (Harper, 1988). The patient or client has questions or concerns about a genetic disorder, and the professional – either a medically trained clinical geneticist or a non-medical genetic counsellor – responds to these questions or concerns by providing information, explanation and support.

The first task of the genetic counsellor, therefore, is to listen to the client – to his or her words and to the gaps between these words – to discover the questions that seek an answer, and the concerns that need to be addressed.

It is usually very helpful to establish the diagnosis of the condition in the family as precisely as possible. This will help to answer at least the technical, factual questions within the constraints of medical science. The conversation may then progress to address the wider concerns of the client. The personal meaning of the disorder for the client may be explored, and the likely significance to the client and her family of any possible future decisions about prenatal diagnosis or predictive testing.

If there is a clear genetic explanation for a child's profound handicap, then the mother may feel relieved of the anxiety that she had caused the problems by something she did in pregnancy. On the other hand, parents or grandparents may be devastated to learn that they have transmitted 'faulty genes' that have caused a serious problem in their child or grandchild. The client may wish to explore her feelings about guilt, blame and responsibility for the problem, and the counsellor may facilitate this. A mother may have sufficient scientific understanding to 'know' that she is not personally at fault for the condition that affects her child, but she may still feel the burden of responsibility at an emotional level (Weil, 1991).

Similarly, the impact on herself and on other family members of a client's decision to have a predictive genetic test for a serious, late-onset dementia (e.g., Huntington's disease) may need to be discussed. How might the various family members respond if the test result is favourable, or if it is unfavourable, or if she decides not to be tested? A similar process may be helpful for couples who are making a decision about prenatal diagnosis and a possible termination of pregnancy for a disorder that affects other family members.

Information Management: Confidentiality
and Autonomy

Just as the core component activity of genetic counselling is the provision of information, so the principal ethical difficulties relate to how this information should be used. Information given to a client may be relevant to other members of the extended family if other individuals are at risk of developing the condition or transmitting it to their children. There may be complications of the condition that can be avoided if the individuals at risk are aware of their situation.

If the client fails to pass on the relevant information, or even just the fact that there is relevant information, then does the genetic counsellor have the duty to do this herself? She may not know the names or addresses of the client's relatives but, where it is possible, should she pass on the potentially important information?

It has been argued that client confidentiality can justifiably be broken in such circumstances, and that guidelines should be drawn up to clarify these circumstances. Against this position, it can be maintained that the drawing up of such guidelines will be unhelpful or even counter-productive, and may devalue the importance of confidentiality (Clarke, 1994).

In almost all cases where an individual initially decides not to pass on important information to other family members, he will in practice change his mind once he has had time to consider the full implications of his decision. Furthermore, it can be argued that the legal duty of confidentiality to the primary client, and respect for the privacy of other family members, make it inappropriate to intervene in these circumstances. If guidelines for professionals are drawn up that legitimize such breaches of confidentiality, then clients will know that genetic information can be passed to other family members without their consent. Even if confidentiality would only rarely be breached in practice, the fear that it may happen could make some clients reluctant to disclose all relevant information, or it may make them reluctant to seek genetic counselling at all.

The importance of client autonomy in decisions about reproduction and about genetic testing is enshrined in the canons of modern bioethics, and is confirmed in numerous policy documents from Britain, Europe and North America. The importance of genetic counsellors adopting a 'non-directive' stance is frequently emphasized and, even if non-directiveness is unattainable in practice, the ethos of genetic counselling is certainly non-prescriptive.

This respect for client autonomy is challenged in two areas. In the context of testing within families, there have been suggestions that genetic testing should be obligatory under certain circumstances if the results would be important for other family members. In the context of genetic screening programmes, there is a danger that individuals will be offered testing in a routinized manner by health professionals who clearly expect them to comply; the clients may participate without having adequately considered the possible consequences.

Breaches of confidence can arise inadvertently in genetic counselling when different members of the same extended family are seen separately. Genetic counsellors must take care to avoid the accidental mishandling of confidential information.

Similarly, genetic laboratories should generate no more information than is needed to answer the questions they have been asked; once information has been generated it can be difficult to contain.

Predictive Genetic Testing

Within genetic counselling, the most intensively studied area of predictive testing has been that for Huntington's disease (HD), a dementia and movement disorder that most often develops in middle life. When predictive testing first became available, it was decided that careful studies and the development of protocols would be needed to ensure that the offer of testing did not cause more harm than good. A wide range of practical problems did arise during the first few years of testing (Morris et al., 1989). More recent experience with follow-up of those given both high-risk and low-risk results has shown that both groups can suffer social and emotional problems. Those given low risks often do not experience the anticipated sense of relief, and may suffer survivor guilt.

Before predictive testing for HD became available, most at-risk individuals indicated that they would want testing. Since then, however, experience has shown that many have decided not to proceed. This serves to emphasize the importance of pre-test counselling, which gives individuals the opportunity to reflect upon the possible consequences of testing and helps them to make appropriate decisions. They can take into account the possible reactions of – among others – family members and partners, employers and insurance companies.

Predictive testing for conditions where patient management is helped by pre-symptomatic testing raises fewer ethical and psychological difficulties, although testing to identify those women at high risk of familial breast cancer (for example) will remain problematic until some medical intervention (screening for tumours, surgery, medication) has been shown to improve their clinical outcome.

Childhood Genetic Testing

Special issues are raised by the genetic testing of children. When the management of a child's health problem depends upon accurate diagnosis, the use of genetic methods to establish the diagnosis is of course in the best interests of the child. Similarly, if a child is at risk of developing a late-onset disorder for which some useful intervention or surveillance is available, which may be of benefit to the individual if started in childhood, then the situation is the same. But if a child is at high risk of a condition that is unlikely to develop until later in life, and if there is no health benefit to the individual from pre-symptomatic diagnosis, then the situation is different.

There are three principal grounds for concern about childhood genetic testing that may lead to a policy of caution. First, testing in childhood removes the individual's future right as an autonomous adult to make their own decision about testing. Second, the confidentiality that would be automatic for any adult undergoing testing will be removed. Finally, genetic testing may lead to harmful social or

217

emotional consequences for the child. The family's expectations of the child may be altered in an unhelpful manner. This could damage the child's educational prospects and their emotional and interpersonal development, and could lead to stigmatization and discrimination. These considerations have led to recommendations that pre-symptomatic testing for HD should *not* be performed on minors and that caution be exercised in other circumstances as well. The fact that so many at-risk adults choose not to be tested does suggest that concern about the child's loss of future autonomy is warranted.

Similar considerations apply to testing children for their carrier status for a recessive disorder. Affected individuals have a double dose of a 'faulty' copy of the gene, whereas an individual who carries a single faulty copy of the gene is perfectly healthy; their single intact copy of the gene is sufficient to avoid disease. Such carriers may have affected children if their partners are also carriers of the same faulty gene. If there are harmful social and emotional effects of carrier testing in childhood, these are unlikely to relate to expectations about the child's future health. Instead, these are likely to be altered family expectations of a proven carrier's future relationships and reproduction as an adult; a girl carrying Duchenne muscular dystrophy, for example, may be brought up in the expectation that she would not have any sons or perhaps any children. These concerns are reinforced by our knowledge that individuals identified as carriers of a genetic disorder – as adults or adolescents – can find this to be burdensome and worrying and can regret being tested. The concerns about the loss of autonomy and confidentiality apply as for predictive testing.

These issues do not arise in the same way if the 'child' is sufficiently mature to take the lead in requesting genetic tests – if (s)he is legally a minor but requests testing and is capable of weighing up the issues. Loss of the child's future autonomy is then no longer an issue.

It may be argued that parents have a right to know the genetic status of their children, but if this is not relevant to health care during childhood then this argument is weak; deciding what is in the best interests of the child would be the most appropriate way of resolving any differences under British law. It may be argued that children accept and adjust to unwelcome information more readily before adolescence than when they are older, but systematic evidence on this point is lacking; there may be more truth in the argument that those adolescents and young adults who have been left free to make their own decisions about testing make the best adjustment to unfavourable results.

There are differences of opinion on these questions, both among health professionals and between professionals and parents, with many professional groups adopting a cautious policy (ASHG/ACMG, 1995). It is difficult to weigh the various considerations against each other – rights against rights, rights against evidence.

Genetic Screening

Genetic screening can be contrasted with genetic counselling in three ways: it is pro-active rather than reactive, it always involves the offer of genetic testing and it is aimed at a whole population or a defined subpopulation rather than individuals and their immediate families.

Four types of genetic screening programme need to be mentioned:

1   Newborn screening, usually for treatable disorders where early diagnosis greatly improves the outlook for an affected child;
2   Carrier screening – to identify carriers of autosomal recessive disorders, who will themselves be healthy but who may have an affected child if their partner is also a carrier;
3   Prenatal screening, usually for malformations (e.g., neural tube defects) or genetic conditions (e.g., Down's syndrome) in the fetus, but sometimes identifying couples who are both carriers of a recessive disorder. These couples have a one in four chance of their child being affected by the condition, but can be offered prenatal diagnosis;
4   Susceptibility screening for genetic predisposition to common diseases such as common cancers, heart disease and Alzheimer's dementia. This type of population screening is not yet technically feasible, although predictive testing is possible within certain unusual, high-risk families.

Informed Consent

In genetic counselling, the clients are actively seeking information about a disease of which they usually already have some knowledge and practical experience. In population screening, on the other hand, the clients may have little knowledge and no experience of the condition for which they are being screened; furthermore, they are being approached by health professionals who usually believe that the test on offer is a good thing. Under these conditions, is the requirement for informed consent actually observed in practice? It is possible to debate the criteria that define informed consent, but it will also be important to conduct empirical research to find out how individuals experience the consent they have given in such circumstances.

Does it matter if the consent obtained is not fully informed, as long as the screening test *is* a good thing? In the context of prenatal genetic screening, such paternalistic arguments lead directly to a new eugenics in which lip service is paid to autonomy and informed consent, but in which these principles are not respected in the reality of everyday clinical practice.

Newborn Screening

Newborn screening began more than thirty years ago with the Guthrie test for phenylketonuria (PKU). Screening for PKU and congenital hypothyroidism is now routine in many countries. In both conditions, an early diagnosis permits effective treatment and results in essentially normal development. Without this, the affected infants would suffer profound mental handicap.

Because the benefits of screening infants for these treatable disorders are so great, programmes of newborn screening have often been instituted with little

219

explanation or information for the parents. Such screening has usually been routinized, and in many states of the USA it is compulsory. Studies of parental knowledge of newborn screening have shown that few parents even know for what conditions their infants are screened. In newborn screening for phenylketonuria, the need for informed and considered parental consent may not be so great.

Newborn screening for other disorders is less widespread because the health benefits for the affected infants are less easily demonstrable, although there is a strong case for introducing tests for some other conditions in specific populations.

One newborn screening programme had to be discontinued because of the adverse impact on families. This was the Swedish programme identifying infants with alpha-1 antitrypsin deficiency, who are at increased risk of chronic lung disease, especially if they are exposed to smoke or dust. The screening programme generated great distress in the families of affected infants. Furthermore, one potential benefit of such screening could have been protection of the susceptible infants from such exposure; it was therefore particularly worrying that more fathers of affected infants smoked than did fathers of control infants (McNeil et al., 1988).

Screening on other grounds – not because of any clear benefit to the affected child – is practised much less commonly. One disorder for which newborn screening is under evaluation in Wales is Duchenne muscular dystrophy (DMD). Entry to the newborn screening programme is optional, on the basis of informed parental consent. DMD is a progressive neuromuscular condition that usually becomes apparent by the age of 5 or 6 years; it leads to the inability to walk by 8–12 years, and to death usually in the late teenage years or early twenties. DMD is inherited as a sex-linked trait, and the mothers of many boys are healthy female carriers with a 50 per cent chance of transmitting the condition to any future son. Other female relatives may also be carriers, so the diagnosis of DMD in one boy may have repercussions for the extended family.

Newborn screening for DMD has potential advantages and disadvantages. One potential advantage is that the family can be offered genetic counselling – they might otherwise unwittingly have a second or third affected son before the first is diagnosed. Other advantages include the avoidance of prolonged uncertainty during the frequently lengthy diagnostic process, and the ability of the family to plan for the future. The principal potential disadvantage is the emotional trauma of such an early diagnosis. The balance between the advantages and disadvantages cannot be determined a priori; this is a clear example of the need for evidence generated by the careful evaluation of a programme in operation. The social evaluation has so far found that most families with an affected child are pleased to have known early – but the duration of follow-up is not yet sufficient for such a programme to be generally recommended.

Carrier Screening

The frequency of carriers for recessive disorders among the general population varies – depending upon the detailed population history of a person's ancestors – but it can be very high. A common recessive disorder in Britain is cystic fibrosis

(CF); one in 25 Britons is a carrier and one in 2,500 children is affected. CF leads to recurrent chest infections that progressively impair lung function and to the mal-absorption of food from the bowel; treatments have improved over the past twenty years so that many affected children now survive into adult life. A common reces-sive disease in West Africa is sickle cell disease; one in four people from some areas carries sickle cell disease and one in 50 is affected. Most 'carriers' of recessive diseases have parents, brothers and sisters who are healthy and have no known 'family history' of the disease in question.

Carrier screening may therefore generate anxieties and concerns in many people who will never 'benefit' from being identified as carriers. It will never be of any significance to them because their partners are not carriers, or they are not plan-ning any further children, or their reproductive plans would anyway not be altered by knowledge of a risk of their having an affected child. Carrier testing may be seen as burdening them with unwelcome information, and so the criteria by which to judge the informed consent procedures of carrier screening programmes must be stringent. In addition, other outcomes of carrier screening – the recall and interpre-tation of test results, the impact on an individual's sense of well-being – must also be evaluated.

How can it be decided whether the modest burden of carrier testing on many people is worthwhile for the sake of a few families who will be pleased to discover their carrier status? From studies of carrier screening programmes in operation it is known that some couples do make use of the knowledge of their carrier status to alter their reproductive plans. But what else has been learned? Are there drawbacks to such screening programmes?

First, it is clear that there can be disadvantages to being identified as a carrier of a recessive disease. Carriers can experience shame, social stigmatization and insti-tutionalized discrimination. Some carriers may have latent concerns about their own health, or may be 'worried' about their carrier status even years after testing and may have concerns about their own future health. Carriers of CF have been found to have lower self-esteem than non-carriers.

Second, we know that many parents, aunts and uncles of children with CF (for example) do not use – or do not intend to use – prenatal diagnosis and the selective termination of affected pregnancies. If there is no consensus among this group, those who know so much about the condition, that carrier screening, prenatal diagnosis and pregnancy termination are worthwhile, then it could be argued that it would be unwise to offer carrier screening on a wide scale to the general popula-tion. In addition, adults affected by CF – the long-term survivors – have differing views about such screening.

Third, while most of those enrolled in carrier screening programmes do not suffer serious distress, some carriers do regret having been tested. Furthermore, experience in Britain and elsewhere suggests that public interest in CF testing is limited. The rate of uptake of testing depends very largely on the way in which the offer is made (Bekker et al., 1993), suggesting that those accepting the test are complying with enthusiastic health professionals but are only weakly motivated.

Those tested in such programmes have a good understanding of their test results shortly after testing, but an increasing proportion of subjects have misunderstandings when asked about the significance of their result some months or years later.

Some professionals have welcomed the prospect of population carrier screening for CF with enthusiasm, seeing it as an opportunity to establish an infrastructure for community genetics which could subsequently broaden to offer screening for other diseases. The financial and opportunity costs of establishing such a programme, however, would be prohibitive if pre- and post-test counselling of high quality were to be included. Some professional and commercial interests may favour the promotion of population carrier screening, but it is still premature to regard population carrier screening for CF and other disorders as being of proven worth.

Pre-natal Screening

The decision of a health-care system or of individual professionals to offer prenatal screening for any condition inevitably conveys a recommendation to pregnant women that accepting the test is the responsible course of action, and that a fetus identified as affected should be aborted. However much the language of reproductive choice, client autonomy and informed consent is employed in discussions with pregnant women, the fact that the screening programme exists will convey this message. This problem is inherent in all screening programmes, but is most acute in the prenatal context.

Those who fail to comply with the 'standard' prenatal screening policy of their hospital may be regarded as irresponsible, and if they have a child affected by a condition that could have been 'prevented' (by termination of pregnancy) they may be regarded as blameworthy. The fear of being blamed may be one potent factor that ensures that most pregnant women do comply. In some health-care systems, parents may be financially liable for the care of a sick child – and if the parents declined prenatal screening then their insurance policies may exclude coverage.

In addition to the effects of prenatal screening programmes on the women involved, they may also have a very negative effect on individuals within society who are affected by the condition that the programme is designed to 'prevent'. Individuals with other disabilities may also feel that prenatal screening programmes are exacerbating society's intolerance of deviations from what is seen as the ideal – the 'normal'.

Susceptibility Screening

Great efforts are being made to identify the genetic factors that contribute to the development of common multifactorial disorders such as colon cancer, breast cancer, diabetes, heart disease, hypertension, Alzheimer's dementia and some psychiatric disorders. Such work could lead to the development of improved therapies, but could also lead to tests that would identify those at increased risk of such disorders without offering any effective means of treatment or prevention. At the very least, there is likely to be a lag of many years between the ability to test for susceptibility to a disease and the ability to treat or prevent it.

'Predictive' genetic testing is possible for single-gene disorders in known families, identifying those who are likely to develop uncommon conditions such as HD or some of the familial cancer syndromes. For the common disorders being considered here, however, such as common cancers and cardiovascular diseases, true predictive testing is most unlikely to be possible. Whether or not someone develops these conditions is influenced by interactions between multiple genetic factors and many environmental variables, only some of which are likely to be under the control of the individual. Genetic tests will identify the relative risk of a person developing a certain disease by a particular age in comparison to the average population risk, but will not be able to make firm predictions about specific individuals. Risk information may or may not be helpful to individuals, and this should certainly not be assumed.

There is a growing trend to account for differences between people in relation to both disease susceptibility and non-disease characteristics such as intelligence and personality in terms of genetic factors. This is known as geneticization. It leads society to seek solutions to its problems through scientific and technological means rather than responding collectively through social, political, economic or environmental change (Alper and Natowicz, 1992; Lippman, 1992). This could lead to demands for genetic susceptibility screening that may be of little health benefit to the tested individuals but may be used by employers, governments or insurance companies.

Genetic tests of susceptibility can generate a sense of fatalism in those at increased risk, and a sense of invulnerability in those at average risk or lower. If there is any scope for lifestyle decisions to modify the disease risk, then both groups may be led to behave inappropriately by indulging in risky behaviours. Labelling individuals as being at risk of disease can also have damaging consequences, sometimes amounting to self-fulfilling prophecy, as seen in screening for high blood pressure and serum cholesterol. To label a substantial proportion of the population as being at increased genetic risk of these common, multifactorial disorders, when there is little benefit in terms of prevention or treatment and a real risk of adverse psychosocial consequences, would seem to be unwise (Clarke, 1995).

Despite these reasons for caution, there may be strong pressures to introduce genetic susceptibility testing on a wide scale. These pressures will include professional enthusiasm, but the most important pressures will be commercial, of three main types. Biotechnology corporations will wish to see genetic testing promoted to increase their profits; pharmaceutical corporations will seek to sell remedies to prevent the diseases to which individuals have been shown to be susceptible; and insurance corporations would like to know any client's risk of disease so as to weight their premiums 'appropriately'. Regulation of such testing and its marketing may be required if society is to avoid some of the serious potential problems.

The benefits to the individual of genetic susceptibility screening remain uncertain. Until effective therapeutic interventions have become readily available – and this may take many years – these benefits will be realized only to the extent that

223

individuals are willing to change their behaviour in response to health promotion, and the message provided by health promotion in the context of genetic testing will be in the form of complex information about relative health risks. Popular under-standings of the influence of lifestyle on (ill)-health differ from professional under-standings, and this may explain the very limited successes of some health promotion programmes. It is unclear how genetic testing will affect the impact of such programmes – they might reinforce the health promotion messages or have paradoxical effects – and different individuals are likely to respond in different ways. Empirical study rather than a priori reflection is required.

Further Information Management

There are other concerns about the possible misuse of genetic information about individuals. Perhaps the area that has generated most debate is that of life and health insurance. It is clearly in the interests of insurance companies to know at least as much about an individual's genetic susceptibility to disease as does that individual. But the social function of insurance would be largely undermined if companies had accurate information about the disease susceptibilities of all their potential clients and used this to set differential premiums. Indeed, there are good grounds for believing this to be morally unfair; insurance would cease to be a form of collective solidarity in the face of infrequent but potentially catastrophic events beyond the control of individuals. Representatives of the insurance industry often reject the assertion that they should choose not to discover as much information relevant to the likely future health of their clients as possible, on the grounds that this would jeopardize the very survival of their industry. As a compromise, it has been proposed that insurance companies should not incorporate genetic informa-tion into their risk calculations for modest levels of insurance cover, while being permitted to do so when providing higher levels of cover.

Such problems are of greater importance in countries where the health-care system is financed through private insurance, and so health care as well as life insurance may be denied to those with unfavourable genetic constitutions. These considerations lend strong support to the organization of health care through a nationalized system, or at least through a universal and state-regulated health insurance scheme.

In addition to these concerns about the use of genetic information by insurance companies, there are other concerns about ways in which genetic information may be used to discriminate against individuals unfairly. The inappropriate denial of insurance cover to healthy individuals with a family history of genetic disease has been documented (Billings et al., 1992). Such examples of the misuse of genetic information strengthen calls to regulate the practice of insurance companies, and also add to the concerns about confidentiality – genetic privacy – in this area. Would employers be able to access such information about potential employees, and select 'the fittest'? Might those with adverse genetic test results, or even just family histories of genetic disorders, become unemployable as well as uninsurable?

Screening for susceptibility to 'occupational' diseases is not yet technically feasible except in the case of A1ATD-associated chronic lung disease, but this may serve as a model disorder for considering the likely future issues. Employers may wish to insist upon screening as a condition of employment, when it may be more appropriate to minimize dust exposure for all employees and monitor them for early signs of the lung disorder (Lappe, 1988).

How can these problems be avoided? In the USA, the Americans with Disabilities Act (1990) may be one means of preventing such genetic discrimination, at least in certain contexts (Natowicz et al., 1992). Fears of discrimination, however, remain. If patients do not trust the health-care system to protect their confidences, they may edit the information they make available to their physicians so that adverse details are not entered in their records; this could then lead to suboptimal care being provided. Society will need to define the types of genetic information that can and cannot be used by employers and insurance companies if these problems are to be avoided.

Goals of Genetic Screening: Public Health vs Individual Choice

The final ethical issue to be raised in the context of genetic counselling and screening relates to the goals and outcomes of such services. What is achieved in genetic counselling and screening? How should this be measured and justified?

There are two broad types of answer to these questions. One approach is to examine the impact on the health-care system of promoting genetics services. This may be termed the 'public health' approach to genetics services. The other approach is to focus on the effects of genetic services on individual clients – the 'client-centred' approach.

The public health approach assesses the outcomes of services in crude measures of the birth incidence of infants with a specific genetic disorder, or the financial costs and benefits of alternative courses of action. The cost of prenatal screening for spina bifida, Down's syndrome or cystic fibrosis and the selective termination of affected pregnancies may be weighed against the cost of caring for affected individuals. The logic of this arguably unjust, resource-sparing approach leads to conclusions that some would regard as ethically offensive, with potential lives being terminated simply because the cost of caring for affected individuals would be greater than the cost of detecting and terminating them prenatally, whether or not their lives might be regarded as 'worthwhile' and whether or not they would entail physical suffering. A system organized with this logic could lead to pressure being applied to clients for them to conform to the system's preferred options – to compliance with prenatal screening programmes and effectively compulsory terminations of pregnancy when 'medically indicated', as in China under its 1995 Maternal and Child Health Law. The question, 'Should society set out to prevent Down's syndrome?' is answered tacitly in the affirmative by society's actions, but the question itself has never been debated comprehensively in public.

The client-centred approach can assess the effect of genetics services by measuring the information gained by individual clients, their understanding of risk infor-

225

mation that has been supplied and the extent to which their reproductive plans, decision-making or behaviour have been facilitated or altered. These measures, however, are not entirely satisfactory, and it may be that the search for readily quantifiable outcome measures for genetics services is inappropriate.

The way in which a genetics service has been structured and the way in which it operates in practice are likely to provide a more valid guide to its true purpose than is provided by its publicly stated objectives. If a service is promoted to the public as being client-centred, but it justifies its existence to the purchasers of health care as saving resources in a crude cost-benefit analysis, then there is likely to be a gap between the public rhetoric and the type of service delivered to clients. The real goals of the service will be manifest in its practice. and they will often reveal the underlying values of those who direct it.

References

Alper, J. S. and Natowicz, M. R. (1992). The allure of genetic explanations [editorial]. *British Medical Journal*, 305, 666.

ASHG/ACMG (American Society of Human Genetics/American College of Medical Genetics) (1995). Points to consider: ethical, legal and psychosocial implications of genetic testing in children and adolescents. *American Journal of Human Genetics*, 57, 1233–41.

Bekker, H., Modell, M., Denniss, G., Silver, A., Mathew, C., Bobrow, M. and Marteau, T. (1993). Uptake of cystic fibrosis testing in primary care: supply push or demand pull? *British Medical Journal*, 306, 1584–6.

Billings, P. R., Kohn, M. A., de Cuevas, M., Beckwith, J., Alper, J. S. and Natowicz, M. R. (1992). Discrimination as a consequence of genetic testing. *American Journal of Human Genetics*, 50, 476–82.

Clarke, A. (1994). Genetic screening: a response to Nuffield. *Bulletin of Medical Ethics*, 94, 13–21.

Harper, P. S. (1988). *Practical Genetic Counselling*, 3rd edn. London: Wright.

Lappe, M. (1988). Eithical issues in genetic screening for susceptibility to chronic lung disease. *Journal of Occupational Medicine*, 30, 493–501.

Light, D. W. (1992). The practice and ethics of risk-related health insurance. *Journal of the American Medical Association*, 267, 2503–8.

McNeil, T. F., Sveger, T. and Thelin, T. (1988). Psychosocial effects of screening for somatic risk: the Swedish alpha-1 antitrypsin experience. *Thorax* 43, 505–7.

Morris, M., Tyler, A., Lazerou, L., Meredith, L. and Harper, P. S. (1989). Problems in genetic prediction for Huntington's disease. *Lancet*, ii, 601–3.

Natowicz, M. R., Alper, J. K. and Alper, J. S. (1992). Genetic discrimination and the law. *American Journal of Human Genetics*, 50, 465–75.

Weil, J. (1991). Mothers' post-counseling beliefs about the causes of their children's genetic disorders. *American Journal of Human Genetics*, 48, 145–53.

Further Reading

Andrews, L. B., Fullarton, J. E., Holtzman, N. A. and Motulsky, A. (eds) (1994). *Assessing Genetic Risks: implications for health and social policy*. Washington, DC: National Academy Press.

226

Annas, G. J. and Elias, S. (eds) (1992). *Gene Mapping: using law and ethics as guides.* New York and Oxford: Oxford University Press.

Bosk, C. L. (1992). *All God's Mistakes: genetic counselling in a pediatric hospital.* Chicago: University of Chicago Press.

Clarke, A. (1990). Genetics, ethics and audit. *Lancet,* 335, 1145–7.

—— (1991). Is non-directive genetic counselling possible? *Lancet,* 338, 998–1001.

—— (1995). Population screening for genetic susceptibility to disease. *British Medical Journal,* 311, 35–8.

Clarke, A., Parsons, E. and Williams, A. (1996). Outcomes and process in genetic counselling. *Clinical Genetics,* 50, 462–9.

Clarke, A. (ed.) (1994). *Genetic Counselling: practice and principles.* London and New York: Routledge. [Volume in Professional Ethics series, series eds R. Chadwick and A. Belsey).

Clinical Genetics Society Working Party (1994). The genetic testing of children. *Journal of Medical Genetics,* 31, 785–97.

Davison, C., Frankel, S. and Smith, G. D. (1992). The limits of lifestyle: re-assessing 'fatalism' in the popular culture of illness prevention. *Social Science and Medicine,* 34, 675–85.

Davison, C., Macintyre, S. and Smith, G. D. (1994). The potential social impact of predictive genetic testing for susceptibility to common chronic diseases: a review and proposed research agenda. *Sociology of Health and Illness,* 16, 340–71.

Duster, T. (1990). *Backdoor to Eugenics.* New York and London: Routledge.

Fost, N. (1993). Genetic diagnosis and treatment: ethical considerations. *American Journal of Diseases of Children,* 147, 1190–5.

Harper, P. S. (1993). Insurance and genetic testing. *Lancet,* 341, 224–7.

Harper, P. S. and Clarke, A. (1990). Should we test children for 'adult' genetic disease? *Lancet,* 335, 1205–6.

—— (1997). *Genetics, Society and Clinical Practice.* Oxford: Bios.

Holtzman, N. A. (1992). The diffusion of new genetic tests for predicting disease. *FASEB Journal,* 6, 2806–12.

Kessler, S. (1989). Psychological aspects of genetic counselling. VI. A critical review of the literature dealing with education and reproduction. *American Journal of Medical Genetics,* 34, 340–53.

—— (1992). Psychological aspects of genetic counselling. VII. Thoughts on directiveness. *Journal of Genetic Counselling,* 1, 9–17.

Lancet [editorial] (1992). Screening for cystic fibrosis. *Lancet,* 340, 209–10.

Lippman, A. (1992). Led (astray) by genetic maps: the cartography of the human genome and health care. *Social Science and Medicine,* 35, 1469–76.

McClean, S. A. M. (1994). Mapping the human genome – friend or foe? *Social Science and Medicine,* 39, 1221–7.

Marteau, T. and Richards, M. (eds) (1996). *The Troubled Helix: social and psychological implications of the new genetics.* Cambridge: Cambridge University Press.

Murray, T. H. (1991). Ethical issues in human genome research. *FASEB Journal,* 5, 55–60.

Nuffield Council on Bioethics (1993). *Genetic Screening – Ethical Issues.* London: Nuffield Council on Bioethics.

Rothman, B. K. (1986). *The Tentative Pregnancy: prenatal diagnosis and the future of motherhood.* London: Pandora.

Royal College of Physicians Committees on Ethical Issues in Medicine and Clinical Genetics (1991). *Ethical Issues in Clinical Genetics.* London.

ANGUS CLARKE

Wertz, D. C. (1992). Ethical and legal implications of the new genetics: issues for discussion. *Social Science and Medicine*, 35, 495–505.

Wertz, D. C. and Fletcher, J. C. (1993). Prcposed: an international code of ethics for medical genetics. *Clinical Genetics*, 44, 37–43.

Wertz, D. C., Fanos, J. H. and Reilly, P. R. (1994). Genetic testing for children and adolescents: who decides? *Journal of the American Medical Association*, 272, 875–81.

PART VII

LIFE AND DEATH ISSUES

23

Medical decisions at the end of life

DAN W. BROCK

No other area of bioethics has captured public interest and concern more than medical decisions at the end of life. In many countries the issues have also been the subject of court cases (Cruzan, 1990; Bland, 1993), government commissions and studies (President's Commission, 1983; the Remmelink Report, Maas, 1991), professional debate and professional policy guidelines (The Hastings Center, 1987). In this chapter I shall develop a general ethical framework for these decisions and focus on a few of the central ethical controversies about them.

An Ethical Framework for Treatment Decision-making

Medical decisions at the end of life are only a subset of medical decisions generally, though one key set of controversies is whether the ethical issues are different when life itself is at stake. Thus, in developing the decision-making framework, we can take as an initial guide the ethical values that should guide all health-care treatment decision-making, guide it both in the sense of determining the proper roles of the typical parties to these decisions, as well as guiding the decision-makers in the content of their decisions. In nearly all countries, historical tradition and practice in medicine, sometimes labelled physician paternalism, saw the physician as the principal decision-maker because of his or her superior knowledge, training and experience regarding the patient's medical condition and prognosis, together with possible treatments that might improve that prognosis. With the enormous increase in recent decades in scientific and medical knowledge and treatment capabilities, we might expect these inequalities between physicians and patients to be greater still today and thus more firmly to support locating decision-making authority with the physician.

Yet a fundamental change in medicine over the last few decades, perhaps most advanced in the United States but present to some degree in many countries, has been the rejection of physician paternalism in favour of shared decision-making between physicians and patients, with a new, more important role for patients in decisions about their treatment. There are many reasons for this historical shift, some external to medicine itself and located in broader societal and cultural changes, some internal to medicine and changes in it. Among the external factors, perhaps the most important have been various consumer-rights movements

231

DAN W. BROCK

and general challenges to established authority. Within medicine, there has been an important change in the conception of medicine's fundamental goals. Traditionally, those goals were understood as the preservation and promotion of the patient's life and health, about both of which it was reasonable to believe the physician, not the patient, possessed the relevant expertise.

In the newer model of shared decision-making, the fundamental values guiding that process are commonly conceived to be two – promoting the patient's well-being and respecting his or her self-determination. How does well-being differ from the older conception of life and health? Health, and in turn how it is best promoted, is typically understood as an objective matter determined by biological and medical science. The concept of well-being is designed to signal the respects in which the fundamental goal of medicine is in part subjectively determined by the particular patient's aims and values. What best serves the patient's well-being depends on which alternative treatment, including the alternative of no treatment, best furthers the patient's overall values and plan of life. The task for the physician is to use his or her medical skills to promote the patient's well-being in this sense, and to do so typically requires the patient's participation in treatment decision-making in order to bring knowledge of the patient's own values and plan of life into the decision-making process. With the increased number of alternative modes of treatment for common disease processes, there is often no one mode of treatment that is best for all patients with a particular medical condition, so the patient's participation in decision-making is necessary to determine which alternative will best serve his or her well-being.

The other fundamental ethical value at stake in treatment decision-making is individual self-determination. Self-determination, as it bears on treatment decision-making, is the interest of ordinary persons in making significant decisions about their lives for themselves, according to their own values or conception of a good life, and in being left free by other persons, at least within limits, to act on those decisions. By the exercise of self-determination, we have substantial control over our lives and the kind of person we become, and thereby take responsibility for our lives. The capacity to direct our lives in this way is the central basis of the moral requirement of respect for persons and the source of human dignity. Patient self-determination is fundamental for health-care treatment decision-making because it is the patient, and the patient's body, that will undergo any treatment; it is the principal legal and moral basis for the requirement of informed consent in health care. It grounds the increasingly broad consensus about patients' rights to decide about treatment, according to the patient's conception of the relative benefits and burdens of different treatment alternatives, and to refuse any treatment. It is important to recognize that sometimes patients may make treatment choices in the exercise of their self-determination that are bad, foolish or irrational and do not best serve their well-being even as determined by their own values. The importance of self-determination implies that even bad choices of competent patients must be respected.

In medical decisions near the end of life, and in particular in decisions about life-sustaining treatment, these values if anything strengthen the general case for

patients' rights to make treatment decisions. In the debilitated and severely compromised condition of many patients near the end of life, patients often become
more concerned with maintaining their comfort, quality of life and dignity than
with extending their lives. Patients sometimes reach a point at which they decide
that the best life possible for them with life-sustaining treatment is sufficiently poor
that it is worse than no further life at all, and so decide to forgo any further life-
sustaining treatment. But there is no objectively correct point for all persons at
which further treatment and the life it sustains are no longer a benefit, but are
instead a burden and without value or meaning. There are only the decisions of
different competent patients about that point.

This ethical framework for treatment decision-making entitles a competent
patient to weigh the benefits and burdens of alternative treatments according to his
or her own values, to refuse any treatment and to select from among available
alternative treatments. However, in many medical treatment decisions at the
end of life, the patient is incompetent, so a surrogate will have to decide for the
patient. For several reasons, common medical practice is to turn to a close family
member to act as the patient's surrogate decision-maker: first, that is usually who
the patient would want to be his or her surrogate; second, that is usually who
knows best what the patient would have wanted and who is most concerned
about the patient's care; third, the family is the social unit in most societies to
which principal responsibility is assigned to care for dependent or incompetent
members. In the case of a previously competent adult patient, there are three
relevant principles to guide surrogate decision-making (see also the essay on advance directives in chapter 26, pp. 261–71). The advance directives principle
requires the surrogate to follow any instructions or preferences relevant to the
treatment choice in the patient's advance directive if one exists. If there is no
advance directive, the substitute judgement principle requires the surrogate to use
his or her knowledge of the patient to attempt to make the decision that the patient
would have made in the circumstances that then obtain, if the patient were
competent. The advance directives and substitute judgement principles respect
the patient's self-determination as much as possible when the patient is incompetent and unable to make decisions for him- or herself. If the surrogate has little or
no relevant knowledge of the patient's concerns and values. then the decision
will have to be guided by the best interests principle which looks to what
most reasonable persons would want in the circumstances. In the case of a patient
who has never been competent, there are no values of the patient to be respected
and the surrogate will have to be guided by an assessment of the patient's best
interests.

There is a general presumption that this framework for all treatment decision-
making for competent and incompetent patients applies in particular to life-
sustaining treatments, but special issues arise which some persons believe place
additional ethical limits on morally permissible treatment decisions when life itself
is at stake. We will explore some of those issues in the rest of this chapter. But first
we will take up a direct challenge to the rights of patients or their surrogates in the
case of futile treatment.

Futile Treatment

Sometimes dying patients or, more commonly, the families of incompetent dying patients, insist on treatment that the patients' physicians believe would be futile. Probably the most common example is insistence that an attempt be made to resuscitate the patient in the case of cardiac or respiratory arrest, but other examples include insistence that a dying patient be placed in the intensive care unit (ICU). Does the decision-making framework we have just sketched require physicians to provide futile treatment when families demand it? In many countries of the world, including developed countries like England and Japan, significant deference to physicians' recommendations makes insistence on futile treatment uncommon. But when it occurs it is crucial to distinguish several different senses of futile treatment. 'Physiological futility' covers treatment that is known with the highest medical certainty cannot produce the physiological effect in the patient for which the patient or family want it. This is an issue on which physicians should be expert and provides the strongest case for their refusing to provide the treatment. but probably few actual cases fit physiological futility. What has been called 'quantitative futility' is when there is only a very low probability, for example, no more than 1 per cent, of a treatment having the hoped-for effect; for example, the possibility of patients with widely metastatic cancer surviving resuscitation to leave the hospital (Schneiderman, 1990). What has been called 'evaluative futility' is treatment that it is agreed is likely to have a particular physiological effect in the patient, but there is disagreement about whether the effect is a benefit for, or would be wanted by, the patient; for example, ICU care for a patient in a persistent vegetative state. The crucial question for physicians refusing to provide a treatment because of quantitative or evaluative futility is why the physician's judgement of whether a benefit is likely enough to be worth pursuing, or whether a particular effect would be a benefit, should override the patient's or surrogate's different judgement and values, since it is the patient who will be most affected by the decision. The policy debate about futile treatment concerns how to restrict physicians' rights to refuse to provide futile treatment to the relatively uncontroversial cases, such as physiological futility, and prevent their denial of patients' or families' right to make treatment decisions according to their own. not the physicians'. values.

Ordinary and Extraordinary Treatment

Traditionally, a distinction was sometimes made between treatments that may be permissibly forgone from those that must be applied, especially in the case of a surrogate deciding for an incompetent patient. In this view, a patient need not accept extraordinary or heroic measures, but ordinary measures must be provided. One issue is how the two kinds of treatments are distinguished. Among the possible interpretations are invasive versus non-invasive, common versus unusual, high technology versus simple, costly versus inexpensive treatments and so forth. Since there are many possible understandings of this distinction, unless it is well-defined, use of it is likely in practice to generate confusion about which treatments are ordinary or extraordinary. However, for interpretations of the distinction like those just cited, it cannot mark a defensible distinction between obligatory and optional treatments. Why, for example, should whether a treatment employs high technology, such as renal dialysis or respirator support, or is relatively simple, such as antibiotics, make the former optional and the latter obligatory. In some circumstances, dialysis or respirator treatment will be on balance clearly beneficial for a patient and so would be wanted, whereas in other circumstances a patient may find the life sustained by those treatments of such poor quality and limited duration that it is without benefit and unwanted. But the same is true of antibiotics which will usually, but not always, be of benefit for patients with treatable infections. What seems morally important and determines whether any treatment should be employed in particular circumstances with a particular patient is not whether the treatment employs high technology or is simple, but whether the patient judges it to be on balance beneficial.

The distinction between ordinary and extraordinary treatment probably originated within Roman Catholic moral theology, where extraordinary treatment is understood as treatment which is excessively burdensome or without benefit for the patient. Since whether a treatment is excessively burdensome depends on whether it produces sufficient benefits to outweigh its burdens, this interpretation of the ordinary–extraordinary distinction does mark a morally important difference between treatments – whether they are on balance beneficial to a particular patient – but adds nothing to the general benefits–burdens ethical framework we developed above. However, since the distinction has so many different interpretations, most of which do not mark morally important differences between treatments, its use can lead to confusion and to giving moral weight to differences between treatments that are not morally important. Moreover, the distinction has suggested to many that it should be possible to classify different treatments, such as nutrition and hydration or dialysis, as always either ordinary or extraordinary, and so as always either obligatory or optional. But on the beneficial–excessively burdensome distinction, any kind of treatment like nutrition and hydration or dialysis will sometimes be ordinary, sometimes extraordinary, depending on a particular patient's condition and values. Since the ordinary–extraordinary distinction can lead to these kinds of confusions, but in its traditional and morally significant interpretation adds nothing to the general benefits–burdens framework, it has been increasingly rejected as not helpful to decisions about life support, at least in secular contexts outside of its origins in Roman Catholicism.

Killing and Allowing to Die

It is widely accepted that physicians must respect their patients' decisions to be allowed to die, but that killing is morally different and rarely, if ever, to be deliberately done. The import of this issue for physician-assisted suicide and euthanasia is addressed in the essay in this volume on 'Voluntary Euthanasia, Suicide and Physician-assisted Suicide' (chapter 27, pp. 272–9), but we shall address here the nature and moral importance of the difference between killing and allowing to die,

235

as well as its application to decisions about life-support. The nature of the difference between killing and allowing to die is morally important if, as many believe, allowing to die can be morally justified in circumstances in which killing would not be; if there is no moral difference between the two it is not morally important how we distinguish between them. Although I will argue briefly that killing is no more seriously wrong than allowing to die, most people believe differently, so I shall first address the nature of the difference and then consider its moral significance. The most common way of differentiating killing from allowing to die is as the difference between acts and omissions resulting in death. A person kills if he or she does an action that causes someone to die who otherwise would not have died; for example, we are in a boat, I know that you cannot swim, so I push you out of the boat and you drown and die. A person allows someone to die if he or she has the ability and opportunity to prevent someone from dying, knows this, but does not act to prevent the death, and the person dies; for example, we are in a boat, you accidentally fall overboard, I know that you cannot swim, but I deliberately do not throw you an available lifebelt, and you drown and die.

Suppose that something close to this distinction between actions and omissions resulting in death correctly captures the difference between killing and allowing to die – is that difference morally significant? It is important to be clear about the meaning of this question because it is easily and often misunderstood. It may be the case that most actual instances of killing, at least outside the medical context, are morally worse, all things considered, than most instances of allowing to die. For example, the motives of most who kill are probably worse than the motives of most who allow to die, and the agent's motives are usually important in our overall moral evaluation of what was done; also the cost to the potential agent in killing is typically less than the cost or burden of not allowing anyone to die. But the moral evaluation, all things considered, of concrete cases of killing or of allowing to die is not what is at issue. Rather, the issue is whether killing is, in itself, morally worse than allowing to die; that is, whether a particular instance of killing is worse, other things being equal, than an instance of allowing to die just because it is killing and not allowing to die. Philosophers who have argued for the moral equivalence of the two have usually used an argument that compares two cases that differ in no other potentially morally relevant respect except that one is killing and the other allowing to die. Here is James Rachels' (1975) well-known example of two such cases:

In the first, Smith stands to gain a large inheritance if anything should happen to his six-year-old cousin. One evening, while the child is taking his bath, Smith sneaks into the bathroom and drowns the child, and then arranges things so that it will look like an accident.

In the second, Jones also stands to gain if anything happens to his six-year-old cousin. Like Smith, Jones sneaks in planning to drown the child in his bath. However, just as he enters the bathroom Jones sees the child slip and hit his head, and fall face down in the water. Jones is delighted; he stands by, ready to push the child's head back under if it is necessary, but it is not necessary. With only a little thrashing about, the child drowns all by himself, 'accidentally,' as Jones watches and does nothing.

Rachels invites us to reflect on whether we believe that what Smith, who kills, does is any worse than what Jones, who allows to die, does. If we decide, as he believes we will, that there is no moral difference between the two cases, then the mere fact that one is killing, the other allowing to die, is not a morally important difference. Moreover, if the descriptive or empirical difference of being killing or allowing to die does not contribute to any moral difference between the two, then it is not clear why it should in any other case, since the descriptive difference will be the same there. Whether killing is any worse morally than allowing to die remains controversial, but since most people believe that all decisions to forgo life-sustaining treatment are cases of allowing to die, it might seem not to matter here whether the moral equivalence thesis is true. Consider a standard case of forgoing life support.

A clearly competent patient with ALS disease (amytrophic lateral sclerosis, or Lou Gehrig's disease) has progressed to the point where she no longer has control over any bodily movements and is completely respirator-dependent for breathing. Her condition is progressive and irreversible; she has made a firm decision that she no longer wants to go on in this condition and asks her physician to remove the respirator and allow her to die.

It is now widely accepted that such a patient's physician may, indeed should, respect her wishes and remove her from the respirator, though it is certain that this will cause her death. Had the patient decided before she was placed on the respirator that she did not want this treatment when she could no longer breathe on her own, this too would typically have been understood as a decision to be allowed to die. Although both not starting and stopping life-support in cases such as these are commonly understood as allowing to die, not killing, I believe that is mistaken and that when the physician removes the patient from the respirator he kills the patient. To see why this is so, consider a case exactly like the last except that:

> the patient with ALS disease has a greedy son who mistakenly believes that his mother will never stop treatment and fears that his inheritance will be used up by her lengthy and costly hospitalization. So he slips into her room while she is sedated, extubates her and she dies. However, the medical staff finds out what he has done and when confronted with having killed his mother, the son replies, 'I didn't kill her, I merely allowed her to die. It was her ALS disease that caused her death.'

I believe that we would and should reject this as transparent sophistry – the son went into his mother's room and deliberately killed her. But he performed just the same physical action that the physician did in the first case, so that if the son kills it seems the physician does so as well.

Now of course this is not to say that there are no important moral differences that make what the son does morally wrong and what the physician does morally justified. The physician acts with the patient's consent, with a good motive to respect the patient's wishes and in a social role in which he is authorized to stop the treatment, whereas the son had no such consent, a bad motive to protect his inheritance and was not in any role that authorized his action. For these reasons

237

DAN W. BROCK

the physician acts rightly and the son acts wrongly, but this does not mean that they do not both kill, only that one kills justifiably whereas the other kills wrongly. One can kill or allow to die with or without the victim's consent, with a good or bad motive and in or not in a social role that authorizes such action; these factors determine whether what was done was morally justified, not whether it is a case of killing or allowing to die.

This argument appeals ultimately to the reader's intuitions about whether the physician kills or allows to die, as tested by the relevant similar case of the greedy son. But we can also apply the act–omission interpretation of the difference between killing and allowing to die directly to what the physician does. When the physician removes the breathing tube that is supplying oxygen to the patient and turns off the respirator he performs an action that causes the patient to die when otherwise she would have continued to live, that is, he kills. On the other hand, suppose the physician had not intubated the patient when she initially went into respiratory distress because of the patient's prior decision to refuse that treatment; then he would have allowed her to die.

Those who construe these cases of stopping life-support as allowing to die usually have something like the following account of the cases in mind. The patient has a potentially lethal disease that is being prevented from causing the patient's death by the physician's intervention with a life-sustaining treatment, such as a respirator. When the treatment is withdrawn, even though that requires a physical action by the physician, the patient is allowed to die because the disease process is allowed to proceed unimpeded to the patient's death. We cannot pursue all the difficulties with this account except to note that it would require us to accept that the greedy son also does not kill, but only allows his mother to die.

Even when both not starting and stopping life-support are considered allowing to die, some patients, families and physicians believe stopping cannot be morally justified in some circumstance in which not starting would be morally justified; in this view, the difference between stopping and not starting life-support is itself morally important, even when all other circumstances are the same. The following case displays the difficulty with this position:

> A very gravely ill patient comes into a hospital emergency room from a nursing home and is sent up to the intensive care unit. The patient begins to develop respiratory failure that is likely to require intubation very soon. At that point the patient's family members and long-standing attending physician arrive at the ICU and inform the ICU staff that there had been extensive discussion about future care with the patient when he was unquestionably competent. Given his grave and terminal illness, as well as his state of debilitation, the patient had firmly rejected being placed on a respirator under any circumstances, and the family and physician produce the patient's living will to that effect. Most would hold that this patient should not be intubated and placed on a respirator against his will. Suppose now that the situation is exactly the same except that the attending physician and family are slightly delayed in traffic and arrive fifteen minutes later just after the patient has been intubated and placed on the respirator. Can this difference be of any moral importance? Could it possibly justify morally a refusal by the staff to remove the patient from the respirator? Do not the very same

238

circumstances that justified not placing the patient on the respirator now justify taking him off it? Do not factors like the patient's condition, prognosis, and firmly expressed competent wishes morally determine what should be done, not whether we do not start, or fifteen minutes later stop, the respirator? Why should the stop/not start difference matter morally at all?

Indeed in practice, there is often an important reason to stop life-support that did not exist earlier not to start it. Often the decision to start a life-sustaining treatment like respiratory support is made in conditions of uncertainty about whether it will provide a hoped for benefit. If it is tried and proves not to provide the hoped-for benefit, the initial uncertainty is removed and there is then reason to stop the treatment which did not exist earlier not to start it. What is morally important is the risks and benefits of a treatment, not whether it is started or must be stopped.

Treating Pain and the Doctrine of Double Effect

With some dying patients, especially cancer patients, it can become necessary to administer increasingly large doses of analgesics to alleviate the patient's pain, which in turn has increasingly higher risks of causing respiratory depression and hastening the patient's death. There is substantial evidence that the pain of dying patients is inadequately treated, and one reason may be the fear that doing so will cause the patient's earlier death, that is, kill the patient. Since it is widely held that it is morally wrong for physicians, or indeed anyone, deliberately or intentionally to kill a patient, is treating pain at the risk of causing the patient's death therefore wrong, or can it be morally justified? Few would hold that patients must be forced to endure and die in agony in order to avoid the possibility of hastening their earlier death, but there is disagreement about why this is so. One line of justification focuses on the physician's intention, which is to relieve the patient's suffering, as distinguished from the possible unintended but foreseen side-effect of hastening the patient's death. This distinction invokes what is sometimes called the 'doctrine of double effect', according to which an action with a bad effect (the patient's death) can be justified if that effect is not intended and is necessary to achieve a proportionately good effect (relief of the patient's suffering) (Bole, 1991). There are cases in which it is difficult to determine whether a bad effect, such as hastening the patient's death, is intended or merely foreseen but unintended (e.g., the patient says that she wants to die and so asks the physician to stop life-support), but at least in the case of pain and symptom control, it seems intuitively clear that the patient's death is not intended, whereas it would be if the physician instead performed euthanasia by deliberately giving the patient a lethal injection. According to the doctrine of double effect, the first action can be morally permissible whereas the latter is morally prohibited.

Critics of the appeal to double effect do not argue that we must leave a dying patient's pain inadequately treated so as to avoid the risk of hastening his or her death, but only that the distinction between whether a death is intended or foreseen but unintended cannot support the great moral difference between permissible and

239

DAN W. BROCK

impermissible killing. In the case of euthanasia, just as in pain and symptom control, critics maintain, the physician's end may be the good one of relieving the patient's suffering. In neither case would death be wanted by the patient or the physician if the suffering could be avoided without it, but both patient and physician may be prepared to accept the patient's earlier death in order to relieve his or her suffering. Although the patient's death in the case of euthanasia may be the necessary means taken in the causal path to relief of suffering, it is the unavoidable side-effect following upon the relief of the patient's suffering in the causal path taken to achieve pain and symptom control. Together these similarities throw into question whether the appeal to intentions in the doctrine of double effect can ground such an important moral difference between permissible and impermissible killing.

Some base the moral difference on the certainty of the patient's death in euthanasia, whereas in pain and symptom control, it only becomes increasingly probable. A difference in the probability of the bad outcome of death is morally relevant in many circumstances, but it cannot help the defender of double effect because it is entirely independent of the distinction at the heart of double effect – whether the bad effect is intended or not. Moreover, sometimes the likelihood of hastening death from adequate pain and symptom control becomes so high that the very small difference between it and the certainty of death in euthanasia could not plausibly support the very great moral difference between permissible and impermissible killing.

An alternative justification for risking hastening death in order to treat pain holds that the physician is morally responsible for all the foreseen consequences of what he does, whether intended or foreseen but unintended; for example, a surgeon is responsible for his patient's unintended death in the course of a high-risk operative procedure. What justifies his operating is the prospect of sufficient benefit from the procedure to warrant undertaking the risk of death after securing the patient's consent to the operation when fully informed of its risks, benefits and alternatives. Likewise, in this view what justifies the measures for pain and symptom control is not a matter of the physician's intentions, but rather the patient's request for pain relief knowing that it risks hastening his death.

Conclusion

There is increasingly widespread agreement about the rights of competent patients, as well as the surrogates of incompetent patients, to decide about life-support – they can refuse any treatment and select from available alternative treatments. But substantial differences remain between different countries in the degree of consensus about these rights, as well as in the degree to which public policy (in the form of law and other professional norms) recognizes and protects them. In every country, substantial work remains to be done to ensure that everyday medical practice respects these rights. Even when it is accepted, the ethical framework for these decisions, which we have sketched here, can only guide decision-makers and decision-making; many of these decisions will remain complex, uncertain and agonizing for the those involved in them. And other debates concerning the care of dying patients, in particular, the debate over physician-assisted suicide and euthanasia, such as practised in the Netherlands and recently legalized for a brief period in one territory of Australia, extend beyond any ethical framework for life-sustaining treatment decisions and are only in their early stages, with their ultimate resolution far from clear.

References

Airedale NHS Trust (Respondents) v. Bland, House of Lords, Judgement, 4 February 1993.

Bole, T. J. (ed.) (1991). Double effect: theoretical function and bioethical implications. *Journal of Medicine and Philosophy*, 16, 467–585. [Special issue.]

Cruzan, V. (1990). Director, Mo. Dept. of Health, 110 S.CT. 2841.

Hastings Center (1987). *Guidelines on the Termination of Treatment and Care of the Dying.* Bloomington: Indiana University Press.

President's Commission for the Study of Ethical Problems in Medicine (1983). *Deciding to Forgo Life-sustaining Treatment.* Washington, DC: US Government Printing Office. .

Rachels, J. (1975). Active and passive euthanasia. *New England Journal of Medicine*, 292/2, 78–80.

Schneiderman, L. J., Jecker, N. S. and Jonsen, A. R. (1990). Medical futility: its meaning and ethical implications. *Annals of Internal Medicine*, 112, 949–54.

van der Maas, P. J. et al. (1991). Euthanasia and other medical decisions concerning the end of life. *Lancet*, 338, 669–74.

Further Reading

Brock, D. W. (1993). *Life and Death: philosophical essays in biomedical ethics.* Cambridge: Cambridge University Press.

Buchanan, A. E. and Brock, D. W. (1989). *Deciding for Others: the ethics of surrogate decision making.* Cambridge: Cambridge University Press.

Kuhse, H. (1987). *The Sanctity of Life Doctrine in Medicine.* Oxford: Oxford University Press.

Lynn, J. (ed.) (1986). *Forgoing Life-sustaining Food and Water.* Bloomington: Indiana University Press.

Steinbock, B. (ed.) (1990). *Killing and Letting Die*, 2nd edn. Englewood Cliffs, NJ: Prentice-Hall.

Weir, R. F. (1989). *Abating Treatment with Critically Ill Patients.* Oxford: Oxford University Press.

24

Severely disabled newborns

EIKE-HENNER W. KLUGE

The birth of a child should be a joyous event. Sometimes, however, it is a tragedy. In particular, this may be the case when the newborn infant suffers from such serious birth defects that it is not expected to live, even with aggressive and sophisticated medical intervention. Under such circumstances, parents or other decision-makers face several choices: to use all available medical means to keep the child alive as long as possible; to let the child die, providing only comfort measures; or actively to terminate the suffering of the child by taking its life as quickly and painlessly as possible.

Similarly, it is tragic when the baby may live if he or she is appropriately treated but there is no reasonable expectation that he or she will grow up to enjoy an acceptable quality of life. Here again, choices have to be made: to take aggressive measures to keep the child alive and ameliorate the effects of the deficits as much as possible; to take whatever medical measures are necessary to keep the child alive but refrain from trying to deal with the deficits because these are perceived to be untreatable; to let the child die, providing only comfort measures; or to terminate the life of the child as quickly and painlessly as possible (Kuhse and Singer, 1985).

The decisions that have to be made in these and similar circumstances are fraught with personal, conceptual and ethical difficulties. The *personal* difficulties centre around the psychological reaction of the parents to the situation. While most prospective parents are aware of the theoretical possibility that an offspring may be severely disabled, this possibility tends not to be taken seriously until it actually occurs. Even when parents know for certain that their offspring may be severely disabled and have made plans for dealing with the situation, the birth itself, and the need to make choices here and now, adds a psychological element that is absent from previous deliberations.

The *conceptual* difficulties cluster around the notions that define the situation itself, particularly the notions of defect, suffering and quality of life. What does it mean to be told that a newborn is 'severely defective', that the child faces a low quality of life and is better off dead? How is 'quality of life' to be understood here, and how is it to be measured? What does suffering mean in these cases, and how is it to be determined? What is meant by saying that the newborn is 'better off dead'?

Ethically, questions of decision-making assume central importance. Who should make such decisions? What criteria should they use? And if it is decided that the newborn is 'better off dead', how should such a decision be put into practice?

Should the baby be allowed to die? Should the baby be made to die? Is there an ethically relevant difference?

Conceptual Issues

'Quality of life'

Beginning with quality of life, it is generally agreed that if the quality of life of a newborn infant will be exceedingly low because of her or his disabilities, then the infant need not be kept alive but may be either made or allowed to die (President's Commission. 1983; Tooley, 1983; Weir, 1984; Magnet and Kluge, 1985; McMillan, Engelhardt and Spicker, 1987; Doyal et al., 1994). It is therefore very important to be clear about what the phrase actually means.

However, its meaning is anything but clear. For instance, some quality-of-life measures define quality of life objectively by focusing on the ability of the individual to function materially in society; others use a subjective approach and focus on the experiences of the individual, and on her or his life satisfaction; still others attempt to combine both subjective and objective elements in order to arrive at what is considered a more balanced scale (Shumaker and Berzon, 1995). However, there is no agreement on which quality-of-life measure is appropriate in general, and for newborns in particular. This presents complications.

The situation is complicated further by the fact that those quality-of-life measures which have a subjective component usually focus on the quality of life as it is *currently* being experienced. While this may be appropriate in most cases, it is arguably inappropriate in the case of newborn children. The reason is that in the case of newborns, focusing on the quality of life as it is currently being experienced takes only their present awareness of the nature and impact of their disabilities into account. Since at this stage of their development, newborns are only aware at the level of sensations, this may lead to the conclusion, in particular cases, that the quality of life is low but within acceptable limits because the newborn experiences no pain.

However, when one broadens the concept of quality of life beyond the momentary and so to speak contemporary viewpoint and expands it to include a longitudinal outlook, then one has to take into account the children's growing awareness, as they mature, of the nature and implications of their disabilities. From this perspective, the conclusion may be entirely different. The children's increasing awareness of their disabilities may have such a severe impact on them that they may experience extreme psychological suffering and wish that they had never been born. No currently available quality-of-life measure takes this evolving parameter of world experience and awareness into account. However, it is arguable that to make a decision about the quality of life of newborns without taking this into account is to operate with a naive and truncated notion of quality of life.

The ability to formulate life plans and expectations, and to experience the world in a cognitively significant fashion, is characteristically human (Tooley, 1983). Therefore, when severely disabled newborns may survive if they are appropriately treated, then the question whether these newborns have the capacity to develop a world-view, or to formulate life plans and to experience the world in a cognitively significant fashion, should form an integral part of any quality-of-life measure that is going to be used to decide whether the quality of their lives is worth living. Some severely disabled newborns will never be able to develop in this direction. Therefore, arguably, such an inability should be seen as an impoverishment of the quality of their lives. Yet these considerations play only an ambiguous and certainly non-standardized role in quality-of-life based decisions about whether severely disabled newborn children should be treated, kept alive or made/allowed to die.

Disability

The notion of disability suffers from similar shortcomings. On one level, the concept is fairly clear. For instance, neonates who are born with an open spine, part of the spinal chord extruded and suffering from incontinence, lower body paralysis, hydrocephalus and severe brain damage are biologically compromised and require medical intervention to stay alive. Such children can never participate in the activities in which children normally engage; and if they survive at all, they will not be able to live the kind of life that most persons can live. They will require constant medical treatment, and need assistance for all their activities of daily living. Therefore in an intuitively obvious sense, such newborns are severely disabled as compared to other persons.

Likewise, a newborn who suffers from something like Tay-Sachs disease – which involves the progressive and irreversible deterioration of the nervous system ultimately leading to death by the age of 6 – suffers from a medically identifiable condition that is disabling in a readily identifiable sense. The same thing is true of an infant who is born without arms and legs, a malformed heart and a blockage in her oesophagus that prevents ingested food from reaching her stomach.

All of these are not merely cases of disability but of severe disability. On the other hand, infants who are born with a cleft palate, rudimentary intellectual capacity or similar conditions are not quite as disabled; and children who are born with impaired vision or hearing, with learning or attention deficits, etc., are disabled, but less severely still. And so on.

Using this sort of approach, one can build up a more or less clear and graduated notion of what counts as a *disability*, what counts as a *severe* disability and what counts as a mere inconvenience. It also becomes clear that the notion of disability has a comparative component which to some degree is tied to the ability of the society into which the child is born to provide remedies for dealing with the problems that are faced by the child.

However, the notion as thus understood requires that the disabling condition manifest itself here and now. It therefore excludes so-called late-onset diseases such as Huntington's disease, where the deterioration of cognitive and bodily functions will not occur until decades later in life. It is arguable that even though the relevant deficits are not experienced immediately, the presence of such genetic determinants also constitutes a disability (Kluge, 1992).

244

Further, some infants are born anencephalic: with an open skull and without any brain except a brainstem. Unless all the technology of modern medicine is used to its fullest extent, this condition is incompatible with life. At first glance, therefore, anencephaly is a prime example of a severe disability. However, while anencephalics are unquestionably human beings in the sense of being members of the species *Homo sapiens*, it is arguable that they are not persons – if by 'person' is meant someone who has the capacity for sentience and cognitive awareness at some level (Tooley, 1983; Kuhse and Singer, 1985; Magnet and Kluge, 1985; Kluge, 1992). Are anencephalic newborns therefore severely disabled *persons* – or are they merely (severely disabled) human beings in a purely biological sense? The issue is important because how it is answered determines whether anencephalics should be the subject of the same ethical considerations that are prima facie relevant in the case of other severely defective newborns.

'Better off dead'

Some have argued that under certain circumstances, a severely disabled newborn may be 'better off dead', while others have countered this by saying that the claim that a newborn would be 'better off dead' is conceptually flawed. Their argument is that, in order to say that someone is better off under one set of conditions rather than another, that person must exist in order for her or his life to be a subject of comparison. However, someone who is dead does not exist and therefore has no life. Therefore how can there be such a comparison (Annas, 1981; Steinbock and McClamrock, 1994)?

The responses to this have been varied. One particulary noteworthy reply has been to accept the argument but to reject its conclusion: it is not that the newborn is better off under one set of circumstances than another but that human life must meet a minimal subjectively experienced qualitative standard (Steinbock and McClamrock, 1994). When this is not possible, then the very fact of living constitutes a continuous injury to the newborn who is being kept alive. To keep the newborn alive is to impose on the child a life that most other persons would not want to live and which, given the chance, they would want to leave. Therefore the decision to end such a life – or to allow it to end – is merely making a proxy decision on behalf of the severely disabled newborn, using quality-of-life criteria that the newborn would be likely to use if she or he were in a position to make a decision. (See also the essay on 'Patients Doubtfully Capable and Incapable of Consent', chapter 43, pp. 452–62.)

Decision Issues

Decision-makers

This of course brings a whole series of other questions in its train. For instance, who should make the decision, using which criteria? There is general agreement that parents, in consultation with physicians, are the appropriate decision-makers

245

because they are assumed to have the best interests of their children at heart. There also is general agreement that this is a rebuttable presumption: that when parents base their decisions on personal values that are not shared by the rest of society, and when the use of these values would disadvantage the newborn compared to other newborns, then the parents are no longer the appropriate decision-makers. The courts should appoint someone else to make the relevant decisions (Gaylin and Macklin, 1982).

Criteria

It is generally agreed that the decision-makers should always have the 'best interests' of their children in mind. Traditionally, it was assumed that 'best interests' were synonymous with life itself. Current thinking accepts that quality-of-life considerations are important, and that newborns should have some capacity for sentient cognitive awareness, enjoyment and the like. Further, a life of unmitigated pain is generally not considered worth living, therefore newborns who look forward only to unmitigated and protracted physical suffering need not be kept alive. In fact, to keep such children alive is to harm them (Engelhardt, 1973; Kuhse and Singer, 1985; Magnet and Kluge, 1985; McMillan, Engelhardt and Spicker, 1987; Steinbock and McClamrock, 1994).

However, agreement on these issues is not universal. Some have argued that this approach devalues people who are disabled by saying that their lives are not worth living; that it introduces an instrumentalistic notion of personhood and sets up standards that someone must meet in order to count as a person. They have also argued that this approach deprives society of the opportunity to develop virtues such as compassion, tolerance and understanding and thereby impoverishes the moral life of society in general (Ashley and O'Rourke, 1982).

Making vs allowing to die

There is also no universal agreement on whether there is an ethically relevant difference between allowing a severely disabled newborn to die and killing the neonate as quickly and painlessly as possible (see also chapter 23, pp. 231–41). One side argues that the two are fundamentally distinct: to bring about the death of a person actively, deliberately and with forethought is to commit murder, whereas to allow a person to die is simply to let nature take its course.

The other side argues that this confuses physics with ethics. Refraining from doing something may determine the eventual outcome just as much as actually doing something (Rachels, 1975). The concept of negligence, and of criminal negligence in particular, rests on this fact. Not using life-saving and/or life-prolonging measures when these could have been used hastens the newborn's death just as surely as killing the newborn by other means. The real issue is not whether the death of the neonate is brought about quickly or slowly through action or inaction but whether attempts should be made to save the child.

Both sides agree that the death of a severely disabled newborn may be appropriate. They differ on the ethical status of the way in which the death is to be brought

246

about. The side favouring letting nature take its course sees nothing morally wrong with not shortening the dying process. It argues that deliberately allowing newborns to die of starvation and dehydration is not to kill them but is simply to allow them to die of their deficits. This, it is said, is morally different from taking active steps to end such children's lives.

The side favouring active termination argues that deliberately starving and dehydrating newborns until they die is not only to kill them, it is to add new elements to their suffering: elements that are distinct from their disabilities and/or the disease processes that affect them. Therefore once it has been decided not to save and/or sustain these newborns, then not to terminate their lives as quickly and painlessly as possible is to behave unethically towards these children.

To this it is sometimes replied that the two cases still differ because the direct agent of death is different in each case. In one case it is the disease process or the condition of the newborns that brings about their death: nature is allowed to take its course. In the other, it is the health-care professional or other relevant agent who is the agent of death (Ashley and O'Rourke, 1982). The reply to this, in turn, is that those who favour inaction and 'letting nature take its course' are merely using the natural course of events – the disease process or the condition of the newborns – as the agent of death, whereas those who favour actively terminating their lives are using some other means. However, agents or tools are morally neutral. The moral difference – if there is any – must lie in the intent with which they are used.

As to intent – so the reply continues – the decision to 'let nature take its course' is not made with the intent of saving the lives of the newborns: it is to allow death to occur. Therefore the intent in both cases is to bring about the death of these children, no matter how artfully or strenuously the decision-maker tries to avoid this realization (Rachels, 1975; Magnet and Kluge, 1985).

Ordinary vs extraordinary means

There is a similar division of opinions about the degree to which medical intervention should be pursued in order to save the lives of severely disabled newborns. Some, like Pope Pius XII (1957) and the Sacred Congregation for the Doctrine of the Faith (1980) have argued that 'ordinary' measures should always be employed to save the lives of severely disabled newborns, but that one is never morally obliged to use 'extraordinary' means. Others, like Ramsey (1970) and Veatch (1976) have argued that the distinction between ordinary and extraordinary means is artificial, question-begging and hopelessly vague. They have argued that whether an intervention is ordinary or extraordinary lies not in the nature of the intervention itself but in the context in which it is employed. Still others (Kluge, 1993) have argued that while the distinction between what is ordinary and what is extraordinary is meaningful, using it in this fashion commits a fundamental error. It is to assume that what is morally obligatory is defined by what is usual or ordinary practice. However, usual or ordinary practice may be morally insufficient. The real question in these cases is not what is usually done, but whether, ethically, attempts should be made to keep the baby alive.

Conclusion

The preceding discussion has dealt with only some of the issues that arise upon the birth of a severely disabled newborn. There are others. For instance, what weight should be attached to the fact that almost invariably, a severely disabled newborn will place a great personal, social and economic burden on the family into which the child is born? What weight should be attached to the burden that the birth of such a child places on the resources that society has at its disposal? Alternatively, what is the moral price that society pays if it does not protect its weakest members, and if it does not go to the limits of what it can do to assist those who cannot help themselves?

These are hard questions. If the current debate over what constitutes appropriate treatment of severely disabled newborn children is any indicator, it will be difficult to provide consistent and, above all, ethically defensible answers. That is not surprising. The birth of a child calls forth our instinctive reactions to save and to protect. The added parameters of disability and need serve only to heighten the intensity of this response, whether it be at the level of the family or at the level of society itself. At the same time, there is also an almost irresistible urge to prevent harm, or at least to minimize its severity and extent.

The challenge, therefore, is to make sure that the needs of the children are not confused with the needs of the parents or of society, and that the values of the latter do not overrule the rights of the children themselves. While there may be conceptual unclarity over many of the issues, this does not mean that the issues should not be clarified; and while there may be competing positions on what weight to accord the different considerations, this does not mean that the issue should not be resolved, lest a tragedy become the occasion for ethical disaster – and with the best of intentions, severely disabled newborns are tortured to life.

References

Annas, George J. (1981). Righting the wrong of 'wrongful life.' *Hastings Center Report*, 11, 1.

Ashley, B. M. and O'Rourke, K. D. (1982). *Health Care Ethics: a theological analysis*. St Louis, MO: Catholic Health Association.

Doyal, L. et al. (1994). Toward guidelines for withholding and withdrawal of life prolonging treatment in neonatal medicine. *Archives of Diseases of Childhood*, 70. [Special issue.]

Engelhardt, H. T. Jr (1973). Euthanasia and children: the injury of continued existence. *Journal of Paediatrics*, 83, 170.

Gaylin, W. and Macklin, R. (eds) (1982). *Who Speaks for the Child?* New York and London: Plenum Press.

Kluge, E.-H. W. (1992). *Biomedical Ethics in a Canadian Context*. Scarborough, Ontario: Prentice-Hall Canada.

Kuhse, H. and Singer, P. (1985). *Should the Baby live? The problem of handicapped infants*. Oxford, New York and Melbourne: Oxford University Press.

McMillan, R. C., Engelhardt, H. T. Jr and Spicker, S. F. (eds) (1987). *Philosophy and Medicine.* Vol. 24. *Euthanasia and the Newborn: Conflicts regarding saving lives.* Dordrecht: D. Reidel.

Magnet, J. E. and Kluge, E.-H. W. (1985). *Withholding Treatment from Defective Newborn Children.* Cowansville, Quebec: Brown Legal Publications.

Pius XII, Pope (1957). Prolongation of life: allocution to an international congress of anaesthesiologists. *Osservatore Romano,* 4.

President's Commission for the Study of Ethical Problems in Medicine and Biomedical and Behavioral Research (1983). *Deciding to Forego Life-sustaining Treatment: A report on the ethical, medical and legal issues in treatment decisions.* Washington, DC: US Government Printing Office.

Rachels, J. (1975). Active and passive euthanasia. *New England Journal of Medicine.* 292, 78–80.

Sacred Congregation for the Doctrine of the Faith (1980). *Declaration on Euthanasia.* Vatican City.

Shumaker, S. A. and Berzon, R. (1995). *The International Assessment of Health-related Quality of Life: Theory, translation, measurement and analysis.* Oxford and New York: Rapid Communications.

Steinbock, B. and McClamrock, R. (1994). When is birth unfair to the child? *Hastings Center Report,* 24/6, 15–21.

Tooley, M. (1983). *An Analysis of Abortion and Infanticide.* Oxford: Clarendon Press.

Veatch, R. (1976). *Death, Dying and the Biological Revolution: our last quest for responsibility.* New Haven and London: Yale University Press.

Weir, R. (1984). *Selective Nontreatment of Handicapped Newborns.* New York: Oxford University Press.

Further Reading

Botkin, J. R. (1990). Delivery room decisions for tiny infants: an ethical analysis. *Journal of Clinical Ethics,* 1/4, 306–11.

Brody, H. and Bartholeme, W. G. (1988). In the best interests of . . . *Hastings Center Report,* 18/6, 37–40.

Hastings Center Research Project on the Care of Imperiled Newborns (1987). Imperiled newborns: a report. *Hastings Center Report,* 17/6, 5–32.

Jonsen, A. R. and Garland, M. (eds) (1976). *Ethics of Newborn Intensive Care.* Berkeley: University of California, Institute of Governmental Studies.

Kuhse, H. (1987). *The Sanctity-of-Life Doctrine in Medicine: A critique.* Oxford: Clarendon Press.

Loewy, E. H. (1991). *Suffering and the Beneficent Community: Beyond libertarianism.* Albany: State University of New York Press.

Nishida, H. (1987). Future ethical issues in neonatology: a Japanese perspective. *Seminars in Perinatology,* 11/3, 274–8.

Qui, R.-Z. (1987). Economic and medical decision-making: a Chinese perspective. *Seminars in Perinatology,* 11/3, 262–3.

Rachels, J. (1986). *The End of Life: euthanasia and morality.* New York and Melbourne: Oxford University Press.

Ramsey, P. (1970). *The Patient as Person.* New Haven and London: Yale University Press.

Veatch, R. M. (1988). Whole-brain, neocortical, and higher brain related concepts. In Richard M. Zaner (ed.), *Death: beyond whole brain criteria.* Dordrecht: Kluwer, 171–86.

25

Brain death, cortical death and persistent vegetative state

JEFF MCMAHAN

Some of us believe that when we die we cease to exist. Others believe that we continue to exist after death, though not in, or in association with, our bodies. Most people seem to agree, however, that when we die we cease to be *here*, though normally our dead bodies remain, for a while anyway. But what is it for one to cease to be here, and how can others tell when one is gone? Again, many people share the conviction that it is necessary and sufficient for one to cease to be here that all possibility of consciousness and mental activity in one's body has been lost. To imagine oneself irreversibly losing all capacity for consciousness or mental activity is, for most of us, to envisage oneself ceasing to be. Similarly, it seems reasonable, on reflection, for those who believe in life after death to accept that one ceases to be with one's body when there ceases to be any possibility of consciousness in one's body. Since the soul is traditionally conceived as the seat of consciousness, the absence of any further possibility of consciousness in the body suggests that the soul has departed. (A conception of the soul that accepts that the soul could exist without the capacity for consciousness may be unappealing, since it raises the possibility of an afterlife devoid of consciousness.)

While we associate or even identify human death with the extinction of consciousness, we also recognize that death is a biological phenomenon that occurs whenever a living being ceases to be alive. The transition from living to non-living may be different in different sorts of living thing – organisms, organs, tissues, cells and so on. In the case of organisms generally, and human organisms in particular, it is widely accepted that death is the irreversible cessation of integrated functioning among the various subsystems that are together constitutive of the organism.

Brain death – the death of the whole brain, or the irreversible loss of functioning in the whole brain – may be understood as a criterion of human death that attempts to capture both of these essential dimensions of death: the irreversible loss of the capacity for consciousness and the irreversible cessation of integrated functioning in the organism as a whole. For the brain functions both to generate consciousness and mental activity and to regulate and integrate the systemic functioning of the organism. Thus it has seemed that, when the whole brain dies, both the capacity for consciousness and the integrated functioning of the organism must disappear without possibility of restoration.

250

There are, or course, other elements in the complete explanation of why brain death has replaced the irreversible cessation of cardiopulmonary functioning as the accepted criterion of death. One is that technologies developed during this century for resuscitating patients in whom respiration and heartbeat have ceased have now rendered the traditional criterion indeterminate in many cases. A person who has lost cardiopulmonary functions may not really be dead if these functions can be restored. So we need to be able to determine when the cessation of these functions can be regarded as irreversible. The best criterion seemed to be the loss of the brain's capacity to sustain them.

There were also practical reasons for the shift to brain death. Respiration and heartbeat can be sustained artificially for a certain period beyond brain death; but, during the interval between brain death and the point at which these functions can no longer be artificially sustained, the body's organs normally deteriorate to such a degree that they become unsuitable for transplantation. The adoption of brain death as the criterion for death allowed physicians to remove patients who met the criterion from respirators, thereby making their organs available for transplantation before they became unusable.

While brain death marks a significant advance beyond the traditional cardiopulmonary criterion of death and has also served reasonably well for purposes of medical and social policy, it is open to serious objections. One significant problem, both for brain death and for other proposed criteria of human death, is that the two essential capacities of the brain noted above – the generation of consciousness and mental activity and the regulation of integrated functioning in the organism – are largely localized in different areas of the brain. It is in the 'higher brain', and in particular the cerebral cortex, which is the outer layer of the cerebrum, that consciousness and mental activity are realized. And it is primarily the 'lower brain', consisting mainly of the brainstem, that coordinates the various somatic functions of the organism. Because the brainstem can survive in a functional state even when the cortex is dead or irreversibly non-functional, the brain can continue to integrate the somatic functions of the organism even when it has lost the capacity to support consciousness and mental activity. When this happens, the organism is said to be in a *persistent vegetative state* (PVS). Similarly, the higher brain can survive and continue to generate consciousness and mental activity even when most of the functional capacities of the lower brain, including most of its regulatory capacities, have been irreversibly lost. Patients in this comparatively rare but horrific condition require intensive life-support and are sometimes described as 'locked in' (Bartlett and Younger, 1988: 205–6). If brain death is the criterion for the death of a human being, then both the patient in a persistent vegetative stage and the locked-in patient remain alive – conclusions that many will find plausible. But notice that this presupposes that neither the capacity for consciousness nor the capacity for internally regulated systemic functioning is essential or necessary for the continued life of a human being. According to the whole-brain criterion, either of these capacities alone is sufficient for continued life. Thus only the loss of *both* is sufficient for death.

One might contend that, since each of these two capacities can occur in the absence of the other, the only appropriate way to recognize the importance of each is to accept what the brain-death criterion in fact implies: for each capacity, it is not that its absence is sufficient for death, but that its presence is sufficient for life. But this misses the metaphysical significance that many of us attribute to the capacity for consciousness. We find it compelling that the capacity for consciousness is *necessary* for our continued existence and thus that when a human being irreversibly loses this capacity, he or she dies or ceases to exist. While brain death is certainly sufficient for the loss of the capacity for consciousness, it is not necessary. Damage to the higher brain can result in the irreversible loss of the capacity for consciousness even while the lower brain remains intact and functional.

The claim that brain death fails to capture the real significance of the loss of the capacity for consciousness is a major objection. Defenders of the whole-brain criterion have typically responded by contending that, while loss of the capacity for consciousness does involve the loss of all that gives life its *value*, it is not the same as the loss of life itself. For them, the continued integrated functioning of the human organism is the *sine qua non* of human life. They then identify the irreversible cessation of integrated functioning with the death of the whole brain, since, as a presidential commission mandated to study this problem put it, 'the brain is the regulator of the body's integration' (President's Commission, 1981: 32). But in fact the irreversible cessation of integrated functioning in the organism is only contingently related to the death of the whole brain.

Brain death is neither necessary nor sufficient for the cessation of integrated functioning in a human organism. It is possible in principle that a person's brain could be surgically extracted and yet kept alive and functional – for example, by being transplanted into a different human organism – while the organism from which it was removed would die. Since in this case integrated functioning would cease even though the brain would not die, brain death cannot be a necessary condition of the irreversible cessation of integrated functioning in a human organism.

Although the brains of animals have been kept alive outside their bodies, the example of a human brain transplant is, for the present, merely hypothetical. But there are actual cases that demonstrate that brain death in human beings is not sufficient for the cessation of integrated bodily functioning. It is now well established, for example, that mechanical ventilation and other forms of support (e.g., nutrition and hydration) can sustain the functional integrity of a human organism for many months beyond a reliable diagnosis of brain death. The functions sustained are sufficiently comprehensive to enable the organism to support fetal gestation (McCullagh, 1993: 35–9).

The 'whole-brain theorists' are, of course, obliged to describe these artificially sustained organisms as ventilated or perfused *corpses* whose operations present only a simulacrum of life (Lamb, 1985: 37). These theorists effectively make it a condition of life not just that the organism function in an integrated way but also that the functions be regulated by the brain. But because new technologies can replace the regulatory functions of the brain to varying degrees, there is a problem about the extent to which the regulation must be carried out by the brain. The whole-brain theorists cannot say that a human being remains alive as long as *any* somatic functions are regulated by the brain; for even after a reliable diagnosis of brain death, the brain in a ventilated organism will continue to regulate some functions (for example, the release of certain hormones (Truog and Fletcher, 1990: 206)). Nor can they say that a human being remains alive only if *all* functions normally regulated by the brain continue to be so regulated; for a conscious patient whose brain is incapable of regulating respiration because of a lesion affecting the respiratory centre in the brainstem is clearly alive. So the whole-brain theorist has to concede that a human organism can remain alive even when the brain is incapable of regulating various important somatic functions. How far can the brain's regulatory capacities deteriorate before one must conclude that the functioning of the organism merely mimics rather than constitutes life?

Matters are brought to a crisis by the case of the locked-in patient. This person's brain lacks virtually all of the normal capacities for regulating somatic functions. It therefore seems wholly arbitrary to say that the functions of the locked-in patient's organism are regulated by the brain while denying that this is true of a ventilated organism that is brain-dead but sufficiently functional to carry a pregnancy to term. Thus, if a brain-dead but artificially sustained organism is dead, then it cannot be by virtue of his integrated bodily functioning that the locked-in patient is alive. (This would be true even if the locked-in patient's brain retains a couple of regulatory functions that a dead brain lacks. A few minor regulatory capacities do not make the difference between life and death, as the whole-brain theorist must acknowledge, since even brains that are officially declared dead retain several regulatory capacities when 'life-support' is provided.) Rather, it is because he retains cortical functions that the locked-in patient is judged to be alive.

It is worth stressing how peculiar the position of the whole-brain theorists is. A human organism that is brain-dead but capable, with assistance, of sustaining a healthy pregnancy is held not to be a living organism. By contrast, the locked-in patient is held to be alive. But the condition of the locked-in patient's *organism* is not relevantly different from that of the brain-dead organism. Both continue to function in an integrated way, though without significant regulation by the brain. The difference is that the locked-in patient's cortex continues to support consciousness. But this cortical activity is not the cause of the integrated functioning of the organism. If the cortex were to die, the state of the organism as a whole would be unaffected. Hence it seems unwarranted for the whole-brain theorists to claim that the locked-in patient is a living organism while denying this status to the brain-dead but artificially supported organism. These theorists therefore face a serious dilemma. For one cannot acknowledge that the brain-dead organism is alive without abandoning brain death as the criterion of death. But it is impossible to believe that the locked-in patient is not alive.

Whole-brain theorists seem, in fact, to have two distinct criteria of life. They insist that, for a human organism to be alive, its various components must function in an integrated way, supervised and regulated by the brain. For this the higher brain is unnecessary. But they also acknowledge that, for an individual to remain in existence, it is sufficient that there be significant activity in the cortex. For this the regulatory functions of the lower brain are unnecessary. In short, brain-regulated, integrated functioning in the organism is sufficient for continued life; but so is the capacity for cortical function. Either is sufficient, but neither is necessary. The problem, however, is that these apparently distinct criteria of human life do not, together, seem to correspond to any coherent conception of what human beings are. What kind of thing is it that can survive as a mindless but living organism (e.g., a patient in a PVS) *or* as a mind housed in an organism that fails to meet the whole-brain theorists' own criterion for being a *living* organism (e.g., a patient who is 'locked in')?

Whole-brain theorists appear to be implicitly distinguishing between the human organism and the human subject (or self, mind or person). And they appear to be offering distinct criteria for the continued life of each (brain-regulated systemic functioning for the one, significant cortical function for the other). Finally, they seem to suggest that we are *both* these things. Yet we cannot be both if they are distinct and independent substances, which in fact appears to be the case. Imagine that your entire brain is removed from your skull and transplanted into the body of your identical twin, whose brain was irreparably damaged and has been removed. Imagine further that surgical techniques have advanced well beyond what is now possible and that all of the various connections between your brain and the nerve pathways in your twin's body have been established. Following the operation, a person is brought to consciousness in your twin's body. That person has your memories, beliefs and character traits and believes him- or herself to be you. Most of us are deeply convinced that that person *is* you. But the organism from which your brain was removed now lies across the room on an operating table. You are not now identical with that organism. But it follows from this that you never were identical with that organism, since a thing cannot cease to be itself and yet continue to exist. (An alternative version of the case involves the transplantation only of your cerebrum, which would be hooked up to your twin's brainstem. In this version, your original organism could remain alive even by the whole-brain theorist's standard; but *you* would be elsewhere.)

Some readers may find this thought experiment too bizarre to provide a firm foundation for the claim that we are not identical with our organisms. There is, however, a very rare but real phenomenon that supports the same conclusion. 'Dicephalus' is a condition in which a human zygote divides incompletely, resulting in twins fully conjoined below the neck: two heads sprouting from a single torso. In these cases, it seems that a single living organism (perhaps with some duplication of internal organs) supports the existence of two distinct persons. It cannot be that *both* these persons are identical with the organism they share. For if *a* is identical with *c* and *b* is identical with *c*, it follows that *a* and *b* are one and the same thing. But conjoined twins are two different people and therefore cannot both be identical with a single organism. There are only two serious options. One is to claim that conjoined twins who diverge at the neck are actually two distinct though overlapping organisms. This is very hard to believe. (Could one die while the other remained alive?) The other is to conclude that neither twin is identical with the organism they share. If this is right, then there are at least some persons who are not organisms. And there is no reason to think that conjoined twins are metaphysically fundamentally different from the rest of us (i.e., that we are organisms while they are some different kind of thing).

If one were identical with one's organism, then of course its death and one's own death would be one and the same event (or process). But if one is distinct from one's organism, then one's own ceasing to exist and the death of one's organism are different. They might coincide, but this would not be a matter of necessity. Thus it is possible that one might die or cease to exist while one's organism would continue to exist and even continue to live. And it is possible in principle (as in the case of the brain transplant) – though not, I believe, in practice – that one might continue to live even after one's organism had died.

It seems, therefore, that we do indeed require two criteria: one for determining when our organisms die, the other for determining when we ourselves cease to exist. These criteria should correspond to two concepts of death (McMahan, 1995: 101–2, 116–17). How we should understand the death of a human organism is primarily a biological issue. And there is general agreement among biologists that a human organism dies when its various components cease to function together in an integrated way. This, of course, leaves certain questions unresolved, such as whether an organism that is brain-dead but continues, with mechanical assistance, to function in an integrated way is still alive. This may be a question that science cannot answer; indeed there may be no objectively correct answer. It seems that we know all the relevant facts – for example, that the organism cannot breathe on its own, but that with mechanical ventilation it will circulate blood, digest food and so on. Whether it is alive is not an *additional* fact, independent of the facts we already know, which might be discovered through further empirical investigation. But it is worth noting, for the record, that consistency suggests that we should consider such an organism to be alive. For the only reason not to regard it as alive is that its integrated functioning is not regulated by its brain. But there are other examples of human organisms that are regarded as indisputably alive even though their somatic functions are not regulated by their own brains – for example, locked-in patients and human embryos and conceptuses. It therefore seems safe to conclude that a human organism's functions need not be regulated by the brain in order for it to be alive.

If this is right, then brain death cannot be the criterion for the death of a human organism. Relatively little hinges on this conclusion, however, since the death of one's organism is not the same as the death of oneself (though they commonly coincide). What is it, then, for one of *us* to cease to exist (or, in the case of the religious, for one of us to cease to exist in association with his or her body)? The answer to this depends on what kind of thing we essentially are. The thought experiment involving the brain transplant should convince us that we are not essentially human organisms. What, then, are we?

'What type of thing are we?' and 'What are the conditions of our ceasing to exist?' are not questions that can be answered by biological science. Science may, for example, tell us many things about human organisms, but it cannot tell us whether *we are* organisms. Many commentators have thought that, because the question 'When has a person ceased to exist?' is not a question of scientific fact, it must therefore be answered by appealing to our values. They have claimed that the question 'When should a person be considered dead?' is reducible to a set of moral questions about when it is permissible to terminate life-support systems, remove a person's organs for transplantation, bury the body and so on. But it is not a value judgement that William Shakespeare is dead. Nor is it a moral question whether the person JM, who was working on this paper yesterday, is still alive today and is the same person who is typing these words now. Similarly, whether one should fear a certain event because it will occur within one's life, or whether one need not fear it because one will have ceased to exist, cannot be determined simply by consulting one's values. Questions about one's own continued existence are primarily neither scientific nor moral. They are instead metaphysical. To answer them, one must engage in reasoning and argument that appeals to our intuitions and judgements about the sorts of changes or losses we could or could not survive, our knowledge of the facts (e.g., about the causal relations between mind and brain), our expectations, attitudes, values and so on. In what follows I will very briefly canvass certain accounts of what we are and what it is for us to die in order both to illustrate how metaphysical reasoning proceeds and to indicate what I think the best account of these matters is.

A common view is that we are souls, non-material substances that somehow inhabit and control our bodies. There are different versions of this view based on different conceptions of the soul, but there is a fairly solid consensus among philosophers that all are untenable, for reasons that are developed in the literature but cannot be rehearsed here (Parfit, 1984: chapters 11 and 12; McMahan, forthcoming, chapter 2) According to another highly influential range of views, we are essentially psychological beings whose continued existence consists in psychological continuity, or the holding of certain continuities of mental life over time. A person twenty years ago and a person today are the same person if and only if the latter is related to the former by an overlapping series of psychological connections, involving memory and the persistence or gradual evolution of a particular set of desires, beliefs, intentions, dispositions of character and so on. Some versions of this view insist that psychological continuity be causally supported by the continued existence and functioning of the same brain, while others hold that the mode of causation is irrelevant. While this disagreement makes no difference in practice, versions of the second sort have implications in certain imaginary examples that many of us find difficult to accept – for example, that one could survive the complete destruction of one's brain if it were replaced by an exact duplicate.

Of the versions that insist that psychological continuity be maintained via the preservation of certain structures in the brain, some presuppose a strong conception of psychological continuity while others accept progressively weaker conceptions. Those based on a strong conception imply, in effect, that we are essentially *persons* – that is, self-conscious beings with mental lives of a high order of unity and complexity. To lose the capacity for self-consciousness is, on such a view, to cease to exist. Versions that deploy a weaker conception of psychological continuity accept that one could survive the loss of personhood; but even these versions hold that there is some level of psychological discontinuity that is equivalent to death. Thus all the versions imply that one could cease to exist even if one's brain were to retain the capacity for consciousness. Even the weakest versions hold that, if one were to suffer progressive dementia (as in Alzheimer's disease), there would be some point before one's brain lost the capacity for consciousness at which one would cease to exist. But, because consciousness and mental activity would persist after one ceased to exist, it seems that one would be supplanted in one's own body by a new and different conscious subject. Indeed, in cases involving radical amnesia and personality change, most versions imply that one would cease to exist and be replaced in one's body by a different *person*.

Most of us find these implications of the psychological continuity theories implausible. Most people's intuitive view is that, even in cases of dementia or of radical amnesia and personality change, one continues to exist as long as one's brain continues to be capable of supporting consciousness or mental activity. Thus if one were in the early stages of Alzheimer's, it would be rational to fear any pain that would be suffered in one's body even during the late stages of the disease. While the *contents* of the later mental life might be radically discontinuous with those of the earlier, the pain would still occur within the same consciousness or mind. From one's present point of view, that future pain would occur within one's own future life.

If this is right, then each of us continues to exist as long as his or her brain retains the capacity to support consciousness or mental activity. One's own death, or ceasing to exist, occurs when one's brain irreversibly loses this capacity. What is the criterion for determining when this has occurred? It seems clear that it is not necessary that the whole brain should die. At a minimum, it is sufficient that the cerebral hemispheres should die. It is likely, however, that the brain can lose the capacity to generate consciousness or mental activity even when certain cerebral functions are retained. Thus most experts agree that the death of the cortex – *cortical death* – is necessary and sufficient for the irreversible loss of the capacity for consciousness or mental activity. If that is right, then cortical death should be our criterion of death.

What is it that dies or ceases to exist when cortical death occurs? It should be stressed that cortical death is *not* the criterion of the death of the human organism. A human organism can remain alive, even in the absence of artificial life-support, following cortical death. It is, rather, *we* who go out of existence. It may be misleading, however, to say that cortical death is the death of the *person*, since this may suggest that we are essentially persons. But it seems that we can survive the loss of personhood (e.g., if we become demented). Similarly, it may also be misleading to say that it is the *human being* that ceases to exist. For one thing, to say that we are essentially human beings is to invite confusion between ourselves and our organisms, which are also human. And in any case it is doubtful that we are in fact essentially human beings (e.g., one could presumably survive if one's brain were transplanted into the body of an ape). It seems that what ceases to exist with cortical death is the *mind*, and that that is what we essentially are. One cannot cease to have a mind without ceasing to exist.

It should also be noted that this account is not confined to human beings but applies to all conscious subjects. Just as I am not identical with my organism, so my dog is not identical with his. My dog will die when his brain loses the capacity to support a mental life, though it is possible that his organism could live on beyond that.

One important implication of this account is that most patients who are in a PVS are dead, though they are outlived by their organisms. There is, however, a limited class of cases in which individuals in a PVS remain alive. These are cases in which the PVS is caused by a lesion to the reticular formation, a configuration in the lower brain that functions rather in the manner of an off–on switch for consciousness. Although mental states are not themselves realized in the tissues of the reticular formation, consciousness cannot occur unless the formation is functional. When the reticular formation is damaged, consciousness is not in practice possible but the individual has not suffered cortical death and it is possible in principle that cortical activity, and therefore the person herself, could be revived. The individual thus remains in existence but, without any possibility of consciousness or mental activity, her life has ceased to be worth living and there seems to be little reason to treat this type of PVS any differently from the type that involves the ceasing to exist of the individual.

The claim that most individuals who lapse into a PVS thereby die suggests that it is permissible to treat their bodies the way we currently treat the bodies of those who are brain-dead. As opponents of the idea of cortical death have pointed out, however, this might lead to the deliberate killing of living human organisms in order to harvest their organs for transplantation. While this is initially shocking, it can, on reflection, be seen to be justified, if the life of a person could thereby be saved. For a mere organism does not have interests and cannot itself be benefited or harmed. To end its life is no more objectionable than it is to kill a plant, provided that what is done does not contravene the posthumous interests of, or manifest disrespect for, the person who once animated the organism. And, for my part, I believe that it would be no more disrespectful for physicians to stop my heart beating after I have ceased to exist than it would be for them to scoop out my organs once those organs had stopped working on their own – which is to say, not disrespectful at all. But, just as people can stipulate that their organs not be used for transplantation, so they could stipulate that their organisms not be killed so long as they continue to function spontaneously. It is, of course, a different question how long an organism in a PVS should be provided with nursing care, given that the resources this would consume could otherwise be devoted to patients who, unlike the mere organism, could benefit from them.

One important objection to treating persistently vegetative patients as dead is that there may be uncertainty about whether they really have lost the capacity for consciousness. It might be claimed, for example, that we can never know that such a patient would not, with proper care, eventually regain full consciousness. But our long experience with this condition, together with advances in techniques for monitoring blood flow to different areas of the brain, make it possible in most cases to determine with virtual certainty when recovery is impossible. There is, however, another worrisome form of uncertainty, which concerns the possibility that corti-cal death is compatible with the presence in other areas of the brain of some residual, primitive form of consciousness or perhaps unconscious mental activity. If this cannot be excluded, then it is possible that the person remains alive, or at least that some vestige or remnant of the person still lingers (which might be articulated by saying that the person remains partially, though not fully, in existence; see McMahan, forthcoming).

While the possibility that some dim, flickering, rudimentary mode of conscious-ness might survive cortical death does provide cause for hesitation in embracing cortical death as the criterion of death, it is not a strong objection to shifting from brain death to cortical death as a matter of policy. The possibility that even inter-mittent, semi-conscious mental activity persists beyond cortical death is very re-mote. Of course, if life in that condition could be good, then even a remote possibility that it persists would be significant. (Here it is important to note that, with ventila-tion, various forms of activity persist in the brain even after a diagnosis of brain death; so the possibility of continued mental activity beyond whole-brain death cannot be completely excluded either.) But it is hard to believe that whatever shadowy, semi-conscious mental activity we might imagine occurring after corti-cal death could contribute to the good of a person's life. Indeed, there are good reasons for thinking that, for most of us, continued existence as what one commen-tator calls a 'manicured vegetable' would be *against* our objective interests (Dwor-kin, 1993: chapter 7). Since the remote possibility of life beyond cortical death is a possibility of life that could scarcely be worth living, the practical significance of this possibility is negligible.

It is worth noting, in conclusion, that a similar point has been advanced by those who believe, contrary to what I have argued, that we are identical with our physi-cal organisms but who nevertheless reject the idea that it is necessary for a person to suffer brain death in order for it to be permissible to remove him from life-support systems, extract his organs for transplantation and so on. These people are im-pressed by the objections that might be urged against the mind–body dualism for which I have argued. For example, if I am not identical with my organism, then there must be two things in the chair in which I am sitting – me and my organism. Applied to all of us, and to animals as well, this reasoning seems to make the world rather more crowded than in fact it is. Moreover, unless there are two self-conscious entities, and thus two persons, where I am now, it seems that we have to deny that organisms have psychological properties. Only I, and not my organism, am conscious, have thoughts, sensations, perceptions and so on. By parity of rea-soning, it may seem that it must be a figurative use of language to attribute my organism's physical properties to me – for example, when we say that *I* weigh 150 pounds. Those who find these implications of the dualism I have advocated to be unacceptable may cling to the idea that we are organisms, hoping that an adequate response to the case of the brain transplant can be found.

But this need not commit them to the view that brain death is death. It is reasonable to believe, as I indicated earlier, that a human organism can remain alive well beyond a reliable diagnosis of brain death. Again, however, this need not

JEFF MCMAHAN

imply that it is morally imperative or even desirable to sustain the lives of human organisms beyond brain death, or even beyond cortical death. For, even if we are organisms and thus remain alive as long as our organisms do. our interest in continued life surely vanishes with cortical death. (Similarly, one has no interest in continued *existence* after death, though if we are organisms we do normally continue to exist for a while, as corpses, after we die.) Thus if we choose to extend an individual's life beyond cortical death, it cannot be for his or her sake that we do so.

References

Bartlett, E. T. and Youngner, S. J. (1988). Human death and the destruction of the neocortex. In R. M. Zaner (ed.), *Death: Beyond whole-brain criteria*. Dordrecht: Kluwer, 199–215.

Dworkin, R. (1993). *Life's Dominion*. New York: Alfred A. Knopf.

Lamb, D. (1985). *Death, Brain Death, and Ethics*. Albany: State University of New York Press.

McCullagh, P. (1993). *Brain Dead, Brain Absent, Brain Donors: human subjects or human objects?* Chichester: John Wiley.

McMahan, J. (1995). The metaphysics of brain death. *Bioethics*, 9, 91–126.

—— (forthcoming). *Killing at the Margins of Life*. New York: Oxford University Press.

Parfit, D. (1984). *Reasons and Persons*. Oxford: Oxford University Press.

President's Commission for the Study of Ethical Problems in Medicine and Biomedical and Behavioral Research (1981). *Defining Death*. Washington, DC: US Government Printing Office.

Truog, R. D. and Fletcher, J. C. (1990). Brain death and the anencephalic newborn. *Bioethics*, 4, 199–215.

Further Reading

Gervais, K. G. (1986). *Redefining Death*. New Haven: Yale University Press.

Green, M. B. and Wikler, D. (1980). Brain death and personal identity, *Philosophy and Public Affairs*, 9, 105–33.

Johnston, M. (1987). Human beings. *Journal of Philosophy*, 84, 59–83.

Lockwood, M. (1984). When does a life begin? In M. Lockwood (ed.), *Moral Dilemmas in Modern Medicine*. Oxford: Oxford University Press, 9–31.

Singer, P. (1995). *Rethinking Life and Death*. New York: St Martin's.

Veatch, R. M. (1988). Whole-brain, neocortical, and higher brain related concepts. In R. M. Zaner (ed.), *Death: Beyond whole-brain criteria*. Dordrecht: Kluwer, 171–86.

[handwritten annotations at top of page]

26

Advance directives

ALEXANDER MORGAN CAPRON

Advance directives for health care are the quintessential topic in bioethics. Advance directives embody the field's commitment to the principle of individual autonomy; they concern decisions about critical illness and death, the aspect of bioethics that touches more lives than any other, given the inevitability of death and the prevalence of medical involvement in the dying process; and they illustrate the movement of bioethics from the bedside into the realm of the law. Yet despite the central place that they have occupied in the field of bioethics over the past several decades, and the great zeal with which they are advocated in some countries, advance directives are conceptually dubious, widely misunderstood, poorly studied and seldom implemented.

What Are Advance Directives and Why Do We Have Them?

Essentially, an advance directive is a statement made in advance of an illness about the type and extent of treatment one would want, on the assumption that one may be incapable of participating in decision-making about treatment when the need arises. Advance directives are usually written though an oral declaration may also suffice; they may name a person to make decisions on one's behalf, give instructions on what treatments should or should not be provided or do both. In theory, advance directives provide a means to express wishes of any sort (for example, that particular treatments be used or not used, or that all possible treatments are to be provided), but they are usually thought of as a means to limit life-prolonging treatment, especially in the United States, where interest in advance directives originated and has been most intense, for reasons that are addressed later in this essay. An attempt to use a directive to insist on 'all possible treatment' is an example of a fairly new problem which is sometimes denominated 'medical futility', namely the insistence of a patient – or, more commonly, family members speaking on behalf of an incapacitated patient – on receiving medical interventions that physicians do not want to provide because they believe the treatments are unlikely to benefit the patient or are too scarce or expensive to be justified, compared to using the same treatment with other patients. The use of a directive does not alter the ethical considerations that must be weighed in resolving disputes over 'futile' treatment, though it may complicate the situation, since the expression of a patient's advance wishes in the document may constrain the ability of inclination of family members to compromise with physicians who are unwilling to utilize the medical interventions the patient appears to have demanded.

Under such names as 'living will', 'durable power of attorney for health care' or 'health-care proxy', advance directives are a familiar part of health care today in many countries. Yet it is worth remembering that they are actually a very recent response to a modern problem, namely the worry of many people that they will become victims trapped by medicine's ever-expanding ability to sustain life indefinitely after they lose the ability to voice their wishes about treatment at the end of life. Of course, physicians do not set out with the purpose of inaugurating endless care of dying, unconscious patients. But treatment begun with a hope – if not necessarily an expectation – of success frequently falls short, especially when the patient has experienced cardiac arrest, stroke or any other injury that has cut off the circulation of oxygenated blood (even for a short period). If the damage that results to the higher centres of the brain is severe enough, consciousness is unlikely to be restored even if the vegetative functions controlled by the lower brain and brainstem persist with supportive care, ranging from mechanical ventilation and drugs to simple feeding through a tube.

In responding to such conditions, decisions must be made about when to provide or to forgo life-sustaining treatment for patients whose medical condition makes them unable to participate in decision-making. Some jurisdictions require very clear proof of what an incompetent patient would have wanted (at least before life-support is discontinued), in which case an advance directive may be legally necessary. And even where the law permits family members or other persons acting on behalf of an incompetent patient to decide with physicians about life-sustaining interventions based either on what they know the patient would have wanted or on what they believe would be in the patient's best interests, surrogate decision-makers and health-care professionals alike may be unwilling to act without clear documentation of the patient's wishes, in which case an advance directive may be a practical (though not a legal) necessity.

The Origins and Limitations of the 'Living Will'

Indeed, advance directives arose initially as a response to the decision-making paralysis, born of guilt and uncertainty, that often occurs when the question is whether to forgo the medical interventions sustaining the life of someone who is no longer able to make his or her own views known. Recognizing that physicians, nurses and other health-care providers, as well as patients' next of kin, often find it difficult to withhold further interventions, much less to withdraw those already being undertaken, Luis Kutner, a Chicago attorney active in a right-to-die organization, in 1967 drafted what he termed a 'living will'. Just as a 'will' signifies a document through which a person leaves instructions for the disposition of his or her estate after death, Kutner's 'living will' allows a person to give instructions for medical care in the final days of life. In particular, through a living will people while still competent are able to state that they do not want their dying process prolonged once they become unable to express their wishes directly.

Living wills were viewed as serving several purposes. First, by executing a living will, a person could lift the burden of decision-making off the shoulders of anxious relatives and diffident physicians. Second, if the wishes expressed in the living will are honoured, a person could in effect participate in treatment decision-making even after he or she has lost the ability to communicate. And third, the existence of living wills – and the interest in many quarters that soon arose about them – helped to educate health-care providers about the public's sense that life-prolonging treatment is not always regarded as a good.

Yet, while living wills were actively promoted by several organizations, first in the United States and then in other countries, only a tiny percentage of the population knew about them, much less signed one. Furthermore, on its face, the original living will – and others that followed its language – candidly admitted its own major limitation, namely that under the common law of agency, it lacked legal effect. The law permits one person (termed the principal) to appoint another (the agent) to carry out instructions on his or her behalf. Commitments undertaken by an agent are binding on his or her principal. If a principal is dissatisfied with an agent, the principal may discharge the agent and notify those relying on the agency that the principal will no longer be bound. Because a person who has become incapable of making his or her own decisions has also lost the ability to discharge an agent or alter his or her instructions, the common law provides that all agents are automatically discharged by operation of law when their principal becomes incompetent, lest a person be bound by the decisions of an agent whom the person was incapable of countermanding. Agents – including those who act under a formal document giving them 'power of attorney' – usually have authority regarding the property rather than the physical person of the principal. (Such an agent is not typically an attorney-at-law but a lay person acting as an 'attorney-in-fact'.) Applied to the medical context, traditional agency law renders instructions in a living will non-binding at the very moment when they are intended to go into effect.

Kutner and other advocates of the living will frankly admitted that it was not legally binding because they believed that its real strength lay in the reassurance – indeed, courage – it could provide to a patient's family, spiritual adviser and physicians to forgo life-prolonging treatment when death was near. But as medicine's powers to sustain biological functioning continued to outpace the health-care professions' ability to draw sensible limitations on the use of these powers throughout the 1970s, some advocates of the 'right to die' became convinced that living wills would only be effective if they could dispel physicians' liability fears. Although the absence of adverse cases should have been enough to reassure physicians that they were at no risk of civil or criminal liability for following a living will, they frequently invoked such risk to justify disregarding these documents. The fear may have been genuine (though erroneous) or merely reflected physicians' discomfort in seeming to 'give up' and admit they were unable to provide an effective cure in the case at hand. In any case, the 'not legally binding' excuse stood in the way of living wills becoming a truly useful and important part of patient care, and living will advocates therefore pressed for legislation that would authorize families and care providers to rely on such directives and immunize them from liability when they did. Yet, while the first 'living will bill' was introduced in 1968 in Florida, the issue did not attract much public attention – and, when it did, it was often intertwined with efforts to legalize physicians taking more active steps to end the lives of dying patients.

Legislatively Authorized 'Instruction Directives'

Ironically. public interest in making living wills valid legal documents was galvanized by the worldwide attention directed to a case in which the patient did not have a living will, the 1976 New Jersey Supreme Court decision regarding Karen Ann Quinlan, a young woman who had slipped into a coma after apparently taking some combination of alcohol and drugs. Her physicians refused to turn off the respirator that they said was needed to support her breathing on the ground that ceasing treatment would amount to criminal homicide. The High Court disagreed and said that it would be reasonable to follow her father's request, provided that an ethics committee convened by the hospital agreed. The plight – both of Ms Quinlan and of her parents – focused attention on the unwillingness of physicians to act without clear legal authority and generated interest in moving living wills from their shadowy existence as hortatory statements to officially recognized instructions from patients expressing their wishes while they were still able to do so.

Within months of the New Jersey decision, California enacted the first statute. As explained by its author in introducing the bill, 'The image of Karen Quinlan haunts our dreams. For many, the ultimate horror is not death, but the possibility of being maintained in limbo in a sterile room, by machines that are controlled by strangers.' Although initially a simple attempt to give legal validity to living wills, the bill was amended dozens of times because many legislators still had severe reservations about discontinuing life-sustaining treatment. The resulting statute, the Natural Death Act, had many flaws, beginning with its name – in this era of wonder drugs and medical miracles almost no death in a health-care facility is 'natural', and each death reflects many human decisions about using or withholding efforts to change the course of illness and prolong life. Yet despite such limitations, the Natural Death Act stimulated legislation across the country, as states either followed the California model or drafted their own versions to overcome some of the problems in the first statute.

As a group, these statutes authorize a type of advance directive sometimes termed an 'instruction directive' because the gist of the document is to instruct physicians and other care-givers about what they should do under particular circumstances. A basic problem with this type of directive is that most people are not able to predict the circumstances of their death with any precision. Therefore, instruction directives – both the original living will and the forms set forth in state statutes – are often written generically, either employing poetic language ('heroic measures') or wording that raises more questions than it answers ('means that only prolong the dying process'). Some physicians suggest using much more specific forms, in which patients indicate on a check list precisely which interventions they would or would not want. Such specificity could prevent arguments over whether a patient intended to forgo only mechanical ventilation or also antibiotics, drugs that maintain blood pressure and the like, and tubes that supply food and fluids. Other commentators object that what is most important to patients is not the particular means used but the results produced, including the probability that some degree of recovery will be achieved and whether the treatment will cause pain or further dehumanize their dying process. Thus, they argue that a living will should be written so as to convey the person's 'values history', a general orientation that would connect issues arising in the dying process with the way the person has lived his or her whole life.

A second basic issue with instruction directives is in knowing when they come into effect. Many versions of the living will are triggered when a 'terminal illness' is diagnosed, but knowing what 'terminal' means is often difficult. Some statutes are written in terms of an illness that would be fatal within six months, while others speak of death being imminent. California's original statute illustrated another problem when it stated that a condition is terminal when it will cause death *whether or not* treatment is provided. If death is about to occur despite treatment, then little need arises for an advance directive because the decision is out of human hands, whereas the reason for using an instruction-type directive is to ensure the death-delaying treatment is halted.

A related problem with the so-called living will statutes is that early versions encompassed only 'terminal illness', while the more frightening prospect for many people is a situation that has no termination in sight, namely prolonged treatment in a vegetative state when death is not imminent because their underlying condition is not a lethal one so long as basic support, such as food and fluids and comfort measures, is continued. Today, some statutes allowing the use of instruction directives either encompass permanent unconsciousness as well as terminal illness as conditions in which the instructions become effective, or they permit the person filling out such a directive to indicate the circumstances under which the instructions take effect. Likewise, the statutes – as well as judicial decisions interpreting them and determining when, if ever, an oral declaration provides a legally effective expression of a patient's wishes to forgo treatment – set forth which treatments are automatically encompassed within do-not-treat instructions and which ones (such as food and fluids by tube) need to be spelled out explicitly by the declarant in order to be valid.

Legislatively Authorized 'Appointment Directives'

Limitations of this sort in instruction-type directives generated interest in finding better means to permit patients to exercise some control over medical decisions even after they lose decisional capacity. As it happened, during the latter part of the 1970s, many jurisdictions adopted statutes that allow people to execute what in the United States is called a 'durable power of attorney' and in Great Britain and some other countries is termed a 'continuing power of attorney'. Such documents are 'durable' or 'continuing' in that they survive the incompetence of the principal; indeed, they may provide that the authority of the agent comes into being only when the principal loses the capacity to make decisions. These laws were enacted to enable people, especially the elderly with small estates, to appoint one of their children or another trusted person to manage their finances and other affairs if they become unable to do so, without the burden of having to seek a formal court appointment of a conservator.

In one of its reports, a US presidential commission on medical ethics in 1983 recommended the adoption of statutes specifically to allow the use of durable powers for health-care decisions. Later that year, California again became the first jurisdiction to enact a statute, the Durable Power of Attorney for Health Care law. All American states save Alaska now have laws that permit the appointment of a health-care agent (and all save three – Massachusetts, Michigan and New York – also recognize a living will or other instructions concerning a patient's wishes about forgoing life-support, thereby permitting people to combine an appointment directive with a set of instructions to guide the agent's decisions).

Typically, organizations in each state make available standard forms that comply with that state's statutory requirements for warnings about the actions covered by the directive (which usually exclude psychiatric treatments, sterilization or abortion) and for who may serve as an agent (which usually excludes health-care providers) and as a witness to the form (which sometimes excludes those who would stand to benefit financially from a patient's death). Although medical associations are often major distributors of the forms, the average person apparently does not think of turning to physicians for assistance regarding advance directives, in part because physicians are seen as committed to life-extending treatment. Rather, those people who have an attorney (for example, to draft a will or to handle business affairs) are more inclined to turn to him or her for assistance in executing a durable power of attorney for health care, even though legal expertise is not needed to fill out the form. In fact, the forms are quite simple to complete, and several lay organizations concerned with the welfare of dying patients also make the forms readily available and provide advice about how to execute them.

Since 1991, a US statute has required all health-care providers to give patients upon admission basic information about their rights under their state's law to make decisions and fill out advance directives. While the timing is bad (the point of admission to a hospital, perhaps in a medical crisis or with the anxiety of imminent surgery, is not the best time for 'advance' planning about end-of-life decisions), there is some evidence that this federal requirement has made the public more aware of advance directives, and the percentage of people who have filled out one has increased, though it still remains quite low.

For persons who have someone they trust to serve as their health-care agent, an appointment-type directive, such as the durable power of attorney for health-care, is regarded by most experts as a more useful document than a living will or other instruction-type directive. The central advantage is that the agent can step into the shoes of the patient and make decisions in the light of the current medical situation

In US, [medical] care is perhaps more aggressive than other countries, but there remains a marked deference to medical opinion

ADVANCE DIRECTIVES

and the advice of the attending physician, whereas instructions may not address the situation or may be so ambiguous as to create more confusion than clarity about what the patient would want done. Experts disagree about whether it is advisable to include instructions in the document appointing an agent. Doing so may increase the ability of the agent to make a decision that accurately reflects what the patient would want, especially since without such instructions neither family members nor health-care professionals turn out to be very accurate predictors of patients' preferences regarding life-sustaining treatment. Yet, to the extent that instructions are unclear or do not directly address the issues that need to be resolved, they can be mischievous, and if a dispute arises between the agent and others, such as other family members or the attending physician, the instructions may be invoked to limit the agent's ability to decide in a way that he or she is convinced best serves the patient's objectives and interests under the circumstances.

Whether or not instructions are written down, all commentators seem to agree that it is advisable for the principal and the agent to talk about what the principal hopes to get from treatment and especially about outcomes or types of treatment that the principal wants to avoid. Ideally, some of these conversations would also involve the principal's regular physician. The physician can thus begin a relation-ship with the agent that will both facilitate good communication if it is ever neces-sary for the agent to become the surrogate decision-maker and ensure that the physician has conveyed to the principal and agent a realistic picture of the kinds of interventions about which decisions may need to be made and the range of outcomes that is likely to flow from using or forgoing these interventions.

Advance Directives Outside the United States

Advance directives not only began as a phenomenon in the United States but to a surprising degree have remained so; aside from Denmark, Germany, the Nether-lands, New Zealand and several Australian and Canadian jurisdictions, they seem not to have made their way into the statute books. One reason may be that care at the end of life has been more aggressive in the US than elsewhere in the developed world, so stronger means to resist over-treatment were felt to be necessary. More-over, legislation on advance directives often came as a response to the pleas of judges in deciding a number of high-profile cases involving physicians' insistence on continuing life-support that patients' families found inappropriate. These cases were themselves an outgrowth of litigation dating to the 1960s that, along with the writings of legal and bioethics scholars, aimed at replacing medical paternalism with patient autonomy through the development of informed consent and related doctrines.

In other countries, not only were medical heroics less likely to be employed but judges were less inclined to diminish physicians' authority to make decisions on behalf of their patients. Thus, legislatures had less reason to develop means by which persons could extend their autonomous choice into a future in which they had lost the ability to exercise such choice. (Also, appointment-type directives were possible, through granting an agent power over one's person as well as property under a 'continuing power of attorney'.) In Great Britain, it was only in 1994 that a House of Lords Select Committee on Medical Ethics recommended that advance directives be formulated and a code of practice be developed to guide health-care professionals in their use, though the committee did not urge legislation to give directives greater force in law. The following year, however, the Law Commission did recommend a Mental Incapacity Bill which provided that a person with capacity to decide about treatment could make an 'advance refusal of treatment' that would take effect 'at any subsequent time when he or she may be without capacity to give or refuse consent'. The bill gave such advance statements (which could be oral or written) only limited effect: 'in the absence of any indication to the contrary', an advance refusal is presumed not to apply when forgoing the treatment would endanger the person's life. In January 1996, the government decided not to pursue this bill. This seems to reflect the basic view of the House of Lords committee about advance directives, namely that patients are better served by relying on physicians' recognized duty to provide only that treatment to an incompetent patient that is both reasonable and in the best interests of the patient.

As late as 1992 in Canada, no court had addressed the validity of living wills, perhaps because physicians were willing to act on the instructions contained in such documents. The Law Revision Commission of Canada did, however, recommend that the criminal code be clarified to ensure that physicians could not be prosecuted for homicide for following the provisions of a living will and withholding all care except palliation of pain. Furthermore, during the 1990s, the provincial legislatures adopted statutes on 'natural death' and on durable powers of attorney of health care (in some cases termed the 'Medical Consent Act'), or in some cases, as in Manitoba, providing for 'health-care directives' through which a person may express his or her health-care decisions or appoint a proxy or both.

In Australia, under revisions to the Medical Treatment Acts (1988) adopted in 1992 in Victoria and 1994 in the Australian Capital Territory, and under the Consent to Medical Treatment and Palliative Care Act 1995 in South Australia, a person may appoint an agent to make treatment decisions, including the refusal of life-sustaining treatment, when the person loses decisional capacity. This refusal may not, however, extend to palliative care, including food and water as well as pain medication. The South Australian Act, and the Natural Death Act 1988 in the Northern Territory, also permit a person to make an advance directive regarding treatment should the person lose the ability to communicate. In South Australia directives to forgo 'life-sustaining measures' are effective if the person is terminally ill or in a persistent vegetative state; the Northern Territory legislation is narrower, allowing people to instruct against the use of 'extraordinary measures' once a terminal illness has been diagnosed. Under regulations issued in 1996 by the Health and Disability Commissioner in New Zealand, consumers' rights to have information about services and to give or refuse consent encompass the use of a written or oral advance directive, which is defined to include choices about future health care not limited to life-sustaining interventions.

268

In the common-law countries, the lack of formal advance directive legislation is sometimes not a true impediment to good decision-making about care at the end of life, since judicial decisions often recognize the right of next of kin to make decisions with physicians about the treatment of incapacitated patients, in the process of which the patients' wishes can be taken into account even if not memorialized in a formal advance directive. Elsewhere, the absence of legal authorization has posed a problem. In some countries, such as Denmark, legislation has been enacted, while in others, such as the Netherlands, advance directives are not recognized.

Conceptual Problems and Practical Difficulties

The emphasis in bioethics on patient autonomy can be seen as a necessary corrective to the excesses of medical paternalism. When it results in a relationship of mutual respect and joint decision-making, it can even improve clinical outcomes, not only because active patients take greater responsibility for their own health but also because they inspire providers to measure the outcomes of medical interventions through the patient's eyes. It is less clear that trying to extend personal autonomy into a future time at which the person has lost the ability for autonomous action is either clinically beneficial or even conceptually sound.

First, even when the instructions in an advance directive are clear, they may reflect misunderstanding on a person's part about the likely results of a medical intervention under particular circumstances. For example, a patient who says 'no mechanical respiration' may be concerned that the use of such devices always leads to a long period of dependence. when in certain circumstances, a ventilator would only be needed for a short period while the person recovers from an injury or from surgery. Second, as the House of Lords medical ethics committee concluded, 'a patient who has made an advance directive could unwittingly be depriving himself or herself of professional medical expertise or of beneficial advances in treatment.' Backing up this objection, some commentators have argued that it is inappropriate to rely on an advance directive in making decisions about patients who have suffered severe and permanent injuries, such as those in a persistent vegetative state. In effect, these patients are no longer the persons they were at the time the directive was executed. This shift in personal identity makes it wrong to dictate the treatment of the patient in the bed by the wishes of the person that formerly occupied this body; rather, treatment should be guided by an assessment of what would be in the best interests of the present patient. To the objection that ignoring an advance directive would trample the interests that a person has in determining the course of what is often his or her final days, these critics reply that since an incompetent person can no longer understand and appreciate any violation of their personal choices, they have no 'autonomy interests' in having those choices respected. Legislators and judges seem largely unmoved by such philosophical objections and adhere instead to the commonsense notion that finds a continuity between a competent person and his or her future self even following a brain injury that obliterates consciousness, memory and self-awareness. Furthermore, particularly when an appointment-type advance directive is used, the health-care agent is

269

usually able to take changed medical circumstances and a current assessment of the patient's best interests into account when participating with physicians and nurses in deciding about the patient's care, rather than being bound in an ironclad fashion by the person's instructions. At the same time, executing an advance directive gives people comfort from the sense that their family and physician will not put them through endless treatment because they are unsure whether stopping treatment accorded with their wishes.

However such conceptual issues are resolved, advance directives remain an unfulfilled dream in many ways. First, advance directives are not yet a routine part of medical care. Few people want to think about their own demise, and many physicians have also been reticent about raising the subject and helping patients to think concretely about how their deaths may occur and the choices that will need to be made along the way. Second, even when an advance directive has been executed, it may not be available when needed. Sometimes, people file their advance directive away with other valuable papers (perhaps even in a safety deposit box in a bank) and the directive is found only after their death; this is another reason why appointment-type directives usually work better, since it is likely that a copy will have been given to the person named as the patient's agent. Sometimes, even when the paper is accessible in the person's home or a copy has been given to the primary physician, the person will be hospitalized while travelling. To overcome such problems, Denmark has a computer registry for advance directives, which can be accessed by health-care providers treating patients who are unable to communicate their wishes regarding treatment, provided of course that the patient has both executed a directive and submitted it to the registry. Similar computerized services are provided for a fee by several organizations in the United States, though they have not been extensively used because they are not well known either among people who fill out directives or among hospital personnel.

Third, the underlying premise of advance directives – that people should have a means to extend their individual autonomy into the future when they would otherwise be unable to control what happens to them – does not correspond to what some people regard as appropriate medical decision-making. Some people feel more comfortable relying on their physician's judgement; issuing any sort of a 'directive' may seem totally inappropriate. For others, social norms may dictate that decisions about treatment do not reside with the individual but with his or her family or community (as embodied in a tribal or religious leader); even if such a person could articulate personal wishes about, for example, limiting death-delaying interventions at the end of life, the person may still want to defer to custom and allow decisions to be made by a spouse or adult offspring, who in turn may feel the need to manifest his or her own love and respect by insisting on maximal treatment.

On a deeper level, advance directive statutes remain only partially effective because, while they furnish means for people of express their wishes, they provide no help in thinking about what those wishes should be. They are neither informative about the clinical realities of the dying process for various diseases nor do they offer spiritual assistance in understanding how one's values could or should shape the arc of one's final days. For such assistance, people must continue to rely on the

270

health-care professionals who take care of them and on the family members and others who care for them. While the long-term value and effectiveness of advance directives remains more an article of faith for many bioethicists and public policy-makers, rather than a matter of empirical proof, it is likely that they will become a more common, albeit still imperfect, part of the medical landscape in the coming years.

Further Reading

Advance Care Planning (1994). *Hastings Center Report*, 24/6. [Special supplement including articles by Dan Brock, Marion Danis, Rebecca Dresser, Linda L. Emanuel, Lachlan Forrow, Dallas M. High, Joanne Lynn, Hilde and James Lindemann Nelson, Robert Allan Pearlman, Greg A. Sachs, Jeremy Sugarman, Joan M. Teno and Terrie Wetle.]

Beltran, Joseph E. (1994). *The Living Will.* Nashville, TN: Thomas Nelson.

Cantor, Norman L. (1993). *Advance Directives and the Pursuit of Death with Dignity.* Bloomington and Indianapolis: Indiana University Press.

Hackler, Chris, Moseley, Ray and Vawter, Dorothy E. (eds). (1989). *Advance Directives in Medicine.* New York: Praeger.

Hornett, Stuart (1994). The legal advance of the advance directive. *Ethics and Medicine*, 10/2, 25–27.

House of Lords Select Committee on Medical Ethics (1993–4). Report. HL 21-L.

Law Commission of Great Britain (1995). Report No. 231. Mental Incapacity. 28 February.

Weir, Robert F. (1994). Advance directives as instruments of moral persuasion. In Robert H. Blank and Andrea L. Bonnicksen (eds), *Medicine Unbound: the human body and the limits of medical intervention.* New York: Columbia University Press, 171–87.

271

Voluntary euthanasia, suicide and physician-assisted suicide

BRIAN STOFFELL

Approved medical practice in the Netherlands, legal initiatives in the USA, the activities of the death-rights activist Dr Jack Kevorkian and the short-lived legislation in Australia's Northern Territory have put voluntary euthanasia and assisted suicide firmly on the public agenda. Yet there is no bioethical issue with a longer philosophical lineage. The place of suicide in a rational life plan drew attention from classical antiquity's major thinkers and philosophical schools. Diogenes Laertius' (7.130) discussion of Zeno's death is typical in its straightforward identification of honourable reasons for a voluntary death (*voluntaria mors*): 'The sage leads himself rationally [eulogos] out of life, namely on behalf of fatherland or friends, also when he suffers from pain which is too fierce, mutilations or incurable diseases.'

This third reason, pain, mutilations or incurable disease, is arguably still the basis for modern requests for euthanasia and assisted suicide, although there is less discussion these days about self-deliverance from such conditions. This is unfortunate, since the classical discussion of the grounds for suicide correctly identifies it as the paradigm case of voluntary death, euthanasia and assisted suicide being morally derivative. Mature reflection on illness, death and choice of exit should begin from suicide as the central case, then move on to requests for help in quitting life. For the sake of this paper, all cases will be taken as motivated by suffering experienced during terminal illness, and all references to euthanasia will be to active voluntary euthanasia.

That bioethical discussion of voluntary death does not normally begin in this way is a function of the period separating us from Greek and Roman debate about *autothanasia* (see Daube, 1972; van Hooff, 1990; Griffin, 1994). Since Josephus in the first century and Augustine in the fifth, the treatment of suicide has been largely negative. Both writers drew on much older traditions of folkore and philosophy in exhibiting an attitude of abhorrence, buttressed by arguments designed to show that suicide is inherently wrong. Despite the largely religious provenance of their arguments – covering the sinful and the impious rather than the immoral – their attitude has had a dramatic impact on our thinking, mediated in the main through religion and law.

This chapter briefly discusses the three modes of voluntary death as they arise in bioethical cases, but treats suicide as the key concept. There are three stages involved. The first identifies the source of some of the traditional attitudes, going on to look at how certain construals are responsible for distorting the structural relationship between the main concepts. The second stage deploys an argument sketch to show how to approach the issues once the distortions affecting suicide and killing are removed. The third stage is more positive, suggesting how voluntary deaths can be assessed and thereby providing a moral basis for public policy on assisted suicide and euthanasia. Establishing the moral status of an act and the moral motivation for policy change is one thing, but it is quite another to evaluate the status of any policy that incorporates the act in law. In the present case I consider only the structure of the public policy debate, indicating where I believe emphasis should be placed.

Traditional Attitudes

All societies have strong prohibitions against certain forms of killing, but it is often mistakenly thought that our Hebrew and Christian traditions enshrine a blanket social prohibition against killing, backed by a fervent religious reverence for human life. The way people view the tribal code of the Hebrews is a prime example, commonly assuming it to contain the commandment, 'thou shall not kill.' The mitzvah at Exodus 20: 13 and Deuteronomy 5: 17 is 'thou shall do no murder,' not 'thou shall not kill.' The crucial Hebrew term for murder is transliterated as *râtsach*. Hebrew is rich in terms for species of killing; for example, when their god Yaweh orders killings done the term used is sometimes *mûwth*, which means both to be made dead, but also worthily so, and sometimes the same term is found in Psalms 10: 8, which has 'in the secret places (of the villages) doth he murder the innocent.' Here the murderer is *hârag*, one who makes slaughter (see also Numbers 31: 17–18). There is no term in Hebrew for suicide. The acts of suicide reported are described in terms of the means employed. For example, Achitophel, in II Samuel 17–23: '[he] put his household in order, and hanged [*chânaq*] himself, and died, and was buried in the sepulchre of his father.' No pejorative taint attaches to the act either here or at any other place in the Hebrew Bible where suicide is described. A similar account holds for the Christian scriptures (see Daube, 1972).

The negative tradition has been eclectic in its assemblage of argument, perhaps in part because its basic texts – Hebrew and Christian – do not support a prohibition on voluntary death (see Schopenhauer, 1970). Equally, how 'sanctity', a word which was first used to denote rather ostentatious ascetic qualities of particular religious lives, became a property of the abstract property, life, needs explanation.

Killing

Nothing of moral significance can be gleaned from the words 'suicide' or 'killing'. Particular acts are amenable to moral evaluation undertaken within the general category of suicide, where 'suicide', like the even broader 'killing', is a morally neutral term awaiting specification of detail (see Kovesi, 1967). The answer to the question, 'what is wrong with killing *per se?*' is, strictly speaking, 'nothing',

273

although it might be charitable to expect that the thrust of the question is really, 'why is murder wrong?' or perhaps, 'are all killings wrong or only some?' To either question a substantial response is required (see Ewin, 1972).

Unhappily, discussions of suicide often start from the assumption that this type of killing needs special justification simply because it is a form of killing, all killing being wrong. This is false. If some suicides – the ones whose grounds connect logically with assisted suicide and euthanasia – are evaluated as either manifesting moral excellence or as morally neutral, as I shall argue, then they are clearly not wrong, and if they are not wrong then it follows that the universal assertion that killing is wrong is false, because these suicides undoubtedly are killings.

A second line of approach supports the conclusion that suicide cannot, for conceptual reasons, be included among the cases of killings that count as murders. This is not to be confused with the weak claim that suicides are bad in so far as they are killings, but excusable; suicides lack the essential element which allows us to specify some killings as wrong.

There is no plausible secular argument to show that suicide is a subset of murder. There cannot be, since there is convincing argument to suggest that 'self-murder' is an oxymoron: injustice to oneself is an incoherent idea, as Hobbes (1845: 137), who explained murder as a species of injustice, so elegantly demonstrated:

> Whatever is done to man, conformable to his own Will signified to the doer, is no Injury to him. For if he that doeth it, hath not passed away his original right to do what he pleases, by some Antecedent Covenant, there is not breach of Covenant; and therefore no injury done him.

Considerations of justice are sufficient to show that suicide cannot be murder, and so cannot figure among the class of morally prohibited killings. We cannot have any blanket moral prohibition against suicide as such. But considerations of justice do not exhaust moral evaluations of suicide. Analysis of individual suicides results in the conclusion that some are tragically misguided – for reasons to do with impulsiveness, irrationality, drugs, depression or spite, for example (some of these being causes addressed in suicide prevention strategies) – while others are not.

Suicide

If reasons for action can be divided into those that are largely self-related and those that are mainly social or other-related, then a planned suicide will normally encompass reasons of both kinds. The solitary person who chooses a quick end to terminal pain may be obliged to consider only reasons of the first sort, but most of us face death accompanied part of the way by family or professional carers. Therefore the reasonableness or otherwise of a particular suicide will normally be a function of assaying both sorts of reasons; but it is plain that choosing to reject unbearable suffering is about as good as reasons for action can possibly get. Whether others are so moved in similar situations is neither here nor there so far as reasonableness is concerned; what matters is that we can appreciate the weight of the reasons for the person. Another person might see their personal suffering as bringing them closer to a realization of their god's plan, whereas a third may brave gross humiliation and suffering, but prefer risking death to loss of salvation through a simple blood transfusion.

The key issue is not suffering *per se*, but its place in the personal scheme of things. This personal scheme of things is best understood in terms of the conscientious commitments that structure a life and allow a person to express an authentic way of life. Too fixed a concentration on the role of pain in terminal illness can occlude this, resulting in a form of moral blindness. We see only the patient's pain, rather than the significance of their pain and anguish within their personal scheme of things. This is why the issue of palliative care and its adequate provision is not central to the discussion of assisted suicide and euthanasia, nor relevant to the case for their legalization. At best it simply reduces the class of those who may choose death. A consideration of what was perceived to be important for the patients aided by Dr Jack Kevorkian supports this point.

There are a number of other reasons that motivate people to suicide, but they do not connect with bioethics in quite the same straightforward way that pain, suffering and debilitation do. When a spy swallows cyanide rather than submit to torture that would result in confession and the subsequent deaths of comrades, her courageous decisiveness is exemplary; but her reasons derive from loyalty rather than amelioration of her situation. A much closer parallel to the bioethical case is provided by the prisoner who suicides by hanging rather than go through some ghastly form of public mutilation and execution. His action exhibits great courage as well as eminent good sense in avoiding a much greater evil. Similarly, wounded soldiers who kill themselves rather than submit to being live bayonet practice for their advancing enemies manifest the same prudence and courage. We are accustomed to admire altruistic suicides but seriously underestimate the moral worth of those carried out for purely self-regarding reasons.

I have suggested that there is nothing morally complex about suicide as such, because it is at best an incomplete moral notion that awaits further specification (see Kovesi, 1967). But there is real moral complexity within suicides, in particular where there are personal reasons for choosing death, but socially related reasons for persevering with life under great adversity. Furthermore, I have outlined cases where suicide is morally admirable because both prudent and courageous. There will also no doubt be cases where suicide might show resolve and courage, but be cowardly or shameful for reasons to do with the abandonment of others. Notice, however, that even in these cases the negative evaluation of the action is in terms of its dereliction or abandonment of those in our care; the fact that this occurs via suicide rather than flight is incidental and morally irrelevant. The moral evaluation of particular acts is all the evaluation that we have available to us here, but it may be extremely difficult to venture very far. Let me explain.

Those among the terminally ill who see suicide as a means of exercising sovereign control over the timing of their death may do so far different reasons. Our access to those reasons would need to be through a deeper knowledge of their life project and how it was conscientiously shaped. There is no guarantee that their aspirations are either easily accessed or understood by those who see them professionally, and it is not uncommon for members of the same family to be in dispute about choices near death. The following case is typical. A woman's resolve to die before all semblance of personality is obliterated by pain or drugs might be flatly at odds with her partner's desire to care for her despite profound dependence and even the obliteration of her old self. To judge the dying woman at fault for denying her partner's wishes is an impertinence of a particularly deep and nasty kind. We have reached a point where two reasonable conceptions of what morality requires – one purely social and the other more existential – part company, and where there is no obvious candidate to arbitrate (see Falk, 1965). Sensitivity requires a non-judgemental silence.

Assisted Suicide and Euthanasia

Both of these modes of voluntary death are morally derivative from suicide, because if there is compelling reason to provide aid in dying, either indirectly or directly, it stems from the sovereign role of the dying patient in determining that their life project is to be completed. The strength of the person's reasons for terminating life through suicide therefore provides whatever reasons there are for helping. Respect for the patient's authentic desires and compassion for their suffering provide the moral case for assisted suicide and euthanasia: they establish a claim – a moral right – to aid in dying, and provide the basis for a charge that any legal structure which impedes access to aid is cruel because it perpetuates unwanted suffering.

Significantly, this moral claim has long been protected in law for a small subset of the dying; namely those who require life-support to stay alive. In many countries there is either a statutory or a common-law right that allows a patient to direct that medical treatments be withdrawn. A person suffering from motor neurone disease who requires intermittent ventilation may determine their time of death by deciding when they will have ventilation withdrawn. This statutory right divides the dying into two classes: those who may achieve their aim of a swift death by refusing further mechanical aid, and those who are at the same stage with their illness but need no mechanical procedures to stay alive. The suffering and anguish may be the same in both cases, but only one group has a death option medically catered for. This form of discrimination is patently unjust.

To avoid the charge of unjust discrimination it would be necessary to argue that the partition among the dying is morally neutral or morally required. This move is implausible if the plight of the patients and their desires are to all intents and purposes the same. Precisely this argument of parity has proved decisive in two recent rulings in the United States. On 6 March 1996, the Ninth Circuit Court of Appeals, sitting in San Francisco (covering nine western states) found that liberty interests based on the Fourteenth Amendment made US law forbidding physician-assisted suicide unconstitutional. Eight of the eleven judges concurred in the judgement that there is a constitutionally protected liberty in determining the time and manner of one's death. On 2 April 1996, the Second Circuit Court of Appeals, sitting in New York (covering three eastern states) came to the same conclusion for slightly different reasons. Relying on the Equal Protection Clause of the Fourteenth Amendment, the court argued that there was no difference between the withdrawal of life-support systems and the prescription of drugs to cause death. This was a unanimous decision of the three judges. Referring specifically to the fact that patients who are machine-dependent have the right to dictate their time of death, two of the judges said that terminally ill patients 'should be free to do so by requesting appropriate treatment to terminate life during the final stages of terminal illness'. Although these judgements were subsequently overturned by the United States Supreme Court, there were many who thought that the Second and Ninth Circuit Court decisions were more convincingly reasoned. Meanwhile, at the time of writing the world's first statute regulating medically assisted suicide, Oregon's Death with Dignity Act (1994), is still in abeyance.

There will predictably be those among the dying who are physically or psychologically unable to enact a suicide even if the means are legally prescribed for them. It follows from the justice argument outlined above that if it is unjust to discriminate against those who are terminally ill but not machine-dependent, then it is equally unjust to discriminate against a subset of them, namely those who are disabled to a point where suicide is not a realizable option or who strongly desire it but for other reasons are incapable of the act.

Australia's Northern Territory has thus far been the only jurisdiction to carry this justice argument to its required conclusion, through the passage of its Rights of the Terminally Ill Act (1995). This Act – later overturned by the Australian Federal Parliament – briefly legalized both physician-assisted suicide and euthanasia, and in so doing closed the last remaining moral loophole. While the Northern Territory legislation followed the practice in the Netherlands, and accepted that euthanasia is the deliberate action to terminate life, by someone other than, and on the request of, the patient concerned, there is still the significant difference that only in the Northern Territory was the act made legal under statute. In 1993 the Dutch passed law which regulated the practice of voluntary euthanasia by setting down statutory guidelines; but under Dutch law voluntary euthanasia remains a criminal offence.

From Morality to Public Policy

It is conventional and correct to point out that our Western liberal polities are pluralist, by which it is meant that they encompass a wide variety of value assumptions, some of which are not compatible (see Engelhardt, 1986) Perhaps the most glaring example of incompatibility can be found in differing evaluations of the fundamental value of life. This contested territory can be described in different ways, but in terms of my remarks about the moral evaluation of killing the locus is sovereignty with respect to one's own life and its termination. The tradition that I have taken – in Zeno – as an emblem for this discussion treats the ceding of such control as akin to slavery, whereas its opposition – in communitarian or religious guise – asserts that control of personal destiny should be limited in the question of the timing of death.

277

The primary public policy question addresses what is to be done in the light of pluralism, and the liberal democratic answer is normally in terms of a harm principle identified by Mill (1960: 73) in the line, 'the only purpose for which power can be rightfully exercised over any member of a civilised community, against his will, is to prevent harm to others.' It would seem that both sides in the public policy debate are therefore obliged to conduct their case in consequentialist mode with societal outcomes as their lingua franca. This must cause some discomfort for people whose primary moral evaluations are often voiced as a rejection of utilitarian morality: do they see public policy argument as non-moral or as a necessary trading in the immoral?

The argument sketched through earlier sections is the usual prima facie case for assisted suicide and euthanasia, and whatever weight it has rests on beliefs about the role of compassion and sovereignty in life. Of course, both sides arrive at the public policy debate with opposed beliefs about what morality requires firmly in hand, so it would seem that if morality alone should dictate public policy then no policy can be stated in any area where unanimity is missing. This is clearly not the case, because the process of public policy-making involves the analysis of moral values and argumentation. In the current case, evaluating courses of action starts from an obvious moral fact: there are many people in our communities who are terminally ill, anguished and suffering, and who seek deliverance via medical help. This fact is not a mere belief, based on scriptural interpretation, dogma or hypothesis about the fabric of our communities.

The fact of real and present suffering inevitably shapes the policy debate, resulting in the following structure: the prima facie case to legalize assisted suicide and euthanasia is confronted with causal arguments that outline unacceptable scenarios (see chapter 28, pp. 280–90). The structure of such arguments is clear. If the arguments against the prima facie position prove unconvincing as causal arguments then the case against legalization dies with them, allowing the prima facie moral case to shape appropriate public policy.

In all of the political contexts where this policy issue has been debated the role of the negative causal arguments has appeared to be critical in the formation of views. I say 'appeared' because the role of basic moral views cannot be easily evaluated in this arena, especially when politicians vote on conscience and where causally shaped arguments about public safety can be cynically aired as a rationale for defending one's idiosyncratic religious values. However, all of these arguments against legalization rest on hypotheses about future states of affairs, against which the real and present plight of many is being balanced and usually discounted at an alarming rate. Joel Feinberg (1992) has argued that these arguments about social dangers and abuse overestimate the risks and seriously underestimate the burden of suffering actually borne by the terminally ill.

Conclusion

Suicide is the key concept in any broadly philosophical discussion of voluntary death, whereas bioethics, because of its narrower concerns, concentrates on responses to suffering and anguish in terminal illness. I have suggested that a component part of our tradition makes moral evaluation of particular suicides either very difficult or impossible, whereas the grounds for such evaluation were well understood and investigated in Greek and Roman philosophy. Conceptual confusion surrounding the morality of voluntary death, derived in the main from the traditional attitudes, thwarts the mature evaluation of suicide, assisted suicide and euthanasia. I then provided some reasons for thinking that whereas we can easily recognize some voluntary deaths as prudent and courageous, it is likely that in other cases morality counsels its own silence.

When we make the step from moral evaluation to law and social policy it is still going to be a moral stance that directs our line of argument. I have suggested that considerations of justice are sufficient to move us from our current protection of a patient's right to refuse therapy all the way through to legalizing voluntary euthanasia, with appropriate safeguards on the model of the short-lived, but pioneering, Northern Territory legislation. Finally, I have indicated the structure of the public policy debate, suggesting that the role of suffering initiates a presumption for change that only a clear causal argument to social harm could rebut.

References

Alvarez, A. (1974). *The Savage God.* Harmordsworth: Penguin.

Daube, D. (1972). The linguistics of suicide. *Philosophy and Public Affairs,* 1/4, 387–437.

Engelhardt, H. T. (1986). *The Foundations of Bioethics.* New York: Oxford University Press.

Ewin, R. E. (1972). What is wrong with killing people? *Philosophical Quarterly,* 22, 126–39.

Falk, W. D. (1965). Morality, self, and others. In H.-M. Castaneda and G. Nakhnikian (eds), *Morality and the Language of Conduct.* Detroit: Wayne State University Press.

Feinberg, J. (1992). *Freedom & Fulfillment.* Princeton, NJ: Princeton University Press. [Chapter 11.]

Griffin, M. (1994). Roman suicide. In K. W. M. Fulford, G. Gillett and J. M. Soskice. *Medicine and Moral Reasoning.* Cambridge: Cambridge University Press.

Hobbes, T. (1839–45). *The English Works of Thomas Hobbes of Malmesbury,* ed. Sir William Molesworth. London: John Bohn. [Volumes III and IV.]

Kovesi, J. (1967). *Moral Notions.* London: Routledge and Kegan Paul.

Kuhse, H. (1987). *The Sanctity-of-Life Doctrine in Medicine.* Oxford: Oxford University Press.

Mill, J. S. (1960). *On Liberty.* London: J. M. Dent. [First published in 1859.]

Schopenhauer, A. (1970). 'On suicide'. In *Essays and Aphorisms.* Harmondsworth: Penguin.

van Hooff, A. J. L. (1990). *From Autothanasia to Suicide.* London: Routledge.

Further Reading

Brandt, R. (1975). The rationality of suicide. In S. Perlin (ed.), *A Handbook for the Study of Suicide.* Oxford: Oxford University Press.

28

The slippery slope argument

GOVERT DEN HARTOGH

An Example

Slippery slope arguments can be used in the context of any discussion whatsoever, but if you are asked to give an example, the odds are that the example which first comes to your mind will be one from a bioethical discussion. In such discussions the argument is used very commonly, mostly in order to object against proposed changes in moral thinking or legislation. To give but one example, chosen almost at random:

> Prenatal diagnostics is wrong in principle, if abortion is the only thing we can do when a genetic defect is found. First a suspicion of Huntington's disease or cystic fibrosis will be counted as a good reason for abortion. Then it will be diabetes, sickle cell anaemia, Down's syndrome. then a club-foot. a harelip. myopia. colour blindness, an extra Y chromosome, left-handedness and finally skin colour. It will be argued that it is in the interest of the future child itself not to be born. But how can we decide that someone's life will not be worth living? People have no right to decide that the life of a handicapped person has no value. To do so is a violation of the basic principle of equality. If we allow ourselves any exceptions to that principle, handicapped people will come to be seen as the products of parental negligence. People will say to them: 'Why are you here? You should have been aborted.' And if these people are consistent, they will in the end believe that the lives of these people should still, in their own interest, be terminated.

The Paradigmatic Form of the Argument

The term 'slippery slope argument' is often used loosely: it is sometimes used for the appeal to a dangerous precedent (see the next section of this article); it is also applied to all kinds of arguments pointing to negative consequences of a proposed action, especially, but by no means exclusively, when the causal chain leading to these consequences consists of several links. So loose is present usage, in fact, that it does not refer to any distinctive form of argument meriting a separate discussion. Instead I will present a characterization of what I take to be the paradigmatic form of the argument, noting by the way some possible deviations from this standard form, but without bothering to decide which of these deviations should and which should not be called slippery slope arguments.

1   The discussion in which the argument is used concerns the question whether a certain class of actions – call them A – should be considered morally acceptable or be legally permitted;
2   The discussion presupposes a status quo position, in which people hold each other, or are held by legal authority, to certain norms of behaviour, prohibiting A;
3   It is proposed to move from the status quo position to a new one, which I will call the top of the slope, in which A will be considered acceptable or be permitted henceforward;

(There is no logical reason why the proposal should not be to prohibit an action which has up to now been accepted, but, remarkably, slippery slope arguments very rarely take this form.)

4   The opponents of the proposal do not question the acceptability of the top position directly. They neither assume that actions of type A are offensive as such, nor suggest that such actions are to be avoided because of their negative consequences (though as a matter of fact they will usually hold one or both of these positions);
5   Instead the opponents argue that a movement will not stop before we have reached the bottom of the slope; unpacking the metaphor, it is alleged that a causal mechanism exists which, once we accept actions of type A will cause us to accept actions of type N as well.

Note that in the paradigmatic form of the slippery slope argument it is not the A-type action itself which is supposed to have negative consequences, but rather the decision to consider such actions acceptable.

6   The causal mechanism referred to has the character of a chain reaction: once we accept A, we will predictably accept B as well, this will cause us to accept C and so on, until eventually we come to accept N.
    What is the nature of the links of the chain? We should consider one possibility in particular. Once we accept A, we have no reason to reject B, and, being reasonable people. we may be expected to realize this fact in due time.

Discussions of the slippery slope argument usually distinguish a logical form of the argument from a causal one. The logical form would simply consist of pointing out that, once we accept A, we are rationally committed to accepting B, C and eventually N. But in practice this logical form is almost always incorporated into a prediction. The opponents assume that even the supporters of the proposal agree that actions of type N are beyond the pale, either for intrinsic reasons, or because of their bad consequences, or both. Most of the time it is silently presupposed that actions of type N, once they are accepted, will be done more often. However, even if this is not the case, it may be alleged that the fact that these bad actions are not only done, but also tolerated, is a bad thing in itself. On the other hand, the opponents may also argue that, whether or not as a consequence of accepting A, actions of type N will be accepted, they will in any case be done more often than they are done at present, and that is what, they suggest, should deter us from accepting A in the first place.

The Appeal to a Pernicious Precedent

I will start my discussion by considering a form of argument which deviates from the paradigmatic one on two points. This is the appeal to a pernicious precedent. It is again conceded that A, on the face of it, has an innocent look. However, it is argued, once we accept A, we have no reason to reject B, which in all relevant respects resembles A. But B is clearly unacceptable. This is not a paradigmatic slippery slope argument, because it does not make any predictions about whether once we accept A we will in fact accept B. The claim is the more limited one that if we accept A we are rationally committed to accepting B.

This is a valid form of argument: the considerations presented, if true, really give us good, if not decisive, reasons, to accept the conclusion. The validity of the argument depends on a well-known characteristic of normative predicates: their *supervenience*. If an action is acceptable, it is always because it has certain other characteristics which make it acceptable. A supervenient predicate is necessarily also a universalizable one, at least in this sense: if, of two action types, one is acceptable and the other is not, it has to be true that they differ in at least one other characteristic. It doesn't follow, however, that if one action-type has a number of characteristics which, taken together, make actions of this type acceptable, all actions which share the characteristics are acceptable as well. They may have other characteristics that make them unacceptable. For this reason moral as well as legal argument is *defeasible*. Even good arguments need not be decisive ones.

This explains how the appeal to a pernicious precedent can be withstood: not only by pointing to a right-making characteristic of A which B doesn't share, but also by pointing to a wrong-making characteristic of B which A doesn't share. The value of the argument is that it lays down the burden of arguing either of these two points (or the acceptability of B) squarely on the shoulders of the defendants.

Slopes of Reason

I said above that the purely logical slippery slope argument can seldom be found in actual use. Nevertheless it is worth discussing, because it can be integrated into a causal argument.

The best-known use of this argument is in the context of abortion. If one considers the killing of a zygote to be acceptable, there is no reason to prohibit the killing of an embryo fourteen days after conception. If that is acceptable, there is no reason to be concerned about the killing of a fetus of three months – and so on. As the development from zygote to child occurs without any sudden jumps, once you have denied protection to the zygote, there is no point at which you can reasonably think it imperative to protect the developing human being. Viability will not do, because it depends on the skills of doctors; nor will birth, which after all doesn't involve any change in the child, but only in its environment.

This argument is similar in form to the one discussed in the last section: it simply repeats the appeal to a precedent, until a clearly pernicious one is reached. If you permit A, you are committed to permitting B: if you permit B, you are committed to permitting C, etc. Therefore, if you permit A, you are committed to permitting N, which clearly is wrong. If the appeal to a pernicious precedent is a valid form of argument, then the logical slippery slope argument, it seems, cannot be an invalid one. We can only say that each step offers the defendants new chances of pointing out relevant differences.

But here is the snag. If the accomplishment of the argument is seen as a shift in the burden of proof, the burden it imposes on the defendants is to identify exactly the point at which they dig in their heels. And that is what they often cannot do.

However, the requirement itself rests on a fallacy, known from ancient times as the Sophism of the Heap (*Sorites*). Consider any person with normal hair growth. Take away one of her hairs. That wouldn't make her bald, would it? Take away another hair. How can one hair make the difference between a bald person and a non-bald person? It cannot. So we take away another hair, and another one, etc. At the end of the process she has no hair left. Still, we are not allowed to call her bald; for we couldn't meet the requirement of pinpointing the exact moment at which she joined the class of bald persons. (It may be objected that only a person with no hair at all is a bald person, strictly speaking, but that is not how we normally use the word.)

It is difficult to explain exactly why this is a fallacy. Logicians still disagree about it. The argument uses three premises:

1   This person has a certain determinate number of hairs;
2   This person isn't bald;
3   If a person with a certain determinate number of hairs isn't bald, a person with one hair less isn't bald either.

The problem is that premises 1 and 2 may be true, premise 3 seems indisputable, and the form of argument which we use in deriving the absurd conclusion that a person with no hairs left isn't bald is clearly a valid one. Perhaps we should hold that the argument form isn't applicable in all cases, in particular not when the relevant predicate ('bald') is a vague term, i.e., a term referring to an indeterminate section of a continuum.

Note that it isn't sufficient to suspend the so-called Law of the Excluded Middle. This is the logical principle saying that for any predicate P, everything in the universe is either P or not-P. It is true that we should suspend the principle in the case at hand. It isn't true that a person is either bald or non-bald: there is a grey area between the two possibilities. However, it doesn't follow that we can reject premise 3, for that would suggest that the boundaries of the grey area are themselves determinate, which they aren't.

It is difficult to explain why Sorites is a fallacy, but it is beyond doubt that it is a fallacy, and that is the important thing. That there is a grey area, and that its boundaries are indeterminate themselves, doesn't imply that we cannot identify points which are definitely at one or the other side of the grey area. For that reason the logical slippery slope argument doesn't succeed in shifting the burden of proof. The requirement to locate the exact stopping-place on the slope should simply be rejected. If you are able to point to a relevant difference between a zygote and a newborn child, it doesn't matter that you are unable to tie the emergence of the difference to an exact point in time. If you are in doubt whether a genetic predisposition for retinitis pigmentosa (an illness which reveals itself in the gradual but eventually complete loss of sight between the ages of 20 and 40) is a good reason for abortion, you are not barred from being sure that Huntington's disease is a good reason for abortion, and colour-blindness is not.

It is true that we are in need of conventional or legal norms locating such a point. For if we allow embryo experimentation or abortion in the first trimester, and forbid infanticide and the use of babies in life-endangering medical experiments, then we have to identify a point at which protection starts, or a series of points at which it gradually increases. If there is no principled way of making this identification, the only reasonable thing to do is to fasten upon an arbitrary point lying safely within the core zone of the grey area. This point will tend to be a 'salient' one, like viability or birth, but, as far as this argument goes, even these points don't have any intrinsic importance. It is sometimes argued that we should aim at 'erring on the safe side', and therefore stay squarely on one side of the grey area. But that suggestion rests on the mistaken idea that, after all, there really exists a clear dividing line between the bald and the non-bald, and the problem is just that we don't know where it is.

In the case of the discussion about abortion, we can illustrate the fatal weakness of the logical slippery slope argument in another way. The proponent of the argument obviously presupposes that the status quo position isn't indeterminate at all: the protection of human life begins at conception. However, fertilization is a continuous process, just like fetal development, only involving a smaller being and a shorter time span. So where exactly do we draw the line: when the sperm contacts the plasma membrane of the oocyte, when it penetrates its zona pellucida, when the second meiotic division is completed, when the male and female pro-nuclei have formed, each with its own membrane or when these membranes break, allowing the chromosomes to mingle? If there is no non-arbitrary answer to this question, does it follow that conception cannot be a morally relevant boundary line?

You will only be able to reject a logical slippery slope argument in this way, if you are able to point to a relevant difference between the Top and the Bottom of the Slope. Some liberals on abortion have a problem here, because the characteristics they believe to be the real basis for protecting the human being (and other animals) are such that they cannot be ascribed to babies. These are the characteristics of persons, most basically an awareness of the self as continuous through time, which in its turn is presupposed in the abilities of having a memory, of making plans, of identifying others and communicating with them. However, that doesn't mean that the logical slippery slope argument is rehabilitated. As I suggested, it can be seen as an elaboration of the appeal to a dangerous precedent, presupposing that, wherever we can draw a continuous line between A and N, such that it is impossible for anybody to identify a clear boundary on the line, A really is a precedent for

284

N. This presupposition is false. But, of course, that doesn't mean that we cannot appeal to the wrongness of N directly in order to argue against the acceptance of A. That argument really succeeds in shifting the burden of proof. Liberals can respond in either of two ways: they can try to find a relevant difference between zygotes and babies after all (for instance, the role of the being in human relations and social conventions) or they can bite the bullet and accept that there are no intrinsic reasons for protecting the life of a baby more than the life of a zygote. Birth is then, they may say, at most a convenient point for drawing the arbitrary dividing line we have to draw anyway.

Slopes of Unreason

In describing the paradigmatic form of the slippery slope argument I said that the causal mechanism it relies upon for its prediction of dire consequences sometimes itself relies on human rationality. In this section I will discuss cases in which the causal mechanism isn't assumed to involve any form of rational commitment.

More specifically, I said that in the first class of cases the causal mechanism relied on human rationality in the following way: once we accept A, we have no reason not to accept B, and, being reasonable people, we may be expected to realize this fact. So we will accept B. Then for the same reason we will accept C, and so on until we reach N. We now see that reasoning in this way is not rational at all, but fallacious. The interesting thing, however, is that this need not impair the force of the prediction. Perhaps this is a kind of fallacy people are particularly prone to commit, as their tendency to be impressed by the logical slippery slope argument testifies. In other words: the only moral boundaries which have any chance of being respected are determinate ones. Morality should eschew the continuum. Very often the use of a slippery slope argument depends on this assumption (see Lamb, 1988, for an example).

The moral psychology behind it is not obviously true. What kind of line will tend to be more respected: a hard and fast but (assumingly) irrelevant one, or a rather indeterminate one which at least has clear instances of morally different cases at both sides of the line? What we know of the development of moral sensibility suggests that people will start their career as moral agents pretty close to the first position, but gradually move away from it. The question then becomes: to what extent are we prepared to treat our fellows as moral adults? It is plausible to assume that assessments of their competence are to a certain extent self-fulfilling.

The assumption is not only a dubious one for its factual presuppositions, it is also in logical trouble. For, to take our illustration again from the abortion debate, it is not difficult at all to identify any determinate point in human development after conception; the problem is that any such point is apparently only an arbitrary one. But this means that it is not enough to show (what is false anyway) that conception is a determinate point; we should also show that it is not an arbitrary one. People who are only asking for determinateness resemble the drunk who is looking for his hat under a lamppost, not because he has lost it there, but because there you have clear sight.

However, a more correct and fair judgement would be to say that people arguing this way actually assume that the status quo position is not an arbitrary one at all, but the only morally defensible one. But then their use of a slippery slope argument will not convince the unconverted.

Even so, it is problematical, not only in the form I have so far discussed in this section, but in any form, in which people are predicted to accept N without good reason, once they have started by accepting A. This is problematical whether or not the prediction is based on the claim that people can't draw a clear dividing line at any point, or on the claim that the intermediate cases form a continuum.

We usually suppose our judgements of moral acceptability to be matters of belief: considering A to be acceptable means believing that it is. The slippery slope argument amounts to saying: once you believe this, you will end up believing N to be acceptable as well, and this is clearly and catastrophically false. But even if that were true, it is no reason at all for not believing A to be acceptable. A proposition isn't any the less true if believing it has undesirable consequences. It isn't any the less true either, if believing it leads people to believe some false things as well, as long as this is not a matter of rational commitment.

In order to make any sense of the argument, we have to move in one of two directions, or both. The first option, which most proponents of a slippery slope argument will hate to take, is to assume that what we are discussing is not a matter of basic moral truth but a matter of human convention. The proposal which the slippery slope argument is meant to refute would then be that we have good reason to change our conventions, from the status quo to the new position.

Even if we conceive it in this way, the argument has a strong smell of paradox. Someone proposes to a certain audience, possibly involving anyone sufficiently interested to read about these matters, that it would be a good thing if people generally allowed each other to do A. The slippery slope argument presents an objection to this proposal to the same audience. The objection is that implementing the proposal would lead people, irrationally, to allow each other to do some really nasty things as well. It is hard to believe that any audience will be convinced by this objection, if the audience consists of a random selection of the very same people who are supposed to be irredeemably subject to the relevant causal mechanism. If they can understand the argument, why can't they correct their reasoning?

So it seems that we have to move in the other direction: suppose that the argument is addressed to a moral elite. The true morality can only be a secret doctrine, revealed to a chosen few. We, the enlightened, know that to enlightened people A would be fully acceptable. However, we shouldn't tell the mob, for they will immediately start to steal the silver from the table.

If the new position we are discussing is a matter of legal provision, rather than of moral acceptance, some of the arguments of this section don't apply. For a legal enactment, even if it should be justified to a large extent by moral belief, is not an expression of that belief. It is really a matter of decision. For that reason it isn't improper to argue that A should not be permitted because it will lead to N being permitted, either by a different authority or by the same one (presumably when staffed by different people). Or, the argument may go, permitting A will lead at least to N being done more often by those subject to the law (Schauer, 1985; van der Burg, 1991).

Furthermore, determinacy has an indisputable value in law. For the question here is not only what kind of boundaries command respect, but also which forms of respect can be intersubjectively verified, for example, by police officers or judges, but also by fellow citizens. Even so, arbitrary boundaries will be most acceptable if they draw a line within a recognizably grey area which has to be drawn anyway. If an arbitrary boundary is chosen for the only reason that it is determinate, even if it prohibits morally innocent behaviour which is important to the people involved, it is questionable whether this boundary should (or will) be respected. So even in this case the effective use of the slippery slope argument presupposes that the status quo position has other moral credentials besides determinacy. Perhaps we may expect a slippery slope argument to have an independent force in this area, in particular in those cases in which it is used to tip the scale in favour of the status quo, when people disagree about whether the status quo or the new position is intrinsically morally superior.

Factual and Moral Plausibility

So far I have established two main points:

1   Of those slippery slope arguments that refer to a slope of reason, the only valid form is that which avoids relying on the construction of a continuum of inter-mediate cases (if it can properly be called a slippery slope argument at all);
2   In the domain of moral argument the slippery slope argument cannot be applied to matters of basic moral truth, but at most to matters of convention.

Which other general conditions, if any, can we state for constructing a sound slippery slope argument? One obvious point is that the causal mechanism we specify should be a plausible one. Given the fact that our knowledge of social psychology is very limited, this is not an easy task. To show that it is not an impossible one, some authors point to past slides down slippery slopes. Some of these examples are more convincing than others. The basic problem with this kind of argument, however, is that while we may be able confidently to explain afterwards why things went wrong, that doesn't mean that we could confidently have predicted this beforehand. We can only conclude that we should be rather modest in our estimation of the probability of bad consequences, if we can give any weight at all to the prediction.

Even if it is then reasonable to give some weight to these considerations, it will not automatically be a decisive weight. In this context the metaphor of the slippery slope is somewhat misleading: slopes incline to one side only. But in discussing actual moral problems we will mostly find that staying at the status quo has its moral costs as well. It may even be the case that some of these costs can be presented in the form of a competing slippery slope argument. John Griffiths, for example, argues that it is only by legally allowing euthanasia and assisted suicide under strict conditions of careful action, that one can succeed in bringing 'a number of

287

socially dangerous medical practices which exist everywhere under a regime of effective societal control', not by 'invoking taboos as if these describe actual practice' (Griffiths, 1995).

It is hard to generalize here. The most we can say is that new conventions and laws almost always open up new possibilities of abuse and mistakes, even if abuse and mistakes are to be identified in terms of the new conventional or legal standard. Whether or not these consequences belong to the area of the slippery slope argument proper (they don't always involve a causal chain, or actions of acceptance as links of the chain), these possibilities have to be taken very seriously (Battin, 1994: chapter 8).

Recently, it was discovered that a nurse in a Dutch hospital for elderly people had killed at least five patients in advanced states of Alzheimer's disease, by giving them overdoses of insulin. She claimed, probably honestly, that she acted from a motive of mercy. According to the psychiatric report she was a very unbalanced person prone to project her own mental sufferings onto others.

It is clear that in terms of the moral consensus and the legal regime concerning mercy killing accepted at present in the Netherlands, her actions were wrong: she did not conform to any clearly expressed will of those patients, there was probably no unbearable suffering, she was not a physician and she acted in a way designed to escape accountability for her actions. Nevertheless, it could be argued, and it has been argued, that she could only have acted in this way because the Dutch moral consensus and legal regime does allow euthanasia in some cases. Believing that mercy could be a good reason for killing, she could come to think, however mistakenly, that it was a good ground in those cases. It is obviously difficult to substantiate a claim like this. It would probably not pass a court of law. Nevertheless, it is not wholly implausible.

On the other hand, people who find their predictions concerning the Dutch experiment with euthanasia confirmed by such events – which to the best of our knowledge occur very rarely – are mostly rather selective in their accounting of the moral costs. They don't attach any weight at all to the fact that, if the option of euthanasia is not available, some people who strongly want to avoid any further suffering will have to go through a prolonged period of severe suffering before they die.

This selectivity in taking account of negative consequences points to another way in which the use of a slippery slope argument usually presupposes the full moral acceptance of the status quo position. Only if taking a life is always wrong, even if it is done to prevent unbearable and hopeless suffering, are we justified in neglecting that side of the balance.

If we take the slippery slope argument as an independent argument, even in cases in which the prediction it makes is not implausible, it will mostly fail to be decisive. That is not in itself a weakness of the argument. Its major weakness can be illustrated by the euthanasia debate again. We assume that the bad consequences the argument predicts follow from people making mistakes in reason, as the Dutch nurse did. (In other words, we are assuming that the bad consequences are not the result of people deriving the right consequences from their acceptance of the new position.) This means that when we use a slippery slope argument in order to argue against the conventional or legal acceptance of voluntary euthanasia, we deny some people their wish to avoid any more of the suffering which for them necessarily is involved in living; and we do so, not because there is anything improper in granting their wish, but because other people will erroneously do unacceptable things if such wishes are granted. But is it fair to require those who urgently want voluntary euthanasia to sacrifice their most vital interests, in order to prevent other people from sinning?

This is a general weakness of all forms of consequentialism which do not systematically distinguish between direct and indirect responsibility. (Indirect responsibility is my responsibility for states of affairs occurring by other people responding in predictable ways to my actions.) It is ironic that this weakness can be found in an argument which is such a favourite with people who generally strongly oppose consequentialist views and insist (for example, in their support of the doctrine of double effect) on the importance of the distinction between what I directly intend and what I merely foresee will happen as a result of my action.

Appearance and Reality

This shows once again that the slippery slope argument cannot stand on its own feet. So far I have taken the argumentative claims of the slippery slope argument at face value. I have found that it can, at best, have some force, hardly a decisive one, within a restricted area of application, when it is made in a tentative way. The most prominent aspect of its use in actual discussion, however, is that these restrictions are seldom honoured: the argument is often used in the context of the discussion of moral fundamentals, and its predictions, especially in this context, are almost always put forward as absolute certainties, and as unreservedly deciding the matter in favour of the status quo position.

It is seldom worthwhile to address such arguments directly. They should rather be taken as expressions of allegiance to the moral superiority of the status quo position, and should be addressed as such. What they mean is this: the one important moral boundary is the boundary between the status quo and the new position. The boundary the defendants suggest exists between the top and the bottom, on the other hand, is not a morally important one at all. Therefore, if we move to the top position, we have crossed the Rubicon, we have entered into a sphere in which the bottom position is really, whatever the defendants believe, no longer a moral impossibility. The prediction – that we will eventually accept the bottom position as well – is only a way of dramatizing this claim. It doesn't add anything substantial to it.

Reconstructed this way, the argument amounts to an appeal to a pernicious precedent. The prediction doesn't matter, the intermediate cases don't matter and the suggestion of detachability from the primary moral controversy is misleading. To return to the example I started with: the real question about prenatal diagnostics is whether the decision to prevent the birth of a handicapped child really is equivalent to saying that handicapped people have no life worth protecting. If it is, then the procedure stands condemned, and the 'consequences' pointed out in the argument I quoted at the beginning don't add to the grounds for this condemnation. They only express it.

The best course for defendants to take in such cases is to ask their opponents squarely whether they believe the slippery slope argument to be independent from their loyalty to the status quo. If they answer that they don't, we can discuss the intrinsic moral merits of the status quo and the new position. If they answer that they do, the defendants most of the time will be able to show that this claim is untenable. Only if it isn't does it make sense to enter into a discussion of the plausibility and force of the argument.

References

Battin, Margaret P. (1994). *The Least Worst Death*. New York: Oxford University Press.
Griffiths, John (1995). Assisted suicide in the Netherlands: the *Chabot* case. *Modern Law Review*, 58, 232–48.
Lamb, David (1988). *Down the Slippery Slope*. London: Croom Helm.
Schauer, Frederick (1985). Slippery slopes. *Harvard Law Review*, 99, 361–83.
Van der Burg, Wibren (1991). The slippery slope argument. *Ethics*, 102, 42–65.
Walton, Douglas (1992). *Slippery Slope Arguments*. Oxford: Oxford University Press.

PART VIII

RESOURCE ALLOCATION

29

Micro-allocation:
deciding between patients

JOHN HARRIS

The necessity for choosing between patients presupposes scarcity of resources. The scarcity may be radical, where there are not enough resources to treat all in need, and the result is that some will be left untreated or die before their turn arrives. Scarcity may be, on the other hand, comparative, where patients have to be prioritized but all will eventually be treated.

That scarcity of resources for health care is a permanent and inescapable condition is usually taken to be axiomatic. Resources, so it is claimed, are after all not infinite, therefore they must be finite, and if finite, then assuming expanding demand, scarcity is inevitable. Two things need to be said about such a claim. The first is that while resources are not infinite, they are not finite either. They are indefinite. Any given budget may be increased if other budgets are traded off against it. This means that priorities can always be reassessed. There are also some grounds for denying the other part of the catechism, namely that demand is increasing and potentially infinite and that this is shown by the increasing problems experienced in public health-care systems. The continuing difficulties that such systems experience in meeting demand is not caused by increasing demand but by diminishing supply (Oppenheimer, 1988a: 17). Moreover, the claim that 'demand for a zero-priced service is bound to be infinite' is, as Peter Oppenheimer, an Oxford economist, has shown, simply 'wild talk'. 'The amount demanded of a free service is determined at the point where customers see no additional benefits to be gained from additional recourse to the service in question. This occurs at modest demand levels for most forms of medical care (as for most public libraries and public lavatories' (Oppenheimer, 1988b).

However, for the rest of this chapter I will assume the necessity to choose between patients and examine the ethics of some of the ways that are usually proposed for coping with scarcity.

What is 'Greater Need' for Health Care?

A common way of prioritizing patients is in terms of their need for treatment. Need is all too often defined either in terms of one conception of the degree of benefit to be obtained from health care, or in terms of the capacity of the patient to benefit, with the implication that the greater the capacity to benefit the greater the need.

There are a number of things that might be meant by 'need' when people argue that priority should be given to those in the greatest need. We might think that the person with the greatest need will be the person who is suffering most, or the person in the worst health state, or the person who will be left in the worst state of health after treatment, or the person who will benefit most from health care, or the person who feels her need for health care most desperately. Here of course we must be careful to distinguish the need for health from the need for health care. Where health care cannot ensure that health is better than it would have been without health care, while there may well be a need for health, there can hardly be an argument for delivering useless and wasteful health care.

The implication is that those in greatest need of health care are those who will benefit most from health care. On this view, the degree of need is the same as degree of capacity to benefit measured in life years or quality-adjusted life years (QALYs) to be gained from treatment. The greater the number of years of good quality life (QALYs) that can be gained from treatment so the argument goes, the greater the need (Williams, 1985).

Is the degree of need for health care equated in any way to the capacity to benefit from it, where capacity to benefit is measured in terms of quality and quantity of life?

The degree of need for health care as has at least three dimensions:

1   The urgency, intensity or importance of the need;
2   The amount of whatever it is that is needed;
3   The capacity of the individual to benefit from what she needs.

If Tom says, 'I badly need a drink' and Dick says, 'I wouldn't mind a drink' they are expressing (probably) different degrees of need in the first sense. If Tom says, 'My thirst won't be satisfied till I've downed ten pints,' and Dick says, 'I'll be happy with a couple of pints,' then again they are expressing different degrees of need in the second sense. If Dick says, having downed his allocation, 'not only has my thirst gone but I feel great,' whereas Tom says, 'my thirst is satisfied but I still feel terrible,' they are expressing different degrees of benefit from need satisfaction. And finally, if Tom says, 'I'll want another ten pints tomorrow and every day thereafter,' and Dick says, 'those two pints will satisfy me for a week,' they are again recording differences in the amount of what they need.

It is not clear that it is plausible to say that Dick has a greater need for beer than Tom because his capacity to benefit is greater in the second two senses, whereas Tom's needs are greater in the first two senses. Just as 'need for greater amounts' is not the same as 'greater need', so neither are 'greater capacity to benefit' nor 'longer satisfaction of need' obviously better measures of degree of need than are 'the urgency, intensity or importance of the need' on the one hand nor 'the amount of whatever it is that is needed' on the other.

It should be noted that I have chosen here an example which uses a subjective notion of need, but this is only to make clear the differences between the different dimensions of need. Those same differences, of course, are also equally present in so-called 'objective' needs, believed to be common for everyone, like the need for food and shelter.

To return to health care, there is a distinction between the need for health and the need for health care, which is relevant only where health care cannot deliver health. If I am ill but there is nothing medicine can do for me then though I need health, I can't be said to need health care. Where it can, then the need for health care cannot legitimately be equated exclusively with *one* measure of the degree to which health care can benefit an individual.

Economists and some utilitarians tend to equate need with capacity to benefit, rather than with other conceptions of need, because they believe they know how to measure capacity to benefit. But, much as we all love economists and utilitarians, they cannot be permitted to hijack the English (or any other) language in order to claim to have provided a way of measuring need. What they may have done is provide a way of measuring one of a sizeable number of *dimensions of need.*

I am not, of course, suggesting that we should not use need as one of the most important criteria for prioritizing people for health care. But what we need to do is decide which dimensions of need plausibly indicate greater necessity for treatment, or a more compelling claim on the resources available for health care.

One plausible candidate for such an indicator is to ask what the patient stands to lose if they are not treated and try to assess the scale of the loss. On such a view, loss of life itself would almost always be a greater loss than diminution in quality of life. But, in the case of loss of life, is the loss greater the more years of life that are lost? Is the claim weaker, the fewer the life years that may be gained by treatment? It is a fallacy to suppose an affirmative answer to such a question is necessarily the right one, though many think it is. Indeed, since no one knows how long she would have lived had she not died at a particular moment, the scale of the loss measured in this way is always speculative.

If the millionaire and his lowly employee both lose all they have in the stock-market crash, on one way of thinking about the loss, each has suffered the same degree of loss, each has lost everything. On another, each has suffered a different quantity of loss measured by the total sum lost. There is no straightforward way of reconciling these different approaches to the assessment of loss. If we are searching for an equitable approach to loss, it is not obvious that we should devote resources allocated to loss minimization to ensuring that the millionaire is protected rather than his more humble employee. Even if it is agreed that resources devoted to health care are resources devoted to minimizing the loss of health or maximizing the health gain, it could not be demonstrated that the person who stands to lose more life years if they die prematurely stands to suffer a greater loss than the person who has less life expectancy. Nor can it be shown that the measure of health gain must be equated with the number of life years, quality adjusted or not, which flow from treatment. Arguments can (and have) been made on both sides, but to define need in terms of capacity to benefit and then argue that the greater the number of life years deliverable by health care, the greater the need for treatment (or the greater is the patient's interest in receiving treatment) is just to beg the crucial question of how to characterize 'need'.

Should the Health-care System Maximize QALYs?

We have seen that among others, the life-years approach to defining health gain (whether or not those life years are adjusted for quality of life considerations) and hence to defining what is to be delivered by health-care systems, is not the obvious answer to the question of which patient is in most need of health care. However, it remains *an answer* to that question. Part of its attraction as an answer is that it dictates a policy of maximizing QALYs – choose the patient and the treatment which will deliver more QALYS per dollar. How good an answer is it? There is much literature on this question (Williams, 1985; Harris, 1987) and justice cannot be done to the complexities of the discussion in this brief space. I will simply summarize some of the problems the QALY style answer has to overcome and leave the judgement as to how successfully it is possible to overcome these problems to the reader.

The use of a QALY approach to micro-allocation tends to bias the health-care system in favour of the young and against the old because, other things being equal, the young have more life years to gain from treatment than the old. This might be thought to amount to ageism and it will be discussed in more detail presently. It also tends to favour patients who have conditions which are at present cheaper to treat. This may pre-empt research and development achieving economies in such treatment and hence not only discriminate against conditions which are initially expensive to treat, but also against groups of citizens identified by their condition, for example, AIDS patients or cancer patients.

Finally it discriminates against those with disability. Imagine twin sisters, one healthy, the other paraplegic from birth. Both now in their thirties have achieved lives they find worthwhile and satisfying. Both are involved in an accident and need the same treatment to restore them to life and to their former health state. QALYs dictate that priority should go to the sister who is not chair-bound. Where resources are scarce, this may mean only the formerly healthy sister will survive. Is this fair and reasonable?

We need now to review the other major considerations which are often used to justify selection between claimants for care. I will first try to identify many of the major sorts of consideration and then, in the brief space left, say something about how we should try to move forward in the face of so many diverse and conflicting considerations.

Choosing between Claimants

We have looked briefly at the concept of a needs-based approach and noted that needs are often cashed out in terms of *quantity of life* and *quality of life*. An idea strongly related to quality of life considerations is that of *the value of someone's life*. When this appears in justifications for treating one person rather than another, three different sorts of appeal are often made. Sometimes the *value to the community* of someone's life is invoked, others lay stress upon a patient's *value to others* nearer to her (children or family perhaps); finally, some believe that the strength of the value an individual attaches to their own life, *value to oneself*, should be taken into account.

Those who equate need with capacity to benefit are often inclined to look at a patient's *prognosis* and argue that those with the best chance of successful treatment should be given priority. Related appeals are often made in terms of someone's *past contribution* to society, or to the health-care system itself in terms of service to it, or payment for it via national insurance contributions. *Future or expected contribution* is sometimes thought relevant, and someone's potential for contribution, in all the above ways and also perhaps, via exceptional skills, to possible medical or scientific advance is often thought to establish a strong claim.

Issues concerning *personal responsibility for health* have been the occasion of much debate about priorities in health care (*British Medical Journal*, 1993; Mclachlan, 1995; De Beaufort, in press). An individual's lifestyle, their eating habits, whether or not they smoke, the dangerous pastimes or sports they indulge in, the danger of not indulging in dangerous sports and becoming unfit and obese, the sexual preferences one has and the frequency with which one indulges them, and with whom and with what care, are all arguably reasonable bases for claims to priority or lack of it in the allocation of health-care resources. Then there are issues that arise from such factors as where people live, the occupational hazards they have to face, how and on or in what people travel; all of these contribute to one's responsibility for ill health and all have been cited in arguments about priority for care.

Moral character and *fault* are also very popular candidates. Should the drunken driver be given the same priority as his victim? If the prison and the hospital are on fire, where should the ambulance go first?

Then there are what we might call *impersonal features.* An individual's illness or treatment may have significance for research purposes for example, or perhaps because there is a useful by-product of their treatment (oocytes for donation, cell lines for development) there may be powerful arguments to prioritize their treatment. Where someone is prioritized because they happen to be part of a larger group and they become part of a strategy of maximizing numbers treated, we might also think of this as an impersonal feature.

I have not tried to be exhaustive. I have failed to mention *triage, compliance*, cases where someone poses an *innocent threat to others* and a number of other considerations. To what extent can we or should we take account of all these things?

Allocation and Liberation

It is a truism that individuals are individual. People are different from one another in a myriad of ways. Among those ways are, of course, ways that make some people better than others, morally, spiritually, existentially. Some are more valuable to society, others better parents, some are healthier and have better life expectancy, others have a quality of life that is enviable and even perhaps envied by the man on the Clapham omnibus. Some people are simply nicer than others and some are even fundamentally nasty.

Of the ways in which it is sometimes thought appropriate to distinguish between candidates for care, many of which we have just reviewed, a substantial number identify moral differences. When we ask whether priority for treatment should be given to the productive executive or to the chronically unemployed, or when we compare the claims of the young mother of four to that of the friendless loner, or when we consider whether the drunken driver or his victim should be treated first, or when we allocate a low priority to smokers, we are making moral assessments. Although these may also have a clinical component they can never be purely matters of clinical judgement. To concentrate on one dimension of this problem: of all the ways in which people may be said to have contributed to their own adverse health state it is usually only the most clearly unpopular candidates that are singled out. Thus although sports injuries, occupational hazards and lifestyle-related illness are all examples of personal responsibility for an adverse health state, anecdotal evidence suggests that discrimination in the allocation of medical resources has tended to concentrate on those who smoke, those who drink excess alcohol and those who are HIV positive.

Moreover, medical needs are seldom simply that. They are often also opportunities to go on living or to be free: free of pain, free or freer in the sense of being mobile or more mobile, more able effectively to operate in the world. Health care is important not simply because we all value health and all want long and healthy lives. It is important also because good health is liberating and poor health is confining.

Since choices between patients as to which will receive the resources required for health care are often choices as to who will be offered the chance to have their life saved, or their pain relieved or their mobility, their freedom restored, three pressing questions arise. They are:

1   Given that we cannot avoid choosing between patients, do we want that choice made in a way that has the ethical evaluation of the patient as a large component of the decision procedure?
2   Where other non-clinical factors are in play, such as the issue of what weight is to be given to the fact that a patient has dependants, the same question arises: do we want evaluation of these factors to determine treatment outcomes?
3   If we are content that we must or should chose between candidates for care in a way that involves the moral evaluation of those candidates or of other non-clinical features of their situation, are we content to leave that evaluation to doctors or health administrators to make on the basis of whatever information just happens to be available at the time?

There are a number of issues here. I think we have good reason to be concerned to avoid making choices that may be life or death decisions on the basis of moral evaluation of persons. But even if we were satisfied that this was a proper thing to do, we should under no circumstances leave such evaluation to untrained medical staff or other health professionals, nor permit such decisions to be made on the basis of necessarily sketchy information. When I talk of 'untrained' medical staff, I mean that while they are medically trained, they are not trained to make the moral evaluations of which we are speaking. Indeed it is doubtful whether such training exists.

Moral Evaluation of Persons

Where decisions about eligibility for treatment or prioritization are made by medical staff or other health-care purchasers or providers and where evaluation of the person plays some part in that decision two immediate problems arise. The first concerns the adequacy of the information on which the judgement is based and the opportunities for fair assessment of all relevant facts. The second concerns problems of measuring degrees of responsibility. In terms of decisions based on the moral evaluation of persons, as we have seen, most of the circumstances in which people are tempted to use moral evaluation as a determinant of the allocation of medical resources turn on cases where the individual is apparently herself wholly or partially responsible for her predicament, for the fact that she needs health care.

For the sake of brevity we will concentrate on the question of whether the person who needs health care because they have over-indulged in alcohol should be given lower priority than candidates who are not apparently responsible for their own adverse health state. There are two good reasons for doing so. The good reasons are that excessive drinking is seen as both voluntary and unnecessary; moreover, its harmful effects are well established and have been long known and well publicized.

One consideration often adduced in favour of discriminating against alcohol abusers, which is of some immediate intuitive force, is the suggestion that when faced with a choice between treating someone whose condition is alcohol-related, and someone who has diligently attempted to protect their own health by avoiding intoxicating beverages, it would be unfair to prefer the drinker. The argument behind this judgement may be that the drinker should not be 'rewarded' for her recklessness while the prudent individual is 'punished' for her care of her own health. A related thought may be that it seems unfair that the non-drinker should be denied the benefit that she has a reasonable expectation would be the just reward for her virtue.

We should remember that it is not entirely true that a non-drinker who is given a lower priority for treatment than a drinker has had the benefit of their virtue negated in some way. Non-drinkers do, other things being equal, get benefit from their virtue; they are less likely to need health care. They do have their fair, deserved advantage over drinkers. They have already been rewarded personally and statistically for their virtue. This is not at issue. The question that must be asked is should they be rewarded *again* by the public health-care system? Does their virtue increase their entitlement to benefit from public health care?

Then there is the suggestion that the drinker should not be *preferred* to the non-drinker, that such a preference would be unfair in that it rewarded vice at the expense of virtue. No one is, I think, suggesting that drinkers should be preferred to non-drinkers; but should they have an *equal* chance of access to health care?

299

If they are given an equal chance of care and treatment then, of course, drinkers will sometimes be treated while non-drinkers are not. It may be unfair in some cosmic sense when the virtuous suffer and the less virtuous prosper. But should we use public resources and even legislation to try to ensure that this does not happen? And if we do so, are we in danger effectively of punishing people for their choice of lifestyle and doing so in a way which not only violates principles of natural justice, as we shall see, but which creates additional and gratuitous injustice.

It is sometimes said that giving a low priority in their allocation of resources for health care to drinkers is justified, not as a punishment for them or a reward for the virtue of abstainers, but because to fail to do so would encourage dangerous and antisocial habits in the community and fail to give a much-needed incentive to people to give up alcohol. However, if the prospect of better health and a longer life on the one hand, and fear of premature death from alcohol-related diseases or injuries on the other, does not act as an incentive, it is surely unlikely that the further fear of failure to get priority in medical care will add much to the incentives and disincentives already in place. If it is right that refusals to treat, or low positions on waiting lists, are unlikely to have much impact on behaviour, then discrimination against drinkers in the allocation of health-care resources will effectively function as a punishment and should be seen as such.

This raises a large issue which we have no space here to tackle adequately. It is the question of the appropriateness of allowing doctors, or indeed the health-care system, to hand out punishments and rewards for behaviour that is quite legal. If this is effectively a form of punishment, and in so far as it is, it would be punishment without a hearing or trial, by individuals who were effectively judge, jury and executioner rolled into one. Moreover, there would be little prospect of appeal or remission of sentence. Not only is there a problem of double jeopardy here, of people being effectively 'punished' twice for the same offence (once by their contracting a condition caused by alcohol and a second time by the refusal to treat that condition), but there is also an insurmountable problem of natural justice.

Moreover, a health-care system which penalized people on the basis of information about their general health state and life expectancy would almost certainly discourage the divulging of information relevant to health and would therefore tend to undermine the public health considerations which are often thought to be part of its attraction.

It can scarcely be necessary to argue the point, but decisions which may involve life or death are as consequential as any decisions can be. Such decisions should clearly only be taken at all under the pressure of overriding necessity. I have suggested at the start of this chapter that such claims may be rather more difficult to sustain than many believe. However, even if it is granted that there is overriding necessity in the form of radical scarcity of resources, clearly some just and impartial procedure must be established for making such decisions. In particular, there must be appropriate mechanisms for establishing the facts on which such decisions are based and an appropriate appeals procedure. Where such 'facts' include judgements as to moral worth, there must at the very least be agreement about, and acceptance of, the appropriate bases for such judgements.

Natural Justice

I believe that most life or death decisions currently taken within public health-care systems that involve choices between patients, where the result is that a patient who could have had his life sustained dies as a consequence of adverse selection, involve violation of the principles of natural justice.

It is well worth while reminding ourselves just what these principles are and what they involve. I will quote from one of the standard texts and most authoritative sources on the question of natural justice:

> The rules of natural justice are minimum standards of fair decision-making, imposed by the common law on persons or bodies who are under a duty to 'act judicially'. They were applied originally to courts of justice and now extend to any person or body deciding issues affecting the right or interest of individuals where a reasonable citizen would have a legitimate expectation that the decision-making process would be subject to some rules of fair procedure . . . All that is fundamentally required of the decision-maker is that his decision . . . be made with due regard for the affected parties' interests and accordingly be reached without bias and after giving the party or parties a chance to put his or their case. (De Smith and Brazier, 1994: 602)

In the absence of agreement about, and acceptance of, the appropriate bases for judgements based on or with a component of moral worth and with no evidence-gathering or checking mechanisms in place, it is surely doubtful whether the first rule of natural justice could be satisfied in micro-allocation decisions. This rule requires *nemo judex in sua causa*, that no one be a judge in his own cause. This means that an adjudicator 'must not be reasonably suspected, or show a real likelihood, of bias'. Equally without affording patients the opportunity of knowing that they have been selected against, and arguing their corner and possibly without an appeals procedure, it is doubtful whether the second rule of natural justice could be complied with. This involves *audi alteram partem*, the right to a fair hearing.

Finally, one other consideration should be mentioned. Even if we could solve the problems of complying with the principles of natural justice, many of the other bases for selection involve information. Responsibility for one's own health state, utility to society or level of past or future contribution, numbers of dependants or friends, membership of some larger group and so on, all involve comprehensive information-gathering and information access and retrieval of a high order. Whenever priorities between patients are set, the appropriate decision-maker would have to have immediate access to a wealth of personal information about all the individuals involved which would include their family details, sexual habits, lifestyle choices, diet, domicile, work, genetic constitution, income levels and much besides. A real question is whether we would want to live in a society that routinely gathered, stored and had instantly retrievable such comprehensive personal information? Moreover, this society would have to license officials (medical staff?) to act on such information instantly, sometimes with life or death consequences. Would we be happy that the information was accurate, had been appropriately assessed and that something crucial was not missing?

Utility to Society

Much the same could of course be said about an individual's utility to society. There are the immense problems of agreeing the appropriate bases for judgements about utility (is a postman more useful than a refuse collector?) and the problems of gathering and having readily available the relevant information which we have noted. Of course there will be cases where fairly complete information on a particular individual may just happen to be to hand. The justice of acting upon it in these cases would share the justice of a tax system which taxed only those on whom tax-relevant information happened to be available, but which had no systematic gathering of information (tax returns, etc.) and no investigative, checking or appeals procedures.

Numbers of Dependants

Many people believe that we should favour those with dependants in the allocation of resources for health care and that the objection that this is unfair 'loses a lot of its force when the preference is justified by citing the interests of dependants rather than the merits of the person selected' (Glover, 1977). There are two major problems with such an approach. The first is that it is not clear why where someone's survival or treatment is dependent on the interests of third parties, the interests of third parties who are dependants should take preference over the interests of third parties who are not. Moreover, it is unclear why only interests *in favour* of treatment should count. Third parties, dependent or not, may have as strong an interest that someone should not be treated and perhaps should not survive as that they should receive treatment. Third parties might stand to benefit financially from someone's death, for example, or might object to treatments such as abortions or fertility treatments.

The second problem is that the feeling that it is somehow more important to treat those with relatives, when elevated to the level of policy, amounts to a systematic preference for those with families over those without. It is not clear how such a policy would avoid the offensive division of people into grades, some more worth saving than others.

Age and Life Expectancy

Implicit in this discussion has been an argument against ageism in the distribution of resources for health care. This argument can be stated thus:

> All of us who wish to go on living have something that each of us values equally although for each it is different in character, for some a much richer prize than for others, and we none of us know its true extent. This thing is of course 'the rest of our lives'. So long as we do not know the date of our deaths then for each of us the 'rest of our lives' is of indefinite duration. Whether we are 17 or 70, in perfect health or suffering from a terminal disease we each have the rest of our lives to lead. So long as

we each wish to live out the rest of our lives, however long that turns out to be, then if we do not deserve to die, we each suffer the same injustice if our wishes are deliberately frustrated and we are cut off prematurely. (Harris, 1985)

An important element of anti-ageism expressed in this way is that it links opposition to discrimination on the basis of chronological age to discrimination on the basis of life expectancy. These are not of course necessarily linked. Some people have defended what might be termed a 'fair innings argument' (Harris, 1985; Callahan, 1990). This suggests that people are entitled to every opportunity to live a fair lifespan (sixty or seventy years?). Up to that point they have equal entitlement to health care; beyond the fair innings they are given very low priority. This argument is tempting because it explains the strong intuition people have that there is something wrong with treating the claims of an octogenarian and those of a 20-year-old as equal. However, the fair innings argument has a number of defects. It assumes that the value of a life is to be measured in units of lifetime, the more the better up to a certain point but thereafter extreme discounting begins. The problem is that people value particular events within their life disproportionately to the time required to experience those events. Although the fair innings argument gives great importance to a life having shape and structure, these things are again not necessarily only achieved within a particular time-span. On the fair innings argument, Nelson Mandela's entitlement to life-sustaining treatment was exhausted before he left Victor Verster prison. And it is not only for such as Mandela that the most important part of their life might well begin after a so-called 'fair innings' had been achieved.

Without the vast detail of each person's life and their hopes and aspirations within that detail, we cannot hope to do justice between lives. I believe the only sensible alternative is to count each life for one and none for more than one, whatever the differences in age and in other quality considerations.

It is this outlook that explains why murder is always wrong and wrong to the same degree. When you rob someone of life you take from them not only all they have but all they will ever have; taking life is an act so different in degree to any other, so radical that it makes for a difference in the quality of the act. However, the wrongness consists in taking from them something that they want. That is why, as has been suggested, voluntary euthanasia is not wrong and murder is.

Those who believe in discriminating in favour of the young or against the old must believe that in so far as murder is an injustice, it is less of an injustice to murder the old than the young, and since they also believe that life years are a commodity like any other, it is clear that in robbing people of life you take less from them the less life expectancy they have.

Fairness and Quality of Life

The same ideas which underpin discrimination against the old on the grounds of fairness would also entail trying to equalize quality as well as quantity of life. The argument here would be that resources required for survival should be distributed

JOHN HARRIS

not only so as to favour the young but also so as to favour those whose quality of life has been relatively poor. Suppose two patients . . . both about 40 years old . . . need a liver transplant but only one suitable liver is available. One of the patients (the first) has had a much worse life than the other. In this case it might be argued that it seems most fair to give the liver to the first person. Again, such a view has some appeal, but it has the same problems concerning information-gathering that we have already noted. We could never make decisions as to how to allocate life-saving or indeed other scarce resources between people until we had their whole (and very complete and detailed) life history. Better surely to treat each person as counting for one and none for more than one than even to embark on the massively invasive (of privacy) data collection which it would be necessary to hold and have instantly available on each and every citizen, and which could never be complete, accurate or proof against abuse.

If it is right to attempt to even out quality of life as between people then we should do so as a matter of public policy throughout society, not simply in the rare cases where resource allocation decisions in health care arise. This might have to include making sure that no one lived longer than the person who has the shortest lifespan and no one was happier than the most miserable. This is likely to be dysfunctional in terms of species survival but we will ignore this problem for obvious reasons.

Ultimately we will be comparing different moral priorities. However, there seems much to be said for taking individual persons and their preferences and fundamental interests as what matters from the point of view of morality. This means that we must recognize that although their lives will all differ in length, happiness and success, in short, in the degree to which their fundamental interests are satisfied, people matter morally despite these differences not because of them, and each person's wish to have the treatment that will offer him the chance of continued flourishing to the extent that his personal health status permits is as urgent and important as that of any other person.

Conclusion

Where consensus about degree of need for health care can be achieved, this should be the basis of choice. Where, as in many cases, this is unlikely to be possible the alternatives are unattractive indeed. The alternative to either complying with the principles of natural justice where decisions between patients are taken or taking such decisions in a way that shows no preference, by lot for example, may be equally daunting. In the light of this, the option of finding a higher level of resources for health care might not seem so unattractive or so onerous.

References

British Medical Journal (1993). Should drinkers be offered coronary bypass surgery? *British Medical Journal*, 306 (17 April), 1047–50.
Callahan, Daniel (1990). *What Kind of Life: the limits of medical progress*, New York: Simon and Schuster.

de Beaufort, Inez (1998). Individual responsibility for health: some thoughts on drinkers, drunken drivers, champagne drinkers and health freaks. In: Charles Erin and Rebecca Bennett (eds), *HIV/AIDS: Who should know?* Oxford: Oxford University Press.

De Smith, Stanley and Brazier, Rodney (1994). *Constitutional and Administrative Law.* 7th edn. Harmondsworth: Penguin.

Glover, Jonathan (1977). *Causing Death and Saving Lives.* Harmondsworth: Penguin.

Harris John (1987). QALYfying the value of life. *Journal of Medical Ethics,* 117–23.

—— (1996a). What is the good of health care? *Bioethics,* 10/4, 269–92.

—— (1996b). Could we hold people responsible for their own adverse health? *Journal of Contemporary Health Law and Policy,* 1, 147–55.

McLachlan, Hugh V. (1995). Drinkers, virgins, equity and health care costs. *Journal of Medical Ethics,* 21, 209–13.

Oppenheimer, Peter (1988a). Economics and the health service. *The Independent,* 7 March, 17.

—— (1988). Economic health and NHS decline. *Health Service Journal,* 19 May.

Williams, Alan (1985). Economics of coronary artery bypass grafting. *British Medical Journal,* 291.

(The author gratefully acknowledges the stimulus and support of the European Commission, CDG XII.)

30

Macro-allocation: dividing up the health care budget

DANIEL WIKLER AND SARAH MARCHAND

'Macro-allocation' of health-care resources involves decisions over the share of a society's total resources which are to be devoted to health, and also the division of the health-care budget between different possible uses. Macro-allocation involves questions of distributive justice because health-care resources are nearly always scarce relative to need. More broadly, 'macro-allocation' also refers to policies which have an impact on health, even if not directly intended to do so, such as decisions about unemployment and the environment.

Determinants of Health

Health status is determined only in part by health care. Longevity and morbidity vary with a variety of social conditions, including education, economic development, class and race. European men live decades longer than men in Bangladesh – and in Harlem, the black district of New York City. The health of the elderly in the former Soviet Union deteriorated alarmingly following its dissolution, due not only to difficulties in access to health care but also, according to observers, to worsened environmental hazards, lower income and social dislocation. Health indices improved greatly in the West during the early decades of this century, for the most part because of better nutrition, sanitation and housing, and only secondarily due to improvements in the science and practice of medicine. The great pathologist Rudolf Virchow, asked to investigate the causes of an outbreak of typhus in a rural district in mid-nineteenth-century Germany, pointed not only to disease-specific pathogens but also to the absence of roads and the failure to separate Church and State.

The greatest injustices in respect to health are reflections of unjust social inequalities within and between nation-states. Because inequalities in health status correlated with social position persist even in countries which have ensured access to health care for all, social policy on health must look beyond the field of health care itself. This article, however, will be largely confined to the latter.

306

Means of Macro-allocation

Macro-allocation can be carried out with varying degrees of detailed planning. A programme of specific allotments to individual health services and categories of illness is usually the work of a government or government agency, but it may also be carried out by a large private health-care company or even an employer paying for health-care benefits. Alternatively, the responsible agency can decentralize allocation by setting budget caps on particular institutions and services, leaving the allocation process to the clinicians and administrators through micro-allocation (see chapter 29, pp. 293–305). Finally, macro-allocators may opt for a market system, leaving consumers to choose health-care resources according to their needs, preferences and ability to pay.

In practice, allocation schemes mix these approaches. Even the most detailed central plan for health must leave many decisions to the clinician at the bedside. Conversely, relatively autonomous hospitals and other health-care institutions working under a global budget must still find resources, such as equipment and specialist physicians, within the pool made available by prior decisions by a central authority. Pure markets, on the other hand, are rare in medicine. Because health-care costs can be catastrophic and unexpected, modern medicine delivered in markets requires health insurance, and in bargaining over the limits of coverage sellers and buyers of insurance jointly make allocation decisions.

These approaches differ in a number of other ethically significant respects. Detailed central planning is generally likely to be less sensitive to individual differences between patients, whereas clinicians operating under global budgets can tailor their micro-allocations to the competing needs of the individuals they care for. Markets may permit a greater role to be played by consumer preferences, though constrained by personal resources, and thus may tailor allocations to the individual in a different way. Detailed planning by a central authority can be made explicit and public, unlike the patterns of decision-making by clinicians in institutions, and can be expected to be more consistent from case to case and institution to institution. Because the choices are explicit, it may also be more feasible to hold the decision-makers accountable for their choices. Rules from above constrain clinicians, but permit them to act as advocates for their patients within these constraints, while institutional budgets requiring rationing at the bedside place clinicians in a dual, and potentially conflicting, role. Markets place physicians in one kind of conflict of interest, with risk of under-treatment if health care is prepaid or capitated and with risk of over-treatment if provided by fee for service.

Principles of Macro-allocation

Determining the overall health-care budget

Countries differ widely in the share of their resources that are devoted to health. Developing countries often devote less than 3 per cent of a relatively tiny gross domestic product (GDP). Among the richest countries, the share of GDP falls between 6 and 14 per cent. The relative share of GDP devoted tó health care tends to mirror a nation's overall relative wealth, a fact which reflects the fact that non-basic health care is an expensive luxury.

Decisions to allocate funds to health care rather than to other ends may reflect formal or informal cost-benefit analyses. Cost-benefit analysis (CBA) attempts to weigh gains in health against other ways of increasing welfare. CBA computes the benefits in monetary terms, permitting the comparison of health benefits to other kinds of benefits, such as education and highways, to permit a reasoned decision on where funds should be spent.

Cost-benefit analysis, an art as well as a science, is open to several important ethical challenges. For example, fixing monetary equivalents of diverse health benefits is typically done by estimates of the beneficiary's willingness to pay. But this in turn reflects ability to pay, and varies according to income level. Moreover, even correcting for income differences, CBA does not necessarily measure the moral importance of health care, which may be based on factors other than its desirability to individuals as measured by their willingness to pay for it. For example, egalitarians believe that provision of health care should be equal, even though willingness to pay is not. In any case, not all health-care expenditures are undertaken in order to maximize overall welfare. The United States, for example, maintains a separate hospital system for veterans of its wars, an allocation of resources which attempts to repay a debt.

Allocation within the health-care budget

No consensus exists on which principle or principles should govern the allocation of resources within the health-care budget. The most widely espoused principle is that of maximization of benefit, or 'value for money'. This principle, however, is anything but straightforward in its application, in part because the notion of 'benefit' in the medical context is itself controversial. Moreover, the principle of maximization is often in conflict with other principles which also seem applicable, such as giving priority to those in the most severe need, or those needed by society, such as workers, soldiers or parents of dependent children. Some moralists have urged that distribution take account of personal responsibility for health, giving lower priority to those whose need for health care stems from risks freely chosen, and many societies permit some health services to be allocated according to ability and willingness to pay.

Health needs and benefits

A strategy of maximizing health benefits is pursued through cost-effectiveness analysis (CEA). CEA, unlike CBA, is designed to permit prioritization among health-related benefits only. Like CBA, it requires that diverse goods be quantified in comparable units. A comparison of treatments for a specific condition, such as hypertension, can use units specific to that condition (in this case, decrease in mmHg). Treatments for different conditions, if they are to be ranked in priority, must use a more general measure, such as net loss or gain in years of life. More fine-grained comparisons take into account not only the quantity of life saved by health-care intervention but also its quality. Highest priority is thus assigned to health-care interventions which involve the lowest cost per unit of health-related quality of life.

The most widely used general unit of measure of medical benefit, the quality-adjusted life year (QALY), discounts life years compromised by symptoms and functional limitations. These are graded on the basis of responses of interviewed subjects who are asked to provide a numerical rating (e.g., between 1 for perfect health, and 0 for death) for a variety of health states, or who may be asked about gambles in which quantity is traded for quality of life. For example, a respondent might be asked how many years of life confined to a wheelchair would be as valuable as five years of perfect health. An alternative measure, the disability-adjusted life year (DALY), relies on experts' estimates of the impact of particular symptoms and functional limitations on the quality of a person's life. These and other health metrics can be used to measure the benefits of health-care interventions, and, in turn, their return of health benefits for money spent.

Ethical issues in measuring health benefits: quantity and quality of life

Any attempt to measure health-related quality of life requires that assumptions be made on a host of ethically sensitive issues. At the most abstract level, a decision must be made whether to measure the benefits of longevity and quality of life in terms of objective features, such as ability to live independently, to hold a job or participate in community affairs. An alternative would involve attempting to measure personal satisfaction with one's life, which may or may not reflect changes in external circumstances. QALYs may be understood as measuring the subjective utility of health states, that is, the value to the individual of being in that health state and how much good this brings to that person. Utility, in this sense, can be estimated by measuring the willingness of individuals in a certain health state to sacrifice longevity for a return to complete health.

Extending a 75-year-old's life by five years, in this view, might represent a smaller benefit to him than the benefit of an additional five years represents to someone 35 years old. This is not because years given to a 35-year-old are more valuable in some moral sense, as judged by us. Rather, years given to a 35-year-old make a much larger difference to (the quality of) his life as a whole than the extra years make to the life of a 75-year-old. The assumption here is that what matters to the individual in determining the value of an extra year of life is the difference that year makes to her life as a whole. The QALY measure counts years as equal in value, so long as the quality of those years is the same. The DALY unit, in contrast, gives less weight to years at the beginning and after young adulthood. The reasoning behind this provision, however, is that young adults often have dependants.

Similarly, QALY arithmetic assumes that two years of life are twice as valuable as one, and that two years of life for one person have the same value to that individual as one year for each of two other people. Again, an alternative understanding of what counts in measuring health benefits focused on value to a person's life as a whole would not necessarily permit a summing of numbers of years to represent the value of quantity of life. But it is questionable whether someone given two extra years would judge her life as a whole to have been made better by twice the amount by which someone else judges his life to have been made better by being given an estra year.

Measurement of the *quality* of life involves further challenges along these lines. The value assigned to a state of health such as mild arthritis or intermittent pain is determined by asking healthy individuals to imagine how bad it would be to be in that state of health, measured, say, by asking the number of years a person would be willing to sacrifice in that condition in order to have fewer healthy years. But a healthy person could be wrong about how bad it would actually be to be in a particular state of health. Healthy people consistently rate conditions such as rheumatoid arthritis as imposing greater burdens than do rheumatoid sufferers themselves. Since it is difficult for the healthy to imagine what their actual experience of a chronic condition would be like, it is problematic to use their utility judgements as the basis for health measurements.

The problem is not fully solved, however, by relying solely on the responses of those who have had experience with the conditions in question. Though they know what it is like to live with this affliction, they may also have made the best of their bad situation, changing their life goals and reducing their expectations of what they might hope to achieve, do and enjoy. While this kind of adjustment to one's real limitations typically enhances the value of life as a whole, having to give up worthwhile pursuits and activities which a disability makes difficult or impossible should count as lowering the objective quality of life, regardless of subjective satisfaction. A satisfactory measure of the utility of health states may require combining objective and subjective evaluations, a task which has not yet been successfully undertaken in health measurement.

Ethical issues in the distribution of health benefits

How should measures of health-related quality of life be used in allocating healthcare resources? One option is maximization of the total sum of units of health-related quality of life; indeed, it is widely assumed that this is the point of the measurement. There are, however, alternative principles of allocation which use these same measures, and defenders of maximization must answer some important ethical challenges.

If we are concerned only about the highest total amount of health benefits, rather than about their distribution among individuals, a patient in severe distress might lose out in competition for health funds to a number of patients in much better condition, providing that the aggregate gain in health-related quality of life of the latter group was greater. In the extreme case, a person with a life-threatening, treatable condition would be allowed to die so that others could enjoy relief from mild discomfort. The total maximizing strategy assumes, controversially, that sufficient amounts of the latter can outweigh the former, but in common moral intuition rescuing people from calamities, or averting them altogether, ought to take priority over lesser forms of aid, even where the latter can be provided to many more people for the same cost.

One apparent virtue of QALYs and other measures of health-related quality of life is their inherent equality. As with utilitarianism, one unit of benefit counts the same no matter who enjoys it. But from a different point of view, maximization of the sum total of benefits does not treat people on equal terms. Those who can be cheaply cured, for example, would always take priority over those whose cure would cost more. Maximization of health benefits treats patients the same if they stand to benefit by the same amount; but in the other view of equality, health-care resources are allocated equally only if patients are treated the same who have the same health-care needs.

Maximization of health benefits measured in QALYs favours the young, since in general they will enjoy the benefits of a particular health service for more years. To some critics, this is unjust on its face. But others hold that under maximization the young are not favoured enough: a 20-year-old person who might be given ten extra' QALYs would lose out to a 65-year-old who might live another eleven QALYs using the same resources. As mentioned above, a measure of benefit which focused on the value to lives as a whole might not count the years of these two patients as offering the same benefits. Even if we adjusted the measure accordingly, however, distributional considerations might prompt us to favour the younger patient, on the grounds that each person should be given an opportunity for 'fair innings', the chance to live at least a good part of the prime of life.

Critics of the maximizing principle have urged a number of alternatives. For example, some priority might be given to the most critically ill, or to other groups whose well-being is of greatest concern. A widely noted rationing programme undertaken by the government of Oregon, in the United States, retreated from an initial maximizing strategy to one which used categories of health-care services ranked by moral importance, with acute life-saving care given highest priority. Another alternative would provide weighted lotteries, with patients given chances for resources in proportion to the amount of benefit they would receive from treatment. In the view of its proponents, this procedure would recognize that patients who would benefit less still have some claim on resources, one which a pure maximization strategy counts for nothing.

Defenders of total maximization have argued that all of these objections can be accommodated within that strategy. One suggestion is that the worst health outcomes be given weights which distinguish them radically from less bad outcomes; this mode of measurement would block the objectionable trade-offs, while still allowing useful comparisons between treatments offering the lesser benefits. A different strategy for blocking these trade-offs involves measuring and counting the strength of preferences of fellow citizens that their neighbours in need be rescued, even at the cost of forgoing a greater quantity of benefit distributed in small amounts over large numbers of people. In effect, their distress at standing by while those with severe health needs go untreated would be added to the suffering of the

311

afflicted person, and the resulting sum might then be larger than the total of small benefits which would otherwise command the scarce resources in question. This adjustment, however, seems to mix health-related benefits with other benefits, which strays from the domain of CEA. In any case, it seems to offer the wrong reason to favour priority for the worst off, which we view as important not because others care but because those in greatest need are entitled to our help.

Even if we accept the thesis that macro-allocation of health-care resources should aim to maximize QALYs, further ethical choices are unavoidable. For example, some insist that future QALYs be given the same value as present QALYs, on the grounds that the moral importance of a healthy life year is independent of when it is realized. Discounting the value of future health benefits merely because they occur in the future, in this view, is nonsensical. But the allocation of health resources is in large part an economic decision, and it is standard practice to discount future expenditures. In CEA, health consequences are usually discounted as well. One reason is that, in their actual spending and budgeting decisions, the public seems to give future health benefits a lower present-day value. Another is that a practice of discounting costs but not benefits arguably leads to paradoxical results: if future benefits can be bought with discounted expenditures, health care interventions should always be postponed. The debate over discounting health benefits within CEA is partly over logic and partly over empirical issues, but its bearing on the allocation of health care resources charges the controversy with ethical significance.

Other principles of allocation

Thus far we have considered allocation principles which are based, in one way or another, on the individual's need for treatment and potential benefit from treatment. Health-care allocations have served other goals, however. In the nineteenth century, advocates of social medicine, which sought to improve health by social and environmental reforms as well as by access to health-care services, argued that the national investment required was justified because it would provide a healthier workforce. The practice of triage in military medicine puts a premium on a wounded soldier's fighting potential.

According to some theorists, the degree of one's responsibility for one's own state of health should sometimes be a factor in deciding how health-care resources ought to be allocated. By adopting healthy habits of living, many people can help themselves more than their doctors can. Those who fail to take the steps necessary to stay healthy, in this view, thereby forfeit some of their entitlement to care. This conclusion is based on the premise that those who take risks should be made to bear the cost themselves, and also on the argument that the basis for entitlement to health care is ordinarily that patients become ill through no fault of their own. When the illness *is* the patient's fault, in this view, there is no entitlement.

Though the theme of personal responsibility for health has been sounded periodically in health-policy debates, it has not been much used as the basis for allocation of resources. One reason is that it is often uncertain whether changes in habits were within the power of the individual in question, be these losing weight, quitting smoking, moderating alcohol intake or reducing stress. Another objection to setting priorities in health care according to the degree of personal responsibility for illness is that individuals can be made to pay their own way. In some jurisdictions cigarette taxes are high enough to ensure that smokers present no net cost to their neighbours. Finally, it has not escaped notice that the 'bad habits' for which individuals are held responsible are largely their sins – gluttony, sloth, lust and the rest – whereas other risks to health, such as child-bearing, are subsidized without complaint. A rare instance of what seems to be allocation according to degree of responsibility for illness is the refusal of some transplant surgeons to provide alcoholics with healthy livers (when non-alcoholics are competing for the same life-saving resource). Even here, however, the explanation given by the surgeons tends to be that alcoholics would enjoy fewer QALYs rather than that these patients have not earned the care.

Democratic Choice

To what extent should macro-allocation of health-care resources be the result of democratic decision-making? Two lines of argument point to a key role.

One consideration in favour of resolving disagreements over macro-allocation through democratic choice is the want of a reasoned alternative. In this view, there is little hope of reaching consensus on principles or patterns of allocation of health-care resources. Intercultural and interpersonal variation in views of justice, and of what justice requires in health care, point to very different macro-allocation policies, and there is as little chance of agreement on the latter as there is of agreement on politics and morality. Since no argument or data will convince everyone to adopt the same position, there is no way to proceed to an acceptable policy of macro-allocation other than to vote.

A second reason to look to democratic participation and decision-making in the macro-allocation of health resources is that these processes might provide a kind of procedural justice. Whether the results of such a process conformed to what any philosophers or health planners considered just, they would still represent the combined preferences of the very population whose care would be governed by the priorities arrived at through democratic choice.

The concept of democratic decisions on the allocation of health-care resources is increasingly attrative, as demands increase for finite resources in the absence of any agreement on principles of allocation. As governments find rationing unpopular, regardless of how it is carried out, democratic procedures promise to shift responsibility away from official allocators. Some governments, such as the American state of Oregon, have encouraged public participation on a mass scale to provide advice to a Health Services Commission. Others, such as New Zealand, have commissioned studies of how individuals from diverse demographic and ethnic groups respond to a series of fictionalized allocation dilemmas. Sceptics have faulted these programmes on the grounds that the citizens participating in these hypothetical choices are often ill-informed, that in any case the degree of democratic involvement is small and, more sweepingly, that these measures are actually subtle marketing campaigns to get the public to accept less provision of health care.

A different sort of democratic decision procedure is a proposal to create a number of health-care plans in the same community, each allocating according to different sets of principles. Individuals would choose to obtain their health care from the plan whose principles matched their own. Resulting allocations would have the active consent of those affected, providing procedural justice. This plan, however, requires an elaborate segregation of the population into different groups of plan members, and a marked differentiation of health-care plans. In actual markets, where the multiplicity of health-care plans make this a possible option, competing plans try to appeal to as many potential clients as possible.

Conclusion

The need for principles of macro-allocation is becoming ever more apparent as costs of health care rise, populations age (in the countries with the costliest health care systems) and the growth of resources fails to keep step. Though physicians have not in general been trained or accustomed to tailor their practices to these principles, those who pay and regulate the physicians turn more frequently to economists and others who offer a rational basis for allocation decisions. 'Rational' allocation aims to achieve value for money, but this cannot be the only goal. The allocation must also be ethically defensible. The ethical assumptions and theories of these allocators will come under increasing scrutiny and analysis in bioethics in the years ahead.

Further Reading

Bell, J. M. and Mendus, Susan (1988). *Philosophy and Medical Welfare*. Cambridge: Cambridge University Press.

Blank, Robert H. (1988). *Rationing Medicine*. New York: Columbia University Press.

Braveman, Paula et al. (1996). *Equity in Health and Health Care*. Geneva: World Health Organization.

Brock, Dan (1993). Quality of life measures in health care and medical ethics. In Martha Nussbaum and Amartya Sen, *The Quality of Life*. Oxford: Oxford University Press.

Churchill, Larry R. (1987). *Rationing Health Care in America: Perceptions and principles of justice*. Notre Dame, IN: University of Notre Dame Press.

Daniels, Norman (1985). *Just Health Care*. Cambridge: Cambridge University Press.

——(1993). Rationing fairly: programmatic considerations. *Bioethics*, 7, 223–33.

Dworkin, Gerald, Bermant, Gordon and Brown, Peter G. (eds) (1977). *Markets and Morals*. New York: John Wiley.

Emanuel, Ezekiel (1991). *The Ends of Human Life: Medical ethics in a liberal polity*. Cambridge, MA: Harvard University Press.

Feinstein, J. S. (1993). The relationship between socioeconomic status and health: a review of the literature. *Milbank Quarterly*, 71, 279–322.

Gold, Marthe R., Siegel, Joanna E., Russell, Louise B. and Weinstein, Milton C. (eds) (1996). *Cost-effectiveness in Health and Medicine*. Oxford: Oxford University Press.

Janovsky, Katja (ed.) (1995). *Health Policy and Systems Development*. Geneva: World Health Organization.

Kamm, F. M. (1993). *Mortality, Morality*. Vol. I. Oxford: Oxford University Press.

McKeown, Thomas R. (1976). *The Role of Medicine: Dream, mirage, or nemesis*. London: Nuffield Provincial Hospitals Trust.

Menzel, Paul (1983). *Medical Costs, Moral Choices: A philosophy of health care economics in America*. New Haven: Yale University Press.

—— (1990). *Strong Medicine*. Oxford: Oxford University Press.

Murray, C. J. L. and Lopez, A. D. (1996). *The Global Burden of Disease*. Cambridge, MA: Harvard University Press.

Strosberg, Martin A. et al. (1992). *Rationing America's Medical Care: The Oregon plan and beyond*. Washington, DC: Brookings Institution.

Wilkinson, Richard (1996). *Unhealthy Societies: The afflictions of inequality*. London: Routledge.

31

Is there a right to health care and, if so, what does it encompass?

NORMAN DANIELS

Is there a Right to Health Care?

Legal vs moral rights to health care

One way to answer this question is to adopt the stance of legal positivists, who claim that there are no rights except those that are embodied in actual institutions through law. We would then be able to reply that in nearly every advanced industrial democracy in the world, there is a right to health care, since institutions exist in them that assure everyone access to needed services regardless of ability to pay. The notable exception is the United States, where many poor and near poor people have no insurance coverage for, and thus no assured access to, medically necessary services, although by law they cannot be denied emergency services.

The legal right to health care is embodied in a wide variety of types of health-care systems. These range from national health services, where the government is the provider of services, as in Great Britain, to public insurance schemes, where the government finances services, as in Canada, to mixed public and private insurance schemes, as in Germany and the Netherlands. Despite these differences in the design of systems, there is a broad overlap in the scope or content of the legal right to health care in these countries. Most cover 'medically necessary' services, including a broad range or preventive, curative, rehabilitative and long-term care for physical and mental diseases, disorders and disabilities. Most exclude uses of medical technologies that enhance otherwise normal functioning or appearance, such as purely cosmetic surgery. The legal rights vary in significant ways, however, for example, in the degree to which they cover new reproductive technologies, or in the types of mental health and long-term care services that are offered.

In the context of rising costs and the rapid dissemination of new technologies, there is growing debate in many countries about how to set limits on the scope of a right to health care. This debate about the scope of rights to health care pushes moral deliberation about such a right into the forefront, even where a legal right is recognized. Legal entitlements, most people believe, should reflect what society is morally obliged to provide by way of medical services. What, then, is the basis and scope of a moral right to health care?

316

Positive vs negative rights

A right to health care is a *positive* as opposed to a *negative* right. Put quite simply, a positive right requires others to do something beneficial or enabling for right-bearers, whereas a negative right requires others to refrain from doing something, usually harmful or restrictive, to right-bearers. To say that others are required to do something or to refrain from doing something is to say they must so act or refrain even if they could produce more good or improve the world by not doing so (Thomson, 1990). For example, a negative right to free expression requires others to refrain from censuring the expression of the right-bearer even if censuring this speech would make a better world. Some public-health measures that protect people against interference with their health, such as environmental protections that protect people against polluters of air, water and food sources, might be construed as requirements of a negative right. More generally, however, a right to health care imposes an obligation on others to assist the right-bearers in obtaining needed and appropriate services. Specifically, claiming a right to health care includes these other claims: society has the duty to its members to allocate an adequate share of its total resources to health-related needs; society has the duty to provide a just allocation of different types of health care services, taking into account the competing claims of different types of health-care needs; each person is entitled to a fair share of such services, where a 'fair share' includes an answer to the question, who should pay for the services? (Daniels, 1985). Health-care rights thus form a part of a broader family of positive 'welfare' rights that includes rights to education and to income support. Because positive rights require other people to contribute their resources or skills to benefit right-bearers, rather than merely refraining from interfering with them, they have often been thought more difficult to justify than negative rights, and their scope and limits have been harder to characterize.

Theories of justice and rights to health care

If we are to think of a right to health care as a requirement of justice, then we should look to more general theories of justice as a way to specify the scope and limits of that right. On some theories of justice, however, there is little basis for requiring people to assist others by meeting their health care or other needs. Libertarians, for example, believe that fundamental rights to property, including rights to personal assets, such as talents and skills, are violated if society coerces individuals into providing 'needed' resources or skills (Nozick, 1974). Libertarians generally recognize an 'imperfect' duty to act beneficently or charitably, but this duty involves discretion. It can be discharged in different ways that are matters of choice. People denied charity have no right to it and have no complaint against people who act charitably in other ways. Though some have argued that the difficulty of coordinating the delivery of charitable assistance might justify coercive measures (Buchanan, 1984), and others have tried to show that even libertarians must recognize some forms of welfare rights (Sterba, 1985), most libertarians resist any

317

weakening of the property rights at the core of their view (Brennan and Friedman, 1981).

A spectre sometimes raised by libertarians against the idea of a right to health care is that such a right is a 'bottomless pit'. Since new technologies continuously expand the scope of 'medical needs', a right to health care would give rise to unlimited claims on the resources of others (Fried, 1969; Engelhardt, 1986). Protecting such an expansive right to health care would thus not be compatible with the function of a libertarian 'minimal state' to assure the non-violation of rights to liberty and property.

Though there remains controversy about whether utilitarians can provide a basis for recognizing true moral rights, there are strong utilitarian arguments in favour of governments assuring access to at least some broad range of effective medical services. Preventing or curing disease or disability reduces suffering and enables people to function in ways that contribute to aggregate welfare. In addition, knowing that health-care services are available increases personal security and strengthens the ties of community. Utilitarians can also justify redistributing the burden of delivering these benefits to society as a whole, citing the decreasing marginal utility of money to support progressive financing of health-care services (Brandt, 1979).

Beneath these quite general arguments, however, there lies a more specific controversy about the scope of utilitarian entitlements to health care. There seems to be little utilitarian justification for investing resources in health care if those resources would produce more net welfare when invested in other things, yet many people believe they have moral obligations to assist others with their health-care needs even at a net cost in utility. For example, some highly expensive and effective medical treatments that most people believe should be offered to people might not be 'cost beneficial' and thus not defensible on utilitarian grounds. Similarly, many forms of long-term care, especially for those who cannot be restored to productive social activity, are also difficult to defend on utilitarian grounds, yet we insist our health-care systems are obliged to provide such services.

Lack of moral acceptance of the distributive implications of utilitarianism makes many uncomfortable with the use of methods, such as cost-effectiveness analysis, that are intended to guide decisions about resource allocation in health care. For example, an assumption of cost-effectiveness analysis is that a unit of health benefit, such as a quality-adjusted life year (QALY), is of equal value or importance regardless of where it is distributed. But this assumption does not capture the concerns many people have about how much priority to give to the sickest patients, or when aggregating modest benefits to large numbers of people it outweighs the moral importance of delivering more significant benefits to fewer people (Nord, 1993; Daniels, 1993).

Two points about a utilitarian framework for a right to health care are worth noting. Recognizing a right to health care is compatible with recognizing limits on entitlements that result from resource scarcity and the fact that there are competing uses of those resources. Consequently, recognizing a right to health care need not open a bottomless pit. Second, just what entitlements to services follow from a right to health care cannot be specified outside the context of a *system* properly designed to deliver health care in a way that promotes aggregate utility. For the utilitarian, entitlements are *system-relative*. The same two points apply to other accounts of the foundations and limits of a right to health care.

Because many people reject the utilitarian rationales for health care (and other welfare) rights, theorists have explored other ways to ground such rights. Some claim that these rights are presupposed as enabling conditions for the exercise of other rights or liberties, or as practical presuppositions of all views of justice (Braybrooke, 1987) or as a way of avoiding vulnerability and exploitation (Goodin, 1988). One approach that has been developed in some detail views a right to health care as a special case of a right to equality of opportunity (Daniels, 1985). This approach shows how the most important contractarian theory of justice, Rawls' (1971) account of justice as fairness, can be extended to the problem of health care, since that theory gives prominence to a principle protecting equality of opportunity (Rawls, 1993). Without endorsing that account here, we shall use it to illustrate further the complexity surrounding the concept of a right to health care.

Equal opportunity and a right to health care

The central observation underlying this account of a right to health care is that disease and disability restrict the range of opportunities that would otherwise be open to individuals. This is true whether they shorten our lives or impair our ability to function, including through pain and suffering. Health care in all its forms, whether public health or medical, preventive or acute or chronic, aims to keep people functioning as close to normally as possible. Since we are complex social creatures, our normal functional capabilities include our capabilities for emotional and cognitive functioning and not just physical capabilities. Health care thus preserves for us the range of opportunities we would have, were we not ill or disabled, given our talents and skills.

The significant contribution health care makes to protecting the range of opportunities open to individuals is nevertheless *limited* in two important ways. It is limited because other things, such as the distribution of wealth and income and education, also profoundly affect equality of opportunity. It is also limited because health care, by restricting its aim to protecting normal functioning, leaves the normal distribution of talents and skills unmodified. It aims to help us function as 'normal' competitors, not strictly equal ones.

Some argue that an equal opportunity account of health care should abandon the limit set by a focus on normal functioning (see Arneson, 1988; G. A. Cohen, 1989; Sen, 1992). They claim our concerns about equality, including equality of opportunity, require us to use health-care technologies whenever doing so would equalize opportunity for welfare or equalizes capabilities. For example, if through medical intervention we can 'enhance' the otherwise normal capabilities of those who are at a competitive disadvantage, then our commitment to equality of opportunity requires us to do so. Obviously, this version of an equal opportunity account would vastly expand the moral requirements on medicine, yielding a right to health care much more expansive than any now embodied in actual systems and, arguably, one that would make administration of a health-care system unwieldy (Sabin and Daniels, 1994).

This expansive version of the appeal to equal opportunity ignores an important fact about justice: our concern for equality must be reconciled with considerations of liberty and efficiency in arriving at the overall requirements of justice (see Sen, 1992; Cohen, 1995; Daniels, 1996). Such a reconciliation seems to underlie the limits we commonly accept when we appeal to equality of opportunity. We generally believe that rights to equal opportunity are violated only if unfair social practices or preventable or curable diseases or disabilities interfere with the pursuit of reasonable plans of life within our society by making us lose competitive advantage. We accept, however, the fact that the natural distribution of talents and skills, working in an efficient market for them, will both enhance the social product and lead to inequalities in social outcomes. A just society will try to mitigate the effects of these inequalities in competitive advantage in other ways than by eliminating all eliminable differences in capabilities. For example, on Rawls' account, transfers that make the worst off as well off as they can be mitigate the effects on equality of allowing the natural distribution of talents and skills to enhance productivity. In what follows, the account of a right to health care rests on a more limited appeal to equal opportunity, one that takes the maintenance of normal functioning as a reasonable limit.

What does a Right to Health Care Include?

System-relative entitlements

By making the right to health care a special case of rights to equality of opportunity, we arrive at a reasonable, albeit incomplete and imperfect, way of restricting its scope while still recognizing its importance. The account does not give individuals a basic right to have all of their health-care needs met. At the same time, there are social obligations to design a health-care system that protects opportunity through an appropriate set of health-care services. If social obligations to provide appropriate health care are not met, then individuals are definitely wronged. For example, if people are denied access – because of discrimination or inability to pay – to a basic tier of services adequate to protect normal functioning, injustice is done to them. If the basic tier available to people omits important categories of services without consideration of their effects on normal functioning, for example, whole categories of mental health or long-term care or preventive services, their rights are violated.

Still, not every medical need gives rise to an entitlement to services. The scope and limits of rights to health care, that is, the entitlements they actually carry with them, will be relative to certain facts about a given system. For example, a health-care system can protect opportunity only within the limits imposed by resource scarcity and technological development within a society. We cannot make a direct inference from the fact that an individual has a right to health care to the conclusion that this person is entitled to some specific health-care service, even if the service would meet a health-care need. Rather the individual is entitled to a specific service only if, in the light of facts about a society's technological capabilities and resource limitations, it should be a part of a system that appropriately protects fair equality of opportunity. The equal opportunity account of a right to health care, like the utilitarian account, makes entitlements to health care system-relative.

Effective treatment of disease and disability

The health care we have strongest claim to is care that effectively promotes normal functioning by reducing the impact of disease and disability, thus protecting the range of opportunities that would otherwise be open to us. Just what counts as 'effective', however? And what should we do about hard cases on the boundary between treatment of disease or disability and enhancement of capabilities?

It is a common feature of public and private insurance systems to limit care to treatments that are not 'experimental' and have some 'proven effectiveness'. Unfortunately, many services that count as standard treatment have little direct evidence about outcomes to support their use (Hadorn, 1992). They are often just customary treatment. Furthermore, it is often controversial just when new treatments or technologies should count as 'safe and efficacious'. What counts as 'reasonably effective' is then a matter of judgement and depends on the kind of condition and the consequences of not correcting it. We might, for example, want to lower our standards for effectiveness when we face a treatment of last resort, or raise them if resource scarcity is very great. On the other hand, we do not owe people a chance to obtain miracles through whatever unproven procedures they prefer to try.

By focusing a right to health care on the maintenance of normal functioning, a line is drawn between uses of medical technologies that count as legitimate 'treatments' and those that we may want but which do not meet our 'health-care needs'. Although we may want medical services that can enhance our appearance, like cosmetic (as opposed to reconstructive) plastic surgery, or that can optimize our otherwise normal functioning, like some forms of counselling or some uses of Prozac, we do not truly need these services to maintain normal functioning. We are obliged to help others achieve normal functioning, but we do not 'owe' each other whatever it takes to make us more beautiful or strong or completely happy (Daniels, 1985).

Though this line is widely used in both public and private insurance practices, it leaves us with hard cases. Some of the hardest issues involve reproductive technologies. Abortion, where there is no preventive or therapeutic need, does not count as 'treatment' because an unwanted pregnancy is not a disease or disability. Some nevertheless insist that requirements of justice, including a right to control one's body, means that non-therapeutic abortion should be included as an entitlement in a health-care system. Some national health-insurance schemes do not cover infertility services. Yet infertility is a departure from normal functioning, even if some people never want to bear children. Controversy may remain about how much social obligation we have to correct this form of impaired opportunity, especially where the costs of some interventions, such as *in vitro* fertilization, are high and their effectiveness is modest. Different societies will judge this question differently, in part because they may place different values on the rearing of biologically related children or on the experience of child-bearing.

Hard cases involve non-reproductive technologies as well. In the United States, for example, many insurers will cover growth hormone treatment only for children deficient in growth hormone, not for those who are equally short but without any pathology. Yet the children denied therapy will suffer just as much as those who are eligible. Similar difficulties are involved in drawing a line between covered and non-covered uses of mental health services (Sabin and Daniels, 1994). As in the cases of reproductive technologies, there is room for different societies to 'construct' the concept of mental disorder somewhat differently, with resulting variation in decisions about insurance coverage.

Rights and limits on effective treatments

Even when some health-care service is reasonably effective at meeting a medical need, not all such needs are equally important. When a disease or disability has little impact on the range of opportunities open to someone, it is not as morally important to treat as other conditions that more seriously impair opportunity. The effect on opportunity thus gives us some guidance in thinking about resource allocation priorities.

Unfortunately, the impact on our range of opportunities gives only a crude and incomplete measure of the importance or priority we should give to a need or service. In making decisions about priorities for purposes of resource allocation in health care, we face difficult questions about distributive fairness that are not answered by this measure of importance. For example, we must sometimes make a choice between investing in a technology that delivers a significant benefit to few people or one that delivers a more modest benefit to a larger number of people. Sometimes we must make a choice between investing in a service that helps the sickest, most impaired patients or one that helps those whose functioning is less impaired. Sometimes we must decide between the fairness of giving a scarce resource to those who derive the largest benefit or giving a broader range of people some chance at getting a benefit. In all of these cases, we lack clear principles for deciding how to make our choices, and the account of a right to health care we are discussing does not provide those principles either (Daniels, 1993). Some methodologies, like cost-effectiveness analysis, are intended to help us make appropriate resource allocation decisions in these kinds of cases. But these methodologies may themselves embody controversial moral assumptions about distributive fairness. This means they cannot serve as decision procedures for making these choices and can at best serve as aids to decision-makers who must be explicit about the moral reasoning that determines the distributive choices they make (Gold et al., 1996).

In any health-care system, then, some choices will have to be made by a fair, publicly accountable, decision-making process. Just what constitutes a fair decision-making procedure for resolving moral disputes about health care entitlements is itself a matter of controversy. It is a problem that has been addressed little in the literature. Our rights are not violated, however, if the choices that are made through fair decision-making procedures turn out to be ones that do not happen to meet our personal needs, but instead meet needs of others that are judged more important (Daniels and Sabin, 1997).

How equal must our rights to health care be?

How equal must our rights to health care be? Specifically, must everyone receive exactly the same kinds of health-care services and coverage, or is fairness in health care compatible with a 'tiered' system? Around the world, even countries that offer universal health insurance differ in their answers to this question. In Canada and Norway, for example, no supplementary insurance is permitted. Everyone is served solely by the national health-insurance schemes, though people who seek additional services or more rapid service may go elsewhere, as some Canadians do by crossing the border. In Britain, supplementary private insurance allows about 10 per cent of the population to gain quicker access to services for which there is extensive queuing in the public system. Basing a right to health care on an obligation to protect equality of opportunity is compatible with the sort of tiering the British have, but it does not require it, and it imposes some constraints on the kind of tiering allowed.

The primary social obligation is to assure everyone access to a tier of services that effectively promotes normal functioning and thus protects equality of opportunity. Since health care is not the only important good, resources to be invested in the basic tier are appropriately and reasonably limited, for example, by democratic decisions about how much to invest in education or job training as opposed to health care. Because of their very high 'opportunity costs', there will be some beneficial medical services that it will be reasonable not to provide in the basic tier, or to provide only on a limited basis, for example, with queuing. To say that these services have 'high opportunity costs' means that providing them consumes resources that would produce greater health benefits and protect opportunity more if used in other ways.

In a society that permits significant income and wealth inequalities, some people will want to buy coverage for these additional services. Why not let them? After all, we allow people to use their after-tax income and wealth as they see fit to pursue the 'quality of life' and opportunities they prefer. The rich can buy special security systems for their homes. They can buy safer cars. They can buy private schooling for their children. Why not allow them to buy supplementary health care for their families?

One objection to allowing a supplementary tier is that its existence might undermine the basic tier either economically or politically. It might attract better-quality providers away from the basic tier, or raise costs in the basic tier, reducing the ability of society to meet its social obligations. The supplementary tier might undermine political support for the basic tier, for example, by undercutting the social solidarity needed if people are to remain committed to protecting opportunity for all. These objections are serious, and where a supplementary tier undermines the basic tier in either way, economically or politically, priority must be given to protecting the basic tier. In principle, however, it seems possible to design a system in which the supplementary tier does not undermine the basic one. If that can be done, then a system that permits tiering avoids restricting liberty in ways that some find seriously objectionable.

A second objection is not to tiering itself but to the structure of inequality that results. Compare two scenarios. In one, most people are adequately served by the basic tier and only the best-off groups in society have the means and see the need to purchase supplementary insurance. That is the case in Great Britain. In the other, the basic tier serves only the poorest groups in society and most other people buy supplementary insurance. The Oregon plan to expand Medicaid eligibility partly through rationing the services it covers has aspects of this structure of inequality, since most people are covered by plans that avoid these restrictions (Daniels, 1991). The first scenario seems preferable to the second on grounds of fairness. In the second, the poorest groups can complain that they are left behind by others in society even in the protection of their health. In the first, the majority has less grounds for reasonable resentment or regret.

If the basic tier is not undermined by higher tiers, and if the structure of the inequality that results is not objectionable, then it is difficult to see why some tiering should not be allowed. There is a basic conflict here between concerns about equality and concerns about liberty, between wanting to make sure everyone is treated properly with regard to health care and wanting to give people the liberty to use their resources (after tax) to improve their lives as they see fit. In practice, the crucial constraint on the liberty we allow people seems to depend on the magnitude of the benefit available in the supplementary tier and unavailable in the basic tier. Highly visible forms of saving lives and improving function would be difficult to exclude from the basic tier while we make them available in a supplementary tier. In principle, however, some forms of tiering will not be unfair even when they involve medical benefits not available to everyone.

References

Arneson, Richard (1988). Equality and equal opportunity for welfare. *Philosophical Studies*, 54, 79–95.

Brandt, Richard (1979). *A Theory of the Good and the Right*. Oxford: Oxford University Press.

Braybrooke, David (1987). *Meeting Needs*. Princeton, NJ: Princeton University Press.

Brennan, Geoffrey and Friedman, David (1981). A libertarian perspective on welfare. In Peter G. Brown, Conrad Johnson and Paul Vernier (eds), *Income Support: Conceptual and policy issues*. Totowa, NJ: Rowman and Littlefield.

Buchanan, Allen (1984). The right to a decent minimum of health care. *Philosophy and Public Affairs*, 13, 55–78.

Cohen, G. A. (1989). On the currency of egalitarian justice. *Ethics*, 99, 906–44.

Cohen, Joshua (1995). Amartya Sen: *Inequality Reexamined. Journal of Philosophy*, 92/5, 275–88.

Daniels, N. (1985). *Just Health Care*. Cambridge: Cambridge University Press.

—— (1991). Is the Oregon rationing plan fair? *Journal of the American Medical Association*, 265, 2232–5.

—— (1993). Rationing fairly: programmatic considerations. *Bioethics*, 7, 224–33.

—— (1996). *Justice and Justification: reflective equilibrium in theory and practice*. Cambridge: Cambridge University Press.

Daniels, N. and Sabin, J. (1997). Limits to health care: fair procedures, democratic deliberation, and the legitimacy problem for insurers. *Philosophy and Public Affairs*, 26/4, 303–50.

Engelhardt, H. Tristram (1986). *The Foundations of Bioethics*. Oxford: Oxford University Press.

Fried, Charles (1969). *An Anatomy of Value*. Cambridge, MA: Harvard University Press.

Gold, Marthe, Siegel, Joanna. Russell, Louise and Weinstein, Milton (eds) (1996). *Cost-Effectiveness in Health and Medicine: recommendations of the Panel on Cost-Effectiveness in Health and Medicine*. New York: Oxford University Press.

Goodin, Robert (1988). *Reasons for Welfare*. Princeton, NJ: Princeton University Press.

Hadorn, David (ed.) (1992). *Basic Benefits and Clinical Guidelines*. Boulder, CO: Westview Press.

Nord, Eric (1993). The relevance of health state after treatment in prioritizing between different patients. *Journal of Medical Ethics*, 19, 37–42.

Nozick, R. (1974). *Anarchy, State, and Utopia*. New York: Basic Books.

Rawls, J. (1971). *A Theory of Justice*. Cambridge, MA: Harvard University Press.

—— (1993). *Political Liberalism*. New York: Columbia University Press.

Sabin, James and Daniels, Norman (1994). Determining 'medical necessity' in mental health practice. *Hastings Center Report*, 24/6, 5–13.

Sen, Amartya (1992). *Inequality Reexamined*. Cambridge, MA: Harvard University Press.

Sterba, James (1985). From liberty to welfare, *Social Theory and Practice*, 11, 285–305.

Thomson, Judith (1990). *The Realm of Rights*. Cambridge, MA: Harvard University Press.

PART IX
ORGAN DONATIONS

32

Organ transplantation

ROSAMOND RHODES

Tissue and solid organ transplantation have been embraced by modern medicine because the technology promises so much good for patients. Transplantation has the capacity to fulfil medicine's central goals: to preserve life, to alleviate suffering, to cure disease, to restore function. However, traditional medical practice also adheres to the principles of 'do no harm,' respect autonomy and provide care for all who come to you in need (see chapter 7, pp. 61–71). Unfortunately, the ethical practice of organ transplantation sometimes requires the thoughtful surgeon to violate each of these central moral tenets. From this alone it is clear that the moral conflicts raised by organ transplantation are complex, compelling and deserving of special careful consideration. Unavoidable characteristics of the transplant surgeon's practice require difficult moral judgements about organ procurement and organ allocation. Questions about advancing the field and extending the treatment to additional groups of patients who might benefit from it provide another array of moral quandaries.

Organ Procurement

Obviously, an organ for transplantation must be taken from either a recently dead cadaver, or a living human donor, or a compatible animal. Taking organs from a cadaver violates certain traditional religious and social attitudes which require us to show respect for the dead by not mutilating the corpse. Taking an organ from a living donor violates the medical dictum, 'do no harm,' because it puts the donor at some risk of serious harm from anaesthesia, intra-operative complications and post-surgical complications. The procedure itself is also certain to harm the donor with disfigurement.

Many people would agree that life preservation or significant life enhancement can justify overriding the moral imperatives that would otherwise prohibit dismembering corpses and harming healthy individuals. However, even though we may decide that, because of the significant good it achieves and the small risk of harm, organ transplantation can be a morally acceptable practice, we still have to answer many weighty ethical questions about removing organs. When is a human being dead? What other criteria must be met before organs can be taken from a corpse? Must family consent be obtained? Can cadaver organs be purchased from the family of the deceased like other inherited property? Should we allow people to sell their own duplicate organs? When can a living donation be accepted? Can we use organs from the nearly dead or the hardly human?

Brain death

Religious and historical tradition had identified death with a permanent cessation of heartbeat and the absence of respiration (see chapter 25, pp. 250–60). But now there are artificial means for keeping hearts beating and lungs pumping even after the brain has totally ceased its function and begun to decompose.

Brain death is now commonly used as the medical standard for defining death. According to the new criteria, when all brain function has terminated, death is declared and organs may be taken even though heartbeat and respiration continue. Brain death has not been accepted as the standard everywhere. No transplants from brain-dead donors can be performed in countries where brain death is not the legally acknowledged standard (as was the case in Japan until 1996).

That the standard for declaring death can be changed by law and that it can be different in different places makes it clear that 'death' is an ambiguous term. Previously death was death. But now technology has allowed biologists to appreciate the physical complexity of declaring a time of death, and it has shown society the gulf between the possibility of sustaining metabolic exchange and the impossibility of restoring brain function. 'Death' has become both a complex philosophical and biological concept and a complex social concept.

The technology that makes it possible to keep alive those who would otherwise be dead becomes a crucial issue in transplantation. Transplant organs must be kept viable by keeping the donor body connected to 'life-support' machines until the organs are removed. Yet it is immoral to kill people in order to transplant their organs. So, if discontinuing the life-support of a brain-dead organ donor is killing then organs cannot be taken from those who are on life-support.

Perhaps a social definition of death tied to the absence of cognitive function would be preferable to a standard based on the absence of any brain function. Consciousness, perception, memory, thought and the initiation of voluntary activity are associated with the activity of the cerebral cortex. If cortical death, rather than whole-brain death, were accepted as a sufficient moral standard for declaring death, organs could be taken for transplantation when the cortex was absent (e.g., from anencephalic infants) or when the cortex had permanently ceased to function (e.g., from those in persistent vegetative states). A cortical standard seems appropriate because any shift from the former whole-body conception of death to a brain-oriented conception of death depends upon accepting the idea that being alive as a person involves cognitive functioning. If thought is the relevant distinguishing characteristic and if it resides in the cortex, then death should be declared based only upon the absence of cortical function. Some of the reluctance to move from a whole-brain to a cortical definition of death is the worry that scientists might be mistaken in their view that no thought is possible without cortical function or that clinicians might inaccurately determine that death has occurred. More of the worry about moving to the weaker cortical standard for declaring death comes from concern about starting onto a slippery slope of deciding that some of us are not entitled to receive care or even to live.

Arguments about the acceptability of the brain death and cortical death standards reflect broader moral positions on personhood and life. Someone who holds that life itself is sacred is inclined to resist any expansion of the death standard. On the other hand, someone who associates personhood or autonomy with the moral demand for respectful treatment can accept brain or cortical death standards. Once the brain, or even the cortex, ceases to function an individual can no longer make choices, act with deliberation or act from principles as an autonomous person could. According to those with a commitment to 'persons', we do not have the obligations to the brain-dead or the cortically dead that we have to those who can still make choices for themselves.

Consent for donation

Regardless of the standard employed for declaration of death, is consent needed before transplantable organs can be removed from the deceased? According to long-standing British common law tradition, the corpse is family property. Furthermore, because religious customs frequently dictate treatment of the dead, commitments to religious freedom have allowed families to make decisions about the disposition of their deceased relatives. The United States currently employs a 'required request' policy in securing permission to use transplantable organs. When a potential donor is identified, the next of kin must be asked about donation; their consent must be given before organs can be removed for transplantation. Yet in the United States, moving from a totally voluntary system with no requirements about approaching families for donation to a 'required request' policy has actually reduced the rate of donation. And even though there has been an increase in the number of people who complete organ donor cards that provide legal authority for using their organs upon death, physician and organ procurement representatives are reluctant to risk contention with reluctant donor families by taking organs based solely upon donor card consent. The current United States policy leaves about two-thirds of those who need transplants without organs. This serious shortfall in organ supply increases the impetus for accepting organs from living donors.

Some countries (e.g., Belgium, France, Austria) follow a 'presumed consent' rule. On this model it is assumed that viable organs will be used for transplantation and they are taken for transplant unless the potential donor previously registered an objection or (in some countries) the family actively exercises their right to object. Because of the serious shortage of transplant organs there have been discussions in several countries about moving to 'presumed consent' or even required donation. While the latter two policies are expected to make more organs available, defenders of the 'required request' status quo in the United States argue that more coercive policies conflict with individual liberty and religious freedom. Prudential

331

arguments also support resisting the more intrusive policy alternatives. For example, in the United States, where segments of the heterogeneous population do not sufficiently trust the medical establishment, the more exacting policies have been counter-productive because they seem coercive.

Using living organ donors

Physicians are committed to act for the good of their patients and to avoid harming them. They are also committed to respecting the personal choices of their patients. Living organ donation is an ethical challenge for medicine because it involves subjecting the donor to some degree of harm. But it also promises significant benefit to organ recipients and, for donors who are eager to give, using them supports their personal choices. If doctors also consider the psychological benefit to a donor from saving a loved one, or significantly improving a beloved's quality of life, or avoiding the guilt of not trying to help, they recognize that donating an organ can be a good to the donor. From this perspective, while subjecting someone to the risks of surgical complications and the certainty of mutilation can never be good, in the context of the totality of what is being achieved, taking an organ from a living donor could be better than the alternative.

In accepting someone as an organ donor the most crucial considerations are the seriousness of the recipient's need, the likelihood of avoiding serious complications for the donor and the quality of the donor's consent. The more pressing the recipient's need, the greater the reason to do some harm to another. The slimmer the chance of serious harm to the donor and the more autonomous the donor's choice, the greater the ethical acceptability of the donation.

Autonomous donor consent is a basic consideration in taking an organ from a donor because it would be an assault and battery to take an organ from someone without her or his consent. Furthermore, in the light of the clear harms that will be done, without the person declaring that the donation would be an overall good there is usually no reason to presume that it is. Since respect for autonomy is one of the most crucial moral imperatives, cooperating with someone's autonomous choice to give provides a prima facie reason for accepting her or him as an organ donor.

Unfortunately, the one who can donate an organ for transplantation may not be autonomous. Small children, the demented and the insane cannot make such decisions for themselves. The autonomy of other prospective donors (e.g., adolescents, those who are being pressed to donate by family members) may be questionable. When you are acutely aware of the moral dimension of taking an organ from a living donor, the ethical acceptability of each prospective donor must be carefully assessed. Furthermore, because the ethical acceptability of living donation relates directly to the likelihood of taking the organ without causing serious harm, at a minimum, each prospective donor must have her or his own medical advocate who is committed to considering the donation only from the perspective of the donor's good.

332

Organ sales

If organs for transplantation can be taken from the deceased and also from living donors, can they be sold? The marketplace serves as an incentive. Since we need more transplant organs to save and improve lives, is it permissible to allow the market to operate and increase the available pool?

One argument against organ sales has been that it would result in unjust distribution of organs – the rich would be able to buy what they needed and the poor would be left without. However, a system could easily be devised to avoid that problem. A national organ-sharing network could be the only buyer and then continue distribution of the more adequate supply according to principles that would not discriminate against the poor. If the distribution of purchased organs were just, would organ sales be acceptable? Those still opposed argue that body parts are the kinds of things that should be given and not sold, that making money the incentive would deprive people of the opportunity to be generous, and that offering money for organs would offend more people than it would inspire. Furthermore, they point out that offering a financial incentive would be unjust to the poor (e.g., Third World poor who might realistically see selling a kidney as the family's route out of poverty) because it would be more likely to coerce them than to affect the decisions of the well-heeled.

Those in favour of allowing organ sales claim that taking organs from the deceased without financial reimbursement is unfair to the family that might be happy to receive some compensation (e.g., burial costs) for their property. It is also argued that refusing to allow the living to sell their own duplicate organs fails to respect their autonomy by refusing to allow people to act on the choices they think best for themselves. Those who argue for lifting the prohibition on organ sales point to the inconsistencies in our attitudes. We do allow people to take much greater risks for financial compensation (e.g., boxing, playing football), and we do allow and even praise people who donate without compensation for taking the same risk. We also accept the use of money as an incentive for the poor to take on the menial jobs that others would prefer to avoid. Perhaps making the amount paid for organs substantial enough to make a significant difference in the life of a poor donor (e.g., $100,000 for a kidney) would make organ sales more acceptable.

Organ Allocation

Once transplant organs are obtained, careful consideration must be given to how they should be allocated. Meeting the needs of all patients will be impossible because there are not enough organs for everyone who needs one. And whenever someone is chosen to receive an organ, those who are passed over and have to wait longer are being harmed as they get sicker and, in some cases, die. Justice and fairness must be considered in distributing the limited organ supply, but what it would take to make an allocation just and fair is not obvious.

333

Distributive justice

Should everyone who needs a vital organ to live or to live a significantly better life be given equal access to organ transplantation? Or are there some considerations that need to be given special consideration in distribution? Should social grounds be taken into account or should only medical factors be considered? What other factors should be counted and how much? Should people be given not more than one organ or should they be allowed multiple organ transplants (e.g., a lung and a heart, a kidney and a pancreas)? And if a transplanted organ immediately fails to function or is ultimately rejected after functioning in the recipient for some period of time, should the recipient be given another organ when others on the recipient list have not yet had a chance?

In some societies (e.g., Israel), organs donated for transplantation were allocated by the institution that acquired them. The individual transplant centre was responsible for creating and implementing its own procedures for allocation. A system of local distribution can aim at a just distribution of organs among its patients; it cannot address the justice of organ allocation across the society.

Other societies develop national distribution systems that try to maximize the justice and efficacy of organ allocation for all prospective recipients. By pooling information about donor organs and recipients, a national system can match organs to the special needs of particular recipients and also be more responsive to urgent situations. Because organs must be transplanted within a short period of time after procurement, distance becomes a limiting criterion for organ sharing. In most cases, the advantages of a speedy transplant mean that organs are directed to a centre that is relatively close to the site of procurement. Urgent need, ideal compatibility or difficulty in finding an organ that will match a particular donor warrants sharing over greater distance. In the United States, a national organ distribution system, the United Network for Organ Sharing (UNOS), works to provide a just and fair distribution of transplant organs. Its rules give priority to urgency of need and then to length of time on the list.

If urgency were always the primary consideration, people with the least likelihood of surviving, including some who were in serious danger of losing a transplanted organ, would be the most likely to receive a transplant. But because fewer patients would survive transplantation if such a policy were adopted, some alternative scheme would be better at maximizing the effective use of organs.

Transplant programmes typically pay most attention to the medical features of gravity and also likelihood of long-term success. Including the likelihood of benefit among their criteria means that transplantation is denied to patients who have some chance of surviving with a transplant, but are so sick that they no longer have a very good chance of surviving. This policy denies treatment to those who need it most, but it also improves the overall utility of the distribution system. While it is painful to remove needy patients from the organ recipient list and to triage them out of the possibility of having an organ transplant, the policy is considered to be just. Reasonable people who might consider the alternatives would perfer a policy that pays attention to the likelihood of benefit over a policy that gives an organ to someone who dies anyway, while the person next on the list also dies because of the lack of an organ. A triage approach uses the same criteria for patients who need retransplantation or multiple organ transplants. At each point of assessment the question is not about providing an equal number of chances but about applying the same allocation standards to everyone who needs an organ regardless of their transplant history. In fact, transplant surgeons consider retransplantation as an essential component of their treatment. The availability of retransplantation as a therapeutic option when a transplanted organ fails to function makes the overall success rate of transplantation high enough for patients to want the procedure.

The usual transplantation criteria can all be considered medical standards and, for the most part, they are the only standards acknowledged as considerations in transplantation decisions. Critics of the current system complain that it is unjust to offer equal access to those who are ill out of bad luck and those whose previous behaviour contributed to their illness. They argue that social criteria, like the patient's previous contribution to society or the patient's future prospects of depleting or contributing to the stock of social resources. should not be overlooked in transplant decisions. They complain about the unfairness of giving some recipients more than one organ while others are still waiting for a first chance. Doctors, who are committed to equal concern about each of their patients, resist social discrimination as anathema to the profession. Unfortunately, as the demand for organs continues to increase, medicine will be pressed to justify not paying more attention to social considerations about possible individual recipients.

Justice between groups

In addition to considering the characteristics of individual organ recipients, questions arise about whether certain categories of individuals should be excluded from the pool of possible organ recipients. Should those who are not eligible to donate or those who would be unwilling to donate be denied access to the limited supply of transplant organs? In other words, should free-riders be allowed to benefit from the kindness of strangers without being willing or able to give anything in return? For example, should those from groups with religious convictions that would rule out members' donations or foreign nationals be eligible to receive organs from a national pool? Offering transplants to them would diminish the already short supply of organs for the pool of those who might be able and willing to give.

On the international scene, countries have refused to allow free-riders to take advantage of others' generosity. For example, through the auspices of the Council of Europe, the nations of the European Community cooperate in an organ-sharing network. Justice considerations, however, moved them to drop countries in which there was a low rate of organ donation. Because those countries did not contribute their fair share. their citizens were made ineligible to receive organs from the common pool.

When transplant organs are allocated by a national distribution scheme, it is easy to draw a line at national boundaries and limit or rule out cadaveric transplants to foreign nationals. Organ scarcity and a concept of fair play explain limiting organ distribution to the national group that donates the organs. Since the same rule gets applied to everyone outside of the designated border, such policies are not obviously unjust. Taking similar action against groups within a community would be harder to justify and impossible to implement. First, it is not groups who need organs, but individuals. So, even if a group trend can be identified (e.g., African Americans in the United States donate organs at a lower rate than other groups), there is no way of knowing whether a particular group member would behave like the majority or not. It would be discriminatory to treat all members of the group as if they would follow the group pattern. Second, individuals can be classified as members of several groups. The same person can be seen an African American, and a woman, and a mother, and a teacher, and a motorcyclist . . . and studies of each of these groups might show different rates of group donation. There is no principled way to determine which group identification gets used for ruling individuals ineligible for a cadaveric organ. Third, the evidence that might support ruling someone out of organ eligibility is not available when the transplant decision has to be made. Intentions are easy to conceal and anyone who signs a donor card now can tear it up later. Furthermore, exploring someone's religious convictions involves a serious invasion of privacy that democratic societies are loath to tolerate. These reasons suggest that while education, campaigns for donor-card completion and systems of rewards can be orchestrated to encourage individuals and groups to donate organs, it would be unacceptable to impose sanctions on individuals who might not be willing to donate.

Excluding foreign nationals from cadaveric transplant eligibility raises different considerations. This kind of exclusion would effectively deny transplantation as a therapy to individuals from developing nations that could not afford to establish transplant programmes of their own. In the United States, UNOS allows transplant centres to provide up to 5 per cent of their transplants to foreign nationals. Centres, however, will provide the treatment only if they are assured of financial payment. Presumably, the economic reality that transplant centres could not afford the cost of providing the treatment without being reimbursed justifies refusal. If financial reality justifies turning away needy foreigners, the mortal reality of domestic patients becoming sicker and dying as they wait on the national list should also justify refusing organs to those who are outside the pool. The value of international goodwill and the high fees that medical centres can charge foreign patients (as opposed to the negotiated lower fees paid by government health insurance or managed care companies) may have something to do with the policy of generosity to foreigners.

Research

Research raises other questions about organ allocation. One research goal is improving transplantation success in the current patient population. Another goal is extending the treatment to patients who are not currently considered transplant candidates. Trying new or modified therapies on patients for whom success is now unlikely challenges the allocation principle of maximizing organ survival. Yet, given medicine's generally accepted duty to pursue new therapies, research that could produce new medical knowledge would justify some overriding of short-term utility considerations. It would not be fair to deny treatment to people with a particular disease only because we had first learned of the treatment's efficacy for another disease. The competing concerns of maximizing effective organ use and advancing transplantation must be prudently balanced in allocating transplant organs. An increasing degree of scarcity may impose increasingly strict limitations on those research projects designed to extend the treatment to a greater pool of patients. At the same time, scarcity considerations might relax restrictions on research that would hold a promise of augmenting the organ supply (e.g., split liver transplantation, xenografts, procuring organs from non-heart-beating donors).

Duties and Debts

The discussion of justice in organ allocation can be understood as an attempt to understand who has a right to transplantation. However, rights are often associated with duties. If some people have the right to a transplant, what does 'the' system' owe them? When a society declares its commitment to transplantation and when an institution advertises itself as a transplant centre, what are patients entitled to expect? What are the duties of the system to the recipient? And what is owed to the rest of society?

By creating, regulating and funding national organ-distribution systems, and by funding the research that has made organ transplantation into a viable therapy for organ failure, governments implicitly proclaim their acceptance of an obligation to provide this therapy. When government support is drawn from the common pool of social resources and when donations of cadaveric organs are solicited from all members of the society and donated through a national distribution network, all (citizens, taxpayers and/or residents) should have equal access to the beneficial therapy. According to this argument, those without the financial wherewithal to pay for transplantation, nevertheless have the right to equal access because of being part of the society that has supported its development. Furthermore, because organ procurement agencies would not refuse cadaveric organ donations from those without health insurance and financial means, monetary considerations should also be irrelevant in organ distribution. Some societies (e.g., Australia, Great Britain, many countries of Europe) have acknowledged the duty to provide their citizens with equal access to transplantation and the essential post-transplant lifelong anti-rejection medication. In other societies (e.g., the United Sates) the uninsured working poor are denied transplantation because they cannot pay. Can it be just for the poor, who can give organs and who may vote their support for transplantation research, to be denied the opportunity to get transplants?

Individual health-care facilities also have duties to transplant patients. Certainly transplant centres are obligated to maintain adequate facilities and staff for performing the surgery and managing the post-surgical care. They should also be prepared to provide pre- and post-transplant education, and necessary psychological and social support. Certainly, transplant programmes are obliged to treat patients with respect by providing sufficient information about the usual experience of living with a transplanted organ, information about the particular complications of the individual's case and information about organ acceptance standards that might be different at other centres so as to allow patients to make autonomous choices about their own lives. As in other areas of doctor–patient communication, the extent of informing that counts as satisfying this obligation is imprecise. Before transplantation must a patient be informed about the donor's age, life and death, the condition of the organs, the sources of blood for transfusion, the surgical experience of members of the transplant team? What must the patient be told about her or his own surgery and subsequent complications? The rule of respect for autonomy requires patients to be given all of the information which would be relevant to their immediate and future decisions. Thoughtful and imaginative assessment must go into determining the parameters of that requirement.

Since special rights usually come with special duties, those who get the right to an organ transplant may also acquire special obligations. Once people are accepted as organ recipients they may owe something to 'the system'? If you get an organ should you be willing to donate your transplantable organs when you die? Should you commit yourself to acting as an organ donation advocate as many recipients have done (e.g., members of Transplant Recipients International Organization (TRIO) and the liver recipient baseball great, former New York Yankee, Mickey Mantel)? Should you authorize an autopsy if your transplant should fail so that something might be learned to help others who come later? While no centre demands that patients fulfil these duties, potential recipients should be made aware of them and encouraged to pay their moral debts.

Organ procurement from 'non-heart-beating donors' is one current issue engaging the transplant community in a heated moral debate. The question is whether it is ethically acceptable to identify organ donors who are not brain-dead but about to die from disease. With appropriate consent, can life-support be removed, death declared once the heart stops, then life-support resumed so that the organs can be removed for transplantation? It seems that the issue here is whether some people's emotional aversion should carry moral weight. A similar question involves the use of tissue (e.g., brain tissue, eggs) from aborted fetuses. That some people feel repugnance at the thought of these procedures cannot alone justify denying transplants to patients who could significantly benefit from them.

Another immediate issue involves transplants with xenografts, tissue or organs from non-human donors. Insulin and heart valves from pigs are already used successfully in humans. From an animal-centred or animal rights point of view, using animal organs as spare parts for humans raises serious moral issues. For those who do not find this use of animals problematic, there is another issue that needs to be considered. While the special characteristics of non-human tissue (e.g., bone marrow from baboons because of their HIV resistance) and the promise of increased organ supply makes the option of using tissue and organs from animals appealing, the transplant community must pay careful attention to the safety of others who might be affected. Here the concern is zoonosis, the possibility of transmitting benign animal viruses to humans where the effects could be devastating.

Generally, the arguments favour using pigs over simians as organ sources because the greater genetic differences between us and the long history of humans living in proximity with pigs as farm animals without disease transmission make zoonosis less likely.

Conclusion

Organ transplantation can save and improve lives. So physicians who are obliged to try to save lives and to act for the good of their patients are morally committed to offering this valuable treatment option to those who can benefit from it. Unfortunately, the serious shortage of transplant organs leaves the medical community to map out and navigate the obscure moral terrain of ethically procuring and allocating organs and conducting research to advance the field. The task in this time of organ scarcity is to draw the moral lines with creative and thoughtful consideration of all those who need transplantation.

References

Annas, G. J. (1989). The transplant odyssey. *Second Opinion*, 12, 33–9.

Childress, J. F. (1989). Ethical criteria for procuring and distributing organs for transplantation. *Journal of Health Politics, Policy and Law*, 14, 87–113.

Diethelm, A. G. (1990). Ethical decisions in the history of organ transplantation. *Annals of Surgery*, May, 505–20.

Singer, P. A. (1990). A review of public policies to procure and distribute kidneys for transplantation. *Archives of Internal Medicine*, 150, 523–7.

Thomasma, D. C. (1992). Ethical issues and transplantation technology. *Cambridge Quarterly of Healthcare Ethics*, 1, 333–44.

Further Reading

Organ Procurement Policy

Caplan, A. L. and Virning, B. (1990). Is altruism enough? Required request and the donation of cadaver organs and tissues in the United States. *Critical Care Clinics*, 6, 1007–18.

Prottas, J. M. (1989). The organization of organ procurement. *Journal of Health Politics, Policy and Law*, 14, 41–55.

Spital, A. (1991). Sounding board – the shortage of organs for transplantation: where do we go from here? *New England Journal of Medicine*, 325, 1243–6.

Veatch, R. M. (1991). Sounding board – routine inquiry about organ donation – an alternative to presumed consent. *New England Journal of Medicine*, 325, 1246–9.

Organ Donors

Kluge, E. H. W. (1989). Designated organ donation: private choice in social context. *Hastings Center Report*, 19, 10–15.

Rhodes, R. (1993). Debatable donors: when can we count their consent? *Mount Sinai Journal of Medicine*, 60, 45–50.

ROSAMOND RHODES

Tomlinson, T. (1993). Infants and others who cannot consent to donation. *Mount Sinai Journal of Medicine*, 60, 41–4.

Organ Sales

Dworkin, G. (1993). Markets and morals: the case for organ sales. *Mount Sinai Journal of Medicine*, 60, 66–9.
Pellegrino, E. D. (1991). Families' self-interest and the cadaver's organs: what price consent? *Journal of the American Medical Association*, 265, 1305–30.

Organ Allocation

American Medical Association Council on Ethical and Judicial Affairs (1993). Report 49 – Ethical considerations in the allocation of organs and other scarce medical resources among patients. *Code of Medical Ethics Reports*, 4, 140–73.
Rhodes, R., Miller, C. and Schwartz, M. (1992). Transplant recipient selection: peacetime vs. wartime triage. *Cambridge Quarterly of Healthcare Ethics*, 1, 327–32.

Research and New Technology

Serge, M. et al. (1992). Partial liver transplantation from living donors. *Cambridge Quarterly of Healthcare Ethics*, 1, 305–26.
Younger, S. J. and Arnold, R. M. (1993). Ethical, psychosocial, and public policy implications of procuring organs from non-heart-beating cadaver donors. *Journal of the American Medical Association*, 269, 2769–74.

PART X

AIDS

33

AIDS: individual and 'public' interests

UDO SCHÜKLENK

AIDS is an acquired immunodeficiency syndrome, the first cases of which were reported in the USA by the Centers for Disease Control in 1981. People with AIDS suffer from a functionally progressively declining immune system; a consequence of this is a greater likelihood of developing opportunistic infections. Patients succumb subsequently to one or more of these infections. The majority of biomedical scientists agrees that a retrovirus, human immunodeficiency virus (HIV) and an unknown number of its mutations, cause AIDS, although the cause of action is so far unknown, and a minority of scientists deny that HIV is the cause of AIDS. Among the supporters of the hypothesis that HIV causes AIDS, it is in dispute whether HIV alone is sufficient to cause AIDS or whether it is only a necessary condition.

There has been enormous interest in AIDS from the media, scientists, healthcare professionals and bioethicists. There were many reasons for this, among them the fact that HIV is sexually transmissible and seems to have the potential to kill an infected person many years after infection. The fascination surrounding AIDS is also related to fact that the majority of people infected in developed countries are gay men and intravenous (IV) drug-users (National Research Council, 1993). The percentage of women in the overall number of people infected in the Western industrialized nations has risen only recently. However, among these a disproportionate number are, in the USA, women of colour who are IV drug users themselves or who have been infected by IV drug-using men. At present the average woman with AIDS in a developed country is more likely to have contracted AIDS through IV drug use than through unprotected heterosexual intercourse. This basic empirical fact has not prevented a number of feminist authors from making claims to the contrary. Some ethicists have suggested that the exaggeration of the real threat of AIDS to women is itself an unethical strategy designed to change the sexual behaviour of women (Mertz, 1996). The assumed course of transmission among users of IV drugs is through sharing of needles.

Bioethicists have been concerned predominantly with the following subject-matter:

- HIV testing;
- Whether HIV infection should be considered harm to others or harm to self;
- AIDS clinical research and access to experimental drugs; and
- The problems surrounding HIV-infected health-care professionals and the duty to treat people with HIV and AIDS.

343

In some religious circles there have been discussions about whether AIDS should be seen as the wrath of God directed against gay men and others committing acts which are considered by some as 'crimes against nature', but bioethicists have generally not taken such arguments seriously.

HIV Testing

Once there was a consensus in the medical profession that a virus (later called HIV) is the cause of AIDS, the possibility of detecting this virus with testing devices was only a question of time. In the early years of the bioethical debate over AIDS-related matters, the issue of voluntary or compulsory HIV testing was prominent. It was recognized, however, that the point of testing lies in the subsequent use of knowledge of the outcome of the test. Indeed, compulsory testing and subsequent isolation of those found positive for antibodies to the cause of AIDS has been suggested and even enacted, for instance, in Cuba. The general consensus among bioethicists seemed to be that mandatory testing is normally only acceptable when there is a successful therapy for the disease available. In an early paper published in 1986 in the *Journal of the American Medical Association*, Bayer and colleagues argued that 'there is no demonstrable public health benefit that justifies universal mandatory screening, given the invasion of privacy involved' (Bayer et al., 1986: 1770). This line of argument, which is based in part on the importance of respect for individual autonomy, has been accepted by those health officials responsible for the AIDS policies of most Western countries. It accepts essentially that until there is a clear benefit to the infected individual from knowing about her infection, there is no paternalistic reason to implement mandatory testing. If there is no benefit for the society at large in knowing that certain individuals are infected, there is no need for mandatory testing. Of course, on this argument the rejection of mandatory HIV testing is conditional upon having no efficient drugs that could either prevent the outbreak of AIDS, prolong the disease-free period or improve the quality of life of a person at risk for AIDS. Combination therapies, including protease inhibitors and nucleoside analogues, have been shown to improve the quality of life of some people with AIDS substantially, and to increase survival. It is not clear, however, what the long-term effects of such drug regimens will be. Some patients have not been able to tolerate these drugs at all, while others have developed serious clinical complications after using them for one or two years. It is unclear whether combination therapy in early HIV infection would be beneficial to patients.

Once the panic of the early years of the epidemic had disappeared, the issue of voluntary testing of selected risk populations was on the agenda. The approval of the chemotherapeutic AZT (zidovudine) in 1987 led a number of bioethicists to argue for broad-scale educational campaigns in favour of voluntary testing. For instance, James F. Childress argued in favour of selective voluntary screening by pointing to the possible benefits to HIV-positive individuals which 'include closer medical follow-up, earlier use of azidothymidine (AZT) (and other treatments), prophylaxis or other care for associated diseases, protection of loved ones, and clearer plans for the future' (Childress, 1991: 58). Until a long-term controlled study in 1994 demonstrated that this drug does not confer survival benefits if taken early, the results of a much smaller short-term 1987 study initiated a shift in the attitude of biomedical ethicists towards voluntary testing. They believed that people with an HIV infection could positively influence the course of their infection by taking early AZT. Several liberal authors warned that some test campaigns conducted by health authorities and AIDS service organizations were of a manipulative nature and ultimately, violated autonomy (e.g., Schüklenk, 1994). Now that AZT intervention in early HIV infection has disappeared as a viable option, the major paternalistic motive for testing has evaporated too. In fact, knowledge of HIV infection *per se* confers no information of clinical relevance at all. All major prophylaxis-related decisions must be based not on HIV status but on immune status (defined by reliable counts of CD4 and CD8 helper cells). This has, however, had no major impact on the arguments of those in favour of testing. Perhaps Hogan is not entirely wrong when he asserts: 'Previous to the advent of AZT, persons in the public health establishment anticipated the use of some effective treatment, and invoked a hypothetical medical benefit of knowing one's antibody status. Once AZT appeared, without doing any kind of critical analysis of whether AZT fulfilled such necessary criteria, they were glad to ascribe unproven value to it, just to rationalize *pre-existent* bias towards testing' (as quoted in Schüklenk, 1994: 254).

In 1994 the issue of mandatory testing for selected groups returned with a new urgency. It is linked again to AZT in AIDS therapy. A study found that the chances of an HIV-positive woman infecting her fetus can be reduced if this drug is administered during pregnancy. There are several ethical issues here. One is whether pregnant women should be forced to test for HIV in order to achieve the best possible treatments for the fetuses. Knowing of the fetuses' infection would automatically lead to information about the mother's HIV status too. If the mother refuses to be tested, does the fetus' interest in potential treatment have priority over the mother's interest not to be tested? Another ethical problem is that again testing itself is not the only issue here, but mandatory treatment is too. Currently only about 10–20 per cent of infected mothers give birth to infected offspring, while the majority of babies remain non-infected. Good general health and nutritional status lead to a reduction of mother–child transmission to 10 per cent, as European studies have shown. Conversely, vitamin A deficiency causes increased transmission rates. The ethical questions to be addressed in this context are these. Should we force all pregnant women to test for HIV? Should we force all women who have tested HIV-positive to take a chemotherapeutic substance which is known to interfere with the replication of their fetuses' rapidly dividing cells (i.e., cells of the central nervous system) even though we know that we can reduce the transmission rate to as low as 10 per cent without using AZT (Murrain, 1997)? AZT would reduce the percentage of infected fetuses to 8 per cent. In other words, under ideal circumstances we would have 8 out of 100 fetuses who have been subjected to AZT HIV-free instead of 10 out of 100 without AZT. The impact of AZT on the human fetus is as yet unknown, but experiments with rats demonstrated that this drug is both embryotoxic and fetotoxic. The medical journal, the *Lancet*, reported in February 1995 that the US National Institutes of Health have aborted a trial among

345

children randomized to various nucleoside analogues. Reportedly the death rate was higher and growth failure, opportunistic infections and neurological and neurodevelopmental deterioration were commoner in the AZT arm. We can therefore assume that this chemotherapeutic has significant potential to harm 98 fetuses, and 100 HIV-infected mothers, for the sake of a reduction of HIV infection by a further 2 fetuses out of 100. Is this ethically justifiable? Michelle Murrain, a neurobiologist and feminist author, suggests that mandatory testing constitutes a violation of women's rights over their own bodies and health. She points out furthermore that 'under the terms of mandatory treatment, once a woman decides to continue pregnancy, she forfeits her right to bodily integrity to ensure fetal health. It [the suggested legislation] gives the right to invade the woman's body to the state' (Murrain, 1997). The US CDC has rejected the idea of mandatory testing of pregnant women.

The advent of combination therapies involving protease inhibitors and nucleoside analogues has led to improvements in patients' survival time and quality of life. This has not re-ignited the debate over mandatory testing. It seems that the arguments in favour of education and voluntariness have triumphed over the idea to compel people to undergo the test, and to compel them to take certain combinations of drugs should they test HIV positive.

The other reason for mandatory testing has classically been seen in cases where unprotected sexual intercourse takes place and HIV infection is considered as harm to others. This issue will be discussed at greater length in the following section of this article.

HIV Infection: Harm to Self or Harm to Others

The moral justification for using the criminal law to interfere with individual choices has traditionally been to prevent harm to others. The use of the criminal law to prevent consenting adults from harming themselves has been seen as much more problematic. In many countries legislators have had to decide whether an HIV infection should be considered harm to self, or whether it should be seen as harm to others. At issue is the fact that most infections that are the result of sexual encounters occur as a consequence of voluntary consensual acts among adults. Libertarians such as Richard Mohr or liberals such as Patricia Illingworth have therefore argued that under such circumstances there is no room for the criminal law. Mohr suggested that AIDS' 'mode of contagion assures that those at risk are those whose actions contribute to their risk of infection, chiefly through intimate sexual contact and shared hypodermic needles' (Mohr, 1987: 38). Mohr's argument for non-intervention in cases of unsafe sexual encounters among autonomously acting consenting adults is this: 'If independence – the ability to guide one's life by one's own lights to an extent compatible with the like ability on the part of others – is, as it is, a major value, one cannot respect that value while preventing people from putting themselves at risk through voluntary association' (Mohr, 1987: 39). In the second part of this section I will get back to positions disagreeing with Mohr's interpretation that HIV infections in most cases occur in sexual encounters among consenting adults and therefore constitute harm to oneself. Obviously, even if one agrees with his interpretation, the option of justifying interventions by health authorities through *paternalistic* strategies remains, and does not look prima facie unreasonable. After all, society interferes often to prevent harm to self (legislation to enforce the use of seat-belts in cars is a good example of this). Why should AIDS be treated differently? Why should we allow people who wish to have unprotected sexual intercourse (in particular when they belong to high-risk groups) to do so? The very nature of sexual acts suggests that most HIV transmissions are acts of *private* harms and at least within a liberal framework 'it would be wrong to adopt policies which would interfere with individual liberty' (Illingworth, 1990a: 11). The classical principle *volenti non fit iniuria* can be utilized to support this point of view.

A few commentators have argued that HIV-positive gay men have a duty to disclose their antibody status to their prospective sexual partners in impersonal sexual encounters. All major AIDS organizations, most of which are run by gay men, have rejected such ideas. The consensus in such groups is that HIV infection constitutes harm to self and that actually such a duty to disclosure might be counter-productive. Empirical research, for instance, has demonstrated that 'the majority of communication in sex is non-verbal,' hence a duty to disclose could not possibly mean that it is a duty on the side of the HIV-positive person to *say* explicitly that he is infected because this would violate the basic 'rule of conduct' in many situations which lead to sexual encounters (Davies, 1993: 49). Those at risk insist on safe sex but not disclosure of HIV status. Illingworth pointed out that a policy of disclosure may have the consequence that uninfected people take fewer precautions to avoid infection. A fictitious example of hers is quite compelling: 'If Sam believes that it is Bob's moral responsibility to inform him of his antibody status, he may construe Bob's silence as an invitation not to practice safe sex' (Illingworth, 1990a: 42). Obviously, such a duty to disclose would only make sense in a society where everybody knows, for instance, because mandatory testing has been introduced, of his or her antibody status *and* where everybody adheres to the rules of this alleged moral duty to disclose. The proposal of mandatory testing of all (known *and* unknown) homosexual men, IV drug users and other members of high-risk groups, however, has already been rejected in Western societies and has, for this reason alone, rendered the idea of a duty to disclose practically useless and, if anything, counter-productive.

As an exception to this general rule ethicists have considered the situation of couples where ethical obligations that are a consequence of friendships apply. Friends generally trust each others, don't harm each other and are supportive of each other. People living in partnerships have prima facie reason to believe that their respective partner is not infected if he does not insist on safe sex because otherwise he would breach the ethical obligation not to hurt his friend or lover. Hence, it has been suggested that people in long-term loving relationships or friendships have a moral obligation to disclose their infection to their partner.

As virtually always in pluralistic societies there is no general consensus that HIV infection primarily constitutes harm to self, not even in those cases where the individuals are autonomous people who are perfectly aware of the risks they take

347

and where these individuals have voluntarily agreed to engage in unsafe sexual encounters with other individuals whose antibody status is unknown to them. Ronald Bayer has recognized that ultimately the question of HIV infection in voluntary sexual encounters is a matter of 'private choices, choices that will be made in the most intimate of settings beyond the observation of even the most thoroughgoing surveillance' (Bayer, 1989: 11). He maintains, however, that any interpretation which would assume that the transmission of AIDS 'between consenting adults [is] belonging to the private realm alone and therefore beyond the legitimate concern of the state would make a serious mistake' (Bayer, 1989: 12). The argument continues that HIV infection must always be considered as harm to others and should be interpreted as a 'public-health' matter. The reasoning behind this interpretation is that the chances of keeping the epidemic under control are good when only a few responsibly acting individuals are infected and the odds turn against societal interests when the level of infection reaches certain saturation levels. Arguments such as these usually conclude that we cannot ignore the collective harmful impact of individual acts which lead to HIV infection. This strategy to justify interventions designed by 'public-health' officials asserts that the health of the public is somehow threatened by consensual unsafe sexual encounters, but its proponents never explain exactly what they mean when they talk about 'public health'. Libertarians have persuasively argued that all known interpretations of 'public health' are either meaningless or totalitarian in their nature (Mohr, 1987: 46–50). Nevertheless, the ethicists invoking a 'public-health' obligation to intervene go to great lengths in criticizing the alleged failure of public-health authorities to close gay bathhouses, in order to enforce the exercise of restraint and responsibility that they request. Liberals have responded to such ideas by pointing out that they violate basic liberal principles on which Western societies are based, and that the interventionists have failed to provide a theoretical defence of such violations. Illingworth adds that furthermore there is reasonable doubt that the closure of bathhouses has the positive 'public-health' effects some hoped it would have: 'gay men who view the option to use gay baths as a hard-won liberty might view their prohibition as an excessively repressive measure which confirms homophobic zeal. In these circumstances, closing the baths might undermine a tendency to cooperate with public health officials' (Illingworth, 1990b: 348).

On a very practical level it won't be possible to prevent such alleged harms to others from occurring, no matter how much we would like to do so. The idea of closing bathhouses is consistent with interpretations of HIV infection as harm to others and the rejection of liberal approaches in favour of 'public-health' policies, without further specification of what the public-health risks might be. It is surprising that proponents of such policies seem not to have considered that such a policy is impossible to implement effectively. Even if we could ignore the significant moral issues surrounding the breach of individual privacy necessary to monitor our bedrooms, or members-only sex-on-venue establishments, in practice it is impossible to enforce such policies without creating Orwell's 1984. Gay bathhouses have been closed in order politically to placate conservatives in the USA, while similar policies have not been introduced in liberal European countries such as Germany or the

Netherlands. Recent reports from San Francisco and Manhattan indicate that gay men were inventive enough quickly to find alternatives to their closed bathhouses. Sex-on-venue premises continue to exist, though perhaps no longer in the *form* of gay bathhouses. It was naive to assume otherwise. The ideology of 'public health' in this sense has failed already in practice.

Access to Experimental Drugs and the Ethics of Research Clinical Trials

Terminally ill people, by definition, have no successful standard treatment available to them. Certain drugs might extend their survival time, but ultimately they will succumb to a disease that is life-threatening and incurable. In contrast to other life-threatening diseases, such as cancer, for instance, people with AIDS tend to be fairly young and unwilling to give up on life easily. Highly sophisticated and creative activist groups such as ACT UP have not only raised public awareness for AIDS with a number of publicity-gaining acts, but have also vehemently criticized the slow response of research agencies to the crisis (Nussbaum, 1990). On ethical grounds they questioned the status quo in two different areas of the testing and availability of drugs. They argued that, given the time involved in the AIDS research establishment's drug testing and approval process, they wanted access to experimental drugs. Their point was that in the case of terminal illness no government has a moral right to prevent patients from taking their chances with experimental agents of their liking. As Martin Delaney, director of the US American AIDS activist group Project Inform, pointed out in his address to the twenty-sixth annual meeting of the US Infectious Diseases Society:

> It is as if I am in a disabled airplane, speeding downward out of control. I see a parachute hanging on the cabin wall, one small moment of hope. I try to strap it on when a government employee reaches out and tears it off my back, admonishing, 'You cannot use that! It does not have the Federal Aviation Administration Sticker on it. We do not know if it will work.' (Delaney, 1989: 416)

This view claims that autonomous terminally ill individuals have a right to take charge of their own lives. The objections are twofold. The first is strongly paternalistic. It concedes that patients are actually aware of the risk they are running when they take unapproved drugs, but maintains that it is not in their best interest and that these patients very probably will harm themselves or will be subject to exploitation by ruthless quacks. As Walters (1988: 601) pointed out, 'unnecessary suffering would be visited on people with HIV infection if they were provided immediate access to ineffective "therapies" or treatments with toxic effects that far outweigh their therapeutic benefits.' This argument constitutes a *petitio principii*. If patients knew that a certain unapproved drug did not work, they surely would not use it. The point is that they do not know, but that they are willing to accept certain risks, given that their very survival is at stake and furthermore that the health care profession has no successful therapy to offer. The second major argument against

349

patient access to experimental drugs has been advanced on the grounds that this constitutes harm to others. Cooper (1989: 2445) suggested that

> The more devastating the disease and less satisfactory the existing therapy, the stronger the disincentive for a patient to enrol in a randomized controlled trial, if the drug can be obtained in some other way. Consequently, a national policy of early widespread availability of unproved experimental agents would slow or even halt the completion of controlled clinical trials through which therapeutic advances are established and then improved on.

This view makes it obvious that there is a conflict between the interests of current patients and those of future patients. At this point the connection between access to experimental agents and the ethics of research clinical trials beomes apparent. Conflicts between participating patients' survival interests and broader research interests seem to be inevitable and are well documented in the literature (e.g., Nussbaum, 1990: 123). Some ethicists have suggested that under such circumstances the recruitment of terminally ill patients as participants in clinical trials exploits these patients' vulnerability in an unethical way. Patients do not really give voluntary (informed) consent to a trial protocol that to some degree neglects their survival interests. They do so only because they are left with no other choice if they want access to an experimental agent they are interested in (Minogue, 1995). The basic question seems to be, therefore, whether we can expect terminally ill people to act altruistically in a way that might even put them at risk of earlier death, should they decide to join a research clinical trial because they have no other way of getting experimental therapies (Schüklenk, 1998). For liberals and libertarians the answer has to be a clear 'no' because the infringements of civil liberties of dying people would be unacceptably high. It seems, however, that even utilitarians would ultimately not try to coerce such people into clinical trials for pragmatic reasons. They would not expect a level of altruism that is superhuman.

An increasing number of people with AIDS do just about everything they can to join a clinical trial. For example, they conceal the fact that they are using other drugs, or they share the experimental agent with other patients who have ended up in the placebo arm of the trial. A consequence of this is that the predictive value of the results of such trials remains in doubt. It has been reported by AIDS researchers in the US that people with AIDS often use concurrent treatments, share drugs with other trial participants and even bribe researchers to get into a certain trial or into a certain trial arm. Those who have been randomized to a placebo drop out quickly and in large numbers (Delaney, 1989). Bioethicists have criticized this patient survival strategy as unethical and suggested that those patients have a moral obligation towards the principal investigator to keep their part of the bargain, that is, to stick to the trial protocol. This claim rests on the assumption that these patients are *real* volunteers. A terminally ill patient who has been robbed of the option to access the drugs he believes might save his life is not acting voluntarily if he joins a clinical trial which offers him only a fifty-fifty chance to get this drug (or an even smaller chance in trials with multiple arms) (Minogue, 1995). Hence it does not seem prima facie unethical for such patients to join trials under false pretences about their use of concomitant drugs, medical history, etc.

HIV Infection in Health-care Professionals and Patients

Attempts have been made to distinguish between the issue of whether health-care professionals should be tested mandatorily for HIV infection and whether their patients should be tested. I cannot see that there is an ethically relevant difference between these situations. Patients of HIV-infected health-care professionals who are having invasive procedures run a *remote* risk of infection and so do health-care professionals from HIV-infected patients. The debate about HIV-infected health-care professionals focuses primarily on whether all health-care personnel should be mandatorily tested for HIV antibodies and, if so, whether those who test HIV-positive should be allowed to continue working as health-care professionals. The heat in the public debate over this issue was turned up significantly after newspaper reports of the first cases of patients who were allegedly infected by in one case a dentist and in another case a physician. So far mandatory testing of health-care personnel has not been recommended by professional medical bodies. The amount written about this issue clearly exceeds its real significance. A 1992 review article reports that unpublished studies looking back at thousands of patients of infected health-care workers have not documented HIV transmission from such professionals to their patients (Weiss, 1992). Some ethicists have nevertheless suggested that there is a significant risk of infection for patients of health-care professionals who perform invasive procedures and that these professionals should refrain from performing such procedures (Gostin, 1990: 308). Gostin believes that such professionals should be required to report their HIV status to their employers (but not to their patients) and 'should be carefully monitored in their performance of their functions' but he leaves it open whether they should refrain voluntarily from performing invasive procedures, or whether they should be forced to do so. Positions such as this were subsequently criticized for suggesting a restriction on the involvement of infected personnel in invasive procedures and for exaggerating the real risk patients face. Feldblum points out that the 'ramifications of his [Gostin's] policy statement for the overall system of health care delivery are so significant that the lack of sufficient data is compelling' (Feldblum, 1991: 136). Indeed, cases of alleged HIV infection in patients caused by infected health-care workers which were reported around the world by the news media turned out to be falsely attributed to the health-care professionals (Dickinson, 1993).

In regard to patients, the question was whether patients should be mandatorily tested for HIV and, if so, should they test HIV-positive, whether there is an obligation for a physician to treat them. Professional medical associations were quick to point out that physicians have a professional obligation to treat HIV-infected people and people with AIDS. Some ethicists have suggested that this duty is a consequence of the special status of the medical profession, which entails accepting certain risks for the health-care providers themselves. Others have argued that there is no such obligation because each individual visit by a patient to a physician should be considered a business deal in which the patient requires certain professional services which the physician agrees to provide for a certain fee. If one of the sides (in this case the physician), for whatever reason, does not wish to enter into the contract, there is no reason to assume that she should be forced to do so. Given empirical evidence that certain subpopulations within the overall number of people with AIDS receive consistently substandard treatments from their physicians in public hospitals and in private, it seems advisable to leave it to physicians to volunteer under such circumstances in order to prevent patients from being subjected to substandard treatments by physicians who are unhappy about having to treat them in the first place (Ayanian, 1994). Obviously, an exception needs to be made for emergency procedures. This problem of racism, sexism and homophobia in the medical profession, which is the cause of such substandard treatments, needs to be addressed by professional associations and teaching institutions alike (Schüklenk, 1997).

Final Remarks

The line-up of issues discussed in this article is far from complete. Due to space constraints I have chosen topics on the basis of two criteria: the quantity of material published by biomedical ethicists on a given subject, and the applicability of my analysis of an issue to related practical problems. The latter allows me to feel more comfortable about the fact that, for instance, I have not discussed the issue of needle-exchange programmes for IV drug users. The analysis of this problem would have employed the frameworks used above, those of paternalism versus autonomy, and at the same time also considered the harm to others argument. I have also not discussed the issue of conflicts between the need for explicit sex education and the availability of condoms, and religious and cultural values which do not condone either sex education mentioning 'immoral' sex acts or the use of condoms. This is dealt with in the second AIDS-related article (chapter 34, pp. 355–65). The reason for this conflict is largely due to the fact that these clashes between health promotional requirements dictated by epidemiological needs versus religious values are much more prevalent and serious in a number of African and South-east Asian countries than they are in secular Western societies.

The bioethical debate over AIDS-related issues has been construed primarily as one of individual liberties versus a supposed 'public interest'. The AIDS debate among biomedical ethicists has not produced any further innovations in the field; rather AIDS has been used as a case study to apply pre-existing philosophical frameworks.

References

Ayanian, J. Z. (1994). Race, class, and the quality of medical care. *Journal of the American Medical Association*, 271, 1207–8.

Bayer, R. (1989). *Private Acts, Social Consequences*. New York: Free Press.

Bayer, R., Levine, C. and Wolf, S. M. (1986). HIV antibody screening: an ethical framework for evaluating proposed programs. *Journal of the American Medical Association*, 256, 1768–74.

Childress, J. F. (1991). Mandatory HIV screening and testing. In F. G. Reamer (ed.), *AIDS and Ethics*. New York: Columbia University Press, 50–76.

Cooper, E. (1989). Controlled clinical trials of AIDS drugs: the best hope. *Journal of the American Medical Association*, 261, 2445.

Delaney, M. (1989). The case for patient access to experimental therapy. *Journal of Infectious Diseases*, 159, 416–19.

Dickinson, G. M., Morhart, R. E. and Klimas, N. G. et al. (1993). Absence of HIV transmission from an HIV-infected dentist to his patients. *Journal of the American Medical Association*, 269, 1802–6.

Feldblum, C. R. (1991). A response to Gostin, 'The HIV-infected health care professional: public policy, discrimination, and patient safety'. *Law, Medicine and Health Care*, 19, 134–9.

Gostin, L. O. (1990). The HIV-infected health care professional: public policy, discrimination, and patient safety. *Law, Medicine and Health Care*, 18, 303–10.

Illingworth, P. (1990a). *AIDS and the Good Society*. London: Routledge.

——(1990b). Review essay. *Bioethics*, 4, 340–50.

Mertz, D., Sushinsky, M. A. and Schüklenk, U. (1996). Women and AIDS: the ethics of exaggerated harm. *Bioethics*, 10, 93–113.

Minogue, B. P., Palmer-Fernandez, G., Udell, L. and Waller, B. N. (1995). Individual autonomy and the double-blind controlled experiment: the case of desperate volunteers. *Journal of Medicine and Philosophy*, 20, 43–55.

Mohr, R. D. (1987). Gays, AIDS and state coercion. *Bioethics*, 1, 35–50.

Murrain, M. (1997). Caught in the crossfire: women and the search for the magic bullet. In N. Goldstein and J. Manlowe (eds), *Gender Politics of HIV*. New York: New York University Press.

National Research Council (1993). *Social Impact of AIDS*. Washington, DC: National Academy Press.

Nussbaum, B. (1990). *Good Intentions: how big business and the medical establishment are corrupting the fight against AIDS, Alzheimer's, cancer and more*. New York: Penguin.

Schüklenk, U. (1994). Against manipulative campaigns by 'community based' AIDS organisations. *Health Care Analysis* 2, 253–61.

—— (1995). *Access to Experimental Drugs in Terminal Illness: Ethical issues*. New York: Howarth.

Schüklenk, U. and Riley, T. (1997). Homosexuality, societal attitudes toward. In R. Chadwick (ed.), *Encyclopedia of Applied Ethics*. San Diego: Academic Press.

Walters, L. (1988). Ethical issues in the prevention and treatment of HIV infection and AIDS. *Science*, 239, 597–603.

Weiss, S. (1992). HIV infection in healthcare workers. *Medical Clinics of North America* 76, 269–80.

Further Reading

Capron, A. M. (1974/5). Informed consent in catastrophic disease research and treatment. *University of Pennsylvania Law Review*, 123, 340–438.

Clark, M. E. (1990). AIDS prevention: legislative options. *American Journal of Law and Medicine*, 16, 107–53.

Davies, P. M., Hickson, F. C. I., Weatherburn, P. and Hunt, A. J. (1993). *Sex, Gay Men and AIDS*. London: Falmer Press.

Feinberg, J. (1984). *The Moral Limits of the Criminal Law: Harm to others*. New York: Oxford University Press.

——— (1986). *The Moral Limits of the Criminal Law: Harm to self*. New York: Oxford University Press.

Gostin, L. O. (ed.) (1990). *AIDS and the Health Care System*. New Haven: Yale University Press.

Gray, J. N., Lyons, P. M. Jr. and Melton, G. B. (1995). *Ethical and Legal Issues in AIDS Research*. Baltimore, MD: Johns Hopkins University Press.

Hunter, N. D. and Rubenstein, B. (eds) (1992). *AIDS Agenda: Emerging issues in civil rights*. New York: Free Press.

34

AIDS: ethical issues in the developing world

UDO SCHÜKLENK, VICHAI CHOKEVIVAT,
CARLOS DEL RIO, SEGUN GBADEGESIN AND
CARLOS MAGIS

Ethical issues of AIDS in developing countries are to some degree similar to those in Western countries, but the problems are different in most matters because of the limited resources available in developing countries for health care. In this article we will be looking at the specific problems encountered in a number of developing countries in Latin America, Asia and Africa. The major ethical problems here are related to justice in the allocation of scarce resources, to discrimination against people with AIDS and to informed consent in research clinical trials.

On an international level the 1948 UN Declaration of Human Rights asserts that 'Everyone has a right to a standard of living adequate for the health and well-being of himself and his family, including . . . medical care.' Clearly there is a huge gap between the ideal explicated in UN papers and the reality in developing countries. One could certainly argue that the developed nations have an ethical obligation to support developing nations on an economic level as well as on the level of know-how in order to reach this goal (Schüklenk, 1998). Until this happens, however, there are difficult choices to be made in developing countries in regard to the question of how to spend the money available for AIDS in an ethical manner.

We have also found that AIDS is used as a pretence by religious and other groups to further their own agenda rather than to support people with AIDS and those at risk of contracting AIDS. Given the much greater influence of, for instance, the Roman Catholic Church in Latin America, when compared to its influence in largely secular Western countries, difficult choices need to be made between adhering to religious values and the health of many citizens of developing countries. Overall, general improvements in regard to civil rights seem to be an important means to a more ethical approach to the AIDS problem in the developing world.

In Latin America, the AIDS epidemic has produced varied reactions. One author has described them as an epidemic of fear, of stigmatization and of usually religious-ly motivated moralizing (Pescador and Bronfman, 1989). As the disease was described in Mexico as predominantly a 'gay disease' it gave society an excuse to persecute the 'risk group'. People were found to be 'suspicious' because of their sexual orientation and not because of their sexual behaviour. As a consequence, the person with AIDS was blamed as the cause of the epidemic, rather than treated as the person affected by an epidemic (Rico et al., 1995a). Attempts were made to protect society through stigmatization, for instance, by limiting the civil rights of a specific 'risk group', mainly gay men. In Latin America one frequently comes across ethically unjustifiable categories such as 'guilty' HIV positive people (i.e., homo- and bisexual men, and IV drug users) and those 'innocent' (i.e., those infected through transfusions and children infected through perinatal infection).

Polygamy in African Societies

A story appeared in a newspaper in the USA about the menace of AIDS in Africa, and the culture that was making the war against it almost unwinnable. The story was as follows. In an East African town, AIDS has been a devastating killer, wiping out families over a period of time. In the particular case of one extended family, the disease had killed a young man, survived by a wife without any children. The wife was still young and was also diagnosed with AIDS. According to tradition, the widowed wife had to be remarried to the junior brother of the deceased, who has the responsibility, not just for taking care of her, but also for sleeping with her so that she could bear children to ensure the immortality of his late brother. The story ended with the conclusion that this young man discharged his traditionally sanctioned duty and contracted AIDS. This story, like many others, perpetuated the myth of Africa as the dark continent. The question is: how true is the story? Even though polygamy is a cultural reality in many African societies it is not traditionally required (Mahmood, 1972). In the case of traditional African societies, it is also true that several proverbs and witty remarks counsel against the dangers of polygamy. If safe sex is not practised under such circumstances, there are grave consequences for the spread of AIDS.

This poses, but does not resolve, an ethical problem. What should be done with those who choose unsafe sex which increases their risks of getting AIDS and increases the likelihood of subsequently infecting others? This touches on the question of autonomy and rationality. Unless it is based on the voluntary agreement of all the parties, any form of prohibition would violate the autonomy of the parties. It should also be realized that, in many cases, one of the parties is an unwilling participant. We cannot see, however, that there are good reasons for suggesting a legal prohibition of polygamous relationships. After all, a monogamous marriage does not prevent either spouse from extramarital affairs which may also lead to disease and infections. Moreover, to prohibit polygamy would be seen as anti-tradition and anti-Islam. For though neither tradition nor Islam requires the practice, it has been identified with both and it is not condemned by them.

Women in the Sex Industry

Women encounter problems in Asian countries which are different to those men have to cope with. Many female sex workers in Nepal, for instance, have been abducted from their native towns or villages, either forcibly or lured with promises of a job in a city in India or marriage (O'dea, 1993). Most of them were abducted or sold by their own next of kin, their parents, husbands, relatives or friends of the family. In addition to that, a large number of women have engaged in sex work in order to provide an income to support their families. Some of this sex work is of a voluntary nature. Commercial sex business has been associated with mass movements of refugees, the breakdown of the family, economic problems, industrialization and the consequent migration to the urban cities (Gosh, 1993). In this climate it cannot be a surprise that the most important factor responsible for the rapid spread of AIDS is the practice of men having sexual intercourse with sex workers. Law-and-order solutions to this problem ignore an important ethical dimension. It is only possible to solve these complex problems by making available alternative careers for women and by empowering those already engaged in it in order to prevent them from taking the risk of acquiring HIV.

Other ethical issues that are special to women are related to abortion rights when HIV-infected women become pregnant. Nothing in this debate, however, differs from the ethical arguments usually put forward by proponents and opponents of women's abortion rights.

Sex Education

A major ethical issue that is prone to create tension between religious values and the fight against AIDS in developing countries is in the area of sex education. It should be noted that AIDS in Africa, for instance, is mostly transmitted through heterosexual contacts, blood transfusion and injection. Western health promoters have argued that educational programmes that promote safe sex are needed. Some religious groups see the promotion of safe sex as an effort to encourage promiscuity, and they would rather teach abstinence. This is true of Catholics, Protestant fundamentalists and some Islamic sects. In a number of developing countries, officials of the Roman Catholic Church went to great lengths to prevent government health officials and non-government organizations informing the public about safe sex. Religiously motivated resistance to health education promoting the use of condoms was reportedly fierce in the predominantly Catholic Philippines and in Uganda (Schüklenk and Mertz, 1993). In Mexico, for instance, the state was criticized for promoting condom use and, since the epidemic is viewed as a disease due to morally improper (sexual) behaviour, campaigns were frequently requested to make society return to more 'traditional sexual behaviour'. Because of pressure from the Church and other conservative groups, governments have been reluctant to develop effective prevention campaigns, designing instead lukewarm campaigns so as not to offend or enrage this powerful sector of society. Prevention campaigns promoting condoms were criticized as 'permissive and conducive to promiscuity' (Rico et al., 1995b). In many countries in Latin America homosexuality is still a criminal offence.

The ethical issue to be discussed in cases such as these is whether adhering to religious teachings is of greater importance than implementing health

357

promotion campaigns designed to save human lives (even at the cost of violating religious values). Clearly, secular ethicists insist that the latter is more important than the former. Christian, ethicists might insist that if people would adhere to the standards of religious teaching there would be no need for the use of condoms because people would not have multiple sex partners. It is common knowledge, however, that even devoted Catholics do not strictly adhere to their Church's teachings when these teachings are not convenient for them. The vast majority, for example, use contraceptives to avoid pregnancy.

Allocation of Health-care Resources

One of the major ethical problems for developing countries appears to be the allocation of resources for fighting AIDS, and obviously this ties up with the perennial problem of resource allocation to the health sector. In situations where less than 2 per cent of the GNP is devoted to health, it is difficult to see how there can be an effective war against disease. Many African countries, for instance, spend a significant part of their income on defence, and corruption is a serious problem which must be combated to free resources for the delivery of adequate health care (Leisinger, 1993). Problems of resource allocation for AIDS programmes can easily be observed in Asia too. The ethical discussion in Latin America has been centred on the high costs of available treatments and the denial of care rooted in discrimination.

Many countries are, for instance, still unable to provide a safe blood supply because they cannot afford to screen all units of blood before transfusion (Laos National Committee for the Control of AIDS, 1994; Myanmar Ministry of Health, 1993). But the issue here is that of micro-allocation within the health sectors. How much ought to be devoted to AIDS cure versus prevention? In Thailand, for instance. some 65 per cent of AIDS funds is available for medical care, while the rest goes into AIDS prevention. The funds available for care can serve only a small portion of the cases in that country (Thailand National AIDS Committee, 1995). It is an argument frequently heard throughout Latin America that, in the absence of a cure, resources for AIDS should be used only for prevention. This position has even found support from international organizations such as the Panamerican Health Organization. This argument is problematic because it often ignores in its equation the indirect costs of AIDS, which are, in some cases, significantly higher than the direct costs of drugs and health care.

The cost of AIDS drugs is prohibitive for the majority of people with AIDS living in developing countries. And, even though many of these countries have health-care systems providing free health care, they are not able to afford the cost of drugs for AIDS victims without a trade-off with other health programmes, including those against malaria and tuberculosis. For instance, in Malaysia only one antiretroviral drug is currently available through the public health-care system. The financial burdens of acquiring other drugs must be borne by the patient or her family and friends. In view of the fact that other areas of the health sector require as much attention as AIDS prevention and cure. the problem of resource allocation cannot be overemphasized. Developments such as the use of combination therapies requiring the long-term use of a variety of expensive drugs make the problem even more acute. Even health-care systems in developed countries such as the UK have problems coping with the costs incurred per patient. Developing countries are unable to provide access to drugs such as protease inhibitors and nucleoside analogues to people with AIDS because these societies' health-care systems would be unable to cope with these costs.

The Kenyan microbiologist Ndinya-Achola argues that when people in developing countries participate in risky vaccine trials, designed by Western developers, there should be some guarantee that they benefit from their participation, such as sharing of profits or access to free health care after the trial, in order to compensate them for the risk they have taken. This point has also been made regarding Brazil, which has been selected for a World Health Organization efficacy trial (Lurie, 1994). The CIOMS International Ethical Guidelines for Biomedical Research Involving Human Subjects (1993) require that 'at the completion of successful testing, any product developed will be made reasonably available to inhabitants of the underdeveloped community in which the research was carried out.'

Another ethical problem related to access to health care is the denial of care which is based on the irrational fear of infection for health-care providers. In Mexico widespread refusal of medical care to those with AIDS can be witnessed (Panebianco et al., 1994).

Universal Ethical Principles

It has been suggested that there are no universally valid moral principles and that therefore we need to look at ethical problems in non-Western countries using different sets of ethical frameworks. Therefore it might be useful to ask if approaches to the AIDS problem in non-Western societies should respect the principles of autonomy, including the primacy of informed consent, privacy and confidentiality, and respect for persons, beneficence and justice. These principles are at the core of Western ethics and bioethics, for very good reasons which have to do with the acceptance of the dignity of the human person as a non-negotiable concept.

However, some authors have insisted that this concept is alien to, for instance, African people, and that these principles 'are not always fully accepted in Africa and may sometimes even clash with other core African values' (Ankrah and Gostin, 1994). Such authors usually do not tell us in detail what such 'other core African values' are.

In reality, these principles have great importance in African societies. This is probably best demonstrated by their ready incorporation in the African Charter on Human and Peoples' Rights ratified by African heads of state in 1986. This document was derived from core African values, according to its authors. It takes into consideration the virtues of African historical tradition and the values of African civilization. Two of its provisions are especially relevant here. First, Article 5 of the charter states that 'every individual shall have the right to the respect of the dignity inherent in a human being and to the recognition of his legal status. All forms of exploitation and degradation of man particularly slavery, slave trade, torture, cruel, inhuman or degrading punishment and treatment shall be prohibited' (Jallow and Hunt, 1991). Second, article 6 provides that 'every individual shall have the right to liberty and to the security of his person. No one may be deprived of his freedom except for reasons and conditions previously laid down by law. In particular, no one may be arbitrarily arrested or detained' (Jallow and Hunt, 1991). These provisions confirm the universality of the principle of respect for the dignity of the person. Jallow and Hunt suggest that, in the light of these provisions, compulsory blood-tests, compulsory quarantine and compulsory internment are unjustifiable. (On this issue see also chapter 3, pp. 24–31.)

Informed Consent in Clinical Trials

Four developing countries have been selected by the World Health Organization for efficacy trials once a suitable vaccine candidate is available. The first reason for choosing these countries is that they have a high rate of infection, which suggests faster results from vaccine trials than would be obtained from trials conducted in countries with a lower prevalence of AIDS. The second reason is that these countries have reliable and capable infrastructures available to conduct these types of study. Utilitarian cost-benefit considerations suggest that this strategy is ethically justifiable, because the impact of the disease in such countries is also quite high and there are few alternative options available. However, there are also less publishable reasons for carrying out such trials in developing countries, namely the costs of the studies and the lower legal responsibility for the manufacturer. Another reason is the primitive state of human rights in such countries.

The issue of informed consent in African countries is one which has caused significant debate among biomedical ethicists, anthropologists and medical researchers. Some commentators have suggested that Western concepts of informed consent, which rely on the principle of respect for the participating research subjects' individual autonomy, are often inappropriate outside the Western world. In particular, it has been argued by Western countries' medical ethicists that in African countries persons often perceive themselves as extensions of the family, rather than as individuals in their own right. Hence it has been suggested that 'the principle of community leader consent may be the only alternative to individual consent' (Christakis, 1988). The community is a core value of many African cultures, but this is not a value that is held at the expense of the individual. Therefore there is no warrant for the claim that 'in Africa . . . the individual is inferior within social groupings' (Ankrah and Gostin, 1994). Obviously, this cannot mean every individual; after all there are kings and queens, chiefs and diviners, herbalists and seers, hunters and griots, professionals of various kinds in traditional societies with tough minds of their own, always demanding and receiving respect from the community. Can the chief order the family head to present himself or a member of his family for a trial protocol against his will? The answer is: no. There have been cases where a 'subject' refused to answer an urgent summons from the king of his village (Osuntokun, 1992).

Furthermore it has been argued that an alleged Western insensitivity towards cultural differences is unacceptable and a cultural analysis a necessary precondition for an ethically designed research clinical trial (Christakis, 1992). Surprisingly, this view has been most strongly rejected by African researchers, for instance, from Kenya, Nigeria and South Africa. They pointed out that to them it is beyond doubt that ethical standards are absolute and argued that they cannot see how such universal standards could possibly be made culturally sensitive (Gilks and Were, 1990). Ebun Ekunwe, a research fellow at the University of Lagos (Nigeria) College of Medicine, proposes a risk-related standard for informed consent procedures. He argues that Western informed consent procedures in the case of standard tests, for instance, are not feasible and not worth the effort. Ekunwe insists, however, that in cases where the proposed procedure is different from routine tests in that it carries risks of complication and/or pain, informed consent must be obtained either verbally or in writing (Ekunwe, 1984). Biomedical ethicists have argued that despite all the known difficulties of obtaining informed consent in, for instance, a number of African countries. informed consent is essential to protect the interests of research subjects in such environments. The South African Carel B. Ijsselmuiden and his US colleague Ruth M. Faden conclude that they 'see no convincing arguments for a general policy of dispensing with, or substantially modifying, the researchers' obligation to obtain first-person consent in biomedical research conducted in Africa' (Ijsselmuiden and Faden, 1992).

It has been pointed out that theoretically this is convincing but practically most African patients suffering from AIDS are poor, illiterate, might speak a local dialect unknown to the researcher and, most problematic, they might have no understanding of modern concepts of disease such as the viral causation of disease theory. Indeed, empirical evidence suggests that about one out of three volunteers in a preventive AIDS vaccine trial in Brazil, sponsored by the United Nations, believe that the experimental drug will successfully prevent them from being infected.

The problem we are obviously faced with is whether it is feasible to achieve a substantial understanding of the matters at stake in research subjects under such circumstances. Peter Lamptey, a native of Ghana and head of an AIDS research organization, is aware of quite a number of studies where, if interviewed, most people in the study would not have understood what they have consented to (Nowak, 1995). This, however, is not a situation which is unique to Ghana. Similar problems have been described for people who have enrolled in clinical research trials in Western countries too, but it has never been accepted as a sufficient reason for doing away altogether with the requirement to obtain first-person informed consent. Instead it has been suggested that informed consent procedures must be improved up to the point where patients have a sufficient understanding of the procedure to which they are giving consent (Kirby, 1983).

Biomedical ethicists agree in general that, if possible, informed consent should be gathered from research subjects in developing countries. Those who seem to accept the necessity of exceptions to this general rule suggest that family members of tribe chiefs might be appropriate alternatives to the concept of first-person informed consent. This has rightly been criticized as a dangerous strategy, given the widespread existence of human rights violations, for instance, in African countries. Since in a number of circumstances it is not feasible to obtain first-person informed consent, it seems reasonable to limit this requirement to situations other than harmless standard procedures. The question is therefore whether clinical AIDS vaccine trials constitute a risk to those subjected to the experimental drug that exceeds the risk research subjects would take if they donated blood in a clinical trial. It seems that at least for some types of AIDS vaccine trials first-person informed consent is a necessary condition for an ethically designed study, given that a number of trials which were scheduled to take place in the USA have been discontinued because they were deemed too risky. The Food and Drug Administration (FDA) committee which decided to pull the plug on these trials in the USA was urged by industry sources 'to cast its recommendations in a more positive light, so that other countries [in the developing world] that were considering sponsoring clinical trials of these candidates wouldn't pull back as well' (Steele, 1994). Ndinya-Achola asked in this context whether developing countries should not insist 'that vaccines be tested in humans in countries of manufacture before large scale trials in other countries'. He suggests furthermore that the only population in African countries suitable for (preventive) vaccine trials currently are children aged 5 to 15 because of the high prevalence of HIV in much of the adult population. This raises further questions related to the ethical problem of prospective trial participants who are unable to give informed consent due to their age (Ndinya-Achola, 1991).

Confidentiality

Confidentiality can often not be preserved in some medical facilities where AIDS cases are separated from other patients. It is often mentioned in ethics textbooks that AIDS and non-AIDS patients should be treated the same so as to keep HIV status confidential and prevent discrimination against patients by the health-service providers. However, it may be unethical to expose AIDS patients who usually have a low immune status to a wide variety of pathogens from the non-AIDS cases, and vice versa. More special services are required for AIDS cases in developing countries. The problem here is often that no funds are available to satisfy demand for such places.

When a person with AIDS dies in a hospital, it is legally required in Thailand accurately to record the cause of death in the death certificate. This requirement will expose the HIV status of the deceased person. Many physicians prefer to put down only the opportunistic disease, for instance, pneumonia or tuberculosis, as the cause of death. Many hospitals in Thailand manage the bodies of the deceased from AIDS and non-AIDS differently. A common practice concerning postmortem management of AIDS patients is to wrap the body of a patient in one or more mostly black plastic bags. Hospital administrators advise the relatives of the dead not to unwrap or open the bag, to shorten the traditional funeral ceremony and to use cremation instead of burial, even though none of this is medically required in order to prevent the spread of AIDS. This practice has created various ethically problematic social consequences, including confidentiality breakdown, discrimination and stigmatization of the family of the dead (Rojanapithayakorn and Ussavathirakul, 1996).

Fear of confidentiality breakdown in Latin America leads to a situation where many AIDS cases are not reported. In Mexico, for instance, in 1995 more than 60 per cent of reported AIDS cases were notified to health authorities by death certificate ascertainment. AIDS cases are frequently reported using name, address and other identifiers to prevent repeated case reporting. This clearly violates the principle of confidentiality and leads to 'epidemiologic persecution' of those affected. People are also frequently illegally tested prior to employment, and their HIV test results are not kept confidential. People with HIV infection are commonly fired from their jobs, even though this is illegal. Since it is their job which provides them with access to social security, the moment they get fired they lose this benefit and thus access to health care.

References

Ankrah, E. M. and Gostin, L. O. (1994). Ethical and legal considerations of the HIV epidemic in Africa. In M. Essex, S. Mboup, P. J. Kanki and M. R. Kalengayi (eds), *AIDS in Africa*. New York: Raven Press, 547–58.

Christakis, N. A. (1988). The ethical design of an AIDS vaccine trial in Africa – another look. *Hastings Center Report*, 18/3, 31–7.

—— (1992). Informed consent in Africa. *New England Journal of Medicine*, 327, 1101–2.

Ekunwe, E. O. (1984). Informed consent in the developing world. *Hastings Center Report*, 14/3, 23.

Gbadegesin, S. (1993). The ethics of polygyny. *Quest: Philosophical Discussions*, 7/2, 3–29.

Gilks, C. F. and Were, J. B. O. (1990). Ethical imperialism. *New England Journal of Medicine*, 322, 200.

Gosh, S. K. (1993). *Women and Crime: crime by women, crime against women and crime for women*. New Delhi; Ashish.

Ijsselmuiden, C. B. and Faden, R. R. (1992). Research and informed consent in Africa – another look. *New England Journal of Medicine*, 326, 830–4.

Jallow, H. B. and Hunt, P. (1991). *AIDS and the African Charter*. Banjul: African Centre for Democracy and Human Rights Studies.

Kirby, M. (1983). Informed consent: what does it mean? *Journal of Medical Ethics*, 9, 69–75.

Laos' National Committee for the Control of AIDS (1994). *External Review of the First Medium-term Plan (1991–1994) for the Prevention and Control of HIV/AIDS*. Vientiane: National Institute of Hygiene and Epidemiology.

Leisinger, K. M. (1993). Bioethics here and in poor countries: a comment. *Cambridge Quarterly of Healthcare Ethics*, 2, 5–8.

Mahmood, T. (1972). *Family Law Reform in the Muslim World*. Bombay: N. M. Tripathi.

Miller, N. and Rockwell, R. (eds) (1988). *AIDS in Africa: the social and policy impact*. Lewiston: Edwin Mellen Press.

Myanmar Ministry of Health (1993). *Myanmar Medium Term Plan Review 1993*. Yangon: Department of Health.

Ndinya-Achola, J. O. (1991). A review of ethical issues in AIDS research. *East African Medical Journal*, 68, 735–40.

Nowak, R. (1995). Staging ethical AIDS trials in Africa. *Science*, 269, 1332–5.

O'dea, P. (1993). *Gender Exploitation and Violence: the market in women, girls and sex in Nepal*. Kathmandu: Printing Support.

Osuntokun, B. O. (1992). Biomedical ethics in the developing world: conflicts and resolutions, In E. Pellegrino (ed.). *Transcultural Dimensions in Medical Ethics*. Frederick, MD: University Publishing Group, 105–43.

Panebianco, S., del Rio, C., Baez-Villasenor, J., Uribe, P. and Morales, G. (1994). Human rights violations and AIDS: two parallel public health epidemics. Abstract No. 206D, X International AIDS Conference, Yokohama 1994.

Pescador, Juan Javier and Bronfman, Mario (1989). Sociedad y SIDA: Viejas reacciones frente a nuevos problemas. In Jaime Sepúlveda (ed.), *SIDA, Ciencua Y Sociedad en Mexico*. Mexico: Fondo de Cultura Economica.

Rico, B., Bronfman, M. and del Rio, Carlos (1995a). Las campanas contra el SIDA Mexico: Los sonidos del silencio o puente sobre arguas turbulentas. *Salud Pública de México*, 37/6, 643–53.

Rico, B., Uribe, P., Pannebianco S. and del Rio, Carlos (1995b). El SIDA y derechos humanos. *Salud Pública de México*, 37/6, 661–8.

Rojanapithayakorn, W. and Ussavathirakul, N. (1996). Postmortem management of AIDS patients in Thailand. Abstract reported at the XI International AIDS Conference, Vancouver, 7–12 July, 1996.

Schüklenk, U. (1995). *Access to Experimental Drugs in Terminal Illness: Ethical issues*. New York: Howarth.

Schüklenk, U. and Mertz, D. (1993). Christliche Kirchen und AIDS. In E. Dahl (ed.), *Die Lehre des Unheils*. Hamburg: Carlsen, 263–79, 309–12.

Steele, F. (1994). AIDS vaccine development hits a sticking point. *Journal of NIH Research*, September.

Further Reading

Ajayi, O. O. (1980). Taboos and clinical research in West Africa. *Journal of Medical Ethics*, 6, 61–3.

Bayer, R. and Ceryl, H. (1989). Controlling AIDS in Cuba: the logic of quarantine. *New England Journal of Medicine*, 320.

Biggar, R. J. (1986). The AIDS problem in Africa. *Lancet*, 79–82.

Conway, D. A. (1994). AIDS and legal paternalism. In L. May and S. Collins Sharratt (eds), *Applied Ethics: A multicultural approach*. Englewood Cliffs, NJ: Prentice-Hall, 399–407.

Faden, R. M. and Beauchamp, T. L. (1986). *A History and Theory of Informed Consent*. New York: Oxford University Press.

Grady, C. (1995). *The Search for an AIDS Vaccine: ethical issues in the development and testing of a preventive AIDS vaccine*. Bloomington: Indiana University Press.

Greeley, E. H. (1988). The role of non-governmental organizations in AIDS prevention: parallels to African family planning activity. In N. Miller and R. C. Rockwell (eds), *AIDS in Africa: the social and policy impact*. Lewiston, NY: Edwin Mellen Press, 131–44.

Green, E. C. (1994). *AIDS and STDs in Africa: bridging the gap between traditional healing and modern medicine*. Boulder, CO: Westview Press.

Kippax, S. and Crawford, J. (1995). Prophylactic vaccine trials: what is different about HIV? *Venereology*, 8, 178–82.

Lewis, M. (1989). *AIDS in Developing Countries: Cost issues and policy tradeoffs*. Washington, DC: Urban Institute Press.

Lurie, P., Bishaw, M., Chesney, M. E. et al. (1994). Ethical, behavioral, and social aspects of HIV vaccine trials in developing countries. *Journal of the American Medical Association*, 271, 295–301.

Schoepf, B. G. (1991). Ethical, methodological and political issues of AIDS research in Central Africa. *Social Science and Medicine*, 33, 749–63.

Tauer, C. A. (1994). AIDS and human rights: an intercontinental perspective. In L. May and S. Collins Sharratt (eds), *Applied Ethics: a multicultural approach*. Englewood Cliffs, NJ: Prentice-Hall, 408–20.

PART XI

EXPERIMENTATION WITH HUMAN SUBJECTS

35

Experimentation on human beings

PAUL M. MCNEILL

History

Webster's dictionary defines an experiment as a 'procedure or policy . . . adopted in uncertainty as to whether it will answer the desired purpose or bring about the desired result'. In this sense ordinary medical treatment is an experiment in that the outcome for any particular patient is not known and, from this perspective, doctors and health professionals have always experimented with their patients. The courts, however, have distinguished experimentation from treatment by the extent of risk to the patients (or human subjects of the experiment) and the relative lack of any therapeutic benefit for them. It is experimentation in this latter sense that I am referring to: the kind of experimentation that offers little or no benefit to the subject and carries with it some risk of harm. It includes informal experimentation conducted to test an idea or a new procedure and experimentation within a formal scientific research programme. While there are isolated historical records of manipulation of human beings solely for experimental purposes, large-scale experimentation is a more recent phenomenon. It coincides with changing perceptions and methods in the late eighteenth and early nineteenth centuries, particularly in the hospitals of Paris, and included the perception of disease as the effect of pathological entities within specific organs and tissues of the body.

Researchers, impressed with this new scientific approach to medicine, deliberately infected human beings with samples of blood and other material taken from sick patients to test their theories without any apparent regard for the harm they inflicted. There are reports in the nineteenth century of the deliberate infection of human beings with syphilis and gonorrhoea. In the United States, other types of experiments included pouring scalding water over slaves as a test of its effectiveness in curing typhoid fever. New techniques in surgery were developed by testing them on slaves. For example, slave women were operated on up to thirty times to practise an operation for correcting vesico-vaginal fistula. There is little in the literature of the time indicating concern for the suffering that resulted from this kind of experimentation. In part this is because experimentation has always been conducted on those with little social standing and few champions (McNeill, 1993).

German and Japanese Atrocities during the War

In the aftermath of the Second World War it became apparent that German doctors and scientists had conducted experiments with a callous disregard for any suffering they inflicted on their human subjects and a denial of any rights that these people might have as human beings. There was a war crimes trial of twenty medical doctors (most of whom had held positions in the medical services of the Third Reich) and three bioscientists. The case is United States v. Brandt (so named after Karl Brandt, who was Hitler's personal physician, and because the trial was conducted under United States military auspices). Of the twenty-three defendants, sixteen were found guilty and seven of these (Brandt included) were hanged for various crimes against humanity and war crimes in the conduct of experiments and programmes of extermination. Many of the experiments had a military objective including 'high-altitude' experiments that were designed to test the limits of human endurance and human existence in low-pressure chambers. In other experiments, humans were held in tanks of ice water for up to three hours as a means for testing various methods for resuscitating pilots who had been severely chilled or frozen after falling into the sea. Experiments with typhus, malaria, jaundice, spotted fever and wounds (deliberately inflicted and infected) were designed to find cures to combat diseases troubling German occupation forces. Experiments in the removal of bone, muscle and nerves from one group of prisoners and their transplantation into others were conducted to assist injured soldiers. Many prisoners died in these experiments and most of them experienced extremes of suffering.

There is an even uglier side. Some of the experiments were part of the Third Reich's programme for 'racial hygiene' which aimed to purify the German peoples by exterminating and sterilizing unwanted groups. Tests on prisoners were made of various methods for sterilizing men and women. There were tests of the effectiveness of various poisons and means for administering poison in killing human beings. Four of the doctors were also accused of developing and carrying out programmes for executing hundreds of thousands of 'useless' people including the aged, insane, incurably ill and deformed children (Annas and Grodin, 1992).

The accused doctors and scientists argued in their defence that they had acted on superior orders; the sacrifice of a few lives was necessary to save the lives of many; that much of the experimentation on human subjects throughout history had been conducted in an ethically questionable manner; and that 'volunteers' in medical experimentation had seldom given proper consent to take part in experiments by medical researchers. While these defences could not justify the horrors they committed in the name of science, it has to be acknowledged that their claims about the conduct of experimentation on human subjects through history were true. In its judgement, the Nuremberg Court specified ten elements that were necessary to justify a medical experiment. These ten points became known as the 'Nuremberg Code' and included the absolute need for the 'voluntary consent of the human subject'; a justification in terms of potential 'fruitful results'; proper design and previous animal experiments; the avoidance of 'unnecessary physical and mental suffering and injury'; the conduct of the experiment by 'scientifically qualified persons'; and the termination of the experiment if it becomes clear that harm will result or if the human subject wishes to bring it to an end.

The Germans were not alone in conducting bizarre and inhumane experiments on human subjects. Williams and Wallace (1989) have given an account of equally horrific experiments conducted by Japanese doctors and bioscientists, largely on Chinese residents and prisoners and also on some prisoners of war. The Japanese atrocities have had very little influence in subsequent developments. This is because they were kept secret for many years after the war as the result of an agreement between the United States government (at the behest of the American Occupation Forces Command in Japan) to give the Japanese experimenters immunity from prosecution in exchange for information about biological warfare. Most of the information about Japanese experiments only became public as the result of freedom of information actions in the United States in the 1980s. The stark contrast between the treatment of some of the principal German experimenters and their Japanese counterparts illustrates the important role politics has played in the development of codes of ethics for the conduct of experimentation on human subjects. Secrecy denied the public an opportunity to react to the Japanese atrocities and diverted the world from giving more attention to the need for humane standards for experimenting on human subjects.

Development of Regulations

Paradoxically, it was Germany that had first developed codes of ethics for experimenting on human subjects. In 1900 a directive from the Prussian Minister of Religious, Educational and Medical Affairs was issued to the directors of clinics. By that directive, medical experiments could only be conducted on competent adults who had consented after a proper explanation of the adverse consequences that might result. Subsequently there were accusations in the German press of the abuse of subjects of experiments, including children. As a consequence the German Minister of the Interior published *Richtlinien* (regulations or guidelines) in 1931 that included requirements for testing on animals, consent based on the provision of appropriate information and the exclusion of any experiments which might endanger children even in 'the slightest degree'. These regulations were in force during the period of the Third Reich but they were obviously flouted.

Although the trial of the Nazi doctors and bioscientists condemned, in the strongest possible way, inhumane experiments on human beings, the Nuremberg Code contained in the court's judgement was not itself very influential. The attitude in the Anglo-American world was that the code was the result of an extreme abuse of human subjects which could only have occurred in the peculiar circumstances of Nazi Germany during the war.

Medical specialist colleges and international medical groups were also reluctant to accept the Nuremberg Code because it included an absolute requirement for consent prior to any experimentation on human subjects. Subsequently, in Rome in 1954, the World Medical Association (WMA) adopted a Code for Research and Experimentation which allowed for proxy consent in experiments on patients who lacked the capacity to consent for themselves. In 1964 the WMA issued another code for research and experimentation, known as the Helsinki Declaration. This code also allowed for experimentation on human subjects including the very young, the unconscious and those who lacked legal capacity such as the mentally ill. While some have criticized the Helsinki Declaration (for watering down the consent provisions of the Nuremberg Code) it gained more publicity than the Nuremberg Code and was more influential within the medical profession.

Unethical Experimentation in the United States

Any complacency within the medical profession about the possibility of inhumane experimentation outside of Nazi Germany was challenged by revelations of unethical experimentation on human subjects within the United States. These scandals prompted the development of regulations within the United States for the conduct of experiments on human subjects. In 1963 doctors had injected live cancer cells into elderly debilitated patients in the Jewish Chronic Disease Hospital. In 1966 an article by Henry Beecher in the *New England Journal of Medicine* drew attention to a number of apparently unethical experiments conducted on human subjects. In one of these, intellectually disabled children were intentionally infected with hepatitis in the Willowbrook State School. Also in the late 1960s, publicity was given to the Tuskegee syphilis case in which 400 poor black men from rural areas in the South, diagnosed with syphilis, had been left without treatment as a part of a study to observe the development of the disease in those men. They were offered no treatment and were simply observed as their condition deteriorated. They had not been informed of their diagnosis nor asked for their consent to take part in any study.

Development of Committee Review

One of the early responses to publicity given to those unethical experiments was a requirement in 1966, by the Surgeon-General of the United States, for committee review of applications for Public Health Service grants. Each applicant was required to state that a committee had considered the risks of the research for any human subjects and had satisfied itself of the adequacy of protection of their rights. Subsequently the US Senate insisted on a national commission to consider human experimentation. The resulting commission published a number of reports, including the Belmont Report identifying basic ethical principles, and the Institutional Review Board Report, which included a survey of the committees known as Institutional Review Boards (IRBs) which were created following the Surgeon-General's request of 1966. The Senate also insisted on the promulgation of regulations covering research on human beings, and those regulations incorporated and strengthened the National Institutes of Health policy requiring that all publicly funded research be approved by a committee.

In 1966 Canada followed the United States' lead and adopted the requirement for review by committee, and the following year the Royal College of Physicians of

London recommended committee review of research proposals within its guidelines for research with human subjects. New Zealand introduced a requirement for committee review in 1972 and a policy of committee review was adopted by the National Health and Medical Research Council in Australia in 1973. Other countries also followed this lead and international codes, such as the Council for International Organizations of Medical Science guidelines, have adopted committee review of research proposals as a major protection for human subjects of experimentation. Within Scandinavia, Sweden has had ethics committee review since the late 1960s, Denmark since the late 1970s and Finland since the early 1980s. In 1984 the Swiss Academy of Sciences recommended advisory bodies on experimentation and, in the same year, the governments of both the Netherlands and Belgium issued decrees requiring ethics committee review. While there are review committees in France, reports indicate that in practice few research proposals are considered. Germany and Japan, the two countries in which there were flagrant abuses of the ethics of experimentation on humans (as discussed above), have been conspicuous in having relatively undeveloped review systems for considering human experimentation, although in the last five years Japan has developed a system of committee review for drug trials. Reports from other countries in Europe, India, the East generally, Africa and Latin America are either non-existent or sketchy and this may indicate the lack of developed systems of review (McNeill, 1993).

Internationally there is very little legislation specifically addressing experimentation on human subjects. The United States was exceptional in issuing governmental regulations covering human experimentation. As indicated above, both the Netherlands and Belgium have issued decrees. Requirements in other countries are usually issued as guidelines (variously called 'codes', 'guidelines', 'statements' or 'standards'). These guidelines have been issued by funding bodies such as the Canadian Medical Research Council, the Australian National Health and Medical Research Council, governmental departments such as the Departments of Health in New Zealand and the United Kingdom and by professional bodies such as the Royal College of Physicians of London.

There are a number of common features of all of these guidelines, standards and regulations. All of them rely on review by a committee of proposals for research on human subjects. The committees are required to consider proposals and decide whether or not they are ethical. Committees have the power to approve a proposal in the form in which it is presented, request modification by the researcher or reject the proposal. Membership of the committees is specified to include some members with expertise in research and one or two community (or lay) members. There are some differences between countries in the other members of committees recommended. Typically the guidelines state the matters that the committee should take into account in deciding whether or not to approve the proposal: for example, the requirement to consider whether the potential benefits of the research justify any risks of harm to the human participants. None of the guidelines includes sanctions against researchers or their institutions for failure to comply. However, a rejection

373

by an ethics committee, or failure to present a proposal for approval by a committee, will often have implications for funding and may lead to the refusal of a journal to publish any results from research programmes that have not been approved.

The following is a more detailed account of the requirements for review of research on human subjects in various countries in the developed world. (For some of the countries not included in the following report see McNeill, 1993.)

Requirements for review in the United States

The United States federal regulations were first published by the Department of Health, Education and Welfare in 1974 and apply to all research funded by the Public Health Service. These regulations were amended in 1981 and amended again in 1991 to create a 'common rule' for all sixteen governmental departments and agencies that conduct, support or in some way administer human subjects research. This policy was designed to lay down a uniform proposal for dealing with publicly funded research or research conducted by federal agencies. Essentially, all federally funded research on human subjects is required to be considered by an institutional review board (IRB). These boards are administrative committees whose principal function is to protect the human research subjects of research conducted within the institution to which the committee is affiliated. The regulations state that IRBs have the power to approve, require modifications in or disapprove any of the research which falls within its jurisdiction as defined by both the federal regulations and the policy of the institution. The IRB must have at least five members, with varying backgrounds so as adequately to review the research activities commonly conducted by the institution. The committees must contain members who are qualified (through their experience and expertise and diversity in their backgrounds) properly to safeguard the rights and welfare of the human subjects, taking into account considerations of racial and cultural heritage, and community attitudes. At least one of the members of the IRB must have his or her primary concerns in scientific areas and at least one member's primary concerns should be in non-scientific areas. The committee must include a member who is not affiliated with the institution. There also needs to be members knowledgeable about institutional requirements, relevant law and standards of professional conduct and practice. Where an IRB regularly reviews research that involves a vulnerable category of subjects, such as children, prisoners, pregnant women or handicapped or mentally disabled persons, it should include members who are knowledgeable about these subjects.

In fulfilling all these requirements, committees typically have many more members (on average fourteen or more) than the minimum five specified. Information on the composition and functioning of IRBs in the United States is somewhat dated, although there is a study being conducted at present. A brief description of the results of a National Commission study in 1978 is included in McNeill (1993: 86). There is still a great deal of research not directly subject to these regulations in the United States. However, the indications are that non-publicly funded research is increasingly being reviewed in a similar manner.

Canada

In Canada, the Medical Research Council has, since 1996, required that proposals for experimentation on human subjects be reviewed by a committee. Guidelines, with different procedures for review, were issued by the Social Sciences and Humanities Research Councils in 1977. These two councils, along with the Natural Sciences and Engineering Research Council, formed a working group in 1994 to develop a unified position on ethical conduct for all research involving humans.

The intention of the working party was to draw from the experience of researchers in a wide variety of fields without imposing any one disciplinary perspective and to develop a common language for the ethics of research. It emphasized the needs of individual research participants in a variety of research settings. It also recognized the important role of committees in educating and supporting researchers in addition to their review function. Its policy (as drafted) required review by a committee including members with expertise in research typically reviewed by that committee, members recruited from the community served by the institution, a member 'knowledgeable in ethics' and (for biomedical research) a member 'knowledgeable in the law'. It is anticipated that a 'Tri-Council Policy Statement' will be published in 1998.

United Kingdom

There are a number of guidelines in the United Kingdom covering research on human experimentation. The principal guidelines were issued by the Royal College of Physicians of London in 1990 and the Department of Health in 1991. The Department of Health guidelines apply to all research projects that take place within the National Health Service (NHS). The College of Physicians guidelines apply more broadly. Membership of research ethics committees is recommended (in both sets of guidelines) to include medical members, nurses and two or more lay members. The College of Physicians guidelines also recommend the inclusion of non-medical workers or scientists (such as psychologists, social scientists and social workers) according to the types of research coming before the committee.

There was concern in the United Kingdom about the effect on research conducted across several localities of numerous local committees with different requirements and inconsistent requirements. In 1995 the Department of Health suggested regional ethics committees to consider multi-centre research proposals. This has reduced to eleven the maximum number of committees to which researchers (such as epidemiologists) need apply to conduct research in more than one locality. Any local committee may be presented with a proposal which has been approved by a regional committee for its area. The local committee has the option of accepting or rejecting a regionally approved proposal (although reasons for refusal must be based on relevant local concerns) and cannot suggest any modifications. The local committee, however, can raise any concern with its regional committee that a major ethical issue has not been properly examined.

Australia

The requirement for review by committee of all research on human subjects is contained in the National Health and Medical Research Council's 'Statement on Human Experimentation and Supplementary Notes'. As its title suggests, this statement includes broad general principles and supporting supplementary notes: on the composition and function of ethics committees, and on specific areas of research such as clinical trials, *in vitro* fertilization, embyro transfer, use of fetal tissue, epidemiological research and gene therapy. The membership guidelines are very specific. Institutional ethics committees (IECs) must include two lay members (a man and a woman), a minister of religion, a lawyer and a medical graduate with research experience. In practice, committees include many more members from the institution conducting the research, along with the required lay persons, lawyer and minister of religion. The Australia Health Ethics Committee has been studying the committee review process in Australia and is expected to present a report in 1996 through the Federal Minister for Health.

New Zealand

The formation of committees in New Zealand was revised radically after the report of an official inquiry in 1988 into an unethical research programme which denied treatment to sufferers of cervical cancer at a major hospital for women in Auckland. The composition and guidelines for committees were included in a report from the Department of Health which was revised in 1991 as a 'Standard for Ethics Committees Established to Review Research and Ethical Aspects of Health Care'. Healthcare ethics committees in New Zealand are required to approve all research investigations involving human participants. They are also required to consider the ethical aspects of new, untried or unorthodox treatment. This explicit extension into the realm of treatment is also beyond the national requirements for review committees elsewhere in the world. It is significant that, after the inquiry, ethics committees were to include a 'lay membership which approximates one half of the total membership of the committee' and that each committee was to be chaired by a lay member. This is a significant increase in the proportion of community members relative to committees elsewhere in the world, with the exception of Denmark. Danish Committees include three lay members and three scientific/medical members with either the chairperson or deputy chair elected from the lay members. Reports from both New Zealand and Denmark indicate that the community members take an active role on their committees; they are not obstructive of research (as had been feared) and are seen as contributing positively both within their committees and to wider community discussion of ethical issues.

Discussion

The response to reports of unethical experimentation on human beings in the United States, in the mid to late 1960s, was the development of review committees which included one or two community members. This response was criticized by Katz (1987) for 'ducking all the important issues' and for putting faith in a procedure (namely review by a committee) without establishing substantive guidelines. Since that time, other countries and international bodies have followed the United States' lead and put their faith in this procedural approach. Guidelines have become better developed and more tailored to particular research situations, but the approach of relying on committee review has its shortcomings. With the exception of committees in New Zealand and Denmark, committees usually have a majority of members from the institution conducting the research. This composition has the potential for biased and inadequate review. Veatch (1975) offered a more radical criticism of committee composition in claiming that it lacks any rationale for combining expert members with lay members on review committees. McNeill (1993) has suggested that combining members in this way serves to disempower the lay members and render them relatively ineffective. Another criticism is that few committees, anywhere in the world, actively monitor research in progress. In effect they are relying on researchers' intentions, as they are stated in research proposals, rather than scrutinizing researchers' actions.

Nevertheless committees continue to be relied on as the best method for ensuring ethical research, yet there is little evidence to show whether or not committees have been successful in protecting subjects of experiments and in ensuring a more equitable share of the benefits of research. There are reports of researchers 'shopping' for a committee to give them a favourable review, not submitting research for review and, in one case, conducting the research prior to seeking approval (McNeill et al., 1992). There are also some disturbing reports of unethical research being approved by ethics committees. This includes the Baby Fae case (Annas, 1985) and the cervical cancer case in New Zealand (McNeill, 1989). It may be that these are exceptional cases that were the result of deficient review. For example, the cervical cancer study was approved by a committee of only three, including the chairman who was a co-investigator of the study and head of the department in which the study was conducted. Such a review would not be regarded as adequate within current guidelines. The fact remains that, in both of these cases, the committees failed to protect the human subjects of those experiments. The review of human radiation experiments in the United States has also highlighted some deficiencies in the system of review (Advisory Committee on Human Radiation Experiments, 1995). Beyond these exceptions there is little evidence that experimentation that has been approved by a committee has been conducted unethically. Most of the grossly unethical studies that have come to light were not reviewed by an ethics committee. Many of these programmes were started in the 1960s (or earlier) before there was any requirement for committee review. It could be concluded, from the very small number of approved experiments that have been shown subsequently to be unethical, that ethics committee review is an effective mechanism for protecting subjects in the vast majority of cases. The exceptions, however, still leave cause for concern about the adequacy of this process.

Perhaps more encouraging is the greater awareness of ethical issues in the research community generally. It is reasonable to postulate that the requirement

377

for review by committee has been responsible in part for this change in the culture. Ultimately it is a change in the attitude and behaviour of researchers that is required. Educational activities, committee review and disciplinary measures can be adopted for the protection of research subjects but, to a large extent, the human participants in experiments rely on the ethical attitude and behaviour of the experimenters themselves. In conclusion, as the history of experimentation on human beings shows, regulations and committee review are not a sufficient safeguard. There is a need for constant vigilance and for a refusal to accept that the desire for knowledge can ever justify inhumane, unethical or inconsiderate treatment in experiments on human beings.

References

Advisory Committee on Human Radiation Experiments (1995). *Final Report*. Pittsburgh: US Government Printing Office, 1995.

Annas, George J. (1985). Baby Fae: the 'anything goes' school of human experimentation. *Hastings Center Report*, 15/1, 15–17.

Annas, George J. and Grodin, Michael A. (eds) (1992). *The Nazi Doctors and the Nuremberg Code: human rights in human experimentation*. New York and Oxford: Oxford University Press.

Katz, Jay (1987). The regulation of human experimentation in the United States – a personal odyssey. *IRB: A Review of Human Subjects Research*, 9/1, 1–6.

McNeill, Paul M. (1989). The implications for Australia of the New Zealand Report of the Cervical Cancer Inquiry: no cause for complacency. *Medical Journal of Australia*, 150, 264–71.

—— (1993). *The Ethics and Politics of Human Experimentation*. Sydney and London: Cambridge University Press.

McNeill, Paul M., Berglund, Catherine A. and Webster, Ian W. (1992). Do Australian researchers accept ethics committee review and conduct ethical research? *Social Science and Medicine*, 35/3, 317–22.

Veatch, Robert M. (1975). Human experimentation committees: professional or representative? *Hastings Center Report*, 31–40.

Williams, Peter and Wallace, David (1989). *Unit 731: Japan's secret biological warfare in World War II*, New York: Free Press.

36

Ethical issues in human experimentation

LEONARDO D. DE CASTRO

Experimentation on human subjects is essential to scientific progress and the promotion of medical well-being. But research risks are unavoidable and the dangers in medicine and health care can be immense. For this reason, the use of human beings as experimental subjects generates ethical concerns. We have to examine its impact on values such as life, autonomy, dignity, justice and happiness, and make a careful assessment of the consequences arising from the procedures involved.

Three types of ethical issues may be identified. One pertains to the accurate assessment of benefits, risks and harm. The second involves questions of autonomy and respect for persons used as subjects. The third relates to justice in the distribution of burdens, use of benefits and other research-related activities.

Weighing Benefits and Risks

Researchers and medical practitioners justify the exposure of human subjects to possible harm associated with medical experimentation in terms of benefits anticipated to be greater than the concomitant risks. The efforts and inconveniences of the subjects (and of the researchers themselves) find their value in the advancement of scientific knowledge and subsequent development of new drugs, technology and procedures that could benefit society.

The theoretical foundations for a benefit-risk evaluation may be found in the principles of beneficence and non-maleficence which assert that our judgement of actions should be governed by the pursuit of happiness and the avoidance of suffering, or perhaps, more broadly, by the enhancement of well-being or the satisfaction of preferences. Indeed, we often justify the rightness of what we do by referring to the happiness or improvement in well-being that it brings. We consider it wrong, other things being equal, to inflict pain or cause suffering. In general, we accept that it is in the interest of human beings that their happiness be promoted and their sufferings be minimized.

But the ethical evaluation of experimental procedures involves more than the assessment of resultant benefits in relation to the concomitant risks and inconveniences. The involvement of human subjects raises concerns about the manner in

LEONARDO D. DE CASTRO

which they are treated in the course of the experiments. Reference is often made to Immanuel Kant's Categorical Imperative: 'Act in such a way that you treat humanity both in your own person and in the person of all others, never as a means only but always equally as an end.' Human beings are not only capable of feeling; they are capable of making decisions for themselves and acting on the basis of those decisions; they are capable of understanding reasons, acquiring values and using these to justify their actions. These capabilities generally are considered indispensable to being human. If they are, they must be taken into account. One way of doing so is to hold that research on human subjects ought to be governed by a principle of respect for human beings that recognizes the importance of self-governance and autonomous decision-making. In the various aspects of experimental work, human subjects must be allowed to use these capacities freely.

Therapeutic and Non-therapeutic

In therapeutic experiments the benefits are intended directly to accrue to the subjects themselves. The risks to be assessed are theirs and so are the anticipated benefits. Respect for human beings dictates that they be allowed to make an individual risk-benefit assessment in accordance with their own ends and the amount of risks they are willing to undertake to enhance their chances of success.

In non-therapeutic experiments, the benefits are expected to be enjoyed by others. Hence, the risks that a particular person undertakes need to be weighed against the benefits intended to accrue to others. The process of evaluation entails a great degree of relativity and subjectivity which could involve unjustifiably giving preference to the interests of some individuals over those of others.

The assessment of benefits and risks is even more complicated in cases where the boundary between therapeutic and non-therapeutic research is obscured. Experiments are characterized as therapeutic or non-therapeutic by their intended effect on a particular subject. One and the same procedure may be therapeutic to some subjects but non-therapeutic to others. But the methodology employed in experiments may confuse some subjects about whether the procedures are therapeutic or non-therapeutic with respect to them.

The possibility that particular subjects may be randomized into a placebo or control group means that those subjects cannot determine whether they are undergoing therapy or not. In the process, crucial information needed for a realistic assessment of personal benefits may be withheld from subjects. While receiving what they take to be therapeutic experiments, they may be temporarily left untreated or placed on a treatment regime that may be inferior to what is currently regarded as the best treatment regime.

In such cases, the imposition of additional risks may be defended on the grounds that it will lead to more scientifically valid results. Assurances may be given that the negative effects of suspended or altered treatment can be corrected. However, it is necessary to make the nature of the entire process sufficiently clear to the subjects. If some form of deception is deemed indispensable, it must be anticipated when the subjects will be provided with full information about the experiment. (See also chapter 42, especially pp. 445–9.)

Exploitation of Human Subjects

Since non-therapeutic experimentation calls for one set of individuals to shoulder risks for the sake of others, the idea that some persons are being 'used' arises. If a person is enrolled as a subject in an experiment the results of which are foreseen to be beneficial only to others, the former is, in effect, being used by the latter to attain their ends.

Admittedly, using other people in this sense is not necessarily wrong. We always find ourselves having to take advantage of the help that others can give us in our effort to serve our purposes. But there is a thin line between taking advantage of help voluntarily given and 'making use of people in a manner that reduces them to objects with no decision-making capabilities.' Because of their vulnerabilities – unfamiliarity with complicated experimental procedures, ignorance of relevant technical information, stress associated with illness, etc. – human subjects of experimentation are more exposed than they are ordinarily to the possibility of exploitation.

This possibility is magnified in non-therapeutic research because it is more difficult to ensure voluntariness of enrolment on the part of subjects who do not have anything directly to gain from the results. They may be coerced into participating; relevant information may be withheld from them; the risks may be more than they are willing to take; or they may not be provided with the safeguards and full technical support necessary for a particular experimental procedure. If so, they are being denied due respect as human beings.

The use of human subjects in research provides a concrete opportunity to clarify what respect means and how it can be – and ought to be – manifested. In experimentation on human subjects, human beings appear to serve as instruments to attain the ends of others. To avoid exploitation, the process must give the subjects an opportunity to make autonomous decisions on the basis of their autonomous value systems.

Consent

The nature and quality of consent given by individual subjects are important in ensuring that exploitation does not take place. Voluntary consent given by adequately informed subjects guarantees that the exercise does not involve the use of human beings merely as a means. By giving voluntary consent the subjects adopt the ends of the experiment as their own and identify with them. If they are used as means at all, it is for ends which effectively have become their own.

Ascertaining the validity of consent is important not only to ensure respect for individual autonomy but also to provide protection against harm, avoid the use of fraud or duress, provide the researchers with a mechanism for self-audit and promote the process of rational decision-making (Downie and Calman, 1987: 232–3).

Ensuring that consent is voluntary

The condition of 'thinghood' to which the research subject submits cannot be redeemed if the voluntary character of consent is compromised (Jonas, 1969: 3–4). The Nuremberg Code defines voluntary consent in terms of the legal capacity to give consent, the ability to exercise free power of choice and the absence of intervention of any element of force, fraud, deceit, or other ulterior form of constraint or coercion. One must add some positive elements that are equally important in ensuring that the decisions made by subjects are truly what they deem compatible with their autonomous values. To enhance the capacity for self-determination, subjects should be able to relate situations to themselves, deliberate about alternatives, relate alternatives to their own values and rank them, select options and understand the consequences of those options. The idea is that voluntariness must be understood in relation to a particular self that retains the integrity of its value system in the process of decision-making.

The human research setting is home to forms of exploitation that are easy to overlook. Historically, the use of prisoners has been a source of controversy. Cast in an environment where their civil rights are suspended, inmates are vulnerable to exploitation perpetrated by some jailers who treat them contemptuously or regard them as means to be disposed of as society pleases. Prisoners already have to contend with many restrictions and coercive forces in their day-to-day life. When there is a 'great disparity in the power of the parties, the opportunity and indeed, temptation, to coercion is always present' (Feinberg, 1986: 260). Examples of ethically dubious experimentation on prisoners include cases where prisoners apparently consented to be exposed to typhoid, malaria, cholera and other diseases (Annas, 1977: 113). The voluntariness of consent thus given is considered suspect because such procedures are not what a reasonable person may be expected to participate in.

The search for the most willing and readily available subjects has also led medical researchers to use their own patients, employees and students. But a relationship of dependence to the researchers endangers the voluntary nature of consent. The possibility of intimidation, whether intended or not, cannot be ruled out even if the readily available subjects are generally motivated by a conscious desire to support the objectives of the medical research at hand. Even when unrecognized, fear or deference to authority may be so strong that they negate or diminish the subjects' ability to make truly free decisions.

The use of compensation and other incentives to attract subjects is also problematic. Exploitation takes place when human subjects are not remunerated adequately for their time and effort (unless they have no desire for remuneration to begin with). But too much compensation could also undermine autonomy by inducing individuals to take levels of risk that are not compatible with their personal thresholds for comfort and safety. They can be victimized by, for instance, appeals to their 'non-rational preferences' (cf. Cocking and Oakley, 1994). This possibility surfaces when compensation becomes the primary tool for inducing subject participation.

As a rule, prohibiting the use of subjects who have a dependent relationship to the researchers seems proper. But exclusion of this sort could be unwarranted if the subjects expect significant therapeutic benefits or if they have a genuine wish to participate, grounded on their appreciation of the nature and purposes of the research, and they are capable of rationally assessing the attendant risks. For some prisoners, participation might be a legitimate vehicle for making amends to society. It needs only to be ascertained that they are sincere in their motivations, their participation is not being forced on them as a form of additional punishment and they have adequate understanding of all pertinent information. If what is crucial to voluntariness is 'the faithful representation of the settled values and preferences of the actor' (Feinberg, 1986: 117) it would be wrong to exclude prisoners who have chosen this method of expressing their commitment to the values of their society.

Ensuring that consent is informed

Adequate information is necessary to validate consent and enhance the subjects' ability to make decisions compatible with self-determined value systems. A subject, according to the Nuremberg Code, 'should have sufficient knowledge and comprehension of the elements of the subject matter involved as to enable him to make an understanding and enlightened decision'. Prospective subjects need to understand the nature, duration and purpose of the experiment as well as the method and means by which it is to be conducted so that they can view the inconveniences, hazards and other effects upon their health in proper perspective. They should have all the information necessary for making a decision that relates the options to the subject's self-determined values. The explanation must suit their level of understanding. Their inability easily to comprehend medical and scientific explanation cannot be an excuse to withhold information and bypass consent requirements.

Notwithstanding these considerations, withholding of pertinent information may be justified in therapeutic experiments when disclosure is likely to have harmful consequences for the subjects. Double-blind trials and the use of placebos also constitute justifiable exceptions provided the non-disclosure is part of the arrangement to which the subjects consent. Even if information is being withheld from them, the subjects' capacity to decide on the basis of self-determined values is not irreversibly compromised provided they fully understand the procedures and their implications.

It is not always easy to determine exactly how much and which information is necessary for an informed and autonomous decision. Respect for human beings requires that subjects be given all the information they want. However, they are not always in the best position to determine what information is relevant. Determination must consider the views of subjects and researchers alike and, generally, as much information must be given as a reasonable lay person would want to have before making a decision. In the end, the competent subjects' sincere preferences

383

must be respected even when they appear to be grounded on non-rational beliefs. After all, human beings do not always have to behave rationally.

Incompetence and proxy consent

Because human beings with diminished ability to think clearly and make rational benefit-cost assessments may be unable to give voluntary and informed consent, they may be excluded from the list of possible subjects of experimentation. Children, people suffering from great pain or under the influence of drugs or narcotics, women in labour and the mentally handicapped are among those who need protection from dangers they may not be able to foresee or evaluate. But medical knowledge that could be extremely beneficial to these special groups may need to be validated by means of experiments involving the participation of some of them as subjects.

If the experiments are intended to be therapeutic, the best interests of the patients dictate a course of action that is calculated to benefit the patient to the greatest possible degree. To deviate from such a course of action in order to attain a result that would be beneficial only to others is to involve the subjects in a non-therapeutic experiment.

When the procedures are not intended directly to benefit such subjects, their inclusion may be permitted only if the risks are totally negligible. In the event, consent must be given for them by a qualified proxy. But as the risks become significant, the validity of a proxy's exercise of substituted judgement becomes questionable, as does the alternative claim that the proxy is acting in the best interests of the subject. The authority to render proxy consent only arises out of the need to protect such subjects. It ends when the need is no longer present. Hence one could not justify decisions to put incompetent subjects at risk when the expected benefits for them are not abundantly significant. (See also pp. 385–7 below.)

We must also take into account the fact that competence is relative to the task at hand. Children and mentally handicapped individuals who are incompetent to make some decisions may be competent enough to make others. Those who have the capacity to understand and process information, and deliberate on the basis of their own values and conception of the good may be in a position to give informed consent. But this has to be balanced against the vulnerability to manipulation and coercion inherent in their dependent relationship.

Incompetence in the case of those who are under stress or under the influence of drugs or narcotics may be transient. If so, respect for autonomy may be guaranteed by prior authorization rather than by recourse to a proxy.

Persons belonging to a community that is the subject of research may pose similar problems but for different reasons. Because of their number, it is often impossible to get their universal and expressed consent. Proxy consent from political representatives is the natural recourse, but it may have to be shown that the risks involved do not go beyond what the members may be presumed to have consented to in electing leaders.

Justice and Human Subjects

Considerations of justice may arise in research on human beings in connection with the distribution of burdens, the availability and use of benefits, the solicitation and compensation of subjects, the provision of compensation for injury and the setting of priorities and directions in the use of research funds and resources.

The recruitment of experimental subjects may be a venue for exploitation in the form of an uneven distribution of risks among different segments of the population. In effect, particular persons and groups that invariably get a bigger share of the risk burden than others are being taken advantage of. And if the lines are drawn along socio-economic levels there may be a form of class exploitation. This form of injustice is perpetrated on a larger scale when dangerous experiments are carried out in some countries rather than in others. (See the essay in chapter 34 (pp. 355–65) on 'Aids: Ethical Issues in the Developing World'.) Provision of overseas funding for drug trials might easily be an instrument for passing the burdens of risk to people who are less likely to enjoy the benefits in the future. Unless health-care costs are adequately subsidized, the benefits of research are less likely to be financially accessible to those who bear the bulk of the burden. When the poor shoulder most of the risks and the rich enjoy most of the benefits, there is an issue of justice that needs to be addressed.

Compensation compromises the voluntary character of consent when it becomes the sole motivation for participation. However, one must look further into the case of those who are motivated by compensation in order to provide for basic needs. It would be unfair not to give them the same chance that is given to the less needy. One may also ask why research compensation should be treated differently from salaries given to people in general, which may deliberately be used to suppress their freedom to accept competing employment offers (de Castro, 1995: 264). Under conditions of socio-economic inequality, the exploitation of human subjects assumes added dimensions. Compensation, rather than being exploitative, could be a subject's opportunity to buy temporary emancipation. Nevertheless, one could only hope effectively to deal with problems of social justice in the context of society at large rather than within the limited environment of medical experimentation.

Ample compensation for damage or injury is also a requirement of justice in the experimental setting. It may be interpreted as some kind of punishment in cases where irresponsibility, negligence, fraud or some other wrongdoing on the part of researchers can be established. However, this view may go against the objective of preventing or minimizing harm to research subjects because of the legal complications involved in proving culpability. Hence, it appears preferable to avoid legal entanglements associated with the establishment of guilt by focusing on the compensatory rather than the retributive aspect of justice. What this entails is a replacement of the 'principle of compensation for injuries caused by the employer's negligence with the concept of compensation for injuries as an inherent cost of the enterprise, regardless of the allocation of fault' (Freund, 1969: xiii).

The setting of priorities and directions in the use of research funds and resources is an important concern that has an impact on large numbers of human beings. Because its effect on individual persons may not be felt directly, its ethical significance is easily overlooked. But there is a need constantly to be aware of the consequences of political and fiscal decisions made by key leaders. The time and effort exerted to ensure that individual research projects do not harm their subjects should be matched by proportionate vigilance in the case of allocation decisions affecting the health and safety of much greater numbers of individuals.

Is there a Duty to Serve as a Subject?

Do human beings have a duty to serve as research subjects? Since the benefits of knowledge derived from biomedical research are useful to everybody in general, it has been suggested that everyone must share in the task of generating such knowledge by serving as research subjects (cf. McDermott, 1967). A cross-generational dimension is provided to this duty-to-serve line of thinking by the argument that present members of society have a quasi-contractual obligation to reciprocate the benefits that have been made available to them through the participation of previous generations in biomedical research. The contention is that this duty ought to be fulfilled by the present generation through their participation as subjects in research that could be of benefit to future generations.

However, it is not true that the benefits of medical research are always available to everybody. If these benefits are available at all, the drugs, procedures or implements that result from successful medical research usually have to be paid for by their users. Hence, those who refuse to serve as subjects cannot be classified as freeloaders. Their payment for medical care constitutes a market-determined compensation for the services rendered (albeit indirectly) by others. Indeed, research costs contribute an increasing proportion to the cost of medical care. Under such circumstances, it would be disingenuous to speak of a duty to serve as a subject of research, arising from society's right to research benefits.

Even in situations where medical care is paid for by the state and the fruits of medical research involving human subjects are truly available to everybody, it has to be shown that a general obligation on the part of the present generation to reciprocate the benefits it has received translates into an obligation that is enforceable with respect to particular subjects. And granting that reciprocation is called for, it does not have to be provided by everyone in the form of service as subjects.

The same response may be given to the argument that human beings are bound by a duty of beneficence to serve as subjects on the assumption that experimentation will maximize benefits for everybody in general. From the existence of a general moral claim it has to be shown with respect to particular individuals that (1) the burden falls particularly on them and not on others (not everybody will have to serve), and (2) their duty lies in serving as experimental subjects and not in other ways of contributing to the common good. In the context of a free and democratic society, it may be more appropriate to speak of a moral claim which calls for a kind of response that is for each individual to determine autonomously. Considerations of beneficence have to be balanced against individual autonomy. Where there is no clear and imminent danger to others, violations of a person's right to self-determination should be avoided.

Confidentiality

Problems of confidentiality in the research environment often relate to the handling of data from retrospective studies where records may be examined without the consent of the subjects. There appears to be no need to require consent provided the subjects' identities are not revealed. However, advances in technology now make it possible to determine genetic groupings and even individual identities. Thus it has been argued that consent should not be automatically waived in research using anonymous tissue samples, as this could lead to labelling and stigmatization of identifiable communities, and the more general loss of control of information about ourselves. The results of DNA tests, taken together with available demographic data, could reveal more information about the subjects than they care to divulge. Moreover, the subjects get no opportunity to decide if they want to participate in the experiment or to learn from the results (Kopelman, 1994).

Using Tainted Knowledge

To some extent, the use of knowledge gained from ethically questionable research procedures may be likened to the use of stolen goods by parties other than the rightful owners. Beneficial information derived from the cruel experiments performed by Nazi researchers provides an extreme example. Assuming that such knowledge is soundly based, and has not been independently discovered using alternative means, is there a responsibility to refrain from its use?

On the one hand, the analogy with tainted goods may be questioned. Tainted knowledge is not privately owned by individual subjects. The notion of ownership may not be applicable at all, since ownership is something that may be both acquired and surrendered. But possession of tainted knowledge cannot be surrendered because even when it is turned over to somebody else it is still retained. Possession of it is very different from possession of material goods that physically may be held, handed over or destroyed.

Moreover, it can be argued that leaving such research findings unused would only underscore the futility of the victimized subjects' sufferings. But the use of such knowledge could show that the subjects did not suffer in vain, provided they are not harmed further and their tormentors are not the ones who are able to take advantage.

On the other hand, the use of tainted research findings by society at large is liable to be seen as condoning the exploitative means by which the findings were arrived at. This is likely to happen if those responsible for the wrongdoing go unpunished. Hence, any attempt to extract beneficial consequences out of the sufferings of the victims in this manner should be undertaken only in a context that sends an unequivocal message of commitment to the implementation of justice by punishing those who are guilty and by strictly implementing regulations designed effectively to deter prospective violators.

Trust and Confidence

The safeguards for technically correct human experiments are as important as the clarification and understanding of key concepts in ensuring ethical soundness. Validation of the procedures and the qualifications of researchers and staff helps ensure that subjects are exposed only to risks and suffering that are truly relevant to the knowledge being sought. But a temptation to focus on form rather than substance must be avoided.

The identification of consent as a key element in ethically sound experimentation has led some people to view it mainly as a legal instrument to protect the subject from harm and preserve autonomy. Others see it as a necessary protection for the researcher. Both approaches carry unacceptable confrontational undertones. More attractive is the view that the researcher, 'because of his superior competence and the trust and reliance placed in him, owes a duty of undivided loyalty and devotion to his client' (Freund, 1969: xiii). What this entails is a relationship built on mutual trust anchored on shared ends.

These shared ends include 'no longer mere protection against harm and the securing of the conditions of our preservation, but active and constant improvement in all the domains of life' (Jonas, 1969: 13) Central to this outlook is the subject's voluntary individual commitment, which is possible only where there is public trust and confidence in a medical community that shows genuine care and concern for its patients and subjects.

References

Cocking, D. and Oakley, J. (1994). Medical experimentation, informed consent and using people. *Bioethics*, 8, 293–311.

De Castro. L. D. (1995). Exploitation in the use of human subjects for medical experimentation: a re-examination of basic issues. *Bioethics*, 9, 259–68.

Downie, R. S. and Calman, K. C. (1987). *Healthy Respect: ethics in health care*. London: Faber and Faber.

Feinberg, J. (1986). *Harm to Self*. Oxford: Oxford University Press.

Freund, P. (1969). Introduction. In P. Freund (ed.), *Experimentation with Human Subjects*. New York: George Braziller, xii–xviii.

Jonas, H. (1969). Philosophical reflections on experimenting with human subjects. In P. Freund (ed.), *Experimentation with Human Subjects*. New York: George Braziller, 1–31.

Kopelman, L. (1994). Informed consent and anonymous tissue samples: the case of HIV seroprevalence studies. *Journal of Medicine and Philosophy*, 19, 525–52.

McDermott, W. (1967). Opening comments to colloquium: the changing mores of biomedical research. *Annals of Internal Medicine*, 67, 39–42.

Further Reading

Annas, G. J., Glantz, L. H. and Katz, B. F. (1977). *Informed Consent to Human Experimentation.* Cambridge, MA: Ballinger.

Barber, B. (1980). *Informed Consent in Medical Therapy and Research.* New Brunswick, NJ: Rutgers University Press.

Barber, B. et al. (1979). *Research on Human Subjects: Problems of social control in medical experimentation.* New Brunswick, NJ: Transaction Books.

Freedman, B. (1987). Equipoise and the ethics of clinical research. *New England Journal of Medicine,* 317, 141–5.

Gray, J. N., Lyons, P. M. and Melton, G. B. (1995). *Ethical and Legal Issues in AIDS Research.* Hampden Station, Baltimore, MD: Johns Hopkins University Press.

Lebacqz, K. (1981). Justice and human research. In E. E. Shelp (ed.), *Justice and Health Care.* Dordrecht: D. Reidel, 179–91.

Levine, R. J. (1981). *Ethics and the Regulation of Clinical Research.* Baltimore, MD: Urban and Schwarzenberg.

McNeill, P. M. (1993). *The Ethics and Politics of Human Experimentation.* Cambridge: Cambridge University Press.

National Commission for the Protection of Human Subjects of Biomedical and Behavioral Research (1978). *The Belmont Report: Ethical principles and guidelines for the protection of human subjects of research.* Washington, DC: Department of Health, Environment and Welfare.

White, B. C. (1994). *Competence to Consent.* Washington, DC: Georgetown University Press.

37

Experimentation on human embryos and fetuses

MARY WARNOCK

The ethical issues arising specifically from research using live human embryos and fetuses are somewhat different from those discussed in other essays in this book that are concerned with experimentation on human beings. In considering these issues I shall inevitably cover again some of the ground covered in chapter 14 (pp. 127–34), since the problems arise not from matters of autonomy or consent but from the status it is thought right to accord to the embryo or fetus itself.

In the Report of the Committee of Enquiry into Human Fertilization and Embryology (HMSO, 1984) the committee attempted to distinguish between pure and applied research, and to separate both from the use of new and untried treatment. It was admitted that these categories overlapped; however, I now think that it was mistaken even to attempt to separate them. In a relatively new science such as embryology, the 'pure' motive for research, to seek further knowledge of the subject, will always exist alongside the motive of new applications of knowledge. And since all the applications are, again, relatively new, those of them that are treatments must inevitably be to a certain extent experimental, being themselves part of a research programme. In any case there is, I believe, a very general moral consensus that no research using humans, however microscopically small and however undeveloped, should be undertaken save for good medical reasons. For in discussing issues in bioethics, one must not forget that, though people hold different moral views on many topics, there exist a number of common values, shared between most humans, binding them, however loosely, in a moral community. It is when these values seem to be in danger that a sense of outrage arises. Indeed, the starting-point of any discussion of the ethics of embryo experimentation is the unquestioned assumption that to use humans for research purposes must not be lightly undertaken. 'Pure' research (what is sometimes scornfully called 'curiosity-led research') using live human embryos would, according to a generally shared moral sense, be even less easy to accept than that which uses laboratory animals.

The question of justification, then, has always been in the foreground of discussions of experiments on live human embryos. We have to remind ourselves how recently this discussion began. For the general public, at least, it began in 1978, with the much publicized birth in the United Kingdom of the first baby in the world to be born by *in vitro* fertilization.

Until that time most people did not know that experiments in fertilizing human eggs in the laboratory had been taking place: but when the experiment succeeded, and not only was the egg fertilized, but implantation in the mother's uterus was also achieved and a healthy baby born, then public debate began. There was still a considerable degree of ignorance among people at large about the early stages of fertilization and the development of the embryo, but at least it became clear that *in vitro* fertilization was a real possibility for the alleviation of certain kinds of infertility. It was the remedying of the often severe misery brought about by infertility that afforded the justification of the original, and indeed much of the subsequent, research.

For the likelihood of success had seemed remote; and the success rate of the procedure was, indeed, at the beginning, very low. If IVF was to be offered as a practical remedy for infertility, then its success rate had to be increased, and this entailed research into the nature of fertilization, and of successful implantation. The Archbishop of York, speaking in the House of Lords in 1989, put it thus: 'I believe that research must continue if *in vitro* fertilization is to continue. One cannot separate them, and I regard as totally unrealistic and indeed immoral any proposal to continue *in vitro* fertilization without a proper backing in research. This is for the simple and basic reason that imperfect techniques without a backing in research are bad practice medically, and, I believe, wrong morally.' To use parents desperate to have children as experimental material for the new techniques, while pretending to offer them therapy, would have been morally wrong, even if it were agreed that no hard line can be drawn between new treatment and research.

In considering where research was needed, we must first try to clarify the early stages of fertilization and embryonic development. In the case of a normal woman, eggs, produced by the ovaries, encounter sperm travelling along the Fallopian tube, and are fertilized there. If the tube is blocked, the egg and sperm cannot meet, and the woman is infertile. It was to meet this kind of case that, in the UK, Patrick Steptoe and Robert Edwards, after years of research using donated eggs, devised a way of removing eggs from a woman's ovary and preparing them for fertilization outside the body, mixing them with male sperm, growing them in a dish for two or three days, in a specially prepared fluid, and finally replacing them in the uterus, in the hope that they would implant in the wall of the uterus. This was IVF.

The egg, when fertilized, spends the first four days making cells. It starts as two, and multiplies during this time to four, sixteen and onwards. The next ten days are occupied with the formation of the placenta, the amnion, the umbilical cord and the other membranes that will be the support-system of the embryo when it is formed. After that comes the clustering of cells together to form what is known as the primitive streak, which will develop fairly rapidly into the spinal column and central nervous system of the embryo (or embryos, for twinning can occur during these first fourteen days by a division of cells). Until the first fourteen days have passed there is no differentiation of cells; any might form part of either, say, the placenta, or of the embryo itself. By eight weeks from fertilization, however, the placenta and all the protective membranes have separated from the embryo, and all the main organs of the body and all the limbs have been formed: from now on the

391

living organism is generally referred to as a fetus rather than an embryo, though there is no strict rule about this.

In what follows I shall concentrate mainly on research using human embryos, rather than fetuses, because it is here that the ethical debate has centred, as a matter of history; and it may have been supposed that any objections to using live embryos would apply with even greater force to the use of more mature fetuses, (though, as far as the law goes, this has not been the case). The areas in which research was needed were various. First, little was known by scientists about the actual process of fertilization and, in particular, the structure of the human egg. Second, it was necessary to experiment with different possible compositions and temperatures of the fluid in which egg and sperm should be brought together in the laboratory; and third, there was a need to discover the factors making for successful implantation.

The ethical issue that arose from the use of embryos was at once seen to be a matter of public rather than private morality. The question was whether people wished to be members of a society which permitted the use of live embryos for research, not whether they wanted to carry out such research themselves. And for this reason it was immediately seen that whether or not such research should be permitted was a question for the law. Advice or guidelines to scientists would not provide enough reassurance to the public. But the law had to be made; there was no existing law that would cover such a wholly novel situation; and any new law would have to reflect, as far as possible, the moral views not merely of Parliament but of the country as a whole. Here lay the greatest difficulty in the beginning. For there was no received wisdom about the use of embryos in the laboratory; there could be none, since the first such embryo had come into existence only a few years before the debate started.

It is generally the presumption of legislation that it should be based on a broadly utilitarian weighting-up of harms and benefits. Most people were prepared to accept that the alleviation of infertility was a major benefit. Moreover, as the debate progressed, other benefits that might flow from research using embryos came to be more clearly perceived. More might usefully be discovered about the cause of spontaneous abortions; new methods of contraception might be discovered; and, finally, the possibility of detecting faulty genes in very early embryos, and even replacing them, came to be regarded as perhaps the greatest benefit from further research. So, in the British Parliament, by the time that the Embryology Bill came to its final stages it was above all on the possibility of detecting and eliminating monogenetic diseases such as Duchenne muscular dystrophy that the argument of those in favour of permitting research was concentrated, and this was true whether they thought of actual genetic manipulation, or of the use of pre-implantation diagnosis, followed by IVF, implanting only healthy embryos, and discarding those with a defective gene. This latter, the most practical option, also involved, as I have argued, the continuation of research, in order to make IVF a more or less routine medical procedure. All these good things seemed to cause no harm or pain to anyone. For the very early embryo, having no central nervous system, could certainly suffer no pain, whatever was done to it in the course of research. The justification of research using human embryos might have seemed overwhelmingly strong on utilitarian grounds, for animals other than humans would not serve as research subjects for the discovery of what was not yet known about human embryology. The processes of fertilization and the development of the embryo differed too much from one species to another.

However, the usual utilitarian arguments were not enough, in this case. It was rightly argued that human embryos, simply because they were human, were quite different from other research material; and there were those who thought that this was the end of the matter. There could be no justification for research which would end in the destruction of the embryo. Other human subjects, it was argued, may be used for research (with their consent) if and only if there is some chance that the research may benefit them personally. Not only can embryos not give consent, but it was generally agreed that any embryo which has been the subject of research must be destroyed, and not implanted in a woman's uterus, for fear that it might have suffered damage. Therefore these embryos were doomed to destruction from the start. The benefit that would come from research would be for others, not the embryos themselves. There were those who argued that it was particularly wrong to fertilize donated eggs especially with a view to research; there were others who, more consistently in my view, held that it made no difference whether the embryo had been created for the sake of research or for the sake of possible implantation, but had been found surplus to the requirements of the woman undergoing treatment: in either case a human embryo must not be doomed to destruction, however useful the outcome of the research.

Such moralists were implacably opposed to research. Some of them, retaining the utilitarian framework or argument, said that the weighing-up of benefits and harms must include the harm done to the embryos that would be used. Though these embryos could not suffer pain, they could and did suffer death, which was worse. In other words, in the calculus of gains and losses, humans who had been born were to be given no priority over those who had just been conceived. It would be generally agreed that to kill some humans to benefit others was not something to be morally condoned; and this was what embryo research amounted to. Others, not inclined to adopt utilitarian arguments, or any other arguments which depended on the consequences of an act, simply asserted that deliberately to take the life of another human was wrong. If it was agreed (as it was) that the embryos in question were both human and alive, then it must be wrong to use them for research and then destroy them. This is the kind of argument most generally used in the United States, and it has made the acceptance of state-funded embryo research impossible there.

There was another argument, sometimes used by itself, sometimes, rather illogically, as an extra to reinforce the arguments just given, and this was the slippery slope argument, which has an immense appeal to people's imagination. This argument held that, even if research using human embryos might be justified by its consequences, it was nevertheless the kind of activity that would inevitably lead to worse activities such as everyone would agree to be wrong. If research using embryos were allowed, then soon it would be research using live fetuses, then neonates, then older babies and finally the Holocaust. It should be noted that there was no suggestion that one of these things followed logically from another; but, human nature being what it is, it is to be supposed that if you give an inch a mile will be demanded.

It is largely in the attempt to meet this kind of argument that legislative regulation of research has been fairly generally adopted. In those countries and states where embryo research is not totally prohibited, it would now take primary legislation to permit research using human embryos of more than fourteen days from fertilization. A barrier has been erected to block descent down the slope.

Fourteen days was decided on as the limit because of the great change in the development of the embryo heralded by the development of the primitive streak. It is only after that that an individual exists with its own now quickly developing central nervous system, its own limbs, its own brain. Even though before that an embryo has a genetic individuality, it has no pattern of human identity, any more than human tissue has. The history of each person who is born can be traced back to the development of the primitive streak and not before. Before that there could have been two or three people formed of the same material. It is because of the enormous change that comes at this stage of development that scientists generally prefer to think of the embryo as actually beginning to exist at this stage. Before that there is the egg and the sperm, and the *conceptus*, that which comes from their conjunction. All these, egg, sperm and conceptus are human (that is, they differ from the eggs, sperm and conceptus of other animals) and are of course alive, but are not yet distinct embryos. Many people are now satisfied with this argument, and are prepared to accept the continuation of research, subject to regulation, with the criminal law in the background. However, it has to be acknowledged that such an approach can do nothing to satisfy those who make no distinction between an embryo immediately after fertilization (a conceptus) and someone who has been born. In their minds research using embryos is murder. The stage of development of the embryo is irrelevant; all human life at whatever stage is to have equal protection.

In practice, however, I believe that most people, even those most sensitive to ethical issues, are gradualists. They grieve less over an early than a late miscarriage; they do not regard it as a moral outrage that at the very beginning of a pregnancy a miscarriage may occur and pass unnoticed. We no longer believe that there is one single identifiable moment when a human being becomes an individual to be separately valued and protected. Aristotle, having no microscopes or any idea of the microscopic, and mostly using guesswork, held that male sperm conveys something called *pneuma* to female menstrual blood, and that this pneuma, which has no permanent life, causes the developing embryo to have a soul or life, first merely vegetative, then such as all animals have, and finally rational, peculiar to man. The rational soul begins in male embryos at about forty days from the entry of the pneuma into the uterus, in females it begins at about ninety days (Aristotle, *History of Animals*, 583b). From then on the fetus has to be protected as potentially human. This doctrine was taken over almost in its entirety by Aquinas, nearly fifteen centuries later. Even Aristotle and Aquinas were gradualists of a kind, and certainly held that the early embryo, however they believed that it came into existence, was less valuable than the later fetus. We, knowing incomparably more, have all the more reason to believe that all biology is a matter of gradual change.

Just as in evolution there was no one single instant in which a hominid became a human, though the differences between them are now profound, so in the case of individual development there need be no instant when a conceptus becomes an embryo, an embryo a fetus, a fetus a baby. And as the development goes on so we accord more importance to that which is developing. We know quite well, for example, that innumerable early embryos are lost through spontaneous abortion (usually those that are in some way defective); but we do not think of these, if we even knew they existed, as so many lost people to be mourned. We know that it is possible for a fetus of, say, twenty-four weeks gestation to have experiences, of pain perhaps, whereas an embryo of less than fourteen days from fertilization can experience nothing, having not even the beginnings of a central nervous system, through which all experiences are transmitted. Indeed, unless one is blinkered by a dogmatic commitment to the idea that all human life is *equally* valuable, it would be difficult to deny that we value the human embryo more the further the pregnancy has lasted.

This is why the idea of research using live human fetuses is so objectionable. After all, if, after a late abortion, the fetus is still alive, or if the late abortion could be so carried out that the life of the fetus was ensured, then immediately we would begin to talk not about a fetus but about a premature baby. It is doubtful whether anyone would seriously propose to use such a premature baby for research purposes, and then destroy it. To advocate such a course would immediately give rise to the sense of common outrage mentioned at the beginning. The treatment given to the baby might be new and untried, and thus in part experimental, but its aim would be primarily to give it a chance of life.

The most controversial research of all, which would inevitably involve the use of live fetuses, would be research into the feasibility of keeping embryos alive right through the normal period of gestation; to invent, that is, an artificial womb within which a fetus could come to term. This is a project that, above all others, induces horror and antagonism in the public at large; and it is easy to imagine the wonderful excitement the press would enjoy if it became possible. I personally would far prefer that a mother who can produce eggs but who has no uterus could have her baby by means of an artificial womb than that she should have recourse to a surrogate, with all the emotional problems that this often involves. But we know too little about the effect of the environment of the womb on the growing fetus to make this likely to be an acceptable area of research at the present time. As long ago as 1983, Peter Singer and Deane Wells (1984) considered dispassionately the arguments for and against ectogenesis. They concluded that the central difficulty of conducting any research in this field was the fear that babies born in this way would turn out abnormal, not physically but mentally and emotionally. The risks might seem too great for the resulting children, if there were any. They suggested that the way forward might be slowly to push back the time of gestation from the other end; to keep smaller and smaller premature babies alive, until knowledge of how to do this developed so far as to make possible a joining of the techniques needed for keeping *in vitro* embryos alive with those needed for keeping alive in-incubator neonates. But they thought, then, that this was a long way off. It still is; and in most countries, there is no doubt that to make it permissible there would be a need for legislation of a kind which is almost unimaginable. For in the question of the ethics of experimentation using human embryos or fetuses, we are essentially concerned with public morality, such as may, if necessary, be translated into law, and so it is impossible to disregard the sometimes unargued spontaneous reaction of members of the public. All are entitled to their own moral opinions; one cannot take this right away, though education, argument, information and time for thought are all helpful in turning gut-reaction into coherent moral sense. But in the end, a kind of consensus has to be reached, otherwise the laws, where they exist, will be unenforceable. Scientists will simply have to turn to other fields of research, for fear of their laboratories being vandalized and even their lives put at risk by the protestors. Consensus morality, though a concept despised both by extreme individualists and fundamentalists of various persuasions, is in fact a necessary foundation for law and the enforcement of law. In the field of medical ethics, and especially in the emotionally charged area of research using live human embryos, consensus, even if it involves compromise, is the very best that can be hoped for, and legally enforced regulation of research the best compromise on offer.

Further Reading

Bertazzoni, Umberto, Fasella, Paolo, Klepsch, Andreas and Lange, Peter (eds) (1988). *Human Embryos and Research*. Frankfurt.

Ford Norman M. (1988). *When did I Begin?* Cambridge: Cambridge University Press.

Singer, Peter, and Wells, Deane (1984). *The Reproductive Revolution*. Oxford: Oxford University Press.

A Question of Life: The Warnock Report on human fertilization and embryology (1985). Oxford: Blackwell.

Walters, W. A. W. (ed.) (1991). *Baillière's Clinical Obstetrics and Gynaecology: human reproduction: current and future ethical issues*. London: Baillière Tindall.

PART XII

EXPERIMENTATION WITH ANIMALS

38

History and ethical regulation of animal experimentation: an international perspective

F. BARBARA ORLANS

Before the nineteenth century, animal experimentation was rare. Among the first recorded uses of live animals was the study of body humours by Erasistratus in Alexandria in the third century BCE. Galen (129–c.210 CE), the most renowned physician of the Roman Empire, used pigs to demonstrate the effects of the severance of various nerves. After Galen's death, medical discovery virtually ceased for many centuries. In the late Middle Ages, a new spark of interest emerged in Europe, and anatomy was keenly investigated by experiments on animals. Notable practitioners were Andreas Vesalius (1514–64) who conducted anatomical experiments on monkeys, pigs and goats; William Harvey (1578–1657) whose studies of live deer contributed to his important discovery of blood circulation; and René Descartes (1596–1650) who asserted that animals are like machines and do not feel pain (a view that persisted until the twentieth century). In the nineteenth century, two renowned physiologists, François Magendie (1783–1855) and his pupil Claude Bernard (1813–78), laid the foundations of scientific experimentation as we know it today.

The animal experiments of Magendie and Bernard were conducted on conscious, restrained animals and provoked much public criticism for their cruelty. Protests came mainly from England, a country with a notable tradition of compassion for animals. In 1876 the first legislation in the world controlling animal experiments was passed. This was the British Cruelty to Animals Act which stood alone as the only national legislation for many decades. The law, which served as a model for other countries, required licensing of investigators and inspection of research facilities. In 1986, the law was revised and significantly strengthened.

The Rise in Animal Experimentation

Since the late 1800s, animal experimentation has increasingly become a major tool of science and the range of uses of laboratory animal has expanded enormously. In Claude Bernard's day, animal investigations were mainly 'basic research' with little or no human clinical relevance. Nowadays, much biomedical research has a primary purpose of improving human health. Diseases such as cancer or infectious diseases are induced in animals to determine the course of the disease, its diagnosis, treatment and prevention. Other purposes include the development of pharmacological agents, the safety testing of consumer products such as cosmetics and detergents and the training of students in experimental methods. Recent advances in human reproductive technology, genetic engineering and organ transplantation have been largely dependent upon animal studies.

Animal experimentation is now carried out not only in Europe but in almost every continent. Many species of animals are used, and an immense commercial enterprise has been established to supply laboratories with mice, rats, hamsters, guinea pigs, rabbits, dogs, cats, pigs and primates.

Millions of animals are bred specially for the purpose every year in order to be used in experimentation, but other animals – such as one-time pets and captured wild animals – are also used. For instance, in the United States, about half the number of dogs used for research are former pets taken from shelters; the other half are purpose-bred. Free-living wild animals (baboons, rhesus and other monkeys) are also captured from their native lands and shipped to laboratories around the world. Sometimes the capture and transport methods are traumatic and animals die before reaching the laboratories.

Purpose-bred animals are preferred to pets or wild animals for ethical reasons. Overall, purpose-bred animals are likely to suffer less; they do not have to make a stressful transition from a free life to a life in captivity. Purpose-bred animals know no other life than living in confined quarters, often singly caged with little or no opportunity to make decisions for themselves over what exercise they take, what they eat, whom they spend time with, etc. But wild animals and former pets are different; they have usually lived rich, social lives where they are used to expressing their own free will, so to lose this freedom can be traumatic. Also, the experimental results are more reliable from purpose-bred animals because, unlike former pets and wild animals, their genetic and health backgrounds are known. This reduces the number of variables that can confound experimental results. However, it is rare for legal restrictions to be made on the source of animals for research.

Chimpanzees, an endangered species, have in past years been captured from the wild for biomedical research. In the 1980s, captive-breeding programmes were established, but not before these animals became extinct in many countries where they used to live. In 1997, there were about 2,500 chimpanzees in laboratories, 1,500 of these in the United States, where a serious problem of surplus chimpanzees has developed. The rest are in Europe, where they are used for AIDS and hepatitis research.

Worldwide, the total number of animals used can only be guessed at. Estimates range from 50 to 100 million animals annually. This wide range indicates how poor the record-keeping is. Relatively few countries keep data on the numbers of animals used and sometimes these data are incomplete. Table 1, which reports on 17 countries, accounts for 41,732,000 animals annually.

It is unclear whether or not the total number of animals used worldwide is declining. For many countries, reliable data do not exist. In the United States, probably the largest user of animals, data do not support the view that the overall numbers of animals used for research are falling, although some have claimed this.

400

Table 1 Number of laboratory animals used in research, by country.

United States (1996)	13,457,000*
Japan (1991)	12,236,000**
France (1991)	3,646,000
United Kingdom (1996)	2,717,000
Germany (1993)	2,080,000
Canada (1995)	1,998,000
Australia (New South Wales, South Australia, Victoria and Western Australia) (1995/6)	1,932,000
Switzerland (1994)	724,000
Italy (1991)	683,000
Netherlands (1996)	652,000
Spain (1991)	559,000
Sweden (1994)	352,000
Denmark (1991)	304,000
New Zealand (1996)	265,000
Portugal (1991)	87,000
Greece (1991)	25,000
Ireland (1991)	25,000
Total	41,732,000

Notes: The annual total of over 41 million animals used is an underestimate. This is because many countries that use animals for experimentation do not count the numbers used. No data are available from several countries in Europe, the Middle East, Africa, South America, Asia and other regions.

The numbers of animals are given to the nearest thousand. Figures in parentheses indicate year of count. Because of different criteria for counting (in the United Kingdom, for instance, procedures are counted rather than number of animals), the figures may not be directly comparable from country to country. Numbers represent official national statistics, except for the United States and Japan; see comments below.

*The United States Department of Agriculture counts only about 10 per cent of all animals used in experimentation. The most used species – rats, mice and birds – are not protected under the relevant legislation and are therefore not counted. In 1996, the number of animals officially counted was 1,345,700. For this table, this figure has been multiplied by ten to achieve approximate comparability with data from other countries.

**Number of animals sold (not necessarily used). Source: Japanese Society of Laboratory Animals.

The number of US research facilities has been increasing, and trends in the numbers of animals used are variable from year to year. There is evidence that the number of dogs and cats used has declined in the United States, but this is probably offset by an increase in other species, such as pigs and ferrets. However, some countries (for instance, Canada, the United Kingdom and the Netherlands) have recently reported a declining trend in animal use.

Countries with and without Laws

Worldwide, by 1998, there were at least twenty countries that had enacted laws requiring certain humane standards for experimenting on animals. Listed alphabetically, these include: Austria, Australia (some states), Belgium, Denmark, France, Finland, Germany, Greece, Iceland, Ireland, Italy, Luxembourg, the Netherlands, New Zealand, Norway, Poland, Sweden, Switzerland, the United Kingdom and the United States. Canada is unusual in having established good voluntary controls (although pressure for a national law exists). In Australia, although there is no federal law, a national code of practice has been adopted and this code is law in all Australian states and territories except Western Australia and the Northern Territory. (A detailed discussion of these laws comes later; see pp. 404–7.)

There is only one country that officially bans all animal experiments – the small principality of Liechtenstein. In neighbouring Switzerland, efforts to ban animal experimentation have repeatedly failed. The Swiss pharmaceutical industry has a strong economic pull, and the combined threats of these companies to relocate outside Switzerland have been sufficient to thwart several public referendums attempting to limit animal experiments.

Also, efforts to ban certain procedures have generally failed. For instance, repeated efforts have been made to outlaw the notorious LD50 test (the lethal dose that painfully kills 50 per cent of the animals) and the Draize test (designed to measure the irritancy of a substance when placed in a rabbit's eye). Nowadays, much progress has been made on a voluntary basis to phase out or modify both these tests. Indeed, the fixed dose procedure, a modified and more humane version of the LD50 test, has now been adopted as the European standard. In 1998 the British government announced its commitment to stop licensing any further testing of cosmetics, alcohol or tobacco products on animals. In addition, their government has banned the use of the LD50 test, any use of chimpanzees and be use of wild-caught primates.

An unusual German law enacted in 1986 forbids the use of animals for certain purposes. Experimentation on animals is forbidden for the development and testing of weapons, and the testing of tobacco products, washing powders and cosmetics.

Several countries, mainly European, are on the verge of enacting legislation. Political pressure has been particularly strong from the European Community on its members. In 1986, the European Parliament issued Directive 86/609/EEC to protect animals used for experimental and other scientific purposes. This directive is legally binding on the (then twelve) member countries of the European Economic Community. While the provisions are not as strong as national legislation already existing in some countries, such as the United Kingdom and the Netherlands, this directive is making significant improvements in those countries that have had little or no legislative controls, such as Spain and Portugal.

Currently, no South American, African or Asian countries have legislation. However, in Mexico, a first step was taken in 1994 when a national declaration of principles for experimentation on animals was published. A 'declaration' has no enforcement provisions, so this is a long way away from an enforceable law that brings sanctions for non-compliance. Cultural factors can present an obstacle to the enactment of animal protective legislation. As Ciro Lomeli, a reform-minded veterinarian in Mexico City, has said: 'It is hard to get any legislation on laboratory animals passed when every Sunday afternoon the most popular public event is the bull fight.'

Cultural factors of a different kind are responsible for Japan's lack of laws governing laboratory animals. It has no formal approval system for animal researchers and research facilities and no system for reviewing experimental protocols. But it does have a long tradition of animal protection, based on the Buddhist teaching against senseless killing as part of its ethical system. Japanese scientists act according to their personal morality. It is typical that biomedical facilities hold annual memorial services for the spirits of the animals killed for biomedical research.

Changing Public Attitudes

Since about the 1970s, there has been an upsurge in public concern about the treatment of animals in research. It stems both from the influence of the animal rights movement and from the scientific discoveries that have widened our appreciation of the capabilities and feelings of animals.

The birth of the modern animal rights movement dates from the 1975 publication of *Animal Liberation* by the philosopher Peter Singer. Other philosophers such as Tom Regan and Bernard Rollin have contributed to this new public awareness about the ethical treatment of animals. This awareness parallels the passage of stronger laws to protect animals.

During roughly the same period, animal behaviourists, ethologists and other scientists have shown that the mental capabilities of many species of animal are far beyond what was previously thought. Primatologists such as Jane Goodall have demonstrated that animals live rich, complex lives with a wide repertoire of behaviours and social interactions. Whereas it was once thought that there was a wide gulf dividing human beings from other primates, the work of modern scientists has complemented the work of Charles Darwin (1809–82) in showing that biological life is a continuum and relationships between animal species can be close.

Human beings and other primate species share many genetic, physiological and mental attributes. For instance, chimpanzees are close relatives of human beings, sharing about 98 per cent of the same genetic material. Language may not be unique to humans as was once thought – it is at least arguable that some great apes use language. Many animal species have remarkable capabilities of communication; even species such as bees and other insects have powerful ways of communicating with each other. Most close observers of animal behaviour now agree that some vertebrate animal species do, to some degree, have significant abilities to intend, understand and communicate. A recent best-selling book, *When Elephants Weep*, has recorded how some species show love, joy, anger, fear, shame, jealousy, sadness, compassion and loneliness (Masson and McCarthy, 1995).

Abilities vary according to species. Generally speaking, there is roughly a descending order of mental ability according to the complexity of the animals' nervous systems. Most complex are primates (human beings, chimpanzees, gorillas, baboons and other monkeys), then other vertebrates (mice, rats, rabbits, birds and fish, etc.) and below that invertebrates (insects, snails, worms and protozoa). Vertebrate species are capable of perceiving pain, and some are also thought to experience mental suffering. It is now acknowledged that a few invertebrate species (such as the octopus) are also capable of perceiving pain, but there is some uncertainty as to where the line should be drawn between those species that feel pain and those which do not.

Laboratory animal protection laws usually cover all vertebrate species (both warm-blooded mammals and cold-blooded fish, reptiles and amphibia). National policies of the UK and Canada are exceptional in that they also protect octopus. It is an anomaly, not found in other countries, that the US law excludes rats, mice and birds, the most commonly used laboratory species.

The reliance of scientists on animal experimentation presents a compelling ethical problem. Those species at the top of the phylogenetic scale (the zoological classification that divides species into various groups) are the most desirable experimental subjects. They have greatest functional similarity to humans. The closer the animal model is to human beings, the more likely it is to replicate the metabolic, physiological, pharmacological and psychological aspects of the human condition. On the other hand, the use of these species gives rise to more acute ethical problems because of their closer kinship to humans, as demonstrated by their heightened ability to suffer. According to the primatologist Roger Fouts, free-living chimpanzees in Africa are not so different from non-technical peoples. 'They live in communities, they hunt, mothers care for their children and children care for their mothers, they use and make tools and, perhaps most important of all, they can suffer emotional as well as physical pain.' If we have an ethical objection to using non-technical people, then is there not an ethical objection to using chimpanzees? Therein lies the ethical dilemma that the laws have yet to address. Efforts to reduce or phase out the use of these higher animals in research have not yet made much progress except in the United Kingdom.

Coverage of Current Legislation

The most important issues covered by current laws in twelve countries are summarized in Table 2 and discussed below. Of the seven provisions listed, the most commonly encountered are those requiring inspection of animal facilities, and control of pain and suffering. The UK and Germany are the only countries where legislation covers all of the provisions discussed. The sequence in which these legal provisions are listed reflects to some extent increasing levels of sophistication in ethical thinking. That is to say, in Table 2, lines 1 and 2 deal with the most basic of issues, (housing and care) whereas the last discussed provision, line 7, addresses the complicated issue of how to justify each specific protocol.

Table 2 Key issues covered by laws governing laboratory animals in various countries.

Provision of law	United Kingdom	Belgium	Denmark	Eire	France	Greece	Germany	Italy	Portugal	Spain	Netherlands	United States
1 Inspection of research and breeding facilities	*	*	*	*	*		*	*			*	*
2 Daily care required	*	*					*				*	*
3 Controls on pain and suffering	*		*	*	*	*	*	*			*	*
4 Competency and licensing of qualified persons	*		*	*	*		*	*		*	*	
5 Monitoring by an independent committee	*	*	*		*		*				*	*
6 Requirement to use available alternatives	*	*	*	*	*		*				*	*
7 Ethical criteria for decision making	*						*				*	

Humane standards of care

A basic ethical concern requires that captive animals be housed and cared for humanely. Standards are maintained by official government inspection of research facilities; in some laws, the provision of daily care is specifically mentioned; see Table 2, items 1 and 2. The frequency and adequacy of inspections vary from country to country, as do the standards required. Usually only minimum standards are mandated, so the tendency has been for animal facilities to conform to the lowest acceptable standards rather than providing ideal housing.

Throughout the 1980s and 1990s, most experimental animals (primates, dogs, cats, guinea pigs and rabbits) have been singly housed in minimally sized cages. Typically, they could be seen huddled in a corner because they have nothing to do, thwarted in their behaviour by the poverty of their environments and deprived of any social interaction with other animals or stimulus from their surroundings.

However, housing standards for captive animals are gradually improving in some countries. Reform has been sparked by research demonstrating that abnormal, stereotypical behaviours (such as pacing, cage-biting, etc.) of laboratory, zoo and farm animals do not occur if the animals are housed in enriched environments – basically as close as possible to those conditions experienced by free-living

405

animals. Demands for better housing conditions for captive animals are now encountered in several countries.

In the United States, a particularly dramatic event happened in 1985 when Congress enacted a law that required promotion of the 'psychological well-being' of primates. At that time, the caging commonly given to laboratory baboons did not allow the animals to walk, stand upright or stretch their arms, all natural postures. Over time, this law has had profound beneficial effects for the animals. Improvements resulting from this law include increased space allocation, group-housing animals of similar species and the addition of branches, toys and exercise apparatus to the cages.

In other countries, too, environmental enrichment for laboratory animals is increasingly being explored. A considerable body of scientific literature now exists describing how to enrich the environments of many common laboratory species such as primates, dogs, cats, rabbits, guinea pigs and rats.

Pain and suffering

Of those countries that have enacted national laws, almost all recognize a moral imperative that every effort be made to reduce or eliminate pain and suffering that result from an experimental procedure. That the degree of animal pain and suffering must be minimized wherever possible is a common thread; see Table 2, line 3. The use of anaesthetics, analgesics or tranquillizers is mandated wherever there is more than trivial pain. As a corollary, specific methods of killing that are rapid and painless are mandated.

Investigator competency and licensing

If animal pain is to be controlled, then at issue is how competent the laboratory personnel are in recognizing and alleviating animal pain. In a few countries, training in humane experimental techniques and animal anaesthesia is a prerequirement before an investigator qualifies for an individual licence to conduct animal experiments. Licensing also helps keeps a check on where the experiments are being conducted. Countries that lack personal licensing provisions (see Table 2, line 4) need to establish alternative ways to control who conducts animal experiments. Independent monitoring committees (line 5) can fulfil this role.

Some recent laws require specific levels of competence from the investigator. For instance, the 1986 German law states: 'Only persons with the requisite expertise may conduct experiments on animals. Only persons who have completed university studies in veterinary medicine, medicine or natural sciences may conduct experiments on vertebrates.' In the Netherlands, a person judged competent to conduct animal experiments must hold a master of science or higher degree in one of the biomedical or biological disciplines. Similar laws requiring college degrees exist in other European countries. However, no such competency provision exists in US law. As a result, improper animal experiments by unskilled high-school students are still encountered, especially in the competitions called 'science fairs'.

406

Monitoring committees

Increasingly it has been recognized that proposed experiments should be reviewed by persons other than the investigator who will conduct the experiments. There are several ways of doing this, including monitoring committees (which may be institutional, regional or national) and to some extent individual licensing. (Line 5 does not distinguish between different types of monitoring committee.) A consensus is emerging that, for project review, institutional oversight committees have many advantages; several countries are now moving to establish institutional review such as that found in the US, Canada and Australia. The purpose of this review is to ensure legal compliance and to approve, modify (to improve the animal's welfare) or disapprove every proposed project.

Ensuring legal compliance does not necessarily mean that ethical debate takes on questioning the fundamental justification of a project. Consideration of ethical justification of each proposed project is not a usual requirement of the laws (for exceptions, see Table 2, item 7, discussed further below). So some oversight committees assume a fundamental justification of a project without further question.·

Each research facility is responsible for establishing its own review body – variously called an Institutional Animal Care and Use Committee or an Animal Ethics Committee. Usually the committee consists of a minimum of a senior scientist experienced in the care and use of research animals, a veterinarian, a non-user of animals and at least one person representing community interests. It is desirable that representatives from humane societies serve in these community positions. The proportional representation of non-animal researchers is important so that animal researchers do not dominate committee membership.

Institutional committees have an advantage over national committees in that the review is local, so the reviewers are likely to be knowledgeable about the quality and humaneness of the laboratory personnel. An additional advantage is that, through the community members, the public has a say in this decision-making, an important issue in matters of social controversy.

Three R alternatives

Many people now believe that there is a moral imperative to apply the three R alternatives wherever possible. These principles of refinement, reduction and replacement were first enunciated by Russell and Burch in 1959. Experimental procedures should be refined to lessen the degree of pain or distress; the numbers of animals used should be reduced consistent with sound methodological design; and where possible, non-animal methods should be used in preference to those that do use animals. The requirement to use available alternatives is written into the law in at least eight countries; see Table 2, line 6.

These laws work well. For instance, in Sweden, the emphasis of the oversight review committee is to work with the investigator on the three R alternatives to determine the research method least harmful to the animal. In the Netherlands investigators cannot legally perform a specific animal experiment if an alternative is available. Furthermore, since 1989, official data is collected in the Netherlands on progress towards adopting alternatives. Each year, research establishments report to the government whether new alternatives to animal experiments have been introduced in their laboratories. In 1993, approximately one-tenth of all reporting establishments introduced new methods aimed at the replacement, reduction or refinement of animal experiments. The introduction of new alternatives is linked to the recent reduction in the numbers of animals used in this country. This Dutch reporting system is a model for other countries to follow.

Alternatives are here to stay. Worldwide, scientists are working on developing alternatives. In the implementation of alternatives, the advances made in toxicity testing procedures and the reduction in numbers of animals used in harmful ways for student training are noteworthy.

Ethical criteria for aspects of decision-making

In general, existing laws do not address the fundamental ethical question, 'Should this particular animal experiment be done at all?' The usual presumption of the law is that animal experimentation is justified and that proposed projects should be approved so long as the investigator believes that useful scientific knowledge might be gained.

But ethical thinking has progressed. A few countries have mandated that the severity of the animal harm must be assessed for each and every project. These systems are variously called severity banding, or invasiveness or pain scales. The investigator and oversight reviewers must ask, 'How much pain and suffering is this animal going to suffer as a result of this experiment? How sick is the animal?'

According to this system, the degree of pain or distress is ranked according to a severity banding of either minor, moderate or severe (Orlans, 1993). As illustrative examples, in the minor category are procedures such as biopsies, or cannulating blood vessels; in the moderate category are major surgical procedures under general anaesthesia, and application of noxious stimuli from which the animal cannot escape; in the severe category are trauma infliction on conscious animals and cancer experiments with death as an endpoint. At some point (according to one's point of view) procedures become unethical because of the severity of animal pain.

Sweden and the Netherlands were the first countries to adopt severity banding as national policy in 1979. Since then Canada, the United Kingdom, Germany, Switzerland and Finland have followed suit. Efforts to enact a pain scale in the United States have so far failed, and in most countries no such provisions exist.

There are many benefits of using severity banding. Emphasis is on how invasive the procedure is from the animals' perspective. Projects that need to be seriously questioned because of the degree of pain are flagged. Also, assessment of the degree of pain is essential if the fundamental justification of a project is to be addressed.

Four countries, UK, Germany, the Netherlands and Australia have gone a step further. Their laws require that a cost-benefit analysis be made, linking the animal pain to the scientific worthiness and social significance of the purpose of the experiment. This means that the ethical costs to the animal are weighed against the human benefits derived from the research results. Although there are problems with weighing animal harms against human benefits, this is the view that has gained mainstream acceptance (see detailed discussion in Smith and Boyd, 1991). The laws in these four countries are the most advanced in this respect because they attempt to give direction to ethical decision-making.

Outlook for Future Laws

Laws to protect laboratory animals are needed in many countries that currently have none. Furthermore, enforcement of many existing laws needs to be strengthened – usually sanctions for non-compliance are weak and rarely imposed. In most countries, new provisions are required governing investigators' competency and training in humane techniques. Public accountability could be enhanced if national record-keeping were improved on the numbers, species and sources of laboratory animals, and the purpose and severity of the animal procedures. Additional efforts are also needed to outlaw the use of former pets and wild-caught animals for biomedical research.

Laws have not yet addressed the major ethical dilemma of using chimpanzees and other primates for research, which proceeds largely unabated. Several recent publications have argued the case for reducing or eliminating laboratory experiments on chimpanzees. For instance, a 1994 book edited by Cavalieri and Singer, *The Great Ape Project*, argues that we should expand the moral community to include all the great apes (humans, chimpanzees and gorillas) – great apes are persons. Also, the case for stopping chimpanzee research has been presented in a series of essays by Jane Goodall and others published in 1995 (see *Poor Model Man*). However, it will take a long time to accomplish these ends.

References

Cavalieri, P. and Singer, P. (1994). *The Great Ape Project*. New York: St Martin's Press.

Fouts, R. (1995). Chimpanzee biomedical experiments: a question of efficacy. *ATLA*, *23*, 585.

Masson, J. M. and McCarthy, S. (1995). *When Elephants Weep: the emotional lives of animals*. New York: Delacorte Press.

Orlans, F. B. (1993). *In the Name of Science: issues in responsible animal experimentation*. New York: Oxford University Press.

Poor Model Man: Experimenting on Chimpanzees, The First PACE Conference. Proceedings of the first PACE (People Against Chimpanzee Experiments) conference on the use of chimpanzees in biomedical research, held 3–4 July 1993, in Brussels, Belgium. These eighteen articles are published in *ATLA*, *23*, September/October 1995, pages 571–651. Available from FRAME, Russell and Burch House, 96–98 North Sherwood Street, Nottingham NG1 4EE, UK.

Singer, P. (1990). *Animal Liberation*, 2nd edn. New York: New York Review of Books.

Smith, J. A. and Boyd, K. M. (eds) (1991). *Lives in the Balance: the ethics of using animals in biomedical research*. London: Oxford University Press.

Further Reading

Francione, G. L. (1995). *Animals, Property, and the Law*. Philadelphia: Temple University Press.

Laboratory Animal Care Policies and Regulations: Canada, Japan, New Zealand, United Kingdom, and United States (1995). A collection of essays by various authors in *ILAR Journal*, 37, 2, 55–78. Available from ILAR, National Research Council, Institute of Laboratory Animal Resources, 2101 Constitution Avenue, NW, Washington, DC 20418.

Midgley, M. (1983). *Animals and Why they Matter*. Athens, GA: University of Georgia Press.

Orlans, F. B., Beauchamp, T. L., Dresser, R., Morton, D. B. and Gluck, J. P. (1998). *The Human Use of Animals: Case studies in ethical choice*. New York: Oxford University Press.

Rachels, J. (1990). *Created from Animals: The moral implications of Darwinism*. New York: Oxford University Press.

Rupke, N. A. (ed.) (1987). *Vivisection in Historical Perspective*. London: Croom Helm.

39

The moral status of animals and their use as experimental subjects

BERNARD E. ROLLIN

For most of human history, society has been satisfied with a very minimalistic ethic for animal treatment. This ethic, which prohibits the deliberate, useless, wilful, sadistic, intentional infliction of pain and suffering or outrageous neglect on animals, reflects both the commonsense empathetic awareness that animals could suffer, and a realization that those who cruelly abuse animals are likely to go on to abuse people. The latter insight has in fact been confirmed by contemporary research (Kellert and Felthous, 1985; Arkow, 1994).

The major reason that such a minimal ethic was socially adequate is that the overwhelming use of animals was agricultural (food, fibre, locomotion and power) and the essence of agriculture was husbandry. Husbandry (etymologically, 'bonded to the house') entailed care of the animals, specifically placing the animals in environments for which they were biologically suited, and augmenting their natural coping attributes with additional food, shelter, protection from predation, etc. The relationship with animals was symbiotic, in that humans in turn benefited from using the animals' products, labour or lives. So powerful was this caring relationship with the animals that the Psalmist in the 23rd Psalm uses it as a model for God's relationship to humans: 'The Lord is my shepherd . . .'

This sort of symbiotic agriculture required that the farmer maximize the animals' basic interests, and not cause the animals harm. Harming the animals meant diminishing the animals' production – if you hurt the animal you hurt yourself, the strongest possible sanction for a self-interested rational person! Thus a minimalistic ethic forbidding cruelty was socially sufficient to deal with those who were sadistic or irrational – the carter who in a rage beats his horse, the sadist who tortures animals for pleasure, the deviant farmer who does not feed or water the animals.

The development of high technology intensive agriculture, 'factory farming', destroyed symbiotic husbandry-based agriculture. Technological 'sanders' such as antibiotics and vaccines allowed us to put animals into environments which harmed the animals while still promoting efficiency and productivity. This new kind of agriculture, coupled with the rise of significant and highly visible research on animals, in essence destroyed symbiotic animal use and forced society out of its long-standing satisfaction with the traditional, minimalistic ethic.

It is patently obvious that research on animals is radically different from husbandry agriculture. Whereas traditional agriculture necessitated inflicting minimal harm on animals, the infliction of pain, suffering, disease, deprivation, fear, injury and various other noxious physical and psychological states upon animals in order to study their effects was essential to research. However, neither factory farming nor research on animals fitted the traditional notion of cruelty, since neither activity was sadistic, purposeless or useless. Although many animal advocates opposed animal research as 'cruel', it was difficult and implausible for society as a whole to equate medical researchers, whose intention was to advance knowledge and cure disease, with the sadists and psychopaths to whom the anti-cruelty ethic was addressed and whose intention was simply to achieve pleasure at another being in pain. (In conjunction with this view of research, virtually all anti-cruelty laws in the United States exempted animal research from their purview, either by statute or by judicial interpretation.) The conceptual limits of the traditional simplistic understanding of our treatment of animals as either husbandry, 'kindness' or cruelty was exposed, and the need for more sophisticated moral evaluation of the burgeoning field of animal research and testing made manifest.

The Moral Critique of Research on Animals

Both Plato and Hegel have argued that at least part of a moral philosopher's job is to help draw out and articulate nascent and inchoate thought patterns in individuals and society. In keeping with this notion, several philosophers, beginning in the 1970s, made explicit a number of moral reservations about human uses of animals in general, including invasive animal use in research and testing, and thereby helped draw out the moral queasiness at such use that had gradually developed in society in general. This task was first engaged by Peter Singer as a chapter in his *Animal Liberation*, wherein he challenged the moral justification for a great deal of animal use, including the moral permissibility of harming animals to advance scientific knowledge. Singer's discussion of research on animals elegantly articulated widespread social reservations about such *use* of animals, and is still in print. In 1982, Bernard Rollin's *Animal Rights and Human Morality* again challenged the morality of hurting animals in research, and also pointed out the inadequacy of the *care and husbandry* provided to such animals, leading to additional suffering which was not only not part of the research, but also, in many cases, inimical to its purposes. Additional work by Tom Regan, Steve Sapontzis, Evelyn Pluhar and numerous others has continued to give prominence to the moral questions of research on animals, aided by a number of scientists such as Jane Goodall, who have come to see the moral issues with clarity.

Although different philosophers have approached the issue from different philosophical traditions and viewpoints, it is possible to find a common thread in their arguments questioning the moral acceptability of invasive animal use. Drawing succour from society's tendency during the past fifty years to question the exclusion of disenfranchized humans such as women and minorities from the scope of moral concern, and the correlative lack of full protection of their interests, these philosophers applied a similar logic to the treatment of animals.

412

In the first place, there appears to be no morally relevant difference between humans and at least vertebrate animals which allows us to include all humans within the full scope of moral concern and yet deny such moral status to the animals. A morally relevant difference between two beings is a difference that rationally justifies treating them differently in some way that bears moral weight. If two of my students have the same grades on exams and papers, and have identical attendance and class participation, I am morally obliged to give them the same final grade. That one is blue-eyed and the other is brown-eyed may be a difference between them, but it is not morally relevant to grading them differently.

Philosophers have shown that the standard reasons offered to exclude animals from the moral circle, and to justify not assessing our treatment of them by the same moral categories and machinery we use for assessing the treatment of humans, do not meet the test of moral relevance. Such historically sanctified reasons as 'animals lack a soul,' 'animals do not reason,' 'humans are more powerful than animals,' 'animals do not have language,' 'God said we could do as we wish to animals,' have been demonstrated to provide no rational basis for failing to reckon with animal interests in our moral deliberations. For one thing, while the above statements may mark differences between humans and animals, they do not mark *morally relevant differences* that justify harming animals when we would not similarly harm people. For example, if we justify harming animals on the grounds that we are more powerful than they are, we are essentially affirming 'might makes right,' a principle that morality is in large measure created to overcome! By the same token, if we are permitted to harm animals for our benefit because they lack reason, there are no grounds for not extending the same logic to non-rational humans, as we shall shortly see. And while animals may not have the same interests as people, it is evident to common sense that they certainly do have interests, the fulfilment and thwarting of which matter to them.

The interests of animals that are violated by research are patent. Invasive research such as surgical research, toxicological research and disease research certainly harm the animals and cause pain and suffering. But even non-invasive research on captive animals leads to pain, suffering and deprivation arising out of the manner in which research animals are kept. Social animals are often kept in isolation; burrowing animals are kept in stainless steel or polycarbonate cages; and in general animals' normal repertoire of powers and coping abilities – what I have elsewhere called their *teloi* or natures (Rollin, 1992) – are thwarted. Indeed, Dr Tom Wolfle, a leading laboratory animal veterinarian and animal behaviourist at the National Academy of Science in the United States, has persuasively argued that animals used in research probably suffer more from the ways in which they are kept for research than from the invasive manipulation they are exposed to within research.

The common moral machinery society has developed for adjudicating and assessing our treatment of people would not allow people to be used in invasive research without their informed consent, even if great benefit were to accrue to the remainder of society from such use. This is the case even if the people being used were so-called 'marginal humans' – infants, the insane, the senile, the retarded, the

413

comatose, etc. A grasp of this component of our ethic has led many philosophers to argue that one should not subject an animal to any experimental protocol that society would not be morally prepared to accept if performed on a retarded or otherwise intellectually disabled human.

There appears in fact to be no morally relevant difference between intellectually disabled humans and many animals – in both cases, what we do to the being in question matters to them, as they are capable of pain, suffering and distress. Indeed, a normal, conscious, adult non-human mammal would seem to have a far greater range of interests than a comatose or severely retarded human, or even than a human infant.

While we do indeed perform some research on marginal humans, we do not do so without as far as possible garnering their consent and, if they are incapable of giving consent, obtaining such consent from guardians specifically mandated with protecting their basic interests. Applying such a policy to animals would forestall the vast majority of current research on captive animals, even if the bulk of such research is non-invasive, given the considerations detailed above concerning the violations of animals' basic interests as a consequence of how we keep them. Steve Sapontzis has further pointed out that we do have a method for determining whether an animal is consenting to a piece of research – open the cages! (Note that an animal's failure to leave the cage would not necessarily assure consent; it might merely demonstrate that a condition like learned helplessness has been induced in the animal.)

The above argument, extrapolated from ordinary moral consciousness, applies even more strongly to the case of animals used in psychological research, where one is using animals as a model to study noxious psychological or psychophysical states that appear in humans – pain, fear, anxiety, addiction, aggression, etc. For here one can generate what has been called the psychologist's dilemma: if the relevant state being produced in the animal is analogous to the same state in humans, why are we morally entitled to produce that state in animals when we would not be so entitled to produce it in humans? And if the animal state is not analogous to the human state, why create it in the animal?

The Uses of Animals in Research

Before examining the response of the animal-using research community to the moral critique presented, it is worth pausing to examine the various ways in which animals are used in research. The different usages are fairly well accounted for by the following seven categories:

1   Basic biological, behavioural or psychological research, that is, the formulation and testing of hypotheses about fundamental theoretical questions, such as the nature of DNA replication, mitochondrial activity, brain functions or learning, with little concern for the practical effect of that research.

2   Applied basic biomedical and psychological research – the formulation and testing of hypotheses about diseases, dysfunctions, genetic defects, etc., which,

while not necessarily having immediate consequences for treatment of disease, are at least seen as directly related to such consequences. Included in this category is the testing of new therapies: surgical, gene therapy, radiation treatment, treatment of burns, etc. Clearly the distinction between category 1 and this category will constitute a spectrum, rather than a clear-cut cleavage.

3   The development of drugs and therapeutic chemicals. This differs from the earlier categories, again in degree (especially category 2), but is primarily distinguished by what might be called a 'shotgun' approach; that is, the research is guided not so much by well-formulated theories that suggest that a certain compound might have a certain effect, but rather by hit-and-miss, exploratory, inductive 'shooting in the dark'. The primary difference between this category and the others is that here one is aiming at discovering specific substances for specific purposes, rather than at knowledge *per se*.

4   Food and fibre research, aimed at increasing the productivity and efficiency of agricultural animals. This includes feed trials, metabolism studies, some reproductive work, the development of agents like BST to increase milk production, etc.

5   The testing of various consumer goods for safety, toxicity, irritation and degree of toxicity. Such testing includes the testing of cosmetics, food additives, herbicides, pesticides, industrial chemicals and so forth, as well as the testing of drugs for toxicity, carcinogenesis (production of cancer), mutagenesis (production of mutations in living bodies) and teratogenesis (production of monsters and abnormalities in embryo development). To some extent, obviously, this category will overlap with category 3, but it should be distinguished in virtue of the fact that 3 refers to the discovery of new drugs, and 4 to their testing relative to human (and, in the case of veterinary drugs, animal) safety.

6   The use of animals in educational institutions and elsewhere for demonstration, dissection, surgery practice, induction of disease for demonstrative purposes, high-school science projects, etc.

7   The use of animals for extraction of drugs and biological products – vaccines, blood, serum, monoclonal antibodies, TPA from animals genetically engineered to produce it in their milk, etc.

For estimates of the numbers of animals used in these activities, see the Orlans article in chapter 38 (pp. 399–410).

The Response of the Research Community to the Moral Critique of Animal Research

Unfortunately for rational moral progress, the research community has had a historical tendency not to engage the moral challenge to animal research, but to sidestep it. Until the mid-1980s, it was not uncommon to hear scientists affirm that 'animal use is not a moral issue, it is a scientific necessity.'

BERNARD E. ROLLIN

The primary reason for researchers taking such a position, a view that in fact flew in the face of social morality, lies in what I have elsewhere called scientific ideology, or the common sense of science, which is to scientific activity what ordinary common sense is to everyday life (Rollin, 1989). Scientific ideology is the set of assumptions and presuppositions taught to nascent scientists as indisputable fact rather than debatable assumptions, along with the data germane to their particular disciplines.

The origin of this ideology lies in the understandable desire to separate science from speculative philosophy and unverifiable notions like 'life force', 'entelechies', absolute space and time and ether, which were plentiful in science at the end of the nineteenth century. Fuelled by the advent of a philosophical movement known as logical positivism, scientific ideology stressed an aspect of modern science prominent since Newton, namely that only claims that can be directly verified by experience or experiment can be legitimately admitted into science.

The effect of this approach on the issue of animal research was profound. In the first place, scientific ideology banished ethical and other value issues from the legitimate purview of science, as moral judgements could not be proven empirically. The result was an almost universal adherence among scientists to the dogma that science was 'value-free' and could not and did not deal with ethical issues in science. Under the influence of positivism, ethical judgements were perceived as exclusively emotive and as such could not be rationally engaged. The fact that many if not most animal advocates couched their opposition to animal research in highly emotional terms further convinced researchers that ethics was simply emotion, and that opposition to animal research on moral grounds needed to be met with emotional appeals based in vivid accounts of human suffering from disease, and the threat to human health that would be occasioned by even regulating animal research, let alone abolishing it.

A second component of scientific ideology strongly buttressed the denial of ethics in science. This involved an agnosticism about the ability of science to study or even know the existence of consciousness in humans or animals. Rooted in the positivistic commitment to allowing only the observable and testable into science, this component expressed itself in the United States and Britain as behaviourism, the movement in psychology which eschewed talk of mental states, and allowed as scientifically legitimate only the study of overt behaviour. The logic of this position can be reconstructed as follows: one should allow into science only what is intersubjectively observable. Mental states are not intersubjectively observable. Therefore mental states are not scientifically able to be studied. Therefore mental states are not scientifically real. Therefore mental states are not of concern to scientists. Felt pain in animals (as opposed to the physiological substratum or machinery of pain) is a mental state. Therefore felt pain in animals is neither scientifically real nor of concern to scientists. (Although this same logic would naturally apply to humans, and behaviourists in fact denied the cogency of talking about consciousness in people, they were clearly unable to act on this ideology in their dealings with humans, since people would hardly accept the claim that their pain was not real!)

416

THE MORAL STATUS OF ANIMALS

Thus scientists were doubly insulated from the moral issue of animal pain and suffering in research and thence from seeing animal research as a moral issue at all by the two components of scientific ideology; first by virtue of the denial of the relevance of moral issues to science, and second by the denial of the scientific reality of animal thought and feeling. Thus scientists were able to see animal use not as a moral issue, but as a scientific necessity, and the moral objections to animal use expressed in society as matters of emotion, not as rational moral concerns.

It is probably for the above set of reasons that there are fewer works defending the use of animals in research than criticizing it. One book, *The Case for Animal Experimentation* by Michael A. Fox, which did attempt to provide a systematic justification for animal use in research, was repudiated by its author within months of publication. None the less, there are certain arguments that are frequently deployed by defenders of animal research.

The argument from benefits   Research on animals has been intimately connected with new understanding of disease, new drugs, new operative procedures, all of which have produced significant benefits for humans and for animals. These significant results and their attendant benefits would have been unobtainable without animal use. Therefore animal research is justified.

Critics of animal research might (and do) attack the argument above in two ways. First of all, one may question the link between premises and conclusion. Even if significant benefits have been garnered from invasive animal use, and even if these benefits could not have been achieved in other ways, it does not follow that such use is justified. Suppose that Nazi research on unwilling humans produced considerable benefits, for example, as some have argued in the areas of hypothermia and high-altitude medicine. It does not follow that we would consider such use of human subjects morally justifiable. In fact, of course, we do not. Indeed, there are significant numbers of people in the research community who argue that the data from such experiments should never be used or even cited, *regardless of how much benefit flows from its use.*

The only way for defenders of animal research to defeat this counter-argument is to find a morally relevant difference between humans and animals that stops our extending our consensus ethic's moral concern for human individuals to animals.

Second, one can attack the argument from benefits in its second premise, namely that the benefits in question could not have been achieved in other ways. This is extremely difficult to prove one way or the other, for the same reasons that it is difficult to conjecture what the world would have been like if the Nazis had won World War II. We do know that as social concern regarding the morality of animal research mounts, other ways are being found to achieve many of the ends listed in our discussion of the uses of animals in research.

The argument that moral concerns of the sort required to question animal research apply only to humans   This approach is, in essence, an attempt to provide what we indicated was necessary to buttress the argument from benefits. Such an attempt was made by Carl Cohen in a *New England Journal of Medicine* article generally considered by the research community to be the best articulation of their position.

One of Cohen's chief arguments can be reconstructed as follows (the argument is specifically directed against those who would base condemnation of animal research on the claim that animals have rights, but can be viewed as applying to our earlier version of the general argument against invasive animal use). Only beings who have rights can be said to have sufficient moral status to be protected from invasive use in research. Animals cannot reason, respond to moral claims, etc. Therefore they cannot morally be said to be protected from invasive use.

The problems with this argument are multiple. In the first place, even if the concept of a right (or of sufficient moral status to protect one from being used cavalierly for others' benefit) arises only among rational beings, it does not follow that its use is limited to such beings. Consider an analogy. Chess may have been invented solely for the purpose of being played by Persian royalty. But given that the rules have a life of their own, anyone can play it, regardless of the intention of those who created the rules. Similarly, rights may have arisen in a circle of rational beings. But it doesn't follow that such rational beings cannot reasonably extend the concept to beings with other morally relevant features. In fact, that is precisely what has occurred in the extension of rights to marginal humans.

To this, Cohen replies that such extension is legitimate since marginal humans belong to a kind that is rational, while extension to animals is not. The obvious response to this, however, is that, by his own argument, it is being rational that is relevant, not belonging to a certain kind. Further, if his argument is viable, and one can cavalierly ignore what is by hypothesis the morally relevant feature, one can turn it around on Cohen. One could argue in the same vein that since humans are animals, albeit rational ones, and other animals are animals, albeit non-rational ones, we can ignore rationality merely because both humans and animals belong to the same kind (i.e., animal). In short, his making an exception for non-rational humans fails the test of moral relevance and makes arbitrary inclusion of animals as rights-bearers as reasonable as arbitrary inclusion of non-rational humans.

Another attempt to provide a morally relevant difference to undercut the argument against invasive animal use is provided by those who argue that scientific ideology is correct and that animals are incapable of pain, suffering and other morally relevant mental states. Such a neo-Cartesian stance has recently been revived by Peter Carruthers and Peter Harrison, and in essence questions the claim that what we do to animals matters to them.

A detailed exposition of and response to such a strategy is impossible to undertake here (Evelyn Pluhar has recently engaged this task in *Beyond Prejudice*). However, the following points can be sketched. First, a heavy burden of proof exists for those who would convince common sense and common morality that animals are merely machines. Even the anti-cruelty ethic took animal pain for granted. Second, such a position would make the appearance of pain and other modes of awareness in humans an evolutionary miracle. Third, the neurophysiological, neurochemical and behaviour evidence militates in favour of numerous similar morally relevant mental states such as pain in humans and animals. Fourth, if animals are truly just machines, devoid of awareness, much scientific research would be vitiated, for example, pain research conducted on animals and extrapolated to people.

One possible way to exclude animals from direct moral status, and thereby justify invasive research on them, is a philosophically sophisticated exposition of the claim we discussed by Cohen (see p. 418) that morality applies only to rational beings. This position, which has its modern roots in Hobbes but in fact was articulated even in antiquity, was more recently thrust into prominence by the work of John Rawls. It has been directly applied to the question of animals' moral status by Peter Carruthers, who was mentioned above as advancing the neo-Cartesian argument, in his book *The Animals Issue*. Interestingly enough, Carruthers' contractual argument is independent of his denial of consciousness to animals. Even if animals are conscious and feel pain, Carruthers believes that the contractual basis for morality excludes animals from the moral status necessary to question the moral legitimacy of experimentation on them.

According to Carruthers, morality is a set of rules derived from what rational beings would rationally choose to govern their interactions with one another in a social environment, if given a chance to do so. Only rational beings can be governed by such rules, and adjust their behaviours towards one another according to them. Thus, only rational beings, of which humans are the only example, can 'play the game of morality', so only they are protected by morality. Animals thus fall outside the scope of moral concern. The only reasons for worrying about animal treatment are contingent ones, namely that some people care about what happens to animals, or that bad treatment of animals leads to bad treatment of people (as Thomas Aquinas argued), but nothing about animals in themselves is worthy of moral status. Further, the above contingent reasons for concern about animal suffering do not weigh heavily enough to eliminate research on animals.

There are a variety of responses to Carruthers. In the first place, even if one concedes the notion that morality arises by hypothetical contract among rational beings, it is by no means clear that the only choices of rules such beings would make would be to cover only rational beings. They might also decide that any rules should cover any beings capable of having negative or positive experiences, whether or not they are rational. Second, even if rational beings intend the rules to cover only rational beings, it does not follow that the rules do not have a logic and life of their own that lead to adding other beings to the circle of moral concern, as indeed seems to be happening in social morality today. Third, Carruthers (1992: 195) seems to assume that according moral status to animals entails that the status be equal to that of humans, 'yet,' he says, 'we find it intuitively abhorrent that the lives and suffering of animals should be weighed against the lives or suffering of human beings.' But it is not at all clear that contractualism, even if true, could not accord animals sufficient moral status to prohibit experimenting on them, yet not say they were of equal moral value to normal humans. Further, as Sapontzis (1993) has pointed out, Carruthers' argument is circular. He justifies such uses as research on animals by appeal to contractualism, and justifies contractualism on the grounds that it renders morally permissible such uses as research on animals.

419

The argument from experimenting on marginal humans   The final defence of research on animals that we shall consider is the utilitarian one advanced by R. G. Frey (1983). Unlike the previous arguments, it is a tentative one, offered up in a spirit of uneasiness.

Frey's argument essentially rests upon standing the argument from marginal humans on its head. Recall that this argument says that animals are analogous to such marginal humans as the retarded, the comatose, the senile, the insane, etc. Since we find experimenting on such humans morally repugnant, we should find experimentation on animals equally repugnant.

Frey's argument reaffirms the analogy, but points out that, in actual fact, many normal animals have richer and more complex lives, and thus have *higher quality* lives, than many marginal humans do. The logic of justifying research on animals for human benefit (which assumes that humans have more complex lives than animals, and thus more valuable lives) would surely justify doing such research on marginal humans who both have lower qualities of life than some animals do and who are more similar physiologically to normal humans, and are thus better research 'models'. If we are willing to perform such research on marginal humans, we are closer to justifying similar research on animals.

Obviously, the force of Frey's argument as a defence of research depends upon our willingness relentlessly to pursue the logic by which we (implicitly) justify animal research and apply the same justification to using humans not different from those animals in any morally relevant way. As Frey himself affirms, there are some 'contingent' (i.e., not logically necessary) effects of deciding to do research on marginal humans as well as on animals that would work against such a decision. He cites the emotional (rather than rationally based) uproar and outrage that would arise (because people have not worked through the logic of the issue), and presumably such other responses as the knee-jerk fear of a slippery slope leading to research on normal humans. But, in the end, such psychological rather than moral/logical revulsion could conceivably be overcome by education in and explanation of the underlying moral logic.

I believe that Frey's argument fails as a defence of research and ends up serving those who originally adduced the argument from marginal humans as a *reductio against* research on animals. If people do see clearly and truly believe that doing research on animals is (theology aside) exactly morally analogous to doing research on marginal humans, they are, in our current state of moral evolution, likelier to question the former than accept the latter. In fact, in my twenty years of working with scientists and animal researchers of all sorts. I have found that the overwhelming majority of them do not, if pressed, feel morally justified in doing research on animals, but tend to focus on the benefits produced and simply ignore the moral perspective, a tack much aided by the scientific ideology described above.

In fact, Frey's argument very likely serves to awaken a primordial component in human moral psychology – revulsion at exploitation of the innocent and the helpless – animals and marginal humans being paradigm cases of both. In a society that increasingly and self-consciously attempts to overcome such exploitation, experimentation on marginal humans, in fact often practised in the past. along with experimentation on powerless humans, is not a living option. In sum then, the force of Frey's argument is not to justify research on animals, but rather to underscore its morally problematic dimension.

Practical Resolution

Whatever the ultimate social-ethical resolution to the question of the moral legitimacy of research on animals turns out to be, it is clear that the arguments against such use have captured a significant moment in social thought, and have helped accelerate the development of an ethic in society that goes well beyond concern about cruelty to concern about all animal suffering, regardless of source. This has in turn resulted in the passage of major legislation in the United States, Britain and elsewhere regulating animal research. In my view, law is, in Plato's phrase, social ethics 'writ large'. While Britain has had a hundred-year history of such regulation, the passage of the US laws in 1985 is especially significant, both because research has essentially hitherto enjoyed a *laissez-faire* status and because the legislation was vigorously opposed by the research community, who threatened significant danger to human health if it were passed.

The passage of laws in the United States bespeaks a society in transition. While society does not wish to see innocent animals suffer, it is also not yet prepared to risk losing the benefits of animal research. As a result, it has stressed the control of pain and suffering of research animals, enriching living environments and generally assuring proper care.

In addition to generating law, the emerging ethic has led to the abandonment of some frivolous research animal use, for example, some of the uses of animals in cosmetic testing; the elimination of many invasive and brutalizing laboratory exercises in undergraduate, graduate, medical and veterinary curricula; and the development of new ways to teach surgery, for example, by way of spay-neuter clinics, cadavers and models for teaching manual skills. Increasing numbers of scientific journals are refusing to publish manuscripts detailing research where severe pain and suffering were involved. And there is far more serious effort than ever before across the scientific community to consider alternatives to animal use, be these a reduction of numbers of animals, refinement of painful procedures (e.g., substituting a terminal procedure for a painful one) and replacement of animals by various modalities (e.g., cell culture, tissue culture, epidemiology).

In my view, there is a new and serious moral issue associated with animal research that has not received sufficient attention. This arises from the advent of genetic engineering technology. By use of this technology one can create animal 'models' for the thousands of gruesome human genetic diseases hitherto not able to be studied in animals. Since many of these diseases involve symptoms of great severity, yet the research community is likely to embrace the creation of such models, a new and significant source of chronic animal suffering is developing. The issue is worsened by virtue of the fact that few modalities exist for controlling chronic pain and suffering. Unfortunately, this issue has hitherto occasioned little discussion.

421

References

Arkow, P. (1994). Child abuse, animal abuse, and the veterinarian. *Journal of the American Veterinary Medical Association*, 204, 1004–6.

Carruthers, P. (1992). *The Animals Issue: moral theory in practice.* New York: Cambridge University Press.

Cohen, C. (1986). The case for the use of animals in biomedical research. *New England Journal of Medicine*, 315, 865–9.

Fox, M. A. (1986). *The Case for Animal Experimentation.* Berkeley: University of California Press.

Frey, R. G. (1983). Vivisection, morals and medicine. *Journal of Medical Ethics*, 9, 94–7.

Harrison, P. (1989). Theodicy and animal pain. *Philosophy*, 64 [January 1989], 79–92.

Kellert, S. and Felthous, A. (1985). Childhood cruelty toward animals among criminals and non-criminals. *Human Relations*, 38, 1113–29.

Pluhar, E. B. (1995). *Beyond Prejudice.* Durham, NC: Duke University Press.

Regan, T. (1983). *The Case for Animal Rights.* Berkeley: University of California Press.

Rollin, B. E. (1982). *Animal Rights and Human Morality.* Buffalo, NY: Prometheus Books. [Rev. edn, 1992.]

—— (1989). *The Unheeded Cry: animal consciousness, animal pain and science.* Oxford: Oxford University Press.

—— (1995). *The Frankenstein Syndrome: ethical and social issues in the genetic engineering of animals.* New York: Cambridge University Press.

Sapontzis, S. (1987). *Morals, Reason and Animals.* Philadelphia: Temple University Press.

—— (1990). The case against invasive research with animals. In B. E. Rollin and M. L. Kesel (eds), *The Experimental Animal in Biomedical Research*, Vol. I. Boca Raton, FL: CRC Press, 3–19.

—— (1993). Review of *The Animals Issue. Canadian Philosophical Reviews*, 13/4, 40–2.

Singer, P. (1975). *Animal Liberation.* New York: New York Review of Books.

Further Reading

Baird, R. M. and Rosenbaum, S. E. (eds) (1991). *Animal Experimentation: the moral issues.* Buffalo, NY: Prometheus Books.

Rollin, B. E. (1985). The moral status of research animals in psychology. *American Psychologist*, August, 920–6.

—— (1990). Ethics and research animals – theory and practice. In B. E. Rollin and M. L. Kesel (eds), *The Experimental Animal in Biomedical Research.* Vol. I. Boca Raton, FL: CRC Press, 19–37.

—— (1995). Laws relevant to animal research in the United States. In A. A. Tuffery (ed.), *Laboratory Animals*, 2nd edn. London: John Wiley, 67–87.

Rowan, A. N. (1984). *Of Mice, Models, and Men.* Albany, NY: SUNY Press.

Russell, W. M. S. and Burch, R. L. (1959). *Principles of Humane Experimental Technique.* London: Methuen.

Smyth, D. H. (1978). *Alternatives to Animal Experiments.* London: Scolar Press.

PART XIII

ETHICAL ISSUES IN THE PRACTICE
OF HEALTH CARE

40

Confidentiality

RAANAN GILLON

One of the oldest codified moral commitments in health care, the obligation to maintain confidentiality is an explicit requirement in the Hippocratic Oath, and remains so in its modern successors such as the World Medical Association's International Code of Medical Ethics. Thus the Hippocratic Oath required doctors to swear that 'Whatever, in connection with my professional practice, or not in connection with it, I see or hear, in the life of men, which ought not to be spoken of abroad, I will not divulge, as reckoning that all such should be kept secret' (British Medical Association, 1993). The International Code of Medical Ethics – a sort of contemporary version of the Hippocratic Oath – even requires that 'A physician shall preserve *absolute* confidentiality on all he knows about his patient, even after the patient has died' (World Medical Association, 1985; British Medical Association, 1993 – emphasis added); and both French and Belgian law defend medical confidentiality as absolute, with transgression a criminal offence (Mason and McCall Smith, 1987); apparently in French law medical confidentiality is regarded as absolute to the extent that patients themselves do not have the right to require their doctors to waive medical confidentiality, even when this would be in the patient's interests (Havard, 1985).

On the other hand, in medical practice in the United Kingdom and in other English-speaking countries medical confidentiality, while still regarded as a fundamentally important medico-moral obligation, is rarely considered to be an absolute requirement, and exceptions are recognized both professionally and legally. The General Medical Council, the medical profession's ruling professional body in the UK, while instructing doctors that as a general principle, 'Patients have a right to expect that you will not pass on any personal information which you have learned in the course of your professional duties, unless they agree' (General Medical Council, 1995: 1) also describes a wide variety of exceptional circumstances in which doctors *may* break medical confidentiality (General Medical Council, 1995: 2). These include (as well as circumstances in which patients give their explicit permission for disclosure) circumstances in which the patient's agreement can be assumed (for example, emergencies); where disclosure even if consent cannot be obtained is deemed to be in the patient's best interests (for example, if a patient is believed to be a victim of serious abuse, or if a doctor believes it would seriously harm a patient to be given information about having a terminal condition but believes relatives should be told); where disclosure is for the purposes of medical teaching, research or audit (for example, in teaching medical students and doctors in training, in medical research in which patient records need to be consulted, and in self-monitoring of the quality of their medical performance by groups of doctors); where disclosure even without consent is required to prevent harm to others (for example, where failure to disclose would expose others to risk of death or serious harm, such as driving when medically unfit, or when a patient refuses to inform a sexual partner that he or she is infected with the HIV virus, or where disclosure is necessary to prevent or detect serious crime); and where doctors are legally obliged to break confidentiality (for example, when ordered by a judge to do so, or where under a statutory obligation to do so, as in notification of abortions, of certain sorts of drug addiction, or of information that would prevent terrorism or materially help police to apprehend terrorists) (Brazier, 1992).

Small wonder, with statements concerning the ethics of medical confidentiality ranging from a requirement of absolute secrecy at one end of the spectrum to such a wide range of exceptions at the other, that in the early 1980s a US physician and ethicist, after finding that between 25 and 100 people at his university hospital would have legitimate access to a patient's *confidential* hospital notes, called medical confidentiality 'a decrepit concept' (Siegler, 1982); and that in the 1990s a UK medical lawyer was still calling the ethics and law of medical confidentiality 'fuzzy and unpredictable' (Brazier 1992).

So what moral sense can be made of the issue? One approach might be to abolish the commitment altogether. Patients would simply come to the doctor and doctors would pass on information about them as and when they saw fit – they 'would give no pretence to the keeping of any secrets – which would leave the patient absolute guardian of his/her own personal privacy and autonomy' in that it would be up to patients to decide whether their privacy or their health was more important. Sometimes people's health would suffer, but it would be 'in a good cause – that of their individual autonomy' (Warwick, 1989).

While this sort of approach to confidentiality is taken in many ordinary life contexts, the problem with it in medical practice – and much other health-care practice – is that in order to do a good job for their patients doctors often need to have information of a sort that people generally regard as private, even secret. Some of the information is merely embarrassing to discuss, some may be positively harmful to the patient or others if it is divulged. Doctors routinely ask a series of questions about bodily functions that people would not dream of discussing with anyone else. When a patient's medical problems may relate to genitourinary functions a doctor may need to know about that patient's sexual activities, sometimes in detail. When a patient's problems are psychological a doctor may need to know in great detail about the patient's experiences, ideas and feelings, relationships past and present, even in some contexts about the person's imaginings and fantasies. In genetics contexts investigations may demonstrate non-paternity – that is, that the putative father of a patient's child is not the genetic father.

Such intrusive medical inquiries are based not on prurience or mere inquisitiveness but on the pursuit of information that is of potential assistance to the doctor in treating and helping the patient. None the less many patients are unlikely to pass on this information unless they have some assurances of confidentiality.

Quite apart from the medical benefits to the patient, maintenance of confidentiality may in some circumstances benefit the health of others. In the context of transmissible diseases, especially sexually transmissible diseases, so long as the patient continues to trust his or her doctor the doctor is left in a position of being able to educate and influence the patient in ways that can reduce the likelihood of the disease being passed on. As soon as confidentiality is broken the trusting relationship is likely to be undermined and the opportunity to help reduce spread of the disease is lost (Boyd, 1992).

Thus the primary moral justification of medical confidentiality seems to be that it produces better medical consequences. It is in order to enable their patients to talk freely about private matters and thus obtain information necessary to practise better medicine and so better help their patients that doctors have for so long assured their patients of confidentiality. Their fundamental Hippocratic moral commitment is to provide medical benefits to their patients with minimal harm. To do so properly they require relevant private and sensitive information about their patients. To overcome people's natural reluctance to reveal such information doctors must establish their patients' trust. A strict professional obligation of confidentiality, known to be enforced on pain of severe professional sanctions, helps to achieve these ends.

This consequentialist defence of medical confidentiality could be generalized further if, as seems likely, the achievement of optimal benefit for patients is likely to contribute to optimizing general welfare, both in the actual provision of medical care and in the prospect of such provision (for we are all potential patients and most of us would wish our medical care to be optimal). Thus a prima facie moral case can be made for claiming that a professional commitment by doctors to maintain their patients' confidences is likely not only to be beneficial to those patients and their health care but also to tend to maximize the general welfare.

Quite apart from such consequentialist justifications, medical confidentiality can also be justified from a variety of other moral perspectives. Respect for autonomy, the fundamental value in Kantian ethics, would also seem to support a commitment to confidentiality, at least if autonomy is understood in its contemporary sense of self-determination, or deliberated or thought-out choice for oneself. For given the imbalance in power between a sick patient and a well and knowledgeable doctor, it seems coercive to say to a patient, as Warwick suggests, 'I need information about your private life and if you don't give it to me you are likely to suffer because my ability to help you overcome your disease is likely to be impaired – but I am not prepared to offer you any assurances of confidentiality.'

This approach offers medical benefits in a way that fails to respect the patient's autonomy at least in that it fails to benefit the patient in the autonomy-respecting empowering way that the patient would probably prefer, assuming that the patient's autonomous preferences would typically be for optimal treatment including disclosure of necessary private information but in a context of confidentiality. The doctor who refuses to agree to confidentiality in providing treatment is somewhat like the surgeon who will operate but refuses to agree to provide an anaesthetic. As Warwick says, the treatment can be given if the patient so chooses, but it is worse treatment and it is treatment that fails to respect a patient's autonomous preferences, generally for no good moral reason (though more about this below).

Once the doctor has accepted the patient's desire for confidentiality and has promised, implicitly or explicitly, to maintain a patient's confidences, then respect for the patient's autonomy becomes an even stronger justification for maintaining confidentiality – for the doctor has promised and the patient is justified in running his or her life on the assumption that the doctor will keep that promise (autonomy literally means self-rule – that is, running one's own life); to break the promise is to infringe the patient's autonomy.

Another common moral perspective is the moral requirement of justice, and from the perspective of rights-based justice it is widely claimed that patients have a right to have their confidences respected by their doctors. Certainly from the perspective of legal justice, such rights to confidentiality are widely entrenched in law, more or less firmly according to the jurisdiction involved.

In addition, preservation of confidentiality may be supported by moral perspectives that emphasize the importance of relationships based on trust and on virtues such as caring, loyalty and faithfulness ('confidentiality' is derived from Latin roots meaning 'with trust' and 'with faithfulness').

Thus, to do away with the norm of medical confidentiality would seem likely to undermine medical care and the general welfare, offend against moral norms of respect for autonomy and respect for patients' rights and undermine moral concerns to preserve and enhance trusting relationships and virtues such as faithfulness, loyalty and care.

Given such strong moral justifications for confidentiality in health care, perhaps we should move to the other end of the spectrum of attitudes and accept medical confidentiality as an absolute obligation, as required by the International Code of Medical Ethics, and as upheld apparently by French and Belgian law. Roman Catholic priests when acting as confessors commit themselves to such absolute confidentiality; and lawyers in the United Kingdom not only consider their communications with clients when preparing for judicial proceedings absolutely privileged, but such privilege is legally protected, unlike the qualified privilege of doctors and priests. Certain types of general moral obligation are sometimes regarded as absolute – Emperor Ferdinand's dictum about justice is often quoted as an example: *fiat justicia, et pereat mundus* – let justice be done though the heavens fall. (See chapter 8, pp. 72–9.)

One of the strongest defences of absolute medical confidentiality is presented by Kottow, in which he argues powerfully that it has to be 'an all or none proposition', 'an intransigent and absolute obligation' and 'a guarantee of fairness in medical actions'. The entire basis of trust between doctors and patients is undermined by any breach of confidentiality; it is a deceit to patients to assure them of confidentiality and then retrospectively disown that assurance; and the putative benefits to society of building in exceptions to medical confidentiality are outweighed by the undoubted harms of breaking it (Kottow, 1986).

Desirable though it might be to maintain an absolute principle of medical confidentiality, unless it is the only absolute moral obligation it runs up against the general problem for plural absolute moral obligations; if there are two or more absolute moral obligations that may conflict then people confronted with such moral conflict are logically unable to act in a morally acceptable way, even where the moral conflict is in no way their responsibility let alone their fault (assuming that, by definition, it must be morally unacceptable to transgress an absolute moral obligation). If the obligation of medical confidentiality were absolute then by definition it could never be morally justified to transgress it. Yet in at least some cases the justification for overriding medical confidentiality seems morally overwhelming.

If a doctor learns in the course of a medical consultation that his patient intends to murder someone – or to make the example even clearer, that the patient is a terrorist, has already murdered at random in the pursuit of his political stance and has now planted a bomb in a busy city centre – 'I'm only telling you this, Doc, because of course I can trust you never to reveal it – but this evening there's going to be mayhem in one of the city squares' – few people, even after the most thorough reflection, would believe that the doctor's moral obligation to maintain medical confidentiality should override the citizen's moral obligations to help protect members of his or her community from being murdered and to obey (morally acceptable) laws and so inform the police.

At a more day-to-day level, what if a patient reveals that he or she, or a spouse or relative, is dangerously abusing a child – physically, mentally or sexually? While protection of the child may in practice be achievable without breaking confidentiality, suppose it is not? Or suppose that it is legally required, as in the United Kingdom, to report such abuse to the social services, who themselves are in certain cases required to inform the police. Are all such putative counter-examples to be overridden by absolute confidentiality? All in all, it seems that maintenance of confidentiality would in some circumstances be wrong, and that therefore an absolute obligation to maintain medical confidentiality in all circumstances and without exception is morally untenable – a position that in a later paper Kottow has come to accept, while maintaining the need for 'stringent and predictable' medical confidentiality, which has moral priority 'over many, perhaps most but not all other considerations' (Kottow, 1994).

It seems then that neither doing away with medical confidentiality nor making it an absolute moral obligation are morally acceptable alternatives. The obvious fall-back position is the one that has in practice been widely accepted and described above – notably that while the obligation is a very important one it is not absolute, and exceptions are justified where maintenance of confidentiality would be too harmful. The problems with this position are equally obvious, for once it is known that confidentiality may be breached by doctors and other health-care workers patients' trust is undermined, and with it, as argued above, individuals' medical care, their general welfare, respect for patients' autonomy, their rights and the doctors' loyalty and fidelity to their patients.

So even if it is accepted that there must be some exceptions to the maintaining of confidentiality, there will remain a tension between the desire for an absolute or near absolute rule of confidentiality that maximizes patients' trust in doctors and thus facilitates good medical practice; and a prima facie rule of confidentiality that

429

allows exceptions when these clearly promote the public welfare, even when the consequent damage that results from undermining trust in doctors is taken into account.

How in practice to maintain this difficult compromise position is far less clear. Some pointers are apparent. It seems highly desirable for doctors and all health-care workers to commit themselves and be committed (for example by their terms and conditions of service) to a strong though not absolute moral obligation of confidentiality to their patients or clients, which should be overridden only where there is a clearly overriding moral justification for doing so. Even then, thoughtful efforts to avoid the need to break confidentiality should always be made before doing so. As Boyd and his working party point out, sometimes even when breaking confidentiality would be justified, it is possible to achieve the desired beneficial effects for others without having to do so. And they also warn that doctors considering the possibility of breaking confidence with a patient should assess carefully the likelihood of actually achieving the protection of others that they are seeking – not only may this fail in the long term, it may also fail in the short term (if, for example, the patient has given the doctor a false name and address, and simply disappears when he or she suspects that the doctor is about to break confidentiality) (Boyd, 1992).

Failure in the long term to protect public health and welfare, even if individuals may be protected in the short term is an important consideration. In this context the maintenance of a strict standard of confidentiality by doctors specializing in the treatment of HIV and AIDS seems particularly important. Porter gives an important 'warning from history' about the dangers of using heavy-handed coercive legal measures to try to control the spread of sexually transmitted disease. While such measures have undoubtedly been effective in controlling infectious diseases such as plague, cholera and typhoid, they were totally ineffective when applied to syphilis in Victorian times. In the case of AIDS, the lesson of history, he argues, is not to make it a compulsorily notifiable disease but to rely on confidentiality and voluntary cooperation between patients and health workers (Porter, 1986).

The final pointer to dealing with the often impossible dilemmas of confidentiality is the need for openness; for the dilemmas are relevant to anyone considering the questions of medical confidentiality, patients, potential patients and health-care workers alike. There seems no plausible way to evade them, but at least let us all acknowledge them openly and indicate the sorts of ways we aim to respond to them. For my part, as a practising doctor I aim to maintain confidentiality to the maximum extent that I can while respecting the morally acceptable laws of my country, refusing to evade opportunities to avert major harms, and exercising common sense both in assessing what my patient would want me to do when I am unable to consult the patient or a proper proxy directly, and in relatively trivial cases where such consultation is likely to appear – and be – simply foolish (Gillon, 1985). But I don't pretend that my approach is or would be acceptable to all, or that other approaches may not be morally acceptable – such, alas, is the nature of genuine moral dilemmas.

430

References

Boyd, K. (1992). HIV infection and AIDS: the ethics of medical confidentiality. *Journal of Medical Ethics*, 18, 173–9.

Brazier, M. (1992). *Medicine, Patients and the Law*, 2nd edn. Harmondsworth: Penguin, 44–67.

British Medical Association (1993). *Medical Ethics Today*. London: BMJ Publishing Group, 326–9.

General Medical Council (1995a). *Good Medical Practice*. London: General Medical Council, 6.

—— (1995b). *Confidentiality*. London: General Medical Council.

Gillon, R. (1985). *Philosophical Medical Ethics*. Chichester: John Wiley, 106–12. [Chapter on confidentiality.]

Havard, J. (1985). Medical confidence. *Journal of Medical Ethics*, 11, 8–11.

Kottow, M. (1986). Medical confidentiality: an intransigent and absolute obligation. *Journal of Medical Ethics*, 12, 117–22.

—— (1994). Stringent and predictable medical confidentiality. In R. Gillon and A. Lloyd (eds), *Principles of Health Care Ethics*. Chichester: John Wiley, 471–8.

Mason, J. and McCall Smith, R. (1987). *Law and Medical Ethics*, 2nd edn. London: Butterworths, 122.

Porter, R. (1986). History says no to the policeman's response to AIDS. *British Medical Journal*, 293, 1589–90.

Siegler, M. (1982). Confidentiality in medicine: a decrepit concept. *New England Journal of Medicine*, 307, 1518–21.

Warwick, S. J. (1989). A vote for no confidence. *Journal of Medical Ethics*, 15, 183–5.

Williams, B. (1973). A critique of utilitarianism. In J. Smart and B. Williams, *Utilitarianism: For and against*. Cambridge: Cambridge University Press, 98–9.

World Medical Association (1985). *The World Medical Association Handbook of Declarations*. Ferney-Voltaire (France): World Medical Association, 4.

41

Truth-telling

ROGER HIGGS

Trusting someone to look after you usually means that you do not expect them to tell you lies. Yet the problem of telling the truth in health care continues to engage us. Most patients have wondered at one time or other whether their own medical advisers are being completely open with them. Anxiety can create frightening shadows. But a policy of openness is a recent innovation in the long history of Western medicine, and in some quarters the revolution has yet to happen. The phrase 'doctor knows best' enshrines a tradition of paternalism which may extend throughout a health service. Some cultures expect that their doctors may not be telling the truth: some doctors feel that proper patient care may sometimes require untruths. Whatever the rhetoric of the modern mission statement or user information sheet, health-care systems still leave control of decision-making and much of the information flow which underpins these decisions firmly in professional hands. In view of this, we need to examine both the traditional approach and the modern insistence on a person's right to be told about the circumstances of their own case. Should health-care professionals always tell the truth, or if not, what exceptions should there be and on what ethical basis?

The Clinical Encounter

Those who work in hospitals or primary care or who have experience as patients will immediately see that this is a field of concern, but others may need to be reminded of the reality. It is not just that dinosaur institutions or individuals have failed to modernize. There are moral issues at stake, which concern us to the deepest levels of our being. The paradigm situation is where the news has to be given to someone that they are suffering from a serious condition from which they will shortly die, in which suffering will be intense or for which there is no cure. This is associated in the modern mind so closely with the diagnosis of cancer that this word has become a metaphor for the hopeless case. Even if many cancers are now curable (and there are many other threats to life), in some way we all dread such a diagnosis. New diseases like AIDS have added further dimensions to the fear. For outsiders, a window to this misery is offered by published accounts, like that by Quill and Townsend (1991) of an interview with a woman telling her that she had recently been infected by her partner with HIV disease; but whatever the condition, similar encounters can be found daily in every health service in every country. To be told this sort of news must be the ultimate horror; to have to do it as part of one's job falls not far short. 'Breaking bad news' seems like a euphemism: no wonder professionals are tempted not to tell the truth. As one of my young colleagues muttered as he walked away from a crying patient, after a long and thoughtful interview, 'I'm sure I didn't sign up for this dreadful sort of job.'

The dramatic should not demean the everyday. Many ordinary decisions can be as difficult. For the professional, when is the possibility of something serious, but unlikely, to be shared with the patient? Screening may unearth something abnormal, but unlikely to affect the patient's life: in a system where patients have access to their notes, how does a health-care worker record possible concerns or incidental findings in such a way as not to cause distress? What about children and families? The mistakes or illness of a colleague may pose dilemmas for health-care staff: when and what should others be told? Advocacy also has its problems: a professional may want to help, and may be asked to add medical weight to a situation where medicine has no expertise. The patient, uncertain about the professional's response, may himself chose to tell a lie to gain such backing. Such questions probe deeply not only into veracity in health care but also into views of the role, goals and boundaries of clinical work. In a multicultural society, it is more than likely that the patient or relatives may have expectations or perceptions which are different from those entertained by the professional. Such complexity may mean we are looking not for 'the best' but 'the better' or even 'the good enough' approach. Community care, public health, teaching, research and management will also all offer us examples where we may need guidelines, rules or principles, but also fine judgement.

Medical Paternalism Re-examined

In the face of such issues, it is not surprising that there has been a tradition within most societies that a doctor can and should withhold the truth under some circumstances. Although the reasoning behind this may be confused, some of the ideas here are too important to be abandoned without careful thought.

The most common confusion is the appeal to *uncertainty*. Because the living body cannot be taken apart, there is always an element of uncertainty about a medical diagnosis. Prognosis too may be based at best on statistics, at worst on well-informed guesswork, while the treatment plan can be judged only by reference to the assessment of others similarly afflicted and treated. Bringing such information together around one patient, when not only that person's future, but also their detailed physical and psychological make-up, their precise social circumstances and their reaction to the illness are largely unknown, means that an encounter can be like a clinical trial of one person. In such circumstances, recordings of interviews often seem like the blind leading the blind. There are so many questions unasked, in both directions. Lawrence Henderson's (1995) response encapsulates the confusion this causes. 'It is meaningless to speak of telling the truth, the whole truth and nothing but the truth to a patient . . . because it is . . . a sheer impossibility. Since telling the truth is impossible, there can be no sharp distinction between what is true and what is false.'

But here is our first point of clarity: such a statement confuses *truth*, as a concept, with *truthfulness*. We are concerned with a truthful exchange between people, not with abstract issues of metaphysics or epistemology. It is our intention which is all-important.

Sissela Bok (1978: 6) sets this out incisively: 'the moral question of whether you are lying or not is not settled by establishing the truth or falsity of what you say. In order to settle the question, we must know whether you intend your statement to mislead.'

Linked to the problem of uncertainty is the concern that *putting across a technical issue may be too difficult*. A patient, untrained in medicine or bioscience, simply cannot understand the issues; so, goes the argument, it's best not to try. The arrogance (or laziness) which lies behind this attitude undermines professional endeavour. Every skilled person who is at the interface with the public must be able to explain what they are up to. Medicine is a good deal less complex than many activities. To dress up simple ideas or uncertainties as mysteries is the sign of the charlatan. One of the key issues in medical ethics is the power gradient between a knowledgeable, confident and healthy professional and an uninformed, anxious and ill person seeking their help. There are risks of all sorts in that situation, from the temptation for the busy professional to take the speedy way, through to the frank abuse of someone who is helpless and in a position of trust. Thinkers since the Enlightenment have been concerned that the individual should be sovereign over her own affairs. Illness threatens a person's autonomy in a number of ways; by restricting her ability to take action, by preventing her being able to think clearly through what is facing her and perhaps by reducing her willpower and energy. The infantilizing effects of illness and health care add to this threat, just as do the temptations for a helper to take over inappropriately. Simply in procedural terms, allowing a doctor to touch requires a person to give consent, and proper consent requires appropriate information. In this line of thinking, enshrined in law in most countries, respecting the autonomy of competent patients requires that they be informed, and that the professional be honest with them in a way that they can understand, about what is wrong, what they are advised should be done and what the risks and prospects are.

It is interesting to reflect how the ethics of personal health care derives from those political concerns of the eighteenth and nineteenth centuries to protect the personal sphere from public intrusion. It is of course precisely because health care crosses this boundary that clear thinking and proper safeguards are in order. It is possible for debates about rising budgets and fears for the health of the next generation to press thinkers on both the welfarist left and the libertarian right to redraw these boundaries: and the arguments about preserving these boundaries need to be rehearsed (Shklar, 1989: 21–38). But it is also possible for a thoroughly respectful physician to take the view that, having crossed that boundary, in some sense she can now see what is best for a patient and the patient is 'better off not knowing'. It is easy to see how in some circumstances a person's life would not be enhanced, and might be ruined, by knowing that something bad lay round the corner which they did not expect. If respect for autonomy is important, so also are the duties to care and to avoid harming the patient. Although disease and illness may be major harms, so too may be anxiety: the person disabled not by disease but by fear of it is sadly common. But the argument that lies are justified to prevent anxiety carries its own rebuttal. The antidote to fear is not silence but open discussion. Sometimes in incurable illness, for instance, sharing of problems in this way is the only therapy on offer. Were trust to decline so that patients did not believe what was being said to them, not only reassurance but also genuine support during an illness would become impossible. We recorded (Higgs, 1982) a case of a woman lied to who wasted what remained of her life waiting for a recovery which could never come. This returns us to the crucial insights of the last paragraph. The presumption remains that competent people must be allowed to choose for themselves. If they do not have the information on which to base a choice, or even a realization that a choice is necessary at all, it seems hard not to see this in itself as a major harm. Of course, we are not crudely balancing harm versus benefit. We may be considering the balance of particular benefits and particular harms: Campbell and Higgs (1982: 83–97) showed how for different people apparently similar harms (or benefits) may have very different values. But in whatever respect the professional has crossed the boundary, and however well she has understood the patient's point of view, unless circumstances make this impossible, the person who should judge the patient's best interest should be the patient.

Examples of such different perspectives abound in clinical decisions at the end of life (Higgs, 1997) but may be even more important at the beginning of an illness. For instance, a very bright but chronically anxious young woman in her last year at school developed symptoms which her doctor thought most likely to be early indications of multiple sclerosis. He decided to share this with her parents, not the patient, because of her personality and the uncertainty of the diagnosis. The parents, although very upset, had high ambitions for her and postponed the discussion so that she would not be distressed during her university entrance exams. The young woman, turned down for life insurance, confronted the doctor who now felt unable to withhold the reason for the insurance company's attitude and the now probable diagnosis. Intensely angry with him and with her parents, the woman left home to live with a boyfriend and in the confusion became pregnant. Her neurological condition worsened dramatically. However difficult decisions might be in such tragic situations, the doctor's almost literally paternalistic initial action had set in train events which deprived the young patient of some of the only effective management strategies in an incurable medical condition – developing confidence in her own abilities to make wise choices about herself, and trust in those around her who could help.

Ethical Frameworks

This justification for dismissing medical secrecy derives its strength from the framework of biomedical principles (as laid out by Beauchamp and Childress, 1994, and by Gillon, 1994: xxi–xxxi), which in turn have their roots both in the duty-based thinking of Kant and in consequentialism, particularly J. S. Mill's utilitarianism. But naturally these two philosophical approaches differ in detail, since a strict deontologist would see being truthful as a primary duty, not to be negotiated, whereas consequentialists might well see other issues impinging on the decision. The same debate might well occur in the clinic or on the wards: is telling the truth an *absolute* duty, or are there occasions when a different approach is justified? Indeed, the acknowledgement of other principles, of beneficence, non-maleficence and justice, competing or requiring to be balanced with respect for autonomy, implies that there *is* this possibility, and may offer a way of resolving an issue. Given the prime importance of open communication between doctor and patient, it seems to place veracity at an inhumanely high level if *no* other considerations can ever be taken into account. Indeed, some have noted that a thoughtless 'dumping' of information on an unprepared person could become a harm in itself: certainly in a medical crisis where life hung in the balance (say, treating the sole survivor of a family just after an accident), there might well be an argument against adding the further stress of receiving tragic news. Absolutist approaches do not seem to express fully the nuances or necessities required in clinical practice. We should look at some of the other reactions against them.

Different Forms of Deception

Honesty can easily appear to have a two-dimensional, 'open and shut' feel to it; the 'tell or not tell' approach has a seductive simplicity, but it actually collapses together unhelpfully (and untruthfully?) the different forms of deception. There are situations in medicine, just as in other walks of life, where information may be withheld for good reasons. In clinical trials, for instance, an informed patient agrees to be kept in the dark; withholding information in other circumstances might be considered justified through arguments about acts and omissions, such as where the information arises as a side issue from other work – an isolated and unexpected abnormal test result in a clinical 'work up' for instance. Here professional competence suggests at least that the clinician should have checked and have some explanation of the result before sharing it with the patient. The philosopher Jennifer Jackson in her (1991) critique of my article (Higgs, 1985: 187–202), concludes that while clinicians have a prima facie duty not to lie, since there are also other forms of intentional deception which should not count as lies, professionals are not duty-bound to avoid these other forms. Further, she notes that by making an inviolable rule, we may be setting our sights too high. Doubting whether 'aiming for the best' is necessary or even intelligible, she suggests that in life in general as people we need the rule against lying 'just so as to get by – whatever particular further aims we happen to have in life. If the rule would still allow us to get by if certain departures were generally allowed, then the departures *can* be allowed. If the rule would only allow us to get by if certain departures were allowed, then the departures *must* be allowed.'

436

Communicating Outside Medicine

If courage to face up to unpleasant truths is required, it is needed more from patients than from professionals. We need to be reminded that outside medicine it would be a normal (and accepted) human reaction to avoid facing up to difficult questions. 'Human kind cannot bear very much reality' was T. S. Eliot's comment (1969: 172). A common argument against telling the truth is that it may destroy hope. For many of us, the hope is that we shall not be reminded of our mortality, rather than that we shall be able to make momentous decisions about our continuing lives. 'Getting by' may involve avoiding the big questions, rather than looking for truthful answers. Socrates thought that the unexamined life was not worth living, but he was by all accounts a remarkable man in every respect. Only the fortunate and gifted minority will have had opportunities to rehearse before it is their life itself which is really examined. It is a brave person who decides to look into the abyss, confronting the reality of their impending death. 'Bad news choosers' often choose to narrow the field of their choice. David Nyberg (1993) takes this one step further, by suggesting that deception is part of our nature, necessary to social life and personal stability as part of our daily lives. This he suggest extends not only to social 'white lies' but also to self-deceptions, which he sees as a mechanism for maintaining mental health in the face of stress.

All this is part of communicating with ourselves and with other people. There are verbal and non-verbal processes at work. People have feelings as well as thoughts, and these feelings may be mixed: ambiguity, the force behind so much great poetry, is also the currency of everyday conversation. Hints, inflection, 'telling' silences, are all part of this form of human intercourse. In the abstract a truth is a hard-edged, clear thing; it is either communicated or not. With this perspective honesty may almost feel like a measurable virtue, unlike, say, courage or prudence. But often in practice a truth, even if clearly delivered, is taken on by the hearer little by little, as Kübler-Ross (1970) points out: sometimes at first apparently not heard, or not fully understood, or initially denied.

All these things suggest that in health care at least *how* a truth is told may be as important as *what* it conveyed. This reminds us not to put unreal requirements on communications between doctors and patients, or to create rules so stringent or exacting that these become self-defeating. It is worth reminding ourselves at this point that although the studies of what patients (and would-be patients) wanted to know from their physicians indicate that the majority do wish to hear the truth about their condition, there is usually a minority, albeit a small one, who do not.

Context, Care and Culture

The absolutist position has come under fire from other directions. Iris Murdoch's call (1970) for further study of 'concerned responsiveness' or 'loving attention' to particular individuals as the basic moral coinage has been developed further (for example, by Blum, 1994). Martha Nussbaum (1990: 66–75) has taken Aristotelian practical reasoning to imply that the *particular*, in the sense of context and/or

437

relationship, should have priority, especially in reasserting the importance of a 'finely tuned concreteness in ethical attention and judgement'. Elsewhere (1986: 316) she talks about a 'flexible movement back and forth between particular and general'. Contextualizing decisions about honesty – talking to *this* person about *this* issue, *now* – may alter the balance of the decision-making. Certainly Nel Noddings (1984) in developing an ethics based on *care* rather than rule or principle, has developed an approach influential in nursing: as an educationalist, she gives an account of a lie from the 'one-caring' to enable the 'cared-for', in this case a child, to stay away from school. The context and the particular relationship indicate that the cardinal virtue at this point should be care for that individual, not a disassociated honesty.

Although these ideas are put forward in contrast to an approach through rules and principles, they may also be seen as another (and for some, more user-friendly) way of dealing with apparent conflict in these principles. But from a *cultural* perspective, human groups set priorities which move their members towards a resolution of these conflicts in a similar way. In some societies, for instance, kindness may be much more important than truthfulness. Veracity in medicine may run counter to deeper assumptions and rules in the society served: Alastair MacIntyre (1981) gives an example of Bantu parents bringing up their children not to tell the truth to strangers since they believe that this could make the group vulnerable to assault by witchcraft. Medical ethics has yet to come to terms with some of the ideas behind modern behavioural sciences (particularly from non-Anglophone thinkers), but it could be said that discussion of ethnic moral relativism says more about power and fear than about human freedom; and arguments derived from relativism in support of deception tell us more about the deficiencies of a particular society than the legitimate moral concerns of the individual within it. Nevertheless, these cultural effects would be felt in clinical context. But if that clinical context is seen in any sense as having a (generally accepted) culture *of its own*, we need to think how sense can be made of the undoubted importance of respecting people by telling the truth, while considering the undoubted importance of the critiques noted above.

One of Alastair MacIntyre's reminders (1967) is that we should put our thinking into historical perspective. Certainly at this time we are seeing great changes in the practice of scientific medicine, in the organization of health care and thus in the doctor–patient relationship too. When little could be done for a patient, in the modern curative sense, perhaps a powerful, mysterious and alien healer was important. Now the position is changing. Clinical relationships are becoming more equal, and potentially deeper. Not only does traditional paternalism reduce a person's autonomy, but it may also maintain someone in a patient role and threaten his recovery. It may be, in Illich's phrase, a 'sickening' process (Illich, 1975). So procedures that ensure that the truth be fully told may be as important a step in clinical care now as the development of asepsis was in surgery. Where a question is asked, it must be answered truthfully. But just as asepsis is not the overriding factor in, say, trauma at the roadside, in critical issues in truth-telling a relationship, a role or a particular context may be of crucial importance and may justify exceptions. Where the relationship changes or the context becomes less medical, clinicians and patients may have developed an open relationship, in which honesty may be part of something deeper.

References

Beauchamp, T. J. and Childress, J. F. (1994). *Principles of Biomedical Ethics*. New York: Oxford University Press.

Blum, I. A. (1994). *Moral Perception of Particularity*, Cambridge: Cambridge University Press.

Bok, S. (1978). *Lying: moral choice in public and private life*, New York: Pantheon.

Campbell, A. V. and Higgs, R. (1982). *In that Case: medical ethics in everyday practice*. London: Darton Longman and Todd.

Eliot, T. S. (1969). Four Quartets: Burnt Norton. In *The Complete Poems and Plays*. London: Faber and Faber.

Gillon, R. (1994). *Principles of Health Care Ethics*. Chichester: John Wiley.

Henderson, L. (1955). Physician and patient as social system. *New England Journal of Medicine*, 212.

Higgs, R. (1982). Truth at the last – a case of obstructed death? *Journal of Medical Ethics*, 8, 152–6.

—— (1985). On telling patients the truth. In M. Lockwood (ed.), *Moral Dilemmas in Modern Medicine*. Oxford: Oxford University Press, 187–202.

—— (1997). Shaping our ends: the ethics of respect in a well led NHS. *British Journal of General Practice*, 47, 245–9.

Illich, I. (1975). *Medical Nemesis: the expropriation of health*. London: Calder and Boyars.

Jackson, J. (1991). Telling the truth. *Journal of Medical Ethics*, 17, 5–9.

Kübler-Ross, E. (1970). *On Death and Dying*. London: Tavistock.

MacIntyre, A. (1967). *A Short History of Ethics*. London: Routledge and Kegan Paul.

—— (1981). *After Virtue*. London: Duckworth.

Murdoch, I. (1970). *The Sovereignty of Good*. London: Routledge and Kegan Paul.

Noddings, N. (1984). *Caring: a feminine approach to ethics and moral education*. Berkeley and Los Angeles: University of California Press.

Nussbaum, M. C. (1986). *The Fragility of Goodness: Luck and ethics in Greek tragedy and philosophy*. Cambridge: Cambridge University Press.

—— (1990). *Love's Knowledge: essays on philosophy and literature*. New York: Oxford University Press.

Nyberg, D. (1993). *The Varnished Truth: truth telling and deceiving in ordinary life*. Chicago: University of Chicago Press.

Quill, T. E. and Townsend, P. (1991). Bad news: delivery, dialogue and dilemmas. *Archives of Internal Medicine*, 151, 463–8.

Shklar, N. (1989). The liberalism of fear. In N. L. Rosenblum (ed.), *Liberalism and the Moral Life*. Cambridge, MA: Harvard University Press.

Further Reading

Beauchamp, T. L. and Walters, L. (1994). *Comtemporary Issues in Bioethics*. Belmont, CA: Wadsworth.

Brody, H. (1992). *The Healer's Power*. New Haven: Yale University Press.

Hattori, H. et al. (1991). The patient's right to information in Japan – legal rules and doctors opinions. *Social Science and Medicine*, 32, 1007–16.

439

Kerr, P. (ed.) (1990). *The Penguin Book of Lies*. London: Viking Penguin.

Reich, W. T. (ed.) (1978). *Encyclopaedia of Bioethics*. New York: Free Press.

Sontag, S. (1978). *Illness as a Metaphor*. New York: Farrer, Straus and Giroux.

Veatch, R. M. (1977). *Case Studies in Medical Ethics*. Cambridge MA: Harvard University Press.

Zeldin, T. (1994). *An Intimate History of Humanity*. London: Minerva.

42

Informed consent and patient autonomy

ROBERT YOUNG

Though the doctrine of informed consent is largely a creation of various court judgements about the health care provided to specific patients, and of the establishment of regulatory standards in connection with medical experimentation, it rests ultimately on a moral foundation. I will first set out that moral foundation; second, highlight some of the landmarks in the development of the legal form of the doctrine; and third, note the exceptions to the doctrine. (For discussion of the giving of informed consent by patients who are at the same time subjects of medical research see chapter 36, pp. 379–89.)

The Moral Foundation

An autonomous or self-determining person is someone who chooses or devises a plan for her life, rather than having one imposed on her by others or allowing circumstances to dictate one, and proceeds to live in accordance with that plan. It should be noted that, in using the term 'plan', I do not have in mind anything like a blueprint. People's life plans can be, and indeed are, subject to revision over time, and occasionally far-reaching revision at that. What is certainly implied by my characterization is that an autonomous person does not merely make choices and decisions about major concerns such as career, lifestyle and fundamental values, but is actively involved in shaping and directing her life so as to realize those choices and decisions (Young, 1986; Brock, 1987; Dworkin, 1988). The following oft-cited remarks of Isaiah Berlin convey very clearly the way in which champions of autonomy consider it to be foundational to our moral agency:

> I wish my life and decisions to depend on myself, not on external forces of whatever kind. I wish to be the instrument of my own, not of other men's, acts of will. I wish to be a subject, not an object; to be moved by reasons, by conscious purposes, which are my own, not by causes which affect me, as it were, from outside. I wish to be somebody, not nobody; a doer – deciding, not being decided for, self-directed and not acted upon by external nature or by other men as if I were a thing, or an animal, or a slave . . . I wish, above all, to be conscious of myself as a thinking, willing, active being, bearing responsibility for my choices and able to explain them by references to my own ideas and purposes. (Berlin, 1969: 131)

441

In a health-care setting, when a patient exercises her autonomy she decides which of the options for dealing with her health-care problem (including having no treatment at all) will be best for her, given her particular values, concerns and goals. A patient who makes autonomous choices about her health care is able to opt for what she considers will be best for her, all things considered. To uphold the importance in health care of obtaining a person's informed consent is to recognize the value of patient autonomy. The seriousness of the recognition is tested, however, whenever a patient autonomously decides on a course of action which runs counter to the judgement made by her health-care advisers about what would be *medically best* for her. For most of the time during which a clinical approach to health care has been taken, the idea has prevailed that health-care practitioners should act so as to do the best for their patients, where doing the best for them was understood in the narrow sense of doing what was medically best. Even if to achieve this it was necessary to deny the patient the information she needed to make an informed choice, it was considered to be in her interests to do so. This practice of paternalism in relation to health care effectively placed a person's interest in her health ahead of her interest in deciding for herself what would be best for her, all things considered.

Now it is, of course, true that autonomy is not the only thing of value, and also true that other values, including those of a person's health and well-being, may sometimes take precedence over autonomy. But if the idea so forcefully expressed in the passage cited earlier from Isaiah Berlin is accepted, that a person's interest in self-determination simply reflects her concern to make important decisions about her own life in accordance with her own aims and values, paternalism in relation to health care should be rejected as long as a patient is able to give her informed consent to a health-care procedure (or to withhold it).

For a patient to be capable of giving informed consent she must be competent, must understand the information disclosed to her and must give (or withhold) her consent freely. I shall elaborate on each of these features in turn. First, it is a working assumption that a normal adult is competent to make judgements about her health care in that she is able to make decisions that reflect her concern for her own well-being (Brock, 1987: 110ff; Dworkin, 1988: 112f; Buchanan and Brock, 1989: chapter 1). Where a person proposes to pursue a course of action which seems likely to have an adverse effect on her well-being, the question will arise as to whether she should (paternalistically) be prevented from pursuing such a course. The effects of injury, illness or medication can increase the probability that a patient will make choices that appear unbalanced and so call into question her competence to make decisions about her health care. This, typically, will occur when a patient's choice about how to proceed is at odds with that of her health-care practitioner. But disagreement as such cannot be taken to signify that the patient is incompetent.

Suppose, for example, an active sportswoman decides, against medical advice, to be given analgesics after an operation intravenously, rather than by means of an epidural, because she wishes to avoid the remote risk of being left paralysed. Here, even though we may presume that the epidural would be medically more efficacious or result in less discomfort, it is clear that because the patient accords great significance to her sporting aspirations there is no reason to doubt the competence of her judgement as to what will be best for her, all things considered. Even cases where life-sustaining treatment is refused do not show that a patient lacks competence. An adult Jehovah's Witness, for example, may competently refuse a life-preserving blood transfusion even though such a refusal is tantamount to accepting death.

To simplify matters, let us assume for the moment that the other elements in informed consent, namely the patient's being informed and choosing freely, are satisfied. Then the following principle is one that should be honoured: in the absence of a reason (and the fact that a patient holds a different view from her health-care advisers on the management of her case is not on its own a reason) for thinking that injury, illness or medication has robbed her of her competence, a patient's decisions about her health care shall be binding. Though this principle may seem very strong it certainly should not be read as precluding care-givers from making reasonable attempts to persuade patients about alternative measures, or even of transferring the case to another practitioner where acceding to the patient's wishes would necessitate a violation of the care-giver's conscience. What it does preclude is a paternalistic overruling of a competent patient's wishes or the paternalistic use of deception to bring about a change of mind on the part of the patient.

The second element in informed consent, the patient's capacity to understand and appraise the information with which she is provided, has perhaps been the most contentious of the three elements. Often health-care practitioners have wished to emphasize the aspect of *disclosure* rather than the patient's *understanding*, the latter being obviously harder to determine. Such a stance makes greatest sense if the concern is to maximize patient sovereignty, since a patient who has been provided with information can exercise her sovereign choice prudently or otherwise. But, if the requirement for informed consent is to be taken seriously, it is the patient's understanding that should occupy centre stage since, at the extreme, failure on the part of the patient to understand the information she has been given, effectively vitiates her choice. For that reason alone the practitioner has an obligation to strive to promote understanding. (For a more comprehensive discussion of the criteria of understanding and some suggestions on ways of satisfying those criteria see Faden and Beauchamp, 1986: chapter 9.)

There is some resistance, even among those health-care practitioners who declare themselves to be opposed to paternalism in health care, to the position which I have just outlined. Sometimes the resistance is grounded in a conviction that health-care professionals, just because they are health-care professionals, bring certain values to their practice that necessarily influence the way in which information is provided to patients. At its crudest this may amount to presupposing that, for instance, more of life is better than less, and so informing patients only about procedures which would lengthen life. What makes this so crude is that it is simply not unqualifiedly true that more of life is better than less – for some patients the truth is quite the opposite.

There is, however, a more subtle idea that can ground the resistance some health-care professionals have to seeing themselves as obligated to ensure that competent patients understand such information as is material to their health and its management. Consider the fact that the way in which information is 'framed', as psychologists say, determines its significance for those (here, patients) to whom it is provided. Thus, for example, if procedures are spelled out in terms of the probability of their resulting in death, rather than the probability of their extending life, there will be a marked difference in the way people evaluate the alternatives. (For references to the psychological literature and discussion see Savulescu, 1995: 328f. Cf., as well, Wear, 1993, especially chapter 6, for a sensitive treatment of related issues.) From this it might be thought that since the values of health-care practitioners will influence the ways in which they frame information to patients, it is unrealistic to think that they can at the same time meet an obligation to promote understanding on the part of patients who do not share similar values. This is most dramatically illustrated in cases where a competent patient who, therefore, is not deficient in her capacity to make decisions for herself, refuses recommended life-sustaining therapy or seeks her doctor's assistance to bring about death. If the obligation to promote the kind of understanding needed for informed consent is to be taken seriously, the practitioner must alert the patient to the values underlying the framing of the information provided. If, having endeavoured to do so, the practitioner cannot rationally dissuade the patient from her chosen course, the practitioner must (as mentioned previously) either withdraw from the case or accept the patient's choice as binding, no matter that it appears mistaken to the practitioner.

To satisfy the third requirement for informed consent, consent must be given freely. If 'consent' is given as a result of coercion or manipulation, or is subject to undue influence, it cannot be considered a genuine authorization even if the patient is fully informed and fully understands. Still, a patient's consent is only likely to be unfreely given as a result of the actions of a health-care practitioner if the information provided to the patient is manipulated. (The manipulation of such information need not be conscious, malevolent or devious for the patient's consent to be unfreely given. Indeed, were a health-care practitioner deliberately to manipulate information, that would affect the consent of even apparently fully informed patients.) With paternalism increasingly out of favour even if not totally rejected everywhere, the likelihood of patients being coerced or subjected to undue influence has been lowered, albeit not eliminated. However, it is not at all unlikely that information might be provided to the patient in a way which will lead to the patient choosing as the practitioner would wish (cf. Brock, 1987: 119). Coercion, or undue influence, by third parties, is another matter altogether. A patient's family, in particular, may well pressure a patient into deciding on a course of action she does not favour. Be this as it may, it is likely that for the purposes of the law it is only when the actions of a health-care practitioner undermine the voluntariness of a patient's choice that there will be any thought of seeking a legal remedy.

If consent is freely given by a competent patient on the basis of an informed understanding, then the moral requirement to respect that person's autonomous decision is satisfied. But it is well to remember that the requirement is one of relatively recent origin (not only in the context of interest to us, health care, but also in others, such as consumer protection). The most important contributions to the formulation of the doctrine of informed consent have, in fact, been made this century and then chiefly in the law. In particular, it is to developments in the law of torts that we must look, if we are to understand the process by which we have reached the present requirement in various jurisdictions for obtaining informed consent from patients. That is not to suggest that there is a single and settled legal position which holds wherever the requirement has come to be recognized. But there have been a number of landmark cases, especially in the English-speaking world, which have contributed greatly to our present understanding of the doctrine. So, while it must be acknowledged that the following discussion is narrowly based as regards the social, political and legal settings from which the cases referred to are drawn, it will provide us with insight into why informed consent has come to be a moral and legal requirement in much of the world, and why there is agitation for it to be so elsewhere.

The Legal Requirement for Consent in Therapeutic Settings

The right of individual self-determination has been the basis for court findings in favour of the informed consent of competent patients to health-care procedures. If competent people have the right of self-determination then, at the very least, they must be able to claim protection against interference with their bodies, including within the health-care practitioner (especially doctor) – patient relationship. Once that is acknowledged, medical judgement and practice cannot be viewed simply in terms of the practitioner acting beneficently (for the good of the patient). For the practitioner not to acknowledge and respect the autonomy of the patient constitutes 'assault and battery'. Such a view was eloquently stated in the judgment of Justice Cardozo in the 1914 American case of *Schloendorff v. Society of New York Hospitals* when finding that surgery ought not have been performed on the patient who had agreed to an abdominal examination under anaesthesia, but had specifically refused an operation. Cardozo declared that 'Every human being of adult years and sound mind has a right to determine what shall be done with his own body; and a surgeon who performs an operation without his patient's consent commits an assault, for which he is liable in damages' [211 N.Y. 128, 105 N.E. 93].

Because it so clearly articulated the central importance of patient self-determination the *Schloendorff* judgement has been seen as critical to the development of the legal doctrine of informed consent. But, in truth, there were quite a few judgements in the early part of this century which made appeal to a patient's right not to be touched without prior consent. In some there was also recognition of the fact that in order to exercise self-determination a patient has to weigh the dangers and risks of surgery, or other medical interventions, against the anticipated benefits. That being so, it makes sense to see later case law as having made more explicit the need not only for consent to be given, but for information to be disclosed to the patient in such a way that the patient's consent can be informed. Hence, the

445

development of the legal doctrine of informed consent has gone hand in hand with the establishment of a duty of disclosure for health-care professionals (though not one of ensuring understanding).

Oddly, the judgement in the American case that is perhaps best known for introducing the phrase 'informed consent', by being the first to insist on the need for it, namely *Salgo v. Leland Stanford Jr University Board of Trustees*, highlights a problem about just what the legal duty of disclosure requires. In *Salgo*, a patient, who had undergone a treatment (which is no longer used) involving puncturing the aorta through the back in order to inject a radio-opaque dye, was left with permanent paralysis of the legs. According to the direction given to the jury 'the physician has . . . discretion [to withhold alarming information from the patient] consistent, of course, with the full disclosure of facts necessary to an informed consent' [317 P.2d 170 (Cal. Ct. App., 1957)].

It is obvious that the direction given to the jury was confused. There simply cannot be any discretion to withhold some information if *full* disclosure is required (Katz. 1984: 60ff). Nevertheless, *Salgo* did highlight the issue of the extent and nature of disclosure required to facilitate informed patient consent even if, for reasons of practicality, disclosure can never be entire and complete. Some subsequent cases were resolved by courts requiring only that disclosure conform to the 'professional practice standard', namely what a reasonable health-care practitioner would do under similar circumstances. To do any less, it was held, would be tantamount to negligence. In other cases, however, such as the landmark US case *Canterbury v. Spence*, in which the patient suffered major paralysis after undergoing a laminectomy, a relatively rare outcome from the operation of which the patient had not been warned, the professional practice standard was held to be inadequate and was replaced by a patient-centred 'reasonable person standard' (Faden and Beauchamp, 1986: 134). By replacing the professional practice standard with a reasonable person standard – in effect, what any reasonable patient would consider it material to know (as against what it might be customary for professionals to disclose) – the court was clearly signalling the right of a self-determining patient to weigh risks and benefits for herself. Given that she would have to make her decision as a lay person, not as a health-care practitioner, the appropriate standard to apply must be the reasonable person standard. The move also had the advantage of overcoming problems occasioned by agreed professional standards being set too low to satisfy the demands of patients for information, of there being no agreed standard for new procedures, and patients being disadvantaged by having to rely upon expert witnesses (normally health-care practitioners) to establish the standard of care (Appelbaum, Lidz and Meisel, 1987: 42f).

By opting for a reasonable person standard, courts were, in reality, demanding of health-care practitioners that they made a greater effort to get patients to participate in decision-making about their own health care, something we have already seen to be morally required. But the courts have never imposed the yet stronger requirement that practitioners must disclose (without qualification or restriction) whatever might come to be considered. To require such a standard would be manifestly unreasonable. The court would have to find for the patient because only the patient's word could settle the matter as to whether she would have consented had she been adequately informed.

We have been considering the evolutionary development of the common law's attempt to protect the autonomy of patients by requiring that health-care professionals satisfy certain standards of disclosure. The standards were developed to help in the determination of whether a particular health-care practitioner (the defendant) had adequately informed the patient (the plaintiff). They were not developed to provide advice for practitioners on what to tell their patients. While case law is about obtaining redress, there has been some legislation in the last couple of decades which has been directed towards the latter task. By putting the judicial opinions and legislative enactments together it is possible to provide guidelines on what has to be disclosed. The so-called *elements* of disclosure needed for informed patient consent can be summarized as involving: the nature of the proposed procedure, its risks, the alternatives to the procedure (including that of not treating) and the benefits of the procedure (Appelbaum, Lidz and Meisel, 1987: 49ff). I shall say a little more about each of these.

The nature of the procedure

Patients should be advised whether a procedure is merely diagnostic or is intended to be therapeutic, given that ordinarily they seek help for the relief of suffering. Other aspects of the procedure which it is considered should be disclosed are whether it is invasive (i.e., involves physically entering some part of the body) and, if so, what part of the body will be entered; what effect, if any, there will be on the part of the body; how long the procedure will take; whether an anaesthetic will be needed; whether an X-ray or scan will be needed; and whether the procedure is experimental.

The risks of the procedure

The nature of the risks associated with a procedure has been the element most emphasized in the courts. While it has to be borne in mind that disclosure of risks is only a necessary not a sufficient condition for obtaining informed consent, patients do need to know about what kinds of risks they face, how likely it is that the risks will eventuate, the effects they would have and when they would occur, if they did eventuate. Of course, these features won't always matter equally for all patients, but it is to be left to the patient to determine how much they matter. Age, life expectancy and occupation are three obvious considerations which could bear directly on how material a risk is to a particular patient.

How likely it is that a risk will eventuate is clearly of importance to a patient. But many practitioners appear to believe that if something (even something serious) is very unlikely to occur, there is no need to disclose the possibility. The finding in a recent court case in Australia (where, as in many other places outside the United States, there had hitherto been a notable reluctance to override a reasonable professional standard in favour of a reasonable patient standard), shows that such a belief is out of step with contemporary ideas about patient autonomy. In *Rogers v.*

447

Whitaker [175 CLR 479 (1992)] the plaintiff, who went to the defendant ophthalmic surgeon for a routine procedure on her bad right eye (in which she had little sight because of a childhood accident), ended up losing the sight in her good left eye as well, as a result of a condition known as sympathetic ophthalmia. Evidence was given that there was a 1 in 14,000 chance of such a result. The plaintiff, unaware of this risk, did not ask about it (although she was insistent about knowing of any risks to her good eye), and the defendant did not inform her of it (though he was aware that it was a remote risk). The High Court of Australia, in finding for the plaintiff, held that where even a fairly remote risk is considered by a patient to be material to her decision about whether to agree to a procedure, she should be advised of that risk so as to be able to exercise her autonomy.

It is important, too, for a patient to know when, if ever, a risk may materialize. The patient can then assess how much weight to put on its possible occurrence. Finally, in addition to disclosing the more serious of the risks to which a patient is likely to be exposed, a health-care practitioner needs to disclose lesser risks and even commonly known risks. As regards the former, it is very important that lesser risks be disclosed, if only because some states represent 'a fate worse than death' for certain patients. As regards the latter, if a reasonable person standard is to apply, health-care practitioners ought to be able to assume that a competent patient knows what a reasonable person could be expected to know.

The alternatives, if any, to the procedure

Where there are other procedures that might be offered to a patient than the one preferred by the health-care practitioner it is important those alternatives be disclosed. As we saw earlier, once it is acknowledged that patients have other interests than their health interests, health-care practitioners are obligated not simply to decide (beneficently) what would be best for the patient. A surgeon's preferred strategy might not coincide with the patient's simply because the patient may wish to give weight to non-medical considerations. (Consider, famously, the way that women have not always been advised of alternative, less disfiguring approaches to breast cancer than radical mastectomy.) It is particularly important that alternatives be discussed when the practitioner's preferred strategy comes down to personal taste (cf. the significance of this consideration in relation to, for example, some procedures in obstetrics like episiotomies and Caesarean sections), or where the professional is not able to offer or perform an alternative procedure.

Benefits of the procedure

Usually if the first three elements have been properly dealt with it will not be necessary to spell out the benefits of the proposed procedure, such as its relieving suffering of one sort or another. However, where the procedure is experimental or where there is reason to think that the suffering will not be fully relieved, the patient needs to know of these things in order to assess the worthwhileness of undergoing the proposed procedure.

These, then, are the four elements in which adequate disclosure consists. But, to reiterate a point previously made, though many practitioners have wished to focus on disclosure, and the courts have frequently appeared content to grant that wish, adequacy of disclosure is only a necessary condition for obtaining informed consent. There can be no truly informed consent without an accurate understanding of what has been disclosed. The need for both disclosure by the practitioner and understanding on the part of the patient shows that informed consent involves the participation of both, even if it is the patient's understanding that is ultimately the more critical. What this entails is that we should insist that a patient understands the nature, risks and benefits of the procedures she is to undergo; this, in turn, will have implications for both institutional practices for obtaining informed consent and for the sort of evidence which might be tendered in a civil court to support a health-care practitioner's belief that a patient did understand information material to her treatment.

The Exceptions

I turn now to the final matter I flagged for discussion, namely the exceptions to the requirement of obtaining informed consent from competent patients. These exceptions have been well set out elsewhere (Meisel, 1979; Appelbaum, Lidz and Meisel, 1987), so I can be brief. There are three kinds of exception to which I shall draw attention: waiver; therapeutic privilege; and emergency.

I have insisted that disclosure of information does not exhaust the idea of informed consent. It is necessary, in addition, that the patient understand and that consent be obtained. The two aspects are required if there is to be genuine participation by patients in health-care decision-making. They are, however, prone to come apart in exceptional circumstances. Consider the situation with a waiver: if a patient has a right to waive disclosure of information she should not be put in a position where she thinks she ought to exercise that right because her health-care practitioner would prefer things that way. We saw earlier that patients can be manipulated into adopting views that have that effect. So while it can be a legitimate exercise of a patient's autonomy for her to waive her right to disclosure, and advice should, therefore, be given to that effect, it would seem best that practitioners not initiate discussions about the exercise of a waiver if they wish to avoid any suggestion of manipulation. Despite their being compatible with respect for a patient's autonomy, waivers should, none the less, be regarded with some scepticism. A patient who is frightened of, or in denial about, her illness may need to be encouraged by her health-care practitioner to reflect openly and fully on the illness rather than resort to waiving her right to participate in the determination of suitable treatment. Further, patients may sometimes waive their right because of a mistaken belief that the practitioner is the one with the relevant expertise and so should make the treatment decisions, when those decisions cannot properly be made without reference to the patient's own values and aspirations. That is not to say that there won't be patients who are made anxious, depressed or confused by having to make decisions about their health care and who, therefore, rightly exercise their waiver. But to limit the risk of well-intentioned misuses of the right of patients to waive making their own decisions, it seems advisable for practitioners, at least at the beginning, to treat waivers sceptically (cf. Wear, 1993: 140ff).

Larger issues arise with the idea of therapeutic privilege. According to this idea, a health-care practitioner may withhold information which would otherwise have to be disclosed if it is judged that it would be likely to lead to harm to the patient were that done. There is a risk that where a practitioner thinks a patient's refusal of treatment is likely to prove harmful that therapeutic privilege may be invoked. This would jeopardize the autonomy of the patient. It would seem best, therefore, initially at least, to set the boundaries for the invocation of therapeutic privilege by reference to whether a patient has competently decided on a course of action, not by reference to whether such a course would probably be harmful. (Related issues are treated in chapters 26 and 27, pp. 261–79.) Some who advocate securing a place for therapeutic privilege urge it in a relatively weak form, namely as defensible where disclosure of *risks* would be likely to lead to harmful consequences (e.g., such as triggering an independent health risk or exacerbating the one being treated). Indeed, such a view was put in the case of *Canterbury v. Spence* mentioned previously. There it was claimed (in relation to disclosure of risks) that 'it is recognized that patients occasionally become so ill or emotionally distraught on disclosure as to foreclose a rational decision' [464 F. 2d 772 (D.C. Cir. 1972) at 789].

With patients already in a vulnerable state because of illness or injury, to entertain a stronger version of therapeutic privilege would surely have the effect not only of jeopardizing patient autonomy but also of making it hard to maintain trust between practitioners and their patients (cf. Dworkin, 1988: 120).

Finally, there is the issue of how to proceed in an emergency. In some emergencies patients will lack competence to consent to any procedure, in others there will be no time to disclose what would be required to achieve informed consent. In the absence of an advance directive, it will be necessary in cases like these to make an exception to the requirement of obtaining informed consent. However, it is plausible to claim that, since reasonable patients would want help in an emergency, especially where a serious risk of mortality or morbidity is involved, the reasonable patient standard is normally not violated when aid is given to, say, an unconscious person.

But matters are much less clear in two other sorts of circumstance (cf. Wear, 1993: 137ff). Consider the use of aggressive life-prolonging treatment in emergency situations involving patients whose death is known to be imminent. In emergencies of this sort it will often not be appropriate to proceed to give such treatment. These cases highlight the importance of holding discussions beforehand with patients at risk. A second troublesome sort of circumstance arises where enough can be disclosed to an apparently still competent patient to make it possible at least to obtain consent to the emergency procedures, even though the consent would not be as well-informed as would otherwise be warranted. While it might seem that to endeavour to obtain such a consent has the merit of seeking to honour the idea of giving a patient the maximum feasible say in what happens to her body, it is doubtful that it is a wise way to proceed. To begin with, though the patient may be competent (despite, perhaps, suffering from shock or loss of blood) her choice will not be a *well-informed* one. Moreover, there is a chance that a patient in such circumstances may, because she lacks adequate information, refuse the emergency procedure. If her refusal to consent is to be taken seriously, treatment would have to be withheld until further discussion, and perhaps even counselling, have taken place. Since that would not be appropriate in an emergency, just to ignore her refusal would make a mockery of the process of seeking her consent. The conclusion to be drawn is that the emergency exception better honours the requirement to obtain informed consent.

References

Appelbaum, P., Lidz, C. and Meisel, A. (eds) (1987). *Informed Consent: Legal theory and clinical practice*. New York. Oxford University Press.

Berlin, I. (1969). *Four Essays on Liberty*. Oxford. Clarendon Press.

Brock, D. (1987). Informed consent. In T. Regan and D. Van De Veer (eds), *Health Care Ethics*. Philadelphia: Temple University Press, 98–126.

Buchanan, A. and Brock, D. (1989). *Deciding for Others: The ethics of surrogate decision making*. New York: Cambridge University Press.

Dworkin, G. (1988). *The Theory and Practice of Autonomy*. New York: Cambridge University Press.

Faden, R. and Beauchamp, T. L. (1986). *A History and Theory of Informed Consent*. New York: Oxford University Press.

Katz, J. (1984). *The Silent World of Doctor and Patient*. New York: Free Press.

Meisel, A. (1979). The 'exceptions' to the informed consent doctrine: striking a balance between competing values in medical decision-making. *Wisconsin Law Review*. 79, 413–88.

Savulescu, J. (1995). Rational non-interventional paternalism: why doctors ought to make judgements of what is best for their patients. *Journal of Medical Ethics*, 21, 327–31.

Wear, S. (1993). *Informed Consent: Patient autonomy and physician beneficence within clinical medicine*. Dordrecht: Kluwer.

Young, R. (1986). *Personal Autonomy: Beyond negative and positive liberty*. London: Croom Helm.

43

Patients doubtfully capable or incapable of consent

CARL ELLIOTT

If the concept of autonomy has played the starring role in the development of bioethics, then the problems of non-autonomous patients have been its supporting cast. For better or worse, the way bioethics has come to see the problems of incompetent and marginally competent patients has been coloured by the way it has seen the problems of competent, autonomous adults. The rights of competent adults were the focus of a considerable amount of the earliest work in bioethics – issues surrounding informed consent, for example, or the patient's right to refuse life-sustaining medical treatment. Moreover, quite a lot of this work got its start in the individualistic, rights-conscious United States. Given this background, it should be no surprise that incompetent patients have presented bioethics with some of its most troubling ethical problems, and that the field is still struggling to find a conceptual framework in which to consider them.

Indeed, the very fact that all incompetent and marginally competent patients are often lumped together in the same category says something about the way the field has evolved. It is only in contrast to more commonly agreed-upon attitudes towards competent patients that incompetence comes to be identified as a morally distinctive feature. Yet identifying it as the most morally relevant feature about a patient downplays the fact that incompetent and marginally competent patients comprise a vastly diverse range of human beings who present very different ethical problems. From an ethical point of view, an anencephalic, a 65-year-old woman with Alzheimer's disease, a violent man with schizophrenia and a 6-year-old with incurable lymphoma are probably divided by more than they share. Not only do different incompetent patients present different ethical problems, they occupy radically different places in our moral and emotional lives. We generally think of children, for example, in ways very different from the ways we think of incompetent adults. While our attitudes towards adults are often centred on respect for the patient's previous values and the narrative of her past life, our moral attitudes towards children are commonly located within notions of dependence, protection, growth and the child's relationship to her parents.

452

Many of the ethical problems associated with paediatrics have developed in situations where there is a divergence between the attitudes of parents and health-care workers towards the care of a child. For example, parents of religious faiths such as the Jehovah's Witnesses or Christian Scientists often have moral and religious objections to certain medical treatments for their children in situations where health-care workers (in agreement with broader Western society) generally regard the treatments as medically necessary for a child's well-being. More generally, conflicts between parents and health-care workers arise over the use of life-sustaining medical interventions such as cardiopulmonary resuscitation, mechanical ventilation or artificial nutrition. Physicians sometimes undertake interventions on a severely ill or disabled child, for example, that the child's parents see as excessively burdensome. On the other hand, parents sometimes demand interventions that physicians see as futile. Some of the starkest conflicts have come with anencephalics or children in a persistent vegetative state whose parents want treatment pursued, regardless of the poor prognosis, out of a belief that even unconscious life should be protected and preserved. In neonatology, such conflicts between parents and health-care workers are complicated still further, because aggressive medical interventions on premature, severely ill or disabled newborns often must be undertaken under conditions of grave uncertainty (Arras. 1984). The outcomes for such newborns often span a great range, from a full cure and normal development, to life with severe mental and physical disability, to death after prolonged and burdensome treatment.

Problems surrounding aggressive or life-sustaining medical treatment also arise for incompetent adults, and often centre around conflicts between the opinions of health-care workers, the patient's previously expressed wishes about treatment and the wishes of various members of the patient's family. Yet the care of incompetent and marginally competent adults has also raised a much broader range of questions. Psychiatrists deal with a number of relatively specialized ethical questions about the care of mentally ill persons, many of which intersect with legal issues: questions about the conditions under which a psychiatric patient accused of wrongdoing is competent to stand trial, or when a psychiatrist is justified in breaching confidentiality, and when he has a duty to warn the victims of a potentially violent patient. Psychiatrists must also consider the question of when it is justifiable to confine or treat an incompetent or marginally competent patient against his (incompetent) expressed wishes – for instance, with antipsychotic drugs, or less commonly, with electroconvulsive therapy. The fact that many mentally ill and disabled patients live in long-term care institutions raises many questions of its own, such as the effects of institutionalization on the quality of informed consent.

While there is still fierce debate on many of these issues, over the past decade or two a fairly broad consensus has emerged in the bioethics literature about two questions that are relevant to many incompetent patients: how competence should be assessed, and how decisions should be made for patients who are incompetent. What I will do here is outline the standard approaches to these questions, and then point out several of the problems that they leave unanswered or unasked.

The Standard Models of Competence and Surrogate Decision-making

Competence (or decision-making capacity, as some writers prefer to call it) is conventionally defined as the ability to perform a task – here, to make decisions about one's medical care, or about taking part in biomedical research (Faden and Beauchamp, 1986: 290). Competent patients, it is widely agreed, generally have the right to make their own health-care decisions, even decisions that others believe are contrary to the patient's interests. However, as a result of illness, disability or immaturity, some patients do not have the mental abilities required to make these decisions. If given the opportunity, many of these patients would make decisions that are risky, dangerous or which they simply would not otherwise make if they were thinking soundly. Assessments of competence protect incompetent patients from the consequences of such decisions, while also protecting the rights of competent patients to make decisions for themselves.

Most writers agree that what is most important for judging competence is how patients reach their decisions, rather than what they decide. Merely because a patient reaches a conclusion that his physician regards as unreasonable – say, refusing effective treatment for a life-threatening illness, or deciding to enrol in a risky research protocol – does not mean that the patient is incompetent. Since different patients have different values and needs, they may reach different conclusions even when presented with the same choice. While it is a matter of debate exactly what mental abilities are necessary for competence, many standards require that a patient have a relatively stable set of goals and values, be capable of understanding the consequences of the decision, including its risks and benefits, and be able to appreciate how the decision will affect them personally (President's Commission Report, 1983; Gutheil and Appelbaum, 1982).

Often patients are clearly not competent, but their families and physicians must still make decisions for them (Buchanan and Brock, 1989). For these patients a hierarchy of decision-making standards has evolved, based largely on commonly held notions of respect for persons. First, when patients have expressed any wishes about the treatment in question while competent (through an advance directive, for example) their surrogate decision-makers should abide by those wishes. Second, when incompetent persons have not expressed any such wishes, surrogates should rely on the 'substituted judgement' standard, according to which decisions are reached according to what patients would have decided if they were able, based on the patients' values, goals and desires. Finally, in the event that a patient has never been competent – a small child, for example – the surrogate must make decisions based on the 'best interests standard'. What the interests of a patient are is often unclear or controversial, but they are generally understood to include, at a minimum, certain basic interests such as avoiding pain and disability and having conscious life extended.

454

The problem of competent irrationality

Some patients understand all the important aspects of their decision, including its risks and benefits, yet still make decisions that seem irrational (Brock and Wartman, 1990). Sometimes these decisions are irrational even from the perspective of the patient's own goals and desires. For example, an apparently competent diabetic patient being asked to consent to the amputation of a gangrenous toe might refuse, even if avoiding death is more important to him than avoiding the amputation, and even if he realizes that his refusal is threatening his life. What are we to make of such a choice? Doctors and nurses, not to mention family members, are understandably reluctant to abide by a patient's decision when that decision is irrational, especially if it is also self-destructive. Yet irrationality is a part of ordinary life. At times we all deceive ourselves, take poor risks, make impulsive decisions, act out of fear or anxiety, downplay future risks or benefits in favour of present ones and otherwise behave in ways that seem unreasonable, idiosyncratic or odd. Should an irrational decision be given the same degree of respect as a rational decision?

A related problem revolves around the question of which mental abilities are relevant to competence, and how high the threshold for competence should be set. For instance, the decisions of children may be influenced by the views of their parents or by other factors to such an extent that a clinician might reasonably question whether that decision is truly the child's own. A 12-year-old child of parents who are Jehovah's Witnesses may refuse a life-saving blood transfusion, and further, may appear capable of understanding both the religious reasons why Jehovah's Witnesses regard blood transfusions as morally wrong and the brute medical facts relevant to that decision. Yet it may still be unclear whether the child's refusal is competent. This is partly because it is unclear where the point lies at which a child's decision becomes truly authentic and autonomous, and partly because it is unclear what sort of factors should cause one to question a child's competence. Some clinicians might see fear, guilt and the influence of the child's parents as reasons to question a child's competence, while others would see them as parts of ordinary decision-making.

A related problem arises for adult patients with severe depression (Elliott, 1997). Depressed patients may be capable of reasoning and deliberating about a decision, yet make very poor decisions, at least partly because of their depression. They may understand the risks of their decision, for instance, yet simply not care about them. The question presents itself: to what degree is a person's emotional state essential to his or her competence? If competence to consent is the ability to make a choice about one's medical care, then the conceptual difficulty is in deciding what counts as that ability.

The problem of personal identity

The standard way of making decisions for incompetent but previously competent patients has come to be the patient's previously expressed wishes. Yet many neurologically damaged or demented patients are not, in some sense, the same persons they were before the damage or dementia. This is especially obvious for patients who are permanently vegetative, where the patient's higher brain functions are absent, but it is also true for patients with other types of cerebral damage, such as stroke or trauma. The patient's personality and values may have changed dramatically; his memory of his past life may be impaired; his intellectual and other mental abilities may be severely damaged. When this broad gap in identity separates the patient's current and past selves, it becomes a matter for debate how much weight should be given to the wishes, values or desires of the patient as he or she was in the past (Robertson, 1991). Should the patient's previously expressed wishes prevail even when they seem to run squarely against his current interests?

Sometimes we may have reason to think that the person would have changed his mind if he could be made aware of subsequent events and developments – for example, a 50-year-old advertising executive in a persistent vegetative state from traumatic injury who, before his injury, had never been sick in his life, who had expressed a lifelong wish to have his life extended as long as possible regardless of the circumstances, but whose family feels would have changed his mind if he had ever been in a hospital intensive care unit. At other times the patient's wishes and values in the past may directly contradict his present wishes and values (Nelson, 1995). Take, for example, a writer who has devoted his life to matters of the mind, and for whom the mental deterioration associated with Alzheimer's disease has always seemed the cruellest way for a life to end. He has told his son that if his mental faculties were to deteriorate, he would rather have euthanasia. What he regards as most humiliating of all is the lack of awareness of one's condition that dementia brings. Yet when his mental faculties eventually deteriorate, he seems perfectly content with his life. He has no memory of his earlier wishes, and as far anyone can determine, he would not now want his life to end. What value should we place on the wishes and values of a patient's previous self, and what should we place on those of the current self?

The problem of involuntary 'altruism'

It is an article of faith in paediatric hospitals that medical decisions for a child should serve that child's best interests. Yet some medical interventions are clearly not in the child's interests, and in fact are designed for other purposes. For example, surgeons often transplant kidneys or bone marrow from children too young to consent, usually matched siblings of the transplant recipient. Unlike the conventional medical interventions for which parents are asked to consent on behalf of a child, transplantation from child donors exposes children to risks that are not balanced by commensurate benefits – or at least not benefits to them personally (Dwyer and Vig, 1995). This problem parallels a problem in certain types of clinical research, where children undergo risks or discomforts not for their own benefit, but to generate scientific knowledge that may eventually benefit others. For example, Phase 1 cancer trials are designed to test the safety (or to put it another way, the toxicity) of new regimens for the treatment of cancer. The subjects in Phase 1 paediatric cancer trials are usually children whose cancer has a very poor prognosis and for whom standard therapy has not been effective. These trials are not designed to test the effectiveness of the new therapy, and the chance that children enrolled in the trials will experience any therapeutic benefit is relatively small. As with parents of living organ donors, parents of potential subjects in clinical research that has a poor risk/benefit ratio are asked to expose their child to risks, harms or discomforts for the sake of someone (or something) other than themselves.

When competent adults take risks or undergo harms for the sake of others, we ordinarily consider their actions not morally obligatory, but altruistic or supererogatory – beyond the call of duty. Certainly they are not things that an adult should be forced to do. Yet if this is true, on what grounds, apart from a crude utilitarianism, can we justify such interventions on young children? Many of the justifications given in the past have a notably ad hoc feel about them. For example, some writers have argued for organ transplantation from living siblings by appealing to the psychological benefit that the sibling would gain from donating. On these grounds a case is made for donation as an intervention that is in the best interests of the donor. Yet while there is no doubt some sense in which a child, at least an older child, might benefit by being volunteered to help his or her brother or sister, it is precisely because undergoing such risks are ordinarily not regarded as being in an adult's interests that they are seen as altruistic.

Other writers have appealed to a sort of hypothetical autonomy, suggesting that a child can be 'volunteered' if at a later point she would come to see the intervention as ethically justifiable, or if the intervention is something for which she would have a moral obligation to volunteer if she were able (McCormick, 1974; Bartholome, 1977). Yet as Ackerman (1979) has pointed out, what a child will come to see as morally acceptable will depend on the interests and character she develops, and often these things cannot easily be predicted. Moreover, at least some of the interventions in question, such as Phase 1 trials, are not generally regarded as something in which adults have a moral duty to take part. If taking part is not obligatory for adults, the argument that it is justifiable for children is weakened. If we admit that an adult stands on solid moral ground in refusing to take part, then the ground for 'volunteering' a child unable to consent seems a little less firm.

The problem of the moral imagination

Deciding what kinds of medical care an incompetent patient ought to receive often means trying to decide what kind of care would be in the patient's interests. How aggressively one should treat a newborn with severe spina bifida; whether a mentally retarded adolescent with cancer should undergo a burdensome course of chemotherapy with uncertain efficacy; determining the point at which a patient with schizophrenia should be treated against his will; deciding whether to treat a pneumonia in a child with cerebral palsy and profound neurological impairment: understanding the interests of such patients requires a kind of imaginative leap. Like anthropologists who must try to understand cultures vastly different from their own, health-care workers must try to understand patients whose lives differ

457

dramatically from theirs by virtue of illness or disability. They must try to imagine what it would be like to have a leg amputated, or never to have heard a sound, or to suffer paranoid delusions about one's parents. Trying to decide what is best for the patient requires trying to see things from the patient's point of view (Elliott and Elliott, 1990).

Imaginatively sharing another person's particular, subjective point of view, however, requires imagining a logical impossibility. It asks the question: what would it be like for me, if I were someone else? And while I may be able more or less to approximate another person's experience by imagining what it would be like for me to undergo that experience, this becomes more and more difficult with patients whose experience is vastly different from mine. The most problematic cases arise when we must imagine what life is like for a person whose mental life appears radically different from our own, as a result of mental retardation, mental disability or mental illness. This kind of imaginative leap requires us to imagine what it would be like not to have the mental abilities that we have, including those by virtue of which we are able to imagine – a difficult leap indeed, and not without its dangers. Adam Smith thought that in imagining what the experience of the mentally impaired is like, a person is tempted to 'imagine what he himself would feel if he were reduced to the same unhappy situation, and what is perhaps impossible, regard it with his present reason and judgement' (Smith, 1982: 12). There are at least two serious dangers here. One danger comes with trying to imagine the experience of the permanently unconscious, such as anencephalic children or permanently vegetative persons. This is the danger of imagining, in Nagel's words, that 'there is something that it is like' to be permanently unconscious, and making a misguided judgement as to the permanently unconscious person's quality of life.

The other serious danger is that of underestimating the quality of a mentally impaired or disabled person's life. The fact that I would not want to live such a life, or the fact that I would not regard my life as worthwhile if I were to lose my mental faculties, says little about the quality of that person's life. For Hauerwas, the 'crucial point is that the retarded do not feel or understand their retardation as we do, or imagine we would, but as they do. We have no right or basis to attribute our assumed unhappiness or suffering to them' (Hauerwas, 1986: 67). The reality of these dangers has been made evident by the willingness of physicians and hospitals to deny treatments to patients on the basis of their mental disabilities, such as the often mild mental handicap associated with Down's syndrome.

The problem of asymmetrical relationships

One serious criticism of the 'best interests' standard of decision-making for children is that by focusing solely on the child it overlooks the role of the family (Nelson and Nelson, 1995). This can leave us with a kind of misplaced individualism, as if the only ethically important considerations are those that have to do with the child himself – intrinsic abilities like his intellect, his awareness, his physical abilities and so on. But this is an odd way to look at children, since what is most striking about children is not their intrinsic abilities but their dependence. Children exist in relationships of dependence on their families, and with time those relationships become deeper and richer and more complex. It seems ungainly to try to consider childrens' interests apart from the interests of their families because their interests are bound up together. This is more than simply saying that parents are best placed to judge the interests of their child; it is saying that very often their interests are the same. It would not be exaggerating to say that very often the worst thing that could happen to parents would be for something to happen to their children.

Because of these kinds of questions, bioethics has begun to pay more attention to families, and has tried to locate our ethical thinking about children within the parent–child relationship. Some writers have argued that what is morally impor- tant about children cannot be reduced solely to their intrinsic capacities, but in- stead needs also to take account somehow of their relationships with others. What matters morally about a child is connected to the fact that they are loved by their parents, and what we value about human beings is not just their intellect but also their capacity for these deep human relationships.

But with some children – for example, those who are left with profound neuro- logical damage from traumatic and anoxic brain injury – these relationships are often completely asymmetrical. Many of these children will never be able to experi- ence the kind of love that they are given, and they will never be able to give it back. Many will never even be able to recognize their parents. What sort of respect and value should we place on these kinds of relationships? Many families seem to have made a place in their lives for such profoundly damaged children, and when it comes to questions about medical care, they want the child treated very aggres- sively, even when the treatment is very burdensome or painful. Here health-care workers are often torn between a desire to respect the parent–child relationship, and the realization that the child is not really a participant in that relationship. Often parents of such children make such tremendous emotional sacrifices for the child, and labour under such guilt about their responsibility for the child's care, that physicians wonder whether it is ethically justifiable to place all the burden of decision-making on the parents.

The problem of meaning and the profoundly damaged child

Human activities and discourse are played out against a backdrop of understand- ings – some widely shared, some rather more fragmented – about what counts as a good life. These are not necessarily a matter of choice for us, or not entirely: they are the framework of tradition and culture within which our choices are made. Part of this framework concerns understandings about what might be called the meaning and significance of life: questions about the way in which we make sense of our lives, what gives our lives significance, beliefs about how one ought to live, stories that we tell ourselves about successful lives and failed ones (Taylor, 1989). Differ- ent cultures and eras have answered these kinds of questions in different ways, of course, and many individuals will answer them differently even within contempo- rary Western culture. Yet some widely shared Western views may call into ques- tion the meaning of the life of a person with profound neurological damage. These questions present deep problems for decisions about the conditions under which such lives should be prolonged.

For example, when we in the West talk about what gives our lives meaning, and the reasons we have chosen to do what we have done with our lives, we often find common ground between us. Many of us talk about the people we love, such as our families, and we also talk about our work – about a calling or a sense of mission, the satisfaction of artistic creativity or taking part in a broader social or political movement. Charles Taylor calls this emphasis on family and work the 'affirmation of ordinary life' (Taylor, 1989). Moreover, this view locates meaning at least in part within the individual himself. That is, we ordinarily think that the meaning of our lives has something to do with us as individuals and the choices we make – with discovering and following a calling, with looking inward and finding one's own special character or talents, with developing a relationship with God and so on.

What is important to realize, however, is that this kind of life is inaccessible to many people with profound neurological damage. If a person is incapable of appreciating and sustaining the emotional bonds of family, and incapable of finding meaning through work, she will not be able to live the kind of life that is widely regarded in our culture as meaningful. It could be otherwise, of course – for example, in a culture in which meaning is found through occupying one's place in the natural order of things, or in which all life is seen as glorifying God, or in any number of other cosmologies. But these are not our Western cosmologies. This may help to explain why such profoundly damaged lives seem so tragic to us, even when we realize that the disabled child is not actually in pain. There is a gap between the kind of life through which the rest of us achieve those goods that make it worthwhile, and what we see as the trajectory that this child's life will inevitably take.

This struggle to find meaning in such profoundly damaged lives places us in a difficult position when it comes to clinical decisions. On the one hand there are very powerful moral ideals in our culture that make us very reluctant to deny these children beneficial medical treatment. Our tradition of rights and equality makes us wary of withholding treatment from a person because of her intelligence. Moreover, we realize that these are the most vulnerable and dependent of human lives, and that they may have deep significance for other people, such as the child's family. Yet these ideals lead us into a kind of ethical double-talk. We feel as if these lives deserve respect, yet at the same time, they fail to meet the criteria by which we count our own lives as meaningful. We want to protect vulnerable lives, yet our own measure of the good life for ourselves does not include a life like this.

This is not to say that we can simply decide to discard or change the broader framework of culture and tradition within which such choices are made. It is only to suggest that we are unlikely to achieve a lasting or ethically satisfying resolution to these choices unless we take these broader questions seriously.

References

Ackerman, T. F. (1979). Fooling ourselves with child autonomy and assent in nontherapeutic clinical research. *Clinical Research*, 27/5, 345–8.

460

Arras, J. D. (1984). Toward an ethic of ambiguity. *Hastings Center Report*, 14/2, 25–33.

Bartholome, W. (1977). The ethics of nontherapeutic clinical research on children. In *The National Commission for the Protection of Human Subjects of Biomedical and Behavioral Research: appendix to report and recommendations: research involving children*. Washington: US Government Printing Office, 31-1–32-2.

Brock, D. W. and Wartman, S. A. (1990). When competent patients make irrational choices. *New England Journal of Medicine*, 322, 1595–9.

Buchanan, A. E. and Brock, D. W. (1989). *Deciding for Others: the ethics of surrogate decision making*. Cambridge: Cambridge University Press.

Dwyer, J. and Vig, E. (1995). Rethinking transplantation between siblings. *Hastings Center Report*, 24/5, 7–12.

Elliott, C. (1997). Caring about risks: are severely depressed patients competent to consent to research? *Archives of General Psychiatry*, 54, 113–16.

Elliott, C. and Elliott, B. (1991). From the patient's point of view: medical ethics and the moral imagination. *Journal of Medical Ethics*, 17, 173–8.

Faden, R. and Beauchamp, T. (1986). *A History and Theory of Informed Consent*. New York: Oxford University Press.

Gutheil, T. G. and Appelbaum, P. S. (1982). *Clinical Handbook of Psychiatry and the Law*. New York: McGraw-Hill.

Hauerwas, S. (1986). Suffer the retarded: should we prevent retardation? In P. R. Dodecki and R. M. Zaner (eds), *Ethics of Dealing with Persons with Severe Handicaps*. Baltimore, MD: Paul H. Brooks, 53–70.

McCormick, R. A. (1974). Proxy consent in the experimentation situation. *Perspectives in Biology and Medicine*, 18, 2–20.

Nelson, J. L. (1995). Critical interests and sources of familial decision-making authority for incapacitated patients. *Journal of Law, Medicine and Ethics*, 23, 143–8.

Nelson, J. L. and Nelson, H. L. (1995). *The Patient in the Family: an ethics of medicine and families*. New York: Routledge.

Robertson, J. A. (1991). Second thoughts on living wills. *Hastings Center Report*, 21/6, 6–9.

Smith, A. (1982). *The Theory of Moral Sentiments*. Indianapolis: Liberty Press.

Taylor, C. (1989). *Sources of the Self*. Cambridge, MA: Harvard University Press.

US President's Commission for the Study of Ethical Problems in Medicine and Biomedical and Behavioural Research (1983). *Making Health Care Decisions: The ethical and legal implications of informed consent in the patient–practitioner relationship*. Washington: US Government Printing Office.

Further Reading

Bloch, S. and Chodoff, P. (eds) (1991). *Psychiatric Ethics*. Oxford: Oxford University Press.

Brody, H. and Bartholome, W. (1988). In the best interests of . . . *Hastings Center Report*, 18/6, 37–40.

Freedman, B. (1975). A moral theory of informed consent. *Hastings Center Report*, 5/4, 32–9.

Hastings Center Task Force (1987). Imperiled newborns: a report. *Hastings Center Report*, 17/6, 5–32.

Lantos, J., Siegler, M. and Cuttler, L. (1989). Ethical issues in growth hormone therapy. *Journal of the American Medical Association*, 261/7, 1020–4.

Lidz, C., Meisel, A., Zerubavel, E., Carter, M., Sestak, R. and Roth, L. (1984). *Informed Consent: a study of decisionmaking in psychiatry.* New York: Guilford Press.

Moore, M. (1984). *Law and Psychiatry: rethinking the relationship.* Cambridge: Cambridge University Press.

Ross, L. F. (1994). Justice for children: the child as organ donor. *Bioethics,* 8, 105–26.

44

Special issues facing nurses

VERENA TSCHUDIN

Nursing has traditionally had a subservient role: physicians prescribe and order, nurses carry out the orders. This role is increasingly unsatisfactory to medicine and nursing alike. Better models are emerging but are not yet clearly defined.

Can Nursing be Autonomous?

Nurses began to consider professional independence in the 1960s when nursing research first began to make an impact. This led to the realization that autonomy meant also greater accountability, and hence professional and legal responsibility for care given. The production of codes of professional conduct, the necessity of nurses to adhere to them and the revolution in nurse education have sharpened the debate about autonomy.

In the view of Affara and Styles, two leading members of the International Council of Nurses (undated, p. 20): 'nursing does seem to be an occupation in transition to mature professional status.' They see university education of nurses and increased capabilities by nurses as decisive factors in modifying and expanding the scope of nursing practice. Nursing cannot and does not strive to be independent of other professions, but seeks to be a body with its own skills and areas of expertise, and with a clear understanding of its responsibilities.

Concentrating on matters of internal regulation and organization seems to have distracted nursing from pursuing a vision or direction. This has been noticed by Johnstone (1994: 509) who urges that 'unless the nursing profession assumes a much higher public and political profile than it has until now, it may, in the final analysis, find that it is in no position to fulfil its broader moral as well as professional responsibilities towards the community at large.'

Nurses as leaders and policy-shapers According to nurse theorist Jean Watson (1989), 'the future of medicine and nursing belongs to *caring* more than *curing*. A more radical thesis is that there is movement out of an era in which *curing* is dominant into an era in which *caring* must take precedence.' This is not understood as nursing doing the 'caring' while medicine is doing the 'curing', with curing having the more effective and prestigious role, but that caring itself is more important than curing. The cost of curing – at least in developed countries – has escalated to the point where it is all but ruining the economy in general. High-cost life-saving treatments will therefore be less and less available; low-cost caring will take precedence. This is where nursing has to offer expertise and leadership.

There are notable nurse leaders in areas such as nursing theory, philosophy and research; however, the transition from theory to practice, research to implementation and from thought to action is as difficult in nursing as it is in other professions.

The lack of visionary and political leadership in nursing, in particular among female nurses, has long been evident. McClure (1978) drew attention to the problem of passivity among nurses and noted that they tended to respond to others rather than take initiatives themselves. Nursing would therefore attract people who do not display ambition; or interviewers deter those who show ambition and leadership. These are serious considerations which are more and more addressed through education.

Nurses can and need to take the lead in areas such as communication between patients and health-care personnel; maintaining and fostering human rights; using and promoting complementary therapies and other aspects of holistic care; promoting health and helping the population at large to maintain health with check-ups and information. These are part of the basic caring role of nursing, but they are also part of the ethical role and include aspects of advocacy, confidentiality and informed consent.

Education   The education of its practitioners has always been considered a vital element in the practice of nursing. In many countries worldwide, managers of units and wards now have to have a first degree. The aim is that nursing generally will eventually be an all-graduate profession. In some countries in Europe (e.g., Belgium) practising nurses are encouraged to hold higher degrees. The proportion of practising ('bedside') nurses who have degrees in philosophy, theology, ethics and economics is growing (Leavitt, 1996). But the use then made of such talents is not yet readily forthcoming, particularly in situations where clearly defined professional roles and hierarchies still exist. The result is disappointment and many nurses move into purely academic careers.

There is still a marked contrast between nurses educated in Western countries, with the emphasis on prolonging life, and those trained in developing countries, with the emphasis on preventing illness. Worldwide epidemics of AIDS, TB and infections due to antibiotic resistance are changing the global need for and of nursing considerably, strengthening also the theory that caring will be dominant in the future in all areas of the world.

The trend worldwide in nurse education is for a core programme of basic studies, after which students branch out into a number of specialties, gaining a diploma or first degree after a minimum of three years. The emphasis in this form of nurse education is on health (rather than illness) and students are schooled equally in community settings as in hospitals. The core curriculum consists of subjects such as health education, ethics, relationships, sociology and communication, as well as life sciences, pathology and sociology.

The need to respond to new economic and political pressures is evident in nurse education. Indeed, the shift to higher education has coincided with the trend to a market economy. With no clear focus of direction at present, however, pressures from outside nursing are strong for more and more caring tasks to be carried out by care assistants rather than nurses. This gives nurse education a stronger incentive to prepare its practitioners for taking responsibility.

Interdependence   One of the possible ways forward for all health care is that some basic education and training of personnel should happen jointly. Medical, nursing, physiotherapy and social-work students should be taught together, particularly in health sciences, communication, ethics, sociology and for discussions of political, economic and social trends in health care. Joint education would remove many of the difficulties created by separate interests and ideologies. Meetings with and discussions among a wide variety of professions in the health-care and law enforcement fields would help to focus communication between the various groups on their responsibilities towards their clients. When boundaries of work and socialization are maintained, it is easy to forget the patient or client who should be at the centre of care and attention.

Many of the problems faced by nurses in the area of patient-centred care stem from the traditional role of nursing as subordinate to medicine. Nurses claim that they are generally closer to patients and clients, both physically and emotionally, than doctors, and therefore know them better and understand their needs better, but they are not consulted on important decisions. Conflict between medical and nursing staff over treatments is therefore frequent and bitter. When nurses have higher and university education, they feel more equal to physicians and they tend to be more respected by them. This development may reduce tension between nursing and medical staff, as decision-making structures change, enabling nurses to play a greater part in decisions.

Professional autonomy in nursing is not a clear-cut issue. While nursing has to become more courageous in leadership in caring policies, in applying these policies, autonomy has to be seen as acceptance of responsibility rather than as an assertion of independence. This may call for sharing of information, awareness of other professionals' contributions and effective patient advocacy.

Should Nursing be Autonomous?

Extended and expanded practice   Assuming that the scenario of the future for health care is valid, nursing needs to be able to take on the role of leader in the field of caring. Nursing is branching into many different extensions of its traditional role, including prescribing in the community, anaesthetizing patients, carrying out minor operations, diagnosing and caring for patients. These are areas where individual nurses and small groups of nurses have made significant steps towards acknowledging new ways of caring. They may be considered to be part of the 'curing' aspect of care, and they need to be made much more widely known. They tend to be local and small-scale projects which have been created by obvious need.

465

The expanded role of nursing has often been seen as applying to the 'caring' aspect of the work, that is, to the less technical side. Expansion is understood to mean the fostering of relationships and human values rather than the acquisition of skills and competencies. But in her understanding of what 'caring' consists of, Roach (1992) lists competence in second place (along with compassion, confidence, conscience and commitment). It is fair to say that the more technical health care becomes, the more it also needs to be aware of the fears and anxieties of patients and clients dependent on the technology. Good and accessible information needs to be given at every stage to allay worry and gain cooperation. Nurses therefore need not only to be skilled in handling increasingly complex technology, but also in relating to and communicating with patients and clients and with other health professionals.

Nurse-led care The quest for extension and expansion of the nursing role has led to some experiments where nurses take the lead in care, in areas such as neonatology, gerontology, hospice care, mental health and rehabilitation. With increasing frequency, nurses are entirely responsible for such services, calling on physicians only when necessary.

Clinics and health stations in developing countries have long known this model. The proven efficiency and cost-effectiveness of nursing development units (Mason, 1994) makes them attractive experiments in a health market which puts high emphasis on value for money in health care.

General practitioners increasingly employ nurses who then run their own clinics for certain medical conditions and for routine health checks. Some hospitals have nurse-led minor injuries clinics in accident and emergency departments. Patients and clients frequently state that they either prefer or at least do not mind being attended by nurses. The impression is often that nurses have more time, give more information in accessible language and are more considerate than doctors.

Nurse specialists exist in many hospital departments or clinics; best-known among them are breast-care nurses and stoma (or enterostomal) therapists (specializing in the care of patients with stomas, that is, artificial orifices from the gastrointenstinal or urinary tract). Other specialties are in dietetics, diabetes, lymphoedema and more generally in paediatrics, oncology, geriatrics and care of the dying. Such nurses advise patients, families and staff. This has increased good care, but does also lead to sometimes acute conflicts of role, where the nurses' professional judgement and autonomy are challenged. Such posts are increasingly often sponsored by firms or companies who ask specialist nurses to use their products (such as stoma products), bringing with them conflicts of interest if the contracts are not clearly negotiated. Sponsorship of many types and kinds is evident in health care, making it more likely that the persons concerned find themselves in situations of professional compromise. For nurses to uphold claims of professional autonomy can then become questionable.

Midwives have traditionally been much more independent of physicians in a number of countries worldwide, in particular in the United Kingdom.

Market pressures on autonomy   The increasing emphasis of market forces in health care has led many nurses to complain that they are not able to exercise professional discretion. Short-term employment contracts and the need to economize at every level mean that nurses are often not in positions to exercise due professional judgement. Most of the evidence for this is anecdotal, as it would be difficult to obtain objective research data. With nurses feeling under pressure, there is less personal involvement, less personal responsibility and more fear of victimization. The sense of duty is dulled, justice is restricted to fairness and the job ceases to be personally fulfilling. With this goes a sense of apathy and professional autonomy becomes merely a theoretical ideal.

The need for economy. efficiency and effectiveness has perhaps become stronger than professional idealism, but it has also made the professions more dependent on each other. In this sense, nursing autonomy can no longer mean professional independence, but a responsibility to produce models for 'caring' in a changing environment. Nursing leadership is called for to shape health care in ways which are both just and fair, effective and compassionate.

Nurses as Patients' Advocates

Nurses have long understood themselves to be the patients' advocates *par excellence*, but patient advocacy has become more of a defined activity in recent times. Above all, nurses are exhorted to foster and maintain the patients' and clients' well-being. What this implies is often not very clear. Curtin (1979) based a philosophy of nursing on the concept of advocacy, stressing the common humanity, the common needs, and the common human rights of both patients and nurses. In this way Curtin moved away from legal concepts of advocacy and defined rights, and described what nurses and patients share. She suggested that because nurses and patients are joined together in common humanity, this commonality compels nurses to act as advocates. This basic stance defines nurses as carers. but at the same time makes them vulnerable because it is their humanity which is called upon, not simply certain skills.

Keeping professional codes and guidelines   The International Council of Nurses (ICN) Code for Nurses (1973) is binding on all nurses. In addition, many countries have their own codes, giving more specific guidance. According to the ICN code, 'the fundamental responsibility of the nurse is fourfold: to promote health, to prevent illness, to restore health and to alleviate suffering.' Problems arise when any of these responsibilities conflict, or when personal values encroach on those demanded by the patient or client, other health carers, employers, the profession or society at large. Nurses working in specific settings, for example, prisons, also have to keep to codes and guidelines produced by those institutions, and demands made by one code (e.g., confidentiality) may be contradicted by another (e.g., disclosure of details to police). Codes can be prescriptive only in general terms, and personal interpretation of specific clauses in particular circumstances will vary. If necessary, nurses should consult with senior personnel or with professional bodies in cases of conflict. This in itself can be controversial, as the lines of management may overlap

467

VERENA TSCHUDIN

for nurses. One way in which nurses exercise their autonomy is by consulting with members of their own profession rather than those of other professions (such as physicians).

Conflicts of interest   Conflicts are caused by the many demands made on nurses. Several have been mentioned already: conflicts of role and culture; demands of efficiency made by employers; professional demands to exercise judgement and being limited by policies; the need to adapt to changes in care with insufficient resources available; demands made by patients and clients for right to be upheld (to which nurses are often unable to respond effectively); the need to extend into other professional fields, and also to expand practice by deepening existing skills.

Such conflicts are well known in professional settings anywhere. The role of caring for people combines both technical and interpersonal skills. This demands a wide range of expertise, experience and stamina. Conflicts arise because of the various spheres of professional and managerial demands made on nurses. Caring intimately for large numbers of ill, sick and vulnerable people who need specific and detailed attention, in a situation which changes constantly, may be seen differently from the point of view of a nurse (who deals with sick people and possibly distraught friends and relations) and a manager (who has to balance a budget).

The professional roles of doctors and nurses increasingly overlap. This is to be welcomed from the point of view of the recipients of care who are thus being treated more holistically. But time and experience for creating team work are often lacking. Although both medicine and nursing aim 'to promote and safeguard the interests and well-being of patients and clients' (UKCC, 1992), in a given situation this is often difficult to maintain. In their area of care, nurses often become very experienced, but they may have to depend on physicians with less experience to prescribe treatments, or carry out decisions which have been taken without being consulted. They may have come to know patients over many months or years of visiting clinics, departments and in the community. This may amount to considerable personal involvement which is both helpful and costly. Some nurse specialists may find that they disagree with treatments prescribed by physicians, but they cannot advise patients and clients of alternatives. Nurses find that they are taken for granted by colleagues but yet have (and want) to treat their patients and clients as unique individuals. They have to uphold the law (e.g., report illegal acts), yet are themselves often pushed to illegal acts (e.g., illicit drug-taking) through stress.

Nurses are obliged to care for patients 'irrespective of their ethnic origin, religious beliefs, personal attributes, the nature of their health problems or any other factor' (UKCC, 1992). Nurses cannot refuse to care for patients, but they can claim conscientious objection to take part in certain procedures which are not considered treatments, such as abortions (in the United Kingdom) and voluntary euthanasia (during the short period in which this was legal in Australia's Northern Territory). When they are therefore confronted with circumstances which they find personally and professionally challenging, conflicts arise which may cause moral distress.

The notion of advocacy has therefore increasingly come to be seen as having the conviction or courage to stand up for a person against a system which is unjust.

468

Whistle-blowing Bringing to light wrongdoing in any area of life – particularly professional life – has come to be known as whistle-blowing. Nursing has produced a number of whistle-blowers. It has also been instrumental in highlighting practices which are of dubious effect or even damaging. One such area – the administration of electroconvulsive therapy (ECT) to children and adolescents – has repeatedly been questioned by nurses (Oxlad and Baldwin, 1995). It is fair to say that the administration of ECT generally has been reduced because of the pressure exerted by nursing staff. Nursing has rightly been credited with the growth of the hospice movement, much of it born of the need for, and nurses' experience with, better care for dying people.

According to Eby (1994), whistle-blowing comprises the specific elements of accountability, loyalty or fidelity, justice and truth or veracity.

The codes of ethics or practice for nurses often contain clauses exhorting them to report matters of concern to appropriate persons in authority. When the problem is one of constant or systematic understaffing, it becomes difficult to respect this exhortation. Accountability to patients and clients demands that nurses should give adequate care. If this is not possible, nurses have to make it known, but the manager may be in an equally impossible position, unable to rectify the situation. Accountability to colleagues, the profession and society all demand that reasonable care be given. The employer is also accountable to patients and clients, as well as to the staff, but may be under pressure from accountants to reduce spending. Pressures may increase for each side to attain what it considers its goal, but the goals differ. For nurses this often means that managers, rather than being helpful, are obstructive. Accountability demands, however, that all possible avenues are exhausted. For nurses the problem may be: to whom are they more accountable? Nurses who have met with attitudes of disregard or hostility from managers or supervisors have taken their grievances to the press. This has cost some nurses their careers, as they could then be accused of breaching confidentiality (Turner, 1992).

The loyalty and fidelity which professionals owe their clients is a first duty. Nurses owe a loyalty to both medical and nursing hierarchies, and loss of that fidelity could result in patient harm through failure of treatment. When considering an act of disloyalty to either colleagues or an organization, conflict is inevitable. It is impossible to guarantee, though, that the wider society will benefit from an act of whistle-blowing. At the time this often cannot be ascertained. An act of whistle-blowing can be considered folly as well as heroism. In the case of nurses, it is more effective and less personally costly if a group of nurses can take action together. It is less easy to dismiss a collection of people than one person.

Justice demands that patients and clients have their rights considered, and therefore anything which infringes rights (such as inadequate care through lack of staff or given by untrained staff) should be questioned. Many nurses feel very keenly that justice is something which it is important to uphold. Loyalty to patients means that nurses may choose to give most attention to those who need it most, regretfully neglecting those who need less specific care, but who may need attention just as much.

469

Whistle-blowing is an accusation by a person against his or her own organization or colleagues. It is often a last effort to get an institution to change. Truth is a fundamental principle in any setting, but what the truth is may be seen differently by people in different positions. A complaint often made by nurses in circumstances when they have grievances is that they were not listened to or were not taken seriously, thus the truth, as they experienced it, was never heard. It may be impossible to know exactly why someone was not taken seriously or not heard. Both sides in a dispute have their reputation to consider, and truth may be that which was said as much as that which was not said. In any case of whistle-blowing, it is vital that documentation is kept carefully and in an accessible way.

The role of advocacy in nursing goes to the roots of the profession in terms of care of others and skills of communication. Whistle-blowing can be regarded as a stand taken by disgruntled people pursuing their own aims, but for the most part it is done in the spirit of one of nursing's primary aims: to ensure that the safety and comfort of patients are safeguarded.

References

Affara, F. A. and Styles, M. M. (undated) *Nursing Regulation Guidebook: from principle to power*. Geneva: International Council of Nurses.

Curtin, L. (1979). The nurse as advocate: a philosophical foundation for nursing. *Advances in Nursing Science*, 1/3, 1–10.

Eby, M. (1994). Whistleblowing. In V. Tschudin (ed.) *Ethics: conflicts of interest*. London: Scutari, 56–84.

ICN (1973). *Code for Nurses*, Geneva: International Council of Nurses.

Johnstone, M.-J. (1994). *Bioethics; a nursing perspective*, 2nd edn. Marrickville: W. B. Saunders.

Leavitt, F. (1996). Educating nurses for their future role in bioethics, *Nursing Ethics*, 3/1, 39–52.

McClure, M. L. (1978). The long road to accountability. *Nursing Outlook*, 26/1, 47–50.

Mason, C. (1994). NDUs: can they fit in a market-led service? *Nursing Standard*, 9/1, 34–6.

Oxlad, M. and Baldwin, S. (1995). Electroconvulsive therapy, children and adolescents: the power to stop. *Nursing Ethics*, 2/4, 333–46.

Roach, Sister M. S. (1992). *The Human Act of Caring: a blueprint for the health professions*, rev. edn. Ottawa: Canadian Hospital Association Press.

Turner, T. (1992). The indomitable Mr. Pink. *Nursing Times*, 88/24, 26–9.

UKCC (1992). *Code of Professional Conduct for the Nurse, Midwife and Health Visitor*. London: United Kingdom Central Council.

Watson, M. J. (1989). New dimensions of human caring theory. *Nursing Science Quarterly*, 2, 175–81.

Further Reading

Benjamin, M. and Curtis, J. (1986). *Ethics in Nursing*, 2nd edn. New York: Oxford University Press.

Chadwick, R. and Tadd, W. (1992). *Ethics and Nursing Practice; a case study approach*. Basingstoke: Macmillan.

Jameton, A. (1984). *Nursing Practice; the ethical issues.* Englewood Cliffs, NJ: Prentice-Hall.

Thompson, I. E., Melia, K. M. and Boyd, K. M. (1994). *Nursing Ethics,* 3rd edn. Edinburgh: Churchill Livingstone.

Tschudin, V. (1993). *Ethics in Nursing; the caring relationship,* 2nd rev. edn. Oxford: Butterworth-Heinemann.

—— (1994). *Deciding Ethically; a practical approach to nursing challenges.* London: Baillière Tindall.

471

PART XIV

THE TEACHING AND PRACTICE OF BIOETHICS

45

Ethics committees and
ethics consultants

JONATHAN D. MORENO

Ethics committee and ethics consultants are among the more interesting phenomena associated with bioethics. Although in some respects both reach back to the
ancient origins of medical ethics, in other ways they are reflections of a 'post-
modern' society that seeks moral resolutions while remaining agnostic about substantive moral absolutes. In the present article I shall describe the history of ethics
committees and ethics consultants, the received view of their functions and uncertainties about their appropriate status. I will conclude with some philosophical
remarks about the nature of ethics committees and ethics consultants, as well as
their implications for the field of bioethics.

Origins and Development

The relationships of ethics committees and ethics consultants to the history of
medicine are quite different. These differences highlight an interesting tension
between the two, even though they are both manifestations of the institution of
bioethics.

The Hippocratic texts (those attributed to a historical personage Hippocrates or
to a cult of male physicians) are explicit about the physician's role as including the
projection to patients and their families of a certain moral standing. In this tradition
the healer's charisma is closely associated with his (at least apparent) wisdom and
personal carriage. The appreciation for the close linkage between the qualities of
wisdom and technical proficiency in the healer's art is remarkably persistent both
historically and cross-culturally, including those that stem from non-Hippocratic
(e.g., Jewish and Islamic) medical ethical traditions. To a large degree, the role of
the ethics consultant is an extension of that of the wise physician.

In other respects, however, the ethics consultant is quite a different figure. Most
obviously, many modern ethics consultants are not doctors of medicine. In fact,
though the Hippocratic authors counselled the use of consultants in hard cases,
they did not seem to anticipate a non-physician consultant whose sole function was
ethical rather than medical assistance (Ackerman, 1989). Further, while the
Hippocratic doctors were guided mainly by the values of non-maleficence and
beneficence, today's ethics consultants concern themselves with other values as
well, such as autonomy and justice. But though the modern ethics consultant is

undeniably a product of the bioethics movement, for which autonomy is the usual ethical 'trump', it is possible that this is less often the case at the bedside than it is for bioethicists who operate in more rarefied settings.

It is not clear who the first modern ethics consultants were, but the occupation can be traced in general terms from several antecedents, including hospital chaplains and theologians who taught medical students in the 1960s, academic philosopher-bioethicists who became interested in the clinical setting in the 1970s and ethics committee members who offered their services for helping with emergent ethical disputes, also during the 1970s (Rothman, 1991). Today ethics consultants often work in tandem with ethics committees, or members of ethics committees who are on call may consider themselves ethics consultants (Wear, 1990). However, there is also a small but vigorous movement of professional ethics consultants who work as independent entrepreneurs, usually in positions supported by hospital receipts.

While the recent origins of ethics committees are more clear than those of ethics consultants, they are notable for the virtual absence of ancient predecessors. The Hippocratic physician was a solo practitioner who, following apprenticeship, did not seek the moral advice of a committee, and certainly not a committee dominantly comprised of non-physicians. Instead, the ethics committee is a creature of a liberal, Western and pluralistic society. It is also indebted to the highly bureaucratized institutional structures of modernity, structures that include working groups known as committees. Moreover, ethics committees are mainly identified with secular bioethical theory, which is dominated by 'mid-level' principles that seek to avoid reference to a single foundational philosophy or to imply that certain actions are ethical and others not (Beauchamp and Childress, 1995). Liberal democratic pluralism, committee systems and mid-level principles all emphasize procedural solutions to social controversy. As a result, ethics committees are process-oriented to the extreme.

The predecessors of ethics committees in the United States were not as determinedly procedural, nor were they at first controlled by non-physicians, though their evolutionary vectors are plain (Moreno, 1995). As part of the eugenic movement early in the twentieth century, sterilization committees were composed mainly of those experienced in the management of the mentally ill (trained neurologists complained there were not enough 'real experts' on these committees). They made what they took to be objective decisions based on the goal of avoiding the social burdens of inherited 'idiocy' through prevention; only much later was it appreciated that few instances of cognitive deficiency are inherited. Until the early 1970s in the United States, abortion selection committees often identified those whose medical or psychiatric condition warranted an elective pregnancy termination. Compared to sterilization decisions, this was a somewhat less 'hard science' judgement. Another ancestor of ethics committees was panels for the determination of which patients suffering from terminal kidney disease should have access to the dialysis machines that were in short supply in the 1960s. Composed in many cases mostly of non-physicians, kidney dialysis selection committees made explicit value choices for the allocation of a scarce life-saving resource. The most famous of these was the 'God committee' at Swedish Hospital in Seattle, Washington, which was the subject of major media coverage in the early 1960s. The publicized experience of this committee was for many people their first exposure to the vexing problem of fairness in the allocation of scarce life-or-death resources (Alexander, 1962).

In a 1974 law review article, the physician Karen Teel reported that many hospitals used ethics committees to help make difficult decisions. Her article was cited by the New Jersey Supreme Court in its landmark ruling on the case of Karen Ann Quinlan. Quinlan was a young woman who fell into a persistent vegetative state (a condition of irreversible unconsciousness) after collapsing at a party. The court found that if the family requested discontinuation of treatment, and if there was no reasonable possibility of Karen Quinlan returning to a 'cognitive, sapient state' and if a hospital ethics committee agreed, then the decision-makers would be immune from civil and criminal liability. The judges' citation of Teel's article was the first great spur for the growth of ethics committees, Ironically, however, the judges seem to have misunderstood the function of ethics committees, confusing them with more traditional and technically driven prognosis committees (Moreno, 1995).

None the less, the New Jersey court's decision was the first of a series of events that gave impetus to the ethics committee movement in the United States in the years since. Another important development was the Reagan administration's attempt, in the early 1980s, to require aggressive treatment of severely disabled newborns, regulations that included reference to 'infant care review committees' (Moreno, 1987). More recently, the Joint Commission for the Accreditation of Healthcare Organizations (JCAHO, 1992) has established as a condition for accreditation that hospitals have a mechanism for addressing ethical disputes, and several states have legislated requirements that their hospitals have ethics committees. As a result, virtually all larger hospitals, and most smaller ones, now claim to have ethics committees in place.

In the United States, ethics committees vary greatly in many of their specific features, but it is a given that they must represent various perspectives, including that of the institution's 'community', and that they should not be dominated by physicians. This is a reflection of the fact that the ethics committee idea is legitimized as an expression of certain themes of democratic liberalism, including especially the notion that moral controversies are best resolved through a process that takes into account multiple perspectives on the nature of the good life. But while ethics committees have an essentially cosmopolitan aspect, the same is not quite true of the idea of ethics consultation, which retains the option of physician dominance. I will return to some of the philosophical implications of ethics committees and ethics consultation later in this article.

One obvious near relation of the ethics committee is the committee for the scrutiny of the use of human subjects in medical research. The idea of prior group review of experiment proposals involving human subjects dates back at least to the late 1940s in the US Atomic Energy Commission's Isotope Distribution Division, though its most famous early manifestation was at the Clinical Center of the

477

National Institutes of Health in Bethesda, Maryland, beginning in 1953 (Advisory Committee for Human Radiation Experiments, 1995). But unlike the ethics committee movement, the current system of local review boards owes its growth mainly to a series of well-publicized 'scandals'. One of these was the infamous Tuskegee Syphilis Study, in which over 400 poor African-American men were medically followed by public health officials for decades without being told their diagnosis, even when effective treatment became available. (See chapter 36, pp. 379–89.) Therefore, in the United States the use of human research subjects is subject to government regulation, and 'institutional review boards' have certain codified legal obligations, while ethics committees do not, at least not at the federal level.

The Functions of Ethics Committees and Ethics Consultants

I have noted that human subjects review panels were largely a response to allegations of investigators' misbehaviour. By contrast, the origins of ethics committees are not nearly so readily identifiable. Thus it is not surprising that their goals are not as clear, for they include assisting physicians in dealing with their ethical dilemmas as well as helping hospitals avoid lawsuits and bad publicity; little reflection is required to register the fact that these goals are not necessarily compatible.

There is broad agreement that ethics committees have three functions: case review, policy advice and staff education. Beyond these functions, and a membership that includes multiple perspectives, there are wide discrepancies among ethics committees. Some report to the hospital's organized medical staff, others directly to administration; some are passive and de-emphasize bedside consulting, others have active leadership and try to assert a presence on the wards; and some include members who are familiar with the bioethics literature and theory, while the members of others have had virtually no previous experience with ethical analysis.

Of the three 'classical' functions of ethics committees, case review has received far and away the most attention, staff education the least. This is perhaps because case consultation is the 'sexiest' of the functions, but it is also the most potentially volatile and the most labour-intensive. The vast majority of committees have operated on what is known as an 'optional-optional' basis for case review. This means that whether a case is brought to the committee is optional, as is whether the attending physician follows the committee's advice.

Not all of the functions of ethics committees were foreseen when they were first organized, and some diverge from the optional-optional model. In some states ethics committees serve to satisfy certain legal requirements. For example, in New York State there is a unique law that mandates the consent of the patient or her appropriate surrogate to a physician's DNR ('do not resuscitate') order. In the event of a dispute between the surrogate and the physician a dispute resolution committee must be formed, and some ethics committees fulfil this function. Dispute resolution mechanisms are also part of some state laws concerning the assignment of durable powers of attorney for health care, and again ethics committees can be convenient venues for this role.

Of the two other classical ethics committee functions, staff education is arguably the most important and the most efficient. A staff that is well-informed about local advance directive mechanisms and actively encourages their use by patients can thereby prevent many problems that might be presented to an ethics committee. However, the practical conditions under which most in-hospital personnel must work make the provision of such 'cognitive' services a low priority.

Policy review and consultation can be of great benefit to the institution's administration, especially if it leads to more reflective and philosophical policy-making than is usually the case when left in the hands of the hospital's attorney. Some committees have drafted truly innovative policies on end-of-life issues, for example, and these efforts have sometimes been made part of a general effort to bring staff together in an educational setting as well. Again, however, these kinds of contributions require a sophisticated ethics committee, which in turn depends upon an initial investment by the institution for the training of committee members. This is especially true of the committee chair, who may also have to be released from some other responsibilities in order to function optimally in this position. If the chair is a physician this could represent a substantial financial commitment by the institution.

In this writer's experience as a member and consultant for numerous ethics committees since 1984, institutional commitments to ethics committees, and their resulting quality, vary widely. Ethics committees are often created amid great excitement and optimism about their anticipated contributions to institutional culture, education and morale, but after the first two years obviously suffer from what the bioethicist John Fletcher calls the ethics committees' 'failure to thrive' syndrome (Fletcher, 1995: 228). In many cases the aetiology of this syndrome turns out to be a passive committee style. The more successful committees tend to be those that actively insert themselves into day-to-day clinical and educational activities, creating relationships with staff members and the sense that the committee is a vital resource for everyone concerned.

For all their remarkable growth and undeniable popularity, there are many unanswered questions about ethics committees. For example, what is the legal status of an ethics committee's non-binding recommendations in a court of law? Should hospital lawyers be voting members of the ethics committee? Who should be able to bring a case to the committee? Should a designated patient advocate sit on the ethics committee? What about the hospital's risk manager? Should an ethics committee record its recommendation in the patient's chart, or only that it discussed the case and offered some assistance?

One possible function of ethics committees that was unforeseen in the mid-1970s is that of resource allocation. As the financial pressures on health-care systems worldwide increase, explicit rationing is a looming possibility. No less a figure than the editor of the *Journal of the American Medical Association* has suggested that ethics committees help develop practice guidelines for their institutions to identify when treatment may be withheld on grounds of (so-called) futility (Lundberg, 1993).

Ethics consultants may work with ethics committees or as independent actors. In either case there is a lively debate in the United States about how they should operate. According to what might be called the 'soft' model, the ethics consultant's job is to bring the parties together, help clarify the issues and arrange a mutually acceptable resolution (Ackerman, 1989). On the 'hard' model the ethics consultant resembles a consulting physician who performs an assessment of the patient's condition, identifies the relevant medical, social, legal and ethical facts and issues a recommendation (LaPuma and Schiedermayer, 1991). The latter model is supported mainly by those who regard formal medical training as a prerequisite for the competent ethics consultant. Although the potential for disciplinary division within the ranks of ethics consultants is ever-present, so far it has been largely contained. Yet if reimbursement for ethics consultation becomes available, one can imagine that the discussion will become less civil. Similarly, the question whether there should be a certification process for ethics consultants is a flashpoint in the practice.

However one approaches this issue, it is plain that the ethics consultant's role is a terribly complicated one, calling for a broader range of skills than can be found in nearly any other field. At a minimum, the competent ethics consultant must speak the languages of medicine, law and ethics, must be interpersonally skilled and cognizant of social-psychological issues and must have the ability to inspire confidence among patients and their families as well as her medical colleagues (Moreno, 1991). So described, ethics consultation perhaps deserves the characterization that was once applied to psychoanalysis as 'the impossible profession'.

Just as there are serious practical questions about the ethics committee phenomenon, the ethics consultant role is also puzzling. Even apart from the problem of which model of consultation to adopt, there is an inherent difficulty with the notion of ethics consultants who are vulnerable to conflicts of interest when they are salaried by the hospital. Short of a version of academic tenure, or at least long-term contracts, the ethics consultant is in a poor position to take a principled stand that is incompatible with administrative goals. Perhaps this is why most who have performed the ethics consultant role have been members of faculties whose primary association is with some associated academic unit, such as the medical school or the philosophy department. The salaried consultant, compensated from hospital revenues, must exercise unusual self-discipline and independence to retain professional integrity. Although this can be done, it presents such an inherently conflictual role that ethics consultation may always be a marginal activity. Though ethics committees are also made up mainly of hospital workers, the group nature of their discourse may provide some more protection than can be true of the 'loan ethicist' on the wards.

One initial obstacle to the establishment of ethics committees and consultants appears to have been dissipated, at least in the United States: the resistance of attending physicians. Especially in the early days of the ethics committee movement, many physicians seemed to take the suggestion of committee involvement as an indictment of their personal moral character. More recently, younger physicians seem to embrace the ethics committee as a source of moral guidance – or, less

480

admirably, as an opportunity to 'turf' a complex and legally ominous issue. The latter is a special concern with respect to ethics consultants, who could easily be viewed as providing 'ethical cover' in tough cases. Thus one reason for the popularity of ethics committees and ethics consultants could be that they provide an opportunity to shift responsibility for decisions that are born in ambiguity and which can provoke anxiety among physicians.

It remains to be seen whether ethics committees and ethics consultants will become permanent fixtures of modern health-care decision-making, or whether they are temporary, transitional arrangements while a new and settled consensus on the use of powerful medical technologies sorts itself out. But then, the same question can be asked of bioethics itself.

The Significance of Ethics Committees and Ethics Consultation for Bioethics

As interesting as the phenomena of ethics committees and ethics consultants are in themselves, they also raise provocative questions about the nature of bioethics as an institution. Elsewhere I have argued at length that bioethics must be understood in the same way social scientists understand any other social institution, namely as a set of social practices (Moreno, 1995). That is, the intellectual and academic origins of bioethics should not obscure its sociological functions. Central among these functions is not only to serve as a multidisciplinary forum for raising interesting value questions about health care and the applications of the life sciences, but also to serve as an agent for certain social forces of which it is itself a product.

In particular, bioethics functions partly as a social reform movement, especially in so far as it has participated in the revolution in the way most people think of doctor–patient relations. Surely no profession has undergone more change in public attitudes in a shorter time than has medicine, and no profession's values have undergone more relentless scrutiny – in spite of the fact that medicine is also the profession that has historically been the most jealous of its prerogatives. Barely thirty years old, the lifetime of bioethics is also the period in which the official values of 'paternalistic' medicine have been shattered.

Bioethics has not only been a foremost voice in the emergence of a new social consensus about doctor–patient relations, it has also established itself as an agent for the development of a new consensus about a myriad of moral questions made pressing by the emerging biomedical technologies. Among the vehicles for the creation of this new consensus have been ethics commissions, operating at regional and national levels, and ethics committees and consultants, operating at institutional levels.

As vehicles for consensus creation in institutions ethics consultants are a mixed bag. What I have called the 'hard' ethics consultation model is an instrument of consensus only in the sense and to the degree that people are likely to defer to expertise. But contemporary scepticism of expert consensus is one of the sources of modern bioethics. The 'soft' model of ethics consultation, which aims at transforming a morally problematic situation into one of relative moral clarity, is perhaps a

481

more promising source of consensus creation. However, it too is limited by the dynamics of intervention by an individual consultant who is too easily viewed as the 'ethics expert'. Ethics experts must, it seems, possess several characteristics, including analytical discernment and a knowledge of medical ethical issues and the relevant literature.

Ethics committees are more promising vehicles for institutional consensus creation. In general, well-integrated groups composed of individuals who are respected within the institution are far more powerful agents of change than any lone consultant could be. But for what sort of change should ethics committees strive? What makes one consensus morally superior to another?

Philosophically, this is surely the root problem for ethics committees and ethics consultants: the fact that there is a certain moral consensus does not imply it is a morally sound one. This appears to be an instance of the fact-value problem, and according to standard analytical philosophy it raises notoriously recalcitrant obstacles to the generation of morally adequate conclusions from social decision processes. There seem to be two ways to deal with this dilemma. One is to accept it as insoluble and conclude that moral truth (however one understands this term) and social consensus coincide accidentally, if at all.

An alternative is to reject a simplistic fact-value dichotomy in favour of a naturalistic moral epistemology in which valuation is viewed as emergent from states of affairs. On this view, morally value-laden conclusions are seen as 'evaluations', literally, 'drawing the value from' state-descriptions. This approach has its *locus classicus* in the work of John Dewey, whose model of 'social intelligence' seems uniquely well-suited to arrangements like ethics committees. Dewey's model was that of an informed citizenry reaching tentative conclusions (or 'hypotheses') together for the solution of common problems, subjecting them to field tests and then revising the hypothesis in light of the results (Dewey, 1958).

The notion of social intelligence, a happy corollary of the scientific method, seems to presuppose a shared culture, or at least shared moral values. However, if the value premises differ among deliberators, there is no guarantee that consensus will be reached, even if there is agreement about the empirical premises. Thus consider two ethics committees faced with problematic cases having identical fact patterns, but one committee operates in a religiously affiliated hospital that caters to patients of that faith tradition, the other operates in a secular hospital. Though the committees may be similar in all other respects, their value-based differences will often generate divergent results.

A somewhat different problem infects the relationship between the committee and the patient community served by the institution. Thus a value consensus reached by a committee composed mainly of well-educated white males may not be shared by many patients or their families. Even the apparently content-free value of autonomy may not be esteemed or understood the same way in all cultures or subcultures.

Of course, the ethics committee itself faces the challenge of achieving internal consensus on the issues it faces. The fact that ethics committees are themselves subject to small group processes has been the source of much criticism of these

482

committees, since interpersonal relations in any group can distort what should be orderly deliberations. This possibility recommends at least that ethics committee processes should be subjected to empirical study.

Some data about ethics committees is already available, and it has interesting philosophical implications. For example, how shall disagreements within ethics committees be resolved? Under what conditions can it be said that the committee has reached an end to its deliberations on a particular matter? Data collected through self-reporting indicates that the vast majority of ethics committees consider themselves to operate according to 'consensus'. Moreover, most committees seem to be uncomfortable about taking explicit votes on substantive questions (Hoffman, 1991). Moral issues, it seems, are not to be settled by recourse to the usual parliamentary procedures.

It might be expected that there would be consensus among ethics consultants, at least on the basic issues of contemporary bioethics, just as we expect consensus among experts on scientific questions. However, what little data are available on this question suggests that is not necessarily the case. In their survey of ethics consultants, Fox and Stocking (1993) found great disagreement concerning several case scenarios. They surveyed 154 ethics consultants for their reactions to a case of a patient in a persistent vegetative state receiving artificially administered food and fluids. Of the several scenarios in which non-treatment was an alternative, the one that specified that the patient had left instructions that she would not want life-prolonging treatment and her family agreed was the only one in which the consultants tended to agree (87 per cent) that the patient should not be treated. The other cases, in which the wishes of the patient and the family were varied, received no more than 50 per cent agreement to stop treatment.

Conclusion

Ethics committees and ethics consultants are among the most visible manifestations of a highly public, social reform-oriented and multidisciplinary field. Yet for all the enthusiasm and wide acceptance that has greeted them in the past few years, beyond some generalizations there is little that can be said with confidence about their functions and goals. Their future seems closely tied to the further evolution of bioethics, especially whether the field continues to be a vigorous presence beyond the academy.

References

Ackerman, T. (1989). Conceptualizing the role of the ethics consultant. In J. C. Fletcher, N. Quist and A. R. Jonsen (eds), *Ethics Consultation in Health Care*. Ann Arbor, MI: Health Administration Press, 37–52.

Advisory Committee for Human Radiation Experiments (1995). *Final Report*. Washington, DC: Joseph Henry Press.

Alexander, S. (1962). They decide who lives, who dies. *Life*, 9 November, 102.

Beauchamp, T. and Childress, J. (1995). *Principles of Biomedical Ethics*, 4th edn. New York: Oxford University Press.

Dewey, J. (1958). *Experience and Nature*, 2nd edn, rev. New York: Dover.

Fletcher, J. C. (1995). Bioethics services in healthcare organizations. In J. C. Fletcher, C. A. Hite, P. A. Lombardo and M. F. Marshall (eds), *Introduction to Clinical Ethics*. Frederick, MD: University Publishing Group.

Fox, E. and Stocking, C. (1993). Ethics consultants' recommendations for life-prolonging treatment of patients in a persistent vegetative state. *New England Journal of Medicine*, 270, 2578–82.

Hoffman, D. E. (1991). Does legislating hospital ethics committees make a difference? A study of hospital ethics committees in Maryland, the District of Columbia, and Virginia. *Low, Medicine, and Health Care*, 19, 111.

Joint Commission for the Accreditation of Healthcare Organizations (1992). Patients' rights. In *Accreditation Manual of Hospitals*. Chicago: JCAHO.

LaPuma, J. and Schiedermayer, D. L. (1991). Ethics consultation: skills, roles, and training. *Annals of Internal Medicine*, 114, 155–60.

Lundberg, G. (1993). American health care system management objectives: the aura of inevitability becomes incarnate. *Journal of the American Medical Association*, 269, 2554–5.

Moreno, J. D. (1987). Ethical and legal issues in the treatment of impaired newborns. *Clinics in Perinatology*, 14, 325–39.

—— (1991). Ethics consultation as moral engagement. *Bioethics*, 5, 44–56.

—— (1995). *Deciding Together: bioethics and moral consensus*. New York: Oxford University Press.

Rothman, D. (1991). *Strangers at the Bedside: a history of how law and bioethics transformed medical decision making*. New York: Basic Books.

Wear, S. et al. (1990). The development of an ethics consultation service. *HEC Forum*, 2, 75–87.

Further Reading

Fletcher, J. C. (1991). The bioethics movement and hospital ethics committees. *Maryland Law Review*, 50, 859–94.

Fletcher, J. C. and Hoffmann, D. E. (1994). Ethics committees: time to experiment with standards. *Annals of Internal Medicine*, 120, 335–8.

Povar, G. (1991). Evaluating ethics committees: what do we mean by success? *Maryland Law Review*, 50, 904–19.

Wolf, S. (1991). Ethics committees and due process: nesting rights in a community of caring. *Maryland Law Review*, 50, 798–858.

46

How bioethics is being taught: a critical review

CATHERINE MYSER

Bioethics is currently taught around the globe – in Africa (including Nigeria and South Africa), Asia (including China, India, Japan, Korea, Malaysia, Sri Lanka and Thailand), Australia and New Zealand, Europe (including Belgium, France, Germany, Greece, Hungary, Italy, the Netherlands, Scandinavia, Spain, the United Kingdom and Yugoslavia), the Middle East (including Israel and Turkey), North America and Latin America (including Argentina, Brazil and Chile) – among other places. Thus, in developing and developed countries alike, educators are taking on the challenges of identifying and developing the most appropriate objectives, content, methods and assessment strategies to teach bioethics. The World Health Organization (WHO) has explicitly endorsed such efforts in medical education, embracing among others the goals of:

> ensur[ing] that universally accepted principles of medical ethics are recognized . . . that a core curriculum in medical ethics that may be applied globally [is developed] . . . and that medical ethics forms an integral part of medical education at undergraduate, postgraduate and continuing education levels in its Member States worldwide. (World Health Organization, 1995: 6)

There is, however, ongoing controversy about why, what, how, when, to whom and by whom bioethics should be taught. Furthermore, there is insufficient international dialogue between those teaching bioethics. For example, in the United States and the United Kingdom, the tendency has been to focus critical reviews almost exclusively on bioethics teaching activities and developments within each of these countries. We are therefore not learning enough from one another.

This ongoing controversy and insufficient international dialogue about the teaching of bioethics challenges the WHO's goals outlined above. I will attempt to achieve more substantive international coverage in this critical review of bioethics teaching, to stimulate more active international dialogue and to determine if there are significant areas of consensus around the globe which might facilitate the achievement of the WHO's goals. To be broader in this regard, however, the scope of this critical review will be limited primarily to exploring the teaching of bioethics in undergraduate medical education, because it is reasonably well-developed around the globe, and thus can be analysed in a broad international context.

Why Bioethics is Taught in Medical Education

Rationale

Over the last three decades, the most common rationale given for teaching bioethics in medical education has been related to the technological revolution in science and medicine, which can both order and disorder our lives. This rationale has been cited in developing (Park, 1985: 139; Babapulle, 1992: 186) and developed (Ewan, 1986: 103) countries alike. Such advances have raised concerns about the Hippocratic Oath, more recent codes and declarations, inculcated professional norms and individual conscience being outrun or outmoded, too vague (Puthucheary, 1980: 86) or otherwise inadequate to meet the ethical challenges of medicine. In some developing countries, an additional concern has been that the intrusion of Western medical models emphasizing scientific and technological training is not only importing Western ethical dilemmas, but is also challenging, eroding and excluding 'traditional values' (Browne, 1972: 64; Qui, 1993: 113–14). Such advances are thus seen to create a need to impart an adequate bioethics knowledge base and adequate clinical ethics skills as one means of enabling medical students or physicians to recognize and manage ethical issues arising from such pervasive scientific, cultural and ethical transformations (Miles et al., 1989: 706).

A second rationale for teaching bioethics in medical education is cultural pluralism within and between nations (Babapulle, 1992: 187). Such pluralism has highlighted additional concerns that existing oaths, codes and declarations are biased according to Judaeo-Christian values, other Western values such as individualism and/or those of medical paternalism. Pluralism is thus seen to create a need to impart bioethics knowledge and skills to medical students and professionals as one means of enabling them to recognize and manage ethical issues in a context in which their own personal and professional values may not be shared by patients, family members, colleagues or the institution or society in which they practise medicine. Thus, they must learn to be more circumspect about themselves and their profession – listening attentively to, critically engaging and even respecting positions and value choices that may differ sharply from their own. An important caveat highlighted by social scientists and others, however, is that the conceptual framework, value system and mode of reasoning of 'Western' (Glick, 1994: 242–3), 'American' (Fox, 1990: 205–10) or European-American bioethics itself appears to be culturally biased, and thus requires that bioethics be similarly circumspect about itself.

Goals and objectives

Although the above reasoning may justify teaching bioethics as part of medical education, it does not specify precise goals and objectives which can frame and direct that endeavour. However, specifying pedagogical goals is arguably the most important step in bioethics teaching in medical education, as from the 'enumeration of specific goals and learning objectives . . . should logically follow . . . content, methods . . . materials' (Fox et al., 1995: 764–5) and specific assessment strategies to guide student learning to achieve those goals. Specifying precise goals and objectives also enables us to address the question of whether bioethics can be taught, because it outlines the knowledge, skills and competencies which must be assessed and/or measured to enable us to answer this question. To these ends, several different kinds of learning goals and objectives have been suggested for bioethics teaching in medical education.

The first are cognitive goals and objectives related to imparting theoretical and conceptual bioethics knowledge and analytical abilities as a framework for recognizing and managing ethical issues in medicine. These cognitive goals and objectives include: (1) to increase sensitivity to and awareness of ethical or value issues in medical practice and research, enabling students to identify and anticipate 'ethical' issues as distinct from 'technical' issues; (2) to promote and enhance critical reflection on the student's own personal and professional values, as well as on the values of patients, family members, other health-care professionals and the institutions and society in which medicine is practised (Ewan, 1986: 104); (3) to identify the value assumptions and substantive ethical principles and concepts underlying clinical decisions; (4) to teach the skills of ethical reasoning, analysis and justification; and thus (5) to provide students with a systematic and critical approach to clinical ethical decision-making (Mitchell et al., 1994).

The second are behavioural or practical goals and objectives related to imparting other 'professional skills' such as bioethics-specific communication and interaction skills, to enable students to implement bioethics knowledge and analytical abilities in a manner consistent with good clinical ethical practice and good patient care. These practical or behavioural goals and objectives, although often not specified beyond 'interaction skills' or 'communication skills', include teaching students how to: (1) bridge the gap between knowledge of ethical theory, principles or concepts and ethical reasoning in clinical practice (Mitchell et al., 1994); (2) facilitate self-expression and shared decision-making by patients, eliciting their 'values, concerns . . . goals' (Forrow and Arnold, 1995: 261) and 'listening to . . . [and] interpreting what [patients] say or do with insight and understanding' (Carse, 1991: 21); (3) break bad news sensitively; (4) obtain a valid consent or a valid refusal of treatment, including how to assess patient competence, communicate to ensure adequate disclosure and understanding and ensure adequate voluntariness; (5) discuss with a terminally ill patient his or her 'do not resuscitate' status or other advance directives; and (6) determine 'when it is morally justified to withhold information from a patient . . . [or] to breach confidentiality' (Culver et al., 1985: 253–5). Clearly this list of bioethics-specific interaction or communication skills is not comprehensive.

Finally, the third are attitudinal or affective goals and objectives related to maintaining, promoting, improving or at least not eroding the 'virtuous' or 'humanistic' character, personality, qualities, emotional capacities and/or behaviour of medical students. These attitudinal goals and objectives, although also not often further specified, and varying somewhat over the last three decades, include maintaining, promoting, improving and/or not eroding: (1) 'high idealism and integrity' (Puthucheary, 1980: 92); (2) 'accountability . . . openness to the criticism of one's ideas . . . a willingness to discuss issues freely . . . and the facility to see the human and personal side of patients' (Jones, 1989: 450, 454); (3) readiness and ability to tolerate ambiguity, disagreement and moral conflict; (4) compassion, empathy, understanding or identification with the patient's perspective; and (5) active attendance to 'the unique . . . features of other persons, our relationship to them, and the circumstances in which we find ourselves with them', involving inequalities in power and dependence, and very real differences in health-care needs due to particular 'factors such as age, gender, class, religion, and sexual orientation' (Carse, 1991: 12, 17, 21).

There is a remarkable consensus around the globe in developing and developed countries alike regarding the appropriateness of the first two kinds of learning goals and objectives for bioethics teaching in medical education, and they are clearly regarded as being linked (Forrow and Arnold, 1995), but the third kind remains a topic of some controversy. Culver and others, for example, claim that bioethics teaching is 'designed not to improve the moral character of future physicians but to provide those of sound moral character with the intellectual tools and interactional skills to give that moral behavior its best behavioral expression' (1985: 253). Miles and others claim furthermore that even 'the dehumanization that occurs . . . during medical training should be addressed through other reforms' (1989: 707). Still, even those who might agree that bioethics teaching cannot improve moral character or prevent its erosion actively attempt to secure medical students of sound moral character who may possess other relevant qualities or abilities, such as empathy and tolerance for ambiguity, relying on medical school admissions selection criteria and interviews with applicants to secure such students (Jones, 1989: 456). However, others go even further to claim that in addition to giving preference to candidates of 'higher moral character' in the admissions process, 'there should be a strong [curriculum] . . . in personality formation' (Park, 1985: 140–1), specifically in the areas of 'compassion . . . empathy, insight . . . sensitivity . . . and identification with the patient' (Glick, 1994: 241). Proponents of 'relational ethics' and/or an 'ethics of care' in particular believe the development of such 'moral capacities' to be essential in bioethics education (Carse, 1991). At any rate, Fox and others refer to a 'plethora of proposals' and strategies for such 'sweeping reforms' (1995: 762–3).

As a small step towards resolving such controversy regarding the third kind of learning goals and objectives for bioethics teaching in medical education, it is worth noting that critics (Forrow and Arnold, 1995: 261) and proponents (Glick, 1994: 241) alike seem to agree that a positive attitude concerning the importance of the humanistic and value-laden aspects of medical care is required to enable students to recognize ethical issues and to motivate them to develop and implement the knowledge base and analytical and interaction skills to manage such ethical issues competently in medical practice. For example, although Miles and others reject bioethics education as an intervention to promote humanistic attitudes or prevent their erosion, they simultaneously argue that 'compassion, empathy, and respect for patients are . . . part of ethical competence' to be considered in attempts to assess the full range of bioethics competence, warning, however, that evaluating ethics education 'necessarily skirts a treacherous distinction between an appropriate evaluation of competence in professional medical ethics and an inappropriate evaluation of the student's . . . moral character' (1989: 707, 710). Thus, what critics and proponents appear to disagree about is whether bioethics teaching or some alternative intervention in medical student selection and/or education is the appropriate way to maintain, promote, improve or at least not erode such positive attitudes. At any rate, proponents and critics alike admit the enormous difficulty of such endeavours.

What Bioethics is Taught in Medical Education

Despite the consensus regarding at least the first two kinds of learning goals and objectives for bioethics teaching in medical education, there does not appear to be a firm consensus about a 'core curriculum' in medical ethics that may be applied globally to achieve these or other teaching objectives. For example, it seems to be agreed that 'core topics' may vary in relevance and evolve or be modified over time in accordance with cultural (Puthucheary, 1980: 92), social (Ewan, 1986: 103), ideological, institutional and even legal and regulatory (Miles et al., 1989: 706) contexts, needs and developments, and in accordance with 'the topic's relative importance to the practice of the majority of physicians', whether in individual physician–patient interactions or in the broader context of health-care resource allocation (Culver et al., 1985: 256). Commentators in developing countries in particular cite the necessity to address 'more diffuse ethical questions . . . additional and superimposed [on Western] medical ethics problems', especially when some ethical issues regarded as relevant in the West can be 'largely irrelevant' in developing countries (Browne, 1972: 64–5). Such commentators also urge consideration of cultural differences in understanding and application of fundamental concepts such as 'personhood', 'causality', 'rights', 'individualism', 'health and life' (Gbadegesin, 1993) and argue, as do some commentators in developed countries, that actual ethical issues related to assisted reproduction, distribution of scarce medical resources, euthanasia, human experimentation, human genetics and transplantation can vary according to differing cultural and religious 'world-views' (Tealdi, 1993), socio-economic contexts and gender or other 'frame[s] of reference' (Park, 1985; Babapulle, 1992: 187). Finally, Qiu (1993: 118) argues that 'we have to recognize that . . . some values or principles . . . are universal to all cultures, and . . . some . . . are relative to each culture,' although he does not address the difficult questions of what these principles are or how they are to be distinguished from one another.

With these and other considerations in mind, various commentators have recommended that bioethics teaching in medical education be adapted or tailored to suit particular cultures (Puthucheary, 1980: 92) and institutional contexts (Fox et al., 1995: 765), especially as it is introduced into developing countries (Gbadegesin, 1993; Tealdi, 1993: 198). Thus, the question of what bioethics content should be taught in medical education – especially when considered in a global context – evokes the universalist/relativist debate, at least at the level of choosing 'core' topics, concepts and principles. Although the broader universalist/relativist debate cannot be resolved within the scope of this article, the international consensus seems to be that cultural and other 'contextual' differences do need to be taken into account in bioethics curriculum design in medical education. Indeed, a radical universalist approach risks a *reductio ad absurdum*, because it does not make sense to proceed from the premise of cultural pluralism to the conclusion that bioethics should be taught as a means of recognizing and managing value differences, and at the same time holds that all elements of the bioethics curriculum can or should be universal in definition and/or application.

The WHO might need to concede, therefore, that its quest for 'universally accepted principles' may not be desirable or achievable in the end. Then again, principles can be accepted as relevant without being balanced or even defined in exactly the same way in every cultural setting. Thus, we need not collapse into radical relativism in terms of curriculum design. For example, Tables 1–3 outline some theory, principles, concepts, ethical analysis and reasoning methods and 'core topics' (including 'topics of special relevance' and 'topics of questionable relevance' suggested by those in developing countries) which do recur in most discussions of 'core content' in developed and developing countries alike. These tables offer, therefore, a loose but useful 'working consensus' with which to begin further discussions aimed at developing a 'core curriculum' in medical ethics that may be applied globally, without requiring a universalist medical ethic or collapsing into radical relativism.

Table 1   Framework for recognizing and managing ethical issues in medicine.

Theoretical and Conceptual Bioethics Knowledge Base
*   Ethical theories: e.g., deontology; situation ethics; utilitarianism
*   Relevant humanities, religious studies and social science theories and concepts
*   Bioethical principles: autonomy; beneficence; justice; mutuality or solidarity or community; non-maleficence
*   Basic bioethical concepts: e.g., best interests; informed consent (including competence, disclosure, understanding, voluntariness); paternalism; personhood; quality of life; rights and duties; slippery slope
*   Relevant laws and public policy
*   Paradigm cases in bioethics

Ethical Analysis and Reasoning Methods:
*   Casuistry; ethics of care; principle-based approaches; virtue theory

490

Table 2   Framework for recognizing and managing ethical issues in medicine.

Core topics:

* **Clinical practice issues:** abortion; AIDS; allocation of scarce medical resources; assessing burdens and benefits; assessing capacity or competence; confidentiality; death and dying; do not resuscitate orders; euthanasia; family role in decision-making; forgoing life-sustaining treatment; genetics; handicapped newborns; informed consent; maternal–fetal conflicts; organ procurement and transplantation; privacy; refusal of treatment; reproductive issues and technologies; right to die; surrogate decision-making; truth-telling; withholding information; withholding and withdrawal of treatment

* **Key relationships:** doctor–patient relationship; doctor–patient–family relationships; doctor–health-care team relationships; doctor–society relationship

* **Professional conduct issues:** abuse of drug privileges; advertising; codes of medical ethics; etiquette; impaired colleagues; doctors' rights and duties regarding colleagues, patients, family members, society and the media; sexual relations with patients

* **Academic practice issues:** authorship; research ethics; social responsibilities of researchers

* **Medical student issues:** academic integrity; revealing student status to patients; challenging medical routine; collusion with non-disclosures by the health-care team; coping with unethical behaviour or demands by supervisors; role on health-care team; student disclosures of new information; student inexperience performing medical procedures and possible harms to patients

How and When Bioethics is Taught in Medical Education

There appears to be significant consensus around the globe about a range of methods employed to advance the goals of imparting theoretical and conceptual bioethics knowledge and analytical abilities, and bioethics-specific communication and interaction skills, to enable medical students in developing and developed countries to implement such knowledge and abilities in a manner consistent with good clinical ethical practice and good patient care. To this extent at least, the answer to the question of whether bioethics can be taught is 'yes'. For example, methods for imparting theoretical and conceptual bioethics knowledge such as that outlined in the tables above – to provide students with a framework for recognizing and managing ethical issues – usually include didactic lectures (Babapulle, 1992: 186) and seminars (Tealdi, 1993), discussion and perhaps student presentations, all of which may also involve hypothetical or actual clinical case analysis, supplemental readings and perhaps videotapes or films (Forrow and Arnold, 1995: 261–

Table 3 Framework for recognizing and managing ethical issues in medicine.

Topics of special relevance in developing countries:
(Browne, 1972; Puthucheary, 1980; Park, 1985; Babapulle, 1992; Gbadegesin, 1993; Qiu, 1993)
Black markets; challenges to autonomy and informed consent due to: (a) lesser emphasis on individualism, and (b) patient and family illiteracy or lack of education; commercialization and exploitation in organ transplantation; competing loyalties of health-care professionals regarding distribution of time, skills, drug supplies, hospital facilities and other scarce resources to family/clan/village/tribe members and others; conflicts between traditional and modern values; duties of patients to live and die cheaply; exploitation in human experimentation, e.g., drug research in developing countries by developed nations; indigenous or traditional versus orthodox or Western medicine; infertility versus overpopulation; internal political and economic strife which can prevent the development of bioethics activities or create bioethics as part of the dominant ideology; benefits and limits of technology; lack of freedom to conduct research and disseminate results; lack of resources for the academic formation of medical ethics; patient rights; poverty; privileged monopolies; resource allocation – curative versus preventative, individual versus societal, urban versus rural; strong paternalism which prevents the recognition and management of bioethical issues and the development of the field

Topics of questionable relevance in developing countries:
(Browne, 1972; Babapulle, 1992; Qiu, 1993)
Advertising; Western codes of medical ethics; individual patient welfare and confidentiality; some advanced technologies

2). These methods are usually emphasized in the pre-clinical years, but may also be employed in the clinical years as the need to reinforce or augment the bioethics knowledge base arises. Methods for developing analytical abilities and bioethics-specific communication and interaction skills usually focus on analysis and discussion of hypothetical or actual clinical cases – and perhaps involve input from communications specialists or liaison psychiatrists, debates, role-playing, video-tapes, interactions with guest patients or other practical exercises (Miles et al., 1989: 707–10) – in small groups, seminars, tutorials, workshops, case conferences (Glick, 1994: 241–2), ward rounds and grand rounds (Puthucheary, 1980: 93). These methods may be employed in both the pre-clinical and clinical years, but are usually emphasized in the clinical years.

Case analysis and case management are increasingly central foci of bioethics teaching during both the pre-clinical and clinical years in medical education. Given that good clinical ethical practice and good patient care are the goals of such teaching, there is widespread consensus that cases should be central, assuming that: (a) a full range of teaching cases is employed, involving 'everyday' as well as 'exotic' ethical issues; and (b) broader contextual (e.g., social, economic, political, interpersonal and/or institutional) questions surrounding such ethical issues are also explored and addressed. There is controversy, however, about whether one should begin with bioethics theory and proceed to clinical ethical case analysis and management, or vice versa. This controversy grows out of the broader debate in bioethics about the relationship between theory and practice. My own view is that 'theory' and 'practice' need not be so dichotomized, and that it is essential to see their relatedness. This is true because theories can illuminate cases and help determine what we ought to do, and cases can be used to test, corroborate and revise theories. The implication of this view for medical ethics education is that the relationship between theory and cases should be made clear from the beginning – by weaving bioethics theory and clinical ethical case analysis and management from the 'pre-clinical' years on – rather than beginning with abstract ethical theory and only afterwards exploring 'applications' to cases, or beginning with cases and hoping to 'induce' useful theories. This is a more effective strategy for teaching medical students because acknowledging the relationship between theory and practice clarifies why learning bioethics theory is important, and thus motivates students to do so. It also enables students to see that bioethics theory can be criticized and revised, like any theory, if it is not useful in illuminating cases or determining what we ought to do. Thus students are encouraged to think more critically about both cases and theory.

Relatively few actual strategies for developing bioethics-specific analytical abilities and communication and interaction skills in medical education have been outlined in the bioethics literature. In some cases this is by design, to acknowledge that 'there is no one specific system by which medical ethics should be taught,' thus allowing for 'continuing innovation and creativity in teaching methods' (Culver et al., 1985: 253–4), but it also seems to be due to a lack of having identified such abilities and skills with sufficient specificity for actual curriculum development. For example, many commentators merely cite the use of 'small group process' as a 'method' for developing analytical abilities and communication and interaction skills (Almy et al., 1992: 572), without specifying what precise strategies or exercises are employed within the small group format to do so, which may lead to less effective learning of such skills by students. Methods specifically aimed at developing analytical abilities which have been outlined in more detail, however, include decision-making skills, clinical handbook and 'professional skills' (Mitchell et al., 1994) approaches. Methods to develop bioethics-specific communication and interaction skills include, generally, behavioural sciences approaches (Ewan, 1986) and, more specifically, various 'doctor–patient relationship' approaches. These are therefore important curricular gaps which remain to be addressed through future educational innovations, especially considering the growing consensus in developing and developed countries regarding the importance of teaching these skills.

Another curricular gap is revealed by the apparently universal consensus around the globe that bioethics teaching in medical education should be integrated

493

horizontally and vertically through every year of undergraduate medical education and beyond, with emphasis on bridging any gaps between appropriate stages of pre-clinical and clinical bioethics instruction. Some reasons underlying this consensus are that: (a) such integration demonstrates the omnipresent nature of ethical issues and conveys that bioethics competence is central to medical practice, and (b) unless continuously reaffirmed, the ethical competence of undergraduate and postgraduate medical students may decline. A recent review of medical ethics education in the United States has suggested that no medical school there 'has fully realized [this] ideal of cohesive, integrated, and comprehensive medical ethics training' (Fox et al., 1995: 764). However, at least one medical school elsewhere has successfully integrated systematic, cohesive and stage-specific bioethics teaching into all five years of its problem-based undergraduate training (Mitchell et al., 1994). There may be other examples, but they have not been cited or described in the international literature to date. Thus, the WHO and others' ideal of integrating bioethics teaching throughout medical education at undergraduate, not to mention postgraduate and continuing education levels, remains an ongoing challenge.

Assessment

Relatively little has been published about strategies to assess bioethics competence among medical students in developed countries, and almost nothing has been published about bioethics assessment in medical education in developing countries. This is a critical gap in bioethics teaching in medical education, because students are likely to structure their learning to acquire the knowledge and skills on which they will be assessed. For example, students who know that their assessment in clinical ethics will include not only exhibiting knowledge, but also demonstrating the ability to apply that knowledge to manage an ongoing clinical case, are more likely to structure their learning priorities towards the acquisition of those additional skills. In this regard, both the curriculum and those aspects of the curriculum selected for assessment determine what medical students learn (Mitchell et al., 1994).

A consensus does appear to be emerging that assessment strategies should be developed to advance specific and measurable cognitive, behavioural and/or attitudinal goals and objectives, in order to develop these multiple components of clinical ethical competence (Miles et al., 1989: 710–11; Fox et al., 1995: 765). Specific strategies used to develop and assess cognitive components of clinical ethical competence, such as knowledge of bioethics theories, principles and concepts, and the ability to recognize and manage ethical issues include: written essays or papers exploring specific topics, issues or cases (Jones, 1989: 452); essay, short-answer, multiple-choice and/or true–false tests (Babapulle, 1992: 186); questionnaires; self-directed learning exercises (Doyal, 1993); simulated clinical case studies; modified essay questions (MEQs) on the step-by-step unfolding of a clinical case (Mitchell et al., 1994); clinical vignettes; participation in small group discussions (Ewan, 1986: 107–8); ethical questions in clinical viva examinations; and oral examination responses to moral dilemmas posed by examiners (Almy et al., 1992: 572–3). Such assessment strategies indicate that cognitive components of clinical ethical competence, such as knowledge of bioethics theories, principles and concepts and the ability to recognize ethical issues, can be taught.

Specific strategies used to develop and assess behavioural components of clinical ethical competence such as bioethics-specific analysis, communication and interaction skills include: simulated or standardized patients (Almy et al., 1992: 573); written and oral case reports on the clinical ethical management of actual patients (Mitchell et al., 1994: 160–3); doctor–patient relationship questionnaires and presentations; audio and/or visual recordings of patient interviews and analysis of transcripts thereof; chart reviews (Fox et al., 1995: 765); objective structured clinical examinations (OSCEs); and direct observation (Doyal, 1993). It is more difficult to determine convincingly through current assessment strategies whether behavioural components of clinical ethical competence such as bioethics-specific analysis, communication and interaction skills can be taught. I suspect they can be, but the jury will be out until we can address some of the curricular gaps addressed in the 'Methods and Timing' section above. Even if we eventually demonstrate through appropriate assessment strategies that the behavioural components of clinical ethical competence can be taught, it will be even more difficult to link this in any meaningful way to gauge actual performance during patient management.

Finally, specific strategies used to develop and assess attitudinal components of clinical ethical competence include: general measures of attitudes related to ethical decision-making and ratings of humanistic qualities by patients, nurses, faculty or peers (Ewan, 1986: 108). For similar reasons to those outlined in the controversy about whether or not attitudinal components can or should be taught as part of a bioethics course, this is the most difficult and problematic component of clinical ethical competence to assess.

To Whom Bioethics Should Be Taught

The primary focus of this critical review has been the teaching of bioethics to medical undergraduates around the globe, for pragmatic rather than normative reasons. Other articles in the education literature have addressed bioethics teaching geared to nursing and allied health students, and less so to law and philosophy students (even those who may some day teach bioethics). An important level of integration apparently not espoused to date by the WHO, however, and only minimally addressed in the bioethics literature, is bioethics teaching to interprofessional groups of various students. This is somewhat ironic, considering that a widespread consensus exists in support of 'interdisciplinary' and 'team' teaching in bioethics, so that faculty from medicine and philosophy, for example, can combine their relevant areas of expertise for more effective teaching, at least of medical students.

This lack of interprofessional bioethics teaching is particularly problematic for medical, nursing and allied health students who may eventually work together to care for patients as members of a health-care team. This lack may be based in part on a decision-making model in which medical doctors remain the primary decision-makers. However, the nursing ethics literature suggests that 'medical ethics' and 'nursing ethics' have little in common, perhaps due to differing perspectives based on distinctions between an 'ethics of justice' and an ethics of care. Although oversimplified, this possible difference in perspectives may be perceived as one kind of obstacle to developing strategies for interprofessional bioethics teaching.

For this very reason it might be beneficial to at least experiment with tailoring bioethics teaching for interprofessional groups of students. Such students could thereby explore early on possible differences in the assumptions, perspectives, values and methods of the different professions, and thus begin to think across disciplines and perhaps approach patient care in a less fragmented manner. This is an enormously difficult challenge, which could be exacerbated in developing countries in which there may be greater disparity in general between the education of medical, nursing and allied health students. However, where possible, such teaching could offer exciting opportunities to make all health-care professionals more effective members of the health-care team.

References

Almy, T. et al. (1992). Health, society, and the physician: problem-based learning of the social sciences and humanities. *Annals of Internal Medicine*, 116, 569–74.

Babapulle, C. J. (1992). Teaching of medical ethics in Sri Lanka. *Medical Education*, 26, 185–9.

Browne, S. G. (1972). Teaching medical ethics in Africa. *Medical Journal of Australia*, 3, 63–5.

Carse, Alisa L. (1991). The 'voice of care': implications for bioethical education. *Journal of Medicine and Philosophy*, 16, 5–28.

Culver, C. M. et al. (1985). Basic curricular goals in medical ethics. *New England Journal of Medicine*, 312, 253–6.

Doyal, L. (1993). A model for teaching and assessing ethics and law within the clinical curriculum. *European Journal of Medicine*, 2, 424–9.

Ewan, C. (1986). Teaching ethics in medical school. *Medical Teacher*, 8, 103–10.

Forrow, L. and Arnold, R. (1995). Bioethics education: medicine. In W. T. Reich (ed.), *Encyclopedia of Bioethics*. New York: Macmillan, 259–64.

Fox, E., Arnold, R. M. and Brody, B. (1995). Medical ethics education: past, present, and future. *Academic Medicine*, 70, 761–9.

Fox, R. C. (1990). The evolution of American bioethics: a sociological perspective. In G. Weisz (ed.), *Social Science Perspectives on Medical Ethics*. Boston: Kluwer. 201–17.

Gbadegesin, S. (1993). Bioethics and culture: an African perspective. *Bioethics*, 7, 257–62.

Glick, S. (1994). The teaching of medical ethics to medical students. *Journal of Medical Ethics*, 20, 239–43.

Jones, D. G. (1989). The New Zealand *Report of the cervical cancer inquiry*: significance for medical education. *Medical Journal of Australia*, 151, 450–6.

Miles, S. H. et al. (1989). Medical ethics education: coming of age. *Academic Medicine*, 705–14.

Mitchell, K. R., Myser, C. and Kerridge, I. H. (1994). An integrated ethics programme in a community-oriented medical school. *Annals of Community-Oriented Education*, 7, 153–66.

Park, P. B. (1985). Teaching medical ethics in the future. *Yonsei Medical Journal*, 26, 139–41.

Puthucheary, S. D. (1980). A curriculum in medical ethics and medical humanities. *Medical Journal of Malaysia*, 35, 86–95.

Qiu, R. (1993). What has bioethics to offer the developing countries. *Bioethics*, 7, 108–25.

Tealdi, J. C. (1993). Teaching bioethics as a new paradigm for health professionals. *Bioethics*, 188–99.

World Health Organization (1995). *Bulletin of Medical Ethics*, 6.

Further Reading

Africa

Editor (1978). Teaching medical ethics. *South African Medical Journal*, 54, 884–5.

Olukoya, A. A. (1983). Attitudes of medical students to medical ethics in their curriculum. *Medical Education*, 17, 83–6.

Asia

Lindbeck, V. (1984). Thailand: Buddhism meets the Western model. *Hastings Center Report*, 24–6.

Australia and New Zealand

Davidson, G. P. and Roberts, F. J. (1977). Relational ethics in medicine. *New Zealand Medical Journal*, 86, 388–91.

Editor (1977). The teaching of medical ethics. *Medical Journal of Australia*, 1, 871–2.

Hays, R. B. and Molodysky, A. (1993). Teaching ethics in the context of general practice. *Medical Journal of Australia*, 159, 33–6.

Mitchell, K. R., Myser, C. and Kerridge, I. H. (1993). Assessing the clinical ethical competence of undergraduate medical students. *Journal of Medical Ethics*, 19, 230–6.

Myser, C., Kerridge, I. H. and Mitchell, K. R. (1995). Teaching clinical ethics as a professional skill: bridging the gap between knowledge about ethics and its use in clinical practice. *Journal of Medical Ethics*, 21, 97–103.

Europe

Allert, G., Sponholz, G., Meier-Allmendinger, D., Gaedicke and Baitsch (1994). Kurze ubersicht uber die lehraktivitaten des Ulmer arbeitskreises fur ethik in der medizin. [Short overview of the different teaching activities of the study-group 'Ethics in medicine' at the University of Ulm.] *Ethik in der Medizin*, 6, 99–104.

Anonymous [Editorial] (1981). Medical ethics and medical education. *Journal of Medical Ethics*, 7, 171–2.

Anonymous [Editorial] (1985). Two concepts of medical ethics. *Journal of Medical Ethics*, 11, 3.

Blomquist, C. (1975). The teaching of medical ethics. *Journal of Medical Ethics*, 1, 96–8.

Burling, S. J., Lumley, J. S. P., McCarthy, L. S. L., Mytton, J. A., Nolan, J. A., Sissou, P., Williams, D. G. and Wright, L. J. (1990). Review of the teaching of medical ethics in London medical schools. *Journal of Medical Ethics*, 16, 206–9.

Calman, K. C. and Downie, R. S. (1987). Practical problems in the teaching of ethics to medical students. *Journal of Medical Ethics*, 12, 153–6.

Clarke, D. D. (1978). The teaching of medical ethics: University College, Cork, Ireland. *Journal of Medical Ethics*, 4, 36–9.

De Wachter, M. A. M. (1978). Ethics for interns. *Journal of Medical Education*, 53, 214.

Downie, R. S. (1991). Literature and medicine. *Journal of Medical Ethics*, 17, 93–6.

Doxiadis, S. A. (1988). The teaching of medical ethics. *Medical Education*, 22, 85–7.

Doyal, L. (1991). Teaching ethics at The Barts and The London. *Bulletin of Medical Ethics*, 19–22.

Gillon, R. (1987). Medical ethics education. *Journal of Medical Ethics*, 13, 115–16.

——(1990). Teaching medical ethics: impressions from the USA. In *Medicine, Medical Ethics, and the Value of Life*. New York: John Wiley, 89–115.

Hope, T. (1991). Teaching medical ethics: healthy variety but are we learning from one another? *Bulletin of Medical Ethics*, 22–3.

Lang, S., Woolhandler, S., Bantic, Z. and Himmelstein, D. U. (1984). Yugoslavia: equity and imported ethical dilemmas. *Hastings Center Report*, 26–7.

Osborne, L. W. and Martin, C. M. (1989). The importance of listening to medical students' experiences when teaching them medical ethics. *Journal of Medical Ethics*, 15, 35–8.

Schubert-Lehnhardt, V. (1992). Teaching medical ethics in Germany. *Bulletin of Medical Ethics*, 13–15.

Seedhouse, D. F. (1991). Health care ethics teaching for medical students. *Medical Education*, 25, 230–7.

Sporken, P. (1975). The teaching of medical ethics in Maastricht, the Netherlands. *Journal of Medical Ethics*, 1, 181–3.

Ten Have, H. (1994). Teaching analysis. *Health Care Analysis*, 2, 173–7.

Terborgh-Dupuis, H. (1984). The Netherlands: tolerance for teaching. *Hastings Center Report*, 23–4.

Von Engelhardt, D. (1994). Ethik in der medizinischen Ausbildung – das Lubecker modell: Grundkurs – Patientenseminar – Studientag. [Ethics in medical education – the Lubeck model: elementary course, patient seminar, teaching day.] *Ethik in der Medizin*, 6, 82–7.

Welbourn, R. B. (1985). A model for teaching medical ethics. *Journal of Medical Ethics*, 11, 29–31.

Wolstenholme, G. (1985). Teaching medical ethics in other countries. *Journal of Medical Ethics*, 11, 22–4.

Wulff, H. (1991). How theory of medicine is taught in Denmark. *Bulletin of Medical Ethics*, 8.

Latin America

Zanier, J. et al. (1990). Present status and prospects of bioethics in Argentina. *Bulletin of PAHO*, 24, 480–90.

Middle East

Carmel, S. and Bernstein, J. (1986). Identifying with the patient: an intensive program for medical students. *Medical Education*, 20, 432–6.

North America

Banks, S. A. and Vastyan, E. A. (1973). Humanistic studies in medical education. *Journal of Medical Education*, 48, 248–57.

Bickel, J. (1987). Human values teaching programs in the clinical education of medical students. *Journal of Medical Education*, 62, 369–78.

—— (1991). Medical students' professional ethics: defining the problems and developing resources. *Academic Medicine*, 66, 726–9.

—— (1993). *Promoting Medical Students' Ethical Development: a resource guide*. Washington, DC: Association of American Medical Colleges.

Capron, A. (1988). A 'bioethics' approach to teaching health law. *Journal of Legal Education*, 38, 505–9.

Chambers, T. (1995). No Nazis, no space aliens, no slippery slopes and other rules of thumb for clinical ethics teaching. *Journal of Medical Humanities*, 16, 189–200.

Christakis, D. A. and Feudtner, C. (1993). Ethics in a short white coat: the ethical dilemmas that medical students confront. *Academic Medicine*, 68, 249–54.

Clouser, K. D. (1980). *Teaching Bioethics: strategies, problems, and resources*. New York: Hastings Center.

Feudtner, C. and Christakis, D. A. (1994). Making the rounds: the ethical development of medical students in the context of clinical rotations. *Hastings Center Report*, 6–12.

Fox, R. C. and Swazey, J. P. (1984). Medical morality is not bioethics – medical ethics in China and the United States. *Perspectives in Biology and Medicine*, 27, 336–60.

Francoeur, R. T. (1984). A structured approach to teaching decision-making skills in biomedical ethics. *Journal of Bioethics*, 145–54.

Friedman, L. D. (1995). See me, hear me: using film in health care classes. *Journal of Medical Humanities*, 16, 223–37.

Hafferty, F. W. and Franks, R. (1994). The hidden curriculum, ethics teaching, and the structure of medical education. *Academic Medicine*, 69, 861–71.

Hebert, P. C., Meslin, E. M. and Dunn, E. V. (1992). Measuring the ethical sensitivity of medical students: a study at the University of Toronto. *Journal of Medical Ethics*, 18, 142–7.

Johnson, A. G. (1983). Teaching medical ethics as a practical subject: observations from experience. *Journal of Medical Ethics*, 9, 5–7.

Lebacqz, K. (1991). Feminism and bioethics. *Second Opinion*, 17, 11–25.

McCullough, L. B. and Ashton, C. M. (1994). A methodology for teaching ethics in the clinical setting: a clinical handbook for medical ethics. *Theoretical Medicine*, 15, 39–52.

Medical Ethics Subcommittee, American Board of Pediatrics (1987). Teaching and evaluation of interpersonal skill and ethical decision-making in pediatrics. *Pediatrics*, 79, 829–33.

Petersdorf, R. G. (1989). A matter of integrity. *Academic Medicine*, 64, 119–23.

Reynolds, R. C. and Carson, R. A. (1976). The place of humanities in medical education. *Journal of Medical Education*, 51, 142–3.

Rezler, A. G. et al. (1992). Assessment of ethical decisions and values. *Medical Education*, 26, 7–16.

Roy, D. J. and DeWachter, M. A. M. (1980). Medical ethics in a medical school education. *Newfoundland Medical Association Journal*, 22, 11–13.

Sanders, C. J. (1994). European–American ethos and principlism: an African–American challenge. In E. R. Dubose, R. Hamel and L. J. O'Connell (eds), *A Matter of Principles? Ferment in US bioethics*. Valley Forge, PA: Trinity Press International, 148–63.

Schwandt, T. A. (1989). Evaluating the medical humanities. *Teaching and Learning in Medicine*, 1, 122–7.

Self, D. J., Baldwin, D. C. and Olivarez, M. (1993). Teaching medical ethics to first-year students by using film discussion to develop their moral reasoning. *Academic Medicine*, 68, 383–5.

Self, D. J., Wolinsky, F. D. and Baldwin, D. C. (1989). The effect of teaching medical ethics on medical students' moral reasoning. *Academic Medicine*, 64, 755–9.

Sidorov, J. J. (1993). Education in medical ethics. *Gastroenterologia Japonica*, 28, 3–10.

Singer, P. A., Cohen, R., Robb, A. and Rothman, A. (1993). The ethics objective structured clinical examination. *Journal of General Internal Medicine*, 8, 23–8.

Smith, S. R. et al. (1994). Performance-based assessment of moral reasoning and ethical judgment among medical students. *Academic Medicine*, 69, 381–6.

Squier, H. A. (1995). The teaching of literature and medicine in medical school education. *Journal of Medical Humanities*, 16, 175–87.

Vastyan, E. A. (1968). Humanities in a medical curriculum. *Pennsylvania Medicine*, 75, 78–81.

Veatch, R. M. (1978). Medical ethics education. In W. T. Reich (ed.), *Encyclopedia of Bioethics*. New York: Free Press, 870–6.

Weisberg, M. and Duffin, J. (1995). Evoking the moral imagination: using stories to teach ethics and professionalism to nursing, medical, and law students. *Journal of Medical Humanities*, 16, 247–61.

Wilson, J. and Blackwell, B. (1980). Relating literature to medicine: blending humanism and science in medical education. *General Hospital Psychiatry*, 2, 127–33.

Index

501